The Canadian Constitution in Historical Perspective

WITH A CLAUSE-BY-CLAUSE ANALYSIS OF THE CONSTITUTION ACTS AND THE CANADA ACT

BAYARD REESOR
Augustana University College

Canadian Cataloguing in Publication Data

Reesor, Bayard William
The Canadian constitution in historical perspective

Includes index.
ISBN 0–13–118761-9

1. Canada – Constitutional law. 2. Canada – Constitutional history. I. Title

JL65.1992 R44 1992 342.71 C91–094316–8

Prentice Hall, Inc., Englewood Cliffs, New Jersey
Prentice-Hall International, Inc., London
Prentice-Hall of Australia, Pty., Ltd., Sydney
Prentice-Hall of India Pvt., Ltd., New Delhi
Prentice-Hall of Japan, Inc., Tokyo
Prentice-Hall of Southeast Asia (Pte.) Ltd., Singapore
Editora Prentice-Hall do Brasil Ltda., Rio de Janeiro
Prentice-Hall Hispanoamericana, S.A., Mexico

ISBN 0–13–118761-9

Acquisitions Editor: Michael Bickerstaff
Developmental Editor: Maryrose O'Neill
Copy Editor: Gail Marsden
Production Editor: Valerie Adams
Production Coordinator: Anna Orodi
Cover Design: Olena Serbyn
Page Layout: Olena Serbyn
Composition: Siegfried Betterman

1 2 3 4 5 RRD 96 95 94 93 92

Printed and bound in the U.S.A. by R.R. Donnelley and Sons.

Part Three: Clause-by-Clause Analysis of the 1867 Constitution Act, 1982 Canada Act, and its Schedule "B," the 1982 Constitution Act *147*

Chapter 7: Clause-by-Clause Analysis — 1867 Constitution Act *148*

Chapter 8: Clause-by-Clause Analysis of the Canada Act, and its Schedule "B," the 1982 Constitution Act 285

Conclusion/Epilogue 410

Appendices

Appendix A: Text of 1867 Constitution Act as Amended 422

Appendix B: Text of 1982 Canada Act and Constitution Act as Amended 437

Endnotes 447

Index of Cases 485

General Index 492

PREFACE

The impetus for this book was the desire to have readily available, in a language appropriate for the undergraduate student of Canadian government, a reasonably concise analysis of what was then the British North America Act. The need for an analysis of the codified part of our constitution was accentuated by the passage of the 1982 Canada Act with its Schedule B, the Constitution Act. That analysis remains the major focus and comprises about two-thirds of the book.

Partly because of the breadth of our constitution, and partly because of the author's belief that a knowledge of history is essential to an understanding of the contemporary scene, the scope of this project rapidly expanded. A brief outline of the book follows.

Part One, entitled "The Road to Independence," focuses on the historical context within which the five major constitutional documents were created between the fall of New France and Confederation. These documents are the 1763 Royal Proclamation, 1774 Quebec Act, 1791 Constitutional Act, 1840 Union Act, and 1867 British North America Act (renamed in 1982 the Constitution Act, 1867). An attempt is made to show how each of these constitutional documents led to the next. In this way we can recognize that the Constitution Act was not created in a vacuum in 1867 but was the product of more than a century of British rule following the collapse of the French Empire on this continent.

This historical part is divided into three chapters. Chapter 1 traces our constitutional development from the fall of New France to the 1837 rebellions in Upper Canada and Lower Canada. Chapter 2 focuses on the struggle for reponsible government during the 1840s. Chapter 3 includes the causes of Confederation, Canada's subsequent territorial expansion, and, because the Constitution Act did not establish an independent country, a notation of the more significant post-Confederation steps in the development of total independence.

Part Two is entitled "The Nature of our Constitution." Chapter 4 considers the basic principles of our constitution—monarchy, rule of law, liberal democracy, responsible government, federalism, and semi-limited government. Chapter 5 acknowledges the multifaceted nature of the constitution. In addition to the 1867 and 1982 Constitution Acts, and the Canada Act, it considers the place of other formal documents, convention, and judicial decisions. Chapter 6 discusses the search by Federal and provincial governments for a formula that would permit Constitution Act amendment entirely within Canada. This search, sporadic and with varying degrees of enthusiasm, lasted for more than half a century and ended with the 1982 Constitution Act.

Part Three (Chapters 7 and 8), the original rationale for the book, makes up the bulk of the volume and consists of a clause-by-clause analysis of the 1867 Constitution Act (as amended) and the 1982 Canada Act and Constitution Act (as amended). Extensive use is made of Supreme Court of Canada rulings through mid-1991. Close attention is also given to some of the decisions of the Judicial Committee of the British Privy Council before 1949, and of our Supreme Court since 1949 (when it became Canada's final appeal body), in cases dealing with the federal distribution of powers between the two orders of government.

In the spring of 1987 the prime minister and the ten provincial premiers met at Meech Lake in the Gatineau Hills to discuss the conditions enumerated the previous year by Premier Bourassa for Quebec to sign the 1981 constitutional agreement. (This agreement had led to the 1982 Canada and Constitution Acts.) The result of the 1987 meeting was the "Meech Lake Accord" which included several proposed constitutional amendments. The eleven first ministers agreed to submit these proposed amendments to their legislatures for approval in accordance with the terms of section 41(e) of the 1982 Constitution Act. As is well known, the proposals were not approved by Manitoba and Newfoundland and so they lapsed on June 23, 1990. Since the death of Meech Lake there has been another flurry of activity by the governments in Ottawa, Quebec, and several other provinces. Some of these developments are noted in the Conclusion/Epilogue.

ACKNOWLEDGMENTS

I am grateful to Augustana University College for providing a sabbatical leave for me to begin this project, and for underwriting the expenses since then. I would also like to acknowledge the Supreme Court of Canada for allowing the use of many cases from *Supreme Court Reports*.

For reviewing the manuscript, I would like to thank Nelson Wiseman (University of Toronto), Patrick Malcolmson (St. Thomas University), Jennifer Smith (Dalhousie), F.L. Morton (Universtiy of Calgary), and Reg Whitaker (York University).

A professor's wife seems destined to spend much time without the companionship that is her due. During my many years of teaching, Sue has shown patience and understanding far exceeding any possible call of duty. I dedicate this book to her as a token of my deep appreciation for this selfless devotion.

INTRODUCTION

The Canadian constitution is rather baffling for it is so difficult to define. For more than a century we have had the British North America Act (in 1982 renamed the Constitution Act, 1867), but that document is of little assistance when we try to understand some of the basic constitutional principles. It explains parts of the political system such as the formal distribution of legislative authority between the Federal government and the provincial governments, but it sheds little light on the actual workings of government. The Act is silent, for example, on the critical principle that the cabinet is ultimately answerable to the House of Commons and cannot retain power if it loses the confidence of the Commons. The Act does not even indicate that the prime minister and cabinet must resign when a different political party wins a general election. Indeed, it fails to acknowledge the existence of a prime minister or cabinet. Neither does the Act contain an amending formula (so that until 1982 we had to ask a foreign government—Britain's Parliament—to make any important changes) or, for people seeking a formal guarantee of rights and freedoms, a bill or charter of rights. The Act is actually misleading in important respects, especially where it appears to attribute almost dictatorial power to the governor general who is the appointed representative of the monarch.

But we now have a "new" constitution, some people say—the 1982 Canada Act, and the Constitution Act which is appended to it. We now have a Charter of Rights and Freedoms and an amending formula, and we need no longer ask Britain to change any part of our constitution. We do indeed have these new documents but they are not a new constitution. They are additions to our existing one. They do add important elements but they do not address the "deficiencies" of the 1867 Constitution Act apart from creating an amending formula and the Charter.

Fortunately, the prime minister understands the principle of responsible government and would not attempt to retain power if defeated on an important matter in the House of Commons or if the party lost a general election. Joe Clark was defeated in the Commons in 1979 on his budget, and when he called an election the voters gave their support to Pierre Trudeau and the Liberal Party. Clark then resigned and Governor General Schreyer invited Trudeau to form the Government. The governor general understands the importance of deferring to his or her ministers and of not exercising most of the legal powers conferred by the Constitution Act.

The question naturally arises: "Why doesn't our constitution include these and other important principles in the operation of government?" The answer is: "It does!" The paradox is explained when we understand that our constitution encompasses far more than the documents noted above. For example, it includes convention. It is convention which dictates that a defeated prime minister must resign. It is convention which determines that the governor general must accept the advice of ministers; nevertheless, as if to create an element of uncertainty, convention also gives to the monarch's representative a "reserve" power to act upon his or her own initiative in extraordinary (but undefined) circumstances. However, failure to act in accordance with conventional rules cannot be challenged in the courts because these rules are not justiciable. The only "court" that can punish those who violate constitutional conventions is the electorate.

Two other basic elements of our constitution are statutes whose subject matter is of constitutional importance (including those establishing government departments, courts of law, voting eligibility, citizenship criteria, or altering Federal-provincial financial relations), and court decisions that adjudicate conflicting jurisdictional claims of the Federal and provincial governments and, since 1982, interpret our new Charter of Rights and Freedoms.

It is useful, therefore, to view a constitution as "the whole body of fundamental rules, written and unwritten, legal and extralegal, according to which a particular government operates."[1] A brief elaboration of this definition reveals several important points. First, the adjective "fundamental" cautions against the inclusion of many laws, regulations, and other rules which, although significant, are of but secondary importance. Constitutional rules set the framework within which other rules are made, interpreted, and applied. Second, fundamental rules are more difficult to change. In a sense this statement is a truism; what may not be self-evident, however, is that the generalization applies even when the difficulty of change is political rather than legal.

Third, constitutional rules need not all be written. The British constitution, for example, relies heavily on the unwritten accumulation of court decisions (the common law) and convention. Some parts of that constitution are indeed written, such as the Magna Carta (1215), Habeas Corpus Act (1679), Petition of Right (1628), Bill of Rights (1689), Act of Settlement (1701), Great Reform Act (1832), and Parliament Act (1911). But in the absence of a single core document the term "unwritten" is frequently applied. By way of contrast the United States constitution is generally regarded as synonymous with the document entitled the "Constitution of the United States" and is therefore classified as "written." There are, nevertheless, significant conventional rules such as those establishing the actual procedure for electing a president and the role of parties in the political process. The convention that a president would serve no more than two terms was formalized (and therefore ceased to be a convention) as a 1951 constitutional amendment following Franklin Roosevelt's election to his fourth term in 1944. Court decisions have also been an important component of United States constitutional rules since 1803 (*Marbury v. Madison*) when the Supreme Court first struck down legislation as being unconstitutional.

Canada is a cross between Britain and the United States: it has always had the core Constitution Act of 1867, to which has been added the 1982 Canada

Act and 1982 Constitution Act, but many of our most important constitutional rules are, as in Britain, unwritten. Using the "written-unwritten" dichotomy our constitution is "partly-partly."

The fourth important point revealed by the above definition follows from the third: the enforcement of some constitutional rules (notably convention) is accomplished only by political means and not through the courts. The term "extralegal" in the definition acknowledges the fact that not all constitutional rules are justiciable.

In spite of their popularity the terms "written" and "unwritten" are really inappropriate to describe constitutions. A "codified-uncodified" classification more accurately expresses the intent, a codified constitution having its essence within a single document. Clearly, then, the British constitution is uncodified, and the United States constitution is codified. What is the Canadian constitution? Unfortunately, these terms do not resolve that problem. The 1982 Canada Act with its Constitution Act certainly strengthens the argument for the adjective "codified" but the degree of codification is far less in Canada than in the United States. We seem to be left with a British-United States hybrid.

The term "constitution" is used in both a narrow and a broad sense depending upon whether or not, or the extent to which, the constitution is codified. The British constitution has meaning only in the broad sense and is frequently spelled with a lower-case "c"; conversely, the United States constitution generally refers to the document bearing that name and is usually spelled with a capital "C." When we come to Canada the distinction between the narrow and broad meanings of "constitution" becomes critical. References in this book to the 1867 or 1982 Constitution Acts and their amendments—the codified parts of our constitution—will use the upper-case "C"onstitution. Reference to the constitutional rules in the broad sense will use the lower-case "c"onstitution.

There is one other use of capitalization which should be noted. Some ambiguity exists with the word "federal" because it means both a characteristic of our political system and the central government in Ottawa. Throughout this book, therefore, the word is spelled with a lower-case "f" when it refers to the system, and with an upper-case "F" when it means the central government.

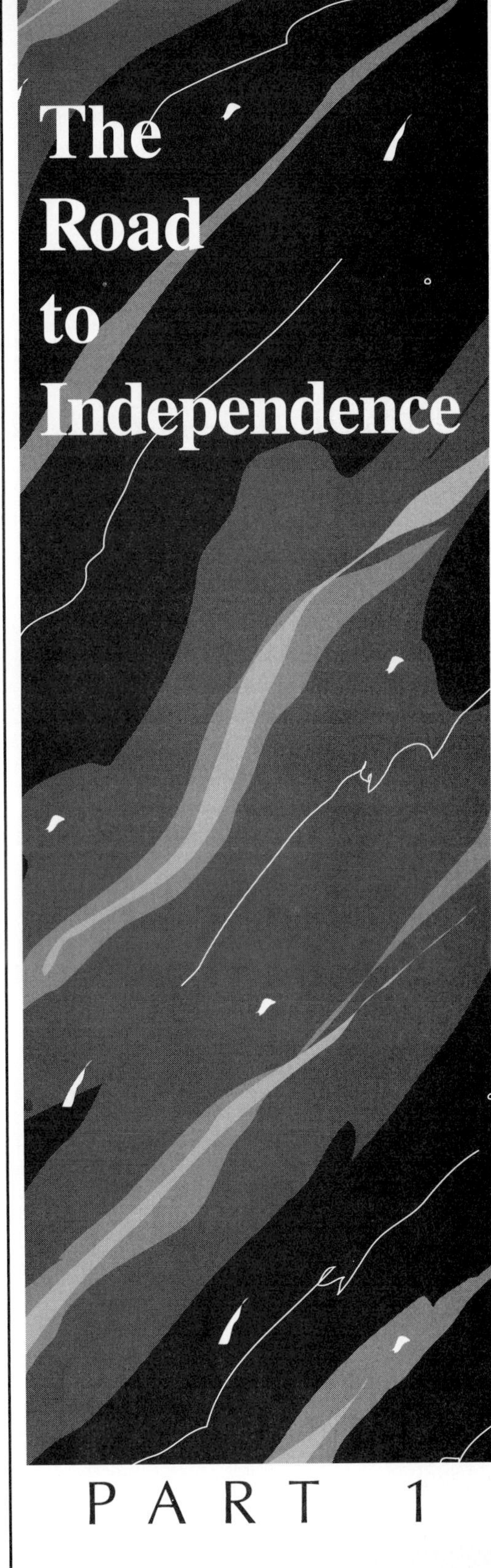

PART 1

CHAPTER 1

From the End of French Rule to Rebellion —1759-1837

1. Introduction
   A. Termination of French Rule, 1763
   B. British Military Rule, 1759-1764
2. Royal Proclamation, 1763
   A. "Settled" and "Conquered" Colonies
   B. "Prerogative" and "Statutory" Constitutions
   C. The Royal Proclamation (and Instructions): Main Provisions
3. Quebec Act, 1774
   A. Main Provisions
   B. Reactions
   C. Consequences
4. Constitutional Act, 1791: Beginning Representative Government
   A. Main Provisions
   B. Reactions
   C. Consequences
5. Rebellions in Lower Canada and Upper Canada, 1837
   A. The Problems in General
   B. Lower Canada
      (i) Racial
      (ii) Economic
      (iii) Political
   C. Upper Canada
      (i) Religious
      (ii) Economic
      (iii) Political

1. INTRODUCTION

A. Termination of French Rule, 1763

By the end of the seventeenth century Britain possessed its colonies along the Atlantic seaboard and, through the Hudson's Bay Company, the lands draining into Hudson Bay. France controlled New France (the territory between these two British possessions from the Atlantic Ocean west to the Mississippi River and south to the Gulf of Mexico), some territory west of the Mississippi, Isle St. Jean (renamed Prince Edward Island in 1799), and Cape Breton Island. Newfoundland and the land south of James Bay were disputed territory. See Map 1.

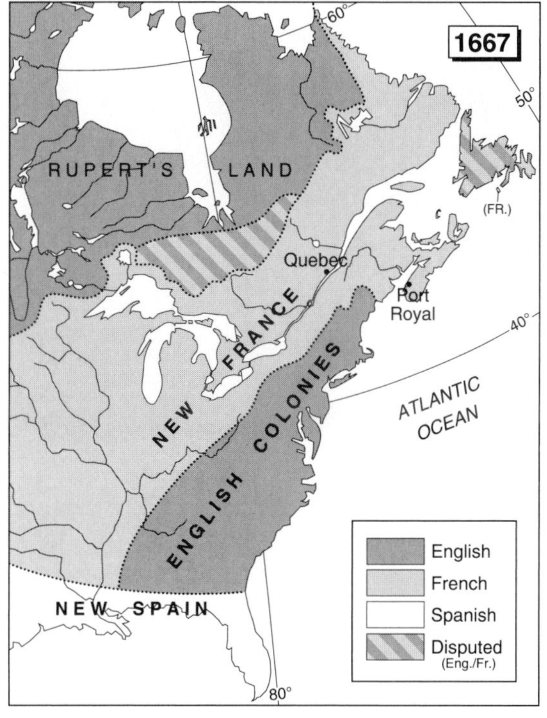

MAP 1

The beginning of the end for France in North America came in 1713 when the Treaty of Utrecht ended the War of the Spanish Succession (Queen Anne's War). By this Treaty, Britain received the Nova Scotia peninsula (although dispute continued over what is now New Brunswick), Newfoundland (along whose north and northeast shores France retained fishing rights), and the islands of St. Pierre and Miquelon off Newfoundland's southern coast. Dispute continued over the boundary between Britain's Hudson Bay region and France's St. Lawrence-Great Lakes territory. See Map 2.

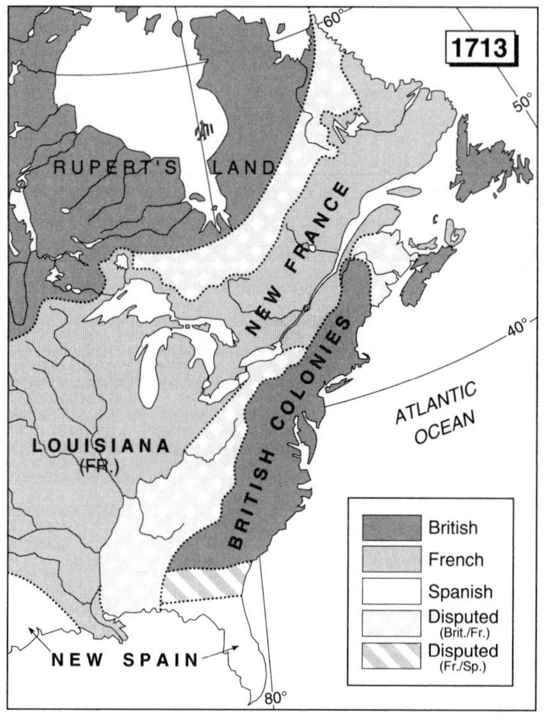

MAP 2

The fall of the towns of Quebec and Montreal to British forces in 1759 and 1760 heralded the virtual end of French rule in North America. This loss was confirmed by the 1763 Treaty of Paris ending the Seven Years' War (known in North America as the French and Indian War). France ceded to Britain all lands in northeast North America—New France, Prince Edward Island, Cape Breton Island (which had fallen in 1758), present-day New Brunswick, and other adjacent islands. France retained her Newfoundland fishing rights under the Treaty of Utrecht, and regained possession of St. Pierre and Miquelon which were to be used as fishing bases and therefore to remain unfortified. In addition, France ceded Louisiana (its territory west of the Mississippi River) to Spain, and (with Spain) land including Florida east of that river to Britain.

B. British Military Rule, 1759-1764

Because New France technically remained French territory until the 1763 Treaty of Paris, Britain established a military administrative system under General Amherst to govern the new possession during the interim following the actual collapse of the French regime.

The Articles of Capitulation[1] which were approved when Montreal surrendered applied to the entire colony and provided for, among other things, "the free exercise of the Catholic, Apostolic and Roman religion." With respect to the legal system the French governor requested that the conquered peoples "continue to be governed according to the custom of Paris, and the laws and usages established for this country, and . . . not be subject to any imposts than those which were established under the French Dominions." General Amherst's reply that the conquered peoples "become subjects of the king" implied that, pending expression of the king's will to the contrary, the laws especially as between subjects would remain as they were—that is, French-Canadian.

During this brief period of military rule there was a deliberate attempt to minimize any dislocation of the social system, including the seigneurial system and the priests' collection of the tithe (although the latter was not enforced by law).

2. ROYAL PROCLAMATION, 1763

Before discussing this first constitutional document it is desirable to note the important distinction between "settled" and "conquered" colonies, and between "prerogative" and "statutory" constitutions.

A. "Settled" and "Conquered" Colonies

Settled colonies were regarded as extensions of Britain in the sense that British subjects took their rights under the common law with them when they moved to the colonies. Among the most cherished of these rights was that to an elected assembly and, therefore, to approve taxes for local purposes. The inhabitants of conquered colonies, on the other hand, had no such rights. The precise nature of their government, therefore, including the rights of the inhabitants, was determined after the conquest. By 1763, all of the American colonies except New York (which had been conquered from Holland) were "settled." Nova Scotia (which by the Proclamation included Cape Breton Island, New Brunswick, and Prince Edward Island) and Newfoundland were also regarded as settled for constitutional purposes, notwithstanding the struggle between Britain and France over some of these lands and, in some cases, obviously prior French settlement.

B. "Prerogative" and "Statutory" Constitutions

The establishment of governments in British colonies, whether the colonies had been acquired by settlement or conquest, required action either by the monarch and privy council or by Parliament. The colonial constitutions were, therefore, either prerogative or statutory. By the end of the seventeenth century there was no doubt about the constitutional supremacy of Parliament over the monarch. Nevertheless, the monarch's prerogative powers continued to exist to the extent that Parliament chose not to interfere. For a long time after the 1688 Glorious Revolution, one such area of non-interference was the establishment and supervision of colonial governments. Once granted by means of the prerogative, however, constitutional rights could be removed only by an Act of Parliament.

C. The Royal Proclamation (and Instructions)

One of these prerogative Constitutions was the Royal Proclamation, issued by King George III on October 7, 1763, eight months after the signing of the Treaty of Paris. This Proclamation created the colony of Quebec (formerly part of New France) and substituted civil for military authority. James Murray, lieutenant governor in command of the town of Quebec during the period of military rule, became the first civil governor. He received his Instructions in December and took command on August 10, 1764. Because of their importance the Instructions should be included with the Royal Proclamation itself as the first Constitution.

The main provisions of these documents are as follows:[2]

(1) The boundaries of the new colony were as shown on Map 3. Basically, Quebec included most of the land draining north and south into the St. Lawrence River (although not quite to the headwaters in the north). The colony's western border was approximately the Ottawa River and a line extending southeast from Montreal; its eastern border was the St. John River and a line extending south past Anticosti Island to the Gaspé Peninsula. Territory north and west of Quebec which had been part of New France was declared to be Indian territory into which settlement was prohibited and within which trade was regulated.

(2) The government of the Colony was located in the town of Quebec and consisted of an appointed governor and his executive council. Because councillors were required to take an oath of loyalty to the king as "defender of the faith" it was certain that no Roman Catholics would be appointed.

(3) An elected assembly—i.e., representative government—was promised for Quebec "so soon as the state and circumstances of the . . . [Colony] will admit thereof," presumably after the anticipated large influx of British settlers was realized.

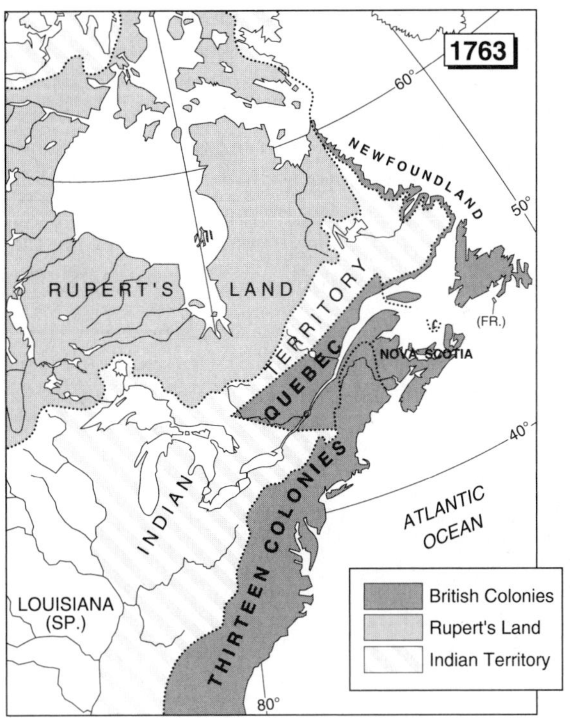

MAP 3

(4) The governor of Quebec was empowered to create courts for hearing both civil and criminal cases "according to Law and Equity, and as near as may be agreeable to the laws of England." Appeal to the British privy council in civil cases was permitted.

(5) The extent of religious freedom for Quebec's Roman Catholics was stated somewhat ambiguously. The promise contained in the Articles of Capitulation has already been noted. This promise was repeated in the Treaty of Paris with the added commitment that the king would "give the most precise and most effectual orders" to ensure religious freedom "as far as the laws of Great Britain permit." The Proclamation was silent on the matter but in his Instructions, Murray was reminded of the earlier commitment. However, the ambiguous nature of Britain's attitude toward Catholics was also evidenced in the Instructions by the requirement that all Catholics, from time to time "as You [Murray] shall think proper, and in the Manner You shall think least alarming and inconvenient to the said [Catholic] Inhabitants, deliver in upon Oath an exact Account of all Arms and Ammunition, of every Sort in their actual Possession." Furthermore, the governor was enjoined "not to admit of any Ecclesiastical Jurisdiction of the See of Rome, or any other foreign Ecclesiastical Jurisdiction whatsoever in the Province."

(6) The governor of Quebec was to take steps to encourage the establishment of the Church of England "both in Principles and Practice."

(7) Prince Edward and Cape Breton islands were joined to Nova Scotia which, as Britain had asserted since the Treaty of Utrecht, included what is now New Brunswick.

(8) The coast of Labrador from the St. John River to Hudson Strait, as well as the islands of Anticosti and Magdalen, were annexed to Newfoundland.

Governor Murray attempted to administer Quebec with as little disruption to its customs as possible, so it was but a matter of time before conflict developed between him and the English merchants. The seigneurial system presented no immediate problem; indeed, some merchants purchased seigneuries. However, in his attempt to conciliate the French inhabitants, Murray decided that the summoning of an assembly (which at that time would exclude Catholics) was inappropriate. Furthermore, he applied French law where possible, permitted Catholic lawyers to practice before the courts, and Catholics to serve on juries inasmuch as their exclusion "would constitute 200 Protestants perpetual judges over the lives and property of . . . 80,000 of the new subjects."[3]

Murray's respect for the orderliness of French society grew, and he suggested that the French were "perhaps the bravest and best race upon the globe, a race, who could they be indulged with a few privileges which the laws of England deny to Roman Catholics at home, would soon get the better of every national antipathy to their conquerors and become the most faithful and useful set of men in this American Empire."[4] But in June 1766 the merchants succeeded in causing Murray's recall and his replacement by Guy Carleton.

Although initially hostile to Murray and his methods, Carleton almost immediately developed Murray's admiration for the French and he came to believe that Quebec required special treatment as a unique colony within the Empire. The local situation was in his view more important than British institutions. In spite of renewed pressure from Britain that the Proclamation's promise of an assembly and British law be implemented immediately, and in spite of suggestions in Britain that Quebec Roman Catholics no longer be excluded from holding office, Carleton reported that "the better sort of Canadians fear nothing more than popular assemblies, which, they conceive, tend only to render the people refractory and insolent." Furthermore, he opined prophetically, Quebec's "long inhospitable winters" ensured that, contrary to the Proclamation's assumption, and "barring catastrophe shocking to think of, this country must, to the end of time, be peopled by the Canadian [i.e., French] race, who already have taken such firm root, and got to so great a height, that any new stock transplanted will be totally hid, and imperceptible among them, except in the towns of Quebec and Montreal."[5]

In view of growing uneasiness in the Thirteen Colonies, Carleton believed that Britain's essential task was to ensure the loyalty of Quebec's natural leaders—the clergy and seigneurs—and therefore to strengthen the customs of Quebec rather than to implement representative government and British laws. Only the British Parliament, however, not the Crown through the prerogative, could revoke the promises made in the 1763 Proclamation.

3. QUEBEC ACT, 1774

Parliament heeded Carleton's suggestions and in June 1774 passed the Quebec Act. This Act was explicit recognition that the anticipated large influx of British settlers was unlikely to occur and that Quebec's population would for the foreseeable future remain predominantly French and Roman Catholic. The Act was designed to ensure that population's loyalty to Britain, or at least its neutrality, in the event of hostility between the mother country and the Thirteen Colonies. Britain assumed that if the clergy and seigneurs were satisfied they would keep the general population under control.

A. Main Provisions[6]

(1) The 1763 Proclamation (insofar as it applied to Quebec) and the governor's Instructions were revoked as of May 1, 1775. They had been found, "upon Experience, to be inapplicable to the State and Circumstances" of the Colony and especially to the Catholic population.

(2) The boundaries of the "Province of Quebec" were extended north to the boundary of Hudson's Bay Company land (basically, to the headwaters of rivers flowing north into Hudson and James bays); west and south to the confluence of the Ohio and Mississippi rivers (although some ambiguity existed as to whether the boundary extended due north from the confluence, or northward along the Mississippi River); and east to include Labrador and the Gulf islands of Anticosti and Magdalen. See Map 4.

(3) Government continued to rest in the hands of an appointed governor and his executive council. However, a special oath of "Allegiance to His Majesty King George" which Catholics were to take made possible the appointment of Catholics to the council. All laws were subject to disallowance by the British government.

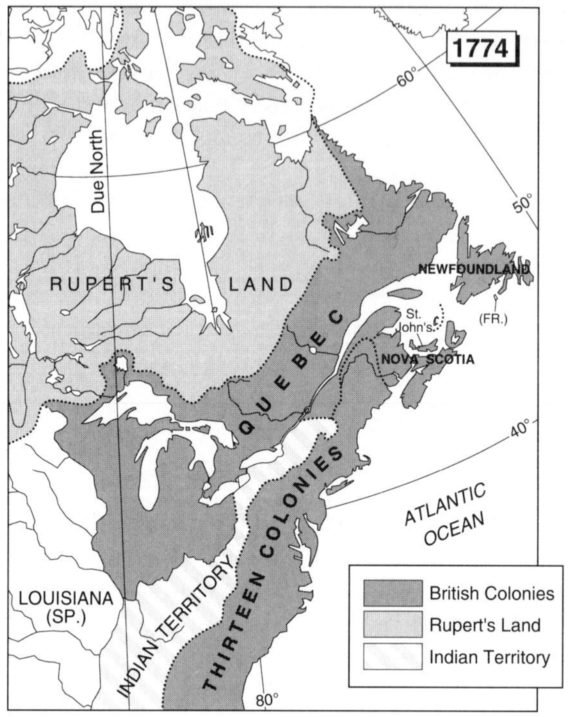

MAP 4

(4) Representative government was rejected as being "at present inexpedient."

(5) Criminal law remained British because of its "Certainty and Lenity . . . and the Benefits and Advantages" resulting from it. Civil law remained French-Canadian.

(6) The seigneurial system was retained, permitting the seigneurs to collect their dues.

(7) Roman Catholics were permitted to "have, hold, and enjoy, the free Exercise of . . . [their] Religion," and the Catholic clergy could "hold, receive, and enjoy, their accustomed Dues and Rights."

(8) Provision was made for the "Encouragement of the Protestant Religion, and for the Maintenance and Support of a Protestant Clergy"—i.e., the tithe.

B. Reactions

Reaction to the Quebec Act was predictable. The English merchants in Quebec were pleased with the westward boundary extension and its implication for the fur trade, but they felt betrayed by the repudiation of British institutions, especially representative government. Governor Carleton ignored the flexibility provided by his Instructions, including the introduction of Habeas Corpus and British civil law in certain instances, which might have conciliated Quebec's English population.

The clergy and seigneurs were comfortable with the basically authoritarian system which the Act perpetuated. Obviously, these leaders could not be expected to be sympathetic toward a concept of political equality. They also supported provisions for the collection of the tithe and feudal dues.

The reaction of the habitants to the Quebec Act is a matter of dispute.[7] Dawson states that the Act was "warmly approved by the French Canadians." McInnis maintains that it reflected an overestimation by Carleton of both the leaders' influence and the habitants' submissiveness, that it left the habitants "in many cases . . . sullen and resentful," and that "it nearly led to the loss" of Quebec. Hilda Neatby suggests that surviving evidence is too fragmentary to determine the general views of the population, and that differing interpretations of that evidence are therefore inevitable.

The Quebec Act was one aspect of a broader controversy between Britain and the Thirteen Colonies. The collapse of the French Empire in North America had removed an immediate threat to those Colonies. This fact coupled with several irritants strengthened the growing desire for total independence. These irritants included the strictures of a mercantile system which the Thirteen Colonies had outgrown, and the imposition of colonial taxes by a British Parliament in which the colonists had no representation. The most famous of these taxes were those levied pursuant to the 1765 Stamp Act (repealed the following year)—one of the so-called "Intolerable Acts."

The Quebec Act, also "Intolerable," accentuated this conflict between Britain and the older colonies. Not only did Quebec's new boundary restrict expansion, but the Act's explicit repudiation of representative government was viewed as an omen of possible tighter British control over the Thirteen Colonies. In fact, Britain did attribute its colonial problems to excessive leniency. Furthermore, the concessions the Act made to the Catholic Church were interpreted by the Thirteen Colonies as an additional threat. The American Congress protested to Britain the protection of "a religion that has deluged our island in blood and dispersed impiety, bigotry, persecution, murder and rebellion through every part of the world."[8]

Although Quebec's French population may not have been enthusiastic about their new Constitution they did not support the American colonists in their Revolution. Rather, they remained basically neutral, for their identity would surely have been submerged were Quebec to become part of an independent American political system. In Carleton's words, "I think there is nothing to fear from them, while we are in a state of prosperity, and nothing to hope for when in distress."[9] The English merchants were anxious to defend Quebec's economy against the threat of American control; furthermore, that economy was still benefitting from the protection of the mercantile system which the older colonies to the south had outgrown.

Nova Scotia, also, rejected rebellion in favour of neutrality in spite of its close economic and family ties with New England. Nova Scotians had grievances, but theirs were different from those to the south. The benefits of the Imperial connection outweighed the burdens.

The Treaty of Paris signed by Britain and the new United States on September 3, 1783, revised the boundary between Quebec and the new country. The significant change was westward from the source of the St. Lawrence River, where the new border followed the middle of lakes Erie, Ontario, Huron, and Superior—basically, the present boundary between Canada and the United States. Britain thus relinquished the bulk of what had once been Indian territory. See Map 5.

By the Treaty of Versailles signed the same day between Britain and France (who had supported the American Revolution), France's ownership of St. Pierre and Miquelon became unconditional and her fishing rights along the Newfoundland coast were shifted to the west.

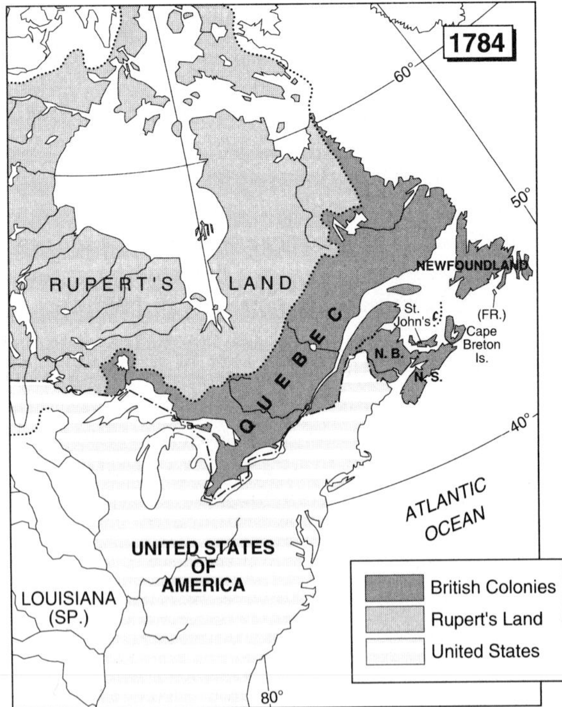

MAP 5

C. Consequences

The main impact of the American Revolution on the constitutional development of the much shrunken British North America resulted from the influx of United Empire Loyalists to Nova Scotia and Quebec. In the Maritimes many of these immigrants settled in the New Brunswick part of Nova Scotia. There was no need for the new arrivals to agitate for their accustomed British institutions inasmuch as these already existed in Nova Scotia and continued after New Brunswick was separated in 1784.

In Quebec the Loyalists were concentrated west of the Ottawa River and the new immigrants lost no time demanding British institutions. This particular concentration of Loyalist settlement enabled the British Parliament to accede to these demands, while at the same time to continue accommodating the French Canadians in the east. In 1791 the Constitutional Act divided Quebec into the two separate colonies of Upper Canada in the west and Lower Canada in the east. However, the English merchants in Montreal, as well as the Loyalists who settled in the east (notably in what are known as the Eastern Townships located south of the St. Lawrence River between Montreal and Quebec City), were not so fortunate as those in the west, inasmuch as they were to remain with the French majority in Lower Canada.

Governor Haldimand (who succeeded Carleton in 1778) questioned whether the Loyalists really wanted the repeal of the Quebec Act: "I have great reason to believe these unfortunate people have suffered too much by committees and houses of assembly, to have retained any prepossession in favour of that mode of government, and that they have no reluctance to live under the constitution established by law for this country."[10]

Carleton, upon his return in 1786 as Lord Dorchester and governor-in-chief of all British North America, also opposed the extension of British institutions and the division of Quebec. Such developments, he asserted, would not be in the interests of the great majority of the population. The main agitation for change came, he said, from the commercial interests in Quebec and Montreal. He maintained, no doubt correctly, that the seigneurs and clergy opposed change; and that the habitants, "having little or no education, are unacquainted with the nature of the question." As for the Loyalists in the west, they "are as yet unprepared for any organization, superior to that of a county."[11]

It is important to note that although the merchants and Loyalists both desired an assembly, a freehold land system, and British law, their economic interests were disparate. Whereas the merchants sought free importation of staples from the United States, the settlers resented this competition. Furthermore, the settlers wanted assistance in the building of roads, schools, and churches—issues of no particular concern to the merchants.

4. CONSTITUTIONAL ACT, 1791: BEGINNING REPRESENTATIVE GOVERNMENT

The opinions of Haldimand and Lord Dorchester were ignored by the British Parliament which concluded that the Quebec Act was now unworkable to govern two societies having such different cultures.

The Constitutional Act, passed on June 10, 1790, and effective December 26, 1791, was the first grant of representative government by the British Parliament. Similar grants to other British colonies had been made by the king—that is, they were parts of prerogative constitutions.

A. Main Provisions[12]

(1) The Act stated the king's intention, which was implemented by order-in-council dated August 24, 1791, to divide the Province of Quebec into two colonies named Upper Canada and Lower Canada. This division occurred along the Ottawa River (see Map 6) although a small area west of Montreal was placed within Lower Canada because of the existing seigneurial system of land tenure. Although not mentioned in the Act, the seats of government were Newark (now Niagara-on-the-Lake) and Quebec. York (now Toronto) became the capital of Upper Canada in 1793.

(2) The executive branch of government within each province was headed by an appointed lieutenant governor although the governor-in-chief of British North America usually performed the functions of lieutenant governor of Lower Canada. (The general term "governor" will be used in this discussion except when the distinction between governor and lieutenant governor is important.) There was also an executive council whose members were appointed by the governor, usually for life although the Act specified no term of office. The Act repealed the provisions of the Quebec Act relating to the executive council.

(3) The legislative branch within each province was bicameral and consisted of an appointed council, and an assembly elected for a term of four years but subject to earlier dissolution by the governor. Annual sessions of the legislature were required. The Act provided for life appointment of councillors who also had to be at least 21 years old. Although provision was made for a hereditary peerage it was never implemented. The minimum age for voting and election to the assembly was 21. The franchise included a modest property qualification although none existed for members of the assembly. Furthermore, although not stated in the Act, voting was restricted to males.

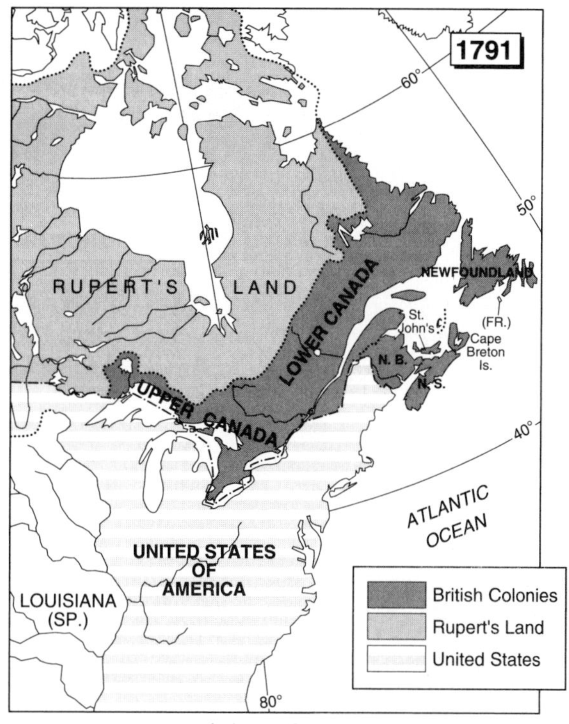

MAP 6

(4) An oath of allegiance to the king "as lawful Sovereign" was require of all members before they could take their seats in either house the legislature. Nothing in the oath precluded membership by Catl olics.

(5) The governor was empowered to give royal assent to legislation, withhold such assent, or to reserve legislation "for the significatic of his Majesty's pleasure thereon." Bills given royal assent were ne ertheless subject to disallowance by the king-in-council within tw years, and bills reserved were not effective unless and until the received royal assent within two years. Sections 55, 56, and 57 of tl 1867 Constitution Act contain similar provisions.

(6) British criminal law applied within both provinces as it had und the Quebec Act. British civil law was optional; Upper Canada adop ed it immediately whereas Lower Canada retained French civil law

(7) The freehold system of land tenure was prescribed for Upper Can da and was made optional with the seigneurial system for futu land grants in Lower Canada.

(8) An amount equal to one-seventh of all land grants to individuals i each province was to be set aside "for the Support and Maintenan of a Protestant Clergy." As will be noted later, the term "Protesta Clergy" was subject to differing interpretations following passage the Act. Indeed, that term may have been deliberately chosen by Parliament to shift to the colonies the inevitable controversy surrounding the distribution of these lands.

(9) The rights of the Catholic Church which had been guaranteed by the Quebec Act were reaffirmed.

The structure of the executive and legislative branches of government created by the Constitutional Act resembled that of our present government; however, there is no *functional* analogy inasmuch as responsible government was in 1791 still a long way off.

Executive: Governor, from Britain and appointed by the British government. This official corresponds to our governor general who now is a Canadian appointed by the Queen of Canada upon our prime minister's advice.
Executive council, appointed locally by the governor. This body corresponds to our ministry (in reality, the cabinet headed by the prime minister) which is appointed by the governor general and (except for the prime minister) upon the prime minister's advice.

Legislature: Legislative council, appointed locally by the governor. This body corresponds to our Senate whose members are appointed by the governor general upon the prime minister's advice.
Assembly, elected on the basis of a wide franchise. The assembly corresponds to our House of Commons.

B. Reactions

Although the granting of representative government was a liberalizing move, it was balanced by additional authoritarian elements such as the appointed legislative council. An inherent conservatism of the French in Lower Canada and the Loyalists in Upper Canada, coupled with a fear of the United States, created at least an acquiescence in the new Constitution provided that authoritarianism was not carried too far. The English merchants in Montreal and Quebec, however, were very disappointed. They had long demanded British institutions but now, although they would have influence in the executive and legislative councils, they would be in a perpetual minority in the assembly they had striven to achieve.

C. Consequences

Paradoxically, although the Constitutional Act was apparently intended to persuade the French Canadians of the superiority of British institutions and therefore to assimilate British culture, it had the opposite effect. By the time Upper Canada and Lower Canada were united in 1841, assimilation was no longer a possibility. The legacy of the Constitutional Act was the abortive 1837 rebellions in the two provinces, the consequent investigation by Lord Durham, and our next Constitution—the Union Act. It is to that legacy that we now turn.

5. REBELLIONS IN LOWER CANADA AND UPPER CANADA, 1837

A. The Problems in General

Within both provinces the main cause of discontent was friction between those who possessed real authority in government and those who did not possess it but thought they should. The Constitutional Act had created a government structure which in fact assured domination by the leaders of society—those in commerce, the hierarchy of the Church of England, and the appointed members of government. The governor was from Britain and, of course, appointed by the British government. Members of the executive council were appointed by, and to advise, the governor who was free to accept or reject their advice. Members of the legislative council, also governor appointees, comprised an upper house somewhat analogous to our Senate except that they not only held, but also frequently exercised, veto power over legislation coming from the elected assembly.

What this government structure meant was that the people were given a formal arena—the assembly—to discuss how they would like to govern, but were denied the power to ensure the implementation of their wishes. In the later words of Lord Durham, "It is difficult to understand how any English statesmen could have imagined that representative and irresponsible government could be successfully combined."[13] With specific reference to Lower Canada it has been bluntly stated that "the system of government . . . could not have been more skillfully contrived to promote friction if such had been its design. Under it, only one result was possible: 1837 was implicit in 1791."[14]

It may well be that the vast majority of the population lacked a clear appreciation of and an interest in the abstract notion of "responsible government." Responsible government would have meant that the governor would choose his advisers (the executive council) from those who could command the support of the assembly, that he would change his advisers when that support was withdrawn, and that he would accept the advice given him. (This constitutional principle is discussed in Chapter 4.) However, the people were very much aware of and interested in the practical significance of "irresponsible" government when their wishes were rejected by the oligarchies who controlled the two provincial governments. These oligarchies were known as the Château Clique in Lower Canada and the Family Compact in Upper Canada.

Sir Francis Bond Head, governor of Upper Canada before the Rebellion, defended the Compact in 1839:

> The "family compact" of Upper Canada is composed of those members of its society who, either by their abilities and character have been honoured by the confidence of the executive government, or who, by their industry and intelligence, have amassed wealth. The party, I own, is comparatively a small one; but to put the multitude at the top and the few at the bottom is a radical reversion of the pyramid of society which every reflecting man must foresee can end only by its downfall.[15]

In a very real sense the nub of the problem was control of the public purse and, therefore, of public policy. This is not surprising, for it is well known that "the one who pays the piper calls the tune." As had been the case in Britain when Parliament struggled for power with the Tudor and Stuart monarchs, so also in the two Canadas: as long as the governor and his supporters in government had access to sufficient revenue to function without having to turn to the assembly for public funds they could govern with impunity. But if the assembly could refuse to vote funds and thereby force the executive to accede to the demands of the people as expressed through their elected representatives, then the assembly could take control of public policy.

Total control of the public purse was not, however, available to the Canadian assemblies at this time. The British government maintained that responsible government was incompatible with the proper relationship between a colony and the mother country inasmuch as a governor could hardly be responsible to both the colonial assembly and London. In his report following the 1837 Rebellions, Lord Durham addressed the issue of responsible government and recommended a solution to the apparent inconsistency which troubled the British government. According to Durham the governor could be responsible to the assembly in local matters while retaining subordination to Britain in Imperial affairs.

B. Lower Canada

It is convenient to discuss the problems within Lower Canada between 1791 and 1837 in terms of racial, economic, and political factors. (The term "race" is used in its customary sense in Canadian history to mean either the French or English cultural group.) Although these factors are considered independently of each other it will be seen that in fact they combined in a struggle essentially between the same two peoples.

(i) Racial: In one sense the racial (or cultural) differences were not themselves a major source of friction in Lower Canada, because on an individual basis the French and English got along well with each other although contact was infrequent. It was the implications that these differences, reflective of entirely different ways of life, had for the economic and the political development of the province that was of great significance, especially because the French greatly outnumbered the English.

(ii) Economic: The economic conflict mirrored the cultural differences. Whereas the French outlook was agricultural, conservative, and reflective of a static society, the English outlook was highly commercial and aggressive. One manifestation of this difference related to immigration. The English sought to encourage the influx of settlers, whereas the French viewed immigration as a threat to their culture. To the French, Lower Canada was already settled.

The best example of the divergence of economic interests related to improvement of the St. Lawrence waterway. The desire of the Montreal merchants, who with those in Quebec comprised the majority of the English population, to use public funds for waterway improvements was opposed by the French on the grounds that only the merchants would benefit. The importance of a navigable Canadian waterway, even though it would be closed for almost half of each year, grew with the competition from the all-winter port of New York. In 1823 that port was linked via the Erie Canal and Hudson River to the United States and Upper Canadian mid-west.

(iii) Political: The absence of responsible government might have been less volatile in Lower Canada than it was west of the Ottawa River because the French Canadians were generally politically apathetic and lacked experience with representative government. Both of these features were traceable to the absolutism of French rule during the Old Regime preceding the fall of New France. However, history demonstrates the ability of French Canadians to turn British institutions to their nationalistic purpose even when they lack the political culture within which these institutions originally developed. In Lower Canada the differences between the oligarchy and the assembly comprised a dichotomy much more fundamental than that in Upper Canada, for underlying the political conflict were the cultural differences of language, religion, law, and basic outlook on life. The Château Clique was predominantly English; a majority of the assembly were French. Within Lower Canada, therefore, the assembly became the focal point for the preservation of French culture.

A word of caution is nevertheless required. As noted at the beginning of this section on Lower Canada it is reasonably accurate and certainly convenient to portray the struggle, whether in racial, economic, or political terms, as one between two homogeneous groups. On the one hand was the conservative, static, agricultural, Catholic, French, represented by the assembly; on the other hand was the aggressive, commercial, Church of England, English, represented by the governor and the two appointed councils. In reality, however, because the Catholic Church had been well treated by the British government, and in view of its own essentially authoritarian form of government, some of the

Catholic hierarchy supported the English oligarchy and warned against the sin of rebellion. In this sense it may be said that "the Quebec Act saved the situation in 1837-1838."[16] Furthermore, some of the English within the Château Clique sympathized with the aspirations of the more moderate French reformers.

Louis Joseph Papineau emerged as the leader of the French Canadians. He was first elected to the assembly in 1812 when he was 26 years old, and he and his followers won a majority in every general election between 1815 and 1837. Papineau was able to strive for responsible government because he was familiar with the thinking of the eighteenth century French philosophers, he understood the principles of the British parliamentary system, and he was Speaker of the assembly almost continuously from 1815 until the Rebellion. Only under responsible government could he achieve his ultimate goal of a strengthened French Canadian culture, for with responsible government the governor would have to choose his advisers from men who supported the will of the assembly with its French majority. Papineau's tactic was to control public finances by refusing to vote funds for salaries and other government expenses. In this effort he was thwarted by the executive's independent control of large amounts of revenue, especially the customs duties under the Quebec Revenue Act passed by the British Parliament in 1774.

Relations between the Château Clique and the assembly steadily deteriorated, and in 1834 the assembly adopted the "Ninety-two Resolutions" which included all of its demands and grievances. In terms of the structure and functioning of government these demands included responsible government, complete assembly control of revenue, and an elected legislative council. However, the extreme and emotional nature of some of the Resolutions alienated Papineau from the moderate reformers. One such reformer made this comment about the Resolutions: "Eleven stood true; six contained both truth and falsehood; sixteen stood wholly false; seventeen stood doubtful; twelve were ridiculous; seven were repetitions; fourteen consisted only of abuse; four were false and seditious; and five were good or indifferent."[17]

The generally tense atmosphere coupled with Britain's rejection of even the more moderate demands for reform precipitated two or three armed clashes in November and December of 1837. This "rebellion," if such it may be called, was without plan, without leadership (Papineau had fled to the United States), without popular support because of the uncertainty of the future position of the Catholic Church under a new regime, and a military failure.

C. Upper Canada

As in the eastern colony so too in Upper Canada, conflict had several foci but ultimately involved the same two groups—the oligarchy and the people as represented in the assembly. The issues were religious, economic, and political. Because virtually the entire population was English there was no "racial" struggle.

(i) Religious: Among the protestant churches in Upper Canada only the Church of England could own property and, until 1831, solemnize marriage. Furthermore, that Church also sought to control education. To the inevitable conflict between the Anglicans and other protestant groups that this situation caused, was added the problem of the Clergy Reserves set aside under the terms of the Constitutional Act for the benefit of the "Protestant Clergy." Predictably, the Church of England claimed the Reserves for themselves even though their numbers were few in relation to other denominations. The Methodists, by 1825 the most numerous denomination, led the struggle against the Church of England. The chief protagonists were Anglican Bishop Strachan, a member of both the executive and legislative councils, and Methodist Egerton Ryerson. The Reserves issue was not settled until 1854 when legislation, intended "to remove all semblance of connexion between Church and State," provided that proceeds from the sale of Clergy Reserves would go to the municipalities after the deduction of pensions for existing clergy.[18]

The economic aspect of this struggle was that the Reserves, consisting of small 200-acre lots scattered throughout the developing parts of the province, remained undeveloped and thus a hindrance to Upper Canada's economic growth.

(ii) Economic: The two main issues involved in this conflict were, on the one hand, the divergence of the economic interests of the pioneer settler and the commercial class, and on the other hand, the "system" (if such a term is appropriate) of land grants. Whereas the ruling oligarchy were primarily interested in canals and commerce, and therefore in spending public funds for these purposes, the settlers' main interest was agricultural and local. The settlers were anxious to gain clear title to their land, to have churches, adequate roads, and schools with qualified teachers.

There was, in fact, no land policy. Large grants of land, as much as several thousand acres each, were given to members of the Compact and their friends. These lands were held for speculative purposes, not settlement and the plough. When the undeveloped Clergy Reserves (perhaps two million acres by 1825) and an equal area of Crown land are also considered, one can readily understand the population sparsity and the consequent frustration of the individual settler with his small lot struggling under a heavy tax burden for roads, churches, and schools. Coupled with this situation was the difficulty faced by the settler coping with red tape in his attempt to secure clear title to his land.

(iii) Political: William Lyon Mackenzie, who came to Canada from Scotland in 1820 when he was 25 years old, emerged as the radical reform leader. In 1824 he established the Colonial Advocate in which he charged that the Family Compact "mould . . . [the governor], like wax, to their will; they fill every office with their relatives, dependants and partisans; . . . they are Paymasters, Receivers, Auditors, King, Lords and Commons!" He claimed, furthermore, that the Compact "has no efficient check from this country to guard the people against its acts of tyranny and oppression."[19]

Mackenzie was first elected to the assembly in 1824. He and other reformers formed their first assembly majority following the 1828 election, but their lack of cohesion prevented a unified attack on the oligarchy. Between 1830 and 1835 the Tories—the "establishment" party—held the majority, but a reform majority returned following the 1835 election. A special committee of the assembly produced its "Seventh Report on Grievances" which, while less extreme than Lower Canada's Ninety-two Resolutions, condemned the inability of the assembly to make its wishes effective and demanded an elective legislative council.

An investigation by the British government in response to this Report and the Ninety-two Resolutions led in 1836 to the appointment of Sir Francis Bond Head as the new governor of Upper Canada. The reformers in Upper Canada hoped that Head's appointment of several reformers, including the moderate Robert Baldwin, to the executive council might lead to the acceptance of some of the reformers' demands—perhaps even responsible government. This hope became short-lived when Head refused to be bound by his advisers or even to consult them on important matters. The council thereupon resigned; the assembly voted non-confidence in the new council and for the first time refused to vote funds. Head then dissolved the assembly. In the ensuing election campaign Head damned the reformers as American and republican and therefore disloyal to the Empire. With the aid of open voting and its attendant opportunities for intimidation, Head easily persuaded the electorate to return a Tory majority on the grounds that it was in the people's best interests to remain on good terms with the governor.

In light of these events, together with Britain's rejection of demands for responsible government and an elected legislative council, the radical reformers realized the impossibility of reform by legal means. This frustration, coupled with the skirmishes in Lower Canada, precipitated a short-lived uprising on December 7 which was even less significant militarily than that in Lower Canada. Mackenzie fled to the United States.

The Rebellions were over.

CHAPTER 2

The Struggle for Responsible Government —1838-1849

1. Lord Durham's Report, 1839
   A. Durham's General Attitude
   B. Recommendations
   C. Reactions
2. Union Act, 1840
   A. Main Provisions
   B. Reactions
3. Responsible Government, 1849
   A. Lord Sydenham
   B. Sir Charles Bagot
   C. Sir Charles Metcalfe
   D. Lord Elgin
4. The Maritime Colonies—East and West
   A. Nova Scotia, Including Cape Breton Island
   B. New Brunswick
   C. Prince Edward Island
   D. Newfoundland
   E. British Columbia and Vancouver's Island

1. LORD DURHAM'S REPORT, 1839

"The blood spilled in the Rebellions . . . accomplished what years of verbal protest had failed to do: it brought decisive action from the government in England. When the news arrived, the authorities were surprised and perplexed. If the Rebellions were not directed against the mother country, what was it Canadians wanted?"[1] The ultimate accomplishment of the Rebellions was responsible government, but not for another decade; the immediate "decisive action" was the appointment of John George Lampton, the Earl of Durham, as governor of British North America. In addition to his overall responsibility for Britain's colonies on this continent, and his specific responsibility to govern Lower Canada (there being lieutenant governors in the other colonies), was his more immediate task to investigate the problems that had precipitated the Rebellions in the Canadian provinces.

A. Durham's General Attitude

By an Act of the British Parliament, the government of Lower Canada reverted to a governor and a special appointed council. No alteration was made to the government of Upper Canada. Lord Durham arrived in Canada in May and stayed for five months, all but two weeks of which was spent in Lower Canada. As a liberal, Durham condemned the system of government that had existed in both provinces under the Constitutional Act; as an Englishman, he believed in the superiority of his culture. Both of these characteristics profoundly influenced his recommendations.

Of Lower Canada, Durham said:

> I expected to find a contest between a government and a people: I found two nations warring in the bosom of a single state: I found a struggle, not of principles, but of races . . . . Every contest is one of French and English in the outset, or becomes so ere it has run its course . . . .
>
> The French could not but feel the superiority of English enterprise . . . . They looked upon their rivals with alarm, with jealousy, and finally with hatred. The English repaid them with scorn, which soon also assumed the same form of hatred.[2]

The English, he added, "have the decided superiority of intelligence on their side."[3]

Although Durham supported the aspirations of the French Canadians for self-government he condemned the motivations which were, he asserted, to maintain "an old and stationary society, in a new and progressive world."[4] As a further condemnation he alleged that "there can hardly be conceived a nationality more destitute of all that can invigorate and elevate a people, than that which is exhibited by the descendants of the French in Lower Canada, owing to their retaining their peculiar language and manners. They are a people with no history, and no literature."[5]

Durham did not familiarize himself with the French Canadian point of view, but he nevertheless maintained that domination of liberal institutions by the English population was essential if the threat of another rebellion, this time by the English, was to be avoided. He quoted a Lower Canadian English spokesman who said that "Lower Canada must be English, at the expense, if necessary, of not being *British*."[6] He concluded, therefore, that the French must not be given more power:

> I entertain no doubts as to the national character which must be given to Lower Canada; it must be that of the British Empire; that of the majority of the population of British America; that of the great race which must, in the lapse of no long period of time, be predominant over the whole North American Continent. Without effecting the change so rapidly or so roughly as to shock the feelings and trample on the welfare of the existing generation, it must henceforth be the first and steady purpose of the British Government to establish an English population, with English laws and language, in this Province, and to trust its government to none but a decidedly English legislature.[7]

In Upper Canada, Durham was critical mainly of the corruption of the Family Compact and the lack of development of the Clergy and Crown Reserves and other large land grants held for speculative purposes. He noted the following comment made by the chief agent for emigrants in Upper Canada: "These blocks of wild land place the actual settler in an almost hopeless condition; he can hardly expect, during his lifetime, to see his neighbourhood contain a population sufficiently dense to support mills, schools, post-offices, places of worship, markets or shops; and without these, civilization retrogrades."[8]

B. Recommendations

Durham made the following recommendations to the British government in February 1839.

(i) Union of Upper Canada and Lower Canada: One of his main recommendations was a legislative union of the two Canadian provinces, representation in the new assembly to be based on population. With 400,000 English in Upper Canada, and 150,000 English plus 450,000 French in Lower Canada, an overall English majority in the legislature would be assured. This majority would increase through anticipated immigration. Union would also, once and for all, ensure the submergence of the French: "I have little doubt that the French, when once placed, by the legitimate course of events and the working of natural causes, in a minority, would abandon their vain hopes of nationality."[9]

Durham would have preferred a federal union of all British North America but he recognized that such a recommendation would have been premature and that a federation, with its attendant regional legislatures, would not likely produce the assimilation of the French. Canadian history since Confederation confirms the accuracy of this conclusion. He did suggest, nevertheless, that legislation uniting Upper and Lower Canada provide for the possibility of a wider union within British North America.

(ii) Responsible Government: Durham's second major recommendation was the immediate implementation of responsible government in the united province. Durham believed that

> every purpose of popular control might be combined with every advantage of vesting the immediate choice of advisers in the Crown, were the Colonial Governor to be instructed to secure the co-operation of the Assembly in his policy, by entrusting its administration to such men as could command a majority; and if he were given to understand that he need count on no aid from home in any difference with the Assembly, that should not directly involve the relations between the mother country and the Colony. This change might be effected by a single dispatch containing such instructions. . . . The Governor, if he wished to retain advisers not possessing the confidence of the existing Assembly, might rely on the effect of an appeal to the people, and, if unsuccessful, he might be coerced by a refusal of supplies.[10]

This statement also indicates that Durham believed local self-government could be reconciled with British control of Imperial matters by distinguishing between these two types of issue.

(iii) Other: Durham also recommended that the Constitutional Act's provisions with respect to the Clergy Reserves be repealed thus placing control in the hands of the legislature; that municipal governments be established both to bring government closer to the people and to serve as training for self-government; and that a permanent civil list be granted by the assembly to ensure the independence of the judiciary and to provide salaries for the executive. He also opposed an elective legislative council on the grounds that an appointed body would be a healthy check on the assembly under a system of responsible government.

C. Reactions

The reformers in both provinces applauded Durham's recommendations, especially his call for responsible government. In Lower Canada the French were outraged by Durham's characterization of their culture, and the English rejected responsible government but approved of union which would mean the end of a French-dominated assembly. In Upper Canada, Durham was criticized for spending so little time in that province that he failed to understand the true situation. The Upper Canadian assembly (then with a Tory majority) and councils opposed union in spite of the commercial advantages that union would provide, and the councils opposed responsible government as well.

Britain responded to Durham's Report by sending Poulett Thomson as governor in the fall of 1839 to secure colonial acceptance of union. In Lower Canada, where the assembly was still under suspension, Thomson persuaded the special council appointed by Durham (largely English in composition) to agree to union. In Upper Canada he secured the acquiescence of the assembly, in spite of opposition from the Compact, by promising financial assistance, public works, and equal representation with Lower Canada in the new legislature. He also gave assurance that the new united Canada would assume the debts of both provinces. Upper Canada was virtually bankrupt, largely the result of expenditures on canals, and its annual revenue no more than covered debt charges; Lower Canada was practically debt-free!

The British government was not prepared to accede to Durham's recommendation of responsible government (which was a relatively new development in Britain itself), for they viewed self-government as proposed by Durham to be incompatible with Britain's parliamentary supremacy. Nevertheless, the seed of responsible government seemed to be planted when Lord Russell (the colonial secretary) advised Thomson that

> the importance of maintaining the utmost possible harmony between the policy of the legislature and of the executive government admits of no question, and it will of course be your anxious endeavour to call to your counsels and to employ in the public service those persons who, by their position and character, have obtained the general confidence and esteem of the inhabitants of the province.

Furthermore, "the Governor must only oppose the wishes of the Assembly where the honour of the Crown, or the interests of the empire are deeply concerned." The practice of lifetime appointments for members of the executive council should be discontinued, Russell added, and councillors "be called upon to retire from the public service as often as any sufficient motives of public policy may suggest the expediency of that measure."[11]

These statements notwithstanding, Russell was already on record during Parliament's debate of the Union Bill that he was "not prepared to lay down as a principle . . . for the future government of the colonies, that we ought to subject the Executive there to the same restrictions as prevail in this country." He told Thomson, therefore, that "you will consider yourself precluded from entertaining any proposition on the subject."[12]

2. UNION ACT, 1840

This Act was passed on July 23, 1840, and came into force on February 10, 1841.

A. Main Provisions[13]

(1) Upper Canada and Lower Canada were united as the Province of Canada. Governor Thomson chose Kingston as the seat of government.

(2) The provisions of the Constitutional Act respecting the assembly and legislative council were repealed, as were several miscellaneous

Acts of the British Parliament including those which had provided for a temporary suspension of the constitution in Lower Canada at the time of the Durham mission.

(3) The Act did not actually provide for an executive branch but assumed the continuation of an appointed governor and his executive council.

(4) The legislative branch was bicameral consisting of an appointed council and an elected assembly. Councillors had to be at least 21 years old and were appointed for life, although in 1856 (pursuant to an earlier amendment) their positions became elective with 8-year terms. The assembly, elected for a term of four years but subject to earlier dissolution by the governor, consisted of an equal number of representatives from the two former provinces. This number was initially 42, but was raised to 65 in 1853. Except for the requirement that members own property of at least £500, the laws relating to qualifications for voting and election within the two former provinces continued until such time as they might be altered by the new legislature.

(5) As under the Constitutional Act, provision was made for the governor to assent to bills, to withhold his assent, or to reserve bills for the signification of the Queen's pleasure; and for the British government to disallow legislation.

(6) The legal and judicial systems of the two former provinces remained as before the union, but were subject to change by the new legislature.

(7) Any law altering the Clergy or Crown Reserves, the rights of the Catholic Church, or otherwise affecting freedom of worship, was to be laid before both houses of the British Parliament for at least thirty days (during which time either House could veto the law) before royal assent could be given.

(8) The language of record was English, although no restriction was placed on French as a language of translation or debate. In fact, both languages were used for debate from the first session. An 1848 amendment placed the two languages on an equal footing for purposes of record.

(9) The revenues of Upper and Lower Canada formed a single Consolidated Revenue Fund, and the new Province assumed the public debt of both regions.

(10) The Crown's revenues were assigned to the Consolidated Revenue Fund of the Province. In return, the assembly was to grant a permanent civil list to be drawn from that Fund to cover salaries and pensions of certain specified officials including the governor; as well as salaries and pensions of judges to ensure their independence.

As expected, the Union Act made no mention of responsible government. On the other hand it must be recognized that responsible government has never rested on statutory authority in Britain or Canada but rather has been a matter of convention. During our colonial days all that was necessary to implement this principle were instructions from the Colonial Office or independent action by the governor.

B. Reactions

Understandably, the French were resentful of the pooling of the public debt, the provision for English as the only official language of record, and the equality of representation in the assembly—"a gigantic gerrymander."[14] It should be noted, on the other hand, that equal representation was likely to work to the advantage of the French in the long run when, as Durham had anticipated and for which reason he had urged against equality, the increase in Canada West's English population made that region larger than Canada East.

3. RESPONSIBLE GOVERNMENT, 1849

The decade of the 1840s was characterized in the Province of Canada by a struggle for responsible government. The primary actors in this constitutional struggle were moderate reform leaders Robert Baldwin and Louis-Hippolyte LaFontaine who had broken with the radical Mackenzie and Papineau before the 1837 Rebellions; and governors Poulett Thomson (elevated to Lord Sydenham following his success in securing colonial acceptance of union), Sir Charles Bagot, Sir Charles Metcalfe, and Lord Elgin.

A. Lord Sydenham: October 18, 1839 - September 19, 1841

Carrying union in Upper and Lower Canada was one thing; dealing with the issue of responsible government, given the views and instructions of Lord Russell, was something else. Sydenham's "success" in relation to responsible government was the result of his political skill and abbreviated term as governor, not his resolution of the issue.

Sydenham's first legislative council consisted of twenty-four members and was divided evenly between Canada East and Canada West. Half of the former were French.[15] His executive council (henceforth to be used interchangeably with the more modern term "ministry") were exclusively English and selected from the assembly but not from a single party. Baldwin was for a short time part of the ministry, but he resigned because Sydenham refused to replace some Tories with reformers following the 1841 election of a reform majority, and because the ministry contained no French Canadians. Baldwin believed that a ministry without representation from such a large segment of the population was impractical.

Sydenham, who was in fact his own prime minister, was able to avoid a showdown over responsible government. This was made possible through skillful manoeuvring (including the gerrymandering of the Quebec and Montreal constituencies to favour the English in the 1841 election); through his appointment of moderates such as Baldwin to the two councils; and with the aid of disunity among the reformers, as well as the good will created by the expenditure of some £1,500,000 on public works.[16]

In response to Baldwin's demand for responsible government Sydenham proposed a compromise that the assembly accepted. While stressing the governor's responsibility to Britain, Sydenham acknowledged the right of the legislature to "exercise . . . a constitutional influence over the Executive Departments," and to legislate "upon all matters of internal Government"; he also acknowledged the obligation of the governor to appoint advisers who "possessed . . . the confidence of the representatives of the people, thus affording a guarantee that the well understood wishes and interests of the people, which our Gracious Sovereign has declared shall be the rule of the Provincial Government, will, on all occasions, be faithfully represented and advocated."[17]

Although a compromise, it was nevertheless one further step in the inevitable movement toward responsible government. Sydenham would surely have had to face the issue head on if death had not intervened, the result of a fall from a horse. But Sydenham died believing that "the Union of the two Canada's is fully perfected," and "the future harmonious working of the Constitution . . . secured."[18] To his credit Sydenham did provide a prerequisite of responsible government—a system of departments, each accountable to a member of his ministry, thus making his ministry a true policy-making body.[19]

B. Sir Charles Bagot: January 12, 1842 - March 29, 1843

Instructions from Lord Stanley (who succeeded Russell as colonial secretary) to Bagot echoed those of Russell to Thomson on the matter of responsible government. Nevertheless, when Bagot left office the following year responsible government appeared to be a fact. All that was needed was a test case.

Bagot believed that a successful government required French Canadians in the ministry and that LaFontaine, the leading French Canadian in the assembly, was essential to the maintenance of assembly support. So much for Durham's prediction of assimilation! LaFontaine accepted his appointment only when Bagot reluctantly agreed to the appointment of several other reformers including Baldwin. The British government approved the appointments even more reluctantly.

Baldwin and LaFontaine, who had been brought together by journalist Francis Hincks, agreed that differences of race must be set aside in the common cause of reform. Indeed, after the 1841 election in which Baldwin won two seats in Canada West (a legal possibility at that time) and LaFontaine was defeated in his Canada East constituency, Baldwin resigned one of his seats and LaFontaine was subsequently elected. In the 1842 election Baldwin, defeated in the West, was elected by the French in Canada East.[20]

The new ministry was able to function with assembly support almost as if it had been appointed from a single united party. But what would happen if the governor wished to reject his ministers' advice or if the ministry lost the support of the assembly? This test of responsible government was yet to be faced, but not by Bagot who was forced to retire in ill health.

C. Sir Charles Metcalfe: March 30, 1843 - November 25, 1845

Metcalfe's intention, under Stanley's instructions, was to stem the tide flowing toward responsible government. He would treat his ministers, he said, "with the confidence and cordiality due to the station which they occupy; . . . consult them not only whenever the law or established usage requires that process, but also whenever the importance of the occasion recommends it, and whenever I conceive that the public service will be benefitted by their aid and advice."[21] Nevertheless, although he would consult he would not compromise his authority. Whether in spite of his intention to consult his ministry, or because of his intention to retain control, Metcalfe's rejection of the full implications of responsible government inevitably led to crisis with his reform ministry. This crisis occurred in November 1843 over the distribution of patronage. Metcalfe complained to Stanley:

> I am required to give myself up entirely to the Council; to submit absolutely to their dictation; to have no judgment of my own; to bestow the patronage of the Government exclusively on their partisans; to proscribe their opponents, and to make some public and unequivocal declaration of my adhesion to these conditions, including the complete nullification of Her Majesty's Government.[22]

Metcalfe was clearly unprepared for responsible government and he could not reconcile internal self-government with loyalty to the mother country.

As a result of the conflict Metcalfe's ministry resigned, the assembly voted confidence in that ministry, and following continuous deadlock between the assembly and the governor's new advisers, Metcalfe dissolved the assembly in September of 1844. The resulting election campaign was marked by violence and corruption. The governor, acting as his own party leader and with the aid of intimidation, won a slim majority mainly through his support in Canada West where the reformers were tainted with charges of republicanism and therefore of disloyalty to Britain.

Metcalfe did not have Sydenham's political skills and he returned to Britain in ill health and with the constitutional crisis still unresolved. Indeed, as parties had become even more clearly defined on the constitutional issue the potential crisis was perhaps greater than ever.

D. Lord Elgin: January 20, 1847 - December 18, 1854

Elgin arrived in Canada with the clear intention, and that of Lord Grey who had succeeded Stanley as colonial secretary, of implementing responsible government. (Elgin was Durham's son-in-law; Elgin's wife—Durham's daughter—was Grey's niece; therefore, Grey was Durham's brother-in-law!)

Instructions from Grey to Lieutenant Governor Sir John Harvey of Nova Scotia expressed the changed attitude of the British government. On November 3, 1846, Grey advised Harvey to refrain from "identifying yourself with any one party, but instead of this, making yourself both a mediator and a moderator between the influential of all parties." While not to give "blind obedience" to his ministry Harvey was told to use "sparingly, and with the greatest possible discretion" his power to reject measures submitted to him. Grey acknowledged that such rejection would likely precipitate the ministry's resignation in which case the governor might appeal to the assembly and even to the electorate. However, he added, "concession to their [the ministry's] views must, sooner or later, become inevitable, since it cannot be too distinctly acknowledged that it is neither possible nor desirable to carry on the government of any of the British provinces in North America in opposition to the opinion of the inhabitants."[23] Finally, lest any doubt might have remained, Grey told Harvey on March 31, 1847: "It appears to me that the peculiar circumstances of Nova Scotia present no insuperable obstacle to the immediate adoption of that system of parliamentary government which has long prevailed in the mother country, and which seems to be a necessary part of representative institutions in a certain stage of their progress."[24]

Lord Elgin as governor-in-chief of British North America received similar instructions. It is not surprising, therefore, given the views of the British government, that Elgin did not interfere with the government of Canada which had been elected during Metcalfe's governorship, and that he took no active part in the January 1848 election. In that election the reform party of Baldwin and LaFontaine won a two-thirds majority in the assembly including a majority in Canada East and in Canada West. The Tory ministry waited to meet the new assembly, a practice which was not uncommon at that time, in order to test their strength. Its defeat was inevitable and Elgin replaced it on March 11, 1848, with a reform ministry. His clear intention was to act according to the principles of responsible government.

The test of responsible government, if one were still necessary, was anticlimactic and came with the passage of the Rebellion Losses Bill. This Bill, introduced in the assembly by LaFontaine in February 1849, was intended to indemnify people in Canada East for property damaged in the 1837 Rebellion. Similar compensation had already been provided for Canada West. The opposition denounced the Bill as a political move to increase support in Canada East and demanded that Elgin refuse royal assent or at least that he reserve the Bill for the British government. However, in spite of his personal doubt about the wisdom of the measure, Elgin assented on April 26 in the belief that his role was to accept his ministry's advice in a purely local matter. A petition asking the British government to disallow the Bill was discussed in the British House of Commons but Elgin's action was upheld. Responsible government, history confirms, had become a reality in Canada.

So strongly did the opponents feel about the Rebellion Losses Bill that rioting broke out in Montreal (where the seat of government had been moved in 1844) and continued for several days. The governor's carriage was pelted with stones and eggs as Elgin left the parliament building following royal assent, members were driven from the assembly, the homes of some of the members who had supported the Bill were attacked, and the parliament building was ransacked and then burned to the ground.

An understanding of some other events occurring in the 1840s is essential if the achievement of responsible government is to be viewed in perspective. One of the results of the Industrial Revolution was a growing influence of the industrialists in Britain who maintained that trade restrictions associated with the mercantile system should be abolished in favour of free trade. However, mercantilism, which the American colonies had found a hindrance to their economic development, was still benefitting the remaining British North American colonies by providing guaranteed markets for their raw materials. These benefits more than offset the restrictions imposed by the Navigation Acts on colonial trade with foreign countries.

Passage of the 1832 Reform Bill, the first major step in the broadening of the British franchise and therefore in the democratization of the House of Commons, led to a reduced influence of the landed aristocracy and an increased influence of the industrialists. Finally, partly in response to the shift in power (although it was precipitated by the Irish potato famine), Britain in 1846 repealed the Corn Laws (the major symbol of mercantilism) and adopted free trade. Also in 1846 the British Parliament authorized the colonies to establish their own customs laws. With this elimination of the economic restrictions as well as the benefits of the mercantile system, it was only logical and a matter of time before the political bond as well would be loosened.

As a result of the difficult economic conditions, the increased power of the French as symbolized by the passage of the Rebellion Losses Bill, and now the refusal of Britain to disallow that Bill, a Tory manifesto urging annexation with the United States was issued in October 1849. The manifesto was signed by several hundred people, but the movement soon collapsed.

Repeal of the Navigation Acts, the other hallmark of the mercantile system, also occurred in 1849. This action, together with negotiation of the Reciprocity Treaty (1854-1866) which provided for free trade of natural products between British North America and the United States, eliminated many of the legitimate grievances resulting from Britain's adoption of free trade.

4. THE MARITIME COLONIES—EAST AND WEST

In one sense it seems inappropriate that the first British North American colony (after the loss of the Thirteen Colonies) to achieve both representative and responsible government should invariably be treated rather summarily by writers of Canadian political history. Nova Scotia was ceded to Britain by the 1713 Treaty of Utrecht. An elected assembly first met in 1758, a year before the fall of Quebec during the Battle of the Plains of Abraham and more than three decades before the Canadas were granted representative government in 1791. Responsible government was achieved in Nova Scotia on February 2, 1848, five weeks before Lord Elgin appointed his first reform ministry in the Province of Canada on March 11, and more than a year before he gave royal assent to the controversial Rebellion Losses Bill on April 26, 1849.

While at first glance it may seem inappropriate, the emphasis placed on Canada compared with the treatment given Nova Scotia can be justified. In the first place it was in Canada that the struggle for constitutional reform was the most vigorous. Indeed, the Canadian struggle for responsible government laid the foundation for the eventual realization of that principle in Nova Scotia as well. It was but a coincidence that, following Lord Grey's directives to Sir John Harvey and Lord Elgin to initiate responsible government, a reform council was appointed in Nova Scotia only shortly before similar action occurred in Canada.

Second, it will be recalled that following the 1791 Constitutional Act the governor of Canada was also governor-in-chief of all British North American colonies in the east, and therefore he was the superior of the several colonial lieutenant governors. Communications between the governor and the colonial secretary frequently addressed the specific problems of Canada, although they carried implications for the other colonies as well. Third, it was in Canada that the most important dramas affecting post-Confederation Canada took place. It was along the St. Lawrence River, for example, that the struggle between our two major cultures began—a struggle which has been the most enduring characteristic of Canadian federalism since 1867. Finally, it was the Province of Canada that took the initiative leading to Confederation and, as the heartland of Canada since 1867, has dominated the political and economic life of the entire country ever since.

A. Nova Scotia, Including Cape Breton Island

Nova Scotia (excluding Cape Breton Island) was ceded to Britain by the 1713 Treaty of Utrecht. Britain claimed that the colony included what later became New Brunswick, whereas France maintained that it included only the peninsula. This dispute became academic in 1763 when France lost all of her North American possessions except St. Pierre and Miquelon. Cape Breton Island was joined to Nova Scotia by the 1763 Royal Proclamation. In 1784 it was separated and promised an assembly which, however, never met. The colony rejoined

Nova Scotia in 1820 and remains part of that province today.

The first assembly in Nova Scotia met in 1758, although effective control of government remained in the hands of the governor and his appointed council which combined the functions of an upper house with those of adviser.

Among the maritime colonies it was in Nova Scotia where the greatest struggle for responsible government occurred. However, apart from isolated disagreements between the assembly and the ruling oligarchy, not until Joseph Howe was elected to the assembly in 1836 did that struggle become continuous. Excited by Lord Durham's Report, and in response to Russell's rejection of responsible government, Howe wrote Four Open Letters to Russell in September 1839.[25] A masterful defence—both profound and humorous—of responsible government, the Letters dismantled Russell's objections with incisive logic. Howe was equally forthright in his demand: "We seek for nothing more than British subjects are entitled to; but we will be contended [sic] with nothing less."

When Russell advised Governor-in-Chief Thomson in October 1839 to reduce his dependence on the executive council by discontinuing the practice of lifetime appointments, and therefore to change the ministry as matters of public policy may require, Howe interpreted this as an invitation to responsible government. However, although Russell instructed Nova Scotia's lieutenant governor to appoint "leading members" of the assembly to the executive council, he advised that Howe be excluded inasmuch as his appointment might "appear a sanction to the opinions of his recent publication" of the Open Letters.[26]

Not until Lord Grey's November 3, 1846 memo (noted above) to Lieutenant Governor Harvey, and the subsequent electoral victory of the reformers late in 1847, was an exclusively reform ministry appointed on February 2, 1848, and responsible government accomplished.

B. New Brunswick

This colony was separated from Nova Scotia in 1784 as a result of the immigration of United Empire Loyalists. The first assembly met in the same year, and the executive and legislative councils were separated in 1832.

By the 1830s, demands for constitutional change were developing slowly because of the sparse population and the absence of a major political centre comparable to Halifax in Nova Scotia. The executive council's control of the revenue from Crown lands with their valuable timber gave that body virtual independence from the assembly. Following an appeal to the colonial secretary this control was transferred to the assembly in 1837 in return for a permanent civil list. From then on there was no agitation for responsible government. The reason for its eventual adoption in 1848 was the change in Imperial policy already noted. The 1848 election produced a reform majority, although the first ministry selected from a single party was not appointed until the middle of the next decade.

C. Prince Edward Island

Prince Edward Island was ceded to Britain under the terms of the 1763 Treaty of Paris and joined to Nova Scotia the same year by the Royal Proclamation. It was separated in 1769 and given its first assembly in 1773.

The major agitation for reform was to gain control of lands awarded to absentee landlords in 1767. These British speculators had failed to improve or to settle their lands as they had promised. Only secondarily was the assembly interested in controlling the governor and his council; indeed, there was no clear-cut distinction between the Tories and the reformers. With even less agitation than in New Brunswick responsible government was introduced in 1851.

D. Newfoundland

Although Newfoundland was discovered and claimed for Britain in 1497 by John Cabot, permanent settlement was forbidden until the early eighteenth century in order to restrict the Newfoundland fishery to ships from British ports. Newfoundland's ports were therefore limited to temporary use by fishing vessels and to the training of British seamen. Settlement developed, nevertheless, as people remained over the winter. During the second decade of the nineteenth century the colony became self-governing and an assembly, granted in 1832, met for the first time in early 1833. Following separation of the executive council from the legislative council, responsible government was implemented in 1855.

In 1934, however, a collapsed economy resulting from the Depression caused Newfoundland to revert to colonial status. Governed directly by Britain the colony lost both responsible and representative government. Newfoundland continued in this condition until it joined Canada in 1949.

E. British Columbia and Vancouver's Island

The development of self-government was slower in the west because of geographic isolation from the rest of British North America and also because of the small European population. In 1803 and 1821 the British Parliament provided for judicial authority in the territory west of Upper Canada and north of the United States. This territory included what later became the colonies of Vancouver's Island and British Columbia.

In 1849 Vancouver's Island became a separate colony with a governor and appointed council; in 1856 it was granted an assembly. In 1858 British Columbia was created with a governor having full legislative power. Because of the colony's cosmopolitan population resulting from the Fraser River gold rush, an assembly was deemed inadvisable.

The two colonies were united in 1866 under a governor, and a council that was partly elected but mostly appointed. In effect, therefore, Vancouver's Island lost its element of popular control. An assembly was created in 1870, and responsible government began with the entry of British Columbia into Confederation in 1871.

To Confederation, Thence to Independence—1840s, 1867, 1931, 1982

1. Causes of Confederation, 1867
   A. Economic
   B. Military
   C. Political Crisis Within the Province of Canada
      (i) Quasi-Federalism, the 1840s
      (ii) Political Realignment, 1848-1854
      (iii) A New Coalition—the Liberal-Conservatives, 1854-1864
2. Conferences and Ratification
   A. Charlottetown Conference
   B. Quebec Conference
   C. Ratification
   D. London Conference
3. A Word About the Term "Confederation"
4. Territorial Expansion, 1870-1949
5. From Confederation to Independence

1. CAUSES OF CONFEDERATION, 1867

The tensions that ultimately brought about Confederation may conveniently be organized as economic, military, and political.

A. Economic

Trade was the key to prosperity for all of the colonies. When Britain abandoned the mercantile system and adopted free trade in the 1840s the colonies lost their guaranteed markets in the mother country and had to make their own way in the commercial world. This dependence on trade, especially the exporting of staples, made the colonies vulnerable to changing world conditions.

Nevertheless, the decade of the 1850s was one of economic prosperity for the colonies. One important reason was the large increase in exports resulting from the Reciprocity Treaty which provided for the free trade of natural products between British North America and the United States. However, the United States abrogated the Treaty in 1866. Anticipating this action the colonies hoped that union which would eliminate intercolonial tariffs might compensate by increasing domestic trade. A second reason for the prosperity of the 1850s was the increased demand for goods resulting from the Crimean War of 1853-1856. Britain and France supported Turkey against the Russian Empire.

A third reason also became the cause of near-bankruptcy for Canada. This was the building of the railways. By the second quarter of the nineteenth century the railway era was under way. The United States initiated this era in North America as it had the age of canals. And as with canals the prize was trade with the continent's interior. Montreal, using the Great Lakes-St. Lawrence water system, attempted to compete with the all-weather port of New York. However, even after the Welland Canal was opened in 1829 most of the trade continued to flow from Lake Erie to New York via the Erie Canal (completed in 1825) and the Mohawk and Hudson rivers. Part of the reason for Montreal's inability to compete was the difficulty of establishing a coherent policy for the St. Lawrence so long as two separate colonies existed along that river. But even after the 1841 union and efforts to improve the waterway, the great bulk of the American West trade continued to flow to New York with its cheaper freight and insurance rates.

The construction of railways in the United States accentuated New York's advantage, and in order to provide Montreal with an all-weather port, the St. Lawrence and Atlantic Railway was built across the State of Maine to Portland. It opened in 1851.

Canada's greatest hopes, however, were pinned on the Grand Trunk Railway which, financed not only by private investors but also heavily from the public treasury, linked Montreal with Toronto in 1856 and with Sarnia in 1860. Intended to supplement the canals, the Grand Trunk competed instead, and both systems suffered. Furthermore, it captured very little trade from the American West. Financial difficulties plagued the Grand Trunk from the start, and more than once additional public funds were poured into the project. It was hoped that a broader union would make that railway more economically feasible, partly by facilitating construction of the much-desired rail link with the Atlantic colonies.

The Maritimes, also, looked to the railway to improve their position in the traffic between Europe and North America. Specifically, they sought a connection with the St. Lawrence, thereby to gain access to the interior to compete with United States ports. A rail link was to become one of the presumed advantages of union with Canada, and it was actually guaranteed by the Constitution Act (s. 145).

Because most of the available fertile land in Canada was occupied, a new frontier was becoming a necessity. With the westward expansion of the United States, Canada realized that the Hudson Bay lands would soon be lost to its southern neighbour unless Canada took steps to open these lands to settlement. Perhaps a broader political union would facilitate this development.

B. Military

Because of the proximity of British North America to the United States, the colonies were in the awkward position of having to bear the brunt of any American antagonism toward Britain. This was particularly true of Canada because of its accessibility. The American Civil War (1861-1865) was a case in point. Canada initially sympathized with the North because of the close social and economic ties resulting from its strong loyalist background, as well as from the increased trade created by the Reciprocity Treaty. However, this sympathy changed to suspicion and fear as friction developed between the North and Britain.

Britain's sympathy lay with the Southern (Confederate) states, the source of cotton for Britain's textile industry. In November 1861 a United States warship stopped the British vessel *Trent* in international waters (the Gulf of Mexico) and forcibly removed two Confederate agents who were on their way from Cuba to seek British aid for the South. This incident, which almost provoked war between Britain and the United States, turned American hostility toward Canada as well. The antagonism was heightened by Confederate plans to use Canada as a base for raids against Northern cities.

Of more immediate frustration for Canada were several raids north across the border by members of the Fenian Brotherhood, an Irish organization formed in the United States in 1857 to gain support in the struggle for Irish independence from Britain. The Fenians created tension along the border from 1866 until 1871.

Although there was fear of invasion by the victorious North, it was the abrogation of the Reciprocity Treaty which reflected United States' hostility. Reasons for cancelling the Treaty included the frustrations noted above, but also Canadian attempts to capture more trade for the St. Lawrence. Furthermore, Canadian tariffs on manufactured goods provoked criticism that the spirit, even if not the letter, of the Treaty was being violated. But beyond these factors was a growing protectionist sentiment in the United States. With the cancellation of the Reciprocity Treaty, Canada also turned increasingly to protection.

The uncertainty and fear caused by the deterioration of Canada-United States relations was accentuated by Britain's reduced commitment to Imperial defence, which accompanied her reduced involvement in colonial economic and political affairs.

C. Political Crisis Within the Province of Canada

It may be that the economic and military problems could have been resolved had the functioning of the Canadian government not ground to a standstill. A political crisis in 1864 forced the immediate reassessment of the political structure.

(i) Quasi-Federalism, the 1840s: The functioning of the Canadian government following the 1841 union reflected Canada's bicultural nature. In the first place, fifteen of the sixteen ministries from Bagot's first LaFontaine-Baldwin ministry (appointed in the fall of 1842) until Confederation had dual leadership.[1] Second, several departments either had both, or alternated between, Upper and Lower Canadian ministers. Of particular significance was the existence of two attorneys general, reflective of the different legal systems in Upper Canada (common law) and Lower Canada (the civil code).

A third quasi-federal characteristic was the result of the Union Act having left untouched much of the cultural distinctiveness of Upper and Lower Canada including the legal systems, the systems of land tenure, the educational systems, languages, and religions. There was a strong desire that laws affecting but one region be passed only with the concurrence of a majority of representatives from that region, and that laws having common interest be passed only with a majority from each region.

In the 1850s, by which time the population balance had swung in favour of Canada West, the West was complaining of interference from the East and was demanding representation by population in the assembly. However, because "rep by pop" in a legislative union would increase the fear of assimilation of the French, some alternative was necessary. A renewal of the "double majority" concept was attempted by John Sanfield Macdonald (who headed a dual ministry between 1862 and 1864), but it could not be sustained. Macdonald himself used a Canada East majority in 1863 to carry a Separate School Bill which affected only Canada West.[2]

In the long run, therefore, the principle of equal representation and the unitary structure of the government were stronger than quasi-federalism. The only alternative would be a federal union.

(ii) Political Realignment, 1848-1854: Alliances forged to accomplish a common purpose are sometimes unable to survive once the immediate objective has been achieved. Differing interests that are readily suppressed for the common good re-emerge with new importance. This was precisely the fate of the reformers following the adoption of responsible government. It will be recalled that the unity of the reform movement in the 1840s had, as one consequence, created a measure of unity among the Tory opponents and thus a *de facto* party system. It is not surprising, therefore, that the disunity which overcame the reform movement had repercussions for the Tories as well. If the result had been the creation of new cohesive parties, required for the proper functioning of responsible or cabinet government, then a stable political system might have characterized the 1850s and 1860s. A new coalition *was* created in 1854 but, for reasons noted below, it was unable to provide the necessary stability. The result, by 1864, was deadlock.

In Canada East the disunity following the achievement of responsible government produced a new radical liberal movement, the Parti Rouge, which had been inspired by Papineau's return to politics in 1848 but which, since his retirement shortly thereafter, had been led by A.A. Dorion. The demands of the Rouges included a broader franchise; the election of more officials; removal of education from church control; abolition of the seigneurial system; and, as a result of the Party's hostility toward Britain and the Act of Union, annexation to the United States—even though such a move would seriously threaten the existence of French culture.

In Canada West at about the same time radical ideas found expression in the Clear Grit Party. "All sand and no dirt, clear grit all the way through," they said of themselves. But whereas the Rouges remained a small minority in the East, the Grits became the majority in the West. The Grit leader was George Brown, although he had originally been a vigorous opponent. "Office-seeking, bunkum-talking cormorants," he had called the Grits.[3] The Grit demands included the secret ballot, a wider franchise, the abolition of property qualifications for members of the assembly, the election of more officials (including the governor and legislative council), abolition of the Clergy Reserves with the proceeds to go to education, and "reform in the representation [in the assembly], based on population," (which by 1857 had become the Party's rallying cry).[4] The 1851-52 census had indicated that, for the first time, the population of Canada West exceeded that of Canada East.

By the time Baldwin and LaFontaine left politics in 1851 they had carried reform as far as they wished. Indeed, it was partly a perception that they were becoming increasingly conservative which contributed to the rise of the Rouges and the Grits whose demands alienated the moderates. As the reform alliance disintegrated, thereby destroying the neat Reform-Tory two-party system, smaller groups were forming on the right as well as the left. Baldwin and LaFontaine were succeeded by a Hincks-Morin ministry which lasted, but with decreasing support, until the 1854 election. By 1854 it had become clear that with the proliferation of parties a new political alignment was needed.

(iii) A New Coalition—the Liberal-Conservatives, 1854-1864: The man of the hour was John A. Macdonald, a politician who "combined a remarkable flexibility with a talent for political effrontery, which left his opponents baffled and raging at his unabashed shifts of policy."[5] He called his new alignment the "Liberal-Conservatives." This name was a stroke of political genius, a sort of political Janus, inasmuch as it was intended to appeal both to those who continued to seek reform as well as to those who believed that progress occurs only slowly and after changes gradually become integrated into society. The major opponents of the new coalition were the Rouges and the Grits.

The first ministry under the new coalition was headed by Augustin Morin (successor of LaFontaine) and Sir Allan MacNab. This was a spectacular illustration of the new realignment: Morin had drafted the 1834 Ninety-two Resolutions and MacNab was "the surviving embodiment of the Family Compact and the scourge of the rebels of 1837."[6] The rationality of this coalition appears when one recalls that the political liberalism of the LaFontaine French Canadians was motivated by a desire for freedom to protect their essentially conservative social and economic order. The coalition would be possible only if the Tories were prepared to accept the French fact, and if the French ceased their opposition to the spending of public money for "economic progress." As a result,

> a group of [French] leaders emerged who . . . combined a championship of French . . . interests with an insistence on a full share in the economic benefits of English capitalism. The powerful influence of the church was enlisted on the side of this dual policy; and pragmatic considerations drew French nationalists and the Catholic hierarchy into a working cooperation with those ancient enemies, the Montreal merchants and the Tories of Canada West.[7]

The participation of the Catholic church was paradoxical, given that church's historic opposition to liberal ideas. The incentive was the church's greater concern about the rise of the radical Parti Rouge as well as the anti-French and anti-Catholic views of the Grits in Canada West.

Among the accomplishments of the first coalition ministry in 1854 was the settlement of the two major issues left outstanding from the Baldwin-LaFontaine/Hincks-Morin era: abolition of the seigneurial system and secularization of the Clergy Reserves. Although the Liberal-Conservative coalition was headed by MacNab and Morin, the real leaders were John A. Macdonald (Attorney General for Canada West) and George-Étienne Cartier. Cartier, who had been a rebel in 1837, succeeded Morin in 1856 as leader of the Canada East Bleus. Cartier possessed the twin qualifications of being a French supporter of Catholic church rights as well as being acceptable to—indeed, part of—the Montreal English commercial establishment by virtue of his promotion of the Grand Trunk Railway.

The four major political parties were:

(1) Grits, led by George Brown, a radical party and the majority in Canada West;

(2) Conservatives, led by John A. Macdonald, a minority in Canada West;

(3) Bleus, led by George-Étienne Cartier, the majority in Canada East;

(4) Rouges, led by A.A. Dorion, a radical party and a minority in Canada East.

Except for four days during the famous "Double Shuffle" of August 1858 the Liberal-Conservative coalition continued in office until Confederation, or at least until the 1864 formation of the "Great Coalition" with the Grits. Nevertheless, given the delicately balanced assembly, political stability could not be achieved. The reason for the instability was twofold. On the one hand there were always a few "independent" members of the assembly—"loose fish" John A. Macdonald called them—who shifted their political allegiance from issue to issue. There were eight ministries during the life of the Liberal-Conservative coalition before it was joined by George Brown in 1864, compared with only two ministries between 1848 and 1854.[8] On the other hand, and paradoxically, the balance between the Liberal-Conservatives and the weak Grit-Rouge alliance became sufficiently even by 1864 so that, given the few loose fish, the result was deadlock which precipitated the Grand Coalition that engineered the 1867 union. The alliance between the Grits and Rouges was weak because the Rouges rejected the Grit cry for "rep by pop" and, of course, condemned Grit views of the French and Catholics.

No consideration of this period of Canadian constitutional history is complete without a discussion of the 1858 "Double Shuffle" which, in addition to its inherent interest, illustrates the political instability of the time. To put the issue in perspective some background information is necessary.

As a general rule, then as now, an individual who holds a position of profit or emolument under the Crown may not also have a seat in the assembly. This rule originated in Britain during the seventeenth- and eighteenth-century struggles between Parliament and the Tudor and Stuart monarchs. The purpose was to ensure that members of the House of Commons would not be improperly influenced by the monarch. Obviously, cabinet ministers holding portfolios (that is, who are heads of departments), and therefore paid as advisers to the Crown, had to be exceptions to this rule. (From 1859 until 1863, however, Prince Edward Island did not provide for this exception, and so all ministers were without portfolios and therefore not paid as ministers.)[9] Until 1931 when cabinet ministers were exempted from the prohibition, Canadian law permitted ministers to regain their seats by successfully running, *as ministers*, in by-elections. Except for any newly appointed ministers, by-elections were not required following a general election that returned the existing ministry because, there having been no resignations, appointments would not be interrupted. A change of ministry between general elections usually meant an adjournment of the House for several weeks while the necessary by-elections were held.

Canadian law also obviated the necessity of by-elections, thus permitting the shifting of ministers among portfolios, provided no more than a month elapsed from the time a minister left one position until he was appointed to the next. It was precisely this provision that became the technicality enabling the Double Shuffle to occur.

The Macdonald-Cartier ministry had been defeated on August 1, 1858, on the question of a permanent capital for Canada. After the 1849 riots and burning of the parliament building in Montreal the seat of government had alternated every four years between Quebec in Canada East and Toronto in Canada West. Rivalry between the two regions had prevented agreement on a permanent site and so Queen Victoria, asked by Macdonald at the urging of Governor Sir Edmund Head (who had replaced Elgin as governor in 1854) to settle the controversy, accepted the governor's recommendation of the small town of Bytown, renamed Ottawa after the river on which it is located. An opposition motion to reject this choice carried when some of the ministry's French supporters defected. Following this defeat and the ministry's resignation, George Brown was invited to form a ministry on Friday, August 2. Dorion joined Brown in the dual ministry which was based upon a policy of representation by population but with constitutional safeguards for Canada East. According to law, the entire Brown-Dorion ministry had to resign their seats and seek re-election. However, rather than follow accepted practice and allow the assembly to adjourn so the by-elections could be held, a Liberal-Conservative motion of non-confidence was moved and carried as soon as the composition of the new ministry was announced to the assembly on the Monday. The governor refused Brown a dissolution and turned to Cartier who, with Macdonald, resumed power the next day (August 6).

In order to avoid a second mass resignation the ministers were initially appointed to portfolios different from those that they had held before their resignation several days earlier. This was the first shuffle. Within a day or two they were reappointed to their original portfolios. This was the second shuffle. Hence the term "Double Shuffle."

The political instability of this period was leading to a crisis. Following three government defeats in two years between May of 1862 and March of 1864, the assembly ground to a halt. Although the political parties were not cohesive enough to provide stability they were sufficiently strong that the few loose fish held the balance of power.

Several times during the nineteenth century, suggestions had been made for a federal union of British North America, most recently by Alexander Galt (a Rouge-turned-Conservative) in 1858. In light of the political problems of the early 1860s, George Brown, who had urged a union in 1859, secured the establishment of an assembly committee in March 1863 to pursue the Galt proposal. The committee reported that there was support for a federal union either of Canada alone or of all British North American colonies in the east.

Given the March 1864 deadlock and rather than dissolve the assembly and call the third election since 1861, Governor Monck urged the Liberal-Conservatives and the Grits to join forces for the purpose of creating a federal union. Dorion's Rouges steadfastly opposed such a scheme. The three prime movers of this Great Coalition were Brown, Cartier, and John A. Macdonald. The solution was Confederation. The pain felt by Brown in crossing the floor rings through his June 22 speech to the assembly:

> Did I conceal from the House that I feel in all its force the painful position I now occupy, I should be deceiving the hon. members. For

> ten years I have stood opposed to the hon. gentlemen opposite in the most hostile manner it is possible to conceive of public men arrayed against each other in the political arena. I am well aware that in dealing with Ministerial coalitions I have used language and spoken in tones such as would forbid my standing in the position I occupy today with any hope of justifying myself before the country had the agreement you have just heard read been signed under the conditions usually attached to political alliances . . . I am free to confess that, had the circumstances in which we are now placed been one whit less important, less serious, less threatening than they are, I could not have approached hon. gentlemen opposite, even with a view to these negotiations. But I think the House will admit that, if a crisis has ever arisen in the political affairs of any country which would justify such a coalition as has taken place, such a crisis has arrived in the history of Canada . . . Mr. Speaker, I have already said that it was not without great pain that I listened to the approaches made by gentlemen opposite. For many years I have been connected with a body of gentlemen from Lower Canada [the Rouges] whom I have learned warmly to esteem—gentlemen who stood by me in times of great difficulty, and whose kindness and friendship I hope never to forget. It is most painful to rend, aye, even to weaken the bonds which have bound me to these gentlemen; but, Mr. Speaker, party alliances are one thing and the interests of my country are another.[10]

By offering the support of the French majority to the scheme, Cartier put his own political future on the line:

> [He] was accepting both the loss of the entrenched French position in the existing union and the establishment of rep by pop within a new federation. It was an act of highest political courage, and, one might add, of undeluded vision. Brown gained new respect and fellow-feeling for Cartier on their joining forces, for, as one sectional leader, he knew what it had cost the other to come to terms. The two of them brought the majority votes, Grits and *Bleus*, that made the Confederation ministry politically viable. It could not have existed or pursued its ends without them both.[11]

2. CONFERENCES AND RATIFICATION

Three conferences were held following the creation of the Great Coalition. The provinces of Canada, Nova Scotia, and New Brunswick attended all of them; Prince Edward Island attended the first two; and Newfoundland attended only the second. The first conference met at Charlottetown on September 1, 1864; the second at Quebec on October 10 of the same year; and the third at London on December 4, 1866. The product of these meetings (plus several changes made in London after the London Conference ended) was the British North America Act passed by the British Parliament on March 29, 1867, and effective on July 1 of the same year.

A. Charlottetown Conference

Maritime union had been proposed off and on for some time, the motivation being the desire to remove intercolonial tariffs, to build an intercolonial railway, and generally to mitigate the effects of isolation. The most recent initiative had come from Nova Scotia Premier Tupper who, with the approval of the Colonial Office, had suggested a September 1864 meeting in Charlottetown to consider a legislative union.

It was to this meeting that Canada, acting through the governor, requested and was granted permission to send unofficial delegates for the purpose of proposing a broader union. The casual approach taken by the host city toward the meeting has been described as follows:

> When the appointed day arrived, members of the Island government as well as the general public were less interested in the arrival of the delegates from the mainland than in the rare presence of a circus in Charlottetown. The delegates from Nova Scotia found no one to welcome them, and the reception to the Canadians took the form of a self-sacrificing provincial secretary rowing out in a small boat to meet the ship in which they arrived.[12]

Twenty-three delegates attended this historic meeting—eight from Canada and five from each of Nova Scotia, New Brunswick, and Prince Edward Island. Of these, the most notable during the pre-Confederation period were Canadians John A. Macdonald, Cartier, Brown, Galt, and McGee; Nova Scotia Premier Tupper; and New Brunswick Premier Tilley.

Once the Canadian proposal had been presented with its well-prepared arguments of economic growth, improved defence, and an intercolonial railway linking Canada with New Brunswick and Nova Scotia, discussion of a maritime-only union was set aside. One reason, in addition to Canada's well-organized presentation, for this turn of events was the lack of unity among the maritime delegations and even within some of them. No doubt the fact that the colonies would retain their separate existence as provinces within a federal union, but not within a maritime unitary structure, was also attractive.

In the absence of official records of the Charlottetown meeting there was some controversy later as to what had been accepted. Nevertheless, there was agreement upon some basic principles including the federal nature of the proposed union (although John A. Macdonald would have preferred a unitary structure as "the best, the cheapest, the most vigorous, and the strongest system of government we could adopt").[13] It was also agreed that residual legislative authority would be vested in the central government; that there would be a bicameral central legislature with representation in the lower house based on population and in the upper house based on the equality of three regions (Maritimes, Canada East, Canada West); and that government would be modelled on the British parliamentary system.[14]

B. Quebec Conference

The major issues occupying the two and one-half weeks of closed meetings in Quebec were representation in the Senate, the division of legislative powers between the central and provincial governments, the division of financial resources between the two orders of government, and the inclusion of guarantees to protect French culture.

One-third of the conference time was devoted to the Senate, viewed by some delegates as a guardian of regional interests. Although there had apparently been agreement at Charlottetown upon an equal distribution of seats among three regions, the shelving of maritime union and the presence of Newfoundland sparked renewed demands for a greater maritime share of the total. However, there was little support for equal *provincial* representation as suggested by one Prince Edward Island delegate. The promise of additional seats in the event Newfoundland joined the union seemed to allay maritime fears. The other area of dispute was the method of choosing senators, but life-appointment by the central government was accepted on condition that the initial selection be from provincial nominations reflecting the major party divisions.

The division of legislative authority caused little controversy. Few delegates seemed concerned about the role of provincial governments in a federal union; indeed, Tupper likened the provincial role to that of Halifax within Nova Scotia. Although this attitude seems surprising today, one must remember that the role of government *per se* was far smaller at the time of Confederation. Furthermore, the essence of the federal principle to most of the delegates at the Quebec Conference lay in the central government and the relation between its two houses; not, as federalism is viewed today, in the division of legislative authority between the two orders of government.

Many of the delegates viewed the Senate and participation in the central cabinet as the first line in the defence of provincial interests; although during the subsequent debate in the Canadian assembly Dorion and Christopher Dunkin challenged, prophetically, the ability of the Senate to protect this diversity. Furthermore, the centralists pointed to the American Civil War then being waged and which they interpreted as the result of excessive decentralization. They suggested, therefore, that powers beyond a specific list of local concerns be placed in the hands of the central government, as well as a general veto power over all provincial legislation.

With the broad grant of power to the central government went unlimited power to tax. The provinces were restricted to direct taxation but, to offset the resultant loss of the bulk of their revenue hitherto derived from tariffs and indirect sales taxes, responsibility for the provincial public debt was assumed by the central government. Special subsidies would also be paid to the provinces.

The most visible provisions to protect French culture were the granting to the provinces jurisdiction over property, civil rights, and education, as well as making French an official language in Quebec and the central government.

When the Quebec Conference ended it had drawn up a set of seventy-two resolutions (the "Quebec Resolutions") which were then submitted, in accordance with Resolution 70, to the several legislatures for consideration.

C. Ratification

Professor Waite makes the revealing comment that

> one of the prevalent assumptions that bespeaks the central Canadian orientation of our history is that the Confederation debates in the Canadian legislature were the Confederation debates. It is sometimes forgotten that there were others in other provinces. Confederation was debated in Newfoundland, in Prince Edward Island, and in Nova Scotia in both the 1865 and the 1866 sessions in substance, if not in form, as it was in Canada. New Brunswick had elections in both these years with Confederation the main issue. Confederation was more controversial in the four Atlantic provinces than it was in the Province of Canada.[15]

Whereas none of the maritime colonies felt any urgency about union, Canada had to resolve its political crisis which would doubtlessly recur should the present scheme fail. Perhaps for this reason, but only after prolonged and lively debate, the Canadian legislature approved the Quebec Resolutions in March 1865 by a vote of 91-33 in the assembly and 45-15 in the council. A double majority (a majority of members from Canada East as well as from Canada West) was achieved in each house. In addition, a majority of French members and of English members (the former by only four or five votes) supported the Quebec Resolutions.[16] Changes in the Resolutions were suggested, but John A. Macdonald's insistence was accepted that the agreement was like a treaty and therefore must be approved or rejected in its entirety. Among the opponents were Dorion, J.S. Macdonald, and Christopher Dunkin. In the following comments Dunkin anticipated a major problem that has plagued the Canadian federation throughout most of its history.

> What is the system we are going to adopt according to these resolutions? What are the relations to be established between our general and local governments? We are told to take for granted that no clashing of interest or feeling need be feared; that the Federal union offered us in name will be a Legislative union in reality. Yet, whoever dislikes the notion of a Legislative union is assured it will be nothing of

> the sort . . . You cannot devise a system that shall have all the advantages of the one and of the other; but it is quite possible that you may devise one that will combine the chief disadvantages of both, and that is, I fear, pretty much what this system does.[17]

John A. Macdonald's own prediction, made to a member of the assembly before the Confederation Debates began, was most clear: "If the Confederation goes on you . . . will see both Local Parliaments and Governments absorbed in the General Power. This is as plain to me as if I saw it accomplished now . . . Of course it does not do to adopt that point of view in discussing the subject in Lower Canada."[18]

In the Maritimes the Resolutions ran into opposition which almost scuttled the entire scheme. Although construction of the Intercolonial Railway was a major inducement, especially for New Brunswick and Nova Scotia, the Maritimes feared that union would mean higher tariffs and a generally higher tax burden. Furthermore, they were not particularly interested in Canada's desire for westward expansion or, of course, in Canada's internal political problems. Also, and understandably, there was no enthusiasm for the inevitable fact that the provinces would lose authority to a central government located beyond the Maritimes.

Prince Edward Island rejected the Resolutions—the legislative council unanimously and the assembly by a large majority. In New Brunswick, where the government was nearing the end of its term, Premier Tilley decided to test the electorate on the issue and was soundly defeated. One charge hurled by his opponents was that he would sell the province to Canada for "eighty cents a head"—a reference to one of the proposed subsidy payments. Nova Scotia Premier Tupper adopted a different course of action. In view of his neighbour's defeat, as well as growing opposition to Confederation led by his political foe and former premier Joseph Howe, he secured the assembly's support not for the Quebec Resolutions but for maritime union.

The Newfoundland government did not put the Resolutions to an assembly vote.

At this point, with Confederation approved only by Canada, the proposal seemed doomed. The British government, however, was determined that union should occur, although rejection by the two island colonies could be countenanced. For one thing, union would strengthen colonial defence and thus assist in the reduction of Britain's responsibility. Furthermore, British investors saw greater financial security in union. Upon Britain's insistence, New Brunswick's lieutenant governor dissolved the recently elected assembly in April 1866. Tilley was then re-elected with the aid of much outside financial assistance and by capitalizing on the abrogation of the Reciprocity Treaty as well as the danger of Fenian raids. The assembly subsequently passed a resolution supporting Confederation, as did the Nova Scotia assembly following the appointment of a governor sympathetic to the scheme.

D. London Conference

Although some alterations were made, the Quebec Resolutions emerged from the London Conference, and following subsequent changes, basically unscathed. The name "Canada" was chosen in preference to Macdonald's "Kingdom of Canada" which Britain rejected in deference to possible negative reaction from the United States. Additions made in London included the right of an aggrieved religious minority to appeal to Ottawa for redress in the event their denominational schools were adversely affected by provincial action (s. 93[3,4]); and the possible appointment of additional senators to break a deadlock between the two houses of Parliament (s. 26). Alterations to the distribution of legislative authority between the two orders of government included the shift of penitentiaries from provincial to Federal jurisdiction; sea coast and inland fisheries from concurrent to Federal jurisdiction; immigration and agriculture from provincial to concurrent jurisdiction with Federal paramountcy; and the inclusion of the solemnization of marriage within provincial jurisdiction.

The B.N.A. Bill was passed by the British government with little apparent interest. Indeed, when the House turned to the next item of business, relating to dog taxes, an observer noticed "a perceptible brightening of the interest of the members."[19] Queen Victoria gave royal assent on March 29, 1867.

No colonial ministry or assembly, to say nothing of an electorate, had the opportunity to discuss or pass judgement upon the work of the London meetings. Nova Scotia, most dissatisfied with Confederation, "ushered in the new Dominion on July 1, 1867, by draping streets in black; and the first Dominion election returned eighteen out of nineteen members pledged to repeal."[20] Following Nova Scotia's first post-Confederation provincial election, which defeated the Tupper Government, the victorious Howe led a delegation to London in an unsuccessful attempt to withdraw his province from Confeder-ation. Nevertheless, by 1869 Howe was a member of John A. Macdonald's cabinet, an appointment he accepted in return for improved financial terms for Nova Scotia.

3. A WORD ABOUT THE TERM "CONFEDERATION"

Canadians are so accustomed to referring to the 1867 union as "Confederation" that many may be unaware that this term, at least with its modern connotation when spelled with a small "c," is a misnomer to describe our union. A small-"c" confederation, as distinct from a federation, is a very loose union in which the central government functions only with the cooperation and consent of the regional governments. The central government cannot act directly upon the people, and so it is dependent upon the regional governments for funds and armies. Furthermore, members of the central government are chosen by, paid by, serve for terms determined by, and therefore represent, the regional governments. For a motion to pass the central government, the support of representatives from all regional governments is generally required. An example of confederation was the American Articles of Confederation (1777), the constitution that preceded the present Constitution of the United States (1787) and under which the Thirteen Colonies fought their Revolutionary War.

Our union was the virtual antithesis of a "confederation" as that term is understood today. Nevertheless, because "Confederation" is now and will remain with us perhaps it can mean precisely whatever we say it means—nothing more than the event which occurred in British North America on July 1, 1867.

4. TERRITORIAL EXPANSION, 1870-1949

The following list quickly identifies the order in which lands were added to Canada, and provinces and territories created, after 1867.[21]

(1) **1870:** Admission of Rupert's Land and the North-Western Territory by British order-in-council, effective July 15, pursuant to Constitution Act section 146; and by the 1868 Rupert's Land Act by which the Hudson's Bay Company surrendered those lands to the Crown in anticipation of their transfer to Canada. The Canadian Parliament's 1869 North-West Territories Act provided for the renaming of these lands, upon their admission, as "The North-West Territories."

(2) **1870:** Formation of the Province of Manitoba from the North-West Territories by the Manitoba Act passed in May. Pursuant to section 1 of the Act, Manitoba was formed on July 15, the date on which Rupert's Land and the North-Western Territory were transferred to Canada. The 1871 Constitution Act amendment confirmed Canada's right to establish provinces from territories admitted to the Dominion and provided also that, once enacted, such statutes could not be amended by Parliament.

(3) **1871:** Admission of British Columbia by British order-in-council, effective July 20, pursuant to Constitution Act section 146.

(4) **1873:** Admission of Prince Edward Island by British order-in-council, effective July 1, pursuant to Constitution Act section 146. Except for Newfoundland (including Labrador) and the Arctic islands, Canada had reached its present boundaries.

(5) **1880:** Admission of "all British Territories and Possessions in North America, and the Islands adjacent to such Territories and Possessions which are not already included in the Dominion of Canada . . . (with the exception of the Colony of Newfoundland and its dependencies)," by British order-in-council, effective September 1. The most notable addition was the Arctic islands.

(6) **1898:** Formation of the Yukon Territory from the North-West Territories by the Yukon Territory Act, June 13.

(7) **1905:** Formation of the Province of Alberta from the North-West Territories by the Alberta Act, effective September 1, pursuant to the 1871 Constitution Act amendment.

(8) **1905:** Formation of the Province of Saskatchewan from the North-West Territories by the Saskatchewan Act, effective September 1, pursuant to the 1871 Constitution Act amendment.

(9) **1949:** Admission of Newfoundland by amendment to the Constitution Act (No. 1, 1949), effective March 31. This amendment confirmed the Terms of Union of Newfoundland with Canada Act which was given royal assent on February 18, 1949. Newfoundland was not admitted by British order-in-council, pursuant to Constitution Act section 146, because that section required the approval of a Newfoundland assembly. As noted in Chapter 2, Newfoundland lost its assembly in 1934 and this made section 146 inapplicable.

5. FROM CONFEDERATION TO INDEPENDENCE

On the morning of the first Dominion Day, Canada was as much a British colony as it had been the night before. All of the colonies forming Canada on July 1, 1867, had participated in unions and separations before. They had also, to all intents and purposes, achieved self-government in local affairs with the coming of responsible government. The main post-Confederation limitations to self-government were of minor importance. These included Britain's power of disallowance, her authority to act in relation to reserved bills, and the potential influence of the governor general who was still responsible to the British government. The only exercise of disallowance occurred in 1873; the governor general's 1878 Instructions deleted the enumeration of types of bills requiring reservation for Britain's consideration; and *de facto* self-government in local matters was complete by the beginning of World War One. Confederation itself marked a watershed in terms of neither independence nor self-government.

In making his distinction between local and Imperial matters for the purpose of responsible government, Lord Durham had suggested that control of only three areas needed to be retained by Britain—the constitution, the disposal of public lands, and the regulation of trade within and without the Empire as well as of foreign relations generally.[22] As to the first of these, the constitution in the form of the Constitution Act was basically the creation of the uniting colonies, although authority to amend the Act remained with the British Parliament until 1982 (but at Canada's expressed request after 1931). Second, the disposal of public lands was not a serious problem.

With respect to Durham's third area, the regulation of trade within the

Empire created no serious problem. As early as 1859, when Canada raised its tariffs on manufactured goods, Finance Minister Galt successfully countered British criticism, perhaps even a veiled threat of disallowance, on the grounds that the Canadian ministry was responsible to the Canadian legislature.

> Self-government would be utterly annihilated if the views of the Imperial government were to be preferred to those of the people of Canada. It is therefore the duty of the present government distinctly to affirm the right of the Canadian legislature to adjust the taxation of the people in the way they deem best, even if it should unfortunately happen to meet the disapproval of the Imperial ministry.[23]

As for trade beyond the Empire, Britain had agreed by the end of the nineteenth century that Canada would not automatically be bound by British trade treaties.[24] The next step for Canada was to secure the right to participate in the negotiation of treaties that were of special significance to her. The 1871 Treaty of Washington began this procedure which culminated in 1923 when Canada both negotiated and signed, without British participation, the Halibut Treaty with the United States.

The realization of control over the political aspects of foreign affairs, however, developed more slowly. More than anything else it was the new relationship between Canada and Britain, established by the extent of Canada's participation in World War One, that led to the formal developments of the 1920s and culminated in the passage of the Statute of Westminster on December 11, 1931. Not until that Statute was passed was Canada (or were the other Dominions) placed in a position of formal equality with Britain. Even then, but at Canada's request, formal control over the 1867 Constitution Act was retained by Britain until 1982.

Some of the more significant events culminating in total independence are listed below:

(1) **1871:** Treaty of Washington. A Joint High Commission was established to settle outstanding issues between Britain and the United States. In recognition of Canada's changing status, Prime Minister Macdonald was appointed a member of the British delegation to represent Canadian interests. These interests included encroachments by United States fishing boats on the Canadian fisheries following the 1866 cancellation of the Reciprocity Treaty, compensation claims for damage caused by the Fenian raids, and claim to the island of San Juan between the mainland and Vancouver Island. Macdonald was in an awkward position inasmuch as he could not control the British side of negotiations and yet he was answerable to the Canadian Parliament. He and other Canadians felt that in the settlement Britain had sacrificed Canadian interests for harmony with the United States.

(2) **1879:** Establishment of the office of Canadian High Commissioner to London, to provide direct contact between governments beyond that which was possible through the governor general. This position is the intra-Commonwealth equivalent of ambassador.

(3) **1887:** First Colonial Conference to facilitate intergovernmental discussion of matters of common concern. At this Conference Britain proposed, and Canada rejected if a reduction of autonomy were involved, the creation of an Imperial council. Conferences were later called "Imperial," and finally "Commonwealth."

(4) **1899:** Beginning of the Boer War. Although the entire Empire was automatically at war, it was the Canadian government that determined the extent of Canadian participation. Opinion was divided between the English who thought Canada should automatically send military support, and the French who disagreed with Canadian participation in what they viewed as essentially a foreign war. Prime Minister Laurier's government compromised for the sake of Canadian unity and sent volunteers who became part of the British army, but the government also stated that this action was not to be regarded as a precedent.

(5) **1903:** Settlement of the Alaska boundary dispute. A British-United States Joint High Commission was established in 1897 to settle Canadian-American disputes, most significant of which was the location of the Alaskan panhandle boundary. For the first time Canadians formed a majority (two of three) of the British commissioners. Although appointees were to be "impartial jurists" who were to make a judicial rather than a political decision, the three Americans were not jurists and were on public record as strongly supportive of their government's position. The lone British member initially supported the Canadian stand, but he swung to the other side probably upon instructions from his government following the threat by President Theodore Roosevelt to settle the issue his own way if necessary.

This British action, coupled with earlier boundary decisions including that in 1871 which gave San Juan to the United States, strengthened the view that Canada should conduct its own foreign affairs.

(6) **1909:** Establishment of the Department of External Affairs.

(7) **1909:** Boundary Waters Treaty which established the International Joint Commission, the first permanent Canada-United States organization. Its purpose was to regulate the use of boundary waters. Although all the "Canadian" commissioners were Canadians, they were formally appointed by the British government.[25]

(8) **1912:** Defeat (by the Liberal-controlled Senate) of Prime Minister Borden's Naval Bill which called for a Canadian contribution to

the British navy as war clouds gathered in Europe. The Bill created much protest that its passage would be the antithesis of self-government. Surprisingly, Laurier's 1910 Naval Bill to create a *Canadian* navy had also been opposed.

(9) **1914:** Outbreak of World War One. As with the Boer War, Britain's declaration of war implicated the entire Empire. As in the previous conflict Canada decided for itself the extent of participation. In this case there was no hesitation (although the conscription issue was later to cause serious problems) and Canada contributed to an extraordinary degree for a country its size. Canadian troops were ultimately under British command, but by 1917 they formed a Canadian corps commanded by Canadian General Currie.

(10) **1917:** Imperial War Cabinet. The first meeting of the Imperial War Cabinet was held in March and consisted of the prime ministers of Britain, the several Dominions, and India—a sort of cabinet of governments—and enabled the participating governments to play a role in establishing a common war policy. Britain hoped that it would also mean a common Imperial voice at the later peace conference, but that was not the wish of the other members and it did not occur. At the 1918 meeting of the Imperial War Cabinet, Britain at first objected to, but later acquiesced in, demands that the Dominions participate in their own right at the peace conference.

(11) **1917:** Imperial War Conference. The Conference met in April of 1917 to establish a procedure formally to alter relationships within the Empire in light of changes which had actually been taking place. Prime Minister Robert Borden was instrumental in proposing the following resolution adopted by the Conference: that an early post-war Imperial conference be called to readjust "the constitutional relations of the component parts of the Empire" so as not only to preserve "all existing powers of self-government and complete control of domestic affairs," but also to give "full recognition of the Dominions as autonomous nations of an Imperial Commonwealth."[26] However, no action was taken until 1926.

(12) **1919:** Treaty of Versailles. Canada and the other Dominions participated in the peace conference and signed the Treaty in their own right, although as members of the Empire and not as independent countries. Canada subsequently became a member of the League of Nations, and in 1927 was elected to a term on the League's Council.

(13) **1922:** Chanak Crisis. Britain warned Turkey that war with Britain would mean war with the entire Empire. This unilateral commitment without prior consultation demonstrated the inadequacy of existing machinery for consultation within the Empire. Prime Minister Mackenzie King responded that the Parliament of Canada, not

Britain, would decide whether Canada went to war. In relation to the subsequent Lausanne Conference (to which the Dominions were not invited) called to negotiate a new peace treaty with Turkey, the Canadian government declared that "in our opinion the extent to which Canada may be held to be bound by the proceedings of the conference or by the provisions of any treaty or other instrument arising out of the same, is necessarily a matter for the Parliament of Canada to decide."[27]

(14) **1923:** Halibut Treaty. Canada had previously been allowed to negotiate trade treaties, but because they were legally British agreements, British representatives had signed. However, at Canada's insistence the British government acquiesced and designated the Canadian Minister of Marine and Fisheries to sign the Halibut Treaty with the United States. There was some debate in the United States Senate about the Treaty's validity because Canada was not an independent country, but the Treaty was ratified nevertheless.

(15) **1926:** Balfour Declaration. It was the 1926 Imperial Conference which gave the Dominions *de facto* independence. In the Report of the Conference, what is usually called the Balfour Declaration described members of the new British Commonwealth of Nations as "autonomous communities within the British Empire, equal in status, in no way subordinate to one another in any aspect of their domestic or external affairs, though united by a common allegiance to the Crown, and freely associated as members of the British Commonwealth."

Furthermore, the Report stated that the governor general was "the representative of the Crown, holding in all essential respects the same position in relation to the administration of public affairs in the dominion as is held by His Majesty the King in Great Britain." The powers of reservation and disallowance as they apply to the relationship between Canada and Britain had therefore become obsolete.

(16) **1927:** Appointment of Canada's first diplomatic representative, independent of the British embassy, to a non-Empire country—namely, the United States. The United States reciprocated in the same year.

(17) **1928:** Appointment of Britain's first High Commissioner to Canada. This had not occurred until the governor general became the representative of the monarch rather than of the British government.

(18) **1931:** Statute of Westminster. With the passage of this Act by the British Parliament on December 11, confirming the 1926 Declaration, Canada and the other Dominions became independent countries. Specifically, no Canadian law would be declared void on

account of conflict with British law, and no British law would apply to Canada except with Canada's express consent. Canada henceforth also possessed the right of extraterritoriality. By this right, a country has authority to legislate for its citizens outside the state so that they are subject to those laws upon their return.

As noted above, one legal restriction was retained at Canada's request—namely, the amendment of the Constitution Act. This restriction did not end until 1982. It has been suggested that some constitutional lawyers might argue that full independence was not achieved until 1939, when Canada declared war for itself a week after Britain's declaration; or until 1949 (see below); or, as "an extreme position," until 1982 (see below).[28]

(19) **1947:** The Letters Patent removed the final legal restriction on the authority of the governor general to exercise the Crown's powers in relation to Canada. This action was mainly symbolic, and for some time there was no essential change in actual practice.

(20) **1949:** The Supreme Court of Canada became the highest court of appeal for Canadians, replacing the Judicial Committee of the Privy Council in Britain. This meant that the Supreme Court would henceforth be the final interpreter of the Constitution Act.

An 1888 amendment to the Canadian Criminal Code had terminated appeals in criminal cases, but this amendment was declared *ultra vires* the Government of Canada in 1926 on the grounds that it conflicted with Britain's Colonial Laws Validity Act. The amendment was re-enacted following passage of the Statute of Westminster. In 1939 the Canadian government sought an advisory opinion as to its ability to abolish all remaining appeals—that is, appeals in civil cases. Both the Supreme Court of Canada and the Judicial Committee of the Privy Council upheld the right, but the matter was set aside at the outbreak of World War Two. Legislation was introduced later and appeals were abolished in 1949.

(21) **1982 (March 29):** Canada Act. This Act declared that no British statute passed after the Constitution Act came into force would apply to Canada. This is the so-called "sign-off" provision. The Constitution Act is attached to the Canada Act as Schedule B.

(22) **1982 (April 17):** Constitution Act. The proclamation of this Act removed the last vestige of British control over the Canadian constitution.

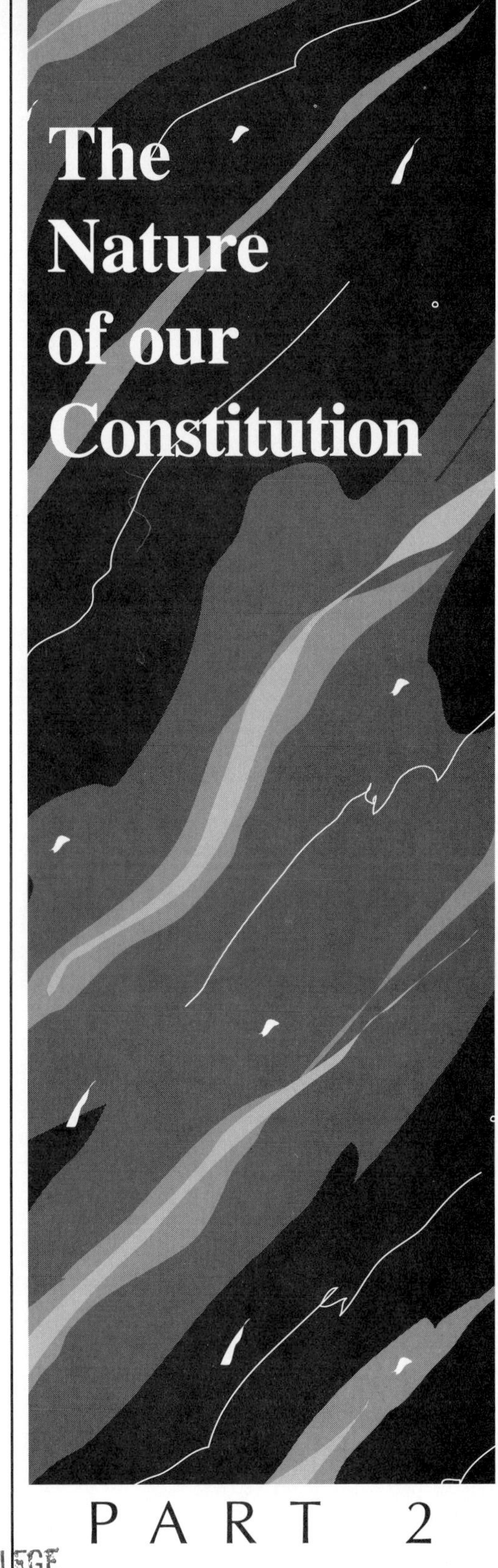

The Nature of our Constitution

PART 2

CHAPTER 4

Principles of the Constitution

1. Monarchy
2. Rule of Law
3. Liberal Democracy
4. Responsible Government
5. Federalism
6. Semi-limited Government

None of our major constitutional documents has rung with the rhetoric of national purpose or, with the possible exception of the new Charter of Rights and Freedoms, of fundamental ideals. And none, including the Charter, has been inspiring literature. A document of "monumental dullness" says Alan Cairns of the 1867 Constitution Act.[1] Compare for example the language of that Act's preamble with the following preamble to the Constitution of the United States: "We the people of the United States, in order to form a more perfect union, establish justice, insure domestic tranquility, provide for the common defense, promote the general welfare, and secure the blessings of liberty to ourselves and our posterity, do ordain and establish this constitution for the United States of America." Better still, compare it with the opening words of the United States Declaration of Independence: "We hold these truths to be self-evident, that all men are created equal, that they are endowed by their Creator with certain unalienable Rights, that among these are Life, Liberty and the pursuit of Happiness." Of course the British North American colonies of 1867 had not fought a revolutionary war; neither were they establishing their independence from the mother country.

It is unfortunate that the framers of the 1982 Constitution Act did not see fit to incorporate some of the spirit of the aborted 1978 Constitutional Amendment Bill (C-60). The preamble to that Bill affirms "the will of Canadians to live and find their futures together in a federation based on equality and mutual respect"; it honours "the contribution of Canada's original inhabitants"; it welcomes "the evolution of the English-speaking and French-speaking communities, in a Canada shaped by men and women from many lands"; and it resolves "that a renewal of the Canadian federation, guided by aims set forth in its constitution, can best secure the fulfilment of present and future generations of Canadians."

Those aims included protecting fundamental rights for the realization of the "legitimate aspirations and essential worth and dignity" of all Canadians; ensuring popular sovereignty, but ensuring also that "neither the power of government nor the will of a majority shall interfere in an unwarranted or arbitrary manner with the enjoyment by each Canadian of his or her liberty, security and well-being"; pursuing "social justice and economic opportunity for all Canadians through the equitable sharing of the benefits and burdens of living in the vast land that is their common inheritance"; and affirming, "through [the] . . . daily lives and governance [of Canadians,] the fundamental proposition . . . that fraternity does not require uniformity nor need diversity lead to division."

The closest that the 1982 Constitution Act comes to inspirational language is the two-line invocation of the supremacy of God (which raises questions about the Charter's guarantee of religious freedom) and the rule of law. The rest is pedantic and legalistic, scarcely likely to enhance Canadian nationalism. Fortunately the existence of constitutional principles does not depend upon rhetoric. The essence of some of the principles described below is to be found within the 1867 or 1982 Constitution Act, but all of the principles depend to some extent upon other parts of the constitution, especially convention. While specific enumerations of Canada's constitutional principles will vary, the following must be included.

1. MONARCHY

> "God save the Queen" really means "God help us to govern ourselves." We are not very good at it sometimes. One reason is the uncertainty of both political leadership and the response to it of the citizenry. The Crown exists to help relieve this difficulty. The anthem goes on, in a later, rarely heard verse, to condemn our enemies: "Confound their politics, frustrate their knavish tricks." The Crown is designed to assist our own politics and compensate for our own tricks.[2]

Although written in lighter vein this opening paragraph of Professor MacKinnon's refreshing and sympathetic *The Crown in Canada* clearly expresses the element of stability that monarchy can bring to a democratic political system. Finer states it this way:

> As a father-image, . . . king or queen stands scatheless, the noble father or mother, while the politicians may be vilified and scourged. This duality is politically comfortable. On the one hand, politics might be red in tooth and claw; on the other royalty reminds the nation of its brotherhood amid their conflicts. The silk gloves are something to be thankful for.[3]

On her Canadian visit during the centennial celebration of the 1864 Charlottetown Conference, Queen Elizabeth stated that the role of a constitutional monarch "is to personify the democratic state, to sanction legitimate authority, to assure the legality of its measures, and to guarantee the execution of the popular will. In accomplishing this task, it protects the people against disorder."[4] These statements of the monarchial ideal notwithstanding, the actual influence of the Crown within the political system today is generally slight, seldom apparent, and at any given time dependent to a large extent upon existing circumstances not the least of which are the personalities and experience of the actors involved.

Section 9 of the 1867 Constitution Act states that "The executive government and authority of and over Canada is hereby declared to continue and be vested in the Queen." Clearly then, Canada is a monarchy and all executive acts are performed if not by the Queen herself then in her name. Although the governor general is now empowered to act in all respects as the Queen's representative in relation to the Government of Canada, our chief of state is the monarch herself. Until the 1947 Letters Patent were issued, there were a few minor exceptions to this generalization. The Queen was commander-in-chief of our military forces (s. 15), she was authorized to determine the location of the seat of the Federal government (s. 16), and she could appoint additional senators (s. 26). Those exceptions disappeared in 1947 when King George empowered the governor general "to exercise all powers and authorities lawfully belonging to Us in respect of Canada."[5] Since then the governor general has legally occupied the same position with respect to the Canadian government as has the monarch in relation to the British government. Nevertheless, until 1978 the Queen continued to receive advice directly from her Canadian ministers regarding our diplomatic relations with other countries, except that the governor general would as in the past appoint high commissioners—the equivalent of ambassadors—to Commonwealth countries. Today, only the issuing of Letters of Credence to our ambassadors involves the Queen directly (although there is no longer a legal requirement), the reason being that these documents are communications between chiefs of state.[6]

The above notwithstanding there is a power remaining with the monarch. This is contained in paragraph XV of the 1947 Letters Patent themselves: "And we do hereby reserve to ourselves, our heirs and successors, full power and authority from time to time to revoke, alter, or amend these our Letters Patent as to us or them seem meet." This includes the power to appoint and remove the governor general, although its exercise would be upon the advice of the Canadian prime minister.

During the sixteenth and seventeenth centuries the British Parliament was engaged in a struggle with the Tudor and Stuart monarchs over control of government. This struggle was not resolved until the 1688 Glorious Revolution when Parliament called the protestant Prince William of Orange and his protestant wife Mary Stuart to reign jointly. (William was the nephew, and Mary the daughter, of the just-deposed Catholic James II; and so the new rulers were first cousins. Mary was also the great granddaughter of the first Stuart [James I]). Parliament passed the Bill of Rights a month before William and Mary ascended the throne in 1689. The 1701 Act of Settlement established the order of protestant succession to the throne, and the 1772 Royal Marriages Act limited the right of the monarch's children to marry without the monarch's consent.

These events marked the watershed ending the monarchial claim to rule by divine right, and establishing parliamentary supremacy and what is generally called "constitutional monarchy." Nevertheless, the real power of the monarch declined only gradually to the point where the Queen now reigns but does not rule. The circumstances surrounding the abdication of Edward VIII in 1936 clearly demonstrated the continued supremacy of Parliament in determining who occupies the throne. The abdication was then confirmed in Britain by His Majesty's Declaration of Abdication Act (1936) and in Canada by the Succession to the Throne Act (1937).

The term "constitutional monarchy" is paradoxical and needs clarification. Most of the important actions of our government are taken by the Crown (by the governor general or, on special occasions and when invited, by the Queen herself) and cannot legally be taken otherwise because they are specified in the Constitution. These include, for example (from the 1867 Constitution Act), the summoning (s. 38) and dissolving (s. 50) of Parliament; the appointing of senators (ss. 24, 26, 32), certain provincial court judges (s. 96), and privy councillors (s. 11); the recommending of money bills to Parliament (s. 54); the assenting to legislation (s. 55); and (from the 1982 Constitution Act) the proclaiming of Constitutional amendments (s. 38[1]). Convention dictates that these powers be exercised only upon the advice of the governor general's ministers. A governor general who acts independently of such advice might be acting legally but also, and at the same time, unconstitutionally. This generalization also applies to the few statutory powers assigned to the Queen. The significance of convention as part of our constitution is considered in the next chapter.

In addition to the Crown's statutory authority is the prerogative power, which Dicey describes as "nothing else than the residue of discretionary or arbitrary authority, which at any given time is legally left in the hands of the Crown. The King was originally in truth what he still is in name, the sovereign, or . . . at any rate by far the most powerful part of the sovereign power."[7] As with statutory powers so also must the greatest part of the royal prerogative be exercised only upon ministerial advice. It is apparent that prerogative powers cannot be increased. They can, however, be diminished by means of statutes. Indeed, most of the Crown's statutory powers in Canada remain part of the prerogative in Britain.

Although convention requires the governor general to accept the advice of ministers in exercising statutory and prerogative authority, there are some powers which under certain circumstances (not always clearly defined) are exercisable upon the governor general's initiative. Paramount among these powers is the responsibility to ensure the existence of a prime minister. Two comments about this personal responsibility are necessary. In the first place the responsibility is personal for the simple reason that no one, including a departing prime minister, has the authority to give constitutional advice as to the appointment of a successor. However, nothing prevents a governor general from seeking that individual's or anyone else's opinion. In the second place the real selection of prime minister is almost invariably made for the governor general by the electorate when they determine the composition of the House of Commons in a general election, or by the House of Commons when it decides whether to support the existing ministry following an indecisive election. If the prime minister suddenly dies or resigns, the governor general will likely consult with ministers and other leading parliamentary members within the ruling party before appointing a successor. Three recent illustrations of the latter situation at the provincial level occurred in Quebec. Lieutenant Governor Gagnon appointed Paul Sauvé following the death of Premier Duplessis in 1959, and Antonio Barrette when Sauvé died four months later; Lieutenant Governor Hughes Lapointe appointed Jean-Jacques Bertrand upon the death of Daniel Johnson in 1968. The responsibility of the governor general or lieutenant governor is in the final analysis always a personal one, but it is of paramount importance that he or she choose someone who is acceptable to the legislature and, of course, the party.

A second discretionary power of the Crown is to advise the government. A century ago Walter Bagehot expressed this power as "the right to be consulted, the right to encourage, the right to warn." He added that "a king of great sense and sagacity would want no others."[8] The usefulness of this three-fold right depends to a great extent upon the personalities of the principals involved, but Canadian experience is less impressive than British. This is doubtlessly because the prestige accompanying a hereditary monarch cannot be matched by an appointed governor general; futhermore, the "term of office" and therefore experience of the monarch generally exceeds that of the representative.

The Crown also possesses a reserve power which is virtually impossible to define. This power exists to cope with a crisis that threatens constitutional government itself and is so intolerable that it cannot await corrective action by other constitutional machinery. Dawson and Ward suggest by way of illustration that the Crown's intervention would be justified, even to the point of dismissal, if a prime minister accepted a bribe and refused to allow Parliament to deal with the issue, or if a prime minister demanded an immediate dissolution of Parliament following an unfavourable general election.[9] A more clear-cut justification, but one not likely to occur, would be the refusal of a prime minister to resign or seek dissolution in the event of a withdrawal of confidence by the Commons. No Canadian prime minister has faced dismissal but five provincial premiers have been dismissed (Quebec in 1878 and 1891; British Columbia in 1898, 1900, 1903).[10] Prime Minister King claimed a right to an immediate dissolution following the October 1925 election which had produced a Conservative plurality, but he wisely chose instead to meet the House. However, during the debate on what was essentially a non-confidence motion in June 1926 King sought, but was refused, a dissolution by Governor General Lord Byng. King immediately resigned, Byng appointed Arthur Meighen as prime minister, Meighen's Government fell on the third day, Meighen sought and received a dissolution, and King won a decisive victory in the general election. The constitutionality of Byng's refusal of King's advice continues to be disputed. Forsey suggests that the entire episode raises at least eight constitutional issues.[11] In December 1979 when Prime Minister Clark advised dissolution seven months into his term, following the defeat of his Government's budget, Governor General Schreyer kept Clark waiting for two hours (presumably to consider his reply) before accepting the advice.

In January 1982 Governor General Schreyer stated publicly that he had considered action "to cause an election to be held and the Canadian people asked to decide" had the Federal-provincial impasse over patriation of the Constitution not been resolved through last-minute bargaining the previous November.[12] It is doubtful that if Schreyer had been unable to persuade Prime Minister Trudeau to advise the dissolution of Parliament the issue would have been so critical as to warrant use of the reserve power. Because the governor general cannot dissolve Parliament without ministerial advice, use of the reserve would have meant the dismissal of Trudeau and the appointment of someone else (presumably Joe Clark, Leader of the Opposition) for the express purpose of advising dissolution. Mallory points out that dissolution requires a proclamation issued under the Great Seal, which is in the custody of a minister of the Crown who would therefore be politically responsible for its use. Other ministers, also, would be involved because an order-in-council is usually needed to issue a proclamation.[13] Furthermore, if Schreyer had proceeded there would have remained the question of how a Federal election would have secured the "provincial" consensus which the Supreme Court of Canada had said was required by convention. If the people were to be "asked to decide" independently of the "provinces," what proportion and what geographic distribution would have been required for a legitimate decision on something so basic as the Constitution? Schreyer was wise not to act and he should have kept his constitutional musings to himself.

Understandably, informed opinion differs as to the propriety of the use of reserve powers. Short of an emergency requiring immediate action, and especially so long as the Government holds the confidence of the House, the caution expressed by Dawson and Ward is well taken:

> The broad rule . . . still holds: the governor general will follow the advice given by his ministers, for they accept the responsibility and with it accept the praise or blame for the decision and its results. The advice given may be bad; it may be short-sighted; it may be foolish; it may be dangerous—these considerations may induce the governor to remonstrate with his ministers and try to win them over to his point of view; but if they persist, his only course is to shrug his shoulders and acquiesce. The decision is not his, but that of his government, and eventually the people and their representatives will deal with those who have proffered the advice. Should the governor set his will against that of the cabinet, his action at once tends to become a political issue and he, whether he likes it or not, finds himself a party leader in the opposition's interests.[14]

In Lord Asquith's terms, by acting unwisely the Crown risks becoming "the football of contending factions,"[15] inasmuch as ministerial action that the Crown believes to be unconstitutional may represent nothing more than disagreement between political parties.

The commentary on section 10 of the 1867 Constitution Act contains a list of our governors general since Confederation.

2. RULE OF LAW

Because a basic constitutional function is to determine the proper relationship between the individual and the state, the definition of this relationship is of critical importance. In our society the rule of law is at the core of that definition. Essentially this principle states that the law is supreme and that it applies to everyone. No one, including the lawmakers, is above the law.

One of the oldest typologies of government was formulated by Plato and Aristotle. Their criteria included answers to the questions "Who rules?" and "In whose interest do they rule?" The second of these relates to rule of law. If governors are bound by constitutional rules rather than capable of acting according to their selfish self-interest, they are governing according to the rule of law. Aristotle's statement is well-known: "He who bids the law rule may be deemed to bid God and Reason alone rule, but he who bids man rule adds an element of the beast; for desire is a wild beast, and passion perverts the minds of rulers, even when they are the best of men. The law is reason unaffected by desire."[16]

Magna Carta (1215) is often regarded as the root of our constitution and especially rule of law. According to section 39 "no freeman shall be taken or (and) imprisoned or disseised or outlawed or exiled or in any way destroyed, nor will we go upon him nor send upon him, except by the lawful judgement of his peers or (and) by the law of the land."[17] Hutchinson and Monahan suggest that by the fifteenth century, the Magna Carta had become "an obscure and hollow proclamation, only later to be romanticized by some modern legal historians," and that it was not until the 1689 Bill of Rights that Parliament had sufficient power over the monarch (its own appointee, William of Orange and his wife Mary Stuart) to enforce its intentions.[18]

The classical expression of the rule of law is undoubtedly Dicey's of a century ago in England:

> "Rule of law," . . . which forms a fundamental principle of the constitution, has three meanings, or may be regarded from three points of view.
>
> It means, in the first place, the absolute supremacy or predominance of regular law as opposed to the influence of arbitrary power, and excludes the existence of arbitrariness, of prerogative, or even of wide discretionary authority on the part of the government. Englishmen are ruled by the law, and by the law alone; a man may with us be punished for a breach of law, but he can be punished for nothing else.
>
> It means, again, equality before the law, or the equal subjection of all classes to the ordinary law of the land administered by the ordinary law courts; the "rule of law" in this sense excludes the idea of any exemption of officials or others from the duty of obedience to the law which governs other citizens or from the jurisdiction of the ordinary tribunals . . .
>
> The "rule of law," lastly, may be used as a formula for expressing the fact that with us the law of the constitution, the rules which in foreign countries naturally form part of a constitutional code, are not the source but the consequence of the rights of individuals, as defined and enforced by the courts; that, in short, the principles of private law have with us been by the action of the courts and Parliament so extended as to determine the position of the Crown and of its servants; thus the constitution is the result of the ordinary law of the land.[19]

Today's complex society, however, increasingly casts doubt upon our ability to realize these "meanings." At least two significant departures must be noted which, if we are not vigilant, may jeopardize the very existence of the rule of law. The first departure is the more serious for it leads inevitably to the second. This is the delegation of vast regulation-making powers by the modern legislature to the executive branch of government—officially to ministers of the Crown (in our system) but in reality to the bureaucracy. The reason for this delegation is the greatly increased government involvement in so many of society's activities. This development, unlikely to diminish significantly in the future, is often described as the rise of the positive state. It is essential, therefore, that people have easy access to regulations for only then can they be fully aware of the legal consequences of their actions. Nevertheless, Dicey's prescription cannot be realized in modern society: that all government action is "bound by rule, fixed and announced beforehand," so that individuals may plan their own activities in full knowledge of the likely consequences.[20]

There are several reasons why legislatures delegate rather than attempt to make regulations themselves. These include the lack of time, lack of technical expertise, and the need for flexibility to meet changing conditions and emergencies. How, for example, are members of Parliament to determine what a hazardous product is for the purpose of a Hazardous Products Act; or to define "blindness" for the purpose of government assistance under a Blind Persons Act? Another reason for delegation reflects the changing emphasis from individual to collective rights which has accompanied the rise of the positive state. Corry has pointed out that "it is easy to prohibit in general terms when you know precisely what you want to discourage. It is impossible to ensure the building of something new for the first time by commanding it in advance in general terms. The desired result can be visualized but the means of achieving it must be determined by the obstacles encountered in daily administration."[21]

Some two-thirds of the Statutes of Canada delegate authority to make rules and regulations. Much of this delegation merely facilitates the administration of statutes. But much is far more general in its scope and embodies vast discretionary power which makes difficult the determination of its legal limits. A major problem associated with the exercise of delegated authority is the danger of abuse—Dicey's "arbitrary power." If "abuse" meant only the exceeding of legal limits, reliance upon the courts might afford sufficient protection. Unfortunately, however, abuse is possible even when legality is maintained, given the breadth of some delegations. We are reminded that "virtue itself hath need of limits."[22]

Undoubtedly the most spectacular example of delegation in Canada was contained in the 1914 War Measures Act (replaced in 1988 by the Emergencies Act).[23] When this statute was invoked the governor-in-council (really the cabinet) was authorized (s. 3[1]) to "do and authorize such Acts and things, and make from time to time such orders and regulations, as he may by reason of the existence of real or apprehended war, invasion or insurrection deem necessary or advisable for the security, defense, peace, order and welfare of Canada." Furthermore, the Act declared that the issuance of the proclamation invoking the Act "shall be conclusive evidence that war, invasion, or insurrection, real or apprehended, exists and has existed for any period of time therein stated, and of its continuance, until by the issue of a further proclamation it is declared that the war, invasion, or insurrection no longer exists" (s. 2). The delegation extended, but was not restricted, to the following (s. 3[1]):

(a) censorship and the control and suppression of publications, writings, maps, plans, photographs, communications and means of communication;
(b) arrest, detention, exclusion and deportation;
(c) control of the harbours, ports and territorial waters of Canada and the movements of vessels;
(d) transportation by land, air, or water and the control of the transport of persons and things;

(e) trading, exportation, importation, production and manufacture;
(f) appropriation, control, forfeiture and disposition of property and of the use thereof.

Little indeed remained beyond the reach of the cabinet.

Whereas the 1960 Bill of Rights stated (s. 6) that any action taken under the War Measures Act "shall be deemed not to be an abrogation, abridgement or infringement of any right or freedom recognized by the Canadian Bill of Rights," such action would after 1982 have been subject to scrutiny under the Charter of Rights and Freedoms. The restrictions actually permitted would have depended upon judicial interpretation of "reasonable limits prescribed by law as can be demonstrably justified in a free and democratic society" (s. 1), as well as the possible invocation of the Charter's "notwithstanding" clause (s. 33) depending upon the rights to be overridden. The Emergencies Act is more moderate than its predecessor, but any restriction of Charter rights will still have to pass muster under section 1. It does not contain the legislative override. For commentary on these sections 1 and 33 see Chapter 8.

Another broad grant of discretionary power was contained in a former Immigration Act. Pursuant to that Act the cabinet was authorized to prohibit or limit the admission of people to Canada on the basis of, among other things, "peculiar customs, habits, modes of life or methods of holding property," or "probable inability to become readily assimilated or to assume the duties and responsibilities of Canadian citizenship."[24]

As a result of the delegation of regulation-making authority by Parliament, many of the "laws" we must obey are in reality subordinate legislation which is neither "ordinary law" nor what Dicey referred to as "established in the ordinary legal manner"—that is, by legislatures. Parliament has recognized the need to strengthen the means of ongoing control or at least scrutiny of the use of delegated power. In 1970 it established the Joint Standing Committee of the Senate and House of Commons on Regulations and Other Statutory Instruments. The Committee's mandate is to review all subordinate legislation (the rules and regulations made pursuant to statutes) on the basis of specific criteria laid down by Parliament.

The second departure from Dicey's formulation of the rule of law is that the "ordinary law courts" have been supplemented by special administrative tribunals or boards for hearing and settling disputes. The reasons for this development include lower costs, greater speed, and greater technical expertise in specific areas of jurisdiction. Furthermore, in an age when collective rights are of increasing importance it may indeed be appropriate to restrict the role of courts. Because of the historical emphasis upon individualism which has characterized the common law (law which has developed over the centuries as the accumulation of judicial decisions), the courts have traditionally stressed the protection of individual and property rights. It is inevitable, however, that the rights of the community advance at the expense of the individual. Significantly, the legal rights enumerated in section 7 of the Charter of Rights and

Freedoms include "life, liberty and security of the person," but not property.

The rule of law may indeed be compromised by the ramifications of the positive state, but whether or not our freedoms are endangered depends upon the vigilance of the population generally and of their elected representatives in particular. "The condition upon which God hath given liberty to man is eternal vigilance; which condition if he break, servitude is at once the consequence of his crime, and the punishment of his guilt."[25]

Dicey's third component of the rule of law appears to eliminate constitutional documents containing declarations of rights, as contrasted with rights produced by the common law. However, Dicey was concerned primarily about declarations that in fact were incapable of enforcement.

> The question whether the right to personal freedom . . . is likely to be secure . . . depend[s] a good deal upon the answer to the inquiry whether the persons who consciously or unconsciously build up the constitution of their country begin with definitions or declarations of rights, or with the contrivance of remedies by which rights may be enforced or secured.[26]

Using this criterion Dicey acknowledged that the rule of law "is as marked a feature of the United States as of England."[27] Presumably, it is also as secure in Canada under the Charter of Rights and Freedoms as it was earlier.

There is a quite different problem associated with the rule of law, although it can be acknowledged here. Hutchinson and Monahan suggest that the historical commitment to rule of law "can no longer be assumed," and they cite several incidents in Canada and elsewhere to illustrate the "extent of popular dissatisfaction with the legal and established order." For example, several times Canadian juries acquitted Dr. Henry Morgentaler in spite of his open and repeated defiance of abortion law. Did these acquittals fly in the face of rule of law, or could they be defended as means to ensure justice (which is after all the essence of rule of law) in spite of the law? Or consider the widespread (though temporary) public support of the New York "subway vigilante" who took the law into his own hands and shot four people who accosted him.[28]

Rule of law is intended to protect individuals from arbitrary action by government and its agencies because it requires government action to be in accordance with law. It would appear, however, that this principle gives no protection to individual freedom in a political system characterized by legislative supremacy; in such a system there is no legal restriction precluding the making of repressive laws. Nevertheless, it must be possible to reconcile rule of law and legislative supremacy because both are basic to the British constitution and were, before 1982, basic to ours as well. If rule of law means nothing more than that all government action is sanctioned by law, reconciliation is easy. But if rule of law involves (as it must) the protection of individual freedom from arbitrary (though lawful) government interference, then the two principles are surely mutually exclusive. Reconciliation comes with the recognition that while legal and constitutional restrictions upon government are not synonymous, the political consequences of a serious violation of constitutional convention may in fact be as much a deterrent as the legal consequences of the violation of a freedom that has been entrenched in a Charter or Bill of Rights.

3. LIBERAL DEMOCRACY

The term "democracy" is one of the most used and abused terms to describe political systems. Indeed, it is sometimes considered to be a way-of-life package, including not only a particular political system but also a particular economic and even religious system. Even when restricted to political systems the term "democracy" is ascribed to countries as diverse as those in pre-1990 Eastern Europe; liberal democracies such as those of Western Europe, Canada, and the United States; and developing countries. As Lewis Carroll's Humpty Dumpty said: "When *I* use a word, it means just what I choose it to mean—neither more nor less." And Crick describes "democracy" with delightful imagery: "She's everybody's mistress and yet somehow retains her magic even when her lover sees that her favours are being, in his light, illicitly shared by many another. Indeed, even amid our pain at being denied her exclusive fidelity, we are proud of her adaptability to all sorts of circumstances."[29]

Until the latter part of the nineteenth century, democracy was a bad word denoting class rule by the masses, rule which would lead inevitably to the end of individual freedom or "liberalism." Liberalism is the notion that there are many aspects of our lives, the privacy of which must be respected by government. Democracy and liberalism were viewed as mutually exclusive concepts with the latter's survival dependent upon some form of aristocratic rule.

The word "democracy" comes from the Greek words *demos* meaning the people, and *kratein* meaning to rule. During the golden age of Athens at the time of Pericles in the fifth century B.C., democracy was direct rather than representative in that decisions were taken at meetings in which all eligible people could participate. Eligibility, however, was restricted to free (perhaps one-third of the total population were slaves), adult, male citizens, both of whose parents also were citizens. These qualifications excluded the vast majority of the adult population.

Because of the size of most modern political units, as well as the complexity of modern government, contemporary democracies are representative rather than direct. For the purpose of this brief description, representative democracy means that government is conducted by majorities of people elected by secret ballot on the basis of universal adult suffrage; that meaningful competition among parties at election time and within the legislature is not restricted; that the qualifications for voters and candidates are essentially the same; and that legitimate input into the political system by the media, interest groups, and the public generally, is encouraged between elections. In other words, representative democracy is intended to ensure that control of government is ultimately in the hands of "the people"—hence the term "popular sovereignty". The concept of universal suffrage may be deemed to imply voting equality and therefore constituencies of approximately equal populations. The commentaries on sections 37, 51, and 52 of the 1867 Constitution Act, and sections 3 and 42(1)(a) of the 1982 Constitution Act, consider the issue of representation by population.

Given the conventional wisdom that the secret ballot is sacred in a liberal democracy, the following view of John Stuart Mill is something to ponder: "The voter is under an absolute moral obligation to consider the interest of the public, not his private advantage," and therefore "the duty of voting, like any other public duty, should be performed under the eye and criticism of the public."[30]

When democracy is also liberal, there is an actual (even if not a legal) limit on majority rule because governments respect, and protect from encroachment by others, privileges or freedoms possessed by individuals and minorities. To the extent that government majorities ignore these privileges and freedoms, the "liberal" aspect of democracy is threatened.

Corry has suggested that the ultimate objective of liberal democracy is "the liberation of and respect for individual personality."[31] This does not mean that as individuals we hold no higher ends in life. It does mean that, because people disagree as to the nature of these ultimate objectives, the main purpose of a democratic system must be the establishment of an environment in which people are free to pursue their own highest goals. For example, Corry asks, "Should not our highest aim be to do the will of God, or to serve Truth and Goodness?" He replies that these questions raise the more fundamental issues of the nature of God's will, truth, and goodness.

> Answers to these questions will turn on religious or philosophical views about the nature of the universe and man's place in it. And when we ask what is the final scheme of things and man's place in it, we meet divergent answers and hot dispute. We are in the midst of the controversies of the ages, and beyond the area in which general agreement is possible in our present state of knowledge.
>
> We cannot frame or hold a common ideal that depends on the prior settlement of questions we cannot presently settle.

Corry concludes that

> from the point of view of democracy, government is a mundane affair, primarily concerned with a framework of order which will serve the concrete needs of an earth-bound humanity. If men will make the adjustments necessary to secure firmly for one another these needs and interests, they are freed in their persons for the pursuit of the various forms of excellence that seem good to them. If one's vision is solitary, he can hitch his wagon to the star of his choice. If he finds others of like mind, they can go forward in voluntary and satisfying fellowship. If the vision fades for some, they need go no

> further. But when government is harnessed to a cosmic purpose, all are required to go in the same wagon to the same star, willy-nilly.

Reality does not necessarily conform to the democratic ideal. One of the obstacles noted in the previous section on rule of law is the extensive delegation of authority by the legislature to the executive—usually, in fact, delegation to officials in the public service. Although such delegation makes it difficult to enforce accountability to the legislature, and ultimately to the people, efforts to do so must not be abandoned. Viewpoints such as the following are unacceptable: "Throughout the length and breadth of our technical civilization there is arising a type of responsibility on the part of the permanent administrator . . . which cannot be effectively enforced except by fellow-technicians who are capable of judging his policy in terms of the scientific knowledge bearing upon it."[32]

In Canada it is an open question whether the problem of enforcing cabinet responsibility to Parliament is an obstacle to popular sovereignty. Not only does the delegation of power contribute to the problem; so also does the existence of disciplined political parties. On the one hand the cabinet is part of Parliament and (except for possible Senate representation) is composed of elected representatives. On the other hand the power which the cabinet possesses greatly reduces effective accountability at least until the next election, and at that time accountability is to the electorate directly rather than to Parliament. The principle of responsible government is considered in the next section.

The qualifications of voters and candidates in Federal elections are established by the Canada Elections Act.[33] Basically, these qualifications are Canadian citizenship and the attainment of age 18. Persons disqualified from voting include the Chief Electoral Officer, the Assistant Chief Electoral Officer, the returning officer in each constituency (except that he or she may vote to break a tie), any judge appointed by the Federal government (except a judge of the Citizenship Court), anyone in a mental hospital, an inmate of a penal institution, and anyone disqualified by any law for "corrupt or illegal practices." Court challenges to the disqualification of judges, or citizens confined to a mental hospital or prison, are noted in the commentary on section 3 of the 1982 Constitution Act. Changes since 1867 in the law defining the franchise are described in the commentary on section 41 of the 1867 Constitution Act.

Persons disqualified from candidacy include anyone who is not an eligible voter; anyone who has been convicted of a corrupt election practice (disqualification is for seven years) or an illegal election practice (disqualification is for five years); any member of a provincial legislature or territorial council; anyone (with minor exceptions) who holds a contract with the Federal government; and any employee of the Crown except a cabinet minister, a part-time member of the armed forces (and a full-time member during wartime), and any public servant on leave without pay for the purpose of seeking election.

4. RESPONSIBLE GOVERNMENT

The struggle for responsible government was an important part of our constitutional development during the first half of the nineteenth century. Responsible government means that the executive branch must yield to the legislature or, more specifically, to the elected assembly. When the governor was active in the political process, he therefore agreed to accept the advice of his executive council who had been appointed from, and who held the support of, the assembly; and to change his council when that support was withdrawn. Now that the governor's leadership has been replaced by that of the council, responsible government means that the cabinet (formally the privy council or the ministry) must accept the will of the House of Commons. Walter Bagehot has described the cabinet, the real executive which formulates policy and is responsible for its administration, as "a combining committee—a hyphen which joins, a buckle which fastens," the legislature to the executive. "In its origin it belongs to the one, in its functions it belongs to the other."[34] The paradox created by ministerial responsibility to both Crown and Commons is resolved by the practical elimination of the former. (For the distinction among privy council, ministry, and cabinet, see the commentary on section 11 of the 1867 Constitution Act.)

Beyond the general statement that responsible government means the cabinet is answerable to the House of Commons, "a clear and succinct account . . . is not easy to give" partly because, as with many conventions, it is "somewhat vague and slippery." Marshall offers this whimsical but important illustration of the problem:[35]

> The slipperiness shows itself when we see that propositions about both types of responsibility [collective and individual] have to be formulated in some such form as: "Ministers generally do or should do X in circumstances Y (but with various exceptions)." Thus:
>
> 1. The prerogatives of the Crown are exercised on the advice of Ministers (except in such cases as they are not).
> 2. The Government resigns when it loses the confidence of the House of Commons (except when it remains in office).
> 3. Ministers speak and vote together (except when they cannot agree to do so).
> 4. Ministers explain their policy and provide information to the House (except when they keep it to themselves).
> 5. Ministers offer their individual resignations if serious errors are made in their Departments (except when they retain their posts or are given peerages).
> 6. Every act of a civil servant is, legally speaking, the act of a minister (except those that are, legally speaking, his own).

Although Marshall is writing for Britain much of this has a familiar ring to Canadians. For example, rarely does a minister resign for maladministration within his or her department, although resignation will likely follow serious personal misconduct. And, although a request for dissolution is an acceptable alternative to resignation when Commons support is withdrawn, there remains the difficulty of determining what, short of a direct non-confidence motion, constitutes "confidence."

Much has been and is being written about the reality or myth of responsible government in Canada. If responsible government means only that the cabinet must retain Commons support then its health is assured: when support fails there is either a resignation or an election. However, if the principle means that the cabinet must constantly woo the Commons lest that support be withdrawn, then responsible government is mythical at least in the short run and when the ruling party possesses a majority. Writing of the British constitution but of matters applicable to Canada as well, Bagehot distinguishes between the "dignified" and the "efficient" parts.[36] The former includes the Crown and the House of Lords (Senate, in Canada); the latter, the Commons and the cabinet. Under a system of tight party discipline, one might speculate whether the House of Commons has joined the dignified section. Indeed, given the power some prime ministers have wielded, leading to the descriptive term "prime ministerial" government, perhaps the cabinet itself has assumed dignified status so that the "hyphen" or "buckle" has become a single person.

This illustrates a paradox. If rigid party discipline produces a virtual dictatorship by the ruling party or by the leadership of that party, a House in which a third party holds the balance of power, or which contains many "loose fish," can produce so much uncertainty that Government long-term planning must be sacrificed in the interest of immediate survival. This uncertainty is reduced to the extent that the third party or uncommitted members fear an election more than they value their political purity. The occasional minority government may be healthy. It has been said that "when a man knows he is to be hanged in a fortnight, it concentrates his mind wonderfully." As a paraphrase Forsey adds: "When a government knows it may be hanged in a fortnight, the knowledge may broaden its mind wonderfully." He continues:

> Having to get support from outside its own party may not only help a government to do good and sensible things but also prevent it from doing bad and foolish things. This . . . is just as important, and may even be more so. The idea that "doing something" is always good, doing nothing always bad, that action is always better than inaction, is a strange, but apparently powerful, delusion. A government with a clear majority may go lickety-split in the wrong direction. A government without a clear majority is more likely to stop, look, and listen. I am not, of course, arguing that minority government necessarily means good government. I am simply arguing that it does not necessarily mean bad government.[37]

Majority government with a substantial opposition, the absence of long periods of same-party rule, or more "free votes"—that is, votes in which party cohesion is not enforced—is no doubt preferable to minority government as a steady diet.

Perhaps in recognition of the apparent cynicism of Canadians toward their politicians, Prime Minister Mulroney acknowledged in the May 1991 Throne Speech the existence of "excessive party discipline and over-zealous partisanship, of empty posturing and feigned outrage." Parliament would be asked, the Speech continued, "to consider new procedures for assessing legislation, for raising grievances on behalf of constituents and for questioning government," in order to strengthen the role of members of Parliament and to "afford them greater independence."[37a] Many people are sketpical of such promises, and will await "proof of the pudding."

There is a structural fusion of the cabinet and Parliament in that all cabinet ministers are required by convention to have seats in Parliament, if not when they are appointed then within a reasonable but unspecified period of time. The record for a minister without a seat in the Canadian Parliament is nine and one-half months. During that time in 1944-1945 General McNaughton, who was Minister of National Defense, made two unsuccessful bids for election, one in a by-election and the other in the 1945 general election. He then resigned from the cabinet. This constitutional requirement really means that ministers must have seats in the House of Commons where they are accountable to the people's elected representatives. Nevertheless, it is now the practice to have a senator in the cabinet to facilitate the conduct of Government business in the upper house. Sometimes several senators may be appointed in order to maintain geographic representation when the ruling party has few or no Commons seats from a large section of the country. Two recent examples are the appointment of three Quebec senators by Prime Minister Clark in 1979, and three senators from Western Canada by Prime Minister Trudeau in 1980.

What happens when there is disagreement between the Government and the House? More specifically, what happens when a Government motion or bill is defeated, or an opposition motion or bill is passed against the cabinet's wishes? If the issue is not a question of "confidence" so that the fate of the Government does not ride on the outcome, then the vote settles the matter and there are no further repercussions. Should a Government decide that a particular defeat is not a matter of confidence, the opposition may remove all doubt by subsequently moving a non-confidence motion.

If the issue is one of confidence then one of two things will happen. The prime minister may submit the Government's resignation and the governor general will call upon someone else, probably the leader of the Official Opposition, to take office. This is a likely alternative only if the Government's defeat follows closely on the heels of an indecisive election and if the formation of an alternative Government without an election seems practicable. The second possibility is that the prime minister will advise the governor general to dissolve Parliament and call a general election. If the Government is victorious at the polls—that is, if the electorate returns a sympathetic House—then it will remain in office without interruption. If the Government is defeated, the prime minister will resign and the governor general will invite the leader of the victorious party to take office. A prime minister will normally prefer an election to immediate resignation because it offers the possibility of retaining power. At first glance, however, dissolution appears to be the antithesis of responsible government in that a defeated Government terminates the life of Parliament. What it actually does is give to the electorate the opportunity to decide which party will rule. It is as if the governor general were saying, "This Parliament sent you here, but I will see if I cannot get another parliament to send some one else here."[38] A prime minister who is dissatisfied with an election's outcome may not then seek the immediate dissolution of the new House in the hope of success the next time around. Nevertheless, as noted earlier in this chapter, Liberal Prime Minister Mackenzie King claimed this right following the election of a Conservative plurality in October 1925.

There may be a third alternative following Government defeat on an important matter. It has but one Canadian precedent. On February 19, 1968, while Prime Minister Pearson was out of the country, the minority Government was defeated 84 votes to 82 on third reading of an amendment to the Income Tax Act. The defeat was entirely avoidable and resulted from Deputy Prime Minister Mitchell Sharp's failure to ensure the presence of sufficient Liberal members before agreeing to the vote. As a general rule the defeat of a money bill cannot be ignored by the Government. Predictably, therefore, there were demands for the Government's immediate resignation or Parliament's dissolution. (Creditiste leader Réal Caouette called for both! He meant, in fact, only the latter.) The crisis was most awkward for the ruling Liberals who were two months away from a leadership convention to replace the retiring Pearson.

The prime minister could not ignore the defeat of a money bill; neither did he resign nor seek dissolution inasmuch as the defeat was a fluke. Instead, following a two-day adjournment (in which Conservative leader Robert Stanfield acquiesced—a questionable political move), he presented a resolution to the House stating "that this house does not regard its vote on February 19th in connection with third reading of Bill C-193 which had carried in all previous stages, as a vote of non-confidence in the government." The Government was sustained (138-119) with the support of the Creditistes who held the balance of power and wanted to avoid an election.[39] There is an interesting footnote to this episode. The 1963 edition of Dawson and Ward's *The Government of Canada* states that third reading "is usually perfunctory," as of course it is; the 1970 edition following closely upon the heels of this event, is somewhat more guarded and comments that third reading "is by no means a formality."[40]

The reality of responsible government is more apparent when political parties are loosely organized as in the early years following Confederation when, Forsey reports, John A. Macdonald's Government "was defeated repeatedly in the House and neither resigned nor asked for dissolution."[41] If sufficient members in the House oppose a Government measure the cabinet must either meet the opposition part way or be defeated. However, with today's disciplined parties a Government with a Commons majority faces no possibility of defeat except in the unlikely event of internal revolt. The party leadership has strong inducements to keep followers quiescent, not the least of which are support during the next election campaign, possible promotion to the cabinet, or (after retirement from active politics) appointment to the Senate or other patronage positions. There are limits to the demands that leaders may place upon the rank and file, and even if these limits are far down the road, their existence must be recognized.

When the ruling party has only a minority of the Commons seats, the reality of responsible government seems greater, for the combined opposition can topple the Government at any time. This assumes that enough of the opposition can agree on an issue for cooperation. It makes the even greater assumption that the opposition parties desire an election. While the Official Opposition may well seek the opportunity to form a Government, the third party holding the balance of power may pay no more than lip service to defeat, inasmuch as it is already in its optimum position. In the next election that party likely has no way to go but down. Of the six minority Governments elected since the Second World War (in 1957, 1962, 1963, 1965, 1972, 1979), three (1962, 1972, 1979) were defeated in the House. However, defeat of the 1972 Liberal Government occurred only after the New Democratic Party had sustained the Liberals for two years. In the ensuing 1974 election the N.D.P.'s representation was halved, its leader (David Lewis) being among the victims. In the election following the defeat of the 1979 Clark Government, the Creditistes were wiped out.

In 1985 Ontario's minority Conservative Government of Frank Miller resigned following its defeat in the legislature. The incoming Liberal Premier David Peterson and N.D.P. leader Bob Rae negotiated and signed an agreement whereby the N.D.P. would support the Government for at least two years. In return, the Government agreed to implement a number of N.D.P. policies and not call an election for at least two years. Such an agreement, which is not legally binding, alters the operation of responsible government by eliminating much of the uncertainty that might otherwise attend a minority government situation.

5. FEDERALISM

Although a federal union of British North America was considered by most politicians to be the only practical solution to the problems of the 1860s, there was virtually no theoretical concept of "federalism" such as has been developed by contemporary writers. As a result, meanings of the term varied among the political leaders. "Federalism" could accommodate Cartier's notion that the essence lay in the protection of French interests through equal regional representation in the Senate and strong representation in the cabinet. It could also accommodate Macdonald's view that provincial governments must be subordinate to the central government. For Macdonald, Parliament represented the entire national interest and part of the provincial interest, whereas provincial legislatures represented only part of the provincial interest. The reason Parliament could represent part of the provincial interest was that its members come from the provinces and are therefore concerned about the provincial impact of national policies. The more modern theoretical concept of federalism, embracing provincial autonomy in local matters, was expressed in embryonic form by the Rouge leader A.A. Dorion, by Christopher Dunkin (Independent Conservative from Canada East), and by the Bleu newspaper *Le Courrier du Canada*.[42]

The earliest developed theoretical formulation of federalism was that of K.C. Wheare who in 1946 defined the "federal principle" as "the method of dividing powers so that the general and regional governments are each, within a sphere, co-ordinate and independent."[43] Wheare called Canada's Constitution "quasi-federal" because of the unitary elements in the Constitution Act (especially Ottawa's powers of disallowance and reservation); its power to appoint and dismiss lieutenant governors and certain provincial court judges; and its "declaratory" power (s. 92[10][c]). He acknowledged, nevertheless, that in its operation our system is "federal." The legalistic nature of Wheare's "classical federalism" has significant shortcomings for it ignores the impact of political parties and interest groups on the relationship between the two orders of government. Furthermore, it fails to recognize the phenomenon Professor Smiley has called "executive federalism"—that the federal balance at any given time is determined mainly by politicians at the ministerial level. This emphasis on political leaders is seen in the numerous multilateral and bilateral agreements which are always portrayed as *faits accomplis* the moment ministers' signatures are appended. Legislatures may be ignored because of the control that the leaders through their parties exercise over them.

One of the most outstanding recent examples of executive federalism in action is the November 5, 1981 constitutional accord, which was announced to the country as the ink was drying. Only Alberta Premier Lougheed (on November 10) and Quebec Premier Lévesque (on December 1) submitted the agreement to their legislatures.[44] But even in those two cases the agreement had already been signed (Alberta) or rejected (Quebec). Even more outstanding was the ill-fated 1987 Meech Lake Accord. It, too, was announced as a *fait accompli*, but there had been almost no prior public knowledge that such a deal was even being discussed let alone concluded behind the closed doors. When the deal finally expired on June 23, 1990, for want of the necessary legislative approval, the prime minister called its demise a betrayal, notwithstanding that the failure was consistent with the Constitutional amending process. (See, however, the commentary on section 39 of the 1982 Constitution Act.)

Political agents of change have become more significant determinants of the federal balance than the formal procedures of constitutional amendment and judicial interpretation, although the role of the courts has increased since the mid-1970s. Judicial review as a constitutional principle is considered in the next section. Formal constitutional amendment and judicial decisions as components of the constitution and agents of change are discussed in the next chapter and, of course, as significant elements of the clause-by-clause analyses in Chapters 7 and 8.

Notwithstanding the federal nature of the constitution there were significant elements in the 1867 Constitution Act that contradicted the federal principle.

(1) Refusal of assent, disallowance, and reservation (ss. 55, 56, 57, 90). Essentially, this is the power of the central government to strike down provincial legislation. Because lieutenant governors are involved in the first and third of these powers they could become agents of the central government.

(2) Appointment, dismissal for cause, and payment, of lieutenant governors by the central government (ss. 58, 59, 60). Furthermore, section 92(1) denied to the provinces authority to change their constitutions "as regards the office of lieutenant governor.".

(3) Appointment and payment of provincial superior, district, and county court judges, and dismissal of superior court judges, by the central government (ss. 96, 100, 99).

(4) Appointment of senators by the central government (s. 24). At first glance it may appear that appointment by the central government does not conflict with the federal principle inasmuch as the Senate is part of Parliament. On the other hand one might argue that the absence of provincial involvement is a denial of federalism, given the original intention that the Senate would protect regional or provincial interests. The nature of these interests, incidentally, has never been defined. Was there an implied right of regional or provincial involvement in policy areas belonging to the central government? Was the Senate to be a watchdog ensuring that the central government did not trespass upon policy areas under provincial control? There are obvious problems with both interpretations; in any event, the Senate has never performed this function.

Furthermore, the Supreme Court has strengthened the notion of the Senate as an integral part of federalism by denying to Parliament the right to alter the upper house unilaterally, notwithstanding the 1949 Constitution Act amendment which permitted Ottawa to change the Act in matters not affecting the provinces. The *Senate Reference* is discussed in Chapter 5 under 1867 Constitution Act amendment by the Federal government. Recent proposals to transform the Senate into a House of the Provinces or to create a "Triple E" Senate are obviously relevant to this question.

(5) The power of Parliament under certain circumstances to make remedial laws which are binding upon a province in the area of education, although education is otherwise under provincial authority (s. 93).

(6) The power of Parliament to legislate in the area of "works" which otherwise are under provincial jurisdiction, by declaring them "to

be for the general advantage of Canada or for the advantage of two or more of the provinces" (ss. 92 [10c] and 91[29]).

(7) The power of Parliament to legislate in the performance of international obligations "of Canada or of any province thereof, as part of the British Empire," arising from "treaties between the Empire" and other countries (s. 132). Because Canada now undertakes treaty obligations as an independent country the central government may not use this section to legislate in areas within provincial jurisdiction. This unitary feature has thus disappeared except for obligations incurred before passage of the Statute of Westminster.

(8) The almost unlimited power of Parliament to levy both direct and indirect taxes (s. 91[3]). (Federal direct taxation is limited to purposes of the Federal government because of the exclusive authority given by section 92[2] to the provinces to impose direct taxes "for provincial purposes.") Excessive use of this power may in fact compromise the provinces' ability to raise money by direct taxation. While Federal and provincial income taxation may coexist because "the Dominion reaps part of the field of the . . . citizen's income [and] the province reaps another part of it," what happens, asks Professor Scott with delightful imagery, if "the poor . . . citizen is reaped right down to his bare stubble"?[45] The answer, given by the Judicial Committee of the Privy Council in 1932, is that "the two taxations, Dominion and Provincial, can stand side by side without interfering with each other, but as soon as you come to the concomitant privileges of absolute priority they cannot stand side by side and must clash; consequently the Dominion must prevail."[46] See the discussion of Federal paramountcy in the commentary on the closing paragraph of section 91 of the 1867 Constitution Act.

(9) The power of Parliament to legislate for the "peace, order, and good government" of Canada (s. 91), whereas the provinces have an enumeration of powers. The real significance of this distinction is determined by the courts and is considered in the final section of the next chapter.

(10) The power of Parliament to spend its money as it sees fit. This is implied by its broad power to tax (s. 91[3]), its power to legislate in relation to the public debt and property (s. 91[1A]), and to spend public funds (s. 106). However, if the spending is within an area under provincial jurisdiction the funds must be taken from the Consolidated Revenue Fund rather than from a special tax levied for this purpose. Furthermore, Federal legislation authorizing such spending within areas under provincial control must not infringe upon provincial jurisdiction—that is, Federal law must not attempt to make compliance by the provinces mandatory. An example is medicare: There has been much discussion about Parliament's

requirement that provinces expecting to receive Federal money under the Canada Health Act must prohibit extra-billing by medical doctors. While Parliament may impose whatever conditions it wishes for the disposition of its money, compliance with those conditions remains voluntary so long as the provinces are prepared to forego the funds.

In 1867 there was none of what has later been called "intrastate federalism" whereby the provinces are represented in national institutions.[47] Canadian senators, and Supreme Court judges after the Court's creation in 1875, were and are Federal appointees. This contrasts with United States senators who were originally appointed by the states and who in turn ratified Supreme Court appointees. It is true that the Constitution Act specifies a federal distribution of senators, that the Supreme Court Act requires three of that Court's judges to come from Quebec, and that ever since John A. Macdonald's first cabinet, prime ministers have paid careful attention to provincial distribution. However, none of these institutions contains provincial representatives as such.

A number of factors in addition to the terms of the Constitution Act itself contributed to the initial centralization.[48]

(1) There was continuity provided by the administrative structure and new parliament buildings which the Dominion government inherited from the former Province of Canada.

(2) The early judicial decisions favoured the Federal government.

(3) The Federal government made liberal use of the powers of reservation (by lieutenant governors) and disallowance.

(4) Politicians could until 1874 hold seats in Parliament and a provincial legislature concurrently. For example, John Sanfield Macdonald, Ontario's first premier, also sat on the Government side in the House of Commons.

(5) The new Ontario and Quebec provincial governments were virtually subservient to the Federal government.

(6) Almost all of the men involved in carrying Confederation opted for Federal politics. Even Joseph Howe and Christopher Dunkin, opponents of Confederation, joined John A. Macdonald's cabinet, and A.A. Dorion later joined the Liberal cabinet of Alexander Mackenzie.

(7) The Federal government acquired the West from the Hudson's Bay Company in 1870 to prevent those lands from falling under United States control. The settlement of the West, together with a system of protective tariffs and the building of the Canadian Pacific Railway, were known as Macdonald's 1878 "National Policy," itself a centralizing force.

Since Confederation the actual balance in Federal-provincial relations has swung between centralization and decentralization, although the general trend has been in the latter direction. The notable exceptions to this trend have been a short period immediately following 1867, the years of World War One and World War Two, as well as brief periods following those wars.

Decentralizing factors began to emerge shortly after Confederation:

(1) Judicial decisions beginning with *Hodge v. R.* (1883) increasingly reflected a more restrictive interpretation of Parliament's powers. This is discussed in Chapter 5.

(2) Politicians with provincial loyalties emerged, notably Oliver Mowat (Ontario premier from 1872 until 1896) and Honoré Mercier (Quebec premier from 1887 until 1891). In 1887 these men called the first interprovincial conference in two decades to discuss what Mercier called the "legitimate fears with regard to the maintenance of our local institutions" in the face of recent "centralizing tendencies."[49]

(3) Some of the financial terms of the Confederation settlement under section 118 were renegotiated within the first two years in spite of their being "in full settlement of all future demands on Canada."

(4) The election of a Liberal Government in 1873, but especially Laurier's Liberal Government in 1896, brought a greater sympathy toward the provinces. However, the Liberals were to become increasingly centralist while the Conservatives espoused provincial rights. This reversal of roles is not surprising in view of the many years of Liberal domination during the twentieth century.

(5) The Compact Theory of Confederation was popular although of at least dubious validity. According to this theory the Confederation settlement was a pact or treaty either among the provinces or between the French and the English (depending upon the version adopted) and therefore required the consent of the participants—governments, not peoples—for revision.

The reason for this decentralization was not hard to find. According to the Rowell-Sirois Commission, Confederation had not shifted loyalties from the colonies to the new Dominion. Rather, "the achievement of Confederation and the spectacular activity of the Federal Government in the early years had merely overshadowed or, at most, temporarily subordinated the separate interests of the distinct regions and communities."[50]

During World War One when the War Measures Act was operative, the federal system became highly centralized. These years were followed by the decade of the 1920s when classical federalism was at its height. The Depression and the economic crisis of the 1930s, coupled with the drought on the prairies, produced additional arguments for centralization; but judicial interpretation of the Constitution Act continued, with brief interruption, to support the provinces.

Following World War Two and the centralized system which accompanied it, the Liberals (the "Government Party")[51] under Mackenzie King expected to continue the wartime centralization. At the 1945 Dominion-Provincial Conference on Reconstruction, the Federal government sought provincial support for three major ("Green Book") proposals.[52]

(1) A commitment to high and stable levels of income and employment. This proposal reflected the influence of the counter-cyclical fiscal and monetary theories of John Maynard Keynes. As a British economist Keynes was naturally thinking in terms of a unitary rather than a federal state and so he was unconcerned about a distribution of legislative authority.

(2) Nation-wide standards of health and welfare services to be achieved by family allowances, an extension of unemployment insurance, and grants-in-aid to the provinces.

(3) A Federal government guarantee of certain levels of provincial revenue through tax rental agreements.

In spite of its failure to secure an overall agreement with the provinces (both Ontario and Quebec rejected the scheme), the Federal government was able to implement most of its proposals piecemeal. Centralization continued into the postwar period largely because of Ottawa's widespread use of its spending power with shared-cost programs, thus blurring jurisdictional lines. This led the Quebec Royal Commission of Inquiry on Constitutional Problems (the Tremblay Commission) in 1957 to condemn the spending power, along with Ottawa's unlimited authority to tax and its reliance on the residual "peace, order, and good government" power.[53]

By the end of the 1950s, however, the federal balance was tilting toward the provinces. The reasons included:[54]

(1) The arrogance of the Liberal Government as symbolized by the 1956 Pipeline Debate.

(2) The subsequent failure of national policies of the Diefenbaker Government to provide economic stability and growth during the 1957-1962 recession.

(3) The increasing relative importance of the provinces in the national economy.

(4) Doubtlessly the single most important factor, the surfacing of Quebec nationalism (the so-called "Quiet Revolution") under Premier Jean Lesage following the deaths of premiers Maurice Duplessis and Paul Sauvé in 1959 and 1960. Although Quebec had once supported the Compact Theory it abandoned this view in the 1960s because Quebec's growing demands for constitutional change clearly would be unacceptable to other provinces.

(5) The extreme flexibility of Prime Minister Pearson in negotiating fiscal matters with the provinces, especially Quebec.

Symbolic of this growing decentralization was the establishment in the 1960s and early 1970s of provincial departments of Federal-provincial or intergovernmental affairs; creation of the Federal-Provincial Relations Office first as part of the Department of Finance and then in 1964 within the Privy Council Office; the summit-like conferences of "First Ministers"; and the emergence of "executive federalism."

Tensions between Ottawa and the provinces in the 1960s and 1970s sparked proposals in the direction of intrastate federalism.[55] A centralist version called for representation by provincial governments in a reformed Senate as well as a provincial role in the appointment of Supreme Court judges. A decentralist version promoted such things as electoral reform along the lines of proportional representation, an elected Senate, or even a place for referenda in the process of constitutional amendment. Decentralization has continued to the present, albeit with greater struggle when Pierre Trudeau was prime minister, so that today Canada has perhaps the most decentralized federal system in the world. In any event the centralizing features of the 1867 Constitution Act are now of little importance when compared to the federal features.

How does the Charter of Rights and Freedoms, or more broadly the 1982 Constitution Act, relate to federalism? On the one hand is the right of a province to opt out of certain constitutional amendments (section 38[3]) and, as noted below, to exempt legislation from some of the Charter's rights. It may be argued on the other hand that the Charter is a unifying force and thereby a centralizing element within federalism. After all it is individual rights which the Charter is to protect, and protection is not intended to depend upon the individual's province of residence. While the Charter shifts no power to the Federal government—indeed, it limits Federal powers as it does provincial authority—it has significant implications for the federal system. As the Supreme Court, at the apex of our judicial system, interprets the Charter it establishes uniform national standards within areas of both provincial and Federal jurisdiction. "Policy directives flowing from Supreme Court decisions on the Charter are transmitted through a single hierarchy of appeals that binds all the courts in the land, and shapes the rights of all Canadians and the powers of all who govern."[56]

Even the use of Charter section 1, which (within limits) enables governments to legislate in contravention of guaranteed rights and freedoms, may "exert a homogenizing influence on provincial policy-making, because variations in provincial laws on the same topic might encourage the courts to hold that the less liberal laws cannot be demonstrably justified in a free and democratic society."[57]

But if the Charter exerts a centralizing force it also has at least the potential for recognizing differing values among the provinces, and that is a basic purpose of federalism. The "notwithstanding" clause (s. 33) allows provincial legislatures (as well as Parliament) to exempt laws from the Charter's fundamental (s. 2), legal (ss. 7-14), and equality (s. 15) rights. Furthermore, the Supreme Court could interpret section 1 in a manner that permitted some variation of Charter rights from province to province in order to recognize the existence of differing values. Before 1982 there had been no such restriction. However, neither the Court's initial consideration of section 1 in *Quebec Association of Protestant School Boards* nor the seeming rigidity of the *Oakes* test was particularly promising. See the commentary on section 1. The question is also explored briefly in the Conclusion/Epilogue.

Had the Meech Lake amendments been approved they would have resulted in greater decentralization of the federal system. There was considerable uncertainty whether the "distinct society" clause would have overridden the Canadian Charter; but regardless of the outcome of that issue, the clause would at least have increased the possibility of a broader interpretation of section 1 to accommodate Quebec's distinctiveness. The distinct society clause provided that "The Constitution of Canada shall be interpreted in a manner consistent with . . . the recognition that Quebec constitutes within Canada a distinct society," and that "The role of the legislature and Government of Quebec to preserve and promote the distinct identity of Quebec . . . is affirmed." The provision for provincial input into the selection of Supreme Court judges and senators (the latter at least until Senate reform might occur), as well as the limitation of Parliament's spending power, would also have had a decentralizing affect. This should not be surprising given Premier Bourassa's conditions for Quebec's political acceptance of the 1982 Accord.

Since the death of Meech Lake and the revival within Quebec of interest in some form of sovereignty, the future of Canadian federalism is once again a lively topic of discussion. Not only the "Quebec question" is of current interest, for that would imply that the rest of the country is satisfied with the existing federal structure. No doubt stimulated by the failure of Meech Lake and the reactions within Quebec, Ottawa and several of the other provinces are formulating their own positions as to a desirable structure of renewed federalism. While post-Meech developments cannot be explored in any detail in the present volume, some are noted briefly in the Conclusion/Epilogue. Regardless of the outcome of this debate there seems no doubt that our federal system is about to undergo significant change, if not some profound overhaul.

6. SEMI-LIMITED GOVERNMENT

One principle of the British constitution is parliamentary supremacy, meaning "neither more nor less than . . . that Parliament thus defined [Queen, House of Lords, House of Commons] has, under the English constitution, the right to make or unmake any law whatever; and, further, that no person or body is recognized by the law of England as having a right to override or set aside the legislation of Parliament."[58] Parliament "can, in short, do everything that is not naturally impossible"; it "can do everything but make a woman a man, and a man a woman."[59] Corry calls the latter assertion an "understatement."[60]

Britain has, therefore, "unlimited" government in the legal sense. One must not conclude that Parliament faces no real limitations in the actual use of its awesome power. Not only do politicians hope to be re-elected; of greater significance is British political culture which requires that certain things just "aren't done." The rights of British citizens are at least as secure as those in the United States in spite of "limited" government in the United States. "Limited government" means that government *per se* is legally prevented from exceeding powers as defined in a constitutional document which itself is "rigid"—that is, whose amendment requires a procedure more difficult than the ordinary law-making process. The United States Bill of Rights (basically, the first ten amendments to the Constitution) limits both Congress and state legislatures.

Where does Canada fit on the continuum? Before the Constitution Act was proclaimed on April 17, 1982, one could with modest rationalization claim the existence of unlimited government by the convenient substitution of "legislative" for "parliamentary" supremacy. The justification was that with few exceptions the distribution of legislative power between the two orders of government was exhaustive. The bulk of this power is conferred by sections 91 and 92 of the 1867 Constitution Act. To these must be added sections 92A, 93, 94, 94A, 95, 101, and 132, of that Act; sections 2 (establishing new provinces from Canadian territories), 3 (altering provincial boundaries with the consent of affected provinces), and 4 (administering Canadian territories not within provinces), of the 1871 Constitution Act amendment; and sections 2 (freeing Parliament from the restrictions of the Colonial Laws Validity Act) and 3 (granting power of extraterritoriality to Parliament) of the Statute of Westminster.[61] In other words the courts acted as a referee between the Federal and provincial governments rather than limited the power of government *per se*. Apart from the absence of a general formula permitting amendment of the Act in Canada, the most obvious exceptions to legislative supremacy include the following sections of the 1867 Constitution Act:

(1) Section 93, establishing rights or privileges of denominational schools,
(2) Sections 96-99, relating to the appointment and tenure of judges,
(3) Section 121, prescribing free trade of goods among provinces,
(4) Section 125, prohibiting the taxing of property belonging to the Federal or provincial government, and
(5) Section 133, establishing language rights in relation to the functioning of the Federal and Quebec governments and courts.

For a consideration of legislative supremacy in relation to pre-Charter Canada see the discussion in Chapter 5 under "Judicial Decisions: Courts and Basic Rights and Freedoms." The 1960 Canadian Bill of Rights as well as the bills of rights enacted by several provincial legislatures apply only within their respective jurisdictions. Furthermore, because they were made by the ordinary law-making process they may be amended or even repealed by the same process.

The Charter of Rights and Freedoms has substantially altered the situation because the courts may now strike down Federal and provincial laws which trench upon protected rights. It is still somewhat early to know the full extent of the changed situation; much depends upon the attitude of the courts, especially the Supreme Court of Canada. Section 1 of the Charter, which invites the courts to determine what "reasonable limits prescribed by law" can be "demonstrably justified in a free and democratic society," probably creates the greatest uncertainty. In any event, legislative supremacy as we have known it is, for good or ill, a thing of the past. Russell characterizes one implication of the Charter as "a further flight from politics, a deepening disillusionment with the procedures of representative government and government by discussion as means of resolving fundamental questions of political justice." He points to the danger that the transfer of social issues (such as obscenity, Sunday closing, and abortion) into technical legal questions to be settled by the adversarial rather than the political process is less likely to produce a social consensus.[62] This is already apparent, especially with respect to abortion.

It would be incorrect to say that Canada now operates under a system of limited government comparable to that in the United States. In the first place there is vagueness in section 1 of the Charter. It should be noted, however, that the absence of a comparable qualifying section in the United States Bill of Rights has not prevented the courts in that country from placing limitations on the unlimited expression of freedoms. In the second place there is section 33. This section permits any of the eleven governments to "expressly declare in an Act of Parliament or of the legislature, as the case may be, that the Act or a provision thereof shall operate notwithstanding a provision included" among the fundamental freedoms, legal rights, or equality rights, which otherwise are protected by the Charter (ss. 2, 7-15). The ultimate effect of the "notwithstanding" clause on legislative supremacy cannot be predicted, but it is likely that Canada will be a reflection of neither the British nor the United States models. Perhaps "semi-supremacy" or "semi-limited government" is an appropriate term to describe what we now have. Russell calls section 33 "that quintessential Canadian compromise." "Perhaps only Canada, still teetering uncertainly between British and American models of government, could come up with legislative review of judicial review." He adds that this compromise might actually provide the best of both worlds—an entrenched Charter and a continuing role for the parliamentary system to handle controversial social issues.[63]

Monahan characterizes section 33 (as well as the authorization of affirmative action under sections 6[4] and 15[2]) as "a concrete commitment to the primacy of politics, and a commitment to the idea that liberty is not the enemy but the product of governmental institutions." It preserves the historic notion, albeit restricted, that the political rather than the judicial process provides the best guarantee of our rights and freedoms.[64] From a different perspective Greene suggests that section 33 "takes the pressure off the judges to solve political crises. . . . Instead, they can concentrate on developing more lasting interpretations of the Charter, leaving the short-term crises to the politicians."[65]

At least until mid-1991 it seems that governments are not ready to make significant use of the override. Quebec is the only jurisdiction to make wholesale use of section 33. It did so because of its rejection of the entire November 1981 constitutional accord, not to violate peoples' rights. The only other use was by Saskatchewan in 1988 (to force striking public servants back to work) pending a Supreme Court ruling which, as it turns out, made that use unnecessary. There are political risks in using the override for the exempted legislation must "expressly declare" its operation notwithstanding the Charter. Opposition parties and the media can be counted upon to make the most of any such exemption.

There has been much debate about the wisdom of an entrenched Charter.[66] For the present purpose suffice it to say that regardless of its presumed merits, the Charter should not be viewed as a panacea to prevent future infringements of our civil liberties. One frequently cited infringement from our past is the displacement of Japanese-Canadians during World War Two. But even in the United States similar action by the government was deemed not to be a violation of the entrenched Bill of Rights.[67]

CHAPTER 5

"constitution," "Constitution," and How They Change

1. Codified: 1867 Constitution Act, 1982 Canada Act, 1982 Constitution Act
   A. 1867 Constitution Act as Part of the Constitution
   B. 1867 Constitution Act Amendment
      (i) Sections That Authorize Their Own Amendment
      (ii) Amendment by the Provincial Legislatures
      (iii) Amendment by the Federal Parliament
      (iv) Amendment by the British Parliament
   C. Canada Act and Constitution Act, 1982
   D. 1982 Constitution Act Amendment
2. Other Formal Documents
   A. British Documents
   B. Statutes of the Federal Government
   C. Statutes of Provincial Governments
   D. Rules of Order
3. Convention
4. Judicial Decisions
   A. The Basis of Judicial Review
   B. The Courts and the Distribution of Power
      (i) 1867-1882
      (ii) 1883-1932
      (iii) 1932-1949
      (iv) 1949-Present
   C. The Courts and Basic Rights and Freedoms
      (i) 1867 Constitution Act
      (ii) Canadian Bill of Rights
      (iii) Charter of Rights and Freedoms

In the Introduction to this book a distinction was made between a country's "c"onstitution and its "C"onstitution. The small-"c" constitution refers to the entire body of fundamental rules, some of them written but many of them not, according to which the country's government operates. The capital-"C" Constitution is the formal or codified document which frequently carries the title "Constitution of. . . ."

What is the Canadian constitution in its broad sense, and how does it change? The following discussion considers four basic components: the codified part of our constitution—the 1867 Constitution Act as amended, and the 1982 Canada Act and Constitution Act as amended; other formal documents—basically, statutes and orders-in-council; conventional rules; judicial decisions.

1. CODIFIED PART OF THE CONSTITUTION: 1867 CONSTITUTION ACT, 1982 CANADA ACT, 1982 CONSTITUTION ACT

A. 1867 Constitution Act as Part of the Constitution

The Constitution Act is not, and was never intended to be, a comprehensive constitutional document describing the workings of government in Canada. What the Act does, essentially, is the following:

(1) Creates the federal union and defines the four original provinces (Parts I-II).

(2) Outlines the structure of the central government (Parts III-IV).

(3) Establishes the office of lieutenant governor, and provides for the initial governments of Ontario and Quebec inasmuch as these provinces had been the single Province of Canada before 1867 (Part V).

(4) Distributes legislative authority between the Government of Canada and the provincial governments (Part VI).

(5) Provides for a judiciary (Part VII).

(6) Establishes the financial arrangements between the two orders of government (Part VIII).

(7) Provides for the admission of additional colonies to the union (Part XI).

(8) Contains a miscellany of provisions such as those respecting the treaty power and language guarantees (Part IX), and (now repealed—Part X) the construction of the Intercolonial Railway.

The Act does not, however, make explicit some of the basic operating principles of government. In this sense it is both misleading and incomplete. (Because of the need to make frequent references to the Government of Canada the terms "Federal government," "central government," sometimes simply "Ottawa," or where appropriate "Parliament," will be used interchangeably with the formal name.)

The Act's preamble states the intent to create "One Dominion" with a constitution "similar in principle to that of the United Kingdom." This statement undoubtedly includes responsible government although that principle is nowhere made explicit in the Act. Indeed, there are provisions in the Act that seem to be the very antithesis of the British constitution. Dawson and Ward have given an excellent account of the misleading nature of the terms describing the executive branch:

> The executive government and authority of Canada is vested in the Sovereign, who is apparently represented by a governor general (sections 9, 10). The latter is assisted by a Council, which he chooses, and summons, and removes (11), and which advises him in his work (12, 13). The Sovereign is commander-in-chief of all naval and military forces in Canada (15). The governor general appoints the Speaker of the Senate (34) and virtually all the judges (96). He appoints all the members of one house of the legislature (24). The other legislative body, the House of Commons, is called together by the governor (38) and this house can be dissolved by him at any time and a new election ordered (50). All money bills must first be recommended by the governor before they can be passed by Parliament (54). The governor may assent to legislation; he may refuse his assent; or he may reserve a bill for the consideration of the Queen-in-Council in Great Britain (55-7); and he may also disallow any provincial act or refuse his assent to any provincial bill reserved for the signification of his pleasure (55-7, 90). The same general powers are exercisable by the provincial lieutenant governors, who are appointed by the governor general, are accountable to him, and may be removed by him (58, 59, 90).[1]

Apparently, then, the Constitution Act prescribes a virtual dictatorship, an executive authority hearkening back to the days preceding responsible government. The legal powers of the Queen in Britain are also broad, although they stem from the royal prerogative rather than a statute. Only when the conventional parts of the constitution are understood does one realize that broad legal power does not express the reality of executive authority in either country. The significance of convention as it affects the governor general's authority is acknowledged by the 1947 Letters Patent advising the Queen's representative to use both statutory and prerogative powers "with the advice of Our Privy Council for Canada or of any members thereof or individually, as the case requires."[2]

Not only is the Constitution Act misleading in some of its provisions; it is also an incomplete document in several important respects:

(1) The Act contains no general or overall amending formula. Because amendment was evidently not an important pre-Confederation issue, one can only speculate as to the reason for its omission from the Act. This is considered below. The search for an amending formula is the subject of Chapter 6.

(2) The Act omits the cabinet (including the prime minister) which is the single most powerful body, the engine of government. The cabinet is the personal "possession" of the prime minister and is identical in membership (although it need not be) to the ministry which itself is the active committee of the privy council. Only the privy council is named in the Constitution Act. The distinction among these three bodies is made in the commentary on section 11 of the Act.

(3) The Constitution Act is virtually silent about civil liberties beyond the rights of denominational schools (s. 93) and language guarantees (s. 133). This omission is doubtlessly explained by Canada's automatic inheritance of the body of common law upon which the rights of British citizens are based. Although the Federal government and several provincial governments have passed bills of rights, such legislation applies only to their respective jurisdictions and may be amended or repealed by the ordinary legislative process. Only in 1982 was an entrenched Charter, applicable to the entire country, added to our constitution.

(4) The Act does not create a Supreme Court, although section 101 authorizes the Federal government to do so. As a colony, Canada relied upon the Judicial Committee of the Privy Council in Britain which was the highest appeal body for the Empire. The role of that body, also, is omitted from the Act.

(5) The Act follows the practice of earlier constitutional documents in assuming the existence of, rather than creating, the office of governor general. This office is created by the Letters Patent issued by the monarch acting upon the advice of her ministers. The first such Letters were issued to Governor General Viscount Monck in 1867 and were combined with his appointment and instructions in a single document.[3] The latest Letters were issued in 1947 except for those of 1952 to permit the resignation of Governor General Lord Alexander.[4]

Why these inaccuracies and omissions? They reflect a similar distinction between law and practice within the British constitution. Furthermore, because the Constitution Act was not creating an independent Dominion—nor, for that matter, was independence contemplated—there was an understanding that the customary ways of governing would continue.

The Constitution Act has also become less accurate over the years as certain sections have ceased to apply even though they remain in the Act without repeal or amendment. To illustrate: section 5 still declares that "Canada shall be divided into four provinces"; and section 71 states that the Quebec legislature will be bicameral and its lower house called the "Legislative Assembly"—notwithstanding that in 1968 Quebec abolished its upper house and renamed its lower house the National Assembly.

B. 1867 Constitution Act Amendment

(i) Sections That Authorize Their Own Amendment: Some twenty-seven sections permit their own amendment with wording such as "until Parliament otherwise provides" or "until the legislature of the province otherwise provides." The content of many of these sections was intended to be temporary, pending Federal or provincial revision once the new Dominion was launched. Consequently, many of the sections have been repealed, have been superseded by ordinary Federal or provincial legislation, or have simply become obsolete. Thirteen of the twenty-seven sections are amendable by Parliament.

- **(1)** Section 12 transfers appropriate pre-1867 governors' powers to the governor general.
- **(2)** Section 35 permits changes in the Senate quorum.
- **(3)** Section 40 establishes electoral districts for national elections in the four original provinces.
- **(4)** Section 41 provides for the application of provincial election laws to national elections.
- **(5)** Section 52 authorizes changes (within prescribed limits) in the size of the House of Commons.
- **(6)** Section 105 allows changes in the governor general's salary.
- **(7)** Section 122 provides for the application of provincial customs and excise laws.
- **(8)** Section 130 provides for the performance of Federal responsibilities (hitherto under provincial jurisdiction) by provincial officers.
- **(9-13)** The remaining sections in this category are 47, 103, 120, 131, and 141.

Ten more may be amended by provincial legislatures. All ten except sections 134 and 135 are in Part V entitled "Provincial Constitutions."

- **(1-8)** Sections 65, 72, 78, 80, 83, 84, 134, and 135 relate to the constitutions of Quebec and/or Ontario and deal with the transition from a single province to two provinces.
- **(9-10)** Sections 64 and 88 apply to Nova Scotia and New Brunswick.

As for the last four:

(1) Section 16 allows the Queen to relocate the seat of the Government of Canada.
(2) Section 68 permits provincial executives to relocate their seats of government.
(3) Section 129 allows Parliament or provincial legislatures to change (within limits) pre-1867 laws, courts, and officers within their respective jurisdictions.
(4) Section 136 authorizes the executives of Ontario and Quebec to alter their provinces' Great Seals and, in the interim, re-establishes the Great Seals of pre-1841 Upper and Lower Canada.

(ii) Amendment by the Provincial Legislatures: There is general authorization in section 92(1)—now replaced by section 45 of the 1982 Constitution Act—for the provinces to amend their own constitutions "except as regards the office of lieutenant governor." The section's main purpose is to give to the original provinces explicit authority to alter parts of their constitutions lying outside the 1867 Constitution Act. It also permits the amendment of those portions of Part V of the 1867 Act not affecting the office of lieutenant governor. Section 92(1) also applied to the constitutional documents (except for restrictions contained therein) of provinces joining Canada after 1867. Those documents are the Manitoba Act, Saskatchewan Act, Alberta Act, Terms of Union of Newfoundland with Canada Act (confirmed by the 1949 Constitution Act amendment [No. 1] admitting Newfoundland), and the British orders-in-council admitting British Columbia and Prince Edward Island.

(iii) Amendment by the Federal Parliament: Following the 1949 (No. 2) amendment to the Constitution Act adding a renumbered section 91(1), the Federal government was authorized to amend "the Constitution of Canada" essentially in matters within that government's jurisdiction—somewhat analogous to the provinces' general amending power in 92(1). Five amendments were made under that provision before its replacement by sections 4(2) and 44 of the 1982 Constitution Act, and (by mid-1991) one amendment has been made since then. Four of these six amendments revised the method of calculating representation in the House of Commons under section 51:

(1) **1952:** Increased the representation of the Yukon Territory and Northwest Territories from one seat (for the two territories combined) to one seat for each territory. It also reintroduced a provision to protect a province with a declining population against an excessive loss of representation.
(2) **1974 (No. 2):** Revised the representation formula. This later became simply the 1974 Amendment because the original 1974 (No. 1) ended up as the 1975 (No. 2) Amendment.

(3) **1975 (No. 1):** Retained the one seat for the Yukon Territory, and increased the representation of the Northwest Territories to two seats.

(4) **1985:** Revised the representation formula.

The other two amendments related to the Senate, one (1965) requiring senators to retire at age 75 and the other (1975 [No. 2]) providing for one senator from each of Yukon Territory and Northwest Territories.

The scope of section 91(1) was the subject of controversy in the 1979 *Senate Reference*. In 1978 the Federal government asked the Supreme Court if Parliament had the authority to alter or repeal sections 21-36 of the 1867 Constitution Act—essentially, to abolish the Senate. In denying this authority the Court stated that the powers conferred by section 91 were upon "Parliament"; that Parliament included the Senate as well as the House of Commons (section 17 of the Act); and therefore that the continued existence of the Senate was required for Parliament to exercise its legislative authority under section 91. Another factor considered by the Court was historical: "a primary purpose of the creation of the Senate . . . [was] to afford protection to the various sectional interests in Canada in relation to the enactment of federal legislation." Because Parliament (including the Senate) is the institution authorized to enact law, "the body which had been created as a means of protecting sectional and provincial interests was made a participant in this legislative process." Therefore, "the Senate has a vital role as an institution forming part of the federal system created by the [1867 Constitution] Act."[5] The Senate has never performed that protective role, the Court's rationale notwithstanding. The significance of the *Senate Reference* as a reference is considered later in this chapter under "Judicial Decisions."

(iv) Amendment by the British Parliament: In all matters not covered by the amending procedures noted above the Constitution Act was until 1982 amendable only by the British Parliament. This included the Act in its most essential respects, such as the distribution of legislative authority between Ottawa and the provinces. One can only speculate why an amending formula was not included in the Act from the outset. One reason is doubtlessly the fact that, the Act being a British statute, amendment required but a simple majority vote by Britain's Parliament. Perhaps, also, the entire Confederation project might have been jeopardized had the question of amendment been raised at the pre-Confederation conferences. Furthermore, John A. Macdonald wished to maintain as much flexibility as possible to ensure provincial subordination to the Federal government; the inclusion of an amending procedure would certainly have reduced this flexibility to the extent that amendment would have involved provincial participation. In any event the omission does suggest that in 1867 an independent Canada was not contemplated. The British Parliament would be the guarantor of provincial and minority rights.

There were seventeen Constitution Act amendments enacted by the British Parliament if the list suggested by Dawson and Ward in 1970 is adopted;

eighteen, if the 1982 Constitution Act is included. Those authors acknowledge that lists vary, depending on the views of the compiler. These amendments are listed below for easy reference. (Section references are to the 1867 Constitution Act.)[6]

(1) **1871:** Constitution Act, confirming the authority of the Federal government to establish provinces, to alter provincial boundaries with the consent of the provinces affected, and to administer territories not included within provinces.

(2) **1875:** Parliament of Canada Act, removing doubts about the privileges, immunities, and powers, of Parliament and its members (s. 18).

(3) **1886:** Constitution Act, authorizing Parliament to provide representation in the Senate and House of Commons for territories not included within provinces.

(4) **1889:** Canada (Ontario Boundary) Act, declaring Ontario's boundaries. Action by the British Parliament was probably unnecessary, given the authority granted by the 1871 amendment.

(5) **1895:** Canadian Speaker (Appointment of Deputy) Act, removing doubts as to the validity of the Canadian Parliament's Speaker of the Senate Act which provided for a Deputy Speaker of the Senate. This Act was repealed by the 1982 Constitution Act.

(6) **1907:** Constitution Act, replacing section 118 with a new grant structure but not, however, formally repealing section 118.

(7) **1915:** Constitution Act, increasing the number and altering the distribution of Senate seats (ss. 22, 28), and establishing the principle (s. 51A) that no province will have fewer seats in the Commons than it has in the Senate.

(8) **1916:** British North America Act, extending the life of the existing parliament by one year, and therefore beyond the maximum life permitted by section 50. The amendment was repealed by Britain's Statute Law Revision Act of 1927.

(9) **1930:** Constitution Act, confirming agreements between the Federal government and the four Western provincial governments. The agreements with Manitoba, Saskatchewan, and Alberta were to transfer ownership of natural resources within those provinces to the provincial governments. The agreement with British Columbia was to return to that province certain Crown lands which had been transferred to the Federal government pending construction of a transcontinental railway.

(10) **1940:** Constitution Act, giving the Federal government jurisdiction (section 91[2A]) over unemployment insurance.

(11) **1943:** British North America Act, postponing the redistribution of House of Commons seats, required after every decennial census in

accordance with section 51, until the end of World War Two. This Act was repealed by the 1982 Constitution Act and so was not renamed.

(12) **1946:** British North America Act, altering the system of representation in the House of Commons by substituting a new section 51. This Act was repealed by the 1982 Constitution Act and so was not renamed.

(13) **1949:** Newfoundland Act, confirming Canada's agreement with Newfoundland for the admission of that colony into Canada. This Act was originally the British North America (No. 1) Act.

(14) **1949:** British North America (No. 2) Act, empowering the Federal government to amend the Constitution Act as provided in the new section 91(1). This Act was repealed by the 1982 Constitution Act and so was not renamed.

(15) **1951:** British North America Act, authorizing the Federal government to make laws in relation to old age pensions (s. 94A), but not so as to conflict with any provincial law in this area. This Act was repealed by the 1982 Constitution Act and so was not renamed. See (17) below.

(16) **1960:** Constitution Act, providing for the mandatory retirement of provincial superior court judges at age seventy-five (s. 99).

(17) **1964:** Constitution Act, extending and clarifying the 1951 amendment (s. 94A).

One of the difficulties encountered in constructing a list is deciding what precisely constitutes an amendment. The following, for example, are not among the seventeen although they are listed as amendments in the 1965 Favreau White Paper entitled *The Amendment of the Constitution of Canada.*[7] Favreau does not, however, recognize the 1889 amendment included above. Obviously, the 1982 Constitution Act, listed below, could not have been part of previous compilations.

(1) Rupert's Land Act, 1868, authorizing the transfer of Hudson's Bay Company lands to Canada. This transfer occurred by British order-in-council in 1870.

(2) Statute of Westminster, 1931, authorizing Parliament to make laws having extraterritorial effect, and authorizing both Parliament and the provinces to repeal any British law (other than the Constitution Act) that formed part of Canada's law. The Statute of Westminster is considered here, however, to be more an independent statute than a Constitution Act amendment.

(3) Statute Law Revision Acts of 1893, 1927, and 1950, repealing some obsolete sections (noted in Chapter 7) of the Constitution Act.

(4) British orders-in-council admitting Rupert's Land and the North-Western Territory (1870), British Columbia (1871), and Prince Edward Island (1873). Favreau does not, however, include the 1880 order-in-council which added the Arctic islands to Canada.

(5) Constitution Act, 1982, containing about five direct amendments including the renaming of all B.N.A. Acts and the addition of section 92A. (The addition of 92A—non-renewable natural resources, forestry resources, electrical energy—is the only amendment that transferred Federal power to the provinces.) The 1982 Constitution Act also has significant implications for other parts of the Constitution Act because of its Charter of Rights and Freedoms and the amending formula. In view of this major impact on the constitution, the Constitution Act is considered here to be an independent statute and not an amendment.

Even among the seventeen amendments listed above, those of 1875, 1889, and 1895, were not originally entitled "British North America Act."

Another problem in identifying amendments is that not all amendments, even among those so titled, "formally add, or replace, or modify a section or a number of sections of previous constitutional documents. They often constitute enactments of their own which supersede existing constitutional provisions or fill in apparent gaps in the original document without embodying their provisions into the latter."[8] This group includes nine Acts—those of 1889 and 1895 just noted, as well as the 1871, 1886, 1907, 1916, 1930, 1943, and 1949 (No. 1) "British North America" Acts as originally titled. (The 1916 and 1943 amendments were, however, temporary.)

These difficulties pale to insignificance, however, when compared with several fundamental questions raised by British involvement in Constitution Act amendment:

(1) What body within Canada must make a request of the British Parliament?

(2) What was the appropriate role of that Parliament upon receipt of such request?

(3) What was the appropriate role of the provinces in the total process?

The first question is the easiest to answer. In every case but two (1875 and 1895, which were initiated by the Canadian cabinet) the request emanated from both Houses of Parliament as a joint address. A 1965 request for an amendment to abolish the Quebec upper house was made by the Canadian cabinet on behalf of Quebec, but British action was pre-empted when Quebec acted alone under section 92(1).[9]

Second, what was the proper role of the British Parliament? When the authority of provincial governments was not affected, or when their authority was affected but consent was given, Britain acted automatically upon Canada's request. But what if provincial powers were affected and prior approval was not obtained? Before the developments leading to the 1982 Canada Act, no proposed amendment involving provincial authority had been transmitted to Britain without the prior agreement either of all provinces or of all the affected provinces. Gérin-Lajoie distinguishes between matters of interest or concern to provincial governments and/or populations, and those affecting the provinces as "bodies politic"—that is, affecting the legal authority of provincial governments.[10] Historically, until the controversy developed in relation to Ottawa's 1981 patriation proposal, every amendment affecting provincial powers had the approval of provincial governments—namely, those of 1930, 1940, 1951, 1964, as well as the 1931 Statute of Westminster (if this is considered to be a Constitution Act amendment).

Essentially, disagreement as to the appropriate role of Britain stemmed from disagreement as to whether or not Britain remained the legal guardian of provincial rights within the federal system following passage of the Statute of Westminster. At one extreme was the "no sniffing at the package" theory.[11] According to this approach, Britain was to accede to any request of the Canadian Parliament even if it meant holding her nose while doing so. At the other extreme was the view that Britain must open the amendment package and determine whether it endangered the federal system, no matter how humiliating an experience that may be for Canada.

The third issue raised by the question of Constitution Act amendment is clearly related to the second. To what extent if any was provincial agreement necessary? This issue was central to the September 1981 decisions of the Supreme Court of Canada in relation to the Federal government's patriation proposal. The Court decided that provincial agreement was not legally required, but that a convention existed which made provincial consent "constitutionally" necessary. The nature of constitutional conventions is developed later in this chapter. The Supreme Court's decisions in the 1981 *Patriation Reference* are noted in Chapter 6.

C. Canada Act and Constitution Act, 1982

Contrary to what many people seem to believe, the Canada Act with its appended Constitution Act is not a new Canadian Constitution. Rather, it adds three important elements to our existing Constitution. In the first place, it patriates the 1867 *Constitution Act* and provides that "no Act of the Parliament of the United Kingdom passed after the Constitution Act, 1982 comes into force shall extend to Canada as part of its law" (Canada Act, s. 2).

Second, it entrenches a Charter of Rights and Freedoms which includes fundamental freedoms, democratic rights, mobility rights, legal rights, equality rights, language rights, and minority language educational rights (1982 Constitution Act, Part I). The significance of this entrenchment for legislative supremacy is considered in Chapter 4. The impact of these rights and freedoms on the Canadian political system becomes apparent only as the courts interpret them when challenges to Federal and provincial laws emerge.

There are, nevertheless, two opportunities built into the Charter for governments to legislate in violation of the "guaranteed" rights and freedoms. Because no rights or freedoms can be absolute, section 1 states that the guarantee is subject to "such reasonable limits prescribed by law as can be demonstrably justified in a free and democratic society." The extent to which this section is permitted to trench upon rights and freedoms will be determined by the courts, especially the Supreme Court of Canada. The second possibility for contravening the Charter is by means of the "notwithstanding" or legislative override of section 33. This section allows any government to declare that a particular statute or part thereof will operate regardless of the existence of fundamental freedoms (s. 2), legal rights (ss. 7-14), or equality rights (s. 15). Provided the requirements of section 33 are met, the only limitation on this power is political.

The third major addition to our Constitution is the amending formula (1982 Constitution Act, Part V). The half-century search which culminated in this formula is the subject of Chapter 6. As a result of the formula, the political system will be more difficult to change especially in those areas requiring the consent of all eleven governments (s. 41). This became painfully evident with the failure of the Meech Lake Accord. However, even the consent of the Federal government and seven provincial governments as required by the general formula may be difficult to obtain. One can understand the concern of people who would have liked to see substantive constitutional reform at the same time the formula was adopted. The degree of inflexibility created by the formula may mean that the system is virtually frozen. On the other hand, if past efforts at constitutional reform are any indication, perhaps the situation has not changed all that much.

The rest of the Constitution Act deals with a variety of subjects.

(1) Part II pertains to the rights of aboriginal peoples.

(2) Part III relates to equalization and regional disparities.

(3) Parts IV and IV.1 require the calling of a constitutional conference within the first year, and two more conferences within the first five years. The agenda of all three meetings must include constitutional matters directly affecting Canada's aboriginal peoples, and representatives of those peoples must be invited to participate. The five years having elapsed, these Parts have now been repealed.

(4) Part VI is the addition of section 92A and its schedule to the 1867 Constitution Act.

(5) Part VII consists of a miscellany of ten provisions.

D. 1982 Constitution Act Amendment

By mid-1991 the 1982 Constitution Act had been amended once. This amendment, made by the Constitution Amendment Proclamation, 1983, affected sections 25 and 35, and created sections 35.1, 37.1 (which comprise Part IV.1),

54.1, and 61. All but the last two sections (which are merely tidying provisions) pertain to the rights of aboriginal peoples. The 1985 amendment to section 51 of the 1867 Constitution Act was made pursuant to section 44 of the Constitution Act because section 91(1) of the 1867 Constitution Act had been repealed. The controversy surrounding the 1985 amendment is discussed in the commentary on section 42 of the 1982 Constitution Act.

2. OTHER FORMAL DOCUMENTS

It is impossible to compile an exhaustive list of documents making up this part of our constitution because there is no definition of "constitution" against which a given document may be measured for congruence. In general one can say only that a document is part of the constitution if its content is constitutional—that is, if it comprises fundamental rules. Unsatisfactory as this generalization may be, there should be little disagreement about including the documents listed below.

A. British Documents

(i) Statutes: The Statute of Westminster is the most significant document in this category (apart, of course, from the 1867 Constitution Act, Canada Act, and 1982 Constitution Act themselves). Its preamble refers to the "established constitutional position of all members of the Commonwealth in relation to one another." That position was summarized by the Balfour Declaration at the 1926 Imperial Conference. The Declaration described members of the new British Commonwealth of Nations as "autonomous communities within the British Empire, equal in status, in no way subordinate one to another in any aspect of their domestic or external affairs, though united by a common allegiance to the Crown, and freely associated as members of the British Commonwealth."[12]

The Statute of Westminster therefore formalized the independence of the Dominions of Canada, Australia, New Zealand, Union of South Africa, Irish Free State, and Newfoundland (s. 1). (As pointed out in Chapter 2, Newfoundland reverted to colonial status in 1934.) In particular, the Statute of Westminster declared that:

(1) No Dominion was denied the right to pass laws which may conflict with those of Britain (s. 2).

(2) Each Dominion had the power of extraterritoriality—that is, the right to exercise jurisdiction over its nationals abroad such that, upon their return, they are made subject to the country's laws (s. 3).

(3) No British law made after the passage of the Statute of Westminster would apply to a Dominion without the latter's consent (s. 4).

(4) At Canada's request, the Constitution Act was exempt from the provisions of the Statute so that Britain retained jurisdiction over that Act's amendment (s. 7).

(ii) Orders-in-council: Because certain territories were joined to Canada after 1867 by means of British orders-in-council, the relevant orders are certainly part of our constitution. They are those admitting Rupert's Land and the North-Western Territory (1870), British Columbia (1871), Prince Edward Island (1873), and all British Territories and Possessions in North America (not already included within Canada) and all Islands Adjacent thereto (except Newfoundland) (1880). These latter territories included the Arctic islands.

(iii) Letters Patent: These documents, issued periodically since 1867 as part of the royal prerogative, created the office of governor general. It will be recalled that the 1867 Constitution Act did not create that office but assumed its existence. The most recent Letters Patent were issued in 1952 to provide for resignation before the expiration of a governor general's term of office (specifically, that of Lord Alexander). However, it is the 1947 Letters which have the greater constitutional significance because through them the monarch delegated all remaining powers with respect to Canada.

B. Statutes of the Federal Government

Three such statutes are not amendable by Parliament inasmuch as they became the primary constitutional documents of three new provinces. This prohibition of amendment is contained in the 1871 Constitution Act. The statutes may be altered only by the respective provincial legislatures, and only to the extent permitted by those statutes—essentially to the same extent as the 1867 Constitution Act authorizes other provinces to amend their constitutions. The three statutes are the

(1) Manitoba Act (1870), validated by the 1871 Constitution Act,
(2) Alberta Act (1905),
(3) Saskatchewan Act (1905).

Other statutes are amendable by Parliament through the ordinary law-making process. What statutes should be considered part of our constitution? This question invites the least consensus. Nevertheless, statutes in the following broad areas are doubtlessly constitutional in nature:[13]

(1) Statutes creating courts of law. The Supreme and Exchequer Courts Act was passed in 1875. The latter Court was replaced by the Federal Court in 1971 and so the original statute is now called the Supreme Court Act. The Federal Court Act would also have a claim for inclusion in the constitution.

(2) Statutes altering provincial boundaries. Most notable among these are the statutes that expanded the boundaries of Manitoba from its original "postage stamp" size; Ontario from an area essentially along the Great Lakes and northward so far as the land drained into those Lakes; and Quebec from the area draining into the St.

Lawrence River. Except for minor adjustments, the boundaries of these three provinces reached their present positions by 1912. (The 1889 definition of Ontario's boundaries was accomplished by an Act of the British Parliament.)

(3) Statutes affecting the franchise. The current statute is the Canada Elections Act.

(4) Statutes altering Federal-provincial financial arrangements. Most important are the series of five-year agreements begun during World War Two and continuing to the present.

(5) Statutes creating government departments. Over the years departments have been created, combined, and eliminated.

To the above categories it seems reasonable to add at least the following specific statutes:

(6) Canadian Citizenship Act (1946). Before the enactment of this statute there was no such thing as Canadian citizenship. Canadians were British subjects only.

(7) Canadian Bill of Rights (1960). The Schedule to the 1982 Constitution Act lists the components of the Constitution of Canada. It also repeals several statutes that are now obsolete. Inasmuch as the Bill of Rights is not included in the Schedule, and therefore is not repealed by the new Act, one must conclude that the Bill of Rights and the Constitution Act coexist. In his comparison of the two documents Hogg concludes that the Charter provides greater protection of rights and freedoms and that with few exceptions it "leaves the Bill with very little work to do."[14] More specifically, see the commentary on section 26 of the Charter.

C. Statutes of Provincial Governments

Provincial governments, also, have enacted statutes of a constitutional nature. For example, Saskatchewan, Alberta, and Quebec have enacted bills of rights.

D. Rules of Order

Mention should be made of the rules of order by which Parliament and provincial legislatures function, although these are not as obviously "formal" as are statutes and orders-in-council. Some of these rules of order are, indeed, statutory in form; they include the sections of the 1867 Constitution Act dealing with Parliament in relation to quorum, voting, the selection of the speaker, and the introduction of money bills. Many rules are written by and for an individual legislature, such as Standing Orders for the House of Commons. Still others are customary in nature.

3. CONVENTION[15]

The importance of convention as part of the Canadian constitution has already been noted. According to the Supreme Court, convention forms "a vital part of the constitution without which it would be incomplete and unable to serve its purpose."[16] Even in 1867 some of the terms of the Constitution Act were intended to operate according to established practice rather than as actually written. This was made clear in the preamble that Canada was to have "a constitution similar in principle to that of the United Kingdom." Probably the most significant of our conventions is responsible government which began in British North America in the late 1840s as the result of instructions from the British colonial office to the governors.

Part of the problem with constitutional conventions is that they are attended by much vagueness. For example, although responsible government is a convention there is much imprecision about the specific content of both collective and individual ministerial responsibility. Marshall's statement to this effect is noted in Chapter 4. Another example relates to the "conventional" relationship between the House of Commons and the Senate. While it may be argued that the upper house is not supposed to (in John A. Macdonald's words) "set itself in opposition against the deliberate and understood wishes of the people" as expressed in the Commons, especially when the Government has a majority of Commons seats, there have been notable exceptions. The 1961 Coyne affair is one: the Senate refused to pass a Commons bill declaring vacant the office of Governor of the Bank of Canada (in reality, firing Governor Coyne). A contemporary illustration was the 1990 attempt of the Liberal-dominated Senate to defeat the Commons bill to enact a Goods and Services Tax—an attempt that failed only when Prime Minister Mulroney appointed eight additional senators pursuant to section 26 of the 1867 Constitution Act.

Sir Ivor Jennings has commented that the individual who considers a constitution without reference to conventions "treats only of bits and snippets of the constitution suspended in thin air."[17] Conventions, therefore, determine the way in which legal authority is to be used. Indeed, conventions may actually contradict the written law, making that law "unconstitutional" although perfectly legal. The term "unconstitutional" can thus be misleading because it applies to the violation of either a legal or a conventional rule. The breach of the former invokes legal sanctions; the breach of the latter is punishable only through the political process.

Can a constitutional convention become part of the law other than through statutory enactment? There is some disagreement among authorities. Hogg, for example, speculates that:

> If a court gave a remedy for a breach of convention, for example, by ordering an unwilling Governor General to give his assent to a bill enacted by both Houses of Parliament, then we would have to change our language and say that the Governor General was under a

> legal obligation to assent, and not merely a conventional obligation. In that event, a convention would have been transformed into a rule of common law.[18]

The Supreme Court disagreed. In the *Patriation Reference* it stated that "it is not for the Courts to raise a convention to the status of a legal principle." The "conflict between convention and law . . . prevents conventions from crystallizing into laws, unless it be by statutory adoption."[19] Marshall acknowledges "there is no doubt that in times past [in Britain] the common law has incorporated into itself rules of constitutional propriety [such as setting limits to the Crown's prerogative powers]. But modern examples of direct conversion or acknowledgement of non-legal rules of law are hard to find."[20]

Our most important constitutional conventions include the following:

(1) The principle of responsible government or ministerial responsibility. This convention is discussed in Chapter 4.

(2) The actual role of the Crown. In accordance with responsible government most of the powers of the governor general (or lieutenant governor or the Queen) are exercised only upon the advice of cabinet or the first minister. The truly discretionary powers are limited to a few extraordinary circumstances. This is discussed in Chapter 4.

(3) The principle of judicial independence. Sections 99 and 100 of the 1867 Constitution Act relating to tenure and salary of certain Federal appointees to provincial courts, and section 11(d) of the Charter referring to an "independent and impartial tribunal," reinforce this independence but the strongest "guarantee" is conventional. (See the commentaries on those sections.)

(4) The existence of the cabinet. In the guise of the ministry (a committee of the privy council) the cabinet is the active part of the privy council to advise the governor general.

(5) The office of prime minister as the chief source of advice to the Crown. The prime minister is mentioned in few statutes such as the Salaries Act and the Official Residences Act. The prime minister is also referred to in sections 35.1, 37, and 37.1 of the 1982 Constitution Act. (The latter two sections are now spent and have been repealed.)

(6) In 1981 a majority of Supreme Court judges decided there was a convention that provincial agreement (but not necessarily unanimity) was constitutionally (but not legally) required for Ottawa to ask the British Parliament for a Constitution Act amendment altering the federal balance. With the passage of the Canada Act and the adoption of a formal amending formula this convention became of only historical interest.

There are other characteristics of our political system which, while perhaps not attaining the status of conventions, are essential to the system's operation as we know it. One of these is the existence and role of political parties which until recently have been almost entirely extralegal. For example, elections are fought on the basis of parties; cabinets are formed from single parties (except when there are coalitions); the membership of parliamentary committees attempts to reflect the relative party strengths in Parliament, and each party chooses its members to serve on these committees; public research funds are distributed among parties; each Wednesday's House of Commons *Hansard* includes party affiliation with the list of members; most patronage appointments by government are to the party faithful. In recent years, however, parties have increasingly become recognized in law.[21] For example, the Broadcasting Act has since 1936 referred to the apportionment of time among "parties" during election campaigns. In 1963 the Senate and House of Commons Act defined "political party" for the purpose of allowances to be paid to party leaders other than the prime minister and leader of the official opposition. Since 1970 the Canada Elections Act has required the registration of political parties and the inclusion of each candidate's party affiliation on election ballots. Contributions to parties are deductible from personal income tax.

A convention is generally established over a period of time as the result of a series of precedents. In this sense it cannot be regarded as an obligatory rule for all time. Changes in convention therefore occur gradually and by the same process in recognition of changing circumstances. An excellent example is that the lieutenant governor's powers of reservation and refusal of assent, and the Federal government's power of disallowance, are no longer to be used although they remain perfectly legal.[22] If they were to be invoked today the provinces would almost certainly demand their repeal.

The election of three successive minority governments within a period of three and one-half years in the 1960s led to speculation that minority government might become the norm. In such a situation some modification of the convention as to what constitutes a vote of non-confidence might be appropriate in order to promote stability and save the electorate from frequent elections. However, with the return to predominantly majority government little is now heard of the suggestion.

Jennings states that although "every act is a precedent . . . not every precedent creates a rule. . . . Precedents create a rule because they have been recognized as creating a rule." One cannot argue, for example, "that if once the House of Lords agrees with the House of Commons it is henceforth bound to agree with the lower House."[23] Jennings's three-part test of a convention is instructive because it emphasizes that the mere existence of precedent (the first part) is insufficient. The second part asks if "the actors in the precedents believe that they were bound by a rule." And third, "Is there a reason for the rule?" He adds that "a single precedent with a good reason may be enough to establish the rule,"[24] but it seems unlikely that this was intended to eliminate the second criterion. Rather, he was probably stressing that a single precedent may sometimes satisfy the first part of the test. An illustration is the principle enunciated, "though against a background of usage," in the 1926 Balfour Declaration that

Britain would not legislate for the dominions without their express consent.[25]

Consideration of Jennings's test in relation to the 1981 *Patriation Reference* facilitates our understanding of the nature of convention. In the first place, what Constitution Act amendments were relevant as precedents in determining whether a convention existed requiring provincial consent to changes that altered the federal balance? There may be conflicting tests for the establishment of a precedent. Are all amendments relevant? Only those amendments of concern to the provinces? Or only those amendments affecting the authority of provincial governments? If the first criterion were adopted then no clear precedent existed. But if the last criterion were appropriate there was a precedent of unanimity—namely, the amendments of 1940, 1951, and 1964 which were approved by all provinces. Furthermore, there was still unanimity if the Statute of Westminster were considered as a Constitution Act amendment.

A majority of the Supreme Court judges in 1981 viewed the amendments of 1930 (which transferred natural resources to the prairie provinces and was approved by those provinces), 1931 (Statute of Westminster), 1940, 1951, and 1964, as the "positive precedents whereby federal-provincial relationships were directly affected in the sense of changing legislative powers." Furthermore, they pointed to what may be called negative precedents whereby one province or two provinces effectively vetoed proposed amendments.[26] A 1951 proposal to allow limited provincial access to the field of indirect taxation was opposed by Ontario and Quebec. In 1961 Saskatchewan "vetoed" the proposed constitutional amending formula. In 1964 Quebec did the same thing. And when Quebec rejected the 1971 Victoria Charter formula the newly-elected Government of Saskatchewan did not bother to register its opinion because it believed the matter to be no longer relevant.

With respect to the second part of Jennings's test, what were the attitudes of the political actors? Several statements of major significance were noted by the judges who formed the majority on the Patriation issue. In 1931 Prime Minister Bennett told the premiers that "there would be no amendment to the constitution of Canada in its federal aspect without consulting the provinces which, it must be remembered had the same powers within their domain that the Dominion has within hers."[27] One should not attach much significance to the reference to consultation rather than provincial consent, for if the Prime Minister had been prepared to act contrary to the wishes of most provinces in seeking amendments affecting the federal balance "then his statement and general performance at this conference must rank as one of the great confidence tricks in modern history."[28]

During Parliament's debate of the 1940 unemployment insurance amendment proposal Prime Minister King stated that

> we have avoided anything in the nature of coercion of any of the provinces. Moreover we have avoided the raising of a very critical constitutional question, namely, whether or not in amending the British North America Act it is absolutely necessary to secure the

> consent of all the provinces, or whether the consent of a certain number of provinces would of itself be sufficient.[29]

(Dawson and Ward comment that "this is a novel way of escaping a constitutional difficulty; for the raising of the compact theory was avoided by conceding all that it demanded, as well as creating another precedent to be stored up for future use.")[30] In 1943 Prime Minister St. Laurent suggested that "it would . . . [be] quite improper to take away from the provinces without their consent anything that they had by the constitution."[31] In the 1965 Favreau White Paper the Federal Government enunciated several principles that it believed had emerged over the years in the process of B.N.A. Act amendment. One of these principles was the following:

> The Canadian Parliament will not request an amendment directly affecting federal-provincial relationships without prior consultation and agreement with the provinces. This principle did not emerge as early as others [noted in the White Paper] but since 1907, and particularly since 1930, has gained increasing recognition and acceptance. The nature and the degree of provincial participation in the amending process, however, have not lent themselves to easy definition.[32]

As for the third part of Jennings's test for the existence of constitutional convention, is there a reason for the rule? Bluntly stated, "The reason . . . is the federal principle." This principle, the Supreme Court continued, "cannot be reconciled with a state of affairs where the modification of provincial legislative powers could be obtained by the unilateral action of the federal authorities."[33]

Is the force of a convention altered through recognition by the courts? Legally, no. However, recognition "may decisively change the situation" if the political disagreement relates to the existence of a convention rather than its binding nature. "Since opposed politicians are rarely likely to convince each other on this point an advisory jurisdiction . . . seems a useful device . . . [to settle] a political argument about the existence of a constitutional rule."[34] The 1981 *Patriation Reference* is a case in point, for the Supreme Court's decision made unilateral Federal action a practical impossibility and led ultimately to the November 5 Accord.

The fact that constitutional conventions may be violated without legal repercussion does not mean that their existence is in constant jeopardy. The political consequences of violating a convention may be as much a deterrent as legal penalties. However, the imposition of political sanctions depends upon a vigilant opposition and, more importantly in the long run, a vigilant electorate.

4. JUDICIAL DECISIONS

In one sense consideration of the courts' impact upon our constitution would entail a complete review of judicial activity in relation to all constitutional documents, especially the 1867 and 1982 Constitution Acts. To the extent that courts have the power of interpretation one may argue that the constitution is whatever the courts say it is. Judge-made law is very much a reality, simplistic statements such as the following by Mr. Justice Roberts in the United States notwithstanding: "When an Act of Congress is appropriately challenged . . . as not conforming to the constitutional mandate the judicial branch of the Government has only one duty,—to lay the article of the Constitution which is involved beside the statute which is challenged and to decide whether the latter squares with the former."[35] If this did reflect reality it would not explain the many split decisions. More accurate, even if somewhat whimsical, is the statement of Jeremiah Smith of the New Hampshire Supreme Court: "Do judges make law? Course they do. Made some myself."[36] Even if a complete review of judicial action were feasible it would be quite inappropriate for the present purpose. What, then, is appropriate for the present discussion? (The commentaries on several sections of the 1867 Constitution Act and especially the 1982 Constitution Act consider many relevant court rulings.)

This topic is divided somewhat arbitrarily into three broad categories. The first is a consideration of the very basis of judicial review. There is merit in providing background so that the reader will understand why the courts have played such an important role in our constitutional development. The second looks broadly at decisions relating to the distribution of legislative authority between Parliament and the provincial legislatures, especially sections 91 and 92 of the 1867 Constitution Act. The third category is a discussion of the courts in relation to basic rights and freedoms.

A possible fourth category would include decisions relating to formal constitutional amendment. Here the 1981 *Patriation Reference* stands alone as a landmark decision of the Supreme Court, although the 1982 *Quebec Veto Reference* is related to it. These cases are discussed in the latter part of Chapter 6. The 1979 *Senate Reference,* also, was significant for constitutional amendment, and was noted briefly earlier in this chapter in relation to Constitution Act amendment by the Federal Parliament.

A. The Basis of Judicial Review

The role of judicial decision making in any democratic system is important, but its significance in a federal state can scarcely be exaggerated. An independent arbiter is essential to adjudicate jurisdictional disputes between the two orders of government. Before the Constitution Act with its Charter of Rights and Freedoms was proclaimed in 1982 the role of the courts was, because of the principle of legislative supremacy, limited basically to the delineation of Federal and provincial powers within the existing Constitution Act. Since 1982 that role has grown because the courts must also consider disputed legislation in relation to rights and freedoms which the Charter has placed beyond the reach of all governments. Viewing the Supreme Court in 1986 Russell concludes not only that the Court is becoming an increasingly significant part of government but also that "it is doubtful if any nation's highest court has as much potential power as the Supreme Court of Canada." He adds that "it is also doubtful that either the Court, the public or the political science community are fully prepared for the Court to exercise this power."[37] Part of the "problem" for Canadians, as it would be in greatly magnified form for the people of Britain, is the seemingly antidemocratic notion of placing in the hands of a non-elective body the ability to overrule the will of an elected assembly.

Until 1949 when the Supreme Court became our highest appeal body (see the commentary on section 101 of the 1867 Constitution Act for the procedure by which this occurred), the final judicial authority for Canada was the Judicial Committee of the British Privy Council. This body is technically not a court but rather a body that advises the monarch. Established in 1833 to consider appeals to the king-in-council from the decisions of courts, the Privy Council makes recommendations to the king (or queen)-in-council who then makes the decisions in the form of orders-in-council. It was possible for Canadian cases to move to the Privy Council from the Supreme Court of Canada or from provincial appeal courts; indeed, half (77 of 159) of all the Privy Council's Canadian cases involving the distribution of powers went directly from provincial courts.[38] Because the Privy Council was a recommending body it spoke with one voice and, therefore, without publicly dissenting opinions. (The significance of this fact in relation to treaty implementation is noted in the commentary on section 132 of the 1867 Constitution Act.) This situation prevented lawyers and lower courts (including our Supreme Court) from building and deciding cases based upon dissent that must have existed within the Privy Council. Since 1966, dissenting opinions have become public. In the following discussion the term *court* is used with reference to both the Privy Council and actual courts.

The reason the task of review devolved ultimately upon the Privy Council was historical because the Constitution Act was silent in this matter. Colonies were forbidden to enact legislation repugnant to the laws of the mother country. The breadth of this prohibition was narrowed by the 1865 Colonial Laws Validity Act which stated that a colonial law could be struck down only if it was "repugnant to the provisions of any Act of Parliament extending to the colony" (s. 2). Furthermore (s. 1), an "Act of Parliament . . . shall be said to extend to any colony [only] when it is made applicable to such colony by the express words or necessary intendment" of the Act. In 1931 the Statute of Westminster exempted the Canadian Parliament and provincial legislatures from the provisions of the Colonial Laws Validity Act except (at Canada's request) insofar as the Constitution Act was concerned. Not until 1982 was this final restriction removed. (See item 17 of the Schedule to the 1982 Constitution Act.)

Both the Supreme Court of Canada and provincial courts of appeal are required by law to hear "references" (as distinct from actual cases) upon the request of the Federal and provincial governments respectively. Appeals from provincial courts to the Supreme Court are a matter of right, so that provincial governments have the same opportunity as has the Federal government to receive an opinion from our highest court. The reference procedure has the advantage of securing judicial opinion before complex and costly administrative machinery is set in place. Two recent examples are the 1976 *Anti-Inflation Act Reference* which upheld Parliament's wage and price control program, and the 1979 *Senate Reference* which rejected the presumption of Parliament's right fundamentally to alter the Senate.[39] Furthermore, in a federal system the quick determination of jurisdiction is most useful so that business interests may know to which order of government they are legally accountable.

More recently, the advisory opinions on the 1981 Patriation Resolution given by the courts in Manitoba, Newfoundland, and Quebec, and especially by the Supreme Court of Canada, had the most profound implications for the ultimate settlement which emerged as the 1982 Constitution Act. Whether some of the questions asked should have been answered is another matter. Indeed, three of the five judges of the Manitoba Court of Appeal declined to answer questions which they believed were "tentative and premature," "not appropriate for judicial response, and, in any event . . . speculative and premature."[40] As for the Supreme Court, not only is it remarkable that every judge answered every question, but the Court went a step further and divided the final question into two parts. That question had asked if provincial consent for certain types of amendment was "constitutionally required." The Court asked (and answered "no") not only whether such consent was legally necessary; it also answered ("yes") a question having strong political overtones—whether consent was required in the conventional sense.[41] In 1982 the Court was asked whether Quebec had a conventional veto over Constitutional amendments affecting Quebec's legislative powers. The Court answered ("no") even though the matter was no longer relevant either legally or constitutionally in the conventional sense.[42] The references associated with the patriation episode illustrate an aspect of the procedure that is especially relevant to federalism. It enables governments to shift emotionally charged issues out of the political forum. As a consequence, however, it adds to the judiciary's political dimension. The 1967 *Offshore Mineral Rights of British Columbia* and 1984 *Newfoundland Continental Shelf* references are two other examples.[43]

It is understandable that courts prefer actual cases to references because hypothetical situations lack the factual content of cases themselves. Indeed, the Supreme Court has claimed a right "to exercise its judgement" whether or not to answer referred questions "if it concludes that they do not exhibit sufficient precision to permit cogent answers."[44] Nevertheless, one-third of all constitutional matters taken to the Privy Council, and from 1949 until 1960 to our Supreme Court, were references. The proportion has since declined although references have included some of the most important decisions.[45]

In the 1979 *Senate Reference* the Court answered four questions and refused to respond to four others "in the absence of a factual background."[46] Could Parliament unilaterally abolish the Senate, alter the proportions of provincial (and territorial) representation in the Senate, provide for direct election of senators, or reduce to a suspensive veto the Senate's authority to withhold legislative approval? The answer was "no." (The rationale is noted above in this chapter under 1867 Constitution Act amendments by Parliament.) Could

Parliament unilaterally change the Senate's name, the qualifications or tenure of its members, or the method of appointing (as distinct from electing) its members? The Court declined to answer.

Courts may answer even when the questions "suffer from excessive abstractness."[47] In *McEvoy* (1983), for example, the Supreme Court rejected New Brunswick's proposal to alter its judicial system, which in the Court's view would involve "the complete obliteration of superior court criminal law jurisdiction." See the commentary on section 96 of the 1867 Constitution Act.

What is the legal force of a court's response to a reference? The Privy Council stated that it is "only advisory and will have no more effect than the opinions of the law officers."[48] In fact, however, reference opinions are treated no differently from judgements.[49]

B. The Courts and the Distribution of Power

Judicial review is but one method of determining the federal balance. Other methods include formal constitutional amendment and political adjustments made by Federal-provincial agreements at the executive level—"cooperative federalism" or the more highly centralized "executive federalism" (a term coined by Professor Smiley). At one time the making of agreements between Federal and provincial wings of political parties was important, especially when the same party was in power in Ottawa and a province. Today, however, parties as between the two orders of government are independent organizations even though they may sometimes have identical names. The New Democratic Party is closest to the earlier type of relationship, but this has not been of much practical significance because the N.D.P. has never formed the Government in Ottawa.

For two decades before 1975 the importance of judicial review as a determinant of the federal balance seemed to decline in relation to political agreements. This led some observers to dismiss the courts as a major factor in establishing that balance. While acknowledging the importance of extrajudicial means, Russell during these decades cautioned against ignoring the courts:

> In any of the issues that arise in federal-provincial relations, those who are responsible for working out the policies and strategies of the governments involved, no matter how pragmatic and flexible they may appear to be in dealing with the division of powers, must always operate on the basis of some assessment of the constitutional power which could be found to sustain the positions they wish to assume. In making these calculations, they will be guided by their awareness of previous constitutional cases and their anticipation of how alternative legislation and administrative schemes would fare if challenged in the courts. The number of major issues that are settled in court should not be regarded as the sole measure of the significance of judicial review.[50]

As a homely analogy "it is not repeated trials of strength between the horse and the fence that keeps the horse in the pasture but the fact that the fence is there and the horse knows it."[51] In any event the number of Supreme Court decisions during the last half of the 1970s increased fourfold over the number during the first half of the decade (from 9 to 36), and it continued to grow (to 42) during the four years from 1980 to 1983. Russell notes retrospectively that this "veritable explosion of constitutional litigation . . . demonstrates how wrong it was to write off the Supreme Court as an important element in the dynamics of Canadian federalism."[52]

What impact have the Privy Council and, since 1949, the Supreme Court had on the constitution? There is no doubt that the Fathers of Confederation intended to create a highly centralized federal system. Unitary elements (but not without ambiguities) of the 1867 Constitution Act are noted in the discussion of federalism in Chapter 4. The distribution of legislative authority between Parliament and the provincial legislatures (essentially sections 91 and 92) comprises one of those elements. The greatest judicial activity in relation to these sections has involved Parliament's broad authority in the opening paragraph of section 91 to legislate for the "peace, order, and good government of Canada" (hereinafter called "p.o.g.g.") in all matters not explicitly assigned to the provinces, and to legislate in relation to the "regulation of trade and commerce" (s. 91[2]). On the provincial side the power to make laws in relation to "property and civil rights in the province" (s. 92[13]) has been the most significant. While 92(16), "generally all matters of a merely local or private nature in the province," is potentially important it has in fact been overshadowed by 92(13). In the mid-1970s the debates surrounding these four powers were "the classic issues of Canadian constitutional law."[53]

Judicial decisions relating to these "classic issues" were the most fundamental, and certainly the most spectacular, judge-made law during the pre-Charter years; that is the rationale for focusing upon them here. Nevertheless, the courts have been called upon to consider other parts of the 1867 Constitution Act as well, and this too has affected the content of our constitution. A number of these court rulings are noted in the commentaries on sections of the Act but the main discussion is here.

Sections 91 and 92 authorize the respective legislatures to make laws "in relation to matters coming within the classes of subjects" assigned to them. Two steps are involved when the courts address a specific challenge brought before them. Put succinctly:

> the first step is to identify the "matter" (or pith and substance) of the challenged law; the second step is to assign the matter to one of the "classes of subjects" (or heads of legislative power). Of course neither of these two steps has any significance by itself. The challenged statute is characterized (or classified) as in relation to a "matter" (step 1) only to determine whether it is authorized by some head of power in the Constitution. The "classes of subjects" are interpreted (step 2)

only to determine which one will accommodate the matter of a particular statute.[54]

There have been numerous issues before the courts that could have been resolved in favour of either order of government. Indeed, the essence of judicial review is precisely the adjudication of disputes about reasonable alternatives. It has been necessary, therefore, for the courts to determine whether the content or subject matter of a challenged law is essentially, or in "pith and substance," one relating to a power assigned to Parliament or to the provincial legislatures. There is, understandably, much room for disagreement because a given statute may pertain in one sense to a matter falling under Federal jurisdiction and in another sense to a matter falling within provincial power. For example, laws governing provincial traffic offences have been upheld under provincial jurisdiction when they relate to "careless driving," and under Parliament's Criminal Code when they are called "dangerous driving." Finkelstein notes the thin line that the courts have drawn in separating these two crimes.[55] The "aspect doctrine" was developed to determine which sense or "aspect" (or, perhaps better, which "matter") is the more relevant in a particular case—i.e., to determine the statute's pith and substance. For example a provincial law may impinge, but only incidentally, upon a Federal power and be upheld because it relates essentially to a subject assigned to the provinces.

On the other hand a provincial law may be struck down because it impacts so severely upon Federal jurisdiction that it effectively nullifies or "sterilizes" Parliament's power in a particular area. (For an illustration of the aspect doctrine with a twist, see the discussion of the 1982 *Exported Natural Gas Tax Reference* in the commentary on section 91[3] of the 1867 Constitution Act.) If legislation appears on the surface to address a provincial (for example) matter but has the clear intent of trenching upon Parliament's jurisdiction, the courts may decide that it is "colourable." See, for example, the note on the *Alberta Statutes Reference* in the commentary on section 91(15) of the 1867 Constitution Act. Hogg considers the fine distinction between rulings based on policy and those based on validity, and he disagrees with the "strong connotation of judicial disapproval" which accompanies the term "colourable." Hogg adds that this disapproval inhibits judicial neutrality, and he contends that colourability should be defined merely as a recognition that (in Abel's words) "form is not controlling in the determination of essential character."[56]

But what happens if conflicting Federal and provincial statutes are equally valid? The doctrine of "Federal paramountcy" resolves the conflict in favour of Ottawa. This is discussed in the commentary on the concluding paragraph of section 91 of the 1867 Constitution Act.

The procedures noted in the preceding paragraphs are raised only to suggest some of the problems facing the courts. The commentaries on several of the powers within sections 91 and 92 of the Constitution Act allude to these procedures.

The purpose of the present discussion is to demonstrate that judicial decisions are indeed a significant component of our constitution. The discussion considers almost exclusively the conflict between p.o.g.g. and property and civil rights, the two competing powers throughout most of the history of judicial interpretation of the Constitution Act. (One may speculate how the course of judicial review would have been different had the full potential of section 94 of the Constitution Act been implemented. That section anticipated the possible unifying of property and civil rights legislation under Federal law throughout the common law provinces.) What became of the apparent breadth of p.o.g.g.? In the hands of the Privy Council p.o.g.g. turned out to be not only subordinate to the enumeration in section 91 but also only an "implied" power which "may" exist, and one that could be invoked only in an emergency such as war, pestilence, famine, or intemperance. It is often claimed that the Privy Council played a dominant, or *the* dominant, role in determining the federal balance of power. However, the caution expressed by Cairns is well taken: "It is impossible to believe that a few elderly men in London deciding two or three constitutional cases a year precipitated, sustained, and caused the development of Canada in a federalist direction the country would otherwise not have taken."[57]

With respect to trade and commerce (91[2]), the other potentially broad Federal power, suffice it to say here that almost from the beginning the courts gave a narrow interpretation and limited Parliament to international trade, interprovincial trade, and trade regulation relating to the entire country. The courts barred Parliament from legislation in relation to intraprovincial trade. The commentary on section 91(2) is a more detailed discussion of this power.

How reverently should the views of people in one age, such as our Fathers of Confederation, be held by people of a later age? Should a codified Constitutional document not be a living thing capable of adaptation to meet changing circumstances? The growth of provincial powers as a result of court decisions was a reflection of other decentralizing forces at work in the country as well. Surely Cairns is right: "It is . . . fallacious to transform the constitutional settlement of 1867 into a measuring rod against which subsequent deviations can be assessed and their perpetrators chastised."[58] The purpose of the present exercise is to demonstrate the courts' role rather than to praise or condemn it.

(i) 1867-1882: During these first few years the courts interpreted p.o.g.g. broadly as a residual power. If the matter involved in the disputed legislation was not found within section 92—property and civil rights not yet being interpreted broadly—then it automatically came within Federal jurisdiction. Reference to the section 91 enumeration was unnecessary.

Russell v. R. (1882) marks the end of this initial period. It was the forerunner of the "aspect doctrine" made explicit the following year. Writing for the Privy Council in *Russell*, Sir Montague Smith said that the pith and substance of the legislation in question (the 1878 Dominion Temperance Act) was in relation to public order and safety rather than property and civil rights. He added in what has become a classic statement:

> Few, if any, laws could be made by Parliament for the peace, order, and good government of Canada which did not in some incidental

> way affect property and civil rights; and it could not have been intended, when assuring to the provinces exclusive legislative authority on the subjects of property and civil rights, to exclude the Parliament from the exercise of this general power whenever any such incidental interference would result from it.

In rejecting the applicability of section 92(16) Sir Montague wrote:

> The present legislation is clearly meant to apply a remedy to an evil which is assumed to exist throughout the Dominion, and the local option, as it is called, no more localises the subject and scope of the Act than a provision in an Act for the prevention of contagious diseases in cattle that a public officer should proclaim in what districts it should come in effect, would make the statute itself a mere local law for each of these districts. In statutes of this kind the legislation is general, and the provision for the special application of it to particular places does not alter its character.

Therefore, "their Lordships having come to the conclusion that the Act in question does not fall within any of the classes of subjects assigned exclusively to the Provincial Legislatures, it becomes unnecessary to discuss the further question whether its provisions also fall within any of the classes of subjects enumerated in sect. 91."[59]

(ii) 1883-1932: In its major rulings relating to the Constitution Act between 1883 and the end of the 1920s, the Privy Council was dominated by the views of Lord Watson and then Lord Haldane. These men moved our federal system toward what may be called the "classical" model, which means that each order of government is considered sovereign within its own sphere of jurisdiction. For the provinces to achieve that status the Privy Council consistently reflected a narrow interpretation of p.o.g.g. and of the trade and commerce power, and a broad interpretation of property and civil rights within the province. It must be stressed, nevertheless, that other events in Canada as well were moving the federal system from the highly centralized model envisaged by John A. Macdonald. Some of the more important decisions of the Watson/Haldane era are noted below.

The shift began with *Hodge v. R.* (1883) which gave explicit formulation to the aspect doctrine: "Subjects which in one aspect and for one purpose fall within sect. 92, may in another aspect and for another purpose fall within sect. 91."[60] The problem was to determine which aspect was relevant in a particular situation, but it was not difficult to find one within section 92 if such were the desire.

By 1896 Parliament's essentially single power (p.o.g.g. plus the "examples"—but note the qualifications in the commentary on section 91's opening paragraph) was divided into two distinct powers and p.o.g.g. was ranked second. In the *Local Prohibition* case of that year Lord Watson characterized p.o.g.g. as being "in supplement of" the enumerated heads of section 91, and he cast doubt upon the existence of even that "supplement" when he commented that "there *may* . . . be matters not included in the enumeration, upon which the Parliament of Canada has power to legislate" (emphasis added). He continued by saying that a broad interpretation of p.o.g.g. "would, in their Lordships' opinion, not only be contrary to the intendment of the [Constitution] Act, but would practically destroy the autonomy of the provinces."[61] This was a clear statement of classical federalism.

Viscount Haldane is known primarily for the "emergency doctrine" which emerged in the 1922 *Board of Commerce Reference.* According to this doctrine, p.o.g.g. could be invoked only in extraordinary circumstances:

> Circumstances are conceivable, such as those of war or famine, when the peace, order and good government of the Dominion might be imperilled under conditions so exceptional that they require legislation of a character in reality beyond anything provided for by the enumerated heads in either s. 92 or s. 91 itself. Such a case, if it were to arise would have to be considered closely before the conclusion could properly be reached that it was one which could not be treated as falling under any of the heads enumerated. Still, it is a conceivable case, and although great caution is required in referring to it, even in general terms, it ought not . . . to be excluded from what is possible.[62]

In 1925 (*Toronto Electric Commissioners v. Snider*) Haldane attempted to fit the 1882 *Russell* decision into the "emergency" mould:

> The evil of intemperance at that time [1870s] amounted in Canada to one so great and so general that at least for the period it was a menace to the national life of Canada so serious and pressing that the National Parliament was called on to intervene to protect the nation from disaster. An epidemic of pestilence might conceivably have been regarded as analogous.[63]

In the opinion of Supreme Court Chief Justice Laskin and two other judges this attempt "did no credit to the judicial process and, in our view, demeaned the Privy Council."[64] The emergency doctrine may be viewed as an extreme form of the aspect doctrine in which the national aspect simply does not exist except in an emergency.

(iii) 1932-1949: The 1932 *Aeronautics Reference* and *Radio Reference* relating to the implementation of international agreements marked a brief return to a broad view of p.o.g.g.[65] The first agreement involved Canada as part of the Empire; the second was an agreement signed by Canada in its own right. In the *Aeronautics Reference* the Privy Council upheld Federal legislation on the basis of section 132 (treaty implementation) of the Constitution Act, although there was a comment (*obiter dictum*) that the national aspect might have justified the use of p.o.g.g. In the *Radio Reference* the Privy Council invoked p.o.g.g. because the implementation of Canadian treaties was not covered by the enumerations of section 92 or 91. That is, treaty implementation constituted a gap in the distribution of enumerated powers—a gap that p.o.g.g. filled.

However, the emergency doctrine returned in 1937 (*Labour Conventions Reference*) when the Privy Council struck down the Bennett Government's 1935 New Deal legislation as trenching upon section 92(13). The economic conditions of the Depression did not constitute an "emergency"! Section 132 was inapplicable because the legislation had been made pursuant to an international agreement signed by Canada in her own right. Furthermore, in an explicit rejection of the *Radio* decision the Privy Council declared:

> For the purposes of ss. 91 and 92 . . . there is no such thing as treaty legislation as such. The distribution is based on classes of subjects; and as a treaty deals with a particular class of subjects so will the legislative power of performing it be ascertained . . . It would be remarkable that while the Dominion could not initiate legislation, however desirable, which affected civil rights in the provinces, yet its government not responsible to the provinces nor controlled by provincial parliaments need only agree with a foreign country to enact such legislation, and its parliament would be forthwith clothed with authority to affect provincial rights to the full extent of such agreement. Such a result would appear to undermine the constitutional safeguards of provincial constitutional autonomy. . . .While the ship of state now sails on larger ventures and into foreign waters she still retains the watertight compartments which are an essential part of her original structure.[66]

The commentary on section 132 of the 1867 Constitution Act speculates about the possible return to the reasoning of the *Radio Reference*.

When, therefore, might p.o.g.g. be used? In normal times, only when the disputed matter did not fall within the enumerated heads of sections 91 or 92. Given the broad interpretation of property and civil rights and, one might add, the narrow interpretation of trade and commerce, there was little likelihood that p.o.g.g. would see the light of day in normal times. The only other opportunity for p.o.g.g. was during an "emergency," when section 92 could be set aside. However, the emergent situation would be determined by the Privy Council and by definition it would be temporary. The only specific clues given by the Privy Council as to what constituted an emergency were war, famine, an epidemic of pestilence or of intemperance. In actual fact, only World War One and the 1870s "evil of intemperance," but not the Depression of the 1930s, had qualified. The residual power had effectively been transferred from Parliament to the provincial legislatures.

In the 1940s the Privy Council returned briefly to the more liberal aspect test, but later decisions were based on the emergency doctrine.[67]

(iv) 1949-Present: What effect has the Supreme Court of Canada had upon the distribution of powers since it became our highest appeal body in 1949?

Russell points out that until the mid-1970s there was a "distinct centralist accent" to Supreme Court decisions relating to p.o.g.g., trade and commerce, property and civil rights, and matters of a merely local or private nature in the province.[68] Over much of that period the Court accepted what has been called the "national concern" or "national dimensions" test for sustaining Federal legislation on the basis of p.o.g.g. This test replaced the emergency doctrine which had been dominant at least since 1922 (*Board of Commerce*) or even 1896 (*Local Prohibition*). The national concern test was first enunciated by Viscount Simon in the Privy Council in the *Canada Temperance Federation* case (1946):[69] What is the "real subject matter" of the legislation? "If it is such that it goes beyond local or provincial concern or interests and must from its inherent nature be the concern of the Dominion as a whole . . . then it will fall within the competence of the Dominion Parliament as a matter affecting the peace, order and good government of Canada." It assumes major importance when the failure of one province to act, such as to control an epidemic disease or marine pollution, might jeopardize the health or safety of people living beyond that province's borders.

In 1976, however, the national dimensions test was rejected in favour of the emergency doctrine to uphold Parliament's Anti-Inflation Act,[70] although the meaning of "emergency" was broadened to include economic conditions. Chief Justice Laskin for the Court majority also suggested that the Act might have been upheld on the basis of Parliament's trade and commerce power (s. 91[2]) if the Federal government had chosen to argue this point rather than p.o.g.g.

By 1985, Russell notes, "the Supreme Court's overall record shows an uncanny balance. In so many areas, the net outcome of its decision-making is to strike a balance between federal and provincial powers."[71] In a sense the Court's 1981 *Patriation Reference* ruling epitomized that balance. The concept of "balance" is rather tricky, and Russell acknowledges the inadequacy of merely counting by wins and losses. Swinton adds that another sense of balance is "the preservation of some kind of overall balance between federal and provincial powers in the federal system so that neither level of government interferes unduly with the other's expectations about legislative autonomy."[72]

C. The Courts and Basic Rights and Freedoms

By the mid-1970s it could be argued that civil liberties cases were receiving greater attention than those dealing with federalism's four "classical issues."[73] And with the Charter of Rights and Freedoms in place the emphasis is even greater. The role of the courts concerning rights and freedoms may be considered in relation to the 1867 Constitution Act, the 1960 Canadian Bill of Rights, and the 1982 Charter of Rights and Freedoms.

(i) 1867 Constitution Act: Two mutually exclusive views are possible. According to one, the principle of legislative supremacy applies in that courts need only to determine which order of government in a particular instance has the authority to violate rights and freedoms or, conversely, to legislate against their infringement. According to the other view there is an implied bill of rights; there are certain fundamental rights or freedoms inherent in the parliamentary system or in the Act's preamble (which refers to our constitution as being "similar in principle to that of the United Kingdom"), and therefore beyond the reach of government *per se*. The problem with this second view is that the parliamentary system and the constitution of the United Kingdom are clearly based upon the principle of legislative supremacy.

Individual judges have supported the notion of an implied bill of rights, the most notable being Supreme Court Justice Duff. In the 1938 *Alberta Statutes Reference* the Court struck down the Alberta Press Bill on the grounds that it conflicted with Federal authority. Duff's reasoning went beyond this. He argued, first, that the implied bill of rights included freedom of speech and of the press. Second, he claimed that the Constitutional requirement of elected legislatures "contemplates a parliament working under the influence of public opinion and public discussion. . . It is axiomatic that the practice of this right of free public discussion of public affairs . . . is the breath of life for parliamentary institutions."[74] This position has since been called the "Duff Doctrine."

The Supreme Court itself, through Justice Beetz, upheld the alternative view of legislative supremacy in *Dupond* (1978): none of the fundamental freedoms which we inherited from Britain (such as speech, assembly, association, press, religion) "is so enshrined in the Constitution as to be above the reach of competent legislation."[75] The significance of this interpretation is that Canadians had no absolute guarantee of civil liberties before the adoption of the Charter of Rights and Freedoms. This situation is similar to that in Great Britain but differs from that in the United States. Canada has had an enviable although by no means perfect record in respecting rights and freedoms. The reason is partly our democratic traditions of free discussion, press, and elections; partly the tradition of an independent judiciary; and partly the common law which tends to support individual rights in struggles with the state. As pointed out in Chapter 4 under "Semi-limited Government" there are exceptions to the concept of an exhaustive distribution of powers between the two orders of government, and hence to the principle of legislative supremacy. Nevertheless, as between this principle and that of an implied bill of rights, this one seems to be the more accurate depiction of the 1867 Constitution Act.

In 1987 (*Ontario Public Service Employees' Union*) Beetz—again for the Court—seemed to reverse his position. (This case did not involve the Charter because the events were pre-Charter.) He quoted with approval both Justice Duff (above) and a 1957 statement of Justice Abbott that the preamble to the 1867 Constitution Act prevented both Parliament and the provincial legislatures from abrogating the "right of free expression of opinions and of criticism, upon matters of public policy and public administration." He then added that the basis of our constitution "contemplates the existence of certain political institutions, including freely elected legislative bodies at the federal and provincial levels . . . I hold that neither Parliament nor the provincial legislature may enact legislation the effect of which would be to substantially interfere with the operation of this basic constitutional structure." He made no reference to his *Dupond* position.[76] Although the Court did not address the Charter issues (ss. 2, 3, 15[1]), these issues would certainly arise in the future. It seems unclear how the court might react if it maintains that certain freedoms are grounded in the preamble to the 1867 Constitution Act, especially if governments become more inclined to use the Charter override (s. 33) from which the preamble is exempt.

(ii) Canadian Bill of Rights: In spite of its name this piece of legislation guarantees no rights or freedoms. It is an ordinary statute of Parliament, although "constitutional" in nature, and therefore freely amendable by Parliament. Furthermore, it is not applicable to the provinces, although several have their own bills of rights. The only case of the Supreme Court using the Bill of Rights to make Federal legislation "inoperative" was *Drybones* (1970).[77] Drybones was an Indian who was found intoxicated off a Reserve in contravention of section 94(b) of the Indian Act. The Supreme Court declared that this section conflicted with the assurance of "equality before the law" (s. 1[b]) in the Bill of Rights. Apart from *Drybones* the history of the Bill of Rights has not been impressive. See, for example, the discussion of the 1974 *Lavell and Bedard* and *Bliss* cases in the commentary on Charter section 15. The principle of legislative supremacy seemed to stand in the way of assigning priority to the Bill of Rights. Furthermore, the significance of the Bill and the comparable provincial statutes has faded since the Charter was enacted in 1982, although the laws remain in force to the extent that their provisions are not covered by the Charter.

There is some awkwardness in determining the status of a law that contravenes the Bill of Rights. Because the Bill and any other Act of Parliament are of equal validity, neither can be used to declare the other "unconstitutional." In our system the usual method of reconciling conflicting laws is for the more recent one to take precedence over the earlier one to the extent of the conflict. In *Drybones* the Court declared section 94(b) of the earlier Indian Act to be "inoperative."

But what is the status of the Bill of Rights in relation to conflicting legislation passed after 1960? The Bill was intended (s. 5[2]) to apply to any law "enacted before or after the coming into force of this Act" unless the Bill's notwithstanding clause was invoked to exempt contrary legislation. Would the courts honour this statement of intent? At least a partial answer was given in *Singh* (1985) when Supreme Court Justice Beetz, for three of the six judges who participated in the unanimous ruling, declared a section of the 1976 Immigration Act "inoperative" on the basis of conflict with the Bill of Rights: "I do not see any reason not to apply the principle in the *Drybones* case to a provision enacted after the *Canadian Bill of Rights*." While the other three judges based their reasons on the Charter, Justice Wilson (who delivered their judgement) commented "there can be no doubt that this statute [Bill of Rights] continues in full force and effect."[78] This has led Greene to the conclusion that the Bill of Rights was "more central" than was the Charter in the Court's ruling, and that the *Singh* ruling was therefore the first since *Drybones* in which the Supreme Court used the Bill to "strike down" legislation.[79]

(iii) Charter of Rights and Freedoms: As noted in Chapter 4 under "Semi-limited Government," Canadian courts in 1982 embarked on an entirely new venture. In addition to their responsibility as arbiter of Federal and provincial jurisdictional disputes they assumed what Justice Estey called "a new dimension, a new yardstick of reconciliation between the individual and the community and their respective rights."[80]

While the Supreme Court has considerable latitude as it approaches the new Charter of Rights and Freedoms, it is also mindful of the precedents that its rulings are establishing. And while decisions of lower courts may be useful, variation in their Charter interpretations means that the Supreme Court must strive toward uniformity to ensure consistency of the Charter's application throughout the country. A major difficulty in accomplishing this uniformity is the Court's ability to hear only a small proportion of cases on appeal from lower courts—not more than one or two per cent by 1988.[81] A different and to some extent contrary consideration is the relationship between the Charter and the recognition of diversity inherent in a federal system. This is noted in Chapter 4 under "Federalism."

According to Justice Wilson "the recent adoption of the *Charter* . . . has sent a clear message to the courts that the restrictive attitude which at times characterized their approach to the *Canadian Bill of Rights* ought to be re-examined."[82] A review of early Supreme Court judgements supports this statement. Until 1986 the Court's activism was demonstrated by the success of 60% of Charter challenges; thirteen of the first fifteen decisions were unanimous. The success rate fell to 25% over the next two years (through January 1988); and unanimity declined to half of the next thirty-two cases. These changes reflect emerging differences in constitutional philosophies. Justices Wilson (who retired at the end of 1990) and McIntyre (who retired in February 1989) dissented the most and in opposite directions—Wilson interpreting the Charter broadly and McIntyre supporting impugned legislation.[83]

The Charter is divided into three main categories—rights and freedoms, application clauses, and interpretation clauses.[84]

(1) Rights and freedoms:

Fundamental freedoms—section 2
Democratic rights—sections 3-5
Mobility rights—section 6
Legal rights—sections 7-14
Equality rights—section 15
Official languages—sections 16-22
Minority language educational rights—section 23

(2) **Application clauses:**

Limitations clause (s. 1)—permits Charter violations if the limits placed on rights and freedoms are "reasonable," "prescribed by law,"and "can be demonstrably justified in a free and democratic society."

Notwithstanding clause (s. 33)—under defined conditions, permits Parliament or provincial legislatures to enact laws that contravene fundamental freedoms, legal rights, or equality rights.

What-it-covers clause (s. 32)—establishes that the Charter applies to all governments—Canada, the provinces, and the territories.

Enforcement clause (s. 24)—authorizes courts to provide remedies when Charter rights and freedoms have been infringed; and permits courts to exclude from proceedings any evidence obtained in a manner that infringes rights or freedoms if its admission "would bring the administration of justice into disrepute."

(3) **Interpretation clauses:**

Aboriginal, treaty, or other rights or freedoms of aboriginal peoples (s. 25)—Charter interpretation must not lead to the abrogation of these rights or freedoms.

Multiculturalism (s. 27)—Charter interpretation must be consistent with the preservation and enhancement of our multicultural heritage.

Sexual equality (s. 28)—Charter rights and freedoms are guaranteed equally to male and female persons "notwithstanding anything in this Charter."

Denominational school rights (s. 29)—the Charter does not diminish the rights guaranteed by section 93 of the 1867 Constitution Act and by analogous provisions of constitutional documents establishing other provinces.

Miscellaneous (ss. 26, 30, 31)—Charter interpretation must not deny any other existing rights; references to provinces include the two territories; the Charter does not add any legislative powers.

Because the Supreme Court is in fact establishing our constitutional law by defining the Charter's rights and freedoms as cases arise, the reader is directed to the commentaries in Chapter 8 where many of the seminal cases are discussed. In addition to judicial interpretations of rights and freedoms is the extremely broad discretionary power given the courts by section 1 to decide what limits to rights and freedoms are reasonable in a free and democratic society, as well as the authority to decide (s. 24[2]) when the admission of evidence brings the administration of justice into disrepute. One thing is certain: the courts are playing a much greater policy role than they have in the past.

Consider for example the relation between Sunday closing, the "right" to strike, and abortion on the one hand, and the freedoms of religion and expression, and the right to life and security of the person, on the other.

There is also the potentially broad power of the legislative override (s. 33). Although it may still be too early to predict the significance of this power, the experience through mid-1991—used only by Quebec and Saskatchewan—suggests that it may be minimal.

CHAPTER 6

Formal Amendment — A Half-Century Search for a Formula

1. 1927 Dominion-Provincial Conference
2. 1935 Dominion-Provincial Conference and 1936 Continuing Committee on Constitutional Questions
3. 1950 Constitutional Conference
4. 1960-1961 Constitutional Conference and the "Fulton Formula"
5. 1964 Constitutional Conference and the "Fulton-Favreau Formula"
6. 1968-1971 Constitutional Conference and the "Victoria Charter"
7. Developments to 1978
   - A. March 1976
   - B. August and October 1976
   - C. January 1977
   - D. June 1978
8. 1978-1979 Constitutional Conference
   - A. October 30-November 1, 1978
   - B. February 1979
9. 1980 Constitutional Conference
10. Events Leading to the 1981 Constitutional Conference
    - A. The Resolution Goes to Parliament
    - B. The Provinces Go to Court
    - C. The Supreme Court of Canada
11. 1981 Constitutional Conference: Success?
12. What About Quebec?

On November 5, 1981, Prime Minister Trudeau and nine of the ten provincial premiers agreed upon five general principles which would be expanded into a resolution to be presented to the Canadian Parliament and, following passage by that body, forwarded to the British Parliament for legislative enactment.[1]

The lone dissenter was Quebec's Premier Lévesque. The major components of the agreement were patriation, an amending formula (perhaps amending formulae is more accurate in that there are five distinct methods of amendment), and a Charter of Rights and Freedoms. Patriation would signal the end of British involvement in matters affecting our Constitution.

This Federal-provincial agreement culminated more than half a century of sporadic searching for an amending formula. That search had been closely linked to the patriation question. Actually, patriation was a non-issue almost from the beginning of Federal-provincial discussions, its desirability virtually unquestioned. There was agreement very early in those discussions that the 1867 Constitution Act should not be "brought to Canada" until an amending procedure was settled; if it were, patriation would either freeze the Constitution Act or place the Act totally under Parliament's control.

Beginning in 1968 the question of an amending formula was part of a broader consideration of Constitution Act reform. The focus of the present chapter remains upon amendment, but the broader issue is acknowledged when necessary to keep the question of amendment in perspective.

1. 1927 DOMINION-PROVINCIAL CONFERENCE

This Conference was a logical consequence of the 1926 Imperial Conference which through the Balfour Declaration had established the principle of sovereignty for the British Dominions. The Federal government proposed in 1927 that British legislation be sought to permit Constitution Act amendment in Canada. The suggestion foundered when it failed to receive unanimous provincial support. According to the Conference *Précis of Discussions* there was no "widespread demand" for a change; if the authority to amend the Act were transferred to Canada "all sorts of demands for changes would be made"; the British government had never rejected a request for amendment; "to submit all sorts of proposals to the provincial governments for approval would stir up local party strife and arouse sentiment and feeling"; and because the Act was a British statute "Canada should go to London for amendments thereto." Amendments should not become "too easy to secure."[2]

2. 1935 DOMINION-PROVINCIAL CONFERENCE AND 1936 CONTINUING COMMITTEE ON CONSTITUTIONAL QUESTIONS

Although the proposals emanating from these meetings produced no action, they did result in the recognition of two basic principles which were generally accepted by succeeding conferences.[3] The first principle, whose frailty became evident on November 5, 1981, was that an amending formula must be agreeable to the prime minister and all provincial premiers before it becomes effective.

(New Brunswick had not agreed to the 1935-1936 proposals.) According to the second principle, suggested in embryonic form in 1927, different amendment procedures are needed for different situations. The procedures suggested in 1935-1936 were as follows:

(1) **Unanimity:** amendments to basic provisions of the Constitution Act. These would require the agreement of Parliament and all provincial legislatures. These provisions were described in the 1965 Favreau White Paper as those directly affecting "the fundamental historical and constitutional relationships between the federal government and the provinces, and in respect of the rights of minorities and the use of the English and French languages. Such matters were considered to be essential to Canadian federalism and Canadian unity."[4]

The specific areas which in 1936 were to be subject to this unanimity rule were the following:

- **(a)** The executive authority of the Queen.
- **(b)** The number of Senate seats and their distribution among the provinces.
- **(c)** Representation in the House of Commons, including the assurance that the number of a province's seats would never be less than the number of its senators—sometimes called the "Senate floor."
- **(d)** Certain of the legislative powers within section 92 (specifically, subsections 4, 5, 8, 12, 14, 15).
- **(e)** Education (s. 93 and the corresponding provisions in the Manitoba Act, Alberta Act, and Saskatchewan Act).
- **(f)** Language (s. 133, and the corresponding provision in the Manitoba Act).

(2) **Parliament acting alone:** amendments to provisions affecting only the Federal government.

(3) **A provincial legislature acting alone:** amendments to that province's constitution. This was already within the Constitution Act.

(4) **Parliament and the legislatures of affected provinces:** amendments to any provision applicable to one or more but not all of the provinces.

(5) **The "general" amending formula:** amendments to provisions affecting the Federal government and the provinces generally. These amendments would be made upon the agreement of Parliament and the legislatures of some proportion of the provinces containing a minimum percentage of the country's population. The 1936 proposal, for example, called for two-thirds of the provinces containing at least 55 per cent of the population, thus ensuring the participation of either Ontario or Quebec.

It was also proposed in 1936 that provinces be permitted to opt out of amendments affecting property and civil rights, or local or private matters, within the provinces (s. 92[13] and [16]). This opting-out notion lay dormant until its revival by Alberta in 1976.

3. 1950 CONSTITUTIONAL CONFERENCE

This Conference was preceded by the 1949 Constitution Act amendment (the new section 91[1]). That amendment enabled the Federal government to amend the "Constitution of Canada" (which was undefined) in matters not affecting the provinces—essentially paralleling section 92(1) which since 1867 had given corresponding authority to the provinces. The 1950 Conference sought agreement upon amending procedures along the lines of the 1935-1936 proposal for those parts of the Constitution Act affecting both orders of government. However, agreement eluded the Conference on the allocation of specific sections among the six categories established—the five noted above as well as one for sections to be repealed. For example, Ontario and Quebec wanted the unanimity rule to apply to the entire distribution of legislative authority.[5]

4. 1960-1961 CONSTITUTIONAL CONFERENCE AND THE "FULTON FORMULA"[6]

Justice Minister Fulton initially proposed that the Constitution Act be patriated without an amending formula. He suggested that until such time as a formula was established the unanimity rule apply to all amendments. This proposal was dropped in view of prevailing optimism that the Conference would have little difficulty settling upon a formula.[7]

The "general" amending formula which emerged specified the consent of Parliament and the legislatures of two-thirds of the provinces containing at least 50 per cent of Canada's population. Furthermore, earlier agreements were reaffirmed, that amendments to provisions of the Constitution which apply to one or more but not all provinces would require the consent of Parliament and the appropriate provincial legislatures. The Conference did not consider sections 91(1) and 92(1) of the Constitution Act.

The Fulton Formula provided, finally, that the unanimity rule would apply to amendments affecting any provision of the Constitution relating to the following seven provisions:

(1) The "Senate floor" for provincial representation in the House of Commons.
(2) The legislative powers of the provinces (thereby meeting the 1950 demands of Ontario and Quebec).
(3) The rights or privileges granted to provincial legislatures or governments.
(4) The assets or property of provinces.

(5) The use of the English and French languages.
(6) Education.
(7) The amending procedure itself.

To mitigate the rigidity created by the unanimity rule the proposal also authorized some delegation of legislative authority between Ottawa and the provinces. Specifically, the Federal government could delegate any of its power to a minimum of four provinces; and a minimum of four provinces (fewer, if the legislation in question affected fewer than four) could delegate to the Federal government their authority within section 92(6), (10), (13), and (16). Any such delegation did not involve the transfer of jurisdiction *per se*, and it could be revoked at any time.

Saskatchewan's N.D.P. government, fearing that the provinces' right of veto implicit in the unanimity rule would create constitutional inflexibility, vetoed the amending formula!

5. 1964 CONSTITUTIONAL CONFERENCE AND THE "FULTON-FAVREAU FORMULA"[8]

This formula was essentially the 1961 proposal to which was added the subject matter of section 92(1) and a modified section 91(1) of the Constitution Act. Named after the two justice ministers involved (Conservative Fulton and Liberal Favreau), the formula was adopted by all first ministers only to be torpedoed five months later by Quebec Premier Jean Lesage. (Saskatchewan had changed its attitude toward unanimity following the 1964 election of a Liberal government in that province.) Lesage noted that parts of the agreement appeared to be subject to differing interpretations. More importantly, with Quebec increasing its demands for fundamental constitutional change, any requirement of unanimity was becoming less a protection than a strait jacket for that province.[9] When Daniel Johnson's Union Nationale was elected in 1966, Quebec demanded a new constitutional document to reflect an equality of the English and French peoples. Johnson's *Equality or Independence*, published the year before the Union Nationale victory, clearly stated the alternatives as Johnson saw them.

6. 1968-1971 CONSTITUTIONAL CONFERENCE AND THE "VICTORIA CHARTER"

Following the 1964 Conference the emphasis broadened from the question of an amending formula to include more substantive constitutional change. Such change included Federal institutions (notably the Senate and Supreme Court of Canada), fundamental rights, and the distribution of legislative authority between Ottawa and the provinces. In a series of meetings beginning February

1968 the discussion of a broad range of issues culminated in the June 1971 agreement known as the Victoria Charter.

The following amending procedures for the "Constitution of Canada" (defined by the Charter's Schedule) were proposed. There was to be no unanimity rule.

(1) Parliament acting alone: amendments in relation to "the executive Government of Canada and the Senate and House of Commons."

(2) A provincial legislature acting alone: amendments to the "Constitution of the Province" (which term was not defined).

(3) Parliament and the legislatures of affected provinces: amendments to any provision applicable to one or more but not all of the provinces. The Senate would have only a ninety-day suspensive veto. Amendments might be initiated by either order of government.

(4) The "general" amending formula: These amendments, which could be initiated by either order of government, would be made upon the agreement of Parliament (the Senate again possessing but a suspensive veto) and the legislatures of a majority of the provinces. However, that majority must include

(a) Every province which according to any previous general census contained at least 25 per cent of the Canadian population (effectively giving Ontario and Quebec permanent vetoes).

(b) Two of the four Atlantic provinces.

(c) Two of the four Western provinces provided that a majority of the population (at the latest general census) of the four provinces was included. This requirement was a concession to British Columbia, for it meant that without British Columbia's concurrence all three remaining Western provinces would have to agree to an amendment.

The general amending formula would be required for amendments relating to

(a) The office of the Queen, governor general, or lieutenant governor.

(b) The requirement of annual sessions of Parliament and of provincial legislatures.

(c) The five-year maximum duration of Parliament and of provincial legislatures, although extensions approved by two-thirds majorities were permitted "in time of real or apprehended war, invasion or insurrection."

(d) The powers of the Senate.

(e) The distribution of Senate seats among the provinces, and the residence qualifications of senators.

(f) The "Senate floor" for provincial representation in the House of Commons.
(g) The principle of representation by population in the House of Commons as prescribed by the Constitution Act.
(h) The language rights included in the Victoria Charter.
(i) The amending formula itself.

It was agreed that the first ministers would report the Charter back to their cabinets, and advise the secretary of the Constitutional Conference within eleven days (by June 28) as to whether or not they were willing to recommend the Charter to their legislatures.[10] By June 23 the prime minister and all provincial premiers, except Quebec's Robert Bourassa and Saskatchewan's Ross Thatcher, had indicated executive approval. On that date, however, Bourassa announced Quebec's rejection of the proposal. His stated reason was the existence of conflicting interpretations of the Charter. It seems more likely that, as in 1966, the objections were more fundamental—that the Premier was reacting to internal opposition to any amending formula that would make the realization of Quebec's constitutional aspirations dependent upon the agreement of other provinces. The same day that Quebec rejected the Charter a new government was elected in Saskatchewan. Evidently the new premier (Allan Blakeney) assumed that any action on his part would now be purely academic, coming as it would after the Quebec announcement, and so the Saskatchewan government did not reply.

7. DEVELOPMENTS TO 1978

For five years after the Victoria Conference there was relative calm in relation to constitutional reform including amendment. Constitutional talks since the beginning of the Quiet Revolution in the early 1960s had centred upon Quebec's demands. "What does Quebec want?" was the familiar cry. The election of Robert Bourassa in 1970 had marked the replacement, at least at the government level, of forces demanding radical change by those of moderate nationalism. Bourassa was definitely a federalist notwithstanding his rejection of the Victoria Charter, and so the immediate incentive for constitutional change diminished. Nevertheless, other issues impinging upon the Canadian federal system came to the fore. The increasing wealth of the West, especially Alberta, resulting from the rapid increase in world oil prices contributed to growing demands for greater decentralization of the federal system.

The major events leading to the 1978-1979 Constitutional Conference may be summarized as follows:

A. March 1976

Prime Minister Trudeau renewed his efforts to achieve agreement with the provinces on a constitutional document. His proposals, based on the Victoria

Charter but modified (except for the amending formula) in the hope of winning Quebec support, still assumed that Quebec nationalism was pivotal to any agreement.[11]

B. August and October 1976

At the conclusion of their August and October meetings when the premiers responded to Trudeau's proposals, it was clear that the Prime Minister had misread the provincial mood. While agreeing in principle with patriation the premiers said that a prior requirement was consensus "on an expansion of the role of the provinces and/or jurisdiction in the following areas: culture, communications, Supreme Court of Canada, spending power, Senate representation and regional disparities."[12]

Some consensus among the premiers was reached on most of the issues, but agreement upon the Victoria amending formula became more elusive. Although eight provinces still supported the formula, British Columbia wanted recognition as a fifth region of Canada with its own veto. Alberta demanded that an amending formula not permit the withdrawal of "rights, proprietary interests and jurisdiction [specifically, matters falling within sections 92, 93, and 109, of the Constitution Act] from any province without the concurrence of that province."[13] Premier Lougheed, elected two months after the 1971 Victoria Conference, was concerned that the Victoria formula could permit the transfer of natural resources from provincial to Federal jurisdiction without Alberta's consent. This demand was essentially a revival of the opting-out idea first expressed in 1936. Quebec did not want to discuss patriation or amending procedures until more substantive constitutional change relating to the distribution of powers had been considered.

The November victory of the Parti Québécois, albeit on a platform of good government rather than separatism, was at first viewed with concern by the other premiers. However, Premier Lévesque's subsequent participation with his colleagues actually strengthened provincial cooperation.[14]

C. January 1977

Trudeau's response to the premiers was that their demands were either too much or too little—too much in that they considerably widened the area of constitutional reform, or too little in that they were limited to issues of provincial concern.

D. June 1978

A broad range of Federal proposals, but not including an amending formula, was released in a White Paper entitled *A Time for Action: Toward the Renewal of the Canadian Federation*. Phase I of these proposals, with an implementation goal of July 1, 1979, was the subject of Bill C-60 (the Constitutional Amendment Bill) and contained matters that the Federal government believed could be achieved unilaterally under section 91(1) of the Constitution Act. These included a reformed Senate ("House of the Federation"), a reformed Supreme Court of Canada, and the entrenchment of a Charter of Rights and Freedoms limited to Federal jurisdiction but available to provinces wishing to opt in. The Supreme Court's subsequent ruling on the *Senate Reference* denied Parliament's jurisdiction over Senate reform. This Reference is noted in Chapter 5 under 1867 Constitution Act Amendment by the Federal Parliament.

Phase II of the proposals included matters that went beyond Parliament's jurisdiction and would be the subject of discussion with the provinces. Assuming agreement on patriation and an amending formula, Phase II matters would be implemented by the British Parliament. The target date for Phase II was July 1, 1981, the fiftieth anniversary of the Statute of Westminster.

Bill C-60 was intended to serve as the basis of discussion among the public, among governments, and of course within Parliament. As a result of opposition within Parliament and from the provinces, however, the Bill died on the order paper when the session ended in October 1978 and was not revived.

8. 1978-1979 CONSTITUTIONAL CONFERENCE

A. October 30-November 1, 1978

At this Conference called to deal with Phase II issues, the first ministers agreed that a fourteen-item agenda proposed by the Prime Minister should be studied over the succeeding three months by a Continuing Committee of Ministers on the Constitution (C.C.M.C.).[15] This agenda included patriation and an amending formula. The Committee was co-chaired by Saskatchewan Attorney General Roy Romanow (Saskatchewan being the host province for the 1978 Premiers' Conference) and the Federal Minister of Justice (initially Otto Lang, but Marc Lalonde by the end of November).

A general amending formula first suggested by Alberta in 1976 gained some support within the C.C.M.C. and ultimately formed the basis of the 1981 Accord. Amendments would require the approval of Parliament and the legislatures of two-thirds of the provinces containing at least 50 per cent of Canada's population. A 1936 proposal was resurrected permitting provinces to opt out of certain amendments; Alberta suggested those affecting provincial powers, property, or natural resources. There would be no unanimity rule except for changes to the amending formula itself.

B. February 1979

When the Constitutional Conference reconvened, patriation and an amending formula were the major stumbling blocks to agreement, although there was some measure of success on several of the other issues. Romanow comments that the "general direction of the negotiations was towards a devolution of federal government authority; it was the assumption upon which all governments [including the Federal government] formulated their positions." When the Conference failed, an exasperated Trudeau commented that "we've almost given up the shop to you people."[16]

By this time the Liberal Government elected in 1974 was nearing the end of its legal term of office. Electoral defeat which had increasingly seemed a possibility was confirmed in the May general election. However, following the interregnum of Prime Minister Clark and the convincing Liberal victory in February 1980 together with the rejection of Premier Lévesque's Sovereignty-Association referendum three months later, a confident Trudeau was ready to reverse his earlier acquiescence in decentralization. He was now prepared to take unilateral action if necessary to achieve patriation of the Constitution Act, the adoption of an amending formula, and the entrenchment of a Charter of Rights and Freedoms applicable to the entire country. But first, one more effort would be made at accommodation with the provinces.

9. 1980 CONSTITUTIONAL CONFERENCE

Following the Quebec referendum, and to fulfill his pledge to the people of Quebec for constitutional renewal, Trudeau took the initiative in another attempt at constitutional reform. He also stated, almost as a portent, that if the separatist Parti Québécois Government refused to cooperate he was prepared to reach agreement with the other nine provincial premiers.[17] At the June 1980 meeting of first ministers the C.C.M.C., again co-chaired by Romanow and the Federal Minister of Justice (now Jean Chrétien), was instructed once more to seek common ground among the eleven governments on a dozen constitutional issues including, of course, an amending formula. The Conference itself would resume in early September. During the summer the C.C.M.C. reconsidered Alberta's proposed amending formula including the opting-out provision. Predictably, the Federal government objected to the formula on the grounds that the right to opt out would produce a constitutional crazy quilt.

A leaked memorandum from the Clerk of the Privy Council (Michael Pitfield) to the Prime Minister reiterated the Federal government's determination to achieve patriation by Christmas of 1980, through unilateral action if necessary. The revelation of this memorandum intensified provincial efforts to reach agreement among themselves on a wide range of constitutional issues before the final meeting of the C.C.M.C. Romanow states that most provinces viewed Ottawa's threat of unilateral action as a bluff and that they considered unilateral action to be both legally and politically impossible.[18] The provinces agreed in principle on the Alberta amending formula, but on most of the other issues consensus was impossible. Of the Continuing Committee's summer meetings Co-chairman Romanow says: "In retrospect, the 1980 C.C.M.C. was successful in one regard: it identified the differences among the governments on all of the issues assigned to it. To this extent, it fulfilled its mandate. It failed, however, to bridge the wide gulfs between governments on contentious issues; in fact, the summer-long process only exaggerated the differences."[19]

Predictably, therefore, the September Conference failed. This failure had virtually been foretold by another leaked memorandum written for the Federal cabinet by Michael Kirby, cabinet secretary for Federal-provincial relations. This memorandum stressed that, if the Conference were to fail, the Federal government must be perceived as having shown flexibility. "The challenge now lies with the federal government . . . to show that disagreement leading to unilateral action is the result of . . . the intransigence of the provincial governments and not the fault of the federal government."[20] Responsibility for failure lay, no doubt, with both orders of government. Romanow acknowledges that the provinces' eleventh-hour attempt to achieve consensus among themselves during the Conference produced only "a wide-sweeping series of provincial proposals which amounted, even in the eyes of many of the provinces, to an unacceptable degree of devolution of federal authority"—indeed, "to a far greater devolution . . . than was ever contemplated in 1979."[21]

The Quebec referendum had demonstrated that people's and governments' wishes may not coincide. To what extent might such incongruity be generalized, and to what extent might it weaken the legitimacy of negotiation between governments? Whose position might it weaken the most? The Federal government's? The provinces'? Which provinces? Is constitution-making by referendum or general convention to be preferred? To what extent might Trudeau's faith in the popularity of his proposals have prompted him to gamble and act unilaterally? Inasmuch as the Trudeau Government had played an active role in the campaign that defeated Sovereignty-Association could his Government have reached beyond the other provincial governments as well and have successfully presented its case directly to the people of Canada?

This raises a fundamental question: Who speaks for Canada—the Federal government, the provincial governments, both orders of government, or indeed the people directly? The legitimacy of a Federal government within which an entire region of the country is virtually unrepresented on the benches of the ruling party, as was the West in the 1980 Trudeau Government, is certainly weakened in the eyes of the provincial governments within that region. This is especially true when the ruling party has a majority in the House. There is no doubt that Federal politicians have been unable adequately to accommodate Canada's regional diversities. On the other hand the legitimacy of provincial premiers speaking for the people is weakened when their position approaches a "confederal" concept of Canada.

10. EVENTS LEADING TO THE 1981 CONSTITUTIONAL CONFERENCE

A. The Resolution Goes to Parliament

On October 6, 1980, a month after the collapse of the Constitutional Conference, the Liberal Government tabled in the House of Commons a resolution containing patriation, an amending formula, and a Charter of Rights and Freedoms applicable to both orders of government. Prime Minister Trudeau intended to use the joint address route to Britain one more time. Unilateral action was becoming a reality. On October 24, following the use of closure in response to determined Conservative opposition, the Commons approved a motion to send the resolution to a special joint committee of the Senate and the House of Commons. The Senate debated a similar motion between October 22 and November 3.

Of the ten provincial premiers only Ontario's William Davis and New Brunswick's Richard Hatfield supported the resolution; the opposing premiers were dubbed the "gang of eight." While the resolution was before the joint committee the "gang" sought agreement among themselves on an alternative patriation package. This agreement, which included Quebec, was finally achieved and publicly announced on April 16, 1981. It included the Alberta amending formula (sometimes called the "Vancouver formula" because of the meeting place where it was proposed) as well as provision for provinces to opt out of amendments adversely affecting provincial powers.[22] There would be fiscal compensation from Ottawa for provinces opting out, the argument being that Parliament would be collecting taxes from the people of all provinces but not providing services uniformly throughout the country.

By supporting the patriation plan Lévesque abandoned his earlier position that more substantive constitutional change must accompany patriation. More significantly he relinquished Quebec's traditional insistence upon a veto over amendments. This latter concession would return to haunt him.

The essentials of Trudeau's proposed amending formula within the Patriation Resolution as it emerged from Parliament in April 1981 are as follows:[23]

(1) As a two-year interim procedure following patriation the unanimity rule would apply to amendments. The only exceptions were amendments which could be made by existing methods such as under sections 91(1), 92(1), and other sections of the Constitution Act providing for their own alteration. Furthermore, amendments to provisions applicable to one or more but not all of the provinces could be made during those two interim years if Parliament and the appropriate provinces agreed.

(2) At the end of the two years a slightly altered Victoria formula would become effective unless an alternative had been proposed by the legislatures of at least seven provinces comprising at least 80 per cent of the population of all provinces.

(3) In the event of such a proposal, either the Federal or the provincial formula would be selected by means of a referendum. (For the purpose of this referendum, Parliament could substitute a formula different from the one noted above.) A majority of the popular vote would determine the referendum's fate. Except for the guarantee of universal adult suffrage Parliament was empowered to determine the rules governing the referendum although those recommended by

a Referendum Rules Commission established for that purpose would have to be "take[n] into consideration."

(4) Regardless of the formula established by the procedure described above, constitutional amendments could be submitted directly to the people through referenda if the following three conditions were met:

   (a) Only the Federal cabinet could initiate the procedure.
   (b) A referendum could be used only to break a deadlock between Parliament and the provinces, and then only a deadlock caused by the failure of enough provinces within a year to support a proposed amendment which had already been approved by Parliament.
   (c) For a proposed amendment to be approved, the referendum had to be supported by an overall majority of the popular vote as well as by a majority of the vote within each of the provinces whose approval would otherwise be required by the general amending formula. Under the modified Victoria formula, for example, this would mean a majority within every province having at least 25 per cent of the country's population, within two of the four Atlantic provinces, and within two of the four Western provinces. (The Victoria Charter requirement that the approving Western provinces must contain 50% of the Western provinces' population had been dropped.) Other rules governing referenda were to be determined in the manner noted above for a referendum to choose an amending procedure.

B. The Provinces Go to Court

While the Patriation Resolution was still before the joint committee the eight dissenting premiers referred its constitutionality to three provincial appeal courts. The Manitoba court was chosen because Premier Lyon was the main opponent of an entrenched Charter and therefore the most anxious to test the Resolution. The Quebec court was chosen because Premier Lévesque was the main opponent of the Resolution generally, and also because a court challenge might create public reaction favourable to the Lévesque Government. The Newfoundland court was chosen because Premier Peckford believed Ottawa's unilateral action to be in violation of Newfoundland's 1949 Terms of Union with Canada.[24]

Because the proposed Resolution, especially the Charter, affected provincial (as well, of course, as Federal) powers the courts were asked if unilateral action was "unconstitutional." Romanow notes that lawyers for the original six opposing provinces (Nova Scotia and Saskatchewan joined later) agreed that "even if there were no legal rule requiring provincial participation for requests to the United Kingdom, there was, they felt, a clear convention to that effect; if the courts were asked to pass on the existence of a convention, the federal government would be hard pressed to argue that no such convention had ever formed."[25] In reality, then, the dissident provinces were counting on judicial confirmation of a convention, more than a legally binding decision, that provincial consent was necessary for certain amendments. It was desirable, therefore, to have the courts' opinions as soon as possible rather than to seek an injunction preventing Parliament from forwarding the Resolution to Britain. It would be even worse to delay a challenge until after the British Parliament had enacted legislation requested by Canada. In both of the latter instances the provinces would have to rely solely upon the legality of their position.

The questions asked of the three courts were basically these:

(1) Does the proposed Resolution affect the Federal-provincial relationship or provincial powers?

(2) Is there a constitutional convention that Parliament will not ask Britain to amend the Constitution in matters affecting Federal-provincial relations or provincial powers without first securing the agreement of the provinces?

(3) Is provincial agreement "constitutionally required" for the types of amendment referred to in question 1? By stating the third question ambiguously— that is, by not stipulating whether it pertained to constitutionality in the legal or conventional sense—the provinces could argue from the point of view of either law or convention.[26]

The courts' responses are shown in Table 6.1:[27]

Table 6.1

Question	Manitoba (February 3)		Newfoundland * (March 31)		Quebec ** (April 15)	
(1)	Yes	2	Yes	3	Yes	5
	Not answered (speculative and premature)	3	No	0	No	0
(2)	Yes	1	Yes	3	Yes	1
	No	3	No	0	No	4
	Not answered (inappropriate for judicial response)	1				
(3)	Yes	2	Yes	3	Yes	1
	No	3	No	0	No	4

* A fourth question related to Newfoundland's Terms of Union with Canada.

** The questions were worded differently, and the one corresponding to a combination of (2) and (3) was phrased to elicit "No" and "Yes" answers where the other courts answered "Yes" and "No." The answers shown above are consistent with the questions as presented to the other courts.

The Manitoba ruling came during the joint committee hearings. The unanimous Newfoundland ruling against the proposed Federal action came during Commons debate following the committee's report to Parliament and effectively stopped that debate. The Liberal Government agreed to refer the issue to the Supreme Court of Canada.

C. The Supreme Court of Canada

On September 28, 1981, the Supreme Court announced its decision on the appeals from the three provincial courts.[28] Questions (1) and (2) were the same as those submitted to the provincial courts. However, the Supreme Court divided question (3) into two parts because the phrase "constitutionally required" has both a conventional and a legal meaning. Question (3a) related constitutionality to convention; question (3b) related it to law. Convention as it applied to the *Patriation Reference* is discussed in Chapter 5 under "Convention." For easy reference the appropriate page numbers of the ruling are included in Table 6.2.

Table 6.2

Question	Number of Judges Answering Yes	No	Supreme Court Reports [1981] 1 S.C.R.
(1)	9 This view was not contested by the Federal government (p. 772)	0	Yes: pp. 762-773, 813
(2)	6	3	Yes: pp. 874-910 No: pp. 849-874
(3a)	6 — "no views being expressed as to its quantification" (p. 909)	3	Yes: p. 909 No: implied by "No" response to q. 2
(3b)	2 — "without deciding at this time, whether the agreement . . . must be unanimous" (p. 848)	7 *	Yes: pp. 809-848 No: pp. 773-809

* These seven included four of the six judges who had formed the majority opinion in question (3a), the remaining three having dissented from the majority opinion of (3a).

The six judges who answered questions (2) and (3a) in the affirmative commented that constitutional conventions cannot be enforced by the courts because they are neither "judge-made rules" nor "statutory commands."

> Perhaps the main reason why conventional rules cannot be enforced by the courts is that they are generally in conflict with the legal rules which they postulate and the courts are bound to enforce the legal rules. The conflict is not of a type which would entail the commission of any illegality. It results from the fact that legal rules create wide powers, discretions and rights which conventions prescribe should be exercised only in a certain limited manner, if at all.[29]

Furthermore, they added:

> This conflict between convention and law which prevents the courts from enforcing conventions also prevents conventions from crystallizing into laws, unless it be by statutory adoption.
>
> It is because the sanctions of convention rest with institutions of government other than courts, such as the Governor General or the Lieutenant Governor, or the Houses of Parliament, or with public opinion and ultimately, with the electorate, that it is generally said that they are political....
>
> It should be borne in mind however that, while they are not laws, some conventions may be more important than some laws.[30]

In the opinion of Canada's highest court, then, the Federal government's proposed Resolution was perfectly legal but at the same time unconstitutional in the conventional sense. The net effect of this ambiguous ruling was to enable each side in the dispute to claim "half a loaf" of victory.[31] It also forced each side to recognize the validity of the other's claim. Russell calls the Court's brinkmanship "bold statescraft, questionable jurisprudence."[32] Had agreement once again eluded the first ministers, and had the Federal government proceeded to Britain unilaterally as it was now legally capable of doing,

> the country would have experienced the worst possible consequences of the court's decision. Patriation with an amending formula and a Charter of Rights would have been achieved, but in a manner which our highest court considered to be unconstitutional. One could scarcely think of a worse way for Canada finally to take charge of her own constitutional affairs and inaugurate a new regime of entrenched rights and freedoms.[33]

That assertion assumes the British Parliament would have acceded to the request of the Federal government. This we shall never know, although Marshall's opinion is that "no majority could have been found in either House of the British Parliament to enact a measure declared by the Supreme Court of Canada to be a violation of the constitutional practice of Canada."[34]

11. 1981 CONSTITUTIONAL CONFERENCE: SUCCESS?

A final conference which opened on November 2 "was convened in a mixed mood of grudging necessity, persistent mistrust, and modest hope."[35] It continued for four days with public, but mainly private, meetings. Once again the amending formula was a major stumbling block—the most contentious aspects being the questions of referendum, opting out, and fiscal compensation. In addition, some aspects of the Charter of Rights and Freedoms, though not the concept itself (except for Manitoba), were controversial.

On November 5, a package reflecting the intense bargaining of the preceding days was accepted by all first ministers except Lévesque. The major concessions made by Trudeau in obtaining the agreement of the nine premiers were:

(1) His abandonment of the referendum option for making constitutional amendments.

(2) His acceptance of the provinces' April patriation package including the "Vancouver" amending formula but without fiscal compensation to provinces which opt out of amendments.

(3) His acceptance of the "notwithstanding" provision, especially its application to the Charter's "fundamental freedoms." Trudeau was adamant, however, in his demand that minority language educational rights (s. 23) be excluded from the legislative override.

Four changes to the Accord were approved by the signatories during the month after November 5. Two of these were an unsuccessful bid to secure Lévesque's support: (1) Ottawa would pay fiscal compensation to provinces opting out of amendments that transfer provincial legislative authority to Parliament in the areas of education and other cultural matters (s. 40), the most critical areas from Quebec's viewpoint, and (2) the "mother-tongue clause" within minority language educational rights would not apply to Quebec until that province agreed (ss. 23[1][a], 59). But the "Canada clause" was not negotiable (s. 23[1][b]). Because these significant moves did not win Lévesque's support one may wonder whether any reasonable compromise would have satisfied the separatist premier. The other two changes (1) excluded sexual equality (s. 28) from the section 33 override, and (2) added aboriginal rights (s. 35[1][2]).

The British Parliament passed the Resolution in the form of the Canada Act, and the Queen gave royal assent on March 29, 1982, exactly 115 years after Queen Victoria assented to the 1867 Constitution Act. The Constitution Act (Schedule B to the Canada Act) was proclaimed by the Queen in Ottawa on April 17, 1982. There remains the paradox that the Canada Act is part of our law only because it was enacted by a foreign legislature.

Although it is an open question whether the Supreme Court should have commented at all upon the Resolution's constitutionality in the conventional sense, it is even more surprising that the Court was willing to consider a totally non-legal question subsequently raised by Quebec. In June 1982 that province asked whether "the consent of the Province of Quebec [is] constitutionally required, by convention," for an amendment affecting the legislative authority of that province. The Court had already established that provincial unanimity was not required, but did Quebec possess a conventional veto, based on a principle of "Canadian duality," in relation to amendments affecting that province's powers? The Court answered in the negative; Quebec had "failed completely to demonstrate compliance with the most important requirement for establishing a convention, that is, acceptance or recognition by the actors in the precedents."[36]

Although the new amending formula is considered in detail in Chapter 8, its essence should be noted here. The term "Constitution of Canada" applies to all of the sections (except 45) below. For discussion of its meaning see the commentary on section 52(2).

(1) Unanimity (s. 41): amendments to the Constitution of Canada in relation to five specific matters—the Crown, "Senate floor," use of the French or English language (subject to s. 43), composition of the Supreme Court, and the amending procedures themselves. Either Parliament or a provincial legislature may initiate an amendment. The Senate has only a 180-day suspensive veto.

(2) Parliament acting alone (s. 44): amendments to the Constitution of Canada "in relation to the executive government of Canada or the Senate and House of Commons." This section is qualified to the extent that the unanimity rule (s. 41) applies or the "general" amending formula (s. 42) is required. The Senate veto is absolute.

(3) A provincial legislature acting alone (s. 45): amendments to the "constitution of the province" (which is not defined), except in matters to which the unanimity rule applies (s. 41).

(4) Parliament and the legislatures of affected provinces (s. 43): amendments to any provision of the Constitution of Canada which applies to one or more but not all of the provinces. Specific mention is made of alterations to boundaries between provinces, and amendments to any provision relating to the use of the English or French language within a province. Either Parliament or a provincial legislature may initiate an amendment. The Senate has only a suspensive veto.

(5) The "general" amending formula (ss. 38, 39, 40, 42): amendments to the Constitution of Canada, which may be initiated by Parliament or a provincial legislature, requiring the concurrence of Parliament and the legislatures of at least two-thirds of the provinces (having at least 50 per cent of the population of all provinces). The Senate has only a 180-day suspensive veto. A province may opt out of an amendment adversely affecting its powers, and if such amendment is in the area of education or other cultural matters the province will receive fiscal compensation from Ottawa (s. 40). Section 42 lists six matters requiring the general formula for amendment.

Table 6.3 summarizes some of the more significant features of the several amending formulae proposed during the past half-century search:

Table 6.3

Year of Proposal	General Formula	Unanimity for Some Amendment	Amendment Permitted By: Ottawa Alone	Amendment Permitted By: Individual Provinces	Amendment Permitted By: Ottawa & Affected Prov's	Fate	Other Features
1935-36	Ottawa & 2/3 of prov's (with 55% of pop.)	yes	yes	yes	yes	New Brunswick veto	opting-out proposed
1950	Failure to agree on allocation of the "Constitution's" sections among the above amending procedures.						
1960-61 "Fulton"	Ottawa & 2/3 of prov's (with 50% of pop.)	yes	not considered		yes	Sask. veto	some delegation allowed
1964 "Fulton/ Favreau"	no change from 1960-61	yes	yes	yes	yes	Quebec veto	no change from 1960-61
1971 "Victoria"	Ottawa & maj. of prov's, incl. all with 25% of pop. & 2/4 Maritime, & 2/4 West having 50% of West pop.	no	yes	yes	yes	Quebec veto	–
1981-82 Success	Ottawa & 2/3 of prov's (with 50% of pop.)	yes	yes	yes	yes	Quebec opp. futile	provincial opting-out allowed

12. WHAT ABOUT QUEBEC?

What changes might be necessary for Quebec to support the 1982 constitutional arrangement? In May 1985 the Lévesque government made several proposals,[37] but these became academic with the defeat of the Parti Québécois and return of the Liberals under Robert Bourassa that December. The following May, Gil Rémillard, Quebec's Minister of Intergovernmental Relations, identified Quebec's five conditions for signing the Accord. These conditions were repeated by Premier Bourassa at the annual Premiers' Conference in Edmonton that August:

(1) A new formula for amending the constitution so that Quebec would have a veto.
(2) Recognition of Quebec as a distinct society.
(3) A greater provincial role in immigration.
(4) A provincial role in the selection of Supreme Court judges.
(5) A limitation on the Federal spending power.

Bourassa was reported to have suggested that the general amending formula be altered to raise from 50 to 75 per cent the portion of Canada's population that must be included in the provinces (minimum of seven) agreeing to an amendment. This change would give the veto to both Quebec and Ontario. "My proposals," Bourassa is reported to have said, "have a Canadian logic in so far as they don't pit any one of Canada's regions against any other. My amendment formula will protect Canada's regions."[38] What he did not say is that two of Canada's regions are single provinces, that the four Western provinces would have to act in concert to exercise a veto, and that the four Eastern provinces gained no protection whatever under the proposal. Not surprisingly, premiers Peckford of Newfoundland and Buchanan of Nova Scotia expressed reservations about the Bourassa formula. Nevertheless, all premiers agreed that their first constitutional priority would be to seek an agreement based on Bourassa's conditions.

On April 30, 1987, Prime Minister Mulroney and the ten provincial premiers reached general agreement on these five issues (although it did not include a change to the general amending formula). This "Meech Lake Accord" was put into legal form as proposed amendments to the 1867 and 1982 Constitution Acts. To become effective the proposal would, pursuant to the 1982 Constitution Act's amending formula, have to be approved by Parliament and all ten provincial legislatures within three years of the date of the first approval (which turned out to be Quebec's on June 23, 1987). The commentary of section 39 of the Act, however, questions this interpretation. During the three intervening years eight provincial legislatures, and Parliament over the Senate's suspensive veto, approved the Accord. These eight included the Newfoundland legislature under Premier Peckford but which rescinded the resolution when Clyde Wells became premier. Manitoba and New Brunswick also changed governments and their new premiers raised serious objections to the Accord. Mulroney called a First Ministers conference at the eleventh hour in June 1990, and following a week of almost continuous bargaining there appeared a reasonable chance that the necessary legislative unanimity would be obtained. But when June 24 arrived the Manitoba and Newfoundland assemblies had not passed the resolution, and the Accord became history.

Since the death of Meech Lake, interpreted by many Quebec francophones as a rejection of Quebec by "English Canada" (presumably the rest of the country), there has been within Quebec a resurgence of interest in some form of sovereignty option. This means that discussion has shifted far beyond the prerequisites for Quebec's acceptance of the 1981 Constitutional Accord. On the one hand is the question of what may become Quebec's terms for remaining within Canada—the 1960s "What does Quebec want?" revisited, but with much higher stakes. On the other hand is the extent to which the rest of the country may be prepared to accept those terms. But the issue is no longer just the "Quebec question," for Ottawa and some of the other provinces are now looking to the broader question of a restructured federal system. The Conclusion/Epilogue briefly considers some of the post-Meech developments.

Clause-by-Clause Analysis of the 1867 Constitution Act, 1982 Canada Act, and Its Schedule "B," the 1982 Constitution Act

PART 3

CHAPTER 7

Clause-by Clause Analysis of the 1867 Constitution Act

Part IX: Miscellaneous Provisions, ss. 127-144
General, ss. 127-133
Ontario and Quebec, ss. 134-144
Part X: Intercolonial Railway, s. 145
Part XI: Admission of Other Colonies, ss. 146-147

A number of questions arise as to the handling of certain sections of the 1867 Constitution Act. In the first place some sections (or parts thereof) of the original Act have been repealed; they are underlined to indicate this status. Other sections are no longer relevant generally because of a built-in time limit; brief comments accompany those sections which are of particular historical interest. Second, some sections have been amended by the British or Canadian parliament. The procedure adopted in this chapter is to comment upon the sections as amended, and then to reproduce the sections in their original forms and make appropriate comments. Earlier amendments are also included, with commentary where this seems advisable. Third, some amendments have not been incorporated into subsequent consolidations. This was noted in Chapter 5. The existence of most of these amendments is acknowledged in the commentary on the appropriate sections of the 1867 Act.

In the fourth place, and as noted in Chapter 5, some sections authorize their own amendment generally by the Parliament of Canada or by provincial legislatures. Such changes take the form of Federal or provincial statutes and do not, therefore, alter the actual text of the Constitution Act. They nevertheless make sections of the Act inoperative or "spent." Changes known to the writer are noted in the commentaries on the relevant sections. Finally, the operation of some sections is modified sometimes to the point of negation by constitutional convention. The more significant instances are noted in the appropriate commentaries. Convention as a component of our constitution is discussed in Chapter 5.

Preamble

An Act for the Union of Canada, Nova Scotia, and New Brunswick, and the Government thereof; and for Purposes connected therewith.

Whereas the Provinces of Canada, Nova Scotia and New Brunswick have expressed their Desire to be federally united into One Dominion under the Crown of the United Kingdom of Great Britain and Ireland, with a Constitution similar in Principle to that of the United Kingdom:

And whereas such a Union would conduce to the Welfare of the Provinces and promote the Interests of the British Empire:

And whereas on the Establishment of the Union by Authority of Parliament it is expedient, not only that the Constitution of the

Legislative Authority in the Dominion be provided for, but also that the Nature of the Executive Government therein be declared:

And whereas it is expedient that Provision be made for the eventual Admission into the Union of other Parts of British North America:

Be it therefore enacted and declared by the Queen's Most Excellent Majesty, by and with the Advice and Consent of the Lords Spiritual and Temporal, and Commons, in this present Parliament assembled, and by the Authority of the same, as follows:

The most significant part of the preamble is the statement that Canada is to be "federally united . . . with a Constitution similar in principle to that of the United Kingdom." The Supreme Court of Canada has noted that a preamble "has no enacting force" but that it can, nevertheless, "be called in aid to illuminate provisions of the statute in which it appears." The "similar in principle" statement, the Court continues, "may well embrace responsible government and some common law aspects of the United Kingdom's unitary constitutionalism, such as the rule of law and Crown prerogatives and immunities."[1]

For a note on an "implied bill of rights" see Chapter 5 under "Judicial Decisions: C. The Courts and Basic Rights and Freedoms."

The enacting clause, underlined above, was repealed by Britain's Statute Law Revision Act 1893.

I. Preliminary

➤ **SECTION 1:** This Act may be cited as the Constitution Act, 1867.

Until amended in accordance with the Schedule to the 1982 Constitution Act this section read as follows:

1. This Act may be cited as the British North America Act, 1867.

➤ **SECTION 2:** The provisions of this Act referring to Her Majesty the Queen extend also to the Heirs and Successors of Her Majesty, Kings and Queens of the United Kingdom of Great Britain and Ireland.

This section was repealed by Britain's Statute Law Revision Act 1893.

II. Union

➤ **SECTION 3:** It shall be lawful for the Queen, by and with the Advice of Her Majesty's Most Honourable Privy Council, to declare by Proclamation that, on and after a Day therein appointed, not being more than Six Months after the passing of this Act, the Provinces of Canada, Nova Scotia, and New Brunswick shall form and be One Dominion under the Name of Canada; and on and after that Day those Three Provinces shall form and be One Dominion under that Name accordingly.

The British Parliament passed the Constitution Act on March 29, 1867. On May 22 Queen Victoria issued a proclamation declaring that the new Dominion would come into existence on July 1, 1867.

➤ **SECTION 4:** The subsequent Provisions of this Act, shall, unless it is otherwise expressed or implied, commence and have effect on and after the Union, that is to say, on and after the Day appointed for the Union taking effect in the Queen's Proclamation; and in the same Provisions, unless it is otherwise expressed or implied, the Name Canada shall be taken to mean Canada as constituted under this Act.

This statement was necessary to avoid confusion with the Province of Canada which had existed before Confederation. The underlined portion was repealed by Britain's Statute Law Revision Act 1893. Some fifteen to twenty sections, most of them within Part VIII, use the term "Canada" to mean the Government of Canada rather than Canada "as constituted under this Act." This meaning is not always "expressed or implied."

➤ **SECTION 5:** Canada shall be divided into Four Provinces, named Ontario, Quebec, Nova Scotia, and New Bruswick.

This section illustrates how some *de facto* amendments are not included in the text of the Act. Canada is now composed of ten provinces and two territories. See Chapter 3 for the instruments used in the expansion. Although section 5 continues to acknowledge the existence of but four provinces, sections 21, 22 and 51(1), dealing with representation in the Senate and the House of Commons, have been altered as the number of provinces and territories has increased.

➤ **SECTION 6:** The Parts of the Province of Canada (as it exists at the passing of this Act) which formerly constituted respectively the Provinces of Upper Canada and Lower Canada shall be deemed to be severed, and shall form Two separate Provinces. The Part which formerly constituted the Province of Upper Canada shall constitute the Province of Ontario; and the Part which formerly constituted the Province of Lower Canada shall constitute the Province of Quebec.

Establishment of provincial boundaries within the new Dominion was necessary. Ontario and Quebec, which had constituted the pre-Confederation Province of Canada, assumed the boundaries of the former colonies of Upper Canada and Lower Canada. Upper and Lower Canada had been established by the 1791 Constitutional Act and continued until their union by the 1840 Union Act.

➤ **SECTION 7:** The Provinces of Nova Scotia and New Brunswick shall have the same Limits as at the passing of this Act.

From at least 1763 until 1784 New Brunswick had been part of Nova Scotia. The territorial development of these two colonies was briefly traced in Chapter 2. Section 7 defines the boundaries of these provinces as those existing immediately before Confederation. New Brunswick therefore remained separate from Nova Scotia. Cape Breton Island, which had been part of Nova Scotia from 1763 until 1784 and again from 1820, remained part of Nova Scotia following Confederation.

➤ **SECTION 8:** In the general Census of the Population of Canada which is hereby required to be taken in the Year One thousand eight hundred and seventy-one, and in every Tenth Year thereafter, the respective Populations of the Four Provinces shall be distinguished.

The decennial census required by this section forms the basis of the redistribution of House of Commons seats in accordance with section 51.

III. Executive Power

➤ **SECTION 9:** The Executive Government and Authority of and over Canada is hereby declared to continue and be vested in the Queen.

Although the preamble's "similar in principle" statement may be assumed to include constitutional monarchy, many sections of the Act appear to provide for something closer to absolute monarchy. See especially sections 9-15, 24, 34, 38, 50, 54-59, 90, and 96. Chapter 4 discusses monarchy as a constitutional principle. Section 9 means that the Queen is Canada's chief of state and that executive power is exercised in her name even if not by the monarch personally.

➤ **SECTION 10:** The Provisions of this Act referring to the Governor General extend and apply to the Governor General for the Time being of Canada, or other the Chief Executive Officer or Administrator for the Time being carrying on the Government of Canada on behalf and in the Name of the Queen, by whatever Title he is designated.

The expectation that the governor general, his or her deputies or the administrator, will be "carrying on the Government of Canada" means that the same deference to ministerial advice applies as it would to the monarch. It has been noted that the 1867 Constitution Act assumes the existence rather than creates the office of governor general. Section 10 also contemplates the exercise of executive authority by some other official "for the time being" under circumstances not defined by the Act. The 1947 Letters Patent provide (para. VIII) that "in the event of the death, incapacity, removal, or absence of Our Governor General out of Canada" for more than one month, or resignation (added by Letters Patent in 1952),[2] all authority of the governor general is transferred to the "administrator." This official is the Chief Justice of the Supreme Court of Canada or, if that person cannot serve, that Court's senior judge. Twice in recent years these powers have devolved upon the administrator: when Georges Vanier died in 1967, and when Jules Léger suffered a stroke in 1974.

Until 1880 the monarch appointed the governor general upon the advice of the British colonial office and prime minister. From 1880 until 1926 there was consultation with the Government of Canada, and since 1926 (consistent with that year's Balfour Declaration) appointments have been made upon the advice of the Canadian prime minister. Although the governor general may be removed by the Queen at the request of her Canadian advisers the term of office is "officially recognized as six years, customarily treated as five years, while on occasion it has been seven years."[3] Since 1952 governors general have been Canadians, and until the appointment of Ray Hnatyshyn they alternated between anglophones and francophones.

Table 7.1 lists our governors general since Confederation with their years in office:[4]

Table 7.1

Viscount Monck (from 1861)	1867-1868	Viscount Willingdon	1926-1931
Sir John Young (Baron Lisgar)	1869-1872	Earl of Bessborough	1931-1935
Earl of Dufferin	1872-1878	1878 Lord Tweedsmuir	1935-1940
Marquess of Lorne	1878-1883	Earl of Athlone	1940-1946
Marquess of Landsdowne	1883-1888	Vis. Alexander of Tunis	1946-1952
Baron Stanley of Preston	1888-1893	Vincent Massey	1952-1959
Earl of Aberdeen	1893-1898	Georges Vanier	1959-1967
Earl of Minto	1898-1904	Roland Michener	1967-1974
Earl Grey	1904-1911	Jules Léger	1974-1979
Duke of Connaught	1911-1916	Edward Schreyer	1979-1984
Duke of Devonshire	1916-1921	Jeanne Sauvé	1984-1990
Lord Byng	1921-1926	Ray Hnatyshyn	1990-

➤ **SECTION 11:** There shall be a Council to aid and advise in the Government of Canada, to be styled the Queen's Privy Council for Canada; and the Persons who are to be Members of that Council shall be from Time to Time chosen and summoned by the Governor General and sworn in as Privy Councillors, and Members thereof may be from Time to Time removed by the Governor General.

The privy council is the body which formally advises the governor general. Except for the prime minister whose selection is the prerogative of the governor general, aided of course by the results of a general election, privy council membership is recommended by the prime minister. Membership carries the title "Honourable" or, for the prime minister, Chief Justice of the Supreme Court, former governors general as well as the governor general at the time, "Right Honourable."

The composition of this body is not conducive to the advisory function. Because appointments are lifetime the privy council contains not only the current set of advisers (which becomes the active part of the council and is called the ministry), but also all living advisers (i.e., ministers) from former governments. In an unusual move, Prime Minister Mulroney had N.D.P. leader Audrey McLaughlin sworn in as a privy councillor in January 1991. This was to enable her to participate in confidential discussions about a Canadian role in the Persian Gulf crisis between the United Nations and Iraq. Liberal opposition leader Jean Chrétien was already a member of the privy council.

Some privy council appointments are strictly honourific and occasionally have included British prime ministers, members of the Royal family, provincial premiers, and others. In 1967, for example, Prime Minister Pearson appointed the ten Canadian premiers in honour of the centennial of Confederation. In 1982 Prime Minister Trudeau did the same thing in honour of the proclamation of that year's Constitution Act. Premier Lévesque, who had opposed the patriation package which formed the basis of the Act, declined the appointment. As of April 1991 there were 221 privy councillors, many more than the typical 100-125.[5]

Obviously, then, the full privy council (or at least the privy council with some non-ministers present) seldom meets except for ceremonial occasions. In recent years it has met to receive the monarch's formal approval of the engagement of the heir to the throne—the 1947 engagement of Princess Elizabeth, and the 1981 engagement of Charles, Prince of Wales. It met in 1952 to hear the proclamation of Elizabeth's succession to the throne when King George VI died. The council has also met with the monarch presiding when the Queen has been in Canada. This occurred at Charlottetown in 1964 as part of the celebrations marking the centennial of the pre-Confederation conferences, and at Ottawa in 1982 when the Queen proclaimed the Constitution Act.

The real executive authority rests with the cabinet, a body having no legal existence but consisting of those members of the ministry (and therefore of the privy council) whom the prime minister selects to meet with him. According to Canadian practice the ministry and cabinet are usually identical in personnel, whereas the British cabinet is generally somewhat smaller than the ministry. The essential distinction between these two bodies lies in their functions rather than their composition. It is the ministry which, acting for the entire privy council, gives formal advice to the governor general and prepares instruments (most commonly, orders-in-council) for signature. Although the term "governor-in-council" is used to indicate when official action is being taken, the governor general in fact no longer meets with the council (ministry) except on formal occasions such as those noted above. The cabinet is more clearly a partisan political body. Its task is, for example, to discuss alternative government policies and to determine how best to secure parliamentary approval of policy with a minimum of political risk. Understandably, the functions of the cabinet and ministry merge imperceptibly.

➤ **SECTION 12:** All Powers, Authorities, and Functions which under any Act of the Parliament of Great Britain, or of the Parliament of the United Kingdom of Great Britain and Ireland, or of the Legislature of Upper Canada, Lower Canada, Canada, Nova Scotia, or New Brunswick, are at the Union vested in or exerciseable by the respective Governors or

Lieutenant Governors of those Provinces, with the Advice, or with the Advice and Consent, of the respective Executive Councils thereof, or in conjunction with those Councils, or with any Number of Members thereof, or by those Governors or Lieutenant Governors individually, shall, as far as the same continue in existence and capable of being exercised after the Union in relation to the Government of Canada, be vested in and exerciseable by the Governor General, with the Advice and Consent of or in conjunction with the Queen's Privy Council for Canada, or any Member thereof, or by the Governor General individually, as the Case requires, subject nevertheless (except with respect to such as exist under Acts of the Parliament of Great Britain or of the Parliament of the United Kingdom of Great Britain and Ireland) to be abolished or altered by the Parliament of Canada.

This section provides for the transfer of executive responsibilities which had belonged to the governors or lieutenant governors of the pre-Confederation colonies. Following Confederation these responsibilities were to be exercised by the governor general to the extent that they pertained to the Government of Canada. The section also provides that Parliament may alter these functions subject to the restriction in parentheses. The prohibition against amending or repealing British laws was removed by the Statute of Westminster except for the Constitution Act itself. That final restriction was eliminated by the 1982 Canada Act.

See section 65 for the analogous provisions applicable to the lieutenant governors of the newly created provinces of Ontario and Quebec.

➤ **Section 13:** The Provisions of this Act referring to the Governor General in Council shall be construed as referring to the Governor General acting by and with the Advice of the Queen's Privy Council for Canada.

The sections that refer to the "Governor General in Council" are 93, 103, 120, 131, and 143. The significance of this section is difficult to determine since the section does not address the question of "advice" in relation to provisions of the Act referring to the governor general acting alone (as distinct from action by the governor general in council). The Act appears to contemplate the governor general acting alone under sections 11, 14, 50, 54, 55, 57, and 96. Furthermore, only the governor general is mentioned in sections 24, 26, 32, 34, 38, and 58, even though action requires use of the Great Seal. Because the Great Seal is in the custody of a minister the political responsibility for its use must be accepted by that minister. In addition, because a proclamation usually involves an order-in-council other ministers as well must consent to the governor general's action.

Are the powers assigned to the governor general to act alone really intended to be exercised without the council as this section would seem to imply? Here convention is of assistance. Dawson and Ward point out (with particular reference to Canada's first half century) that in many cases

> no difficulties occurred, for the governor tended to follow advice, but there were some powers which were questionable. The power of the governor to disallow provincial legislation, to dismiss a lieutenant governor, to make statements on public questions, to exercise the prerogative of mercy, to dismiss ministers, to refuse prorogation or dissolution, to reject appointments suggested by his cabinet—all these were at some time under discussion or were raised by concrete issues, and in the majority of cases the decision was in favour of the governor accepting the advice of his cabinet. The emphasis of the argument was not placed so much on the exact working [wording?] of the British North America Act or of the prerogative instruments involved, but on the broad intent and on precedents in Canada, Great Britain, and the other dominions.[6]

McConnell suggests that this section "says either too much or too little, is not supported by practice if it means what it appears to mean [that council participation is unnecessary except where explicitly required], and would seem to be redundant."[7]

➤ **SECTION 14:** It shall be lawful for the Queen, if Her Majesty thinks fit, to authorize the Governor General from Time to Time to appoint any Person or any Persons jointly or severally to be his Deputy or Deputies within any Part or Parts of Canada, and in that Capacity to exercise during the Pleasure of the Governor General such of the Powers, Authorities, and Functions of the Governor General as the Governor General deems it necessary or expedient to assign to him or them, subject to any Limitations or Directions expressed or given by the Queen; but the Appointment of such a Deputy or Deputies shall not affect the Exercise by the Governor General himself of any Power, Authority or Function.

The authorization anticipated by this section was given by Queen Victoria in the Letters Patent appointing Viscount Monck in 1867. First among the governor general's deputies is the Chief Justice of the Supreme Court of Canada, the role of deputy not to be confused with the Chief Justice's role as the administrator. The other justices of the Supreme Court may also be appointed as deputies. Deputies may be assigned any of the duties of the governor general except the dissolving of Parliament or, in all likelihood, the appointing of a prime minister.[8] It is usual for a deputy to give royal assent to bills, to prorogue Parliament, and to extend to members of the House of Commons the ceremonial summons to the Senate before the election of the Commons speaker at the opening of a new Parliament.

➤ **SECTION 15:** The Command-in-Chief of the Land and Naval Militia, and of all Naval and Military Forces, of and in Canada, is hereby declared to continue and be vested in the Queen.

By the time of Confederation the British North American colonies had basically become self-governing in their internal, although not their external, affairs. It is not surprising, therefore, that Canadian military forces remained under British control. As in the case of the British military the Queen was commander-in-chief. Canadian forces outside of Canada were part of the British forces until 1931, although by 1917 they were under the command of Canadian officers. With the achievement of control over our own external affairs the designation of the Queen as commander-in-chief merely recognized one role of Canada's chief of state acting as Queen of Canada and upon the advice of her Canadian ministers. Since 1931, letters patent have referred to the "Office of Governor General and Commander-in-Chief."

➤ **SECTION 16:** Until the Queen otherwise directs, the Seat of Government of Canada shall be Ottawa.

The seat of government of pre-Confederation Canada had been variously located at Kingston, Montreal, Toronto, and Quebec (alternating between the last two locations following the Montreal riots at the time of the 1849 Rebellion Losses Bill). In 1857 Queen Victoria was asked to settle what had become a controversial issue and to choose the capital. She selected the small town of Ottawa, formerly called Bytown.

IV. Legislative Power

➤ **SECTION 17:** There shall be One Parliament for Canada, consisting of the Queen, an Upper House styled the Senate, and the House of Commons.

It is commonplace to equate "Parliament" with the House of Commons or with the Commons and Senate together, but it is not generally understood that Parliament includes the monarch. The passage of legislation requires the agreement of all three components. Although the governor general retains the statutory authority to withhold royal assent or to reserve a bill for the Queen's pleasure (ss. 55, 57), these powers long ago fell into disuse as did the power of the Queen-in-council (i.e., the British government) to disallow Canadian statutes (s. 56). See the commentaries on sections 55, 56, and 57.

The legal power of the Senate is virtually equal to that of the House of Commons. The only restrictions are that money bills must originate in the Commons and, since 1982, that the Senate may under specified conditions (see section 47 of the 1982 Constitution Act) be bypassed in the making of certain constitutional amendments. The first of these restrictions is inconsequential given the Senate's unlimited amending authority—notwithstanding the House of Commons denial of this power in relation to money bills. This controversy between the Senate and House is considered in the commentary on section 53 of the 1867 Constitution Act. It is too soon to assess the significance of the second restriction; the Senate has been bypassed only once and that was in relation to the Meech Lake Accord.

The Senate's actual authority is considerably less than that of the elected Commons, the Senate rarely standing in the way of a determined lower house.

➤ **Section 18:** The privileges, immunities, and powers to be held, enjoyed, and exercised by the Senate and by the House of Commons, and by the Members thereof respectively, shall be such as are from time to time defined by Act of the Parliament of Canada, but so that any Act of the Parliament of Canada defining such privileges, immunities, and powers shall not confer any privileges, immunities, or powers exceeding those at the passing of such Act held, enjoyed, and exercised by the Commons House of Parliament of the United Kingdom of Great Britain and Ireland, and by the Members thereof.

The original section 18 (quoted below) had restricted the "privileges, immunities, and powers" possessed by the Canadian Parliament and its members to those held by the British Parliament and its members "at the passing of this Act." That is, they were frozen at the 1867 British level. The amended section only prevents Canadian privileges, immunities, and powers from exceeding those in Britain at the time those in Canada may be expanded. This latter restriction disappeared with the 1949 Constitution Act amendment which added the new section 91(1) enabling the Canadian Parliament to alter, with certain exceptions, "the Constitution of Canada."

An 1873 Act of the Canadian Parliament, duly assented to by the governor general, had provided for the examination of witnesses under oath by parliamentary committees. This Act was subsequently disallowed by Britain (the only Canadian Act ever to suffer this fate) on the grounds that British committees did not possess this privilege in 1867 (although the privilege had been granted by 1871). The amended version of this section was enacted in 1875 at Canada's request.

Parliamentary privilege has been defined as

> the sum of the peculiar rights enjoyed by each House collectively as a constituent part of the High Court of Parliament, and by members of each House individually, without which they could not discharge their functions, and which exceed those possessed by other bodies or individuals. Thus privilege, though part of the law of the land, is to a certain extent an exemption from the ordinary law.[9]

Those who enjoy this privilege are thus, to that extent, exempt from the ordinary law of the land. When the Speaker of the House of Commons claims of the governor general all of Parliament's "undoubted rights and privileges," what really is being claimed? Privileges of individual members are those which prevent interference with parliamentary responsibilities and include freedom (during the session) from arrest or imprisonment arising from civil (but not criminal) action, freedom (also during the session) from jury duty or subpoena as a witness, and freedom to speak without the fear of prosecution arising from speeches in or publications of Parliament. The collective privileges of Parliament include the right to establish internal rules of order and discipline and to take action for breaches of privilege emanating from outside

Parliament. A member who breaches the privileges of Parliament may be called to order, "named" (in which instance the member is suspended), or even expelled. Breaches of privilege from outside Parliament may be punished by reprimand, fine, or imprisonment. Rarely has the matter of privilege been an issue in Parliament beyond the occasional "naming" of a member and his or her consequent suspension for perhaps the rest of the day.

The 1875 amendment to section 18 illustrates two points made in Chapter 5. Although all parties went on record during the debate of the 1871 proposed amendment that a joint address of the Senate and House of Commons was the proper mechanism for requesting Constitution Act amendments from Britain, the 1875 request proceeded from the ministry. Prime Minister Mackenzie defended the procedure although he acknowledged that "it might have been better . . . to have proceeded by address."[10] The second point which the amendment illustrates is that not all direct amendments to the B.N.A. Act carried the "British North America Act" title; in this case the amendment was called the "Parliament of Canada Act."

As originally enacted section 18 read as follows:

> 18. The Privileges, Immunities, and Powers to be held, enjoyed, and exercised by the Senate and by the House of Commons and by the Members thereof respectively shall be such as are from Time to Time defined by Act of the Parliament of Canada, but so that the same shall never exceed those at the passing of this Act held, enjoyed, and exercised by the Commons House of Parliament of the United Kingdom of Great Britain and Ireland and by the Members thereof.

➤ **SECTION 19:** The Parliament of Canada shall be called together not later than Six Months after the Union.

This section became spent when the first Parliament met on November 6, 1867.

➤ **SECTION 20:** There shall be a Session of the Parliament of Canada once at least in every Year, so that Twelve Months shall not intervene between the last Sitting of the Parliament in one Session and its first Sitting in the next Session.

This section was repealed by the 1982 Constitution Act, and its substance re-enacted as section 5 of that Act which was made applicable to the provincial legislatures as well.

The Senate

➤ **SECTION 21:** The Senate shall, subject to the Provisions of this Act, consist of One hundred and four Members, who shall be styled Senators.

The Senate originally had 72 members, 24 from each of the three divisions of Canada—Ontario, Quebec, and the Maritime provinces of Nova Scotia and

New Brunswick which received 12 each. The increase to the present 104 members (excluding the eight additional senators appointed in 1990 under section 26) has occurred as shown in Table 7.2:[11]

Table 7.2

Year	Total	Reason for Increase
1867	72	Original terms of the Constitution Act.
1870	74	Manitoba: 2 seats under the Manitoba Act.
1871	77	British Columbia: 3 seats under the Terms of Union.
1873	77	Prince Edward Island: 4 seats in accordance with section 147 of the Constitution Act. Also according to section 147, the new province was deemed to be part of the Maritime division and so Nova Scotia and New Brunswick were reduced to 10 seats each through attrition. There was, therefore, no overall change in the size of the Senate.
1882	78	Manitoba: 1 additional seat (making a total of 3 seats) because of increased population, under the Manitoba Act.
1887	80	Northwest Territories: 2 seats under the 1886 Constitution Act.
1892	81	Manitoba: 1 additional seat (making a total of 4 seats) because of increased population, under the Manitoba Act.
1903	83	Northwest Territories: 2 additional seats (making a total of 4 seats), under the 1886 Constitution Act.
1905	87	Saskatchewan and Alberta: 4 seats each, under the Saskatchewan and Alberta Acts. Because the Northwest Territories already had 4 seats the net addition was 4. Northwest Territories representation was eliminated.
1915	96	A fourth division consisting of the four western provinces was established by the 1915 Constitution Act. Each province was to have a total of 6 seats, giving an overall increase of 9 seats—2 for Manitoba, 2 for Saskatchewan, 2 for Alberta, and 3 for British Columbia.
1949	102	Newfoundland: 6 seats in accordance with the 1915 Constitution Act which increased the number from the 4 stipulated in section 147 of the 1867 Act.
1975	103	Northwest Territories: 1 seat under the 1975 Constitution Act (No.2). Note: The Act also declared that for its purposes the term "province" included each of the two territories. This is of significance in relation to the qualifications and disqualifications of senators.
	104	Yukon Territory: 1 seat under the 1975 Constitution Act (No. 2). See also the note immediately above.

As originally enacted section 21 reads as follows:

> 21. The Senate shall, subject to the Provisions of this Act, consist of Seventy-two Members, who shall be styled Senators.

➤ **SECTION 22:** In relation to the Constitution of the Senate Canada shall be deemed to consist of Four Divisions:—

1. Ontario;
2. Quebec;
3. The Maritime Provinces, Nova Scotia and New Brunswick, and Prince Edward Island;
4. The Western Provinces of Manitoba, British Columbia, Saskatchewan, and Alberta;

which Four Divisions shall (subject to the Provisions of this Act) be equally represented in the Senate as follows: Ontario by twenty-four senators; Quebec by twenty-four senators; the Maritime Provinces and Prince Edward Island by twenty-four senators, ten thereof representing Nova Scotia, ten thereof representing New Brunswick, and four thereof representing Prince Edward Island; the Western Provinces by twenty-four senators, six thereof representing Manitoba, six thereof representing British Columbia, six thereof representing Saskatchewan, and six thereof representing Alberta; Newfoundland shall be entitled to be represented in the Senate by six members; the Yukon Territory and the Northwest Territories shall be entitled to be represented in the Senate by one member each.

In the Case of Quebec each of the Twenty-four Senators representing that Province shall be appointed for One of the Twenty-four Electoral Divisions of Lower Canada specified in Schedule A. to Chapter One of the Consolidated Statutes of Canada.

The changes noted in the commentary on section 21 are incorporated into this section. The requirement that Quebec's seats be distributed among the twenty-four electoral divisions (which had at one time been represented in the legislative council of Lower Canada) has existed since Confederation. The purpose of the requirement was to ensure Senate representation for Quebec's English-speaking minority.

The emphasis placed upon the Senate as central to the federal system—as the guardian of regional interests against hasty action by the House of Commons—during the 1864 Quebec Conference was noted in Chapter 3. (That the Senate has never fulfilled the guardianship role is another matter.) This emphasis led to the principle of regional equality, with two of the four original provinces defined as regions, although there were proposals from some maritime delegates for provincial equality. Equality, however defined, was intended to offset the inequality which representation based on population was to create in the Commons. There has been renewed interest in provincial equality in the Senate, this time expressed mainly by the western provinces and especially Alberta.

Over the years since Confederation there have been many proposals for Senate reform, the only tangible result being the 1965 innocuous imposition of mandatory retirement at age 75. Once in power, political parties have hesitated to act perhaps because of a reluctance to disturb the usefulness of the Senate as the plumb of patronage appointments. Only the New Democratic Party has consistently maintained a policy of reform—abolition. The 1979 *Senate Reference* illustrates a Government's desire to determine the extent of reform it could take unilaterally. See the discussion in Chapter 5 under "1867 Constitution Act Amendments by the Federal Parliament."

A prior question relating to reform must surely ask the intended purpose of a reformed upper house. However, reform which strengthens the Senate vis-à-vis the House of Commons must be viewed with skepticism because the principle of responsible government does not include the Senate. Nevertheless, in this day of popular government it is doubtful that a non-elective Senate responsible to no one but itself should be permitted to retain power to block the will of the peoples' representatives. The most recent spectacular attempt to block that will was in relation to the 1990 Goods and Services Tax bill. The Liberal-dominated Senate might have succeeded had Prime Minister Mulroney not created additional senators pursuant to section 26 of this Act. Britain resolved part of the problem with their House of Lords in 1911 by eliminating the veto for money bills and otherwise by substituting a suspensive veto for the absolute veto; in 1949 the maximum period of veto was reduced.

As originally enacted section 22 read as follows:

> 22. In relation to the Constitution of the Senate, Canada shall be deemed to consist of Three Divisions:
>
> 1. Ontario;
> 2. Quebec;
> 3. The Maritime Provinces, Nova Scotia and New Brunswick;
>
> which Three Divisions shall (subject to the Provisions of this Act) be equally represented in the Senate as follows: Ontario by Twenty-four Senators; Quebec by Twenty-four Senators; and the Maritime Provinces by Twenty-four Senators, Twelve thereof representing Nova Scotia, and Twelve thereof representing New Brunswick.
>
> In the case of Quebec each of the Twenty-four Senators representing that Province shall be appointed for One of the Twenty-four Electoral Divisions of Lower Canada specified in Schedule A. to Chapter One of the Consolidated Statutes of Canada.

➤ **SECTION 23:** The Qualification of a Senator shall be as follows:

(1) He shall be of the full age of Thirty Years:

(2) He shall be either a natural-born Subject of the Queen, or a Subject of the Queen naturalized by an Act of the Parliament of

Great Britain, or of the Parliament of the United Kingdom of Great Britain and Ireland, or of the Legislature of One of the Provinces of Upper Canada, Lower Canada, Canada, Nova Scotia, or New Brunswick, before the Union, or of the Parliament of Canada, after the Union:

(3) He shall be legally or equitably seised as of Freehold for his own Use and Benefit of Lands or Tenements held in Free and Common Socage, or seised or possessed for his own Use and Benefit of Lands or Tenements held in Franc-alleu or in Roture, within the Province for which he is appointed, of the Value of Four thousand Dollars, over and above all Rents, Dues, Debts, Charges, Mortgages, and Incumbrances due or payable out of or charged on or affecting the same:

(4) His Real and Personal Property shall be together worth Four thousand Dollars over and above his Debts and Liabilities:

(5) He shall be resident in the Province for which he is appointed:

(6) In the Case of Quebec he shall have his Real Property Qualification in the Electoral Division for which he is appointed, or shall be resident in that Division.

The idea of popularly controlled government was viewed with suspicion before the twentieth century. This explains not only the existence of upper houses but also their intended conservatism as checks on potentially irresponsible elected assemblies. The conservative characteristics of the Canadian Senate are the relatively high age and property qualifications. The age requirement assumes that with age comes maturity, wisdom, and hence conservatism. The property qualification assumes that people with a vested interest in the impact which government policy has on property will view change with particular care. It should be noted that this latter qualification is twofold. Not only must a senator have clear title to property with a value of at least $4,000; he or she must also have a total net worth of at least $4,000.

It is of interest, although probably of no practical importance, that while election to the House of Commons is now open only to Canadian citizens, appointment to the Senate remains open (according to this section) to all subjects of the Queen. Nevertheless, if the second disqualification in section 31 is read in the light of the current meanings of "Foreign Power" and "Subject or Citizen," non-Canadians may in fact be precluded from appointment; at least they would immediately become disqualified should the Senate so decide under section 33.

➤ **SECTION 24:** The Governor General shall from Time to Time, in the Queen's Name, by Instrument under the Great Seal of Canada, summon qualified Persons to the Senate; and, subject to the Provisions of this Act, every Person so summoned shall become and be a Member of the Senate and a Senator.

Although Senate appointments are made by the governor general it is the prime minister who makes the recommendations—almost always from among the party faithful. It is customary for the governor general to accept these recommendations, although this constitutional convention is (as are so many conventions involving the Crown) subject to the governor general's nebulous reserve power. For example, in 1896 following his electoral defeat but before his resignation, Prime Minister Tupper recommended several Senate (and judicial) appointments. The governor general refused to make the appointments on the grounds that the Prime Minister, although still the Crown's chief advisor, no longer enjoyed the confidence of the newly elected House or of the people.

In 1928 a unanimous Supreme Court of Canada ruled that the term "persons" used in this section included only males.[12] Part of the reasoning was that in 1867 when the Constitution Act was passed, women were not "persons" able to hold public office under British law. However, the British Privy Council reversed this decision in 1930, in part on the grounds that changing circumstances must be recognized.[13] Both males and females, therefore, could be appointed to the Senate. Although the first woman (Cairine Reay Wilson) was appointed in 1930, by 1969 there were still only five women in the upper house. As of April 1991 there were fifteen including two of the eight additional senators appointed in 1990 under section 26.[14]

The Meech Lake Accord established an interim procedure for filling Senate vacancies until such time as agreement might be reached on Senate reform. This procedure was followed until Meech Lake died on June 23, 1990. When a Senate vacancy occurred the appropriate provincial government submitted a list of nominees to the Federal cabinet. The person selected from the list had to be acceptable to the cabinet. In an effort to force a move toward an elected Senate the Alberta legislature enacted a law providing for an election, held in October 1989, to fill Alberta's existing Senate vacancy. Prime Minister Mulroney objected to this procedure and delayed the appointment of the victorious candidate until June 11, 1990, two weeks before the death of Meech Lake.

➤ **SECTION 25:** Such Persons shall be first summoned to the Senate as the Queen by Warrant under Her Majesty's Royal Sign Manual thinks fit to approve, and their Names shall be inserted in the Queen's Proclamation of Union.

It was agreed at the 1864 Quebec Conference that the first senators would be appointed from the major parties in each of the pre-Confederation provinces and that the several premiers would make the nominations. The provinces have not since been involved except for several appointments made under the interim procedure contained in the Meech Lake Accord as described in the commentary on section 24 above.

This section was repealed by Britain's Statute Law Revision Act 1893.

➤ **SECTION 26:** If at any Time on the Recommendation of the Governor General the Queen thinks fit to direct that Four or Eight Members be added to the Senate, the Governor General may by Summons to Four or

> Eight qualified Persons (as the Case may be), representing equally the Four Divisions of Canada, add to the Senate accordingly.

This section was added at the 1866 London Conference upon the suggestion of the British government. The intention was to provide a mechanism for breaking a deadlock between the two houses of Parliament. Originally providing for the appointment of an additional one senator or two senators for each of the three regions, the section was amended in 1915 to reflect the creation of the fourth region. Given the generally large party imbalance in the Senate, however, seldom would the appointment of an additional four or eight senators suffice to break a deadlock.

Britain, which knows neither a "rigid" constitution nor the concept of regional balance demanded by a federal system, has resolved deadlock between the House of Lords and the House of Commons by the simple expedient of the Government appointing, or threatening to appoint, enough additional peers sympathetic to the wishes of the Commons. The former procedure was adopted for the 1832 Reform Act; the latter for the 1911 Parliament Act which abolished the upper house veto of money bills and replaced the absolute with a suspensive veto for other legislation.

Authority to appoint additional senators under section 26 was given to the monarch rather than the governor general. In the years following Confederation, while Canada was still a colony, such appointments would ultimately have been made upon the advice of the monarch's British advisers after a recommendation from the Canadian government to the governor general had been transmitted through the colonial secretary. With the achievement of Canadian independence, appointments would be made by the monarch (in reality by the governor general) solely upon the advice of Canadian ministers.

This section establishes no criteria for determining the circumstances which might warrant additional appointments, nor for determining which province(s) within a region would receive the additional senator(s). On the first point Mallory notes three occasions when use of the section was discussed by Canadian prime ministers and the colonial office (in 1873-74, 1900, and 1912), but apparently only in the first instance was there a formal request—and rejection.[15] Liberal Prime Minister Mackenzie had argued, first, that agreement upon the "equitable distribution of its [the Senate's] political power between the two political parties" which had governed the initial appointments in 1867 had been "seriously disturbed" by subsequent Conservative appointments; and second, that "the new Administration should have an opportunity of seating some of the prominent supporters of its policy . . . for the purpose of having able advocates of the Government measures in the House." The colonial secretary replied that approval would be granted only when conflict of opinion between the Commons and the Senate was "of so serious and permanent a character that the Government could not be carried on without Her [the Queen's] intervention, and when it could be shown that the limited creation of Senators allowed by the Act would apply an adequate remedy."[16]

The sole use of this section was Prime Minister Mulroney's appointment of eight additional senators in September 1990 in an effort to ensure passage by the Senate of the Goods and Services Tax (GST) bill. The Liberal Senate majority had vowed to kill the bill (or, as they said, to "axe the tax"). With the extra appointees the Conservatives still lacked a majority, the balance of power resting with several independents, but they were able to secure passage in December in time for the proposed January 1, 1991, effective date.

The irony of this episode was what seems to have been the entirely unforeseen (at least by the Government) constitutional implication of the appointments. With two new senators from the Maritime "division" it was inevitable that at least one province would end up with one Commons seat fewer than its Senate seats. Prince Edward Island and New Brunswick each had the same number of Commons and Senate seats—four and ten respectively. Nova Scotia had eleven Commons and ten Senate seats. Following the appointments Nova Scotia had eleven of each but New Brunswick had ten and eleven, an apparent violation of section 51A of this Act which declares that a province is entitled to as many seats in the Commons as it has in the Senate, "notwithstanding anything in this Act." The new situation was immediately challenged but courts in Ontario, New Brunswick and British Columbia upheld the appointments.[17] The Ontario court said section 51A was not intended to prevent the operation of section 26. The British Columbia ruling denied that non-use of section 26 had established a legally binding rule. The New Brunswick court focussed on that province's shortfall in the Commons rather than its extra senator and ruled that New Brunswick was entitled to one more seat in the Commons. The awkwardness of this solution is apparent: when the number of senators drops to ten through attrition (s. 27), Commons representation would likewise have to fall according to the redistribution formula. If a new section 51 formula (containing the same no-reduction guarantee as in subsection [2] of the present formula) were implemented sometime in the future, New Brunswick could presumably claim the continuation of its eleven seats!

Section 26 as originally enacted read as follows:

> 26. If at any Time on the Recommendation of the Governor General the Queen thinks fit to direct that Three or Six Members be added to the Senate, the Governor General may by Summons to Three or Six qualified Persons (as the Case may be), representing equally the Three Divisions of Canada, add to the Senate accordingly.

➤ **SECTION 27:** In case of such Addition being at any Time made, the Governor General shall not summon any Person to the Senate, except upon a further like Direction by the Queen on the like Recommendation, to represent one of the Four Divisions until such Division is represented by Twenty-four Senators and no more.

Following the use of section 26 the usual method of appointment provided by section 24 must await the drop of a division's representation to the normal

24 senators. It seems possible, therefore, for a province within a division to fall below its quota as the division itself drops to its normal complement of 24 senators, and to remain underrepresented until the division falls below 24.

As originally enacted section 27 read as follows:

> 27. In case of such Addition being at any Time made the Governor General shall not summon any Person to the Senate except on a further like Direction by the Queen on the like Recommendation, until each of the Three Divisions of Canada is represented by Twenty-four Senators and no more.

Did this original section preclude appointments under section 24 until every division had fallen to 24 senators? If so, then one division could actually fall below 24 while awaiting the drop to 24 by another. In any event the question is academic inasmuch as the current wording eliminates possible ambiguity.

Section 27 was amended at the same time as were sections 26 and 28

➤ **SECTION 28:** The Number of Senators shall not at any Time exceed One Hundred and twelve.

The number 112 is the normal 104 plus the 8 permitted under section 26. As originally enacted this section provided for the then normal 72 plus 6 authorized by the original section 26, and read as follows:

> 28. The Number of Senators shall not at any Time exceed Seventy-eight.

➤ **SECTION 29:** (1) Subject to subsection (2), a Senator shall, subject to the provisions of this Act, hold his place in the Senate for life.

(2) A Senator who is summoned to the Senate after the coming into force of this subsection shall, subject to this Act, hold his place in the Senate until he attains the age of seventy-five years.

Whereas senators were originally appointed for life, subject to earlier resignation (section 30) or becoming disqualified (section 31), the 1965 Constitution Act amendment made retirement mandatory at age 75 for new senators. Senators appointed before the amendment became effective on June 1, 1965, could either retire at age 75 (or immediately if they were already at least that age) or continue under the life terms for which they had been appointed. With mandatory retirement, senators became covered by the Members of Parliament Retiring Allowances Act.

As originally enacted section 29 read as follows:

> 29. A Senator shall, subject to the Provisions of this Act, hold his Place in the Senate for life.

➤ **SECTION 30:** A Senator may by writing under his Hand addressed to the Governor General resign his Place in the Senate, and thereupon the same shall be vacant.

A total of 100 senators resigned between 1867 and 1975, one-third of them since 1964. Of the 100, 22 left to become lieutenant governors, 10 to seek election to the House of Commons, and 10 to accept judgeships.[18]

➤ **SECTION 31:** The Place of a Senator shall become vacant in any of the following Cases:

(1) If for Two consecutive Sessions of the Parliament he fails to give his Attendance in the Senate:

(2) If he takes an Oath or makes a Declaration or Acknowledgement of Allegiance, Obedience, or Adherence to a Foreign Power, or does an Act whereby he becomes a Subject or Citizen, or entitled to the Rights or Privileges of a Subject or Citizen, of a Foreign Power:

(3) If he is adjudged Bankrupt or Insolvent, or applies for the Benefit of any Law relating to Insolvent Debtors, or becomes a public Defaulter:

(4) If he is attainted of Treason or convicted of Felony or of any infamous Crime:

(5) If he ceases to be qualified in respect of Property or of Residence; provided, that a Senator shall not be deemed to have ceased to be qualified in respect of Residence by reason only of his residing at the Seat of the Government of Canada while holding an Office under that Government requiring his Presence there.

The reasons for a Senate seat becoming vacant are quite straightforward, although one or two remarks seem to be in order. It is an interesting but sad commentary even to contemplate an absence of two consecutive sessions. McConnell notes but one disqualification, that of an original senator, for non-attendance.[19] In view of the imprecision of "felony or . . . infamous crime" the Senate would have to make its own judgement in individual cases—much as the United States Congress must decide what constitutes "high crimes and misdemeanors" for impeachment and conviction under the United States Constitution.

➤ **SECTION 32:** When a Vacancy happens in the Senate by Resignation, Death or otherwise, the Governor General shall by Summons to a fit and qualified Person fill the Vacancy.

Although the governor general is required to fill Senate vacancies, no time limit is imposed. Prime ministers have frequently left seats vacant until a short time before an election in order to encourage maximum effort and loyalty from all who aspire to the Senate. A notable recent exception occurred when an overconfident Prime Minister St. Laurent left sixteen vacancies for a grateful John Diefenbaker to fill in 1957.

➤ **SECTION 33:** If any Question arises respecting the Qualification of a Senator or a Vacancy in the Senate the same shall be heard and determined by the Senate.

This section provides the mechanism for dealing with questions about qualifications and vacancies in individual cases. It might also permit the Senate to turn a blind eye to possible disqualifications.

➤ **SECTION 34:** The Governor General may from Time to Time, by Instrument under the Great Seal of Canada, appoint a Senator to be Speaker of the Senate, and may remove him and appoint another in his Stead.

The speaker of the Senate is chosen from the Government party (even though that party may be the Senate minority) and appointed by the governor general upon the prime minister's recommendation.

The Constitution Act does not provide for a deputy speaker of the Senate, although section 47 permits the election of such an officer for the House of Commons. In 1894 Parliament passed the Speaker of the Senate Act enabling the Senate to select a deputy speaker, although doubts were expressed about Parliament's authority to enact such legislation. (Section 91[1] authorizing Parliament to amend certain parts of the Act was not enacted until 1949.) Because of the uncertainty and at the request of the Canadian cabinet, the British Parliament passed the Canadian Speaker (Appointment of Deputy) Act in 1895 "for removing doubts as to the validity" of the Canadian legislation. This amendment was one of only two to be requested by the cabinet rather than Parliament although, in this case, Parliament was unanimous in supporting an amendment if such were necessary.[20] The British Act was repealed by the 1982 Constitution Act.

➤ **SECTION 35:** Until the Parliament of Canada otherwise provides, the Presence of at least Fifteen Senators, including the Speaker, shall be necessary to constitute a Meeting of the Senate for the Exercise of its Powers.

The quorum is still fifteen senators. There is no flexibility for the House of Commons quorum; section 48 sets that quorum at 20.

➤ **SECTION 36:** Questions arising in the Senate shall be decided by a Majority of Voices, and the Speaker shall in all Cases have a Vote, and when the Voices are equal the Decision shall be deemed to be in the Negative.

Unlike the Commons speaker, the speaker of the Senate votes on all issues. As a consequence a tied vote is considered to be a negative decision.

The House of Commons

➤ **SECTION 37:** The House of Commons shall, subject to the Provisions of this Act, consist of two hundred and ninety-five members of whom ninety-nine shall be elected for Ontario, seventy-five for Quebec, eleven for Nova Scotia, ten for New Brunswick, fourteen for Manitoba, thirty-two for British Columbia, four for Prince Edward Island, twenty-six for Alberta, fourteen for Saskatchewan, seven for Newfoundland, one for the Yukon Territory and two for the Northwest Territories.

Section 8 of this Act prescribes a decennial census. Section 51 establishes the rules for redistributing seats among the provinces and territories. Application of the most recent set of rules (established in 1985) to the 1981 census created a House of 295 members.

The original section 37 read as follows:

> 37. The House of Commons shall, subject to the Provisions of this Act, consist of one hundred and eighty-one members, of whom Eighty-two shall be elected for Ontario, Sixty-five for Quebec, Nineteen for Nova Scotia, and Fifteen for New Brunswick.

Since 1867 a number of adjustments have been made both in the size of the House and in the method of distributing seats among provinces and territories. These adjustments resulted from new provinces joining Confederation and population shifts among provinces, as well as from attempts to balance the principle of representation by population with what might be called "meaningful" representation. These changes are outlined in the commentary on section 51.

Although the Constitution Act is silent as to the method of determining constituency boundaries within provinces and territories following each decennial census and redistribution, it seems appropriate to comment upon the procedures which Parliament has adopted from time to time. Three periods may be delineated. From 1867 until 1903 a Government bill introduced the proposed changes after each census. This meant, in effect, that the ruling party was able to redraw boundaries to its own political advantage. All three bills during this period (1872, 1882, and 1892) contained gerrymanders, the most blatant of which was the 1882 gerrymander of half of Ontario's 92 constituencies.

Between 1903 and 1964, boundary adjustments were determined by a House select committee representing all parties. Although massive gerrymandering was eliminated, this procedure allowed for some "skillful butchery" because provincial subcommittees attended to the details and produced "close in-fighting among the parties which happened to be strong in that particular province."[21]

In 1964 the House of Commons relinquished its historic role by passing the Electoral Boundaries Readjustment Act which created independent electoral boundaries commissions—one commission for each province and one for the Northwest Territories following the 1975 increase in its Commons representation from one member to two members. Each commission redraws constituency boundaries according to the Act's guidelines which require that populations be as equal as possible. The commission is directed to consider "(i) the community of interest or community of identity in or the historical pattern of an electoral district in the province, and (ii) a manageable geographic size for districts in sparsely populated, rural or northern regions of the province." In so doing it may depart from the arithmetic mean (the "electoral quotient") up to a maximum of 25% above or below that mean. A 1985 amendment to the Electoral Boundaries Readjustment Act (Part II of the 1985 Representation Act) permits the 25% limit to be exceeded in "circumstances viewed by the commission as being extraordinary."[22] Professor Courtney notes that this provision reflects the pressure of parliamentarians to reduce the sizes of northern and otherwise sparsely populated constituencies, but that it also bucks the trend of the commissions which have since the 1960s reduced the extent of deviation from provincial means. He adds that commissions took advantage of the increased flexibility in only five constituencies,[23] but Sancton cautions that only time will determine whether the use of this new power expands.[24]

Each commission has three members: a judge appointed by the provincial or territorial chief justice from the court over which the chief justice presides, and two members appointed by the speaker of the House of Commons. The latter are typically "legislative clerks, provincial election officials, and academics."[25] A Representational Commissioner sat on all commissions until the office was abolished in 1979. The preliminary reports of the eleven commissions are published within their respective areas to allow for public reaction. Following any alterations which the commissioners may make, and not later than one year from the time they began their work, the reports are forwarded to the House of Commons and thence to a committee which considers any objections raised by members of the House. These objections together with the committee's minutes of proceedings are then returned to the commissions no later than two months from the time the commissions reported to the House. The commissions then decide whether or not to make additional changes. The final step is approval by order-in-council.

Since the establishment of the boundary commissions in 1964 the time required for the total redistribution process has ensured the fighting of elections on outdated constituency boundaries. Courtney makes this startling comment: Constituency boundaries for the 1988 election were thirteen years old, and had that year's election been called before the July 14, 1988, effective date of the 1987 redistribution, "fully one-third of all electoral districts would have exceeded the plus or minus 25 per cent margins—some with populations more than 200 per cent above their province's electoral quota."[26]

➤ **SECTION 38:** The Governor General shall from Time to Time, in the Queen's Name, by Instrument under the Great Seal of Canada, summon and call together the House of Commons.

This is another illustration of authority assigned to the governor general but in reality exercised upon the advice of the prime minister. The sole legal time restraint is that no more than one year may elapse between the end of one session and the beginning of the next (section 20, replaced by section 5 of the 1982 Constitution Act).

➤ **SECTION 39:** A Senator shall not be capable of being elected or of sitting or voting as a Member of the House of Commons.

This proscription does not affect the possibility of a senator being appointed to the cabinet and even administering a government department. Such a senator is nevertheless prevented from sitting, and therefore speaking and defending his department, in the House. A number of senators have held cabinet positions, including John Abbott and Mackenzie Bowell who were prime ministers in the 1890s.

➤ **SECTION 40:** Until the Parliament of Canada otherwise provides, Ontario, Quebec, Nova Scotia and New Brunswick shall, for the Purposes of the Election of Members to serve in the House of Commons, be divided into Electoral districts as follows:

1.—Ontario.

Ontario shall be divided into the Counties, Ridings of Counties, Cities, Parts of Cities, and Towns enumerated in the First Schedule to this Act, each whereof shall be an Electoral District, each such District as numbered in that Schedule being entitled to return One Member.

2.—Quebec.

Quebec shall be divided into Sixty-five Electoral Districts, composed of the Sixty-five Electoral Divisions into which Lower Canada is at the passing of this Act divided under Chapter Two of the Consolidated Statutes of Canada, Chapter Seventy-five of the Consolidated Statutes for Lower Canada, and the Act of the Province of Canada of the Twenty-third Year of the Queen, Chapter One, or any other Act amending the same in force at the Union, so that each such Electoral Division shall be for the Purposes of this Act an Electoral District entitled to return One Member.

3.—Nova Scotia.

Each of the Eighteen Counties of Nova Scotia shall be an Electoral District. The County of Halifax shall be entitled to return Two Members, and each of the other Counties One Member.

4.—New Brunswick.

Each of the Fourteen Counties into which New Brunswick is divided, including the City and County of St. John, shall be an Electoral District. The City of St. John shall also be a separate Electoral District. Each of those Fifteen Electoral Districts shall be entitled to return One Member.

The constituencies defined in this section were altered for the first time in 1872 following the first census and redistribution. As noted in the commentary on section 37, constituency boundaries are now established by order-in-council which implements the reports of the several electoral boundaries commissions. Section 40 provided for two members to represent the County of Halifax. Indeed, between 1872 and 1892 there were at least ten two-member ridings. The last of these (Queens in Prince Edward Island, and Halifax in Nova Scotia) were abolished by the 1960s redistribution.[27]

The First Schedule, pertaining to Ontario, lists forty-three "existing" electoral divisions consisting of nine "counties"; twenty-five "ridings of counties"; and nine "cities, parts of cities, and towns." It also identifies thirty-nine new electoral districts.

➤ **SECTION 41:** Until the Parliament of Canada otherwise provides, all Laws in force in the several Provinces at the Union relative to the following Matters or any of them, namely,—the Qualifications and Disqualifications of Persons to be elected or to sit or vote as Members of the House of Assembly or Legislative Assembly in the several Provinces, the Voters at Elections of such Members, the Oaths to be taken by Voters, the Returning Officers, their Powers and Duties, the Proceedings at Elections, the Periods during which Elections may be continued, the Trial of controverted Elections, and Proceedings incident thereto, the vacating of Seats of Members, and the Execution of new Writs in case of Seats vacated otherwise than by Dissolution,—shall respectively apply to Elections of Members to serve in the House of Commons for the same several Provinces.

Provided that, until the Parliament of Canada otherwise provides, at any Election for a Member of the House of Commons for the District of Algoma, in addition to Persons qualified by the Law of the Province of Canada to vote, every Male British Subject, aged Twenty-one Years or upwards, being a Householder, shall have a Vote.

This was an interim measure, now spent, pending the establishment of Dominion election laws. The franchise for Federal elections has had a chequered history. Five distinct periods of time may be identified.[28]

1867-1885: Provincial laws applied during this period. Two developments led to the establishment of Federal election laws. First, some provincial governments, most of them Liberal, began to disfranchise Federal employees many of whom had received patronage appointments from Conservative Governments in Ottawa. The second development was the removal of property qualifications and the establishment of full manhood suffrage by some provinces, a move which Prime Minister Macdonald opposed. A further consideration in the enactment of Federal legislation was the fact that such laws would require Federal voters lists which would mean additional patronage jobs. During this first period of time the Conservatives under Macdonald were in power except from November 1873 until October 1878.

Although provincial laws applied during this period, Parliament introduced the secret ballot for Federal elections in 1875. The secret ballot had been used in Halifax municipal elections as early as 1849 and in New Brunswick provincial elections by 1855.[29]

1885-1898: This was a period of Federal franchise. Voting was restricted to male British subjects who were at least 21 years old and met a low property qualification. Laurier opposed the centralization which a uniform Federal law implied.

1898-1917: The Liberals under Prime Minister Laurier repealed the Federal law upon their return to power in 1896 and re-established provincial franchise with the stipulation that neither Federal nor provincial employees could be disfranchised.

1917-1920: During these few years there was a combination of Federal and provincial franchise laws. In 1917 the coalition Union Government passed the Military Voters Act and the Wartime Elections Act, the clear purpose being "to give the vote to those who would support the government, to take it away from those who would oppose it, and to create a floating military vote, a large part of which would almost certainly be given to government candidates."[30] These Acts enfranchised everyone on active service including, therefore, people who would otherwise be ineligible to vote—women, Indians, and all other people less than twenty-one years old. They also extended the right to vote to female relatives of servicemen overseas. On the other hand, conscientious objectors were disfranchised, as were people naturalized after 1902 but who were born in or who customarily spoke the language of an enemy country.

In 1918 all women who were otherwise qualified were enfranchised.

1920-Present: A uniform Federal franchise characterizes this period. Under the Canada Elections Act passed in 1970, the voting age was reduced from 21 to 18 and (as of 1975) eligibility was restricted to Canadian citizens and not merely to British subjects. Indians living on reservations, and therefore ineligible to vote, were enfranchised in 1960.

Other statutes relevant to subjects mentioned in this section 41 are the Dominion Controverted Elections Act, Parliament of Canada Act and the 1982 Constitution Act (section 3 of which guarantees the right to vote and to hold public office).

The reason for the specific mention of Algoma in the second paragraph of the present section is that the area was not part of any pre-Confederation province but was joined to Ontario at the time of Confederation.

➤ **SECTION 42:** For the First Election of Members to serve in the House of Commons the Governor General shall cause Writs to be issued by such Person, in such Form, and addressed to such Returning Officers as he thinks fit.

The Person issuing Writs under this Section shall have the like Powers as are possessed at the Union by the Officers charged with the issuing of Writs for the Election of Members to serve in the respective House of Assembly or Legislative Assembly of the Province of Canada, Nova Scotia, or New Brunswick; and the Returning Officers to whom Writs are directed under this Section shall have the like Powers as are possessed at the Union by the Officers charged with the returning of Writs for the Election of Members to serve in the same respective House of Assembly or Legislative Assembly.

This was of a transitional nature and was repealed by Britain's Statute Law Revision Act 1893.

➤ **SECTION 43:** In case a Vacancy in the Representation in the House of Commons of any Electoral District happens before the Meeting of the Parliament, or after the Meeting of the Parliament before Provision is made by the Parliament in this Behalf, the Provisions of the last foregoing Section of this Act shall extend and apply to the issuing and returning of a Writ in respect of such vacant District.

This section, also, was transitional and repealed by Britain's Statute Law Revision Act 1893. The Parliament of Canada Act now provides for the filling of vacancies.

➤ **SECTION 44:** The House of Commons on its first assembling after a General Election shall proceed with all practicable Speed to elect One of its Members to be Speaker.

The speaker is the presiding officer of the House of Commons, and it is he or she who ensures that the business of the House is conducted in accordance with the House rules (called Standing Orders). The speaker is also in charge of the House of Commons staff and responsible for the House estimates.

The procedure for choosing a speaker is bound up with the ceremony that attends the opening of a new Parliament. On the morning of the day appointed for the opening of Parliament the members of the House of Commons assemble, with the clerk of the House (who is the permanent head of the House staff) in the chair. The Gentleman Usher of the Black Rod knocks three times on the door of the House and, when admitted, announces that the deputy governor general requires the members' attendance in the Senate chamber. Lacking a speaker, the members move to the Senate in an obviously unorganized fashion. Upon learning that the House has not yet selected its speaker, the Speaker of the Senate with the following words (1988, when Jeanne Sauvé was governor general) sends the members back to the House to make their selection.

> I have it in command to let you know that Her Excellency the Governor General of Canada does not see fit to declare the causes of her summoning the present Parliament of Canada until a Speaker of the House of Commons shall have been chosen, according to law; but this afternoon, at the hour of four o'clock, Her Excellency will declare the causes of her calling Parliament.[31]

Although formally elected by the entire House, the speaker was, before a 1985 amendment to Standing Orders, the nominee of the prime minister and chosen from among the Government backbenchers. A member of the cabinet or the leader of the Official Opposition usually seconded the nomination. The first use made of the new procedure was the election of John Fraser in the early morning hours of October 1, 1986. The occasion for the election was the resignation of Speaker John Bosley. Basically, the new procedure (Standing Order 4 [November 1988]) is election by secret ballot from among all members of the House except ministers of the Crown, party leaders, and any other members who have indicated their wish not to be considered.[32] Balloting continues until one member receives a majority of the votes. Following each ballot the member(s) with the fewest votes is (are) eliminated, and any other members may voluntarily withdraw. One major disadvantage of the new procedure is the length of time that might be required for the election. For example, Fraser's election took eleven hours and eleven ballots even though there were only thirty-nine names on the first ballot.[33] On December 12 following the 1988 election, on the other hand, Fraser was declared elected within an hour or so on the first ballot which had only twelve names. Whether some modification in the procedure may be necessary will likely be unknown until the incumbent does not stand for re-election.

Once elected the new speaker is led, protesting, to his chair. The reason for feigned reluctance is that, in early Britain, speakers were known to be punished, occasionally by death, by a monarch whose will was being opposed by the House of Commons. The speakership has generally alternated between English-speaking and French-speaking members of the House, although it is apparent that the new procedure will not ensure this result. For example, both Bosley and Fraser are anglophones. The deputy speaker is required by Standing Order 7(2) (November 1988) to have a "full and practical knowledge of the official language which is not that of the Speaker."

It has been Canadian practice to elect a different speaker for each Parliament, although seven speakers have been elected to second terms and two to third terms. The three-term speakers are Lemieux (1922-1930) and Lamoureux (1966-1974).[34] In 1979, Prime Minister Clark renominated Speaker (and former Liberal) Jerome. The only other occasion when the speaker has not been of the ruling party was the continued service of Speaker Lemieux during the brief Meighen Conservative Government which took office—and was defeated three days later—upon the resignation of Mackenzie King in June 1926. In that instance the Parliament for which Lemieux had been elected did not end until dissolution following Meighen's defeat at the polls in early July.

➤ **Section 45:** In case of a Vacancy happening in the Office of Speaker by Death, Resignation, or otherwise, the House of Commons shall with all practicable Speed proceed to elect another of its Members to be Speaker.

There have been six resignations during the term of a Parliament, the latest (before Speaker Bosley's) being Jeanne Sauvé's in 1984 to become governor general.[35]

➤ **Section 46:** The Speaker shall preside at all Meetings of the House of Commons.

A distinction must be made between the House sitting as the House and sitting as the Committee of the Whole House. In the first instance the presiding officer is the speaker; in the second it is the Chairman of Committees of the Whole (who doubles as the deputy speaker). The speaker is not only expected to preside over the House with impartiality; he must also divest himself of all party contact during his term in office. He neither participates in House debates (whether or not he is presiding at the time) nor occupies a seat on the floor of the House (when he is not presiding) as an elected member of Parliament.

> ➤ **SECTION 47:** Until the Parliament of Canada otherwise provides, in case of the Absence for any Reason of the Speaker from the Chair of the House of Commons for a Period of Forty-eight consecutive Hours, the House may elect another of its Members to act as Speaker, and the Member so elected shall during the Continuance of such Absence of the Speaker have and execute all the Powers, Privileges, and Duties of Speaker.

In 1885 Parliament passed The Speaker of the House of Commons Act which provides for the "Chairman of Committees, or, in his absence, . . . any member of the House, to take the chair and to act as deputy speaker." At the beginning of each Parliament, therefore, the House elects both a speaker and a Chairman of Committees of the Whole. The House also chooses, for each session, a Deputy Chairman of Committees of the Whole and an Assistant Deputy Chairman of Committees of the Whole (Standing Order 8 [November 1988]). Any of these officials may be called upon to preside in the absence of the speaker.

> ➤ **SECTION 48:** The Presence of at least Twenty Members of the House of Commons shall be necessary to constitute a Meeting of the House for the Exercise of its Powers, and for that Purpose the Speaker shall be reckoned as a Member.

At the beginning of each sitting the speaker determines whether or not a quorum is present. During the sitting the initiative rests with individual members to call attention to the absence of a quorum. Whereas section 35 permits Parliament to alter the Senate quorum, section 48 does not provide such flexibility for the House.

> ➤ **SECTION 49:** Questions arising in the House of Commons shall be decided by a Majority of Voices other than that of the Speaker, and when the Voices are equal, but not otherwise, the Speaker shall have a Vote.

It is rare for the speaker to be called upon to break a tie. McConnell notes that, as of the mid-1970s, there had been only two occasions—in 1870 and in 1889.[36] As noted in the commentary on section 36 the Senate speaker votes on all issues. With the existence of disciplined political parties in today's Parliaments a tied vote in the House is most unlikely, and it would probably indicate a House so evenly divided that the conduct of business would be virtually impossible. A general election would then be the only solution.

> ➤ **SECTION 50:** Every House of Commons shall continue for Five Years from the Day of the Return of the Writs for choosing the House (subject to be sooner dissolved by the Governor General), and no longer.

Election writs are returned to the chief electoral officer with the official election results about one month after the election date. The date the writs are returned begins the five-year statutory maximum life of Parliament. Although the next dissolution may occur no later than five years hence, it is more likely that a prime minister will advise dissolution before that time expires in order to retain maximum flexibility to go to the polls when it is politically the most expedient. It would be technically possible, nevertheless, for a period of about six years to elapse between elections: one month after the first election before the writs are returned; plus five years following the return of the writs; plus almost a year after automatic dissolution, allowing only enough time for the second election to be held and the new Parliament to meet within a year of dissolution (as prescribed by section 20 of this Act—now section 5 of the 1982 Constitution Act).

It is customary to speak of four years between elections as the norm, although in the thirty-one years between 1957 and 1988 there were eleven elections (including 1957 but not 1988) for an average of 2.8 years between elections. The fact that six of these elections produced minority governments no doubt contributed to the relatively short parliaments; indeed, there were on average 4.4 years between elections for the five majority governments. By contrast, in the thirty-one years from 1926 to 1957 there were only seven elections (including 1926 but not 1957), all of which produced majority governments for an average of 4.4 years for each parliament.

The 1916 B.N.A. Act, repealed by Britain's 1927 Statute Law Revision Act, extended by one year the life of the Twelfth Parliament which had been elected in September 1911 and was due to expire in October 1916. The 1949 Constitution (No. 2) Act, which added the new section 91(1) to the original statute, permitted Parliament to extend its own life "in time of real or apprehended war, invasion or insurrection" provided such extension is supported by a two-thirds majority of the House of Commons. This provision, now section 4(2) of the 1982 Constitution Act, has never been invoked.

The substance of the present section was re-enacted as section 4(1) of the 1982 Constitution Act, but there seems to be no explanation why section 50 itself was not repealed.

The governor general cannot dissolve parliament upon his own initiative because the proclamation must be issued under the Great Seal of Canada. As noted in the commentary on section 13 the Great Seal is in the custody of a minister of the Crown who must accept political responsibility for its use. In fact, several ministers would likely be involved because an order-in-council is the normal vehicle for issuing a proclamation. Only by dismissing his ministry and appointing one that was prepared to advise dissolution could a governor general attempt to force an election. See the discussion of monarchy in Chapter 4 for reference to the possibility of this course of action in relation to the 1981 patriation controversy. No Federal ministry has been dismissed since Confederation, although five provincial ministries have been dismissed.

The governor general may legally refuse to act upon the prime minister's advice to dissolve Parliament, although such refusal would be most unusual. The celebrated King-Byng crisis of 1926 is our outstanding example.

➤ **SECTION 51:** (1) The number of members of the House of Commons and the representation of the provinces therein shall, on the coming into force of this subsection and thereafter on the completion of each decennial census, be readjusted by such authority, in such manner, and from such time as the Parliament of Canada from time to time provides, subject and according to the following Rules:

1. There shall be assigned to each of the provinces a number of members equal to the number obtained by dividing the total population of the provinces by two hundred and seventy-nine and by dividing the population of each province by the quotient so obtained, counting any remainder in excess of 0.50 as one after the said process of division.
2. If the total number of members that would be assigned to a province by the application of rule 1 is less than the total number assigned to that province on the date of coming into force of this subsection, there shall be added to the number of members so assigned such number of members as will result in the province having the same number of members as were assigned on that date.

(2) The Yukon Territory as bounded and described in the schedule to chapter Y-2 of the Revised Statutes of Canada, 1970, shall be entitled to one member, and the Northwest Territories as bounded and described in section 2 of chapter N-22 of the Revised Statutes of Canada, 1970, shall be entitled to two members.

The redistribution formula in subsection (1) was enacted by the Constitution Act, 1985 (Representation), which is Part I of the 1985 Representation Act. It replaced the formula created by the 1974 Constitution Act. The new formula establishes an initial 279 seats to be allocated among the ten provinces as follows. The total population of the provinces—that is, excluding the territories—at the most recent decennial census (24,274,287 in 1981) is divided by 279. Each province's representation is then determined by dividing its population by that quotient (87,005). If the remainder exceeds .5 an additional seat is assigned to that province. It is possible, therefore, that the number of seats so obtained may not be precisely 279; indeed, as indicated in column (3) of Table 7.3 the above calculation for the 1980s redistribution produced 280 provincial seats. If, as a result of the foregoing calculation, a province would have fewer seats than immediately preceding this redistribution it is given additional seats to prevent that reduction.

Table 7.3 shows for each province (with territorial seats noted for completeness):[37]

In column (1), the number of seats it had under the 1974 formula and based upon the 1971 census.

In column (2), the number of seats it would have received under the 1974 formula following the 1981 census—that is, if a new formula had not been established.

In column (3), the number of seats it did receive under the new formula based on the 1981 census but before the no-reduction and Senate floor (s. 51A) guarantees were applied.

In column (4), the number of seats it has actually received under the new formula.

In column (5), the electoral quotient for each province, based on the number of seats in column (4) and the overall quotient of 87,005.

Table 7.3

Province		**Number of Seats**			**Quotient**
	(1)	(2)	(3)	(4)	(5)
Alberta	21	27	26	26	86,066
B.C.	28	33	32	32	85,765
Manitoba	14	15	12	14	73,303
New Brunswick	10	10	8	10	69,640
Newfoundland	7	8	7	7	81,097
Nova Scotia	11	12	10	11	77,040
Ontario	95	105	99	99	87,122
P.E.I.	4	4	1	4	30,627
Quebec	75	79	74	75	85,845
Saskatchewan	14	14	11	14	69,165
	279	307	280	292	
NWT	2	2	2	2	
Yukon	1	1	1	1	
Total	282	310	283	295	

Representation for the two territories, authorized by the 1886 Constitution Act, began in 1946 when one seat was assigned to the Yukon Territory and Northwest Territories combined. Each of these territories was given one seat in 1952 and the Northwest Territories gained its second seat in 1975. The first Parliament based upon the 1985 formula was elected in 1988. Because of the ratchet effect (no-loss guarantee) created by this system, the House will increase in size following each decennial census. However, the increase is expected to be much less than that which would have occurred under the 1974 formula.

Appearing before the House of Commons Standing Committee on Privileges and Elections during study of Bill C-74 (which became the 1985 Representation Act), Courtney commented that "the doctrine of representation by population . . . has never been greatly respected in Canada." For example, every province that joined Confederation after 1867 received more seats than it "should" have had—such as Manitoba which got four seats rather than one seat, and British Columbia which got six instead of two. Furthermore, Courtney pointed out, during the fifty-one days of debate leading to the 1964 Electoral Boundaries Readjustment Act "there was virtually no support by any of the Members of Parliament for the cause of reforming the redistribution process and setting up independent electoral boundary commissions on the grounds of the one-man one-vote principle."[38] Given these facts it is not surprising that whereas the electoral boundary commissions have moved closer to equality within the provinces (see the commentary on section 37) Parliament has moved in the opposite direction. This departure from a strict representation by population rule began with the "one-twentieth" rule in 1867, continued with the "Senate floor" in 1915, the "fifteen per cent" rule in 1952 (see the commentary below on this section), and was compounded by the no-reduction guarantee in 1985 which according to the 1980s redistribution established a protection for four of the ten provinces—Manitoba, Nova Scotia, Quebec, and Saskatchewan (see Table 7.3). New Brunswick and Prince Edward Island were already protected by the Senate floor. The principle of representation by population seems therefore to be honoured at least as much in the breach as in the observance! The commentaries on section 52 of the present Act and section 42 of the 1982 Constitution Act note the legal challenge to the 1980s redistribution.

Before the introduction of the 1985 redistribution formula there had been since Confederation three distinct formulae.

1867-1946: Redistributions through the 1930s

During this time Quebec had a fixed number of 65 seats. The number of seats assigned to each other province was determined by dividing Quebec's electoral quotient into each province's population. The total size of the House was therefore not constant.

Section 51 originally read as follows:

> 51. On the Completion of the Census in the Year One Thousand eight hundred and seventy-one, and of each subsequent decennial Census, the Representation of the Four Provinces shall be readjusted by such Authority, in such Manner, and from such Time, as the Parliament of Canada from Time to Time provides, subject and according to the following Rules:
>
> (1) Quebec shall have the fixed Number of Sixty-five Members:
>
> (2) There shall be assigned to each of the other Provinces such a Number of Members as will bear the same Proportion to the Number of its Population (ascertained at such Census) as the Number Sixty-five bears to the Number of the Population of Quebec (so ascertained):

(3) In the Computation of the Number of Members for a Province a fractional Part not exceeding One Half of the whole Number requisite for entitling the Province to a Member shall be disregarded; but a fractional Part exceeding One Half of that Number shall be equivalent to the whole Number:

(4) On any such Re-adjustment the Number of Members for a Province shall not be reduced unless the Proportion which the Number of the Population of the Province bore to the Number of the aggregate Population of Canada at the then last preceding Re-adjustment of the Number of Members for the Province is ascertained at the then latest Census to be diminished by One Twentieth Part or upwards:

(5) Such Re-adjustment shall not take effect until the Termination of the then existing Parliament.

Britain's 1893 Statute Law Revision Act altered the opening words of the section to read "On the completion of each decennial Census" because the 1871 census was no longer relevant.

The purpose of subsection 4 above (sometimes called the "one-twentieth rule") was to prevent a province from losing seats because of a declining population relative to Quebec, but only if the province was *not* declining in relation to the population of the country as a whole. The effect of the provision was cumulative, so that a province whose representation had been preserved following one redistribution could have the same "artificially" high representation preserved again following the next redistribution. The one-twentieth rule actually benefited Ontario, the largest province and arguably the one least in need of having its relative impact in the House of Commons strengthened. As a result, Ontario's 82 seats in 1914 were preserved following the redistributions of the 1920s and 1930s and would have been through the 1940s as well had the system not been changed. Based upon its population in relation to that of Quebec, Ontario's representation "should" have fallen to 74 seats by the 1940s.[39]

Section 51A was added in 1915 to establish an absolute minimum representation for a province equal to that province's number of senators. This is the "Senate floor" to which reference has already been made.

The 1943 B.N.A. Act postponed that decade's redistribution until after World War Two.

1946-1974: The Redistributions of the 1940s, 1950s, and 1960s

During these years the total size of the House was fixed—first at 255, then at 262 (pursuant to the Terms of Union of Newfoundland with Canada Act, s. 4) when Newfoundland joined Confederation in 1949, and finally at 263 in 1952 when the Yukon Territory and the Northwest Territories were assigned one seat each. The total size of the House following any redistribution could, however, vary slightly as a result of the formula's application.

The formula established by the 1946 B.N.A. Act was as follows:

51. (1) The number of members of the House of Commons shall be two hundred and fifty-five and the representation of the provinces therein shall forthwith upon the coming into force of this section and thereafter on the completion of each decennial census be readjusted by such authority, in such manner, and from such time as the Parliament of Canada from time to time provides, subject and according to the following rules:

1. Subject as hereinafter provided, there shall be assigned to each of the provinces a number of members computed by dividing the total population of the provinces by two hundred and fifty-four and by dividing the population of each province by the quotient so obtained, disregarding, except as hereinafter in this section provided, the remainder, if any, after the said process of division.
2. If the total number of members assigned to all the provinces pursuant to rule one is less than two hundred and fifty-four, additional members shall be assigned to the provinces (one to a province) having remainders in the computation under rule one commencing with the province having the largest remainder and continuing with the other provinces in the order of the magnitude of their respective remainders until the total number of members assigned is two hundred and fifty-four.
3. Notwithstanding anything in this section, if upon completion of a computation under rules one and two, the number of members to be assigned to a province is less than the number of senators representing the said province, rules one and two shall cease to apply in respect of the said province, and there shall be assigned to the said province a number of members equal to the said number of senators.
4. In the event that rules one and two cease to apply in respect of a province then, for the purpose of computing the number of members to be assigned to the provinces in respect of which rules one and two continue to apply, the total population of the provinces shall be reduced by the number of the population of the province in respect of which rules one and two have ceased to apply and the number two hundred and fifty-four shall be reduced by the number of members assigned to such province pursuant to rule three.
5. Such readjustment shall not take effect until the termination of the then existing Parliament.

(2) The Yukon Territory as constituted by Chapter forty-one of the Statutes of Canada, 1901, together with any Part of Canada not comprised within a province which may from time to time be included therein by the Parliament of Canada for the purposes of representation in Parliament, shall be entitled to one member.

In accordance with this formula a province's representation was determined by the relationship of its population to that of all of the provinces combined. Furthermore, the Yukon and the Northwest Territories were together represented by one member.

The 1952 B.N.A. Act increased the size of the House to 263. The only other change was the reintroduction of a provision to protect a province from a large reduction in representation. That provision read as follows:

> 5. On any such readjustment the number of members for any province shall not be reduced by more than fifteen per cent below the representation to which such province was entitled under rules one to four of the subsection at the last preceding readjustment of the representation of that province, and there shall be no reduction in the representation of any province as a result of which that province would have a smaller number of members than any other province that according to the results of the then last decennial census did not have a larger population; but for the purposes of any subsequent readjustment of representation under this section any increase in the number of members of the House of Commons resulting from the application of this rule shall not be included in the divisor mentioned in rules one to four of this subsection.

The operation of this provision was not cumulative as was the earlier one-twentieth rule. The provision did not, therefore, preclude a reduction of more than fifteen per cent in a province's representation at any one redistribution. Rather, it only prevented more than a fifteen per cent reduction in the number of seats to which the province was entitled exclusive of any "inflated" number that may have resulted from the application of paragraph 5 during the previous redistribution. For example, Saskatchewan dropped from 17 seats following the 1950s redistribution to 13 seats after the 1960s redistribution—a reduction of 23.5 per cent. Based upon its population, Saskatchewan had been "entitled" to only 15 seats at the time of the 1950s redistribution but was assigned 17 seats—a drop of 15 per cent from its 20 seats resulting from the 1940s redistribution. The drop from 15 to 13 was only 13 per cent.

1974-1985: The Redistribution of the 1970s

This virtually incomprehensible formula enacted by the 1974 Constitution Act was as follows:

> 51. (1) The number of members of the House of Commons and the representation of the provinces therein shall upon the coming into force of this subsection and thereafter on the completion of each decennial census be readjusted by such authority, in such manner, and from such time as the Parliament of Canada from time to time provides, subject and according to the following Rules:
>
> 1. There shall be assigned to Quebec seventy-five members in the readjustment following the completion of the decennial census

taken in the year 1971, and thereafter four additional members in each subsequent readjustment.

2. Subject to Rules 5(2) and (3), there shall be assigned to a large province a number of members equal to the number obtained by dividing the population of the large province by the electoral quotient of Quebec.
3. Subject to Rules 5(2) and (3), there shall be assigned to a small province a number of members equal to the number obtained by dividing
   - (a) the sum of the populations, determined according to the results of the penultimate decennial census, of the provinces (other than Quebec) having populations of less than one and a half million, determined according to the results of that census, by the sum of the numbers of members assigned to those provinces in the readjustment following the completion of that census; and
   - (b) the population of the small province by the quotient obtained under paragraph (a).
4. Subject to Rules 5(1)(a), (2) and (3), there shall be assigned to an intermediate province a number of members equal to the number obtained
   - (a) by dividing the sum of the populations of the provinces (other than Quebec) having populations of less than one and a half million by the sum of the number of members assigned to those provinces under any of Rules 3, 5(1)(b), (2) and (3);
   - (b) by dividing the population of the intermediate province by the quotient obtained under paragraph (a); and
   - (c) by adding to the number of members assigned to the intermediate province in the readjustment following the completion of the penultimate decennial census one-half of the difference resulting from the subtraction of that number from the quotient obtained under paragraph (b).
5. (1) On any readjustment,
   - (a) if no province (other than Quebec) has a population of less than one and a half million, Rule 4 shall not be applied and, subject to Rules 5(2) and (3), there shall be assigned to an intermediate province a number of members equal to the number obtained by dividing
     - (i) the sum of the populations, determined according to the results of the penultimate decennial census, of the provinces (other than Quebec) having populations of not less than one and a half million and not

more than two and a half million, determined according to the results of that census, by the sum of the numbers of members assigned to those provinces in the readjustment following the completion of that census, and

(ii) the population of the intermediate province by the quotient obtained under subparagraph (i);

(b) if a province (other than Quebec) having a population of

(i) less than one and a half million, or

(ii) not less that one and a half million and not more than two and a half million does not have a population greater than its population determined according to the results of the penultimate decennial census, it shall, subject to Rules 5(2) and (3), be assigned the number of members assigned to it in the readjustment following the completion of that census.

(2) On any readjustment,

(a) if, under any of Rules 2 to 5(1), the number of members to be assigned to a province (in this paragraph referred to as "the first province") is smaller than the number of members to be assigned to any other province not having a population greater than that of the first province, those Rules shall not be applied to the first province and it shall be assigned a number of members equal to the largest number of members to be assigned to any other province not having a population greater than that of the first province;

(b) if, under any of Rules 2 to 5(1)(a), the number of members to be assigned to a province is smaller than the number of members assigned to it in the readjustment following the completion of the penultimate decennial census, those Rules shall not be applied to it and it shall be assigned the latter number of members;

(c) if both paragraphs (a) and (b) apply to a province, it shall be assigned a number of members equal to the greater of the numbers produced under those paragraphs.

(3) On any readjustment,

(a) if the electoral quotient of a province (in this paragraph referred to as "the first province") obtained by dividing its population by the number of members to be assigned to it under any of Rules 2 to 5(2) is greater than the electoral quotient of Quebec, those Rules shall not be applied to the first province and it shall be assigned a number of members equal to the number obtained by dividing its population by the electoral quotient of Quebec;

(b) if, as a result of the application of Rule 6(2)(a), the number of members assigned to a province under paragraph (a) equals the number of members to be assigned to it under any of Rules 2 to 5(2), it shall be assigned that number of members and paragraph (a) shall cease to apply to that province.

6. (1) In these Rules,

"electoral quotient" means, in respect of a province, the quotient obtained by dividing its population, determined according to the results of the then most recent decennial census, by the number of members to be assigned to it under any of Rules 1 to 5(3) in the readjustment following the completion of that census;

"intermediate province" means a province (other than Quebec) having a population greater than its population determined according to the results of the penultimate decennial census but not more than two and a half million and not less than one and a half million;

"large province" means a province (other than Quebec) having a population greater than two and a half million;

"penultimate decennial census" means the decennial census that preceded the then most recent decennial census;

"population" means, except where otherwise specified, the population determined according to the results of the then most recent decennial census;

"small province" means a province (other than Quebec) having a population greater than its population determined according to the results of the penultimate decennial census and less than one and half million.

(2) For the purposes of these Rules,

(a) if any fraction less than one remains upon completion of the final calculation that produces the number of members to be assigned to a province, that number of members shall equal the number so produced disregarding the fraction;

(b) if more than one readjustment follows the completion of a decennial census, the most recent of those readjustments shall, upon taking effect, be deemed to be the only readjustment following the completion of that census;

(c) a readjustment shall not take effect until the termination of the then existing Parliament.

This formula attempted to strike a proper balance between representation by population and what may be called "meaningful" representation. Under the previous system half of the provinces would have suffered reduced representation in the House even though they had population increases; and Ontario would have received the same number of additional seats as British Columbia even though its population increase was, in absolute terms, three times that of British Columbia.[40] The formula

(1) Assigned a specific number of seats to Quebec (initially 75, but increasing by 4 after each decennial census).

(2) Guaranteed that no province would lose seats in a redistribution, or have fewer seats than a smaller province.

(3) Determined a province's representation in relation to that of other provinces of comparable size.

To accomplish the third purpose the provinces (other than Quebec) were divided into three groups. "Large" provinces had populations of at least 2 1/2 million (Ontario); "small" provinces had populations of less than 1 1/2 million (Newfoundland, Prince Edward Island, New Brunswick, Nova Scotia, Manitoba, Saskatchewan); and "intermediate" provinces had populations between 1 1/2 and 2 1/2 million (Alberta and British Columbia).

The representation of a large province was determined by the relation of its population to that of Quebec. The representation of a small province was determined by dividing the average constituency size of all small provinces, based on the previous redistribution, into the province's population at the latest census. The representation of an intermediate province was determined by dividing its population by the new small-province average constituency size, and then (because of the relatively small divisor) halving any representation increase.

It is obvious that with the representation of the base province (Quebec) increasing for each redistribution the total size of the House would grow rapidly. Indeed, by the first decade of the twenty-first century the size was projected to rise from 282 following the 1970s redistribution to 354 or even 381 depending upon the population projection.[41]

Table 7.4 shows the representation of the provinces and territories in the House of Commons since 1867.

Table 7.4

Representation in the House of Commons, as at Federal General Elections 1867-1988

Source: 1990 Canada Year Book, Table 19.3, p. 19-21.
(Reproduced with the permission of the Minister of Supply and Services Canada, 1990)

<table>
<tr><th>Prov./Territory</th><th>1867</th><th>1872</th><th>1874
1878</th><th>1882</th><th>1887
1891</th><th>1896
1900</th><th>1904</th><th>1908
1911</th><th>1917
1921</th><th>1925
1926
1930</th><th>1935
1940
1945</th><th>1949</th><th>1953
1957
1958
1962
1963
1965</th><th>1968
1972
1974</th><th>1979
1980
1984</th><th>1988</th></tr>
<tr><td>Ontario</td><td>82</td><td>88</td><td>88</td><td>92</td><td>92</td><td>92</td><td>86</td><td>86</td><td>82</td><td>82</td><td>82</td><td>83</td><td>85</td><td>88</td><td>95</td><td>99</td></tr>
<tr><td>Quebec</td><td>65</td><td>65</td><td>65</td><td>65</td><td>65</td><td>65</td><td>65</td><td>65</td><td>65</td><td>65</td><td>65</td><td>73</td><td>75</td><td>74</td><td>75</td><td>75</td></tr>
<tr><td>Nova Scotia</td><td>19</td><td>21</td><td>21</td><td>21</td><td>21</td><td>20</td><td>18</td><td>18</td><td>16</td><td>14</td><td>12</td><td>13</td><td>12</td><td>11</td><td>11</td><td>11</td></tr>
<tr><td>New Brunswick</td><td>15</td><td>16</td><td>16</td><td>16</td><td>16</td><td>14</td><td>13</td><td>13</td><td>11</td><td>11</td><td>10</td><td>10</td><td>10</td><td>10</td><td>10</td><td>10</td></tr>
<tr><td>Manitoba</td><td>—</td><td>4</td><td>4</td><td>5</td><td>5</td><td>7</td><td>10</td><td>10</td><td>15</td><td>17</td><td>17</td><td>16</td><td>14</td><td>13</td><td>14</td><td>14</td></tr>
<tr><td>British Columbia</td><td>—</td><td>6</td><td>6</td><td>6</td><td>6</td><td>6</td><td>7</td><td>7</td><td>13</td><td>14</td><td>16</td><td>18</td><td>22</td><td>23</td><td>28</td><td>32</td></tr>
<tr><td>Prince Edward Is.</td><td>—</td><td>—</td><td>6</td><td>6</td><td>6</td><td>5</td><td>4</td><td>4</td><td>4</td><td>4</td><td>4</td><td>4</td><td>4</td><td>4</td><td>4</td><td>4</td></tr>
<tr><td>Saskatchewan</td><td rowspan="2">—</td><td rowspan="2">—</td><td rowspan="2">—</td><td rowspan="2">—</td><td rowspan="2">4</td><td rowspan="2">4</td><td rowspan="2">10</td><td>10</td><td>16</td><td>21</td><td>21</td><td>20</td><td>17</td><td>13</td><td>14</td><td>14</td></tr>
<tr><td>Alberta</td><td>7</td><td>12</td><td>16</td><td>17</td><td>17</td><td>17</td><td>19</td><td>21</td><td>26</td></tr>
<tr><td>Newfoundland</td><td>—</td><td>—</td><td>—</td><td>—</td><td>—</td><td>—</td><td>—</td><td>—</td><td>—</td><td>—</td><td>—</td><td>7</td><td>7</td><td>7</td><td>7</td><td>7</td></tr>
<tr><td>Yukon Territory</td><td rowspan="2">—</td><td rowspan="2">—</td><td rowspan="2">—</td><td rowspan="2">—</td><td rowspan="2">—</td><td rowspan="2">—</td><td rowspan="2">1</td><td rowspan="2">1</td><td rowspan="2">1</td><td rowspan="2">1</td><td rowspan="2">1</td><td rowspan="2">1</td><td>1</td><td>1</td><td>1</td><td>1</td></tr>
<tr><td>Northwest Terr.</td><td>1</td><td>1</td><td>2</td><td>2</td></tr>
<tr><td>Total</td><td>181</td><td>200</td><td>206</td><td>211</td><td>215</td><td>213</td><td>214</td><td>221</td><td>235</td><td>245</td><td>245</td><td>262</td><td>265</td><td>264</td><td>282</td><td>295</td></tr>
</table>

➤ **SECTION 51A:** Notwithstanding anything in this Act a province shall always be entitled to a number of members in the House of Commons not less than the number of senators representing such province.

As long as the prevailing redistribution formula guarantees that no province will lose Commons seats (and as long as no province receives additional Senate seats) section 51A has no practical significance. This was the case in 1974 and 1985, but there is no assurance that it will continue for future redistributions. Furthermore, section 41 of the 1982 Constitution Act provides that any Constitutional amendment which reduces the number of Commons seats below the Senate floor requires the consent of all eleven legislatures.

This section was the basis of several unsuccessful provincial court challenges to Prime Minister Mulroney's 1990 appointment of eight additional senators under section 26 which resulted in New Brunswick having one Commons seat fewer than its Senate seats. See the commentary on that section.

➤ **SECTION 52:** The Number of Members of the House of Commons may be from Time to Time increased by the Parliament of Canada, provided

> the proportionate Representation of the Provinces prescribed by this Act is not thereby disturbed.

Parliament is authorized to increase the size of the House of Commons provided that the "proportionate representation of the provinces prescribed by this Act" (presumably by section 51) is not thereby altered. Because there have been significant changes to section 51 over the years the actual significance of section 52 as a limiting device seems unclear.

Section 42(1) of the 1982 Constitution Act provides that an amendment "in relation to . . . the principle of proportionate representation of the provinces in the House of Commons" can be made only under the general amending formula of section 38—that is, with the concurrence of two-thirds of the provinces as well as Parliament. Parliament apparently considered itself free to continue its practice of redistributing seats, inasmuch as the 1985 overhaul of section 51 was enacted by Parliament alone pursuant to this section or section 44 of the 1982 Constitution Act. However, in 1987 that redistribution was challenged, albeit unsuccessfully, in the British Columbia courts as being contrary to the principle of "proportionate representation of the provinces" within section 42 of the 1982 Act. See the commentary on that section.

Money Votes; Royal Assent

> ➤ **SECTION 53:** Bills for appropriating any Part of the Public Revenue, or for imposing any Tax or Impost, shall originate in the House of Commons.

This section, requiring that supply (spending) and taxation bills originate with the House of Commons, is one of only two legal distinctions in legislative power between the House and the Senate. (The other is the suspensive veto power described in section 47 of the 1982 Constitution Act.) On the basis of the present section, nevertheless, the House claims that the Senate is also precluded from amending money bills. Standing Order 80(1) (November 1988) reads as follows:

> All aids and supplies granted to the Sovereign by the Parliament of Canada are the sole gift of the House of Commons, and all bills for granting such aids and supplies ought to begin with the House, as it is the undoubted right of the House to direct, limit, and appoint in all such bills, the ends, purposes, considerations, conditions, limitations and qualifications of such grants, which are not alterable by the Senate.

The Senate rejects this position on the grounds that the 1867 Constitution Act would have explicitly barred the upper house from making amendments if such had been the intent. The Senate has in fact amended money bills; it is, nevertheless, precluded by section 54 from increasing dollar amounts of spending bills inasmuch as such increases would require the governor general's recommendation.

Depending upon the nature of a Senate amendment, and especially if the Commons is pressed for time, the Commons may reluctantly agree to the change rather than to "insist on its privileges in respect thereto, but . . . the waiver of the said privileges in this case be not however drawn into a precedent."[42]

➤ **SECTION 54:** It shall not be lawful for the House of Commons to adopt or pass any Vote, Resolution, Address, or Bill for the Appropriation of any Part of the Public Revenue, or of any Tax or Impost, to any Purpose that has not been first recommended to that House by Message of the Governor General in the Session in which such Vote, Resolution, Address, or Bill is proposed.

Not only must money bills (both spending and taxation) originate in the House of Commons; spending bills must also be recommended by "Message" of the governor general. It is the cabinet, of course, that prepares the message and a minister who introduces it in the House. Custom requires that bills which increase taxes must also be introduced by a minister. Any member may propose a decrease in spending or taxation, but there is little chance of such a proposal being approved by a House in which the Government has a majority of the seats.

The significance of sections 53 and 54 is that the cabinet must accept total responsibility for the government's financial policy.

➤ **SECTION 55:** Where a Bill passed by the Houses of the Parliament is presented to the Governor General for the Queen's Assent, he shall declare, according to his Discretion, but subject to the Provisions of this Act and to Her Majesty's Instructions, either that he assents thereto in the Queen's Name, or that he withholds the Queen's Assent, or that he reserves the Bill for the Signification of the Queen's Pleasure.

There are three possible courses of action which the governor general may take in relation to legislation duly passed by Parliament. The normal action is to give royal assent in the monarch's name. Alternatively, the governor general may refuse assent or reserve the bill for a decision by the monarch (really, in 1867, the British government).

In fact, no governor general has ever refused assent. Writing before Confederation, and of Britain, Bagehot stated that the Queen "has no veto. She must sign her own death-warrant if the two Houses unanimously send it up to her. It is a fiction of the past to ascribe to her legislative power."[43] The same may be said of the governor general in Canada. Twenty-one bills have been reserved, the last in 1878.[44] Because a reserved bill would now be acted upon by the Queen upon the advice of her Canadian ministers, reservation would merely direct the legislation back to the cabinet which probably introduced it in the first place. More significant is the fact that the governor general is unlikely to act contrary to the wishes of Parliament. The power of reservation was declared obsolete at the 1930 Imperial Conference.

It is surprising that the power of reservation, together with that of disallowance in section 56, were not repealed at the time the 1982 Constitution Act was drafted. Their abolition had been part of the 1971 Victoria Charter.

➤ **SECTION 56:** Where the Governor General assents to a Bill in the Queen's Name, he shall by the first convenient Opportunity send an authentic Copy of the Act to one of Her Majesty's Principal Secretaries of State, and if the Queen in Council within Two Years after Receipt thereof by the Secretary of State thinks fit to disallow the Act, such Disallowance (with a Certificate of the Secretary of State of the Day on which the Act was received by him) being signified by the Governor General, by Speech or Message to each of the Houses of the Parliament or by Proclamation, shall annul the Act from and after the Day of such Signification.

The power of disallowance, declared obsolete at the 1930 Imperial Conference, was used only once (in 1873). The circumstances are described in the commentary on section 18. The sending of bills to Britain was "quietly discontinued" in 1942.[45]

➤ **SECTION 57:** A Bill reserved for the Signification of the Queen's Pleasure shall not have any Force unless and until, within Two Years from the Day on which it was presented to the Governor General for the Queen's Assent, the Governor General signifies, by Speech or Message to each of the Houses of the Parliament or by Proclamation, that it has received the Assent of the Queen in Council.

An Entry of every such Speech, Message, or Proclamation shall be made in the Journal of each House, and a Duplicate thereof duly attested shall be delivered to the proper Officer to be kept among the Records of Canada.

The monarch, meaning (in 1867) the British government, could take up to two years to decide the fate of a reserved bill. Inaction by the end of that period voided the bill.

V. Provincial Constitutions

Executive Power

➤ **SECTION 58:** For each Province there shall be an Officer, styled the Lieutenant Governor, appointed by the governor general in Council by Instrument under the Great Seal of Canada.

The Constitution Act is unclear whether appointment of lieutenant governors by the governor general in council (that is, by the Federal cabinet) meant that these provincial officers represented the Crown or the Federal government. The answer to this question was significant because if they represented Ottawa then all executive authority including the prerogative would belong ultimately to the central government. The issue was resolved by Lord Watson for the Privy Council in 1892:

> There is no constitutional anomaly in an executive officer of the Crown receiving his appointment at the hands of a governing body who have no powers and no functions except as representatives of the Crown. The act of the Governor-General and his Council in making the appointment is, within the meaning of the statute, the act of the Crown; and a Lieutenant-Governor, when appointed, is as much the representative of Her Majesty for all purposes of provincial government as the Governor-General himself is for all purposes of Dominion government.[46]

Appointment of lieutenant governors is the prerogative of the prime minister who is in no way bound to consult with provincial premiers. Any such consultation is but a matter of courtesy. Lieutenant governors might also to some extent be Federal officials especially in relation to their use of the power of reservation under section 90. This is discussed in the commentary on that section.

➤ **SECTION 59:** A Lieutenant Governor shall hold Office during the Pleasure of the Governor General; but any Lieutenant Governor appointed after the Commencement of the First Session of the Parliament of Canada shall not be removeable within Five Years from his Appointment, except for Cause assigned, which shall be communicated to him in Writing within One Month after the Order for his Removal is made, and shall be communicated by Message to the Senate and to the House of Commons within One Week thereafter if the Parliament is then sitting, and if not then within One Week after the Commencement of the next Session of the Parliament.

The term of office of a lieutenant governor is not specified in the Constitution Act; instead, the lieutenant governor holds office "during the pleasure" of the governor general. Nevertheless, that "pleasure" must endure for at least five years subject to earlier dismissal "for cause assigned." Saywell notes that two dismissals have occurred, those of Quebec's Letellier by the Macdonald Government in 1879, and British Columbia's McInnes by the Laurier Government in 1900. He adds that "these two cases of dismissal stand alone and as far as one can tell the federal government never again considered dismissing a Lieutenant-Governor. They proved beyond all doubt that the central government possessed the unrestricted power to dismiss."[47] In restrained understatement McConnell comments that both dismissals occurred during unusual circumstances. Both men were "strong-minded lieutenant-governors having a somewhat defective understanding of the working of the relevant constitutional conventions and operating in conditions of more than the usual political turbulence."[48]

➤ **Section 60:** The Salaries of the Lieutenant Governors shall be fixed and provided by the Parliament of Canada.

Salaries are authorized by the Salaries Act. Expenses are the responsibility of the provincial governments.

➤ **Section 61:** Every Lieutenant Governor shall, before assuming the Duties of his Office, make and subscribe before the Governor General or some Person authorized by him Oaths of Allegiance and Office similar to those taken by the Governor General.

No comment is needed.

➤ **Section 62:** The Provisions of this Act referring to the Lieutenant Governor extend and apply to the Lieutenant Governor for the Time being of each Province, or other the Chief Executive Officer or Administrator for the Time being carrying on the Government of the Province, by whatever Title he is designated.

This is analogous to section 10 which pertains to the governor general. Of interest, but perhaps of no significance in view of Lord Watson's 1892 statement (see section 58 above), are the concluding words of this section which refer to the chief executive officer "carrying on the government of the province." In section 10 the chief executive officer carries on the Government of Canada but "on behalf and in the name of the Queen."

➤ **Section 63:** The Executive Council of Ontario and of Quebec shall be composed of such Persons as the Lieutenant Governor from Time to Time thinks fit, and in the first instance of the following Officers, namely,—the Attorney General, the Secretary and Registrar of the Province, the Treasurer of the Province, the Commissioner of Crown Lands, and the Commissioner of Agriculture and Public Works, within Quebec, the Speaker of the Legislative Council and the Solicitor General.

This was transitional. The executive councils of Ontario and Quebec are now established by provincial legislation.

➤ **Section 64:** The Constitution of the Executive Authority in each of the Provinces of Nova Scotia and New Brunswick shall, subject to the Provisions of this Act, continue as it exists at the Union until altered under the Authority of this Act.

This is analogous to section 63 except that the previous section had to provide for the executive governments of two new provinces. Section 64 merely states that the existing ministries of Nova Scotia and New Brunswick would continue until altered by those provinces. The phrase "subject to the provisions of this Act" invokes section 92(1) which essentially has become section 45 of the 1982 Constitution Act. Section 92(1) not only permitted provinces to amend their own constitutions; it also precluded their tampering with "the office of lieutenant governor."

A provision similar to this section was included in the instruments admitting British Columbia, Prince Edward Island, and Newfoundland. The Manitoba Act, Alberta Act, and Saskatchewan Act, provided for the executive governments of those newly created provinces.

➤ **SECTION 65:** All Powers, Authorities, and Functions which under any Act of the Parliament of Great Britain, or of the Parliament of the United Kingdom of Great Britain and Ireland, or of the Legislature of Upper Canada, Lower Canada, or Canada, were or are before or at the Union vested in or exerciseable by the respective Governors or Lieutenant Governors of those Provinces, with the Advice or with the Advice and Consent of the respective Executive Councils thereof, or in conjunction with those Councils, or with any Number of Members thereof, or by those Governors or Lieutenant Governors individually, shall, as far as the same are capable of being exercised after the Union in relation to the Government of Ontario and Quebec respectively, be vested in and shall or may be exercised by the Lieutenant Governor of Ontario and Quebec respectively with the Advice or with the Advice and Consent of or in conjunction with the respective Executive Councils, or any Members thereof, or by the Lieutenant Governor individually, as the Case requires, subject nevertheless (except with respect to such as exist under Acts of the Parliament of Great Britain, or of the Parliament of the United Kingdom of Great Britain and Ireland,) to be abolished or altered by the respective Legislatures of Ontario and Quebec.

This is analogous to section 12 which provided for the transfer, to the governor general, of authority respecting the new Dominion as had been exercised by pre-Confederation governors and lieutenant governors. Section 65 establishes the authority of the lieutenant governors of the new provinces of Ontario and Quebec. Nova Scotia and New Brunswick are omitted because they were continuing provinces whose executive authority was confirmed by section 64.

The restriction noted in parentheses, prohibiting the alteration or repeal of British statutes insofar as they applied to Canada, was removed by the 1931 Statute of Westminster except for this Constitution Act itself.

➤ **SECTION 66:** The Provisions of this Act referring to the Lieutenant Governor in Council shall be construed as referring to the Lieutenant Governor of the Province acting by and with the Advice of the Executive Council thereof.

This is analogous to section 13 which refers to the governor general in council, and it is similarly confusing.

➤ **SECTION 67:** The Governor General in Council may from Time to Time appoint an Administrator to execute the office and Functions of Lieutenant Governor during his Absence, Illness, or other Inability.

Sections 10 and 62 refer to the existence of an "administrator" who may "for the time being" carry on the Federal or a provincial government. This position within the Federal government is created by letters patent and is filled as necessary by the Chief Justice of the Supreme Court of Canada. For provincial governments the administrator is appointed by the Federal cabinet which is not restricted in its selection.

➤ **SECTION 68:** Unless and until the Executive Government of any Province otherwise directs with respect to that Province, the Seats of Government of the Provinces shall be as follows, namely,—of Ontario, the City of Toronto; of Quebec, the City of Quebec; of Nova Scotia, the City of Halifax; and of New Brunswick, the City of Fredericton.

Whereas the seat of the Government of Canada may be moved by the Queen (section 16), provincial capitals may be changed by provincial cabinets. Although this section names only the four original provinces, the instruments which added the remaining provinces either contained the same provision (Manitoba, Alberta, and Saskatchewan) or implied this authority by stating that the terms of the Constitution Act applied to the new provinces (Prince Edward Island, British Columbia, and Newfoundland). There have been no changes in the locations of provincial governments.

Legislative Power

1. Ontario

➤ **SECTION 69:** There shall be a Legislature for Ontario consisting of the Lieutenant Governor and of One House, styled the Legislative Assembly of Ontario.

Because the pre-Confederation Province of Canada was reconstituted as the new provinces of Ontario and Quebec, provision had to be made for their legislatures. Their executive governments were established under section 63. Sections 69-87 establish the legislatures and some of their rules of operation. By contrast, only one section (s. 88) was needed for the continuing provinces of New Brunswick and Nova Scotia. When the remaining provinces joined Confederation they either retained their existing legislative machinery (Prince Edward Island, British Columbia, and Newfoundland) or were provided with legislatures by the enacting statutes (Manitoba, Alberta, and Saskatchewan).

Section 69 establishes a unicameral legislature for Ontario, the only one in 1867 Canada. In John A. Macdonald's view, "for a subordinate Legislature acting under authority of a general government, having in fact the character of a municipal body, one chamber had been considered sufficient."[49] Quebec was given a bicameral legislature in 1867; Nova Scotia and New Brunswick, as well as the new provinces of Prince Edward Island and Manitoba, had bicameral legislatures at the time of union. All five provinces have since abolished their upper houses: Manitoba in 1876, New Brunswick in 1891 (effective in 1893), Prince Edward Island in 1893, Nova Scotia in 1928, and Quebec in 1968.[50]

➤ **SECTION 70:** The Legislative Assembly of Ontario shall be composed of Eighty-two Members, to be elected to represent the Eighty-two Electoral Districts set forth in the First Schedule to this Act.

This section is now spent, with representation provided by provincial legislation.

2. Quebec

➤ **SECTION 71:** There shall be a Legislature for Quebec consisting of the Lieutenant Governor and of Two Houses, styled the Legislative Council of Quebec and the Legislative Assembly of Quebec.

In 1867 a bicameral legislature was viewed as an additional safeguard against the Federal government. The Bertrand government abolished Quebec's upper house at the end of 1968. At the same time, and consistent with the nationalistic fervour of the 1960s Quiet Revolution, it renamed its legislature the National Assembly.

In view of the move to a unicameral legislature this section as well as sections 72-79 are now spent.

➤ **SECTION 72:** The Legislative Council of Quebec shall be composed of Twenty-four Members, to be appointed by the Lieutenant Governor, in the Queen's Name, by Instrument under the Great Seal of Quebec, One being appointed to represent each of the Twenty-four Electoral Divisions of Lower Canada in this Act referred to, and each holding Office for the Term of his Life, unless the Legislature of Quebec otherwise provides under the Provisions of this Act.

In view of the 1968 abolition of the Legislative Council this section is now spent. The twenty-four divisions referred to are the same as those established for Quebec's representation in the Senate (section 22). The reason for the divisions was to ensure representation by the English-speaking minority.

➤ **SECTION 73:** The Qualifications of the Legislative Councillors of Quebec shall be the same as those of the Senators for Quebec.

In view of the 1968 abolition of the Legislative Council this section is now spent. Qualifications were identical to those specified for Quebec senators in section 23.

➤ **SECTION 74:** The Place of a Legislative Councillor of Quebec shall become vacant in the Cases, *mutatis mutandis*, in which the Place of Senator becomes vacant.

In view of the 1968 abolition of the Legislative Council this section is now spent. Disqualifications were patterned upon those for senators in section 31.

➤ **Section 75:** When a Vacancy happens in the Legislative Council of Quebec by Resignation, Death, or otherwise, the Lieutenant Governor, in the Queen's Name, by Instrument under the Great Seal of Quebec, shall appoint a fit and qualified Person to fill the Vacancy.

In view of the 1968 abolition of the Legislative Council this section is now spent.

➤ **Section 76:** If any Question arises respecting the Qualification of a Legislative Councillor of Quebec, or a Vacancy in the Legislative Council of Quebec, the same shall be heard and determined by the Legislative Council.

In view of the 1968 abolition of the Legislative Council this section is now spent. Note that, as for the Senate (section 33), the Council itself would decide questions related to qualification in individual cases.

➤ **Section 77:** The Lieutenant Governor may from Time to Time, by Instrument under the Great Seal of Quebec, appoint a Member of the Legislative Council of Quebec to be Speaker thereof, and may remove him and appoint another in his Stead.

In view of the 1968 abolition of the Legislative Council this section is now spent. It is analogous to section 34 which pertains to the Speaker of the Senate.

➤ **Section 78:** Until the Legislature of Quebec otherwise provides, the Presence of at least Ten Members of the Legislative Council, including the Speaker, shall be necessary to constitute a Meeting for the Exercise of its Powers.

In view of the 1968 abolition of the Legislative Council this section is now spent.

➤ **Section 79:** Questions arising in the Legislative Council of Quebec shall be decided by a Majority of Voices, and the Speaker shall in all Cases have a Vote, and when the Voices are equal the Decision shall be deemed to be in the Negative.

In view of the 1968 abolition of the Legislative Council this section is now spent. It is analogous to section 36 which pertains to the Senate.

➤ **Section 80:** The Legislative Assembly of Quebec shall be composed of Sixty-five Members, to be elected to represent the Sixty-five Electoral Divisions or Districts of Lower Canada in this Act referred to, subject to Alteration thereof by the Legislature of Quebec: Provided that it shall not be lawful to present to the Lieutenant Governor of Quebec for Assent any Bill for altering the Limits of any of the Electoral Divisions or Districts mentioned in the Second Schedule to this Act, unless the Second and Third Readings of such Bill have been passed in the Legislative Assembly with the Concurrence of the Majority of the Members representing all those Electoral Divisions or Districts, and the Assent shall not be given to such Bill unless an Address has been presented by the Legislative Assembly to the Lieutenant Governor stating that it has been so passed.

This section is spent, representation in the National Assembly now being governed by provincial legislation. The Second Schedule contains the names of eleven counties and one town, all in the Eastern Townships which at the time of Confederation had predominantly English-speaking populations. The intent was to guarantee representation for the English-speaking minority.

3. Ontario and Quebec

➤ **SECTION 81:** The Legislatures of Ontario and Quebec respectively shall be called together not later than Six Months after the Union.

This section was an interim measure and repealed by Britain's Statute Law Revision Act, 1893.

➤ **SECTION 82:** The Lieutenant Governor of Ontario and of Quebec shall from Time to Time, in the Queen's Name, by Instrument under the Great Seal of the Province, summon and call together the Legislative Assembly of the Province.

Lieutenant governors summon their provincial assemblies upon the advice of their first ministers.

➤ **SECTION 83:** Until the Legislature of Ontario or of Quebec otherwise provides, a Person accepting or holding in Ontario or in Quebec any Office, Commission, or Employment, permanent or temporary, at the Nomination of the Lieutenant Governor, to which an annual Salary, or any Fee, Allowance, Emolument, or Profit of any Kind or Amount whatever from the Province is attached, shall not be eligible as a Member of the Legislative Assembly of the respective Province, nor shall he sit or vote as such; but nothing in this Section shall make ineligible any Person being a member of the Executive Council of the respective Province, or holding any of the following Offices, that is to say, the Offices of Attorney General, Secretary and Registrar of the Province, Treasurer of the Province, Commissioner of Crown Lands, and Commissioner of Agriculture and Public Works, and in Quebec Solicitor General, or shall disqualify him to sit or vote in the House for which he is elected, provided he is elected while holding such Office.

Although the subject matter of this section is now covered by provincial legislation, the restrictions on Crown employees were analogous to those which created Prime Minister Meighen's problems when Meighen assumed office in 1926 during the King-Byng constitutional crisis. Members of the ministry had to resign their assembly seats upon their appointment to the ministry, and to seek re-election while holding office.

➤ **SECTION 84:** Until the Legislatures of Ontario and Quebec respectively otherwise provide, all Laws which at the Union are in force in those Provinces respectively, relative to the following Matters, or any of them, namely,—the Qualifications and Disqualifications of Persons to be elected or to sit or vote as Members of the Assembly of Canada, the Qualifications or Disqualifications of Voters, the Oaths to be taken by Voters, the Returning Officers, their Powers and Duties, the Proceedings at Elections, the Periods during which such Elections may be continued, and the Trial of controverted Elections and the Proceedings incident thereto, the vacating of the Seats of Members and the issuing and execution of new Writs in case of Seats vacated otherwise than by Dissolution,—shall respectively apply to Elections of Members to serve in the respective Legislative Assemblies of Ontario and Quebec.

Provided that, until the Legislature of Ontario otherwise provides, at any Election for a Member of the Legislative Assembly of Ontario for the District of Algoma, in addition to Persons qualified by the Law of the Province of Canada to vote, every male British Subject, aged Twenty-one Years or upwards, being a Householder, shall have a vote.

This section providing for the continuation of the election laws of the pre-Confederation Province of Canada has been superseded by provincial legislation. The District of Algoma was not part of pre-Confederation Canada but was added to Ontario in 1867.

➤ **SECTION 85:** Every Legislative Assembly of Ontario and every Legislative Assembly of Quebec shall continue for Four Years from the Day of the Return of the Writs for choosing the same (subject nevertheless to either the Legislative Assembly of Ontario or the Legislative Assembly of Quebec being sooner dissolved by the Lieutenant Governor of the Province), and no longer.

Both Ontario and Quebec enacted legislation to lengthen the maximum duration from four years to five years. All other provinces except Newfoundland have done so as well.[51] Section 4 of the 1982 Constitution Act specifies a five-year maximum for all provinces, subject to extension (if two-thirds of the assembly approve) "in time of real or apprehended war, invasion or insurrection." As for Parliament the period is counted from the day the election writs are returned.

➤ **SECTION 86:** There shall be a Session of the Legislature of Ontario and of that of Quebec once at least in every Year, so that Twelve Months shall not intervene between the last Sitting of the Legislature in each Province in one Session and its first Sitting in the next Session.

Section 5 of the 1982 Constitution Act generalizes this requirement for all provinces and includes Parliament as well. As an interesting footnote the comparable provision in the present Act (section 20) which governed Parliament, as well as one in the Manitoba Act governing that province, were repealed by the 1982 Act; the present section was not. (See items 1 and 2 in the Schedule to the 1982 Act.)

➤ **SECTION 87:** The following Provisions of this Act respecting the House of Commons of Canada shall extend and apply to the Legislative Assemblies of Ontario and Quebec, that is to say,—the Provisions relating to the Election of a Speaker originally and on Vacancies, the Duties of the Speaker, the Absence of the Speaker, the Quorum, and the Mode of voting, as if those Provisions were here re-enacted and made applicable in Terms to each such Legislative Assembly.

This section requires no comment. See sections 44-49 for the provisions applicable to the House of Commons.

4. Nova Scotia and New Brunswick

➤ **SECTION 88:** The Constitution of the Legislature of each of the Provinces of Nova Scotia and New Brunswick shall, subject to the Provisions of this Act, continue as it exists at the Union until altered under the Authority of this Act.

A transitional final part of this section repealed by Britain's 1893 Statute Law Revision Act read as follows:

> and the House of Assembly of New Brunswick existing at the passing of this Act shall, unless sooner dissolved, continue for the Period for which it was elected.

The situation existing in Nova Scotia at the time of Confederation was covered by section 89.

5. Ontario, Quebec, and Nova Scotia

➤ **SECTION 89:** Each of the Lieutenant Governors of Ontario, Quebec and Nova Scotia shall cause Writs to be issued for the First Election of Members of the Legislative Assembly thereof in such Form and by such Person as he thinks fit, and at such Time and addressed to such Returning Officer as the Governor General directs, and so that the First Election of Members of Assembly for any Electoral District or any Subdivision thereof shall be held at the same Time and at the same Places as the Election for a Member to serve in the House of Commons of Canada for the Electoral District.

This transitional section was repealed by Britain's 1893 Statute Law Revision Act.

6. The Four Provinces

➤ **SECTION 90:** The following Provisions of this Act respecting the Parliament of Canada, namely,—the Provisions relating to Appropriation and Tax Bills, the Recommendation of Money Votes, the Assent to Bills, the Disallowance of Acts, and the Signification of Pleasure on Bills reserved,—shall extend and apply to the Legislatures of the several

> Provinces as if those Provisions were here re-enacted and made applicable in Terms to the respective Provinces and the Legislatures thereof, with the Substitution of the Lieutenant Governor of the Province for the Governor General, of the Governor General for the Queen and for a Secretary of State, of One Year for Two Years, and of the Province for Canada.

This section extends the application of sections 53-57 of the present Act to the provinces. Reference to "appropriation and tax bills" in section 53, requiring money bills to be initiated in the lower house, is no longer relevant for the provinces because they all have unicameral legislatures.

Of much greater significance is the fact that section 90 converts the relationship between the Government of Canada and that of Britain (as stated in sections 55-57) to a relationship between the provincial governments and the Government of Canada. Specifically, this section authorizes lieutenant governors to assent to bills passed by provincial legislatures, to withhold their assent, or to reserve bills for the pleasure of the governor general—in effect, of the Federal cabinet. Furthermore, the Federal cabinet may disallow any provincial bill. The time limit for Ottawa to act on a reserved bill, or to disallow a bill which has been passed by the provincial legislature, is one year.

Sections 55-57, as modified by section 90, read as follows:

> 55. Where a Bill passed by the House or Houses of the Legislature [of a Province] is presented to the Lieutenant-Governor of the Province for the Governor General's Assent, he shall declare, according to his Discretion, but subject to the Provisions of this Act and to the Governor General's Instructions, either that he assents thereto in the Governor General's Name, or that he withholds the Governor General's Assent, or that he reserves the Bill for the Signification of the Governor General's Pleasure.
>
> 56. Where the Lieutenant Governor of the Province assents to a Bill in the Governor General's Name, he shall by the first convenient opportunity send an authentic Copy of the Act to the Governor General, and if the Governor General in Council within One Year after Receipt thereof by the Governor General thinks fit to disallow the Act, such Disallowance (with a Certificate of the Governor General of the Day on which the Act was received by him) being signified by the Lieutenant-Governor, by Speech or Message to the House, or, if more than one, to each of the Houses of the Legislature, or by Proclamation, shall annul the Act from and after the Day of such Signification.
>
> 57. A Bill reserved for the Signification of the Governor General's Pleasure shall not have any Force unless and until within One Year from the Day on which it was presented to the Lieutenant-Governor for the Governor General's assent, the Lieutenant-Governor signifies by Speech or Message to the House, or, if more than one, to each of the Houses of the Legislature or by Proclamation, that it has received the Assent of the

Governor General in Council.

An Entry of every such Speech, Message, or Proclamation shall be made in the Journal of the House or of each House, if more than one, and a Duplicate thereof duly attested shall be delivered to the proper Officer to be kept among the Records of the Province.[52]

It was primarily these powers of refusal of assent, reservation, and disallowance, which prompted K.C. Wheare to call our "C"onstitution (i.e., the 1867 Constitution Act) "quasi-federal" although he acknowledged that the federal principle as he defined it was indeed fully operational in terms of our "c"onstitution (in the broad sense). According to Wheare's federal principle, "the general and regional governments are each, within a sphere, co-ordinate and independent."[53] By the 1940s, when Wheare gave his blessing to our constitution as a true example of federalism in action, these essentially unitary features had all but fallen into disuse. This is not the place to discuss the many ways in which the two orders of government interact, but the discussion of federalism as a constitutional principle in Chapter 4 acknowledges the absence of watertight compartments.

Since Confederation, lieutenant governors have refused assent to about 27 bills; only two refusals have occurred since 1924 (actually, in 1945).[54] Provincial bills have been disallowed 112 times, none of them since 1943. All of the last 12 disallowances occurred against Alberta legislation and, of these, 11 were against Social Credit bills.[55] Lieutenant governors have reserved 70 bills—59 before 1900 and 4 since 1920. The last reservation occurred in 1961 and involved Saskatchewan legislation. Of the 70, assent was subsequently given to 14.[56]

In 1882 John A. Macdonald instructed lieutenant governors through a minute-in-council to exercise their power of reservation only upon instructions from Ottawa: "It is only in a case of extreme necessity that a Lieutenant-Governor should without such instructions exercise his discretion as a Dominion Officer in reserving a bill. In fact, with the facility of communication between the Dominion and provincial governments, such a necessity can seldom if ever arise."[57] Nevertheless, only eight of the reservations have resulted from Federal instructions.[58] Thus, when in 1961 Saskatchewan's Lieutenant Governor Bastedo reserved Bill 56 entirely on his own initiative and without prior consultation with Ottawa, an angry Prime Minister Diefenbaker erred when he announced that "the reservation by lieutenant governors have [sic] been generally accepted as dependent on a request from the governor in council."[59]

The legality of the powers of refusal of assent, reservation, and disallowance remains intact. This position was upheld by the Supreme Court in the 1938 *Power of Reservation and Power of Disallowance Reference,* and again in the 1981 *Patriation Reference.*[60] Nevertheless, as the Court declared in 1981, these powers "have, to all intents and purposes, fallen into disuse." Indeed, it is surprising that they were not abolished at the time the 1982 Constitution

Act was created. Abolition of disallowance and reservation had been part of the 1971 Victoria Charter and was proposed by Prime Minister Trudeau in the 1978 Constitutional Amendment Bill (Bill C-60). Mallory comments that the powers of reservation and refusal of assent "are prone to unskillful and inappropriate use by Lieutenant-Governors who, as a class, are not likely to be versed in constitutional law or rich in political experience." As a result, he continues, and except for the reservation of three Alberta bills in 1937, the issues that have provoked reservation and refusal of assent since the mid-1930s "are almost frivolous and acutely embarrassing to the federal government."[61]

VI. Distribution of Legislative Powers

Powers of the Parliament

➤ **SECTION 91 (OPENING PARAGRAPH):** It shall be lawful for the Queen, by and with the Advice and Consent of the Senate and House of Commons, to make Laws for the Peace, Order, and good Government of Canada, in relation to all Matters not coming within the Classes of Subjects by this Act assigned exclusively to the Legislatures of the Provinces; and for greater Certainty, but not so as to restrict the Generality of the foregoing Terms of this Section, it is hereby declared that (notwithstanding anything in this Act) the exclusive Legislative Authority of the Parliament of Canada extends to all Matters coming within the Classes of Subjects next hereinafter enumerated; that is to say,—

This paragraph authorizes Parliament to legislate for the "peace, order, and good government of Canada" (p.o.g.g.) in matters not assigned to the provinces. The phrase "p.o.g.g." is best understood as one broad delegation rather than as a delegation to be interpreted word for word. It was commonly used by Britain in colonial constitutions including the Quebec Act, Constitutional Act, and Union Act, where it was phrased as "peace, welfare, and good government." The 1871 Constitution Act authorized Parliament to legislate for the peace, order, and good government of lands within Parliament's jurisdiction. The judicial history of p.o.g.g. has been thoroughly discussed in numerous publications, and is considered as part of the "Judicial Decisions" component of our constitution in Chapter 5.

This opening paragraph goes on to state that the following enumeration is intended "for greater certainty, but not so as to restrict the generality" of the residual p.o.g.g. power. This does not mean that the enumeration is excess baggage adding nothing to Parliament's authority—that it is merely illustrative of p.o.g.g. Although there has been dispute in this matter it seems that were it not for the enumeration, the breadth of "property and civil rights in the province" (s. 92[13]) would have led the courts to assign to the provinces trade and commerce (91[2]), banking (91[15]), bills of exchange and promissory notes (91[18]), interest (91[19]), bankruptcy and insolvency (91[21]), patents of invention and discovery (91[22]), copyrights (91[23]), and marriage and divorce (91[26]).[62] Unemployment insurance (91[2A]) was added to the enumeration in 1940 precisely because it had been deemed to be part of property and civil rights. From this point of view p.o.g.g. is a residual power only after the section 91 enumeration as well as provincial powers have been acknowledged.

Under what circumstances has p.o.g.g. been applied as a residual power—that is, when the courts have not used one of the enumerated heads of section 91?[63] Three broad areas may be noted: when there is a "gap" in the distribution of powers between the two orders of government, when a matter is of "national concern," and when there is an "emergency." Each of these areas is considered below.

A "Gap" in the Distribution of Powers[64]

P.o.g.g. has been used when the subject matter has been deemed not to fall within one of the enumerated classes of subjects (heads of power). As noted in Chapter 5 the broad interpretation of "property and civil rights" has narrowed p.o.g.g.'s potential application. This use of p.o.g.g. is illustrated by the following cases.

Citizens Insurance Co. v. Parsons (1881). The Privy Council stated that Parliament could incorporate companies except those "with provincial objects" which fall within provincial jurisdiction under section 92(11).

Radio Reference (1932). The Privy Council upheld Parliament's authority to legislate for the implementation of Canadian (as distinct from British Empire) treaties. The "gap" in the distribution of legislative power between Parliament and provincial legislatures resulted from section 132's application only to treaties affecting Canada as part of the Empire. However, the existence of the gap was denied by the Privy Council five years later in the *Labour Conventions Reference.*

Newfoundland Continental Shelf Reference (1984). The Supreme Court held that because the Continental Shelf lies beyond Newfoundland's boundary it does not come within section 92. Legislative jurisdiction belongs, therefore, to Parliament under p.o.g.g. The same reasoning applied to the *Offshore Mineral Rights of B.C. Reference* (1967), although the ruling mentioned the "national concern" rationale (below) as well.

"National Concern"[65]

The concept of "national concern" was first stated in the *Canada Temperance Federation* (1946) case. Some definition of "national concern" is obviously needed because many issues are of concern to the entire country, including some such as education which clearly fall within provincial jurisdiction. Concern becomes truly national when the failure of one province to act, such as to control an epidemic disease or marine pollution, will endanger the health or safety of people living beyond that province's borders. This use of p.o.g.g. is illustrated by the following cases.

Johannesson v. West St. Paul (1952). The Supreme Court ruled that provincial governments—in this case the Manitoba government—could not regulate the location of aerodromes.

Munro v. National Capital Commission (1966). The Supreme Court upheld authority granted to the National Capital Commission by the National Capital Act to expropriate lands for the purpose of "the development, conservation and improvement of the National Capital Region in order that the nature and character of the seat of the Government of Canada may be in accordance with its national significance" (ss. 10, 13).

Crown Zellerbach Canada Limited (1988). The Supreme Court upheld Federal legislation regulating the dumping of any substance "at sea" (defined to include Canadian inland waters other than fresh waters)—in this case, within British Columbia. Ocean pollution was deemed to be of national concern.

"Emergency"

The "emergency" doctrine is considered in Chapter 5 under "Judicial Decisions."

There is another point which needs comment. Apart from non-renewable resources (92A), old age pensions (94A), and agriculture and immigration (95), the Constitution Act does not explicitly address the general issue of paramountcy when a conflict exists between otherwise-valid Federal and provincial laws. Conflicts have in fact been resolved through the doctrine of Federal paramountcy which is considered in the commentary on the closing paragraph of this section.

In addition to the legislative authority conferred by section 91, several other sections of the Constitution Act as well as other Acts assign legislative authority to Parliament:

- **(1)** 1867 Constitution Act: sections 92(10), 92A(3), 93(4), 94 (with provincial consent), 94A (although provincial laws have paramountcy), 95, 101, 132.
- **(2)** 1871 Constitution Act: sections 2-4, 6. These sections authorize Paliament to
  - **(a)** establish new provinces from lands within its jurisdiction;
  - **(b)** provide for, but not subsequently to alter, constitutions for such newly created provinces;
  - **(c)** alter provincial boundaries (with provincial consent);
  - **(d)** legislate for the "administration, peace, order, and good government" of lands within its jurisdiction (and thus not within provinces).

The establishment of new provinces from, and the extension of existing provinces into, territories under Parliament's jurisdiction can now be accomplished only by use of the general amending formula which is section 38 of the 1982 Constitution Act. See section 42 of that Act.

(3) 1886 Constitution Act: section 1. Parliament may provide for representation, in the Senate and/or House of Commons, of any territory under its jurisdiction.

(4) 1931 Statute of Westminster: section 3. Parliament is given the power of extraterritoriality.

(5) 1982 Constitution Act:

- **(a)** Constitutional amendments proposed under sections 38, 41, 42, and 43, may not be proclaimed unless they have been approved by Parliament.
- **(b)** Constitutional amendments under section 44 may be made by Parliament acting unilaterally.

➤ **SECTION 91(1):** The amendment from time to time of the Constitution of Canada, except as regards matters coming within the classes of subjects by this Act assigned exclusively to the Legislatures of the provinces, or as regards rights or privileges by this or any other Constitutional Act granted or secured to the Legislature or the Government of a province, or to any class of persons with respect to schools or as regards the use of the English or the French language or as regards the requirements that there shall be a session of the Parliament of Canada at least once each year, and that no House of Commons shall continue for more than five years from the day of the return of the Writs for choosing the House: provided, however, that a House of Commons may in time of real or apprehended war, invasion or insurrection be continued by the Parliament of Canada if such continuation is not opposed by the votes of more than one-third of the members of such House.

This subsection, added by the 1949 B.N.A. (No. 2) Act, was repealed by the 1982 Constitution Act, and its substance was re-enacted in sections 4(2) and 44 of the 1982 Act. Section 91(1) granted to Parliament an amending power analogous to that of the provinces in section 92(1). The explicit exclusions from Parliament's authority are sections 92, 93, 133, 20, and (although an escape provision was included) 50. This section 91(1) was added at the initiative of the St. Laurent Government (without prior consultation with the provinces) immediately before the 1950 Constitutional Conference. Because that Conference was to seek an amending formula St. Laurent's move was no doubt part of a bargaining strategy with the provinces.

Five amendments were made pursuant to this section before 1982, and by mid-1991 one amendment had been made under section 44 of the 1982

Constitution Act. These six, as well as questions concerning possible Senate amendment, are identified in Chapter 5 under "1867 Constitution Act Amendment by the Federal Parliament."

➤ **SECTION 91(1A):** The Public Debt and Property.

The "public debt" in 1867 included the financial obligations assumed by the Federal government at the time of Confederation, such as the salaries of the governor general (s. 105), judges appointed by Ottawa (s. 100), lieutenant governors (s. 60), and public servants (s. 106). It also included the financial obligations assumed in relation to the provinces under sections 104, 111, 116, 118, and 119. Since Confederation, Ottawa has borrowed heavily for many purposes, one of the more significant being the financing of World War Two. Not only may the Federal government legislate to incur debt; it also has the responsibility to legislate for the purpose of controlling that debt.

"Property" includes conventional types such as public works, including works transferred from the provinces at Confederation under section 108, and also (and of much greater significance in terms of Canadian federalism) money raised by taxation. It is the disposition of these moneys, Parliament's "spending power," which has been controversial. The Federal government claims the right to dispose of its property, including its money, as it sees fit. Opponents of this view say that by offering the provinces money for areas within provincial jurisdiction, and especially by attaching conditions to the gifts, Ottawa is able to accomplish indirectly what it legally is prevented from doing directly through legislation. In this way, say the critics, the federal balance is altered. Perhaps the best articulated opposition to conditional grants is the 1956 Report of Quebec's Royal Commission of Inquiry on Constitutional Problems (the Tremblay Report). Commissioner Tremblay expressed vigorous opposition to what he called the "New Federalism"—the centralization created by the Federal government's presumed spending power coupled with its broad power to tax (s. 91[3]) and its residual p.o.g.g. authority.[66]

Arguments in opposition to the spending power notwithstanding, the exercise of this power has gone unchallenged in the courts. The Supreme Court has ruled, nevertheless, that "while Parliament may be free to offer grants subject to whatever restrictions it sees fit, the decision to make a grant of money in any particular area should not be construed as an intention to regulate all related aspects of that area." A recent case was *YMHA Jewish Community Centre of Winnipeg v. Brown* (1989), in which the Court ruled that the Federal grant to YMHA did not remove the jurisdiction of provincial labour law over the job-creation project.[67]

The spending power is unrestrained so long as the financing of the grants is from the Consolidated Revenue Fund rather than from a separate tax levied for the purpose, and so long as Parliament does not attempt to make compliance with conditions attached to such grants mandatory. Non-compliance may, of course, lead to the withdrawal of these grants. A recent illustration is Ottawa's withholding medicare grants under the Canada Health Act from provinces which permitted medical doctors to extra-bill their patients in violation of conditions laid down in the Federal legislation. A direct tax levied by Parliament explicitly for some "provincial purpose" would conflict with the provinces' exclusive authority (s. 92[2]) to do so.

Unconditional grants by Ottawa to the provinces have existed since Confederation. See especially sections 111, 116, 118, and 119, for those required by the 1867 Constitution Act. Conditional grants have been part of Federal-provincial financial relations since 1912, but have been of major significance since World War Two.

This subsection was originally number (1), but was renumbered (1A) when the new number (1) was added by the 1949 B.N.A. (No. 2) Act.

➤ **SECTION 91(2):** The Regulation of Trade and Commerce.

This topic has been the subject of much litigation, the courts having to adjudicate between the Federal power and provincial jurisdiction over "property and civil rights" (s. 92[13]). There is no doubt that were the phrase "trade and commerce" to be interpreted literally and as broadly as it suggests there would be little room for the provinces. In fact the courts have restricted Parliament's jurisdiction essentially to interprovincial and international trade and commerce, leaving intraprovincial trade for provincial legislation. This broadly expressed trade power may be compared with the much narrower expression of authority assigned by the United States Constitution to the central government "to regulate commerce with foreign nations, and among the several states." Whereas Ottawa's authority has been severely constrained by the courts notwithstanding the broad terminology, Washington's jurisdiction has been broadened notwithstanding the much narrower wording. It is as though the wordings of the two constitutional statements had been interchanged.

Consideration of judicial interpretation of our trade and commerce power begins with the Privy Council ruling in *Citizens Insurance Company v. Parsons* (1881).[68] While acknowledging that a literal rendering of the power could include "every regulation of trade ranging from political arrangements in regard to trade with foreign governments, requiring the sanction of parliament, down to minute rules for regulating particular trades," the Privy Council concluded that such was not the intent of the Act's framers. Had it been otherwise, the Privy Council added, there would have been no need to specify in section 91 certain other Federal powers such as banking (15), weights and measures (17), bills of exchange and promissory notes (18), interest (19), and banking and bankruptcy (21). The Privy Council's conclusion was that trade and commerce encompasses "political arrangements in regard to trade requiring the sanction of parliament, regulation of trade in matters of interprovincial concern, and it *may* be that they would include general regulation of trade affecting the whole dominion" (emphasis added). The power would not extend to the regulation of intraprovincial trade (such as fire insurance contracts—the case then before the Privy Council) which belongs to the provinces. The important determination in individual cases is the point at which intraprovincial regulation becomes (1) interprovincial or international regulation, or (2) sufficiently "general" to be caught by section 91(2). (International trade has not presented a significant problem.) The rest of this commentary is a consideration of these two possibilities.

When does trade and commerce become "interprovincial"? Before 1949 when the Privy Council was the final decision-maker for Canadian cases, this power was interpreted narrowly. Essentially, the Privy Council denied Parliament the authority to legislate the control of a particular trade, even when that trade contained a significant interprovincial component, "in which Canadians would otherwise be free to engage in the provinces."[69] When the Supreme Court in 1925 struck down a Federal attempt to regulate the grain trade (*Eastern Terminal Elevator Co.*)[70] on the grounds that the regulation of grain elevators (which was only part of a broader regulation scheme) infringed provincial jurisdiction over "local works" (s. 92[10]), Parliament invoked the declaratory power. See the commentary on section 92(10)(c). In effect, "trade and commerce" had become only an ancillary to some other Federal power.

Although the trade and commerce power has (in Chief Justice Dickson's words) "enjoyed an enhanced importance"[71] since 1949, there seems to be no clear trend as to what is "interprovincial."[72]

When does trade and commerce become "general"? (This is sometimes referred to as the "second branch" of the trade and commerce power.) This criterion is even more vague than that for describing trade as interprovincial, and so little may be said that is conclusive. In 1983 Justice Dickson reviewed previous litigation. He noted that despite affirmations by individual judges of the existence of a second branch, only twice (in 1915 and 1937) had this interpretation been applied by a final appellate court. He added that "the correctness of even these decisions has been widely doubted," and that with those two exceptions "the potential applicability of the general . . . power has been considered and rejected in a string of final appellate court decisions" from 1916 to 1980.[73]

Following a tentative statement of the second branch in *Parsons* (1881) the Privy Council moved in 1915 (*John Deere Plow v. Wharton*) to a broad approach: "if it be established that the Dominion Parliament can create such [Federally-incorporated] companies, then it becomes a question of general interest throughout the Dominion in what fashion they should be permitted to trade." At the other extreme was the *Board of Commerce* (1922) decision (which did not distinguish between the "interprovincial" and "general" criteria) that trade and commerce was only an ancillary power. In Dickson's view the correct interpretation, the true balance between the competing "trade and commerce" and "property and civil rights" powers, lay between these two extremes.[74]

In 1977 Chief Justice Laskin listed three criteria to be satisfied before the second branch would uphold impugned Federal legislation: (1) the legislation must be part of a general regulatory scheme, (2) the scheme must be monitored by a Federal regulatory agency, and (3) the legislation must be concerned with trade generally rather than with a particular industry.[75] Chief Justice Dickson (for a unanimous court) added two more in 1989: (4) the legislation should be beyond provincial power to enact, and (5) the failure to include one or more provinces in the scheme would jeopardize the scheme nationally. Quoting from an earlier ruling he continued:

> The above does not purport to be an exhaustive list, nor is the presence of any or all of these *indicia* necessarily decisive. The proper approach to the characterization is still the one suggested in *Parsons*, a careful case by case assessment. Nevertheless, the presence of such factors does at least make it far more probable that what is being addressed in a federal enactment is genuinely a national economic concern and not just a collection of local ones.[76]

The 1989 case (*General Motors of Canada v. City National Leasing*) upheld the constitutionality of a section of the Combines Investigation Act. That section permitted an individual to sue for recovery if he or she had suffered loss or damages resulting from price discrimination or pricing designed to lessen or eliminate competition. The Combines Investigation Act had already been upheld as criminal law under section 91(27), but with the expansion of the powers of the Restrictive Trade Practices Commission in the mid-1970s, including provision for civil action, the development of a "double aspect" was important. In this instance both aspects pertained to Federal power—criminal law and the general trade and commerce power.

➤ **SECTION 91(2A):** Unemployment insurance.

In 1935 the Bennett Government passed several statutes known collectively as the Bennett New Deal. Among these was the Employment and Social Insurance Act. The Liberal opposition won the ensuing 1935 election and, believing the New Deal legislation to be unconstitutional, asked the Supreme Court for an advisory opinion. That Court in 1936, and the Privy Council the following year, declared much of the legislation (including the Employment and Social Insurance Act)[77] *ultra vires* Parliament, on the grounds that it transgressed provincial property and civil rights authority.

With the consent of all of the provinces, and in response to a recommendation of the Royal Commission on Dominion-Provincial Relations (the Rowell-Sirois Commission), Parliament subsequently requested and Britain enacted the 1940 Constitution Act which transferred unemployment insurance jurisdiction to Parliament.

➤ **SECTION 91(3):** The raising of Money by any Mode or System of Taxation.

This subsection is part of the overall 1867 financial settlement between Ottawa and the provinces. In 1867 Ottawa was assigned the major and (at the time) more costly functions. Consequently, the distribution of taxing powers favoured the Federal government. Parliament is authorized by this provision to impose both "direct" and "indirect" taxes. Although there is more than one way to distinguish between direct and indirect taxation it is John Stuart Mill's approach which the Privy Council in 1887 adopted for the Constitution Act. According to Mill:

> Taxes are either direct or indirect. A direct tax is one which is demanded from the very persons who, it is intended or desired, should pay it. Indirect taxes are those which are demanded from one person in the expectation and intention that he shall indemnify himself at the expense of another; such as the excise or customs. The producer or importer of a commodity is called upon to pay a tax on it, not with the intention to levy a peculiar contribution upon him, but to tax through him the consumers of the commodity, from whom it is supposed that he will recover the amount by means of an advance in price.[78]

Speaking for the Privy Council, Lord Hobhouse added that this definition "seems . . . to embody with sufficient accuracy for this purpose an understanding of the most obvious indicia of direct and indirect taxation, which is a common understanding, and is likely to have been present to the minds of those who passed the Federation [Constitution] Act."[79] An income tax, for example, is a direct tax. A sales tax imposed upon the ultimate consumer is also a direct tax even if it is collected by the seller; however, a tax imposed on the seller is an indirect tax because its burden will be shifted to the consumer. In spite of what appears to be a clear distinction, judicial interpretation of specific tax laws has been necessary over the years. In one sense, of course, all taxes (whether direct or indirect) levied upon businesses will be passed on, inasmuch as prices charged for goods and services must recover all costs of production if businesses are to survive.

Except for section 92A, the provinces are restricted (s. 92[2]) to direct taxation. Before Confederation the provinces collectively had gained more than 80% of their revenues from indirect taxes, primarily customs duties (taxes on the importation of goods) and excise taxes (taxes on the manufacture or distribution of goods).

Parliament entered the direct tax field relatively late, a fact which has periodically led to the erroneous claim by some provincial politicians that the provinces have exclusive authority over direct taxation. In 1916 Parliament instituted a war profits tax and in 1917 an income tax, both intended as temporary wartime expedients. Subsequent litigation led the Privy Council in 1924 to delcare (*Caron v. R.*) that "there is nothing in s. 92 to take away the power to impose any taxation for Dominion purposes which is prima facie given by head 3 of s. 91. It is not therefore ultra vires on the part of the Parliament of Canada to impose a Dominon income tax for Dominion purposes."[80] Federal succession duties did not emerge until 1941. Although Ottawa has abandoned the latter tax, Federal income tax remains very much with us. On January 1, 1991, a Federal Goods and Services direct sales tax was introduced, and within three months a challenge was under way in the Alberta courts by the provinces of Alberta, British Columbia and Ontario. The bases of the challenge were sections 92(3) and 92(13).

Understandably, some of the provinces levied direct taxes soon after Confederation. British Columbia introduced property and personal income taxes in 1876, and Prince Edward Island in 1894. In 1892 Ontario became the first province to impose succession duties. Quebec established a corporation tax in 1882. Gasoline taxes arrived in the 1920s.

Although the Parliament is precluded from levying direct taxes for provincial purposes, it must be acknowledged that there is in fact no distinction between direct and indirect tax revenue in the Consolidated Revenue Fund. This plus the fact that Ottawa transfers large sums of money to the provinces both conditionally and unconditionally means that there is much *de facto* direct Federal taxation for provincial purposes.

All governments are precluded (s. 125) from taxing "lands or property belonging to Canada or any province" and (s. 121) from imposing interprovincial customs duties.

The relationship between section 125's prohibition, and the Federal government's authority to tax (s. 91[3]) and to regulate trade and commerce (s. 91[2]), was the subject of the 1982 *Exported Natural Gas Tax Reference*.[81] The Supreme Court was asked whether a proposed Federal tax on natural gas owned by the Province of Alberta was constitutional. At issue were the three sections just noted. Was the tax intended to raise revenue? To regulate trade and commerce? Both? The Court majority held that, within the context of Ottawa's 1980 National Energy Program and its budget, the proposed tax was clearly intended to raise revenue rather than to regulate. But it was not an export tax because it applied to all gas "and only incidentally reaches exports." The Federal government had argued that as an export tax it was in the nature of a customs duty, and therefore not a tax on lands or property within the context of section 125. Rather, the Court ruled, it was a tax under section 91(3), subject to section 125, and therefore unconstitutional.

The Court added that "while s. 125 restricts the federal taxing power, it does not limit the exercise of other heads of power found in s. 91. Thus, federal legislation in the form of taxation may yet be binding on a province if it is primarily enacted under a head of power other than s. 91(3)" including, presumably, trade and commerce. This case illustrates the aspect doctrine with a twist. This doctrine has generally been important only to determine which order of government has authority in a particular matter. Here it was important to distinguish between two heads of Federal power within section 91. The reason was that section 125 limited taxation but not trade and commerce.

➤ **SECTION 91(4):** The borrowing of Money on the Public Credit.

Governments borrow money when their expenditures exceed their revenues. Governments are also expected to use the tools of fiscal and monetary policy to help regulate the economy. This entails the running of deficits in times of recession in order to stimulate investment and employment; and, conversely, surpluses in times of inflation to control the demand for goods and services. Regulating the economy is not this simple, for we have discovered that unemployment and inflation may coexist and thus send mixed signals as to the appropriate corrective action.

The unlimited nature of this power to borrow money on the public credit has led to a massive public debt. The most rapid growth of the debt took place during World War Two, but there is much concern about the debt's rise in recent years. There are important questions which must be addressed. For example, when does the debt become "too large"? Who bears the burden of the debt, the present generation or future generations? What effect do interest payments raised through general taxes to service the debt have on the distribution of income? To what extent do interest payments increase the difficulty of reducing the debt? To what extent does a large deficit today make more difficult the use of fiscal policy to meet the next recession?

➤ **SECTION 91(5):** Postal Service.

In October 1981 the Canada Post Corporation Act created the Canada Post Corporation, an "agency" Crown corporation. Before this reorganization the postal service had operated as a department under direct authority of a cabinet minister (the Postmaster General).

➤ **SECTION 91(6):** The Census and Statistics.

Responsibility for conducting the decennial census and for compiling statistics on many different topics lies with Statistics Canada which was established in 1918 as the Dominion Bureau of Statistics. This Federal power does not preclude other organizations, including provincial governments, from collecting statistics which are relevant to them. Nevertheless, the minister of justice in 1873 noted that a British Columbia law requiring the registration of births, deaths, and marriages within that province could contravene Federal authority over "statistics."[82]

➤ **SECTION 91(7):** Militia, Military and Naval Service, and Defence.

In 1922 the Department of National Defence was established. It replaced the Department of Militia and Defence (created in 1867), the Department of the Naval Service (created in 1910), and the Air Board (created in 1919).[83] In 1968 the Royal Canadian Navy, Canadian Army, and Royal Canadian Air Force were combined into the single Canadian Forces.

The Supreme Court ruled in 1980 that this subsection authorizes the enacting of legislation such as the National Defence Act "for regulation and control of the behaviour and discipline of members of the service, and this in turn includes the making of provision for the establishment of courts to enforce such legislation."[84]

➤ **SECTION 91(8):** The fixing of and providing for the Salaries and Allowances of Civil and other Officers of the Government of Canada.

The principle enunciated by this subsection is clear—the Federal government is responsible for determining the salaries and allowances paid to its employees. The machinery for determining these payments is complicated by the existence of different categories of employees. The most obvious group are departmental employees who are hired under the supervision of the Public Service Commission (created in 1908 as the Civil Service Commission). Salaries of the Commissioners themselves are determined by Parliament. The salaries of departmental employees are determined through collective bargaining between staff bargaining agents (who are certified by the Public Service Staff Relations Board) and the Treasury Board. The Treasury Board was assigned this "employer" role by a 1951 amendment to the Financial Administration Act. The bargaining process is conducted in accordance with the Public Service Staff Relations Act but it excludes deputy ministers (who are appointed by the cabinet), as well as managers, part-time staff, and casual staff. Before the Public Service Staff Relations Act was passed in 1967 there was no collective bargaining; salaries were determined through "consultation" between the government and the unions (or "staff associations").

In addition to government departments there are more than 400 Crown agencies (Crown corporations, regulatory bodies, and administrative tribunals). These agencies exhibit differing methods of establishing employee salaries and working conditions. There are also members of the Canadian Forces and the R.C.M.P.; political advisers to the prime minister (the Prime Minister's Office) and to other cabinet ministers; and the employees of Parliament.

➤ **SECTION 91(9):** Beacons, Buoys, Lighthouses, and Sable Island.

Perhaps the most interesting of the items named in this subsection is Sable Island, a crescent-shaped visible part of the continental shelf located some 300 kilometers southeast of Halifax. This treeless sandbank, 38 kilometers long and 1.5 kilometers wide at its widest point, is home to about 200 wild horses. Although it has never been settled, the Island has periodically been occupied by shipwrecked sailors, convicts, and pirates. The Canada Shipping Act provides for a possible jail term of up to six months for anyone who attempts to reside on the Island without a licence issued by the minister of transport. The purpose of this restriction may be to control the search for wreckage.[85] The only inhabitants are Federal weather-station and navigation-station personnel.

In view of the many shipwrecks in the area the Federal government in 1873 built two lighthouses on the Island. Originally manned, these light houses were automated in the 1960s.

➤ **SECTION 91(10):** Navigation and Shipping.

This is but one of several Federal powers relating to water travel and transport, the others being authority to legislate with respect to:

(1) beacons, buoys, and lighthouses (91[9]),
(2) ferries connecting a province with territory beyond that province (91[13]),
(3) ships, railways, canals, telegraphs, and other works extending beyond a province (the exceptions contained in 92[10]),
(4) specified public works and property belonging to the pre-Confederation provinces, and now owned by the Federal government. These include canals "with lands and water power connected therewith," harbours, lighthouses and piers, steamboats, dredges, public vessels, and rivers and lake improvements (s. 108 together with the Third Schedule to the 1867 Constitution Act).

This is an impressive list of powers within the broad area of navigation and shipping. In 1926 the Judicial Committee of the Privy Council stated that "there is no doubt that the power to control navigation and shipping . . . is to be widely construed."[86] Hogg lists the following specific areas of Federal jurisdiction all based on litigation: "navigable waters, works of navigation, harbours, and a far-reaching body of maritime or admiralty law, which includes laws regarding liability for loss or delay of a ship's cargo, liability for loss of life or personal injury caused by a ship, marine insurance, the sale, purchase and ownership of ships, the construction, repair and maintenance of ships, and pilotage and towage."[87] As in the case of trade and commerce (s. 91[2]), the broad language of this subsection has not been deemed to extend Federal jurisdiction to intraprovincial activity.[88]

➤ **SECTION 91(11):** Quarantine and the Establishment and Maintenance of Marine Hospitals.

The Quarantine Act provides for the detention of ships, aircraft, and other means of transport arriving from other countries; and for the inspection of crews and passengers for diseases such as cholera, smallpox, and yellow fever. Quarantine stations, originally the "marine hospitals," are now located at major seaports and airports.[89]

With this exception public health falls under provincial jurisdiction.

➤ **SECTION 91(12):** Sea Coast and Inland Fisheries.

This authority includes the right to legislate for the protection of fish by "prescribing the times of year during which fishing is to be allowed, or the Instruments which may be employed for the purpose,"[90] or by preventing the addition (to waters frequented by fish) of substances which are deleterious to fish or their habitat. However, provincial authority over property and civil rights within the province (s. 92[13]) prevents the Federal government from using section 91(12) to legislate for the control of pollution in waters frequented by fish, unless the substances deposited are harmful to the fish.[91]

Section 91(12) may be used to illustrate that proprietary rights do not accompany legislative authority. This was made clear in the 1898 *Fisheries Reference* when the Privy Council declared that "the distinction . . . must be borne in mind. . . . It was the latter only which was conferred" by section 91.[92] This distinction is even clearer with respect to banking and the incorporation of banks: section 91(15) does not bestow ownership upon Parliament. The distinction between ownership and legislative authority may nevertheless be tenuous if legislation imposes significant restrictions upon the owner's right to use property. The courts may in such circumstances be called upon to determine whether legislation is essentially in relation to ownership or in relation to fisheries (or banking, and so on). If the former, the legislation will be found to violate provincial jurisdiction over property and civil rights.

Although Parliament has not been given a general power to expropriate property, the Supreme Court has noted that "no difficulty has ever arisen in the constitutional cases with respect to the absolute right in appropriate circumstances of the federal government to take over the lands of a province where such is a necessity in order properly to discharge the constitutional responsibilities of Parliament."[93] For example, in 1966 the Supreme Court upheld Parliament's grant of authority (under p.o.g.g.) to the National Capital Commission to expropriate lands for the "development, conservation and improvement" of the National Capital Region.[94] Perhaps Parliament could also expropriate a "local work" after declaring it to be "for the general advantage of Canada or for the advantage of two or more provinces" (s. 92[10][c]).

➤ **SECTION 91(13):** Ferries between a Province and any British or Foreign Country or between Two Provinces.

It is important to distinguish between ferries operating beyond the bounds of a province and those operating solely within the province. The latter fall within provincial jurisdiction.

➤ **SECTION 91(14):** Currency and Coinage.

This is the first of seven subsections within section 91 which, collectively, give Ottawa exclusive control over banking, money, and credit. The others are (15), (16), (18), (19), (20), and (21).

In one sense anything that is accepted in exchange for goods can be called money, and over human history many objects have in fact been used. Because durability and stability of value are prime requisites, gold and silver have always held a special place as money. The first coins were made of pure metal, but with their value stamped to obviate the necessity of weighing at the time of each transaction. However, the practice of rubbing and clipping led first to the development of milled edges and finally to the introduction of fiduciary money—coins the value of whose metal content is relatively insignificant in relation to the stamped value. The value of paper money is based solely on trust, especially if (as now) the paper cannot be exchanged for precious metal such as gold.

Before Confederation a variety of coins (including French, Spanish, and English) circulated, their values differing among the colonies and sometimes even within colonies.[95] Not until 1858 was there Canadian (i.e., Province of Canada) coinage or standard money. Following Confederation a uniform currency was established for Ontario, Quebec, New Brunswick and, in 1871, Nova Scotia.

The Currency Act authorizes the issue of gold coins, and other coins in denominations of one dollar, fifty cents, twenty-five cents, ten cents, five cents, and one cent. The metallic content (gold, silver, copper, tin, bronze) of all coins may be altered as necessary. Coins are struck at the Royal Canadian Mint (a Crown corporation).

In 1868 Dominion paper money replaced that issued by the provinces. When the Bank of Canada was created in 1935 it began to issue its own paper money which replaced Dominion notes. The issuing of paper money by the chartered banks, begun in 1822, ceased in 1945. In 1950 the Bank of Canada assumed the liability for outstanding bills of the chartered banks. Until recently Canada's paper money contained the statement that "The Bank of Canada will pay to the bearer on demand" the face value of the bill. Payment could originally be demanded in gold, but when convertibility was abolished the statement meant only that the bill could be exchanged for another or for fiduciary coins. Our paper money now says merely that "This note is legal tender."

➤ **Section 91(15):** Banking, Incorporation of Banks, and the Issue of Paper Money.

What is "banking"? What are "banks"? The courts have defined "banking" widely enough "to embrace every transaction coming within the legitimate business of a banker." Furthermore, the definition expands as the type of transaction undertaken by banks expands.[96] There are, then, no functions which are peculiar to "banking." An institutional rather than functional approach was confirmed by the Supreme Court in 1980.[97] Banking is thus the activity performed by the institutions called "banks" under the Bank Act. The implication is that "banking" activities could be redefined by Parliament if it chose to redefine the concept of "bank." There are presently about a dozen such banks although the largest five have some 90% of the total assets—Royal Bank, Canadian Imperial Bank of Commerce, Bank of Montreal, Bank of Nova Scotia, and Toronto-Dominion Bank.

There are other institutions, sometimes called "near-banks," performing functions generally associated with the business of banking, such as holding savings and chequing deposits and making loans. Among these institutions are trust companies, caisses populaires, credit unions and, to a much lesser degree, mortgage companies. Because they are often provincially incorporated (s. 92[11]), and therefore provincially regulated, they cannot be called "banks."

This is not a serious impediment inasmuch as there are no exclusively "banking" functions. Trust and mortgage companies incorporated by the Federal government are regulated by Ottawa but not, of course, under the Bank Act.

Provincial legislation in relation to one of the heads of section 92 will be *intra vires* the province if it has only an incidental effect upon the chartered banks. However, if its pith and substance relates to banks or banking the law will be *ultra vires*. For example, in the 1930s Alberta's Social Credit Government imposed a heavy tax exclusively upon the banks. The Privy Council struck the law down in the 1939 *Alberta Statutes Reference*, on the grounds that it was in relation to banking rather than the raising of revenue by direct taxation.[98] This point may be generalized as the "sterilization" principle: a province (in this case) may not pass legislation which ostensibly falls within its jurisdiction if it impairs the ability of Parliament to legislate under one of its powers. The term "colourable" is sometimes applied to such legislation which has as its intent the invasion of (in this case) Federal jurisdiction. In the case at hand the Privy Council concluded that the legislation was not "in any true sense" taxation to raise revenue but rather part of a scheme to prevent the legitimate operation of banking institutions in the province. A similar principle was enunciated by the United States Supreme Court in *McCulloch v. Maryland* (1819): "A power to create implies a power to preserve . . . A power to destroy, if wielded by a different hand, is hostile to, and incompatible with, these powers to create and preserve." The power to tax, said the Court, involves the power to destroy.[99]

The principle of Federal paramountcy (noted in the commentary on the closing paragraph of section 91) will also result in "valid" provincial laws being made inoperative if they conflict with the Bank Act. In *Bank of Montreal v. Hall* (1990),[100] for example, the Supreme Court decided there was a conflict between a provision of Saskatchewan's Limitation of Civil Rights Act and Parliament's Bank Act. The provincial law required a creditor to serve notice on a debtor of its intention to foreclose on property upon default of a loan repayment, whereas the Bank Act contained its own definition of the rights and obligations of banks and borrowers including the right of immediate seizure. The Court acknowledged the constitutionality of Saskatchewan's law under property and civil rights; however, because of the conflict with the Bank Act the Court declared the former "inoperative" to the extent of the conflict.

Canada's central Bank of Canada was created in 1935. Its major functions are to control the money supply, to issue paper money, to act as a bank to the chartered banks, to act as the Federal government's bank, and to influence some of the activities of the chartered banks. Because the chartered banks are private institutions there is no assurance, Federal regulation notwithstanding, that they are immune from serious financial problems and collapse. In 1985 two Alberta-based banks, the Canadian Commercial and the Northland, were liquidated. Until these failures, only one Canadian chartered bank had failed—the Home Bank in 1923.

➤ **SECTION 91(16):** Savings Banks.

The Province of Alberta Treasury Branches (established in 1938) and the Province of Ontario Savings Office (established in 1922) are provincially owned but were established under Federal legislation. The Montreal City and District Savings Bank was established in 1846 and has been under a Federal charter since 1871. All of these institutions report monthly to the Department of Finance in Ottawa.

➤ **SECTION 91(17):** Weights and Measures.

The object of this subsection is to ensure standardization throughout the country. In 1971 the Preparatory Commission for Metric Conversion was established for the purpose of phasing in the metric system by the early 1980s. Although conversion has taken place in many areas, opposition to metrification continues.

➤ **SECTION 91(18):** Bills of Exchange and Promissory Notes.

A bill of exchange (or draft) is an unconditional written order to pay. It is addressed by one person to another and signed by the addresser, requiring the addressee to pay on demand or at a stated future time the amount of money indicated. Payment is either to order or to the bearer. An ordinary cheque drawn on a bank is an example of a bill of exchange.

By contrast, a promissory note is an unconditional written promise to pay. It is made by one person to another and signed by the maker, promising to pay on demand or at a stated future time the amount of money indicated. Payment is either to order or to the bearer. Bank of Canada notes at one time stated that the Bank will pay to the bearer on demand the face amount of the note. This originally meant payment in gold, but when Canada left the gold standard the statement came to mean payment only in other Bank of Canada notes. Today, Bank notes say merely that "This note is legal tender."

Both bills of exchange and promissory notes are used widely for payments between business firms.

➤ **SECTION 91(19):** Interest.

"Interest" is one of the clauses of section 91 which must be regarded as more than but an illustration of p.o.g.g.—in this instance, a qualification of property and civil rights assigned under 92(13) to the provinces. In the event of conflict between Ottawa and the provinces, therefore, it is necessary to determine whether the pith and substance of the impugned legislation is in relation to interest or in relation to property and civil rights.

Two cases illustrate the dilemma. In 1949 the Privy Council upheld a decision of the Supreme Court that the Saskatchewan 1944 Farm Security Act, which provided what amounted to interest adjustment, infringed upon the exclusive jurisdiction of the Federal government to legislate in relation to interest.[101] The Act had provided that during a period of crop failure the amount of principal owing would be reduced by the amount of interest. The amount of interest was left unchanged. Speaking for the Privy Council, Viscount Simon pointed out that such an alteration "is necessarily to increase the rate [of interest] on the principal outstanding . . . It is obvious that the language used [in the legislation] has been ingeniously chosen in an endeavour to avoid a conflict with Dominion powers . . . , but in the view of their Lordships the endeavour is not successful."

In announcing the Committee's decision Viscount Simon commented:

> Contractual rights are, generally speaking, one kind of civil rights and, were it not that the Dominion has an exclusive power to legislate in relation to "interest," the argument that the provincial legislature has the power, and the exclusive power [under s. 92(13)], to vary provisions for the payment of interest contained in contracts in the province could not be overthrown.

Furthermore, the Privy Council rejected arguments that the pith and substance of the Saskatchewan Act was property and civil rights or, alternatively, agriculture in the province (section 95). In the case of agriculture it was also argued that the Act did not violate any Federal legislation, and therefore it did not run afoul of the Federal paramountcy provision of section 95.

In 1963 the Supreme Court gave a narrow meaning to the concept of interest and upheld Ontario's Unconscionable Transactions Relief Act as being in relation to property and civil rights. The Act

> is not legislation in relation to interest but legislation relating to annulment or reformation of contract on the grounds . . . (a) that the cost of the loan is excessive, and (b) that the transaction is harsh and unconscionable. The wording of the statute indicates that it is not the rate or amount of interest which is the concern of the legislation but whether the transaction as a whole is one which it would be proper to maintain as having been freely consented to by the debtor.[102]

Such is the dilemma facing legislatures and, indeed, the courts. McConnell adds that "if policy were the sole guide, it would seem that farmers on the prairies suffering during the thirties . . . were just as much entitled to judicial consideration as the beleaguered debtors" in Ontario.[103]

➤ **SECTION 91(20):** Legal Tender.

The Currency Act defines legal tender as consisting of gold and other current coins, as well as Bank of Canada paper money. Although gold coins and paper money may be used for payment in any amount, other coins may not. For example, pennies are legal tender to a maximum of 25 cents. The Act also recognizes Newfoundland coins, issued before that province joined Canada, as legal tender. However, "no coin that is bent, mutilated or defaced, or that has been reduced in weight otherwise than by abrasion through ordinary use, shall pass current."

➤ SECTION 91(21): Bankruptcy and Insolvency.

McConnell suggests that the problem of distinguishing between Federal jurisdiction under this subsection and provincial jurisdiction under section 92(13) and (16) results from their being

> a gradual continuum of transactions ranging from simple debtor-creditor relationships at the one end of the spectrum to complete financial collapse at the other, the provinces having jurisdiction over the first and the Dominion over the second. Whether a specific statute applying to a complicated fact situation is a matter of local contract falling under s. 92(13) and (16), or a matter of "bankruptcy and insolvency" turns, in borderline cases, on where a fine line is drawn.[104]

There is an analogy, therefore, between the nicety of this distinction and that noted in relation to "interest" in section 91(19).

➤ SECTION 91(22): Patents of Invention and Discovery.

The Patent Act gives inventors exclusive right to market their inventions.

➤ SECTION 91(23): Copyrights.

The operative legislation is the Copyright Act which has been influenced by several international conventions on the subject.

➤ SECTION 91(24): Indians, and Lands reserved for the Indians.

The term "Indian" is defined by Parliament in the Indian Act. It is based upon kinship, descent being established through the male line, "and traces Indian status from particular bands whose Charter members were normally determined at the time of the establishment of a reserve or the making of a treaty."[105] These "status Indians" are the only people who have a right to live on Indian reserves.

This subsection 24 includes status Indians and probably other ("non-status") Indians, whether full-blooded or not, who are excluded from the Indian Act—Métis and Inuit (Eskimo) people, Indians who relinquish their status by "enfranchisement" and, until the mid-1980s, Indian women who married non-Indian men.[106]

While it is not entirely clear to what extent Parliament may legislate in relation to Indians in areas otherwise within provincial jurisdiction, the Indian Act does contain sections relating, for example, to education and property.[107] Section 88 of the Indian Act is nevertheless particularly relevant:

> Subject to the terms of any treaty and any other Act of the Parliament of Canada, all laws of general application from time to time in force in any province are applicable to and in respect of Indians in the province, except to the extent that such laws are inconsistent with this Act or any order, rule, regulation or by-law made thereun-

> der, and except to the extent that such laws make provision for any matter for which provision is made by or under this Act.

However, as in so many other matters, the relevant question asks what is the pith and substance of disputed legislation. Is it in relation to Indians or, for example, education?

Provincial laws which apply only to Indians or their lands—that is, which are not of general application in the province—would likely be invalid. Provincial laws of general application could be struck down on the basis of the sterilization principle—that is, if their application would seriously impair Parliament's ability to legislate in respect of Indians or Indian lands. Similarly, provincial laws that conflict with Parliament's authority, but which are otherwise valid, could be declared unconstitutional because of the doctrine of Federal paramountcy. (The concept of Federal paramountcy is considered in the commentary on the concluding paragraph of section 91.) It was the paramountcy doctrine which led to a 1986 Supreme Court ruling that British Columbia's Family Relations Act, insofar as it dealt with the division of property at the time of a marriage break-up, could not apply to lands on an Indian reserve. The conflict was between (a) the Indian Act which provided that an Indian lawfully in possession of lands on a reserve (that is, who possesses a Certificate of Possession) may transfer the right to possession only if the Minister of Indian Affairs approves; and (b) the Family Relations Act which authorizes a court of law to declare the transfer of property.[108]

A law of Manitoba, Saskatchewan, or Alberta, which purported to deprive Indians of the right to hunt and fish for food, would be unconstitutional insofar as it contravened the Federal-provincial natural resources agreements effected by the 1930 Constitution Act which is now part of the Constitution of Canada. Each of these agreements includes the following statement:

> In order to secure to the Indians of the Province the continuance of the supply of game and fish for their support and substance, Canada agrees that the laws respecting game in force in the Province from time to time shall apply to the Indians within the boundaries thereof, provided, however, that the said Indians shall have the right, which the Province hereby assures to them, of hunting, trapping and fishing game for food at all seasons of the year on all unoccupied Crown lands and on any other lands to which the said Indians may have a right of access.[109]

This statement does not protect Indians from the application of Federal laws.[110]

What effect might the equality rights (s. 15) of the 1982 Charter of Rights and Freedoms have upon the constitutionality of the Indian Act? The courts may well uphold the Act under the affirmative action clause of section 15 or as a reasonable limit to equality rights under section 1 of the Charter.

"Lands reserved for the Indians" date back to the 1763 Royal Proclamation which set aside land west of Quebec as Indian territory into which settlement was prohibited. Since then, other lands have been reserved, and they fall within the jurisdiction of this subsection. Now that aboriginal rights have been entrenched in Charter section 35(1), this section 91(24) must be read with the new 35(1).[111]

➤ **SECTION 91(25):** Naturalization and Aliens.

Canadian citizenship is not mentioned in the 1867 Constitution Act because the concept did not exist in 1867. A Canadian Citizenship Act was first enacted in 1946, effective in 1947.

Is discrimination against aliens by provincial legislation constitutional? A province may control foreign ownership of land. In 1975 the Supreme Court upheld a Prince Edward Island statute limiting property ownership by any person "who is not a resident of the province." Hogg comments that "the decision would have been more difficult if the discrimination had been against aliens," although he acknowledges that because authorities are divided on the subject, provincial discrimination against aliens might be upheld "as a valid property law."[112]

Because of the principle of legislative supremacy, the authority of Parliament or provincial legislatures to discriminate on the basis of characteristics now protected by the Charter of Rights and Freedoms was not in doubt before 1982. The only question was which order of government had the authority to discriminate or, alternatively, to legislate against discrimination. In the case of aliens, authority clearly lay with Parliament, unless provincial legislation could be defended on the grounds that the impact on aliens was necessarily incidental to the legislation which clearly fell within provincial jurisdiction.

➤ **SECTION 91(26):** Marriage and Divorce.

A distinction must be made between the "marriage" component of this subsection and "the solemnization of marriage in the province" (s. 92[12]). Most laws relating to marriage are provincial. Because the courts have given a liberal interpretation to provincial authority the Federal power has remained basically undefined. The only (proposed) Federal law to be brought before the courts was declared *ultra vires* by the Privy Council in 1912 on the grounds that the "conferring on the provincial Legislature the exclusive power to make laws relating to the solemnization of marriage in the province operates by way of exception to the powers conferred as regards marriage by s. 91, and enables the provincial Legislature to enact conditions as to solemnization which may affect the validity of the contract."[113] The current situation stemming from this and later decisions has been summarized as follows:

> It is clear that a province has power to stipulate pre-ceremonial requirements, such as, the issue of a licence or the publication of banns, and to stipulate the qualifications of the person performing the ceremony, even if breach of the stipulations renders the marriage a nullity. These are matters closely associated with the perfor-

mance of the ceremony—the solemnization. Much less clearly associated with the ceremony is a requirement of parental consent to the marriage of a minor; but in two cases the Supreme Court of Canada has held that a province may enact that parental consent is a condition of a valid marriage. These cases were decided on the dubious ground that parental consent was a "formality" of marriage rather than a matter governing the capacity of the parties. Laws governing the capacity of the parties are outside provincial power, for example, a law prescribing the prohibited degrees of consanguinity and affinity, or a law prescribing the capacity of divorced people to remarry.[114]

Until Parliament enacted the Divorce Act in 1968 divorce law varied among the provinces. The reason was that section 129 provides for the continuation of pre-Confederation laws pending Federal legislation in areas (such as divorce) which in 1867 were brought under Parliament's jurisdiction. Because there were no divorce procedures in Newfoundland and Quebec (and Ontario before 1930) every divorce within those provinces could be granted only by an individual Act of Parliament. It was the Senate through two full-time standing committees that performed the necessary work for divorce bills. This work, essentially judicial in nature, included the identification of grounds and collection of supporting evidence. Following passage in the Senate these bills were rubber-stamped without debate, and in wholesale lots, by the House of Commons. In order to protest Parliament's involvement with divorce bills a few members of the House decided to debate each bill to call attention to the situation and hopefully to force a procedural change. As a result, the rules were altered in 1963 to eliminate House involvement. With passage of the Divorce Act in 1968 total responsibility for the granting of divorces fell to provincial courts.

In addition to stipulating the grounds for divorce, the Divorce Act legislates in the consequent areas of alimony, child maintenance and custody, which formerly had been covered by provincial legislation. Russell notes, however, that if these matters are associated with marriage separation rather than divorce, they fall within provincial jurisdiction under section 92(12).[115]

➤ **SECTION 91(27):** The Criminal Law, except the Constitution of Courts of Criminal Jurisdiction, but including the Procedure in Criminal Matters.

Canada has essentially (but by no means completely—see the commentary on section 96) a system of provincially created inferior and superior courts of original and appellate jurisdiction which administer both provincial and Federal law. The system culminates in the Supreme Court of Canada which was created by Parliament under section 101 of the present Act. Section 92(14) authorizes the provinces to create courts having jurisdiction in both criminal and civil matters. Nevertheless, Parliament is empowered by 91(27) to establish the procedure to be followed by provincial courts in criminal matters. The Criminal Code establishes these rules of procedure and the Canada Evidence Act establishes the rules of evidence. Section 92(14) gives the provinces jurisdiction over procedure in civil matters. There is some question whether Parliament may create courts of criminal jurisdiction. Section 91(27) explicitly forbids it, but section 101 authorizes the establishment, "notwithstanding anything in this Act," of "any additional courts for the better administration of the laws of Canada."

The bulk of our criminal law is to be found in the Criminal Code; other statutes finding their justification in this subsection include the Food and Drugs Act, Hazardous Products Act and (until it was struck down by the Supreme Court in *Big M Drug Mart*), the Lord's Day Act.[116]

➤ **SECTION 91(28):** The Establishment, Maintenance, and Management of Penitentiaries.

Although this subsection places "penitentiaries" under Federal jurisdiction, and section 92(6) assigns "reformatory prisons" to the provinces, the Constitution Act does not distinguish between these two types of institution. The Criminal Code makes the distinction on the basis of the length of prison term. Terms of at least two years are served in Federal institutions and therefore in "penitentiaries." Terms of less than two years are served in provincial institutions and therefore in "prisons."[117]

➤ **SECTION 91(29):** Such Classes of Subjects as are expressly excepted in the Enumeration of the Classes of Subjects by this Act assigned exclusively to the Legislatures of the Provinces.

Specifically, this subsection transfers to the Federal government legislative authority in relation to "local works and undertakings" covered by section 92(10)(a)(b)(c).

➤ **SECTION 91 (CONCLUDING PARAGRAPH):** And any Matter coming within any of the Classes of Subjects enumerated in this Section shall not be deemed to come within the Class of Matters of a local or private Nature comprised in the Enumeration of the Classes of Subjects by this Act assigned exclusively to the Legislatures of the Provinces.

If the closing paragraph of section 91 is read as it is grammatically written, it appears to give the enumerated heads of section 91 priority over 92(16) alone—that is, the "*class* of matters of a local or private nature comprised in the enumeration of the *classes* of subjects" assigned to the provinces (emphasis added). This seems to have been the Privy Council's interpretation in 1881.[118] Alternatively, and this was the 1896 interpretation, "it appears . . . that the language of the exception in s. 91 was meant to include and correctly describes all the matters enumerated in the sixteen heads of s. 92, as being, from a provincial point of view, of a local or private nature."[119] Whichever interpretation is adopted the concluding paragraph does not enable Parliament's p.o.g.g. to trench upon provincial jurisdiction. Indeed, the opening paragraph of section 91 explicitly prohibits such trenching. "Exceptions" to this prohibition which are based upon the concept of national concern, or which depend upon judicial determination of the pith and substance of the disputed laws, or which depend upon the existence of an emergency, are considered in the commentary on section 91's p.o.g.g., and in Chapter 5 under "Judicial Decisions."

The commentary on p.o.g.g. also raised the question of Federal paramountcy in the event of conflict between provincial and Federal laws. This doctrine was clearly stated by Lord Watson in the *Local Prohibition* case (1896): "It has been frequently recognized by this Board [the Privy Council], and it may now be regarded as settled law, that according to the scheme of the British North America Act the enactments of the Parliament of Canada, in so far as these are within its competency, must override provincial legislation."[120] Upon what is the paramountcy doctrine based? According to Laskin it rests upon the "effective operation of the federal system fortified explicitly by the *non obstante* clause [the notwithstanding clause in the opening paragraph] of section 91 and also [more generally] by the concluding clause."[121] The doctrine is common among federal states[122] and is explicit, for example, in the constitutions of the United States and Australia. According to Article VI of the Constitution of the United States, "This Constitution, and the Laws of the United States which shall be made in Pursuance thereof . . . shall be the supreme Law of the Land; and the Judges in every State shall be bound thereby, any Thing in the Constitution or Laws of any State to the Contrary notwithstanding." Section 109 of the Commonwealth of Australia Constitution Act states that "When a law of a State is inconsistent with a law of the Commonwealth, the latter shall prevail, and the former shall, to the extent of the inconsistency, be invalid."

What is an inconsistency or conflict between a Federal and a provincial law? This is a significant question and so the answer adopted by the courts is critical. A broad definition of inconsistency or conflict has the effect of expanding Federal power, whereas a narrow definition gives greater protection to provincial power. The Supreme Court has adopted the latter: "In principle, there would seem to be no good reason to speak of paramountcy and preclusion except where there is actual conflict in operation as where one enactment says 'yes' and the other says 'no'; 'the same citizens are being told to do inconsistent things'; compliance with one is defiance of the other."[123] Several actual situations illustrate the point. There is a contradiction when court orders made under Federal and provincial laws assign custody of the same child to the wife and to the husband who are separated; or when a Federal law demands equal employment opportunities to Japanese and Canadian citizens within Canada, and a provincial law prohibits the employment of Japanese in mines. See also the commentaries on sections 91(15) and 91(24) which note two Supreme Court cases.

A potential application of Federal paramountcy lies in the area of direct taxation. While Parliament may raise money "by any mode or system of taxation" (s. 91[3]) its power is limited by the provinces' exclusive authority to impose direct taxes "for provincial purposes" (s. 92[2]). In the 1932 *Silver Brothers Reference* the Privy Council ruled that "the two taxations . . . can stand side by side without interfering with each other, but as soon as you come to . . . absolute priority they cannot stand side by side and must clash; consequently the Dominion must prevail."[124] Although the courts have not been called upon to consider the question of paramountcy, one wonders what combined Federal-provincial income tax rate (for example) would be needed to force the issue. Presumably it would not exceed 100 percent!

When paramountcy is involved, Federal legislation prevails to the extent of the conflict, but the provincial law is not thereby repealed; it is only made inoperative. If at some future time the Federal law is altered such as to eliminate the conflict, the provincial law automatically becomes operative.

Exclusive Powers of Provincial Legislatures

➤ **SECTION 92 (OPENING PARAGRAPH):** In each Province the Legislature may exclusively make Laws in relation to Matters coming within the Classes of Subject next hereinafter enumerated; that is to say,—

Section 92 gives to the provinces a list of specific powers, the residue going to Parliament under section 91's p.o.g.g. However, the expansion of "property and civil rights in the province" (92[13]) by the courts provides some justification for referring to 92(13) as a residual power. This was noted in the commentary on section 91's opening paragraph and developed in Chapter 5 under "Judicial Decisions."

➤ **SECTION 92(1):** The Amendment from Time to Time, notwithstanding anything in this Act, of the Constitution of the Province, except as regards the Office of Lieutenant Governor.

This subsection was repealed by the 1982 Constitution Act and its substance re-enacted as section 45 of that Act. The prohibition against tampering with the office of lieutenant governor is now contained in section 41 of the new Act. Provinces are now officially involved in the broader amending process as well; see the commentaries on sections 38, 41, 42, and 43, of the 1982 Act. Although section 92(1) has been repealed, relevant comments are made here because the authority and restriction contained in this subsection have been diffused in the new Act.

The exception of the office of lieutenant governor from the provinces' amending power has led to several court cases involving provincial legislation authorizing the direct participation of the electorate in the law-making process.[125] In 1919 the Privy Council struck down Manitoba's 1916 Initiative and Referendum Act on the grounds that, although it was an amendment to Manitoba's constitution, it went beyond the bounds permitted by section 92(1) because the law-making process envisioned by that Act excluded the lieutenant governor. The Act authorized the electorate to petition for the enactment of a proposed law or the repeal of an existing law. If the legislature did not act upon this "initiative" a referendum on the petition was required. A simple majority of those voting was sufficient to enact or repeal the law so that neither the assembly nor the lieutenant governor was involved. It was the omission of the lieutenant governor which was the basis of the Privy Council's decision.

In 1913 the Alberta government enacted the Direct Legislation Act which, differing from the Manitoba law, stipulated that following initiation by the electorate and subsequent passage in a referendum, the proposed law "shall be enacted by the Legislature at its next session without amendment . . . and . . . shall come into force upon receiving royal assent." Both the legislature and the lieutenant governor were therefore involved. Preservation of the latter persuaded the Privy Council in 1922 to uphold the 1916 Alberta Liquor Act which had been enacted with the machinery established by the Direct Legislation Act.

There have, of course, been many amendments to provincial constitutions over the years. Part V of the present Act (excluding those sections pertaining to the office of lieutenant governor), as well as other provisions of the Act which apply "until the province otherwise decides," have been changed under the authority of section 92(1). For example, the upper houses of all five provinces which at one time had bicameral legislatures have been abolished, and the maximum duration of provincial assemblies was extended from four years to five years by every province except Newfoundland. See the commentaries on sections 69 and 85.

In 1979 the Supreme Court ruled (*Blaikie*) against Quebec legislation making French the only language of that province's legislature and courts, and on the same day it ruled (*Forest*) against similar Manitoba legislation making English the official language. The Court reasoned that language rights were really part of the Constitution of Canada rather than the constitution of a province. See the commentary on section 133 of this Act.

Chief Justice Dickson noted in *Ontario Public Service Employees' Union* (*OPSEU*, 1987) "the difficulty of assigning a precise content to the concept" of "the constitution of a province," and Justice Beetz (for the Court) spent some time examining the concept within the context of Ontario's ban on certain types of political activity by its public servants:[126]

> The constitution of . . . [a province] is not to be found in a comprehensive, written instrument called a constitution. An enactment can generally be considered as an amendment of the constitution of a province when it bears on the operation of an organ of the government of the province, provided it is not otherwise entrenched as being indivisibly related to the implementation of the federal principle or to a fundamental term or condition of the union, and provided

> of course it is not explicitly or implicitly excepted from the amending power bestowed upon the province by s. 92(1), such as the offices of Lieutenant-Governor and of the Queen.

The case at hand involved a challenge to provisions of the Ontario Public Service Act which prevented a public servant from running for public office, soliciting funds for a political party or candidate, or expressing through the spoken or written word views on any matter relating to a party's platform, without first securing a leave of absence from the service. Nor could a public servant canvass on behalf of a candidate. Although these proscribed activities applied to both Federal and provincial elections the case related only to the former.

The impugned provisions were held to be *intra vires* the provincial legislature because (1) they bore on an organ of the provincial government—the public service as part of the executive branch; (2) they imposed duties on members of a branch of the provincial government—they forbade participation in certain activities; and (3) they had as their objective the implementation of a principle of government—the impartiality of the public service being essential to responsible government. The issue raised the question of the extent to which a legislature could interfere with freely elected legislative bodies without affecting the federal principle, and therefore trenching on the Constitution of Canada rather than merely amending its own constitution. The Court ruled that the impact on the federal principle was only "incidental."

A broader issue raised by *OPSEU* was whether certain freedoms were placed beyond the reach of both Parliament and the provinces by the "similar in principle" wording of the preamble to the 1867 Constitution Act. The following statement suggests that Beetz clearly believed so. Additional statements made by Beetz and others are noted in Chapter 5 where the question of an implied bill of rights is discussed. (See especially the section on "Judicial Decisions: The Courts and Basic Rights and Freedoms.")

> The fact that a province can validly give legislative effect to a prerequisite condition of responsible government [in this instance, ensuring the impartiality of its public servants] does not necessarily mean it can do anything it pleases with the principle of responsible government itself. Thus, it is uncertain, to say the least, that a province could touch upon the power of the Lieutenant-Governor to dissolve the legislature, or his power to appoint and dismiss ministers, without unconstitutionally touching his office itself. The principle of responsible government could, to the extent that it depends on those important royal powers, be entrenched to a substantial extent. The power of constitutional amendment given to the provinces by s. 92(1) does not necessarily comprise the power to bring about a profound constitutional upheaval by the introduction of political institutions foreign to and incompatible with the Canadian system.

➤ **Section 92(2):** Direct Taxation within the Province in order to the raising of a Revenue for Provincial Purposes.

Three limitations are imposed upon the provinces: taxes must be "direct," they must be within the province, and their purpose must be to raise revenue for provincial purposes. Furthermore, section 125 precludes the taxing of government property by any government. (Section 92A authorizes provincial indirect taxation of resources.)

The distinction between direct and indirect taxation was noted in the commentary on section 91(3). This distinction itself provides a reason to limit the provinces to direct taxation because taxes must be within the province. Indirect taxes are passed on to consumers who may reside beyond the province imposing the tax. This would conflict with the principle that provincial legislation (including tax legislation) may apply only within the province. There would also be a basic problem if governments were permitted to tax people whom they do not serve and to whom they are not responsible—a sort of taxation without representation. In 1978, for example, the Supreme Court ruled that Saskatchewan's royalty surcharge on oil production was both an indirect tax and, because most of the consumers were beyond Saskatchewan's borders, not a tax "within the province."[127] Although direct taxes, also, are passed on as part of production costs, that is a condition of economic survival and different from the situation which characterizes indirect taxes.

The third limitation (that the intent of taxation must be to raise revenue for provincial purposes) means that a province may not levy a direct tax for the purpose of regulating that which is taxed. This is of particular significance if the tax is imposed upon institutions falling within Federal jurisdiction, for the tax law may be in pith and substance a transgression of Parliament's authority. Alberta's attempt to tax the chartered banks in the 1930s was noted in the commentary on section 91(15). The significance of the phrase "for provincial purposes" is unclear inasmuch as provincial governments have spent money in areas beyond their legislative jurisdiction. The purchase of Pacific Western Airlines by the Alberta government was an example.

The more obvious direct taxes are personal and corporate income tax, property tax, retail sales tax, business tax, and succession duty or inheritance tax. An estate tax, however, is indirect because it is levied upon the executor of the estate and therefore recouped from the beneficiary; furthermore, because estates frequently exist beyond the province in which the deceased lived, a provincial estate tax would be unconstitutional as not being "within the province."[128]

Charges which are not "taxes" under section 92(2) may be levied by a province without regard to the direct/indirect test, but they must be valid under some other provincial powers. These charges may be proprietary or regulatory in nature.[129] As to the former,

> a province may levy charges in the form of licence fees, rents or royalties as the price for the private exploitation of provincially-owned natural resources; and a province may charge for the sale of books,

> liquor, electricity, rail travel or other goods or services which it supplies in a commercial way. Some of these charges are undoubtedly indirect, but they are valid nonetheless, because they are not taxes.

Regulatory charges are permissible

> if they are taken in payment for a specific governmental service, and if they bear a reasonable relation to the cost of providing the service—whether it be the issue of a licence, the registration of a deed, the provision of a bridge, or the supply of water. These charges are not taxes because their purpose is to defray expenses, not to raise revenue. Even if a charge proves to be too high and produces a surplus of revenue which is available for general governmental purposes, the charge will still not be characterized as a tax so long as the court is satisfied that it is not a colourable attempt to levy indirect taxation.

The commentary on the opening paragraph of section 91 noted that a broad grant of power may be limited to the extent that portions of it are given to the other order of government. This is especially true of each province's power to legislate in relation to property and civil rights in the province, a power limited by some eight of the enumerated heads of section 91. Another example is the limitation on "marriage and divorce" (s. 91[26]) imposed by the "solemnization of marriage in the province" (s. 92[12]). This reasoning applies to the taxing power only to the extent that Parliament may not levy direct taxes explicitly for provincial purposes. Apart from that restriciton, direct taxation may be viewed as a concurrent power.

➤ **SECTION 92(3):** The borrowing of Money on the sole Credit of the Province.

No limit to the amount or source of borrowing is specified. It is common for provinces to borrow on the international market, and several provinces borrowed from Alberta's multi-billion dollar Heritage Trust Fund.

➤ **SECTION 92(4):** The Establishment and Tenure of Provincial Offices and the Appointment and Payment of Provincial Officers.

There are two major exceptions to the generality of this subsection. In the first place lieutenant governors fall within Federal jurisdiction under sections 58-60. Because the original intention was that lieutenant governors would in certain respects act as Federal officials, this exception is understandable. But today, given the formal nature of the lieutenant governor's role, it seems reasonable that these Crown representatives should be appointed upon the recommendation of the premiers.

The second exception is the Federal power (ss. 96, 100) to appoint and pay judges of provincial superior, district, and county courts. See the commentaries on those sections. The tenure of these judges is discussed in the commentary on section 99. This Federal power notwithstanding, it is the province under section

92(14) which establishes the courts and determines the number of judges for each court.

The appointment and tenure of provincial public servants, judges below district and county courts, as well as the establishment of appointment criteria, are all within provincial jurisdiction. When the Supreme Court upheld (*OPSEU*, 1987) Ontario's restrictions on political activity by Ontario public servants its rationale was based on section 92(4) as well as 92(1). See the commentary on 92(1).

➤ **SECTION 92(5):** The Management and Sale of the Public Lands belonging to the Province and of the Timber and Wood thereon.

When the Constitution Act assigned indirect taxes to the Federal government, provincial revenues were reduced by more than 80% for the four provinces combined (because the provinces had previously relied heavily upon customs duties and excise taxes—both indirect taxes). This reduction was offset to some extent by the system of grants to be paid to the provinces by Ottawa (ss. 111-119). Furthermore, what were then considered the most costly government functions were assigned to Parliament. As the role and expenses of the provinces have grown over the years so has the need for revenue. Beginning within two years of Confederation provincial finances have continued to be a topic of Federal-provincial negotiations.

Section 109 of the present Act confers ownership of land resources upon the provinces. Ownership was extended to the three prairie provinces in 1930. This, together with section 92(5) authorizing the sale of resources by provinces as proprietors, has provided important additional sources of revenue. In recent years Alberta was able to establish a multi-billion dollar Heritage Trust Fund from the sale of oil and natural gas rights. Alberta and British Columbia have retained ownership of some 80% of their natural resources, and as a result, have benefitted from royalties more than Saskatchewan and Manitoba which in some oil and gas-producing regions have retained as little as 25%. Where resources are privately owned only the direct tax (and since 1982 the indirect tax as authorized by section 92A) is available as a revenue source.[130]

➤ **SECTION 92(6):** The Establishment, Maintenance, and Management of Public and Reformatory Prisons in and for the Province.

The absence of a precise distinction between prisons (under provincial jurisdiction) and penitentiaries (under Federal jurisdictions) was noted in the commentary on section 91(28).

➤ **SECTION 92(7):** The Establishment, Maintenance, and Management of Hospitals, Asylums, Charities, and Eleemosynary Institutions in and for the Province, other than Marine Hospitals.

This represents one of the best illustrations of the impingement of the Federal spending power on provincial jurisdiction. Two of the largest conditional grants have been those for hospital insurance and medicare. Hospital insurance as a joint-cost plan began in 1958 but did not include all provinces until 1961. Shared-cost medicare began in 1968 and was effective throughout Canada by 1972.[131]

➤ **SECTION 92(8):** Municipal Institutions in the Province.

Municipalities fall under the jurisdiction of the provincial governments, even though the sizes and economic impact of some of them exceed those of our smaller provinces. But it is only the provinces (as well as the Federal government) which have guaranteed existence under the Constitution Act. Furthermore, some departments of the Federal government are involved in matters such as housing and school financing which directly affect municipal governments. Because of the political and economic impact of our larger cities there is periodic discussion of ways to involve the municipal level in Federal-provincial conferences. Understandably, provincial governments are cautious about tri-level conferences.

➤ **SECTION 92(9):** Shop, Saloon, Tavern, Auctioneer, and other Licences in order to the raising of a Revenue for Provincial, Local, or Municipal Purposes.

The significant phrase is "in order to the raising of a revenue," indicating that this subsection does not sanction provincial legislation relating to licences for the purpose of regulating business. Regulatory legislation must find its justification under a different subsection such as (8), (10), (13), (16), or section 92(A)(1).

➤ **SECTION 92(10):** Local Works and Undertakings other than such as are of the following Classes:—

(a) Lines of Steam or other Ships, Railways, Canals, Telegraphs, and other Works and Undertakings connecting the Province with any other or others of the Provinces, or extending beyond the Limits of the Province;

(b) Lines of Steam Ships between the Province and any British or Foreign Country;

(c) Such Works as, although wholly situate within the Province, are before or after their Execution declared by the Parliament of Canada to be for the general Advantage of Canada or for the Advantage of Two or more of the Provinces.

The basic intent of subsection 10, and especially of paragraphs (a) and (b), is clear—to assign jurisdiction over local works and undertakings to the provinces while giving authority to Ottawa in relation to interprovincial and international works and undertakings. It is the Federal jurisdiction which is the more noteworthy. As already stated in its commentary, section 91(29) explicitly assigns authority in relation to paragraphs (a), (b), and (c) to Parliament, just as if these works and undertakings had been enumerated in section 91. Nevertheless, here as elsewhere, legislative authority does not imply proprietary rights.

It should also be noted that provincial laws affecting works or undertakings within Parliament's jurisdiction are valid if their pith and substance is deemed to lie within provincial powers—that is, if the laws do not have a sterilizing or crippling effect on Federal authority. See the commentary on section 91(15). In *Bell Canada v. Quebec (Commission de la Santé et de la Sécurité du Travail* (1988)[132] the Supreme Court ruled that "although the objective of the [Quebec] *Act respecting occupational health and safety* is the elimination, at the source, of dangers to the health, safety and physical well-being of workers, a detailed analysis of the whole of its provisions demonstrates that the pith and substance of the Act is working conditions, labour relations and the management of an undertaking"—in this case a Federal undertaking. (In 1882 Parliament had declared Bell Canada to be a Federal undertaking under section 92[10][c].) The Quebec legislation was therefore inapplicable.

"Works" have been considered by the courts to be "physical things not services," whereas an "undertaking" has been viewed as "not a physical thing, but an arrangement under which . . . physical things are used"—more an "organization" or "enterprise."[133] In 1989 the Supreme Court was asked if a job-creation program funded by a Federal grant was a Federal undertaking. If it were, the labour relations part of the program would presumably be subject to Federal rather than provincial jurisdiction. The Court noted that section 92(10)(a) and (b) relate only to transportation and communication, and that the Federal government had not expressed any desire to assume control of labour relations in the program by means of a subsection (c) declaration.[134] Had there been such a declaration the Court would doubtlessly have been asked if the program were indeed an "undertaking."

Paragraph (a): This includes ship lines, railways, canals, and telegraphs. "Other works and undertakings" have been deemed to include road transportation as well as radio and television broadcasting.

The regulation of aeronautics, on the other hand, has not been placed under 92(10)(a) by the courts; rather, it falls under p.o.g.g. The reason is historic. The first Federal law in this area was enacted to implement an Empire treaty and, although the legislation was upheld on the basis of the treaty power (s. 132) in the 1932 *Aeronautics Reference*,[135] the Privy Council commented that p.o.g.g. might also have applied. In 1952, by which time section 132 was virtually obsolete because Canada was entering into treaty arrangements as a sovereign state, the Supreme Court in *Johannesson v. West St. Paul*[136] upheld Federal authority (both intraprovincial and interprovincial) on the basis of p.o.g.g. as being of national concern. Why not 92(10)(a)? According to Hogg "no court has ever asked or answered this question."[137]

Companies which engage in the communication or transportation business having both intraprovincial and interprovincial segments are deemed to be involved in a single undertaking, and they are subject in their entirety to Federal regulation when the interprovincial segment is significant, provided of course that the business is in fact a single undertaking. A company that crosses a provincial boundary unnecessarily to evade provincial regulation will not come within the purview of section 92(10)(a).

Before the privatization of Alberta Government Telephones that utility presented an interesting situation. Although the utility was an interprovincial undertaking within the meaning of section 92(10)(a) (and therefore lay exclusively within Federal jurisdiction), it was also a provincial Crown agent (and therefore not within the regulatory authority of the Canadian Radio-television and Telecommunications Commission [CRTC] pursuant to the Railway Act.) The reason for this absence of CRTC jurisdiction was the failure of Parliament expressly to bind the Crown in the Railway Act. The reason section 92(10)(a) applied to AGT was partly the interconnection of its facilities with those in other provinces, but especially the Company's commercial agreements enabling it "to play a crucial role in the national telecommunications system and so provide to its local subscribers services of an interprovincial and international nature."[138] In a companion case the Court held that the Canada Labour Code was inapplicable to AGT. The Court acknowledged the possible hiatus in labour legislation caused by the inability of the provincial government to regulate a Federal work or undertaking and, on the other hand, the inability of the Canada Labour Code to regulate the provincial Crown, but it could only suggest that it was Parliament's responsibility to address the situation.[139]

If an undertaking involves more than one business both Federal and provincial regulation may be involved. An example is the 1950 *Empress Hotel Reference* in which the Privy Council held the intraprovincial operation of this Victoria C.P.R. hotel to be separate from the interprovincial railway operation of the Company.[140] On the other hand, two or more people may own and operate two closely-linked undertakings in different provinces, and yet the courts may consider the business to be a single undertaking for the purpose of section 92(10)(a). An example of this situation is the 1955 *Stevedores Reference* in which the Supreme Court ruled that the local operations of the company in each port were part of a broader interprovincial operation and therefore subject to Federal regulation under paragraph (a).[141]

Additional legislative authority in relation to communication and transportation is assigned to Parliament by section 91(5), (9), (10), and (13)—postal services; beacons, buoys, and lighthouses; navigation and shipping; and ferries between a province and other countries or between provinces. However, and unlike the United States commerce clause, the courts have not interpreted the trade and commerce power (s. 91[2]) as granting authority over communication and transportation.[142]

Paragraph (b): This paragraph requires no comment.

Paragraph (c): This is the extraordinary "declaratory" power—extraordinary because it permits Parliament unilaterally to assume legislative jurisdiction over any "works" (but not "undertakings") located entirely within a province merely by declaring such works to be "for the general advantage of Canada or for the advantage of two or more of the provinces." Whether or not an "advantage" actually exists is not justiciable, for the Supreme Court has said that "Parliament is the sole judge of the advisability of making. . . [a] declaration as a matter of policy which it alone can decide."[143] Furthermore, no reasons for a declaration need be given although there may be a political imperative to provide a rationale. The courts may, of course, determine what is a "work."

The origin of this power is obscure, but Laskin suggests that "what clues there are to its purpose come down to a concern that 'national works' like the Welland Canal or the St. Lawrence canals should come under federal control."[144] It is evident that the actual power goes well beyond that intent. "Undertakings" are not included. Nevertheless, Laskin points out that:

> If anything can be gathered from what has been done under s. 92(10)(c), as well as from what has been said about it, the result of a declaration of a "work" to be for the general advantage of Canada must surely be to bring within federal authority not only the physical shell or facility but also the integrated activity carried on therein; in other words, the declaration operates on the work in its functional character . . . Services as such are clearly outside of the category of "works," yet if function is involved in a declaration there are services connected with the operation of the work. May Parliament then declare a hospital to be a "work"? Or a school, or a university? Or a retail store?

The answer to this broad question seems uncertain.

Paragraph (c) permits Parliament to make a declaration in respect of works not yet constructed. This raises the question as to the degree of specificity required. The Supreme Court upheld a declaration in the Canada Grain Act which included "all [grain] elevators in Canada heretofore or hereafter constructed," and one in the Canada Wheat Board Act extending to "all flour mills, feed mills, feed warehouses and seed cleaning mills, whether heretofore constructed or hereafter to be constructed."[145] The declaration in the Grain Act was in response to a Supreme Court decision denying the applicability of the trade and commerce power (s. 91[2]) to Federal efforts to regulate the grain trade, notwithstanding the obvious fact that most of our grain is consumed beyond the province of production. Indeed, most is exported.[146]

A declaration does not change the ownership of the work—it is not an act of nationalization. However, because Parliament may generally expropriate property over which it has legislative jurisdiction, it is likely that Parliament could "expropriate or authorize the expropriation of what it has brought within its jurisdiction" by means of section 92(10)(c).[147]

As of 1969 some 470 declarations had been made. Of these, none was more recent than 1961 and only nine occurred since 1950. Most instances have related to local railways, but others involved tramways, canals, bridges, dams, tunnels, harbours, wharves, telegraphs, telephones, mines, mills, grain elevators, hotels, restaurants, theatres, oil refineries, and factories.[148] In 1946, for example, the Atomic Energy Control Act declared works "for the production, refining or treatment of prescribed substances," which included uranium, to be for the general advantage of Canada.

In 1981 during the oil-pricing dispute between the governments of Alberta and Canada there was a veiled threat that Parliament might invoke the declaratory power in some way. The definition of "work" could have been of considerable significance although it would not likely have included the oil itself.

➤ **SECTION 92(11):** The Incorporation of Companies with Provincial Objects.

The significant phrase is "with provincial objects" for it has been judicially determined that Parliament's p.o.g.g. power extends to the incorporation of companies whose objectives extend beyond the bounds of a province.[149] The only explicit authorization for Ottawa to incorporate companies is section 91(15) in relation to banks. Although a province may not give to a company which it incorporates a legal existence beyond the boundaries of that province, it may authorize the company to accept such existence bestowed by another province or a territory.[150]

There seems to be no functional limitation upon the power of incorporation—that is, a provincially incorporated company need not be confined to matters which under the Constitution Act lie within provincial jurisdiction. Consider, for example, companies that perform banking functions. Although Parliament possesses exclusive power to incorporate "banks," there has been no serious questioning of the provinces' ability to create "near-banks" such as trust companies, credit unions, and caisses populaires.[151]

➤ **SECTION 92(12):** The Solemnization of Marriage in the Province.

See the commentary on section 91(26) which considers the relation between these two subsections. This subsection is an illustration of carving a narrow power from a broader one, thus limiting the scope of the latter.

➤ **SECTION 92(13):** Property and Civil Rights in the Province.

The impact of judicial review on this power has been considered under "Judicial Decisions" in Chapter 5. Many of the disputes have revolved around this subsection in competition with the Parliament's p.o.g.g. or trade and commerce powers.

The term "property and civil rights" goes back in Canadian constitutional history to the Quebec Act which stated (s. 8) that "in all matters of controversy, relative to property and civil rights, resort shall be had to the laws of Canada [i.e., French civil law existing before Britain's defeat of New France], as the rule for the decision of the same." The phrase also appeared in Upper Canada's first statute following the Constitutional Act's division of Quebec into Upper Canada and Lower Canada: the laws of England were to be substituted for French civil law in settling disputes relating to property and civil rights.[152] In these documents, as in the present Act, the phrase was intended as a broad description of the private law which governs the relationships between individuals, as distinct from public law which pertains to the relationships between people and their government. Hogg points out, however, that

> the original distinction between private and public law has tended to break down for constitutional purposes, as governments have increasingly intervened to regulate the economic life of the nation. Labour relations, once a private matter between employer and employee, is now so extensively regulated that it may be thought of as a branch of public law. Much business activity is no longer governed simply by contract, but by statutory rules and the decisions of government officials. These governmental interventions in the marketplace, if they could not be fitted rather clearly into a particular head of legislative power, have for the most part been allocated by the courts to property and civil rights in the province. In other words, the evolution of our laws has now swept much public law into the rubric which was originally designed to exclude public law.[153]

As noted in the commentary on section 91's opening paragraph, certain aspects of "property and civil rights" were explicitly assigned to Parliament in 1867.

➤ **SECTION 92(14):** The Administration of Justice in the Province, including the Constitution, Maintenance, and Organization of Provincial Courts, both of Civil and of Criminal Jurisdiction, and including Procedure in Civil Matters in those Courts.

The commentary on section 91(27) pointed out that Canada has basically a system of provincial courts which hear cases arising from, including the constitutionality of, both Federal and provincial law. Nevertheless, sections 96-101 impose significant centralizing features.

Although provincial governments create their own hierarchy of courts, the judges of "superior, district, and county" courts are Federally appointed under section 96. Quebec never had district or county courts, and only British Columbia, Nova Scotia, and Ontario have retained them. For "superior" courts every province now has a trial court and a court of appeal. Trial courts (in addition to the district and county courts where they still exist) are variously called "Court of Queen's Bench" (Alberta, Manitoba, New Brunswick, Saskatchewan), "High Court of Justice" (Ontario), "Trial Division of the Supreme Court" (Newfoundland, Nova Scotia, Prince Edward Island), "Supreme Court" (British Columbia), or "Superior Court" (Quebec). Appellate courts are called "Court of Appeal" or, where a Supreme Court has two divisions, "Appeal Division of the Supreme Court." Half of the provincial appeal courts (or appellate divisions) have been established since 1966. Ontario's in 1874 was the first; Prince Edward Island's in 1985 was the last.[154]

Provision for Federal appointment of "section 96 judges" has significant implications for provincial authority in assigning responsibilities to lower ("inferior") courts, and therefore for the "administration of justice" and the "organization" of provincial courts. See the commentary on section 96. Judges, sometimes called magistrates or justices of the peace, of these other ("inferior") courts are provincially appointed. (Inferior courts are often called "provincial," thus creating ambiguity within the context of all courts established by provincial legislatures. In the present discussion this narrower meaning of "provincial" is avoided.) Unfortunately, the existence of provincial courts staffed by both Federal and provincial appointees has created a two-status system, and this hinders recruitment of inferior court judges even though they hear the overwhelming majority of criminal cases as well as civil cases.[155]

The difficulty of interpreting section 92(14) is further complicated by the fact that Parliament has jurisdiction (s. 91[27]) in relation to criminal law and procedure within provincial courts. As in so many areas the problem is one of pith and substance. Is an impugned law in relation to the constitution of courts having criminal jurisdiction (s. 92[14]) or in relation to procedure in criminal matters (s. 91[27])? In 1980, for example, the Supreme Court ruled that a Nova Scotia statute permitting judges within eight months of leaving office to "give judgement or grant an order in any proceeding previously tried or heard before him" was within provincial jurisdiction.[156]

Provincial jurisdiction over the administration of justice includes policing and prosecution. Provinces have the power, therefore, to establish their own police forces—Ontario and Quebec have done so—and to authorize municipalities to establish their own forces. Provinces and municipalities may instead hire the R.C.M.P. to perform policing services. When the R.C.M.P. is used, both Federal and provincial governments become involved and this can create grey areas of jurisdiction. In the "administration of justice" the R.C.M.P. operates under provincial authority although that authority does not extend to the discipline, organization, and management of the R.C.M.P.[157] The police are subject to the Royal Canadian Mounted Police Act, and to the Commissioner who is responsible to the solicitor general.

Although the provinces have jurisdiction over the administration of justice and enforce both Federal and provincial law, the Supreme Court has ruled that the authority to enforce the Federal criminal law is not exclusive. Rather, it rests "only on the abstention of the federal authorities from intervening in the prosecution of federal offences." Chief Justice Laskin elaborated:

> Although s. 92(14) grants jurisdiction over the administration of justice, it narrows the scope of the s. 91 criminal law power only with respect to "the Constitution, Maintenance, and Organization of Provincial Courts . . . of Criminal jurisdiction" and could not be con-

strued as including jurisdiction over the conduct of criminal prosecutions. Further, the general administration of justice power cannot be preferred over the special criminal law and procedure power; neither the language of s. 92(14), nor logic, would support such a construction.[158]

It is inconceivable that inadequate provincial enforcement could be allowed to paralyze the operation of Federal legislation.

➤ **SECTION 92(15):** The Imposition of Punishment by Fine, Penalty, or Imprisonment for enforcing any Law of the Province made in relation to any Matter coming within any of the Classes of Subjects enumerated in this Section.

This power would likely have been judicially established had it not been made explicit, because provinces must have the means to enforce their laws.[159] However, the offence must be against a provincial law. No limit is specified as to the amount of fine, severity of penalty, or length of imprisonment. Laskin suggests that "'penalty' would presumably include forfeiture of property and hard labour as an adjunct of imprisonment, but would not include capital punishment."[160]

➤ **SECTION 92(16):** Generally all Matters of a merely local or private Nature in the Province.

This may be considered a type of residual power for local or provincial matters. In a sense, therefore, it is comparable to section 91's p.o.g.g. which was intended to give Parliament the authority to legislate in relation to matters that could not be assigned under any other grant of legislative power.

The potential breadth of 92(16) has been usurped by the broad judicial interpretation of "property and civil rights in the province" (s. 92[13]), leaving subsection 16 with little work except, upon occasion, to be cited as an alternative justification of provincial legislation. In *Schneider* (1982),[161] however, this subsection was the sole justification for upholding British Columbia's Heroin Treatment Act which provided for compulsory detention and treatment of heroin users. The pith and substance, the Supreme Court said, was medical treatment of heroin addicts and not "punitive or . . . a colourable attempt" to invade Parliament's criminal law jurisdiction. Justice Dickson added that "the problem of heroin addiction neither reached a state of emergency giving rise to federal competence under the residual power nor went beyond provincial concern and become by its nature of national concern." The question of Federal paramountcy did not arise, inasmuch as Part II of Parliament's Narcotic Control Act ("Preventive Detention and Custody for Treatment") had not yet been proclaimed.

Non-Renewable Natural Resources, Forestry Resources and Electrical Energy

➤ **SECTION 92A: (1)** In each province, the legislature may exclusively make laws in relation to

(a) exploration for non-renewable natural resources in the province;

(b) development, conservation and management of non-renewable natural resources and forestry resources in the province, including laws in relation to the rate of primary production therefrom; and

(c) development, conservation and management of sites and facilities in the province for the generation and production of electrical energy.

(2) In each province, the legislature may make laws in relation to the export from the province to another part of Canada of the primary production from non-renewable natural resources and forestry resources in the province and the production from facilities in the province for the generation of electrical energy, but such laws may not authorize or provide for discrimination in prices or in supplies exported to another part of Canada.

(3) Nothing in subsection (2) derogates from the authority of Parliament to enact laws in relation to the matters referred to in that subsection and, where such a law of Parliament and a law of a province conflict, the law of Parliament prevails to the extent of the conflict.

(4) In each province, the legislature may make laws in relation to the raising of money by any mode or system of taxation in respect of

(a) non-renewable natural resources and forestry resources in the province and the primary production therefrom, and

(b) sites and facilities in the province for the generation of electrical energy and the production therefrom,

whether or not such production is exported in whole or in part from the province, but such laws may not authorize or provide for taxation that differentiates between production exported to another part of Canada and production not exported from the province.

(5) The expression "primary production" has the meaning assigned by the Sixth Schedule.

(6) Nothing in subsections (1) to (5) derogates from any powers or rights that a legislature or government of a province had immediately before the coming into force of this section.

The Sixth Schedule is as follows:

Primary Production from Non-renewable Natural Resources and Forestry Resources

1. For the purposes of section 92A of this Act,
   (a) production from a non-renewable natural resource is primary production therefrom if
      (i) it is in the form in which it exists upon its recovery or severance from its natural state, or
      (ii) it is a product resulting from processing or refining the resource, and is not a manufactured product or a product resulting from refining crude oil, refining upgraded heavy crude oil, refining gases or liquids derived from coal or refining a synthetic equivalent or crude oil; and
   (b) production from a forestry resource is primary production therefrom if it consists of sawlogs, poles, lumber, wood chips, sawdust or any other primary wood product, or wood pulp, and is not a product manufactured from wood.

This section with the Sixth Schedule was added as an amendment by sections 50 and 51 of the 1982 Constitution Act—the sole change made by that Act to the distribution of legislative authority between the two orders of government. It is an attempt to give greater control over resource development to the producing provinces. It establishes concurrent jurisdiction over interprovincial trade of natural resources and permits the provinces to levy indirect taxes on these resources.

Controversy between the producing provinces (especially Alberta and Saskatchewan) and the Federal government characterized much of the 1970s. In the early years of that decade a world energy crisis resulted in the quadrupling of the international price of oil. The Federal government imposed controls on the export of crude oil, established an oil export tax to subsidize imports of expensive oil, and moved to reduce oil imports by expanding the market for domestic oil into Quebec and the Atlantic provinces.[162] It also decided to hold the price of domestic oil below the world price—in effect to subsidize the large consumers in central Canada—and eliminated (but later modified) the deductibility of royalty payments from corporate income for tax purposes. Meekison and Romanow, key players in the negotiations which ultimately produced section 92A, comment that "in the aggregate, these policies were considered by the oil- and gas-producing provinces of western Canada to be an attempt to wrest resource management and control from the provincial governments." This concern was reinforced, they add, by Finance Minister Turner's May 1974 budget statement that "a provincial resource is also a national resource, and the federal government has a responsibility to see that a reasonable portion of this gain is shared by all Canadians."[163] At the October 1978 First Ministers Conference, Saskatchewan Premier Blakeney wanted to know why the revenues from oil but not from other commodities were to be shared nationally. Why should Ottawa impose an export tax, the proceeds to be shared nationally, on western oil "while exports of hydro-electricity from Ontario and Quebec enrich those provinces alone[?] . . . Financing our federation is something that must be done by all sides in a fair manner, not by singling out for special federal levies the particular resources of a specific region."[164]

The urgency of a solution was heightened when the Supreme Court struck down two Saskatchewan laws in 1977 and 1978 which had attempted to strengthen provincial control over resources and to increase resource revenue.[165] In *Canadian Industrial Gas & Oil Ltd.* (*CIGOL*, 1978) the Court declared unconstitutional the province's mineral income tax and its royalty surcharge which had been imposed to capture some of the windfall profit resulting from the sky-rocketing world oil price. The Court ruled that the "mineral income tax," levied on oil from private land, was not a tax on income "as that term is understood" (which would be a direct tax). Rather it was an indirect per barrel commodity tax imposed on the seller who would pass it on as part of the price to the consumer. As for the "royalty surcharge" the Court decided that it could not be a royalty. The province had expropriated private lands in order to impose royalties on the newly acquired Crown lands. However, the leases were not expropriated and, because the amount of royalty was fixed by the terms of the lease, the additional charge could not be a royalty but must be a tax. Justice Martland, who delivered the Court's majority ruling, concluded that "the royalty surcharge made applicable to these Crown leases was not a royalty for which provision was made in the lease agreement. It was imposed as a levy upon the share of production to which, under the lease, the lessee was entitled, and was a tax upon production"—a tax "of the same nature as the mineral income tax." Furthermore, because the legislation enabled the minister to establish the price which Saskatchewan oil companies would receive on their export sales (there being practically no local market), an authority not belonging to the provinces, it trenched upon Parliament's power to regulate trade and commerce (s. 91[2]).

In *Central Canada Potash* the Court ruled that Saskatchewan's restriction of potash production and establishment of a minimum price was not legislation to conserve natural resources. The province claimed that its "Potash Conservation Regulations" had indeed demonstrated the intent of resource conservation and therefore the legitimacy of provincial action. According to studies quoted by Chief Justice Laskin, Saskatchewan's reserves could satisfy world needs for some 1500 years. Therefore, the pith and substance was "the regulation of the marketing of potash through the fixing of a minimum selling price." Because "the only market for which the schemes had any significance was the export market" the Court used the *CIGOL* reasoning and ruled that the legislation effectively regulated export prices and therefore interfered with Parliament's trade and commerce power. Hogg disagreed with the ruling, noting significantly:

> The purpose of the controls was not to reduce the export trade (though that was certainly their effect), but to protect the local mining industry. The Court's reasoning produces the unfortunate consequence that those provinces that, like Saskatchewan, are mainly primary producers have less control over their natural resources than those provinces that, like Ontario, have more integrated economies.[166]

According to Meekison and Romanow these two rulings "coloured all future constitutional negotiations on resources."[167] When the Continuing Committee of Ministers on the Constitution (C.C.M.C.) was established at the 1978 First Ministers' Constitutional Conference, resources were one of the fourteen agenda items. The major resource issues were a definition of "natural resources" (should the concept include both renewable and non-renewable resources? water?), a definition of "primary production" (where should the line be drawn with manufacturing?), the Federal trade and commerce power in relation to natural resources, the ability of provincial governments to levy indirect taxes in relation to natural resources, and the Federal declaratory power (s. 92[10][c]) in relation to natural resources. The C.C.M.C. recommended the definitions that finally emerged in section 92A and the Sixth Schedule; concurrent Federal-provincial jurisdiction over interprovincial and international trade of non-renewable resources; and Federal paramountcy over both international and interprovincial trade, except that in the latter situation the Federal law would have to serve a "compelling national interest" (a test for which remained an outstanding issue). The provinces would be able to levy indirect taxes to raise resource revenue. Exercise of the declaratory power would require provincial consent.[168]

An aging and weakened Trudeau Government accepted these proposals at the February 1979 Constitutional Conference. However, after the 1980 election victory following the short-lived Clark Government, and the defeat in the same year of the Quebec sovereignty-association referendum, an emboldened Trudeau became less flexible. The original patriation resolution presented to Parliament in October 1980 contained no natural resources amendment, but one was added in a deal to secure the support of the Federal New Democratic Party (minus the support of most of Saskatchewan's M.P.'s). The result was the present amendment. Ottawa had rejected concurrency in international trade of resources, limitation of Federal paramountcy in interprovincial trade, and restriction of its declaratory power.

Subsection (1): It is doubtful that this changes the law; legislation in relation to (a), (b), and (c), would likely have been upheld under section 92(5), (10), (13), or (16).[169] However, the amendment's detail, far greater than in the section 91 and 92 enumerations, removes any lingering doubt by its specific application to resources. The courts may have to establish definitions of some key terms such as "development," "conservation," and "non-renewable."

Subsection (2): This is a new provincial power now held concurrently with Parliament inasmuch as interprovincial trade has always been deemed by the courts to fall within section 91(2). Because this subsection is limited to trade within Canada, it adds little authority in relation to resources such as Saskatchewan potash most of which is exported to the foreign market. The restriction also raises a question about legislation affecting resource production destined for both the rest of Canada and beyond. Finally, price discrimination between the producing provinces and the rest of Canada is expressly prohibited.

Subsection (3): This makes Federal paramountcy explicit in the event of conflict between provincial legislation under subsection (2) and Federal legislation under section 91(2) or 92(10)(c).

Subsection (4): Provinces have hitherto been limited to direct taxation. Now they may levy indirect taxes in relation to matters stipulated in paragraphs (a) and (b) of this subsection, provided that such taxes do not discriminate between production exported to another part of Canada and that consumed within the producing province. The phrase "to another part of Canada" leaves open the possibility of tax discrimination between production exported beyond Canada and that consumed within the producing province, unless the courts interpret such discrimination as a foray into international trade and therefore Parliament's jurisdiction. The restriction in section 92(2) that provincial taxation be "within the province" is not reproduced here; indeed, the present subsection explicitly authorizes provincial taxation "whether or not such production is exported in whole or in part from the province." Without this relaxation there would have been little benefit to an exporting province, given the CIGOL ruling that Saskatchewan's tax was unconstitutional in part as not being "within the province."

Subsection (5): The Sixth Schedule defines the term "primary production" used in subsections (1), (2), and (4).

Subsection (6): This ensures that section 92A does not reduce provincial powers under section 92(5), (10), (13), or (16).

The gains made by the producing provinces are reinforced by the Constitutional amending formula which (s. 38[3] of the 1982 Act) permits a province to opt out of an amendment which derogates from the province's legislative power (now explicitly including natural resources) or proprietary rights.

Education

➤ **SECTION 93:** In and for each Province the Legislature may exclusively make Laws in relation to Education, subject and according to the following Provisions:—

(1) Nothing in any such Law shall prejudicially affect any Right or Privilege with respect to Denominational Schools which any Class of Persons have by Law in the Province at the Union:

(2) All the Powers, Privileges, and Duties at the Union by Law conferred and imposed in Upper Canada on the Separate Schools and School Trustees of the Queen's Roman Catholic Subjects shall be and the same are hereby extended to the Dissentient Schools of the Queen's Protestant and Roman Catholic Subjects in Quebec:

(3) Where in any Province a System of Separate or Dissentient Schools exists by Law at the Union or is thereafter established by the Legislature of the Province, an Appeal shall lie to the Governor General in Council from any Act or Decision of any Provincial Authority affecting any Right or Privilege of the Protestant or Roman Catholic Minority of the Queen's Subjects in relation to Education:

(4) In case any such Provincial Law as from Time to Time seems to the Governor General in Council requisite for the due Execution of the Provisions of this Section is not made, or in case any Decision of the Governor General in Council on any Appeal under this Section is not duly executed by the proper Provincial Authority in that Behalf, then and in every such Case, and as far only as the Circumstances of each Case require, the Parliament of Canada may make remedial Laws for the due Execution of the Provisions of this Section and of any Decision of the Governor General in Council under this Section.

Although this section assigns legislative authority in relation to education to the provinces, it also protects a denominational school system (as defined in the section) that exists "by law" within a province "at the union or is thereafter established by the legislature of the province." This protection takes the form of granting authority to the Federal government to act in support of an aggrieved minority within a province that passes legislation prejudicial to that minority. The Federal government may require the province to redress the grievance or, failing compliance, it may pass remedial legislation binding upon the province.

This section was made directly applicable to British Columbia and Prince Edward Island through the orders-in-council admitting these provinces. Those orders made the Constitution Act applicable "as if the Colony . . . had been one of the Provinces originally united by the said Act." Similar provisions with appropriate adjustments to meet local conditions were written into the constitutional documents admitting the remaining provinces. Because Manitoba had a separate school system in practice but not in law at the time of union, the Manitoba Act (s. 22) substituted "by law or practice" for "by law." For the Alberta Act and Saskatchewan Act the words "in law" in section 17 referred to chapters 29 and 30 of the 1901 Ordinances of the Northwest Territories. In the case of Newfoundland, protection was extended (by Term 17 of the Schedule to the Terms of Union of Newfoundland with Canada Act), but without the right of appeal to the Federal government, to "denominational schools, common (amalgamated) schools, or denominational colleges."

Subsection 4 of this section has never been implemented, but it came close as a result of Manitoba legislation (1890) which replaced the system of denominational schools with a single tax-supported non-denominational system. The Catholic minority appealed to the Federal government; this was a difficult decision because most of Manitoba's Catholics had come from Quebec and were reluctant to invite Federal intervention in provincial matters. The Conservative Government of Prime Minister Bowell on March 21, 1895, instructed the Manitoba government to provide redress to the Catholic minority, but the Manitoba government procrastinated and finally rejected the order in December 1895.[170] Remedial legislation was introduced in Parliament in February 1896, but Parliament's statutory five-year time limit ran out as the Liberals filibustered. Following the victory of Laurier and the Liberal Party in the June 1896 election a compromise arrangement was worked out with the Manitoba government. That arrangement did not include the reinstatement of a tax-supported separate school system.

It should be noted that the protection given by this section is to schools, not languages. A challenge to Ontario's 1913 "Regulation 17," which curtailed the use of the French language in Catholic schools, was rejected by the Privy Council which affirmed that the protection of section 93 extended to "a class of persons determined according to religious belief, and not according to race or language."[171] The importance of this distinction between denominational and non-denominational aspects of education in denominational schools was made explicit in *Greater Montreal Protestant School Board* (*GMPSB*, 1989) and *Mahe* (1990).[172] In these cases the Supreme Court interpreted the reference to the rights and privileges of "denominational schools" in section 93(1) of the present Act (and, by analogy, provisions of other constitutional documents forming or admitting the other six provinces) to mean rights and privileges of (1) the denominational aspects of education in denominational schools, and (2) any non-denominational aspects necessary to give effect to denominational rights. The protection does not, therefore, extend to any non-denominational aspects of education in denominational schools which are not necessary to give effect to denominational rights.

In *GMPSB* this meant that the Quebec government may establish curricula for Protestant schools so long as they avoid the content of moral and religious education. "By carving out the denominational content of curriculum and leaving it in the hands of the Protestant Committee of the Conseil, the province has conformed to the law in effect at the time of the Union." In *Mahe* it meant that granting powers of management and control over minority language education to minority language trustees on the Edmonton Catholic Separate School Board, in accordance with Charter section 23, does not "affect any rights in respect of the denominational aspects of education or related non-denominational aspects."

What might be non-denominational aspects of education which affect the rights of denominational schools and which, therefore, should be protected? In *Greater Hull School Board* (1984),[173] the Court ruled that a proposed new system of school funding for Quebec which failed to specify that grants would be distributed to denominational schools on a proportionate basis—the basis existing by law in 1867—prejudicially affected the rights guaranteed by section 93. However, in *GMPSB* the claim of the Protestant appellants was rejected. This claim was that Quebec's underlying educational philosophy prejudicially affected the rights of Protestant schools. For example, the number of required courses made impossible the teaching of electives; the only course in Canadian history (which was also required), entitled "History of Quebec and Canada," ignored post-1929 Canada beyond Quebec; teaching English as a second language before grade 4 was prohibited. In making its ruling the Court held that to accept the Protestant School Board's claim would be to cast the section 93(1) guarantee net much too broadly:

> By associating the content of the constitutional guarantee with a Protestant educational philosophy founded upon pluralism, the appellants would give to the Protestant community a right or privilege to determine the curriculum used in denominational schools which is completely incompatible with the exercise of a general regulatory power of the province over matters of curriculum which fall outside religious and moral education.[174]

In 1987 (*Ref. re Bill 30, an Act to Amend the Education Act [Ont.]*)[175] the Supreme Court upheld the authority of the Ontario legislature to provide full funding for Roman Catholic separate high schools under section 93. This case is discussed in the commentaries on Charter sections 15 and 29.

Uniformity of Laws in Ontario, Nova Scotia and New Brunswick

➤ **SECTION 94:** Notwithstanding anything in this Act, the Parliament of Canada may make Provision for the Uniformity of all or any of the Laws relative to Property and Civil Rights in Ontario, Nova Scotia, and New Brunswick, and of the Procedure of all or any of the Courts in Those Three Provinces, and from and after the passing of any Act in that Behalf the Power of the Parliament of Canada to make Laws in relation to any Matter comprised in any such Act shall, notwithstanding anything in this Act, be unrestricted; but any Act of the Parliament of Canada making Provision for such Uniformity shall not have effect in any Province unless and until it is adopted and enacted as Law by the Legislature thereof.

This provision for the uniformity of laws and court procedures excludes Quebec. The reason is that all of the provinces except Quebec have common-law traditions. No attempt has been made to create the uniformity envisioned by this section and, despite obvious benefits which would accrue to our increasingly mobile society, there seems little likelihood that provincial governments would be willing to relinquish their jurisdiction to Ottawa.

If the potential of this section had been implemented, much of the litigation over the years involving property and civil rights in competition with p.o.g.g. would have been avoided. One consequence would have been a centralized federal system.

Old Age Pensions

➤ **SECTION 94A:** The Parliament of Canada may make laws in relation to old age pensions and supplementary benefits, including survivors, and disability benefits irrespective of age, but no such law shall affect the operation of any law present or future of a provincial legislature in relation to any such matter.

Section 94A as originally enacted by the 1951 B.N.A. Act authorized Parliament to make laws "in relation to old age pensions." The current section, enacted by the 1964 Constitution Act, broadens possible Federal involvement to include survivor and disability benefits. The 1951 Old Age Security Act provided for pensions to be funded entirely by Ottawa. The contributory Canada Pension Plan was established in 1966 and operates in nine provinces. Quebec has its own parallel plan, the result of Federal legislation permitting provinces to opt out of certain cost-sharing schemes and to receive either tax abatements or Federal grants in return for the establishment of similar programs.

Old age pensions are the only area of concurrent jurisdiction having provincial paramountcy. Concurrent jurisdiction with Federal paramountcy exists in relation to non-renewable natural resources, forestry resources, and electrical energy (s. 92A); agriculture and immigration (s. 95); and, for practical purposes, direct taxation. For the doctrine of paramountcy generally, see the commentary on the closing paragraph of section 91.

As originally enacted section 94A read as follows:

> 94A. It is hereby declared that the Parliament of Canada may from time to time make laws in relation to old age pensions in Canada, but no law made by the Parliament of Canada in relation to old age pensions shall affect the operation of any law present or future of a Provincial Legislature in relation to old age pensions.

Agriculture and Immigration

➤ **SECTION 95:** In each Province the Legislature may make Laws in relation to Agriculture in the Province, and to Immigration into the Province; and it is hereby declared that the Parliament of Canada may from Time to Time make Laws in relation to Agriculture in all or any of the Provinces, and to Immigration into all or any of the Provinces; and any Law of the Legislature of a Province relative to Agriculture or to Immigration shall have effect in and for the Province as long and as far only as it is not repugnant to any Act of the Parliament of Canada.

In spite of the preponderance of agriculture in the Canadian economy, especially at the time of Confederation and on the western prairies since then, there has been relatively little judicial action dealing with agriculture *per se*.[176] Agriculture has been more of a by-product of controversy involving Federal powers relating to "interest" and "bankruptcy and insolvency," and provincial authority regarding "property and civil rights." This controversy was noted in the commentary on section 91(19) and (21).

There is an obvious relationship between agriculture and immigration in a sparsely settled country whose main occupation is farming. Our first Federal minister of agriculture noted the intimacy of this relationship in 1868:

> The Dominion Government having no land can make them [immigrants] no grants of land, that being in the possession of the local [provincial] governments. Therefore it was important for us to know what steps the Dominion Government have taken in this matter, and to know whether the local governments are willing to cooperate with them in order to settle the country.[177]

Although the criteria for entry into Canada is a Federal matter and governed by the Immigration Act, the encouragement of settlement in the provinces, including measures to ease the problems associated with movement to a strange land, falls within provincial jurisdiction. If the Meech Lake amendments had been approved, the provinces would have played a more formal role with respect to immigration although Federal paramountcy would have been retained.

VII. Judicature

➤ **SECTION 96:** The Governor General shall appoint the Judges of the Superior, District, and County Courts in each Province, except those of the Courts of Probate in Nova Scotia and New Brunswick.

The implications of this section go far beyond mere appointment of provincial court judges. Indeed, it may be argued that section 96 together with sections 97-101 create a unified judicial system under significant Federal control. Supreme Court Justice Pigeon pointed out in 1979 that "while it is usual to refer to these [section 96] courts as provincial, they are so only in a limited sense. Under s. 96 the federal government plays the most important role in their establishment."[178]

What was the purpose of section 96? The section attracted little attention in the discussions at the time of Confederation, but the Privy Council and the Supreme Court have since attached considerable importance to it. It could have been argued in 1867 that Federal appointment of provincial judges was necessary to ensure a judiciary free of provincial political interference. The Privy Council adopted that view in the 1930s when it characterized Federal appointment together with the tenure and salary provisions (ss. 99, 100) as "three principal pillars in the temple of justice . . . not to be undermined,"[179] and "at the root of the means adopted by the framers of the . . . [1867 Constitution Act] to secure the impartiality and independence of the Provincial judiciary."[180] Today this rationale is antiquated. Nevertheless, although provincial governments are naturally concerned about appointments to their section 96 courts, there is no systematic consultation by Ottawa.[181]

The significant unitary features of the 1867 Constitution Act, as well as the subsequent decentralization toward a more classical federalism, were noted in Chapter 4. Not until the mid-1970s, however, did the centralizing feature of section 96 become an important topic of judicial review and political criticism. Between 1975 and 1982 section 96 was involved in eleven Supreme Court cases—more than any other constitutional issue.[182] By the end of the 1970s the provinces sought authority to appoint all judges to their courts.[183] Indeed, current discussion challenges Ottawa's exclusive right to appoint judges even to the Supreme Court of Canada. If the integrating effect of section 96 is to be acceptable to provincial as well as Federal politicians it seems that a change in the appointment process to involve both orders of government is inevitable.[184]

The importance which the Supreme Court has attached to section 96 was expressed by Justice Dickson for a unanimous Court in the *Residential Tenancies Act Reference* (1981). He noted that the broad provincial authority to legislate in relation to the administration of justice (s. 92[14]) was limited by sections 96-100. Together, he said, these powers assigned to the two orders of government

> represent one of the important compromises of the Fathers of Confederation. It is plain that what was sought to be achieved through this compromise, and the intended effect of s. 96, would be destroyed if a province could pass legislation creating a tribunal, appoint members thereto, and then confer on the tribunal the jurisdiction of the superior courts. What was conceived as a strong constitutional base for national unity . . . would be gravely undermined. Section 96 has thus come to be regarded as limiting provincial competence to make appointments to a tribunal exercising s. 96 judicial powers and therefore as implicitly limiting provincial competence to endow a provincial tribunal with such powers.[185]

This statement highlights the controversy. To what extent does the Federal appointing power frustrate provincial attempts to assign judicial functions among courts and administrative bodies for the better administration of justice under section 92(14)? According to the Supreme Court the provinces may not tamper with the functions normally performed by their superior, district, or county courts; unfortunately, however, those functions have not been precisely defined (although Dickson suggested a three-step test in 1981).[186] The fact remains that the restriction places a significant limitation on the ability of provinces to exercise their section 92(14) authority. The *Residential Tenancies Act* decision, for example, denied the cheaper and quicker access to Ontario's Residential Tenancy Commission which possessed expertise in the specific area of landlord-tenant disputes.

However, in the 1990 *Young Offenders Act (P.E.I.) Reference* the Court used the *Residential Tenancies Act Reference* to sustain Prince Edward Island's Young Offenders Act. That Act gave to the province's (inferior) youth courts jurisdiction over young persons. The Court's rational was that this function had not been exercised by superior courts at the time of Confederation. Indeed, in 1867 there was no comprehensive scheme recognizing the "special situation and special needs of young offenders."[186a]

In another case the attempt by British Columbia to unify all family law under a single family court (staffed by provincial appointees) was frustrated by the Court's ruling in the *B.C. Family Relations Act Reference* (1982).[187] The province could confer upon its family court jurisdiction "respecting guardianship of the person of the child and custody of or access to the child," but it must leave to the superior (section 96) courts jurisdiction "respecting orders concerning occupancy and use of the family residence and the making of non-entry orders."

In *McEvoy* (1983),[188] the Supreme Court denied Parliament's authority to unify criminal law under inferior courts. Until that decision it appeared that restrictions in assigning section 96 functions to inferior courts applied only to the provinces. The unanimous *McEvoy* ruling declared that

> Parliament can no more give away federal constitutional powers than a province can usurp them . . . The effect of this proposal to transfer the present superior court criminal jurisdiction over indictable offences to a provincial court [or, the Court added, to give such court concurrent jurisdiction with superior courts] would be to deprive the Governor General of his power under s. 96 to appoint the judges who try indictable offences. . . . This section bars Parliament and the provincial legislatures from altering the constitutional scheme envisaged by the judicature sections of the *Constitution Act, 1867* which guarantee the independence of the Superior Courts from both levels of government.

The proposal would amount to a "complete obliteration of superior court criminal law jurisdiction" through an unconstitutional transformation of inferior into superior courts under colour of legislation in relation to section 92(14). Section 96 is an "insuperable obstacle to any such endeavour." The Court added that "there is . . . a cardinal difference between mere alteration or diminution of criminal jurisdiction and complete exclusion of such jurisdiction." Finkelstein questions the significance of such a distinction unless there exists a definitive body of criminal jurisdiction within section 96.[189] Russell adds that the *McEvoy* ruling "is not easily squared with Parliament's assignment over the years of a vast jurisdiction in criminal matters" to inferior courts.[190]

Apart from a decision to unify jurisdiction under section 96 courts, the only means of overcoming the Supreme Court restrictions would seem to be a Constitutional amendment. Such an amendment proposed by the Federal government in 1983 (which has not been pursued) would have permitted a provincial legislature to delegate a section 96 function to an administrative body such as a "tribunal, board, commission or authority, other than a court . . . concurrent or exclusive jurisdiction in respect of any matter within the legislative authority of the Province." Decisions of such a body would be "subject to review by a superior court of the Province for want or excess of jurisdiction."[191] While such an amendment would doubtlessly remove much of the present uncertainty, the exclusion of inferior courts from the delegation would create the additional judicial task of deciding what or when is a "court."

➤ **SECTION 97:** Until the Laws relative to Property and Civil Rights in Ontario, Nova Scotia, and New Brunswick, and the Procedure of the Courts in those Provinces, are made uniform, the Judges of the Courts of those Provinces appointed by the Governor General shall be selected from the respective Bars of those Provinces.

The purpose of this section is presumably to ensure that only lawyers who are familiar with a province's law will be appointed to the superior, district, and county courts. Had the uniformity of law contemplated by section 94 been realized there would doubtlessly have been pressure for the appointment of judges from each province's bar.

➤ **SECTION 98:** The Judges of the Courts of Quebec shall be selected from the Bar of that Province.

This provision recognizes Quebec's distinctive civil law inherited from France and derived from the 1804 Napoleonic Code, which itself may be traced back to Roman Law. Legal systems in the other provinces are based on the common law.

➤ **SECTION 99:** (1) Subject to subsection two of this section, the Judges of the Superior Courts shall hold office during good behaviour, but shall be removable by the Governor General on Address of the Senate and House of Commons.

(2) A Judge of a Superior Court, whether appointed before or after the coming into force of this section, shall cease to hold office upon attaining the age of seventy-five years, or upon the coming into force of this section if at that time he has already attained that age.

The purpose of tenure "during good behaviour" and removal "on address" of both houses of Parliament is to prevent the removal of judges for political reasons. Nevertheless, the principle of judicial independence from political pressure cannot be realized by security of tenure alone. Removal for political reasons is blatant interference; attempts to influence judges can be very subtle.

The 1976 "judges affair" provides a recent example. According to a letter from Quebec Superior Court Justice MacKay to Federal Justice Minister Basford, four Federal cabinet ministers had interfered with the course of justice during the previous half dozen years, a practice "all too prevalent amongst your colleagues." As a result of the episode, Prime Minister Trudeau announced in the House of Commons that "in future no member of the Cabinet may communicate with members of the judiciary concerning any matter which they have before them in their judicial capacities, except through the Minister of Justice, his duly authorized officials, or counsel acting for him."[192]

When is "good behaviour" breached? In common law, says Russell, it is "confined to an improper exercise of the office, neglect or refusal to perform the duties of the office, or conviction for a serious criminal offence involving moral turpitude."[193] Dawson and Ward say basically the same thing but then add:

> A judge may be stupid, and make scores of wrong decisions; he may be indolent, and neglect his work; he may be, at least to a degree, biased and unfair, yet there is every likelihood that he will be retained in office. The government would certainly not punish him for stupidity, for over that he has no control. Nor is it at all likely that the government would take any action against him for the above, and many other, faults for which he is definitely to be blamed. While his conduct may be shocking and the administration of justice may suffer, the lesser evil is to leave him alone; for an attack and a removal for any but the most flagrant and scandalous offences would have a detrimental effect on the work, security, and peace of mind of all the other members of the judiciary.[194]

A 1971 amendment to the Judges Act established the following somewhat more precise, yet still broad, criteria for dismissal:[195]

(a) age or infirmity
(b) having been guilty of misconduct
(c) having failed in the due exercise of his office
(d) having been placed, by his conduct or otherwise, in a position incompatible with the due exercise of his office.

Since the Constitution Act's 1960 amendment which added part (2) of this section 99, compulsory retirement at age 75 has helped to resolve problems resulting from old age. Methods of inducing some judges to accept early retirement include a substantial pension upon resignation after fifteen years of service, and (after prescribed steps have been followed) the stoppage of salary when, pursuant to the Judges Act, a judge has "become incapacitated or disabled from the due execution of his office." The latter inducement has evidently not been used, although it has been threatened successfully and its constitutionality questioned.[196]

Section 99 provides security of tenure for judges appointed to superior, but not district or county, courts. Because the section does not explicitly identify the superior courts as provincial there has been speculation as to whether the Supreme Court and Federal Court are "superior" and therefore caught by this section. Tenure provisions, including compulsory retirement, for Supreme Court and Federal Court judges were determined by ordinary Act of Parliament, whereas compulsory retirement at age 75 for "superior" court judges was accomplished by formal Constitutional amendment. Perhaps the question is academic, but it would be strange if our two highest courts have less constitutional protection than some provincial courts.[197] Had the Meech Lake Constitutional amendments been approved, the guarantees of sections 99 and 100 of this Act would have been extended to the Supreme Court. The commentary on section 52(2) of the 1982 Constitution Act notes that the constitutional status of the Supreme Court is somewhat ambiguous for other reasons as well.

The tenure of district and county court judges is also "during good behaviour," but because it is established by legislation (the Judges Act) it may be altered by Parliament. Compulsory retirement at age 75 was established in 1987.[198] Provincially appointed judges, whose retirement age is generally 65 or 70, are protected by similar provisions in provincial legislation.[199] As in other areas of employment the stipulation of a compulsory retirement age may be challenged under section 15 of the Charter as age discrimination. On December 6, 1990, the Supreme Court upheld compulsory retirement provisions for university professors as a valid limitation on the Charter's equality rights. That issue is noted in the commentaries on Charter sections 15 and 32.

Does section 99 provide one method or two methods of removal? In other words, are removal for bad behaviour and removal by joint address independent of each other? This question may be academic in view of the strong tradition of judicial independence. In fact, no superior court judge has been removed since Confederation.[200]

➤ **SECTION 100:** The Salaries, Allowances, and Pensions of the Judges of the Superior, District, and County Courts (except the Courts of Probate in Nova Scotia and New Brunswick), and of the Admiralty Courts in Cases where the Judges thereof are for the Time being paid by Salary, shall be fixed and provided by the Parliament of Canada.

This section is intended to support the concept of an independent judiciary. The cabinet appoints the judges (s. 96) but Parliament, which must authorize the expenditure of all funds, establishes their salaries through the Judges Act. There may be no difference in the outcome, given the cabinet's control of Parliament, but Parliamentary action ensures public scrutiny.

➤ **SECTION 101:** The Parliament of Canada may, notwithstanding anything in this Act, from Time to Time provide for the Constitution, Maintenance, and Organization of a General Court of Appeal for Canada, and for the Establishment of any additional Courts for the better Administration of the Laws of Canada.

A bill to create the Supreme Court was introduced in the House of Commons in 1869 and again in 1870. These efforts were abandoned mainly because of Quebec's concern that the Court, which would be part of the central government machinery, might lack objectivity in Ottawa's disputes with the provinces over legislative jurisdiction.[201] This concern has been expressed by some provincial governments since then, but studies have not substantiated those fears.[202] Upon its creation in 1875 the Supreme Court was given appellate jurisdiction in civil and criminal cases with respect to both Federal and provincial laws. The legislation also allowed appeals from provincial courts to bypass the Supreme Court and go directly to the Privy Council.

The size of the Supreme Court was increased from six to seven judges in 1927 and to nine in 1949. An appointee must either come from a provincial superior court or be a lawyer with at least ten years of experience. Representation from Quebec rose from two in 1867 to three in 1949. Although Quebec's presence on the Court is the only "federal" characteristic required by law, a definite pattern of regional representation has developed. In recent years three judges have come from Ontario, two from western Canada, and one from Atlantic Canada. It is usual to include on a panel judges from the region involved when the full Court is not sitting. Regional representation is not, of course, intended to create regional or provincial bias in disputes between the two orders of government, but it does enable a judge who is familiar with a province's laws to bring expertise to cases involving that province or region. The Supreme Court Act requires judges to retire at age 75; tenure is during good behaviour.[203]

Although the Supreme Court was created as the "general court of appeal for Canada," the British Privy Council remained the final appeal body for Canadian cases. An 1888 amendment to the Criminal Code terminated these appeals in criminal cases, but the legislation was struck down when it was challenged in 1926 as being in conflict with British law which was paramount by virtue of the Colonial Laws Validity Act.[204] Section 129 of the 1867 Constitution Act permitted Canada to alter domestic law and (among other things) judicial authority, but a parenthetical restriction within that section prevented Canadian legislation from contravening certain British laws and, as it turned out, from eliminating appeals to the Privy Council. See the commentary on section 129. The 1926 ruling was one reason for the 1926 Imperial Conference which produced the Balfour Declaration that the dominions were equal with Britain in status.

In 1933, two years after the Statute of Westminster confirmed the Balfour Declaration and repealed the Colonial Laws Validity Act with respect to Canada and the other dominions, the 1888 legislation was re-enacted and upheld by the Privy Council.[205] Because of uncertainty whether Ottawa could act alone to eliminate appeals proceeding directly from provincial courts to the Privy Council in matters under provincial jurisdiction, appeals in civil cases remained until 1949. In the 1937 *Labour Conventions Reference* the Privy Council struck down Prime Minister Bennett's New Deal legislation, notwithstanding the real emergency of the Depression. This action was a powerful motivating force to abolish appeals, although there were provincial— especially Quebec—fears that the elimination of appeals would lead to greater centralization of the federal system. (The Supreme Court of Canada had divided evenly on this Reference.)[206] In the *Privy Council Appeals Reference* (1947) the Privy Council agreed that section 101 of the Constitution Act included the authority "to deny appellate jurisdiction to any other court."[207]

There is some ambiguity as to the current Constitutional status of the Supreme Court. On the one hand the Court is a creature of Parliament and not a "Constitutional court" whose existence could be protected by the Constitution Act. Indeed, the Schedule to the 1982 Constitution Act does not include the Supreme Court Act as part of the "Constitution of Canada." On the other hand, the Constitution Act's amending formula denies Parliament the authority to alter unilaterally the Court's composition and, depending upon the significance of the Supreme Court Act's omission from the Schedule, perhaps other aspects of the Court as well. It is even possible that the very existence of the Court is subject solely to Parliament's discretion. (See the commentary on section 52[2] of the 1982 Act.)

Had the Meech Lake amendments been approved, Supreme Court judges would henceforth have been selected by the Federal cabinet from lists of qualified individuals submitted by provincial governments and acceptable to the cabinet. To be qualified an appointee would have been a judge of any Canadian court, or a member of the bar of any province or territory, for at least ten years. The current statutory provision requiring three of the nine Supreme Court judges to come from Quebec would have been entrenched. Finally, sections 99 and 100 of the 1867 Constitution Act would have been extended to include Supreme Court judges.

In addition to the establishment of a general court of appeal, section 101 authorizes the establishment of "any additional courts for the better administration of the laws of Canada"—that is, the laws of the Government of Canada. Under this authority the Federal government created the Exchequer Court at the same time as the Supreme Court. The Exchequer Court was a court of original jurisdiction essentially to hear revenue cases involving the Crown. Jurisdiction was increased over the years until, by the time of the Court's replacement by the Federal Court in 1971, it extended far beyond fiscal matters to include copyright, trademarks, patents, admiralty, tax, and citizenship—all relating to Federal laws.[208] Appeals were heard by the Supreme Court as a matter of right in cases involving more than $500. The Supreme Court and the Exchequer Court were initially composed of the same judges, but in 1887 the latter court was reduced to a single judge independent of the Supreme Court. This number was increased to seven by 1971.

The Federal Court has jurisdiction over matters formerly heard by the Exchequer Court, as well as authority to review decisions of Federal boards and commissions. Because it has both trial and appellate divisions the new Court has relieved the Supreme Court of a major source of appeals. Appeals from the

Appeals Division may nevertheless be heard at the discretion of the Supreme Court. The Federal Court may also determine the constitutionality of Parliament's laws and regulations made pursuant to them, but this does not exclude the jurisdiction of provincial superior courts. In fact, the Supreme Court has ruled that Parliament "lacks the constitutional authority to strip the provincial superior courts of the power to declare a federal statute beyond Parliament's competence." The power of these courts "to consider the constitutionality of federal statutes is fundamental to the federal system established by the Constitution."[209] The Federal Court Act provided for mandatory retirement at age 70, but that Court's Trial Division declared this to be in violation of the Charter's section 15 equality rights. Legislation has since established retirement at age 75 for all Federally appointed judges not otherwise required to retire at that age.[210]

The Federal Court began with twelve judges (eight on the Trial Division and four on the Appeal Division) including four from Quebec. By 1985 there were twenty-five (fourteen on the Trial Division and eleven on the Appeal Division) of whom eight were from Quebec.[211] Cases before the Trial Division are generally heard by a single judge; those before the Appeal Division by a panel of at least three judges.

Other "additional courts" established under section 101 include citizenship courts, the Court Martial Appeal Court, the Tax Court (which was the conversion of an existing administrative tribunal), and courts for the Yukon Territory and the Northwest Territories. This section would also enable Parliament, if it chose, to move considerably in the direction of an entire system of courts to handle Federal law, and therefore to parallel the present set of provincial courts.[212]

VIII. Revenues; Debts; Assets; Taxation

➤ **SECTION 102:** All Duties and Revenues over which the respective Legislatures of Canada, Nova Scotia, and New Brunswick before and at the Union had and have Power of Appropriation, except such Portions thereof as are by this Act reserved to the respective Legislatures of the Provinces, or are raised by them in accordance with the special Powers conferred on them by this Act, shall form One Consolidated Revenue Fund, to be appropriated for the Public Service of Canada in the Manner and subject to the Charges of this Act provided.

This section provides for the establishment of the Consolidated Revenue Fund. Revenue which constitutes the Fund comes from all sources except those reserved by the Constitution Act to the provinces.

➤ **SECTION 103:** The Consolidated Revenue Fund of Canada shall be permanently charged with the Costs, Charges, and Expenses incident to the Collection, Management, and Receipt thereof, and the same shall form the First Charge thereon, subject to be reviewed and audited in such Manner as shall be ordered by the Governor General in Council until the Parliament otherwise provides.

Once the Consolidated Revenue Fund is established according to section 102, the first charge upon it is the expenses associated with its collection and management.

➤ **SECTION 104:** The annual Interest of the Public Debts of the several Provinces of Canada, Nova Scotia, and New Brunswick at the Union shall form the Second Charge on the Consolidated Revenue Fund of Canada.

According to section 111 the Federal government assumed responsibility for the provinces' public debts as part of the overall financial settlement at the time of Confederation. Section 104 provides that the interest on these debts is to be the second charge on the Consolidated Revenue Fund.

➤ **SECTION 105:** Unless altered by the Parliament of Canada, the Salary of the Governor General shall be Ten thousand Pounds Sterling Money of the United Kingdom of Great Britain and Ireland, payable out of the Consolidated Revenue Fund of Canada, and the same shall form the Third Charge thereon.

The governor general's salary is now provided for by the Governor General's Act. This salary is the third charge on the Consolidated Revenue Fund.

➤ **SECTION 106:** Subject to the several Payments by this Act charged on the Consolidated Revenue Fund of Canada, the same shall be appropriated by the Parliament of Canada for the Public Service.

Parliament has jurisdiction over the Consolidated Revenue Fund except for the charges already provided for by the Constitution Act, such as by sections 103, 104, 105, 116, 118 (not repealed, but made obsolete by the 1907 Constitution Act), and 119.

This section together with section 91(1A)—authority to legislate in relation to the public debt and property—constitutes Parliament's spending power. This power is related to Ottawa's broad power to tax (s. 91[3]). See the commentaries on those sections.

If the Meech Lake amendments had been approved, provinces would (as at present) have been able to opt out of national shared-cost programs established by Parliament in areas of exclusive provincial jurisdiction. However, a province that opted out would at the same time have received "reasonable" compensation if it established a program that was "compatible" with "national objectives." Because the meanings of these key words were undefined there was uncertainty as to the extent of provincial flexibility which the amendment would have created. There was also controversy as to how much flexibility would be desirable in certain areas such as medicare.

➤ **SECTION 107:** All Stocks, Cash, Bankers' Balances, and Securities for Money belonging to each Province at the Time of the Union, except as in this Act mentioned, shall be the Property of Canada, and shall be taken in Reduction of the Amount of the respective Debts of the Provinces at the Union.

This relates to the transfer of property (in this case funds) from the pre-Confederation provinces to Ottawa at the time of Confederation. The value of the specified items reduced the sizes of the provincial debts assumed by the Federal government pursuant to section 111.

The term "Canada" means the Federal government.

➤ **SECTION 108:** The Public Works and Property of each Province, enumerated in the Third Schedule to this Act, shall be the Property of Canada.

The Third Schedule is as follows:

1. Canals, with lands and Water Power connected therewith.
2. Public Harbours.
3. Lighthouses and Piers, and Sable Island.
4. Steamboats, Dredges, and public Vessels.
5. Rivers and Lake Improvements.
6. Railways and Railway Stocks, Mortgages, and other Debts due by Railway Companies.
7. Military Roads.
8. Custom Houses, Post Offices, and all other Public Buildings, except such as the Government of Canada appropriate for the Use of the Provincial Legislature and Governments.
9. Property transferred by the Imperial Government, and known as Ordinance Property.
10. Armouries, Drill Sheds, Military Clothing, and Munitions of War, and Lands set apart for general Public Purposes.

The term "Canada" means the Federal government.

➤ **SECTION 109:** All Lands, Mines, Minerals, and Royalties belonging to the several Provinces of Canada, Nova Scotia, and New Brunswick at the Union, and all Sums then due or payable for such Lands, Mines, Minerals, or Royalties, shall belong to the several Provinces of Ontario, Quebec, Nova Scotia, and New Brunswick in which the same are situate or arise, subject to any Trusts existing in respect thereof, and to any Interest other than that of the Province in the same.

The four original provinces retained control of their natural resources ("lands, mines, minerals, and royalties") at Confederation. The provinces of British Columbia, Prince Edward Island, and Newfoundland kept control of their resources when they joined Canada. However the resources of Manitoba,

Saskatchewan, and Alberta were retained by the Federal government when these provinces were created from Federally owned Rupert's Land and the Northwest Territories. Not until the 1930 Constitution Act was passed were the resources turned over to the prairie provinces.

The ownership of natural resources has been one of the major factors in the development of provincial power in this century; not surprisingly it has also been a major source of Federal-provincial friction. The extent of provincial ownership is limited by section 91(24)—Lands reserved for Indians. Furthermore, in view of the 1967 *Offshore Mineral Rights of British Columbia* and 1984 *Newfoundland Continental Shelf* references, it excludes mineral resources off provincial coasts.[213]

➤ **SECTION 110:** All Assets connected with such Portions of the Public Debt of each Province as are assumed by that Province shall belong to that Province.

Although the public debts of the several provinces were taken over by Ottawa in accordance with section 111, the assets associated with them were retained by the provinces.

➤ **SECTION 111:** Canada shall be liable for the Debts and Liabilities of each Province existing at the Union.

The 1867 Federal-provincial financial settlement was a comprehensive agreement involving taxing powers, provincial debts, and grants. The grants (which are unconditional) are now a minuscule part of Federal unconditional payments to the province and are collectively referred to as the "statutory subsidies."

Because they were excluded from indirect taxes the provinces were immediately deprived of more than 80% of their revenues—those from customs duties and excise taxes. Although the Constitution Act assigned to Ottawa the major (and it was thought the more expensive) legislative powers to offset this revenue loss, financial compensation for the provinces was still needed. This was accomplished primarily by Ottawa's assumption of provincial debts (s. 111) coupled with the debt-adjustment formula (ss. 112, 114, 115, 116), as well as by payment to the provinces of subsidies specified in sections 118 and 119. The total subsidy package accounted for 80-90% of the anticipated revenue of Nova Scotia and New Brunswick. Because Quebec and Ontario had additional sources of funds the subsidies represented only 50-65% of their revenue.[214]

The term "Canada" means the Federal government.

➤ **SECTION 112:** Ontario and Quebec conjointly shall be liable to Canada for the Amount (if any) by which the Debt of the Province of Canada exceeds at the Union Sixty-two million five hundred thousand Dollars, and shall be charged with Interest at the Rate of Five per Centum per Annum thereon.

Sections 112, 114, 115, and 116 may be considered together.

It was agreed at the Quebec Conference that, in response to Ottawa's assumption of each province's public debt, each province (Ontario and Quebec being treated as a single unit) whose debt exceeded a sum equal to $25 per person would pay in perpetuity to Ottawa annual interest of 5% of the difference. Ottawa would pay in perpetuity to each province whose debt was less than an amount equal to $25 per person annual interest of 5% of the difference. The $25 figure was the approximate per capita debt of New Brunswick and Nova Scotia ($7 million and $8 million respectively) based on the 1861 census, so that no interest was payable by or to those provinces. Because the per capita debt of pre-Confederation Canada (Ontario plus Quebec) exceeded $25 those provinces jointly were assessed interest on the difference. Given the practical difficulty of dividing the responsibility between Ontario and Quebec these interest payments were never made. Instead, the debt-adjustment allowance was modified so that the Ontario-Quebec indebtedness was eliminated, and New Brunswick and Nova Scotia received interest payments.[215]

As other provinces were created or joined Canada they were given generous debt-adjustment allowances even when, as for the three prairie provinces formed from Federally owned land, they had no public debt.

➤ **SECTION 113:** The Assets enumerated in the Fourth Schedule to this Act belonging at the Union to the Province of Canada shall be the Property of Ontario and Quebec conjointly.

The Fourth Schedule lists twenty-one assets: three are court houses; twelve are "funds," "grants," "accounts," "loans," or "trusts"; and the remaining six are lunatic asylums, a normal school, Upper Canada Law Society, Royal Institution, Upper Canada Agricultural Society, and "Education-East."

➤ **SECTION 114:** Nova Scotia shall be liable to Canada for the Amount (if any) by which its Public Debt exceeds at the Union Eight million Dollars, and shall be charged with Interest at the Rate of Five per Centum per Annum thereon.

See the commentary on section 112. "Canada" means the Federal government. The obligations contained in sections 114, 115, and 116, as well as those created in relation to newer provinces, have been enacted by the Provincial Subsidies Act.

➤ **SECTION 115:** New Brunswick shall be liable to Canada for the Amount (if any) by which its Public Debt exceeds at the Union Seven million Dollars, and shall be charged with Interest at the Rate of Five per Centum per Annum thereon.

See the commentaries on sections 112 and 114. "Canada" means the Federal government.

➤ **SECTION 116:** In case the Public Debts of Nova Scotia and New Brunswick do not at the Union amount to Eight million and Seven million Dollars respectively, they shall respectively receive by half-yearly

Payments in advance from the Government of Canada Interest at Five per Centum per Annum on the Difference between the actual Amounts of their respective Debts and such stipulated Amounts.

See the commentaries on sections 112 and 114.

➤ **SECTION 117:** The several Provinces shall retain all their respective Public Property not otherwise disposed of in this Act, subject to the Right of Canada to assume any Lands or Public Property required for Fortifications or for the Defence of the Country.

This section gives to the Federal government limited power of expropriation. "Canada" means the Federal government.

➤ **SECTION 118:** The following Sums shall be paid yearly by Canada to the several Provinces for the Support of their Governments and Legislatures:

	Dollars
Ontario	Eighty thousand.
Quebec	Seventy thousand.
Nova Scotia	Sixty thousand.
New Brunswick	Fifty thousand.
	Two hundred and sixty thousand;

and an annual Grant in aid of each Province shall be made, equal to Eighty Cents per Head of the Population as ascertained by the Census of One thousand eight hundred and sixty-one, and in the Case of Nova Scotia and New Brunswick, by each subsequent Decennial Census until the Population of each of those two Provinces amounts to Four hundred thousand Souls, at which Rate such Grant shall thereafter remain. Such Grants shall be in full Settlement of all future Demands on Canada, and shall be paid half-yearly in advance to each Province; but the Government of Canada shall deduct from such Grants, as against any Province, all Sums chargeable as Interest on the Public Debt of that Province in excess of the several Amounts stipulated in this Act.

Section 118 provided for two types of annual grant—lump sum grants and 80-cent per capita grants. The latter were based on the 1861 census, except that for New Brunswick and Nova Scotia they were to be based upon the populations at each decennial census to a maximum population of 400,000 per province. (New Brunswick's 1861 population was 252,000; Nova Scotia's was 331,000.) The per capita grants were exaggerated for some provinces by assuming fictitious populations. For example, Manitoba's 12,000 population was assumed to be 17,000 in 1870, and 150,000 rather than the actual 64,000 in 1882. When British Columbia joined Canada in 1871, its population was deemed to be 60,000 rather than the actual 34,000.[216]

Although section 118 grants were to be "in full settlement of all future demands on Canada"—that is, on the Federal government—an additional subsidy was granted to Nova Scotia within two years of Confederation. This addition was relevant to the question of Ottawa's spending power, for it immediately raised the question whether Parliament could spend (in this case to give to the provinces) beyond the statutory requirement. So far as the Federal government of the day was concerned the section 118 grants were the maximum required and did not prevent Parliament from spending additional funds if it wished to do so. This broader issue raised by the spending power has not been tested in the courts.

The 1907 Constitution Act established a new grant structure which "shall be substituted for the grants or subsidies" provided by section 118, and the Act stated that section 118 "shall cease to have effect." Although that section thereby became obsolete it was not formally repealed until passage of Britain's 1950 Statute Law Revision Act. This is an excellent illustration of a *de facto* Constitution Act amendment which left the original terms of the 1867 Act intact.

The relevant provisions of the 1907 amendment are stated below. They are still operative but of little significance in terms of the totality of transfer of payments made by Ottawa in accordance with present-day Federal-provincial agreements.

> 1. (1) The following grants shall be made yearly by Canada to every province, which at the commencement of this Act is a province of the Dominion, for its local purposes and the support of its Government and Legislature:—
>
> (a) A fixed grant—
>
> - where the population of the province is under one hundred and fifty thousand, of one hundred thousand dollars;
> - where the population of the province is one hundred and fifty thousand, but does not exceed two hundred thousand, of one hundred and fifty thousand dollars;
> - where the population of the province is two hundred thousand, but does not exceed four hundred thousand, of one hundred and eighty thousand dollars;
> - where the population of the province is four hundred thousand, but does not exceed eight hundred thousand, of one hundred and ninety thousand dollars;
> - where the population of the province is eight hundred thousand, but does not exceed one million five hundred thousand, of two hundred and twenty thousand dollars;
> - where the population of the province exceeds one

million five hundred thousand, of two hundred and forty thousand dollars; and

(b) Subject to the special provisions of this Act as to the provinces of British Columbia and Prince Edward Island, a grant at the rate of eighty cents per head of the population of the province up to the number of two million five hundred thousand, and at the rate of sixty cents per head of so much of the population as exceeds that number.

(2) An additional grant of one hundred thousand dollars shall be made yearly to the province of British Columbia for a period of ten years from the commencement of this Act.

(3) The population of a province shall be ascertained from time to time in the case of the provinces of Manitoba, Saskatchewan, and Alberta respectively by the last quinquennial census or statutory estimate of population made under the Acts establishing those provinces or any other Act of the Parliament of Canada making provision for the purpose, and in the case of any other province by the last decennial census for the time being.

(4) The grants payable under this Act shall be paid half-yearly in advance to each province.

(5) The grants payable under this Act shall be substituted for the grants or subsidies (in this Act referred to as existing grants) payable for the like purposes at the commencement of this Act to the several provinces of the Dominion under the provisions of section one hundred and eighteen of the *British North America Act, 1867*, or of any Order in Council establishing a province, or of any Act of the Parliament of Canada containing directions for the payment of any such grant or subsidy, and those provisions shall cease to have effect.

(6) The Government of Canada shall have the same power of deducting sums charged against a province on account of the interest on public debt in the case of the grant payable under this Act to the province as they have in the case of the existing grant.

(7) Nothing in this Act shall affect the obligation of the Government of Canada to pay to any province any grant which is payable to that province, other than the existing grant for which the grant under this Act is substituted.

(8) In the case of the provinces of British Columbia and Prince Edward Island, the amount paid on account of the grant payable per head of the population to the provinces under this Act shall not at any time be less than the amount of the corresponding grant payable at the commencement of this Act, and if it is found on any decennial census that the population of the province has decreased since the

last decennial census, the amount paid on account of the grant shall not be decreased below the amount then payable, notwithstanding the decrease of the population.

The 1907 revision tied the fixed grant for the support of government to a province's population, extended the 80-cent per capita grant until that population reached 2 1/2 million at which point the grant was reduced to 60 cents for any additional population, and provided a ten-year annual grant to British Columbia.

➤ **SECTION 119:** New Brunswick shall receive by half-yearly Payments in advance from Canada for the period of Ten years from the Union an additional Allowance of Sixty-three thousand Dollars per Annum; but as long as the Public Debt of that Province remains under Seven million Dollars, a Deduction equal to the Interest at Five per Centum per Annum on such Deficiency shall be made from that Allowance of Sixty-three thousand Dollars.

This section, now spent, was intended to recognize New Brunswick's particularly acute financial situation. The $63,000 figure was the estimate of the difference between that province's income and expenditure.[217]

The term "Canada" means the Federal government.

➤ **SECTION 120:** All Payments to be made under this Act, or in discharge of Liabilities created under any Act of the Provinces of Canada, Nova Scotia, and New Brunswick respectively, and assumed by Canada, shall, until the Parliament of Canada otherwise directs, be made in such Form and Manner as may from Time to Time be ordered by the Governor General in Council.

This section needs no comment except, perhaps, to note that "Canada" (in reference to the assumption of liabilities) means the Federal government.

➤ **SECTION 121:** All Articles of the Growth, Produce, or Manufacture of any one of the Provinces shall, from and after the Union, be admitted free into each of the other Provinces.

Because one of the purposes of Confederation was the strengthening of colonial economies the prohibition of interprovincial customs duties was a logical part of the 1867 settlement. There remains a question, however, whether section 121 precludes other devices restricting the flow of goods between provinces. The view that the section applied only to customs duties was rejected in 1971 by the Manitoba Court of Appeal. When Quebec imposed restrictions on the movement of eggs into that province from other provinces, the Manitoba government tested the constitutionality of the restriction by referring for judicial interpretation a similar, but hypothetical, Manitoba restriction. The Manitoba court ruled that the restriction would conflict with Parliament's trade and commerce power (s. 91[2]), but added that it would also "have the effect of impeding the free flow of trade between Provinces and therefore runs counter to s. 121 of the B.N.A. Act, 1867."[218] The Supreme Court concurred in this decision but used only section 91(2).[219]

Although the courts have considered section 121 only in relation to fiscal impediments, a 1958 statement by Justice Rand suggesting a broader interpretation was supported by Chief Justice Laskin for the Supreme Court in 1978. According to Rand, section 121 is "aimed against trade regulation which is designed to place fetters upon, or raise impediments to, or otherwise restrict or limit, the free flow of commerce across the Dominion as if provincial boundaries did not exist . . . What is forbidden is a trade regulation, that in its essence and purpose is related to a provincial boundary." Laskin added that "the application of s. 121 may be different according to whether it is provincial or federal legislation that is involved because what may amount to a tariff or customs duty under a provincial regulatory statute may not have that character at all under a federal regulatory statute." In the case at hand, for example (*Agricultural Products Marketing Act Reference*), Laskin found nothing in the Federal marketing scheme "that, as a trade regulation, is *in its essence and purpose* related to a provincial boundary. To hold otherwise would mean that a federal marketing statute, referable to interprovincial trade, could not validly take into account patterns of production in the various Provinces in attempting to establish an equitable basis for the flow of trade." [220]

Provincial impediments to trade have not yet been struck down on the basis of this broader interpretation. Indeed, it has been reported that Canadian manufacturers count some three hundred barriers to interprovincial trade. For example, a brewery must build a plant in a province in which it wishes to sell beer or face price discrimination within that province (although this trade restriction was reported in February 1991 to be on the way out), and British Columbia reportedly applies as much as a 20-30% markup (presumably as a direct tax) on Ontario wine. Some provinces allow a 10-15% margin for local companies bidding on provincial projects. All this notwithstanding section 121's "free trade" requirement. New Brunswick Premier McKenna has bluntly stated that if other provinces want access to the New Brunswick market they must allow New Brunswick access to their markets.[221] At their annual meeting in August 1990 the provincial premiers agreed to move toward freer trade. As reported, the agreement includes almost all government purchases, and seeks to free the markets under provincial control, "with no impediments to business in other provinces or preferential treatment of their own."[222]

In June 1991 the full cabinets of New Brunswick, Nova Scotia, and Prince Edward Island met to begin negotiations for "freer trade" among their provinces.

➤ **SECTION 122:** The Customs and Excise Laws of each Province shall, subject to the Provisions of this Act, continue in force until altered by the Parliament of Canada.

The provinces were prohibited by section 92(2) from levying indirect taxes, although section 122 as a transitional measure perpetuated provincial customs and excise laws (both of which were indirect taxes) until Parliament enacted its own legislation. Interprovincial customs taxes were precluded by section 121. Federal legislation was passed during the first session of Parliament thus making sections 122 and 123 obsolete.[223]

➤ **SECTION 123:** Where Customs Duties are, at the Union, leviable on any Goods, Wares, or Merchandises in any Two Provinces, those Goods, Wares, and Merchandises may from and after the Union, be imported from one of those Provinces into the other of them on Proof of Payment of the Customs Duty leviable thereon in the Province of Exportation, and on Payment of such further Amount (if any) of Customs Duty as is leviable thereon in the Province of Importation.

This section applied to goods imported into one province from beyond Canada, and which then moved into a second province—both provinces having customs duties. The duties levied by the first province had to be paid before goods moved to the second province. If the duties of the second province exceeded those of the first province, the excess had to be paid when the goods moved into the second province. As noted in the commentary on section 122, Federal legislation made this section obsolete during the first session of Parliament.

➤ **SECTION 124:** Nothing in this Act shall affect the Right of New Brunswick to levy the Lumber Dues provided in Chapter Fifteen of Title Three of the Revised Statutes of New Brunswick, or in any Act amending that Act before or after the Union, and not increasing the Amount of such Dues; but the Lumber of any of the Provinces other than New Brunswick shall not be subject to such Dues.

New Brunswick was permitted to continue its export duty (existing since the 1840s) on lumber, but the duty could not be increased. These "Lumber Dues" were terminated in 1873 and, as compensation for the loss of revenue, Ottawa paid an annual subsidy (which is still in effect) of $150,000.[224] This concession to New Brunswick was made notwithstanding the general prohibition of provincial indirect taxes (s. 92[2]) and the right given to Parliament (and exercised during its first session following Confederation) to legislate customs duties.

➤ **SECTION 125:** No Lands or Property belonging to Canada or any Province shall be liable to Taxation.

One government may not tax the property of another government. (The term "Canada" means the Federal government.) There may be difficulty in specific cases distinguishing between a charge intended primarily to raise revenue for general government purposes and one whose purpose is essentially regulatory. The courts will interpret the first charge as a tax, and therefore declare it unconstitutional, but the second one will not be subject to section 125. This point is considered in relation to the 1982 *Exported Natural Gas Tax Reference* in the commentary on section 91(3).

Section 125 does not prevent a government from submitting voluntarily to payments in lieu of taxes. With the expansion of government and therefore of government property, this is particularly significant for municipalities (especially the seats of government) containing many government buildings on choice land. Because municipalities may not levy property taxes against a senior government, governments now make payments in lieu of taxes, and in amounts approximating the taxes that otherwise would be payable. While the net result may be similar to that if a tax were paid, the principle enunciated in section 125 remains intact.

A government may tax its own Crown corporations. Since 1952 "proprietary" Crown corporations of the Federal government (basically, those competing with private companies) have paid income taxes on the same basis as private corporations.

> **SECTION 126:** Such Portions of the Duties and Revenues over which the respective Legislatures of Canada, Nova Scotia, and New Brunswick had before the Union Power of Appropriation as are by this Act reserved to the respective Governments or Legislatures of the Provinces, and all Duties and Revenues raised by them in accordance with the special Powers conferred upon them by this Act, shall in each Province form One Consolidated Revenue Fund to be appropriated for the Public Service of the Province.

This section provides for the establishment of a Consolidated Revenue Fund for each province.

IX. Miscellaneous Provisions

General

> **SECTION 127:** If any Person being at the passing of this Act a Member of the Legislative Council of Canada, Nova Scotia, or New Brunswick to whom a Place in the Senate is offered, does not within Thirty Days thereafter, by Writing under his Hand addressed to the Governor General of the Province of Canada or to the Lieutenant Governor of Nova Scotia or New Brunswick (as the Case may be), accept the same, he shall be deemed to have declined the same; and any Person who, being at the passing of this Act a Member of the Legislative Council of Nova Scotia or New Brunswick, accepts a Place in the Senate, shall thereby vacate his Seat in such Legislative Council.

The original appointees to the Senate were not permitted at the same time to be members of provincial legislative councils—that is, of the upper houses of provincial legislatures. The Province of Canada is omitted from the latter part of this section because its government (including, therefore, the legislative council) was replaced by the two provincial governments of Quebec and Ontario. The question of retaining a seat in an upper house which ceased to exist could not arise.

This section was repealed by Britain's Statute Law Revision Act 1893.

➤ **SECTION 128:** Every Member of the Senate or House of Commons of Canada shall before taking his Seat therein take and subscribe before the Governor General or some Person authorized by him, and every Member of a Legislative Council or Legislative Assembly of any Province shall before taking his Seat therein take and subscribe before the Lieutenant Governor of the Province or some Person authorized by him, the Oath of Allegiance contained in the Fifth Schedule to this Act; and every Member of the Senate of Canada and every Member of the Legislative Council of Quebec shall also, before taking his Seat therein, take and subscribe before the Governor General, or some Person authorized by him, the Declaration of Qualification contained in the same Schedule.

The Oath of Allegiance contained in the Fifth Schedule is as follows:

> I, *A.B.* do swear, That I will be faithful and bear true Allegiance to Her Majesty Queen Victoria.
>
> *Note: The Name of the King or Queen of the United Kingdom of Great Britain and Ireland for the Time being is to be substituted from Time to Time, with Proper Terms of Reference thereto.*

The Declaration of Qualification in the Fifth Schedule is as follows:

> I, *A.B.* do declare and testify, That I am by Law duly qualified to be appointed a Member of the Senate of Canada [*or as the Case may be*], and that I am legally or equitably seised as of Freehold for my own Use and Benefit of Lands or Tenements held in Free and Common Socage [or seised or possessed for my own Use and Benefit of Lands or Tenements held in Franc-alleu or in Roture (*as the Case may be*),] in the Province of Nova Scotia [or as the Case may be] of the Value of Four thousand Dollars over and above all Rents, Dues, Debts, Mortgages, Charges, and Incumbrances due or payable out of or charged on or affecting the same, and that I have not collusively or colourably obtained a Title to or become possessed of the said Lands and Tenements or any Part thereof for the Purpose of enabling me to become a Member of the Senate of Canada [*or as the Case may be,*] and that my Real and Personal Property are together worth Four thousand Dollars over and above my Debts and Liabilities.

Section 73 states that the qualifications of Quebec's legislative councillors are the same as those of Quebec's senators. Because Quebec no longer has a legislative council, the reference to Quebec in this section is now spent.

➤ **SECTION 129:** Except as otherwise provided by this Act, all Laws in force in Canada, Nova Scotia, or New Brunswick at the Union, and all Courts of Civil and Criminal Jurisdiction, and all legal Commissions, Powers, and Authorities, and all Officers, Judicial, Administrative, and Ministerial, existing therein at the Union, shall continue in Ontario, Quebec, Nova Scotia, and New Brunswick respectively, as if the Union had not been made; subject nevertheless (except with respect to such as are enacted by or exist under Acts of the Parliament of Great Britain or of the Parliament of the United Kingdom of Great Britain and Ireland), to be repealed, abolished, or altered by the Parliament of Canada, or by the Legislature of the respective Province, according to the Authority of the Parliament or of that Legislature under this Act.

This section provides for the continuation of pre-Confederation laws, courts, commissions, powers, authorities, and officers. The purpose was to avoid a vacuum especially until Parliament enacted laws in areas which fell within its jurisdiction after Confederation. After 1867 the laws, courts, and so on, could be changed or abolished by the provinces or the Federal government according to the distribution of legislative authority established by the Constitution Act.

The parenthetical restriction extended to British laws whose application to the colonies was protected by the 1865 Colonial Laws Validity Act. This Act in effect permitted colonies to enact legislation which contradicted British laws only if such British laws did not explicitly state (or necessarily imply) their application to the colonies. (As noted in the commentary on section 101, section 129 had preserved the right of appeal to the Privy Council.) The restriction was removed by the Statute of Westminster except for the Constitution Act itself. Because the Statute of Westminster states (s. 7[1]) that "nothing in this Act shall be deemed to apply to the repeal, amendment or alteration of" the 1867 Constitution Act, it could have been argued that the 1931 Statute left section 129 fully operative with the parenthetical restriction. However, this interpretation was not supported by the courts.[225] Passage of the 1982 Canada Act removed this remaining qualification.

As new provinces were created or joined Canada, similar provisions were included in the enacting documents.[226]

➤ **SECTION 130:** Until the Parliament of Canada otherwise provides, all Officers of the several Provinces having Duties to discharge in relation to Matters other than those coming within the Classes of Subjects by this Act assigned exclusively to the Legislatures of the Provinces shall be Officers of Canada, and shall continue to discharge the Duties of their respective Offices under the same Liabilities, Responsibilities, and Penalties as if the Union had not been made.

This section, now spent, was an interim measure to provide for the continued performance of functions which became the responsibility of the Federal government at Confederation.

➤ **SECTION 131:** Until the Parliament of Canada otherwise provides, the Governor General in Council may from Time to Time appoint such Officers as the Governor General in Council deems necessary or proper for the effectual Execution of this Act.

This interim section needs no comment.

➤ **SECTION 132:** The Parliament and Government of Canada shall have all Powers necessary or proper for performing the Obligations of Canada or of any Province thereof, as Part of the British Empire, towards Foreign Countries, arising under Treaties between the Empire and such Foreign Countries.

In 1867 Canada's independence from Britain was not anticipated and so the trappings of sovereignty, including the treaty-making power, were not included in the Constitution Act.

Section 132, which pertains to treaty-implementation rather than treaty-making, gives to Parliament "all powers necessary or proper" to perform Canada's obligations under treaties between the British Empire and foreign countries and which affect Canada as part of the Empire. This authority is granted regardless of the Constitution Act's distribution of legislative authority between the two orders of government. In other words, that distribution is inoperative with respect to Empire treaties—the only treaties affecting Canada in 1867. The first treaty actually signed by Canada was the Versailles Treaty ending World War One, but we signed as part of the British Empire. The 1923 Halibut Treaty was the first treaty signed in our own right with a foreign country—in this case the United States.

Legislative authority to implement Canadian (as distinct from Empire) treaties is not covered by the Constitution Act. In the 1932 *Aeronautics* and (especially) *Radio* references the Privy Council suggested that treaty-implementation fell within Ottawa's jurisdiction as part of the residual p.o.g.g. In the 1937 *Labour Conventions Reference*, however, the Privy Council rejected this interpretation. (The Supreme Court of Canada had divided evenly on the Reference.) The absence of treaty legislation as a subject within sections 91 and 92 does not invoke p.o.g.g. according to the Privy Council: The distribution of legislative authority "is based on classes of subjects; and as a treaty deals with a particular class of subjects so will the legislative power of performing it be ascertained." Furthermore,

> There is no existing constitutional ground for stretching the competence of the Dominion Parliament so that it becomes enlarged to keep pace with enlarged functions of the Dominion executive [e.g., treaty making] . . . In other words, the Dominion cannot, merely by making promises to foreign countries, clothe itself with legislative authority inconsistent with the constitution which gave it birth.[227]

In 1955 Lord Wright, a member of the Privy Council panel which decided the *Labour Conventions Reference*, stated that he disagreed with the decision.[228]

There has also been a suggestion that the panel had split 3-2, and that "we are left with the fascinating, but rather disturbing, possibility that one of the most important cases in Canadian constitutional law was determined by the vote of Sir Sidney Rowlatt, a 'taxation judge,' who, I am told, sat throughout the 1937 hearings in his overcoat making neither note nor comment."[229] Be that as it may, the 1937 decision means that Federal-provincial cooperation is of utmost importance before Ottawa involves the country in treaty obligations, the honouring of which may require provincial legislative action.

Recent statements of Supreme Court judges suggest a possible return to the reasoning of the *Radio Reference*. For example, in 1956 Chief Justice Kerwin speaking for himself and Justices Taschereau and Fauteux (each of whom later became Chief Justice) opined that "it might be necessary . . . in the future to consider" the *Labour Conventions* decision.[230] Chief Justice Laskin seemed to suggest the same thing in 1977.[231] And Justice Rand in 1960 proposed that "the totality of treaty-making action" is "a discrete and entire subject matter" whose "only place of reception [is] in the residual power of the Dominion."[232]

The authority of the Federal government to make treaties with foreign countries is not in doubt. During the debate surrounding the then-proposed Canada-United States "free trade" agreement Prime Minister Mulroney insisted, as well, that Parliament possessed the authority to enact any legislation necessary for that treaty's implementation. For a time it seemed that this "totality of treaty-making action" might have become a matter for judicial decision rather than speculation. In any event there seems little doubt that, until the courts are called upon for additional rulings, the *Labour Conventions* decision is most inconvenient for us in the modern world.

➤ **SECTION 133:** Either the English or the French Language may be used by any Person in the Debates of the Houses of the Parliament of Canada and of the Houses of the Legislature of Quebec; and both those Languages shall be used in the respective Records and Journals of those Houses; and either of those Languages may be used by any Person or in any Pleading or Process in or issuing from any Court of Canada established under this Act, and in or from all or any of the Courts of Quebec.

The Acts of the Parliament of Canada and of the Legislature of Quebec shall be printed and published in both those Languages.

Any consideration of language rights in Canada must include not only those in this section but also the analogous guarantees applicable to Manitoba (section 23 of the Manitoba Act), New Brunswick (sections 16-19 of the Canadian Charter) and, until 1988, Saskatchewan and Alberta (sections 16 of the Saskatchewan Act and the Alberta Act in relation to section 110 of the North-West Territories Act). Language is also an intimate part of the Charter's guarantee of minority language educational rights (s. 23) and has been important in relation to the Charter's guarantee of the fundamental freedom of expression (s. 2[b]). The nature of these latter guarantees and the litigation associated with them are considered in the appropriate commentaries. The commentary on the present section is divided into four parts: (1) a general discussion of the content of and litigation relating to section 133, and by extension to the analogous provisions noted above; and consideration of court cases uniquely applicable to (2) Quebec, (3) Manitoba, and (4) Saskatchewan and Alberta.

The Basic Meaning of Section 133 and the Analogous Sections of Other Statutes

This section is sometimes thought to make Canada officially bilingual. Although there is some truth to that view, a cursory reading of the section reveals that bilingualism is not carried very far; and a closer look at its details in the light of judicial interpretation reveals that bilingualism may be carried for a much shorter distance than many people believe. Perhaps the following remarks of Supreme Court Justice Beetz in *MacDonald v. City of Montreal* (1986), which upheld a French-only summons issued by a Quebec court, state the essence of the section's guarantee:

> Section 133 has not introduced a comprehensive scheme or system of official bilingualism, even potentially, but a limited form of compulsory bilingualism at the legislative level, combined with an even more limited form of optional unilingualism at the option of the speaker in Parliamentary debates and at the option of the speaker, writer or issuer in judicial proceedings or processes. Such a limited scheme can perhaps be said to facilitate communication and understanding, up to a point, but only as far as it goes and it does not guarantee that the speaker, writer or issuer of proceedings or processes will be understood in the language of his choice by those he is addressing.[233]

The section has three basic components. In the first place it applies only to the governments of Canada and Quebec (although its essence is extended to some of the other provinces as noted above). Second, it requires that Acts, Records, and Journals of the two governments be printed in both English and French. In the third place it provides that either of these two official languages may be used by any person in the legislative debates and in the "pleading or process in or issuing from" any court within the two jurisdictions.

What this third part of the section really says is that although either language may be "used" by a person in debates or in court, no one has a right to be understood in the language of his or her choice or to understand the language of another person's choice. This comes as no surprise with respect to the legislatures, for no member claims the right (and certainly not under section 133) to hear in his or her choice of language. Otherwise, the member speaking would have lost the right of choice—even assuming that the member was bilingual. The provision of simultaneous translation is a service to members and not a section 133 right.

Section 133 does not guarantee the right to a trial in the accused's choice of language. The wording of this section with respect to court proceedings is essentially the same as for legislative debates and protects only the speaker. In other words, the defendant has no right under this section to understand what is being said by others or even to be understood by the judge at his or her own trial! Chief Justice Dickson and Justice Wilson disagree with their Supreme Court colleagues on this point. Wilson believes "there is an obligation on the state by virtue of the right conferred on the citizen." The nature of the obligation, which in her view is prescribed by section 133, starts with the premise that "the essence of language is communication and that implicit in the notion of language rights in the context of court proceedings is the ability both to understand and to be understood."[234] According to Dickson, "the right to 'use' French or English in the courts embraces the right to be understood. . . . What good is a right to use one's language if those to whom one speaks cannot understand?"[235]

Furthermore, section 133 does not guarantee the issuance of court documents such as parking tickets and summonses in the language of the recipient—this would present practical difficulties—or in both languages. Rather, the section provides that any "pleading or process in or issuing from" a Quebec court or a court established by Parliament under the present Act may be in either official language. According to the Supreme Court,

> if there is a right to use either language, there can be no obligation or duty to use the other. In judicial proceedings in the courts covered by s. 133, the language rights protected are those of litigants, counsel, witnesses, judges and other judicial officers who actually speak, not those of parties or others who are spoken to; and they are those of the writers or issuers of written pleadings and processes, not those of the recipients or readers thereof.[236]

Wilson again dissented, maintaining that the section 133 right of a litigant to use his or her own language "imposes a correlative duty on the state to respect and accommodate that right" if there is to be meaningful access to the courts by both anglophones and francophones.

So much for the guarantees of section 133! However, everyone has the common law right, and now the Charter right, to a fair trial which includes the right to be informed of the charge and to understand the proceedings. Section 14 of the Charter requires the provision of interpreters to facilitate communication, but that right exists regardless of the language spoken or understood by the individual and has nothing to do with Canada's official languages. The disagreement which Dickson and Wilson have with their colleagues is therefore not so much with the totality of rights but with those which may be ascribed to section 133. Nevertheless, Wilson has stated that Charter section 19(2)—analogous to part of the present 133—does afford a litigant "something more than the fair hearing rights accorded by [Charter] ss. 7 and 14."[237]

Section 133 does not preclude a government from extending language rights beyond the requirements of that section. This is now made explicit by Charter section 16(3) but it had been established by the Supreme Court which declared in 1974, in upholding Ottawa's Official Languages Act, that section 133 did not prevent "the conferring of additional rights or privileges or the imposing of additional obligations respecting the use of English and French, if done in relation to matters within the competence of the enacting Legislature."[238]

Quebec and Section 133

In 1977 the Quebec National Assembly enacted the Charter of the French Language (Bill 101) making French the sole official language of the province, including "the language of the legislature and the courts of Quebec" (ss. 7-13). In the 1979 *Blaikie* case a unanimous Supreme Court struck down these sections as being contrary to section 133. Quebec had based its argument on section 92(1) of the present Act, which allows provinces to amend their own constitutions "notwithstanding anything in this Act." In reply, the Court declared that section 133 is an "entrenched provision,"

> is not part of the Constitution of the Province within section 92(1) but is rather part of the Constitution of Canada and of Quebec in an indivisible sense, giving official status to French and English in the Parliament and in the Courts of Canada as well as in the Legislature and Courts of Quebec.[239]

Because the Quebec legislature already had "unofficial" English translations of statutes passed subsequent to its Charter, the task of enacting them in English was relatively simple.

In a second *Blaikie* case, in 1981, the Court affirmed that section 133 applied to "regulations which constitute delegated legislation and to rules of practice enacted by the courts and quasi-judicial bodies" as extensions of the legislative power. The section did not, however, extend to the by-laws of municipalities or school boards. Because municipal bodies were in existence long before Confederation, and because section 92(8) empowers provinces to make laws in relation to municipal institutions, "the absence of any reference to them in s. 133 cannot be viewed as an oversight."[240] In 1990 the Court ruled that the tabling of sessional papers in the Quebec National Assembly only in French was a violation of section 133.[241]

Manitoba and Section 23 of the Manitoba Act

When the Province of Manitoba was created in 1870 the French-speaking population outnumbered the English. In spite of section 23 the Manitoba legislature passed the Official Languages Act in 1890, by which time the English-speaking population was in the majority. This Act declared that "the English language only shall be used in the records and journals of the Legislative Assembly of

Manitoba, and in any pleading or process in or issuing from any court in the Province of Manitoba . . . [and the] Acts of the Legislature of Manitoba need be printed and published only in the English language."

County courts ruled the Act unconstitutional in 1892 and 1909 but the decisions were not reported, not appealed, and not heeded by the Manitoba government. Furthermore, the Act was not disallowed by the Federal government. A similar decision by a county court in 1976 led Manitoba's attorney general to declare that the ruling was unacceptable to the government! A subsequent challenge resulted in the Supreme Court's 1979 *Forest* decision that the Act was unconstitutional. The reasoning was the same as in *Blaikie*, delivered the same day regarding Quebec's Bill 101: the Manitoba government could not unilaterally repeal section 23 of the Manitoba Act.[242]

This decision immediately raised a question which the Court had not addressed. What was the validity of all Manitoba statutes passed only in English since 1890? Unlike Quebec, Manitoba had no unofficial translations in the second language. Furthermore, the Manitoba government did nothing to re-enact its statutes in the French language, and as late as 1984 it was still enacting some only in English. In 1985 in response to a Federal government reference (*Re Manitoba Language Rights*) the Supreme Court declared "the unilingual Acts of the Legislature of Manitoba to be invalid and of no force and effect." It added, however, that this declaration "without more, would create a legal vacuum with consequent legal chaos in the Province." Therefore, unilingual laws passed before the June 13, 1985, date of the judgement would be deemed "temporarily valid . . . from the date of this judgement to the expiry of the minimum period necessary for translation, re-enactment, printing and publishing." However, temporary validity "will not apply to unilingual Acts of the Legislature passed after the date of this judgement."[243]

On November 4, 1985, after receiving recommendations from the affected parties, the Court ordered that the period of temporary validity would last until the end of 1988 for certain documents, and until the end of 1990 for the rest. It also allowed for possible extension "in the case of necessity upon further application, supported by such evidence as may be required."[244]

Saskatchewan and Alberta and Section 110 of the North-West Territories Act

This situation is unique in that language rights which the Supreme Court found in *Mercure* (1988) to apply to Saskatchewan (and, in *Paquette* [1990], to Alberta)[245] were enacted as part of the North-West Territories Act before those two provinces were created in 1905. The relevant section (s. 110) reads, in part: "Either the English or the French language may be used by any person in the debates of the Legislative Assembly of the Territories and in the proceedings before the courts; and both those languages shall be used in the records and journals of such Assembly; and all ordinances made under this Act shall be printed in both those languages."[246] These rights and obligations are the same as those in section 133 of the 1867 Constitution Act, the Manitoba Act, and the Canadian Charter. They were made applicable to Saskatchewan and Alberta by either or both section 14 and 16 of each of the statutes establishing those provinces.[247] According to section 14:

> Until the said Legislature [of Saskatchewan or Alberta] otherwise determines, all the provisions of the law with regard to the constitution of the Legislative Assembly of the Northwest Territories . . . shall apply, *mutatis mutandis*, to the Legislative Assembly of the said province.

Section 16 states:

> All laws and all orders and regulations made thereunder . . . existing immediately before the coming into force of this Act in the territory hereby established as the province of Saskatchewan [or Alberta], shall continue in the said province as if this Act and The *Alberta* [or *Saskatchewan*] Act had not been passed; subject, nevertheless, . . . to be repealed, abolished or altered by the Parliament of Canada, or by the Legislature of the said province.

However, unlike the rights and obligations applicable to Parliament, Quebec, Manitoba, and New Brunswick, these were not entrenched. Territorial laws applied "until the legislature otherwise determines" or (from section 16) "subject . . . to be repealed, abolished or altered by the . . . legislature." In response to an argument that the requirements of section 110 had lapsed because French had not been used in Territorial debates, statutes, and court proceedings since 1882, Justice La Forest (for the Court majority in *Mercure*)[248] commented that "statutes do not . . . cease to be law from mere disuse." He added: "It does not strike me as a particularly attractive argument to put before a court of justice that a majority can destroy the rights of a minority by simply acting in violation of those rights."

The Court held, as it had for Manitoba, that Saskatchewan's unilingual statutes were invalid but that reasonable time would be allowed for the province to translate, enact, print, and publish them in French. Noting the irony La Forest stated Saskatchewan's alternative to "resort to the obvious, if ironic, expedient of enacting a bilingual statute removing the restrictions imposed on it by s. 110 and then declaring all existing provincial statutes valid notwithstanding that they were enacted, printed and published in English only." Before the year was out both Saskatchewan and Alberta had removed the restrictions.

The case itself resulted from a speeding charge against Father Mercure. Mercure had sought to enter a plea in French, have his trial conducted in French, and to have the proceedings delayed until the relevant statutes, validly enacted in French, were produced. The Court agreed with the first request but denied the other two. The right to use a particular language did not mean a right to understand or to be understood.

Ontario and Quebec

➤ **SECTION 134:** Until the Legislature of Ontario or of Quebec otherwise provides, the Lieutenant Governors of Ontario and Quebec may each appoint under the Great Seal of the Province the following Officers, to hold Office during Pleasure, that is to say,—the Attorney General, the Secretary and Registrar of the Province, the Treasurer of the Province, the Commissioner of Crown Lands, and the Commissioner of Agriculture and Public Works, and in the Case of Quebec the Solicitor General, and may, by Order of the Lieutenant Governor in Council, from Time to Time prescribe the Duties of those Officers, and of the several Departments over which they shall preside or to which they shall belong, and of the Officers and Clerks thereof, and may also appoint other and additional Officers to hold Office during Pleasure, and may from Time to Time prescribe the Duties of those Officers, and of the several Departments over which they shall preside or to which they shall belong, and of the Officers and Clerks thereof.

This section was made necessary by the division of the Province of Canada into Ontario and Quebec and, therefore, by the necessity of immediately establishing two sets of government officers. The legislatures of both provinces have enacted legislation in this area and so the section is now spent.

➤ **SECTION 135:** Until the Legislature of Ontario or Quebec otherwise provides, all Rights, Powers, Duties, Functions, Responsibilities, or Authorities at the passing of this Act vested in or imposed on the Attorney General, Solicitor General, Secretary and Registrar of the Province of Canada, Minister of Finance, Commissioner of Crown Lands, Commissioner of Public Works, and Minister of Agriculture and Receiver General, by any Law, Statute, or Ordinance of Upper Canada, Lower Canada, or Canada, and not repugnant to this Act, shall be vested in or imposed on any Officer to be appointed by the Lieutenant Governor for the discharge of the same or any of them; and the Commissioner of Agriculture and Public Works shall perform the Duties and Functions of the Office of Minister of Agriculture at the passing of this Act imposed by the Law of the Province of Canada, as well as those of the Commissioner of Public Works.

This transitional section, now spent, states that until the legislatures of Ontario and Quebec otherwise provide, the officials appointed by the lieutenant governors of those provinces in accordance with section 134 will continue to have the authority of the corresponding officials under the former Province of Canada.

➤ **SECTION 136:** Until altered by the Lieutenant Governor in Council, the Great Seals of Ontario and Quebec respectively shall be the same, or of the same Design, as those used in the Provinces of Upper Canada and Lower Canada respectively before their Union as the Province of Canada.

This section needs no comment.

➤ **SECTION 137:** The words "and from thence to the End of the then next ensuing Session of the Legislature," or Words to the same Effect, used in any temporary Act of the Province of Canada not expired before the Union, shall be construed to extend and apply to the next Session of the Parliament of Canada if the Subject Matter of the Act is within the Powers of the same as defined by this Act, or to the next Sessions of the Legislatures of Ontario and Quebec respectively if the Subject Matter of the Act is within the Powers of the same as defined by this Act.

Any unexpired temporary statutes of the Province of Canada continue in force, until their intended expiration, as statutes under the authority of Parliament or of the legislatures of Ontario or Quebec, as appropriate.

➤ **SECTION 138:** From and after the Union the Use of the Words "Upper Canada," instead of "Ontario," or "Lower Canada" instead of "Quebec," in any Deed, Writ, Process, Pleading, Document, Matter, or Thing shall not invalidate the same.

This section ensures that the change in name from "Upper Canada" to "Ontario," and from "Lower Canada" to "Quebec," does not alter the validity of documents bearing the former names.

➤ **SECTION 139:** Any Proclamation under the Great Seal of the Province of Canada issued before the Union to take effect at a Time which is subsequent to the Union, whether relating to that Province, or to Upper Canada, or to Lower Canada, and the several Matters and Things therein proclaimed, shall be and continue of like Force and Effect as if the Union had not been made.

This section, also, is transitional and is intended to ensure the continued validity after Confederation of proclamations issued by the Province of Canada before Confederation.

➤ **SECTION 140:** Any Proclamation which is authorized by any Act of the Legislature of the Province of Canada to be issued under the Great Seal of the Province of Canada, whether relating to that Province, or to Upper Canada, or to Lower Canada, and which is not issued before the Union, may be issued by the Lieutenant Governor of Ontario or Quebec, as its Subject Matter requires, under the Great Seal thereof; and from and after the Issue of such Proclamation the same and the several Matters and Things therein proclaimed shall be and continue of the like Force and Effect in Ontario or Quebec as if the Union had not been made.

This transitional section authorizes the issuance of proclamations after Confederation pursuant to pre-Confederation legislation of the Province of Canada.

➤ **SECTION 141:** The Penitentiary of the Province of Canada shall, until the Parliament of Canada otherwise provides, be and continue the Penitentiary of Ontario and of Quebec.

Because penitentiaries are now covered by Federal legislation this section is spent.

➤ **SECTION 142:** The Division and Adjustment of the Debts, Credits, Liabilities, Properties, and Assets of Upper Canada and Lower Canada shall be referred to the Arbitrament of Three Arbitrators, One chosen by the Government of Ontario, One by the Government of Quebec, and One by the Government of Canada; and the Selection of the Arbitrators shall not be made until the Parliament of Canada and the Legislatures of Ontario and Quebec have met; and the Arbitrator chosen by the Government of Canada shall not be a Resident either in Ontario or in Quebec.

The division to which this section refers having been made, the section is spent.

➤ **SECTION 143:** The Governor General in Council may from Time to Time order that such and so many of the Records, Books, and Documents of the Province of Canada as he thinks fit shall be appropriated and delivered either to Ontario or to Quebec, and the same shall thenceforth be the Property of that Province; and any Copy thereof or Extract therefrom, duly certified by the Officer having charge of the Original thereof, shall be admitted as Evidence.

This section is probably spent. Two orders were issued on January 24, 1868.[249]

➤ **SECTION 144:** The Lieutenant Governor of Quebec may from Time to Time, by Proclamation under the Great Seal of the Province, to take effect from a Day to be appointed therein, constitute Townships in those Parts of the Province of Quebec in which Townships are not then already constituted, and fix the Metes and Bounds thereof.

This section needs no comment.

X. Intercolonial Railway

➤ **SECTION 145:** Inasmuch as the Provinces of Canada, Nova Scotia, and New Brunswick have joined in a Declaration that the Construction of the Intercolonial Railway is essential to the Consolidation of the Union of British North America, and to the Assent thereto of Nova

Scotia and New Brunswick, and have consequently agreed that Provision should be made for its immediate Construction by the Government of Canada; Therefore, in order to give effect to that Agreement, it shall be the Duty of the Government and Parliament of Canada to provide for the Commencement, within Six Months after the Union, of a Railway connecting the River St. Lawrence with the City of Halifax in Nova Scotia, and for the Construction thereof without Intermission, and the Completion thereof with all practicable Speed.

A railway to link the maritime colonies with Lower and Upper Canada had been proposed as early as 1839 by Lord Durham, and it became a condition of Confederation. Built in stages, some before Confederation, the railway joined Halifax and Rivière-du-Loup in 1876. In 1879 the Intercolonial Railway acquired part of the Grand Trunk Railway west of Rivière-du-Loup, and in 1889 it secured running rights over the Grand Trunk Railway to Montreal. The Cape Breton Railway was added to the system in 1891. The Intercolonial has been part of the Canadian National Railways since 1919.[250]

This section was repealed by Britain's 1893 Statute Law Revision Act.

XI. Admission of Other Colonies

➤ **SECTION 146:** It shall be lawful for the Queen, by and with the Advice of Her Majesty's Most Honourable Privy Council, on Addresses from the Houses of the Parliament of Canada, and from the Houses of the respective Legislatures of the Colonies or Provinces of Newfoundland, Prince Edward Island, and British Columbia, to admit those Colonies or Provinces, or any of them, into the Union, and on Address from the Houses of the Parliament of Canada to admit Rupert's Land and the North-western Territory, or either of them, into the Union, on such Terms and Conditions in each Case as are in the Addresses expressed and as the Queen thinks fit to approve, subject to the Provisions of this Act; and the Provisions of any Order in Council in that Behalf shall have effect as if they had been enacted by the Parliament of the United Kingdom of Great Britain and Ireland.

All of these territories have been added to Canada: Rupert's Land and the North-western Territory in 1870, British Columbia in 1871, Prince Edward Island in 1873, and Newfoundland in 1949. The Arctic islands were added in 1880.

Because Newfoundland had no legislature at the time of union, it could not be admitted solely under the authority of this section which specified an address from Newfoundland's legislature. As noted in Chapter 2, Newfoundland in 1934 was forced to revert from Dominion to colonial status and in so doing relinquished both responsible and representative government. Newfoundland's admission to Canada was therefore effected by British statute (B.N.A. Act [No. 1], 1949—renamed the Newfoundland Act in 1982).

➤ **SECTION 147:** In case of the Admission of Newfoundland and Prince Edward Island, or either of them, each shall be entitled to a Representation in the Senate of Canada of Four Members, and (notwithstanding anything in this Act) in case of the Admission of Newfoundland the normal Number of Senators shall be Seventy-six and their maximum Number shall be Eighty-two; but Prince Edward Island when admitted shall be deemed to be comprised in the Third of Three Divisions into which Canada is, in relation to the Constitution of the Senate, divided by this Act, and accordingly, after the Admission of Prince Edward Island, whether Newfoundland is admitted or not, the Representation of Nova Scotia and New Brunswick in the Senate shall, as Vacancies occur, be reduced from Twelve to Ten Members respectively, and the Representation of each of those Provinces shall not be increased at any Time beyond Ten, except under the Provisions of this Act for the Appointment of Three or Six additional Senators under the Direction of the Queen.

The 1915 Constitution Act added a fourth Senate division consisting of the four western provinces, and in so doing increased the number of senators to 96. It provided, further, that upon the admission of Newfoundland to the union, that province would receive six Senate seats (rather than four as specified in this section) and that the size of the Senate would therefore rise from 96 to 102. Reference to the appointment of "three or six additional senators" is to section 26. The commentary on section 21 includes a table showing the increases in the size of the Senate.

This section is now spent.

CHAPTER 8

Clause-by-Clause Analysis of the Canada Act, and its Schedule "B," the 1982 Constitution Act

Contrary to what some people seem to believe, the 1982 Canada Act with the Constitution Act (the latter being Schedule B to the Canada Act) is not a new Canadian Constitution. It does not replace the 1867 Constitution Act although it amends several sections of that Act; rather, it is an addition—an extremely important addition—to the codified part of our constitution. Basically, the Canada and Constitution Acts accomplish three major things.

First, they "patriate" our Constitution in the sense that the British Parliament no longer has even formal jurisdiction over the 1867 Constitution Act or, of course, over the two new Acts. It will be recalled that section 7 of the Statute of Westminster had exempted the 1867 Act from Britain's total withdrawal from Canada's constitutional affairs. (The continued role of the Privy Council until 1949 as Canada's highest appeal body in civil cases is not relevant to the current discussion.) Patriation is accomplished by section 2 of the Canada Act.

The second accomplishment is the Charter of Rights and Freedoms which is Part I (ss. 1-34) of the new Constitution Act. It is applicable to both orders of government so that, subject to sections 1 and 33 (see the commentaries below), its rights and freedoms are placed beyond the reach of government *per se*. The Charter is amendable in accordance with the new formula contained in the 1982 Constitution Act.

Third, then, is the amending formula which is Part V of the Constitution Act. For the first time in our history the codified parts of our constitution may be altered entirely within Canada.

CANADA ACT, 1982

➤ **PREAMBLE:** An Act to give effect to a request by the Senate and House of Commons of Canada.

Whereas Canada has requested and consented to the enactment of an Act of the Parliament of the United Kingdom to give effect to the provisions hereinafter set forth and the Senate and the House of Commons of Canada in Parliament assembled have submitted an address to Her Majesty requesting that Her Majesty may graciously be pleased to cause a Bill to be laid before the Parliament of the United Kingdom for that purpose.

Be it therefore enacted by the Queen's Most Excellent Majesty, by and with the advice and consent of the Lords Spiritual and Temporal, and Commons, in this present Parliament assembled, and by the authority of the same, as follows:

The 1926 Balfour Declaration had enunciated the constitutional convention that the British dominions (which included Canada) "are autonomous communities within the British Empire, equal in status, in no way subordinate to one another in any aspect of their domestic or external affairs." The 1931 Statute of Westminster had formalized this independence by stating (s. 4), pursuant to a recommendation of the 1930 Imperial Conference, that henceforth no Act of the British Parliament would apply to a dominion "unless it is expressly declared in that Act that that Dominion has requested, and consented to, the enactment thereof."

According to section 7(1) of the Statute of Westminster this requirement of request and consent did not apply to the "repeal, amendment or alteration" of the 1867 Constitution Act. The 1982 Constitution Act does make several amendments to the 1867 Act, but it does not of itself (and neither does the Canada Act) constitute a "repeal, amendment or alteration" of the 1867 Act. While there may be an interesting question whether the request and consent contained in the preamble to the Canada Act was legally necessary, it is of no practical import. Suffice it to say that request and consent has been the norm, and the preamble is a reminder that the historic vehicle for changes to our Constitution was a joint Senate-House of Commons address to the monarch requesting legislative action by the British Parliament. (The absence of any reference to provincial approval is also the norm.) In any event, sections 4 and 7(1) of the Statute of Westminster are repealed, insofar as they apply to Canada, by item 17 of the Schedule to the 1982 Constitution Act.

It is unfortunate that neither the Canada Act nor the Constitution Act received any special treatment by a Canadian legislature. Request by joint address, even with the support of provincial premiers, is not unique. Surely there would have been some value, even if only symbolic, in the approval of these new documents by eleven (or even ten, until Quebec concurs) legislatures.

➤ **SECTION 1:** The *Constitution Act, 1982* set out in Schedule B to this Act is hereby enacted for and shall have the force of law in Canada and shall come into force as provided in that Act.

Although an Act becomes law when it receives royal assent it does not necessarily come into force at that time. Some statutes provide that they will come into force only when proclaimed by the Crown. The Canada Act (including the Constitution Act) became law, therefore, when it was given royal assent on March 29, 1982. The Canada Act, exclusive of the Constitution Act, came into force immediately. Section 58 of the Constitution Act provides that that Act would come into force when proclaimed by the Queen or governor general. The Queen issued the proclamation on April 17, 1982.[1]

➤ **SECTION 2:** No Act of the Parliament of the United Kingdom passed after the *Constitution Act, 1982* comes into force shall extend to Canada as part of its law.

This provision patriates our Constitution. Complementing this section is the repeal, noted above, of sections 4 and 7(1) of the Statute of Westminster. Because this final step of independence was taken by British rather than Canadian legal action, and because the enactment of section 2 of the Canada Act cannot bind a sovereign British Parliament, one might speculate (even if only momentarily) as to the legal consequences of a repeal by Britain of the Canada Act (and, for that matter, of the 1867 Constitution Act). If Britain were to enact legislation which purported to extend to Canada, our courts would reject it on the grounds that our legal system denies the authority of any other country to legislate for Canada.

➤ **SECTION 3:** So far as it is not contained in Schedule B, the French version of this Act is set out in Schedule A to this Act and has the same authority in Canada as the English version thereof.

The Canada Act was passed by the British Parliament in both English and French. The French version constitutes Schedule A of the Act and "has the same authority" as the English version. The Constitution Act also, having been appended to the Canada Act, was passed in both English and French thus making both versions of equal authority. Nevertheless, and presumably unnecessarily, section 57 of the Constitution Act reiterates this equality.

What if the English and French versions appear to have slightly different meanings? The problem did not arise in relation to the 1867 Constitution Act or the amendments enacted by the British Parliament, because the only official version was the English. In the event of a perceived difference between the English and its French translation the former prevailed. Section 55 of the new Constitution Act requires the enactment of official French versions of the "Constitution of Canada." Pursuant to section 133 of the 1867 Act, as well as section 18(1) of the 1982 Constitution Act, all legislation passed by the Canadian Parliament (including amendments to the 1867 Act that were made in Canada) have been enacted in both official languages. Therefore, the danger of linguistic inconsistency created by the 1982 Canada and Constitution Acts is not new. The issue is not considered in this book, although an occasional passing reference is made to illustrate potential problems of interpretation that the courts must address. See, for example, discussion of the phrase "minority language educational facilities" in the commentary on Charter section 23(3)(b).

➤ **SECTION 4:** This Act may be cited as the *Canada Act 1982*.

This section needs no comment.

CONSTITUTION ACT, 1982

Part I: Canadian Charter of Rights and Freedoms

The existence of the Charter of Rights and Freedoms adds a constitutional dimension hitherto unknown in Canada, for the courts must now address issues from the perspective of entrenchment in addition to those relating to federalism.

Although about 175 cases were decided by the Supreme Court of Canada during the first nine years of the Charter—actually, in only seven years following its first case—"Charterland" (to use Professor Russell's term) is still in the early stages of being charted. Because the Charter becomes in a real sense what the courts say it is, the following analysis draws heavily upon judicial decisions. And because the final word rests with the Supreme Court of Canada, it is that Court's decisions which, with few exceptions, are used. Justice McIntyre cautions, however, that

> the *Charter* should not be regarded as an empty vessel to be filled with whatever meaning we might wish from time to time. The interpretation of the *Charter*, as of all constitutional documents, is constrained by the language, structure, and history of the constitutional text, by constitutional tradition, and by the history, traditions, and underlying philosophies of our society.[2]

Because the meaning of the Charter has been unfolding before our eyes during the years since 1982, an effort has been made in the following commentaries to use the words of Supreme Court justices as they explain their interpretations of the Charter's provisions. In this way the reader is able to sample first hand the reasoning that supports judicial decisions.

The Supreme Court has ruled that the Charter does not have retrospective application to events occurring before April 17, 1982, even if the trial takes place after that date. In announcing this decision for the Court majority Justice Le Dain quoted with approval Associate Justice Tarnopolsky of the Ontario Court of Appeal: "One applies the law in force at the time when the act that is alleged to be in contravention of a Charter right or freedom occurs" and "it is important that actions be determined by the law, including the Constitution, in effect at the time of the action."[3]

Some two-thirds of all Charter cases throughout Canada have involved claims of Charter violations by public officials.[4] These include, for example, the use of unreasonable search methods or the failure to advise detainees of the right to counsel. This new emphasis on procedural safeguards may increase respect for the individual among public officials; it also risks the possibility that the guilty will go free. Section 24(2) of the Charter attempts to balance these two effects by asking whether the admission of evidence gained in a manner that infringes Charter rights will bring the administration of justice into disrepute.

A question that should probably be addressed at the outset is the meaning or meanings of the following terms: "everyone" (ss. 2, 7, 8, 9, 10, 12, 17); "any person" (ss. 11, 19); "any member of the public" (s. 20); "anyone" (s. 24); "every individual" (s. 15[1]); and "citizen" (ss. 3, 6, 23). Specifically, do any or all of these terms include artificial persons such as corporations as well as natural persons, and do they include fetuses? Hogg addressed this question in 1982 with respect to corporations and concluded that the first four above are intended to be synonymous; and that they include corporations except where the context of the section suggests otherwise—e.g., sections 7, 9, 10, 11(e). The term "every individual" would not likely apply to a corporation; this interpretation is supported by the change from "everyone" in the original 1980 Patriation Resolution to "individual." Finally, "citizen" (at least as defined in the Canadian Citizenship Act) would exclude corporations.[5] Supreme Court rulings have been consistent with this interpretation, although the Court has added that a corporation which is the "any person" charged with an offence (s. 11) cannot be a witness in judicial proceedings; however, its employees may be witnesses.[6]

In *Tremblay v. Daigle* (1989) the Supreme Court declared that a fetus is not a "human being" under the Quebec Charter. It also noted that in "Anglo-Canadian law a foetus must be born alive to enjoy rights" but, because the case involved two private individuals and therefore did not invoke the Canadian Charter, the Court declined to speculate as to the potential applicability of section 7's right to life.[7] In March 1991 a unanimous Supreme Court ruled that a fetus is not a human being under the Criminal Code, but it was not called upon to decide the question within the framework of the Canadian Charter.[8]

➤ **Preamble:** Whereas Canada is founded upon principles that recognize the supremacy of God and the rule of law:

The absence of stirring language and enunciation of great principles was noted at the beginning of Chapter 4. The preamble to the 1982 Constitution Act, such as it is, is the best we have. The principle of the rule of law was considered in Chapter 4. One may wonder how a declaration of the supremacy of God can be reconciled with freedoms of religion and belief which are guaranteed in section 2(a) and (b), especially when preambles, though not legally binding, may be used as guides to interpretation.

Guarantee of Rights and Freedoms

➤ **Section 1:** The *Canadian Charter of Rights and Freedoms* guarantees the rights and freedoms set out in it subject only to such reasonable limits prescribed by law as can be demonstrably justified in a free and democratic society.

This section establishes the "guarantee" of the Charter's rights and freedoms—namely:

(1) Fundamental freedoms (s. 2).
(2) Democratic rights (ss. 3-5).
(3) Mobility rights (s. 6).
(4) Legal rights (ss. 7-14).
(5) Equality rights (s. 15).
(6) Language rights (ss. 16-22).
(7) Minority language educational rights (s. 23).

However, section 1 makes each of these rights and freedoms subject to "such reasonable limits prescribed by law as can be demonstrably justified in a free and democratic society." It is a potentially useful device enabling provinces to adapt their laws to their peculiar requirements so long as infringements of Charter rights and freedoms are "reasonable," and so long as the Supreme Court is prepared to consider reasonableness in the light of provincial needs. Romanow thought that the courts might be encouraged to interpret "reasonable limits" broadly, adding that "from the perspective of those who were opposed to entrenchment, the limitation clause was, in some ways, superior to a *non obstante* [notwithstanding] clause" because it did not involve the political risk of an explicit declaration that guaranteed rights were being overridden.[9]

Before considering this basic question of what "reasonable" means it is useful to look at the other requirements of section 1. In the first place the limits must be "prescribed by law"—that is, not be arbitrary. The "law" will normally be statutory, but subordinate legislation made pursuant to enabling statutes will also qualify. Furthermore, the limitation may result "by necessary implication from the terms of a statute or regulation or from its operating requirements. The limit may also result from the application of a common law rule."[10] See the commentary on section 10(b). However, section 1 is not available for the two-thirds of Charter cases claiming violations by public officials. For example, if a police officer fails to inform an individual of the right to "retain and instruct counsel without delay" (s. 10[b])—i.e., before "detaining" the person by requiring him or her to accompany the officer to the police station for a breathalyzer test—this violation of section 10 cannot be saved by appeal to section 1 because the violation was not prescribed by law.[11]

Second, limits must be "demonstrably justified." The burden of justification rests with the government seeking the limitation. It is apparent that the application of section 1 is at least potentially available every time a court determines that a Charter right has been violated. However, a court considers reasonableness only when the author of the offending law attempts to justify it.

As to the essentials of a "free and democratic society" Chief Justice Dickson for the Supreme Court stated that

> the values and principles essential to a free and democratic society embody, to name but a few, respect for the inherent dignity of the human person, commitment to social justice and equality, accommodation of a wide variety of beliefs, respect for cultural and group identity, and faith in social and political institutions which enhance the participation of individuals and groups in society.[12]

In its first draft, section 1 provided that a limitation to the Charter's guaranteed rights and freedoms had to be (1) "reasonable" but not necessarily prescribed by law, (2) "generally accepted" rather than demonstrably justified, and (3) accepted "in a free and democratic society *with a parliamentary system of government*" (emphasis added). It is obvious that on all three counts the possibility of limiting rights and freedoms has been restricted by the final version. The third of these is of particular interest for at least two reasons. In the first place the United States would not have qualified as a society that the courts might consider in their deliberation. In the second place, and to the extent that other parliamentary systems (especially the British) are characterized by legislative supremacy, the courts may have been more lenient with governments seeking to limit the Charter's rights and freedoms.

The basic question remains, however: "What is 'reasonable'?" We now turn to that question. A related question asks whether "reasonableness" might be interpreted so as to recognize variations among the provinces, but in its first encounter with an argument of "reasonableness" (*Quebec Association of Protestant School Boards*, 1984) the Court avoided the issue by claiming the limitation was really an amendment to Charter rights. The case involved an alleged violation of the Canadian Charter's minority language educational rights (s. 23[1][b]) by Quebec's Charter of the French Language (better known as Bill 101). The so-called "Quebec clause" of Bill 101 restricted the right of English-language education to children whose parents or older siblings had been educated in English within Quebec, whereas the Canadian Charter's "Canada clause" guarantees the right to the children of Canadian citizens who have been educated in English anywhere in Canada. According to the Supreme Court, the Quebec clause was not a "limit" upon, but rather a redefinition of, the right. That is, it was a redefinition "of the class of persons who are entitled to instruction in the minority language, and has the effect of creating an exception to s. 23 and of amending the *Charter*. Whatever their scope, the limits which s. 1 allows cannot be equated with exceptions to the rights and freedoms guaranteed by the *Charter*."[13] Such a restrictive interpretation of "limits" has not been repeated but it could increase the uncertainty of section 1's meaning. It is also significant in terms of the recognition of differences inherent in a federal system. This is noted in Chapter 4 under "Federalism."

The Supreme Court's criteria of "reasonableness" were stated in *Oakes* (1986), although they emerged in embryonic form the previous year in *Big M Drug Mart*[14] which was a successful challenge to the Sunday-closing provision of the Lord's Day Act. The Federal government had argued that the restriction on Sunday opening was reasonable because the need for a universal day of rest was generally accepted, and that the choice of Sunday accorded with the Christian majority population. Justice (as he then was) Dickson for the Court rejected the second argument as "no more than an argument of convenience and expediency and is fundamentally repugnant because it would justify the law on the very basis upon which it is attacked for violating s. 2(a)" of the Charter. While accepting the need for a day of rest, he rejected the argument presented because the purpose of the Lord's Day Act was religious rather than secular. (The commentary on section 2[a] notes the significance of "purpose" in establishing constitutionality relating to freedom of religion.) The point to note here is Dickson's more general statement that

> not every government interest or policy is entitled to s. 1 consideration. Principles will have to be developed for recognizing which government objectives are of sufficient importance to warrant overriding a constitutionally protected right or freedom. Once a sufficiently significant government interest is recognized then it must be decided if the means chosen to achieve this interest are reasonable—a form of proportionality test. The court may wish to ask whether the means adopted to achieve the end sought do so by impairing as little as possible the right or freedom in question.

This broad guideline was given greater precision in *Oakes*. It is quoted in full below because of the Court's subsequent reliance upon it whenever section 1 is invoked. Nevertheless, the Court clearly has much discretionary authority.

> To establish that a limit is reasonable and demonstrably justified in a free and democratic society, two central criteria must be satisfied. First, the objective, which the measures responsible for a limit on a *Charter* right or freedom are designed to serve, must be "of sufficient importance to warrant overriding a constitutionally protected right or freedom." The standard must be high in order to ensure that objectives which are trivial or discordant with the principles integral to a free and democratic society do not gain s. 1 protection. It is necessary, at a minimum, that an objective relate to concerns which are pressing and substantial in a free and democratic society before it can be characterized as sufficiently important.
>
> Second, once a sufficiently significant objective is recognized, then the party invoking s. 1 must show that the means chosen are reasonable and demonstrably justified. This involves "a form of proportionality test." Although the nature of the proportionality test will vary depending on the circumstances, in each case courts will be required to balance the interests of society with those of individuals and groups. There are, in my view, three important components of a proportionality test. First, the measures adopted must be carefully designed to achieve the objective in question. They must not be arbitrary, unfair or based on irrational considerations. In short, they must be rationally connected to the objective. Second, the means, even if rationally connected to the objective in this first sense, should impair "as little as possible" the right or freedom in question. Third, there must be a proportionality between the *effects* of the measures which are responsible for limiting the *Charter* right or freedom, and the objective which has been identified as of "sufficient importance."
>
> With respect to the third component, it is clear that the general effect of any measure impugned under s. 1 will be the infringement of a right or freedom guaranteed by the *Charter*; this is the reason why resort to s. 1 is necessary. The inquiry into effects must, however, go further. A wide range of rights and freedoms are guaranteed by the *Charter*; and an almost infinite number of factual situations may arise in respect of these. Some limits on rights and freedoms protected by the *Charter* will be more serious than others in terms of the nature of the right or freedom violated, the extent of the violation, and the degree to which the measures which impose the limit trench upon the integral principles of a free and democratic society. Even if an objective is of sufficient importance, and the first two elements of the proportionality test are satisfied, it is still possible that, because of the severity of the deleterious effects of a measure on

> individuals or groups, the measure will not be justified by the purposes it is intended to serve. The more severe the deleterious effects of a measure, the more important the objective must be if the measure is to be reasonable and demonstrably justified in a free and democratic society.[15]

In summary, then, the following questions must be answered:

(1) Is the government's objective important enough to justify the infringement of a Charter right?

(2) Are the means used to override the right justifiable—i.e., are they proportional to the objective? Specifically,

- **(a)** Are the means likely to achieve the objective? Is there a rational connection between the means and the objective?
- **(b)** Do the means infringe the Charter right "as little as possible" in achieving the objective?
- **(c)** The foregoing notwithstanding, is the achievement of the objective worth the price of allowing the Charter violation? This seems redundant. If the impugned law has survived to this point, what possible consideration could strike it down? Indeed, this stage of analysis has never been reached.

In *Oakes* the Federal government sought exemption of the "reverse onus" provision in the Narcotic Control Act. ("Reverse onus" presumes guilt under certain conditions until the accused proves his or her innocence. It clearly runs into the presumption of innocence guaranteed by Charter section 11[d]). The provision in *Oakes* survived the first criterion—the objective of protecting society from the evils of drug trafficking—but foundered on the first component of the proportionality test in that there was not, in the Court's view, a rational connection between the fact of possession and the presumed fact of possession for the purpose of trafficking.

The Supreme Court has consistently accepted the purpose of government policy in its interpretation of section 1, with a possible exception in which the justices disagreed among themselves even as to whether the impugned regulation was prescribed by law.[15a] Otherwise, it would be venturing even more into the political realm. Even so, Russell suggests that the Court cannot avoid the political by restricting itself to means:

> To reject legislative means, it must compare them, more or less explicitly, to "better" alternatives. But political controversy is as often about means as it is about ends, and the legislative choice of means may be carefully deliberated rather than careless. In such cases, some will consider the judicial evaluation of alternative means to be no less a matter of second-guessing policy wisdom than is the evaluation of objectives.[16]

What can be said about attempts to invoke section 1? By mid-1991 the Supreme Court actively considered the limitations clause in about fifty cases involving fourteen Charter rights and freedoms. The most frequent appeals to this limitations clause were government efforts to override sections 2(b), 11(d), and 7:

> Section 2(b) (freedom of expression): overridden in eight of the twelve attempts.
>
> Section 11(d) (mainly the presumption of innocence element): overridden in only six of the thirteen attempts. Four of the seven cases in which 11(d) prevailed were decided concurrently.
>
> Section 7 (life, liberty, security of the person): overridden in none of the four attempts. Because the Supreme Court has stated that violations of legal rights (sections 8-14) infringe section 7 guarantees as well, the half dozen attempts to override section 7 together with another legal right have been excluded from the total. Note the Court's statement quoted at the end of the commentary on section 7.

If a trend is discernible it is that appeals to section 1 have fared much better since the beginning of 1988. Before that time, the limitations clause overrode the Charter only once in almost a dozen attempts. The case was *Edwards Books and Art* (1986)[17] and the freedom was conscience and religion (s. 2[a]). Since then, section 1 has sustained limitations to Charter rights and freedoms in well over half the cases involving that section; this may suggest an increasing deference to government. Unsuccessful appeals to section 1 have foundered in almost every instance on the second part of the *Oakes* "proportionality test" requiring that government action in violation of the Charter "should impair as little as possible the right or freedom in question." The Supreme Court's treatment of section 1 is noted for many of the cases in the following commentaries.

Fundamental Freedoms

➤ **SECTION 2:** Everyone has the following fundamental freedoms:

(a) freedom of conscience and religion;

(b) freedom of thought, belief, opinion and expression, including freedom of the press and other media of communication;

(c) freedom of peaceful assembly; and

(d) freedom of association.

Even before the Charter, these fundamental freedoms were recognized by the Canadian Bill of Rights and several provincial bills of rights, although they were not entrenched in the sense of being beyond the reach of the ordinary law-making process. As Charter freedoms they are subject to the legislative override of section 33, their "fundamental" nature notwithstanding.

Subsection (a): Freedom of conscience and religion

In its first freedom of religion case (*Big M Drug Mart*, 1985) the Supreme Court attempted to give meaning to this freedom within the broader concept of freedom itself. Speaking for the Court, Justice (as he then was) Dickson said:

> A truly free society is one which can accommodate a wide variety of beliefs, diversity of tastes and pursuits, customs and codes of conduct. A free society is one which aims at equality with respect to the employment of fundamental freedoms and I say this without any reliance upon s. 15 of the *Charter*. Freedom must surely be founded in respect for the inherent dignity and the inviolable rights of the human person. The essence of the concept of freedom of religion is the right to entertain such religious beliefs as a person chooses, the right to declare religious beliefs openly and without fear of hindrance or reprisal, and the right to manifest religious beliefs by worship and practice or by teaching and dissemination. But the concept means more than that.
>
> Freedom can primarily be characterized by the absence of coercion or constraint. If a person is compelled by the state or the will of another to a course of action or inaction which he would not otherwise have chosen, he is not acting of his own volition and he cannot be said to be truly free. One of the major purposes of the *Charter* is to protect, within reason, from compulsion or restraint. Coercion includes not only such blatant forms of compulsion as direct commands to act or refrain from acting on pain of sanction, coercion includes indirect forms of control which determine or limit alternative courses of conduct available to others. Freedom in a broad sense embraces both the absence of coercion and constraint, and the right to manifest beliefs and practices. Freedom means that, subject to such limitations as are necessary to protect public safety, order, health, or morals or the fundamental rights and freedoms of others, no one is to be forced to act in a way contrary to his beliefs or his conscience.[18]

Given the breadth of the concept of freedom, the Court will have to decide the extent to which the guaranteed freedom will legitimize activities that otherwise conflict with Canadian law. This is the purpose of section 1 of the Charter. Some activities clearly are unacceptable in our society and could be prevented by invoking section 1. Among these are human sacrifice, polygamy and, as decided in December 1990 (*Keegstra*—see the commentary on 2[b] below), the dissemination of hate literature. Others, which may have no overriding social implications, could be permitted without creating serious problems even if they involve exemption from the ordinary law. Would Alberta's Communal Property Act (repealed in 1972), for example, which required cabinet approval for the expansion of Hutterite colonies or the creation of new colonies, have survived Charter section 2? It was upheld by the Supreme Court of Canada in 1969 on the grounds of provincial jurisdiction over property even though it related to Hutterite religious practice: "The Act is not directed at Hutterite religious belief or worship, or at the profession of such belief. It is directed at the practice of holding large areas of Alberta land as communal property, whether such practice stems from religious belief or not."[19]

The inclusion of freedom of conscience as well as religion acknowledges the freedom of agnostics, atheists, and the followers of certain cults which may not be considered "religions."

Four cases relating to freedom of religion (three of them to Sunday closing) under the Charter had been decided by the Supreme Court by mid-1991. These were *Big M Drug Mart* (1985), *Plantation Indoor Plants* (1985), *Edwards Books and Art* (1986), and *Jones* (Alberta, 1986). In the first two (decided the same day), challenges to the Sunday-closing requirement of the Lord's Day Act were upheld. The Court declared that the first point to be determined is the Act's purpose, and only if the Act passes the purpose test is it necessary to consider the effects in relation to religious freedom. Simply stated, if the purpose violates the Charter, the possibility of "reasonable limits" under section 1 does not arise. In the two cases at hand the Court stated that

> since the acknowledged purpose of the *Lord's Day Act*, on long-standing and consistently maintained authority, is the compulsion of religious observance, that Act offends freedom of religion and it is unnecessary to consider the actual impact of Sunday closing upon religious freedom. Legislation whose purpose is found to violate the *Charter* cannot be saved even if the effects were found to be inoffensive . . . *The Lord's Day Act* to the extent that it binds all to a sectarian Christian ideal, works a form of coercion inimical to the spirit of the *Charter*. The Act gives the appearance of discrimination against non-Christian Canadians . . . The protection of one religion and the concomitant non-protection of others imports a disparate impact destructive of the religious freedom of society.[20]

In contrast, Justice Wilson argued that the Charter is effects-oriented rather than purpose-oriented. This point in relation to discrimination is noted in the commentary on section 15.

The significance of "purpose" became evident in the *Edwards Books and Art* challenge to Ontario's Retail Business Holidays Act.[21] This Act, also, required that stores be closed on Sundays (among other specified days defined as "holidays"). Exceptions to this requirement were made for stores not exceeding a certain size and who closed on Saturdays—in effect a concession to people who observed a Saturday sabbath. The Supreme Court decided that the purpose of the Act was to provide uniform holidays for retail workers; it was not "a surreptitious attempt to encourage religious worship." This difference in pith and substance also accounts for the jurisdictional difference between this Act and the Lord's Day Act. This one falls within provincial jurisdiction under section 92(13) of the 1867 Constitution Act, whereas the Lord's Day Act came under section 91(27) of the 1867 Act. In effect, Sunday-closing legislation was now a provincial responsibility so long as its purpose remained secular. Given this ruling (and as an interesting footnote) it seems that, had the Federal government been able successfully to argue a secular purpose for the Lord's Day Act in *Big M Drug Mart*, the Court would have declared the Act in violation of provincial jurisdiction.

The Court acknowledged that the Ontario legislation infringed upon the religious freedom of non-exempt retailers, as well as customers, who were Saturday observers. However, this infringement constituted "reasonable limits" under Charter section 1. Chief Justice Dickson moderated his *Oakes* position. In *Oakes*, the impugned legislation had to impair a Charter right "as little as possible"; in *Edwards Books and Art*, "as little as is *reasonably* possible" (emphasis added).[22]

The impact of the Act upon retailers who observe no weekly religious holiday was deemed to be secular rather than religious in nature, and therefore of no significance in relation to section 2(a): "While freedom of conscience necessarily includes the right not to have a religious basis for one's conduct, it does not follow that one can rely upon the Charter protection of freedom of conscience to object to an enforced holiday simply because it happens to coincide with someone else's sabbath."[23]

Because of the currency of the Sunday-closing issue, Chief Justice Dickson's rationale for accepting the objective of the Ontario Retail Business Holidays Act is a classic statement:

> A family visit to an uncle or a grandmother, the attendance of a parent at a child's sports tournament, a picnic, a swim, or a hike in the park on a summer day, or a family expedition to a zoo, circus, or exhibition—these, and hundreds of other leisure activities with family and friends are amongst the simplest but most profound joys that any of us can know. The aim of protecting workers, families and communities from a diminution of opportunity to experience the fulfilment offered by these activities, and from the alienation of the individual from his or her closest social bonds, is not one which I regard as unimportant or trivial. In the context of the fast-growing trend toward wide-scale store openings, I am satisfied that the Act is aimed at a pressing and substantial concern.[24]

In *Jones* (Alberta 1986), the Court was divided on the question whether the Alberta School Act constitutes a violation of religious freedom. The Act requires that children attend schools whose instruction has been approved by the Department of Education; alternatively, that children have official certificates stating that they are "under efficient instruction at home or elsewhere." Most schools are operated by elected boards in accordance with the School Act, but private schools are allowed if they meet with Departmental approval. In the case at hand Jones, the pastor of a fundamentalist church, was teaching his and others' children without seeking approval for his private school. Because he did not seek exemption for his own children from attending the regular public school he was charged with truancy. According to Jones, the requirement that he apply for an exemption was a violation of his religious belief that God rather than the government had authority over the education of his children. Four justices said that the School Act, in providing for the approval of alternative schools, was actually accommodating religious freedom, and that the Act did not violate freedom of religion. Three others agreed that religious freedom was violated but, "considering the compelling interest of the province in the 'efficient instruction' of the young," the requirement that home instruction be certified "constitutes a reasonable limit on a parent's religious convictions concerning the upbringing of his children."[25]

Subsection (b): Freedom of thought, belief, opinion, and expression, including the media

Without freedom of expression the freedoms of thought, belief, and opinion have little meaning, inasmuch as these activities cannot easily be controlled except by regulating access to others' ideas through censorship of the written and spoken word. It is the guarantee of expression, therefore, which is the critical part of section 2(b). In the words of John Stuart Mill: "If all mankind minus one were of one opinion, and only one person were of the contrary opinion, mankind would be no more justified in silencing that one person, than he, if he had the power, would be justified in silencing mankind."[26] Or, as United States President Thomas Jefferson said in this unique way: "If there be any among us who would wish to dissolve this Union or to change its republican form, let them stand undisturbed as monuments of the safety with which error of opinion may be tolerated where reason is left free to combat it."[27] The tradition of free speech and assembly in London's Hyde Park is testimony to this belief.

One might add that without the freedoms of thought, belief, opinion, and expression, freedoms of peaceful assembly and of association (s.2[c][d])—indeed the democratic rights of sections 3, 4, and 5, as well—would be meaningless. Clearly, then, these freedoms are at the very core of liberal democracy. Judges of the Supreme Court have often spoken in this vein. For example:

> Freedom of expression is not . . . a creature of the *Charter*. It is one of the fundamental concepts that has formed the basis for the historical development of the political, social and educational institutions of western society. Representative democracy, as we know it today, which is in great part the product of free expression and discussion of varying ideas, depends upon its maintenance and protection.[28]

The importance of this freedom may explain why it has provoked the most frequent appeal to the limitations clause (s. 1). Paradoxically, freedom of expression was sacrificed to section 1 eight of the twelve times the limitations clause had been actively considered by the Supreme Court until mid-1991. This success of section 1 demonstrates that no matter how important these freedoms may be they cannot be absolute. One can understand that laws against libel and slander, sedition, obscenity, contempt of court, and false advertising, for example, find general acceptance within society notwithstanding practical difficulties in their application. And in the December 1990 *Keegstra* case the Supreme Court ruled that hate propaganda cannot be protected by section 1.

Keegstra, a former Alberta high school teacher, was convicted of willfully promoting hatred against an identifiable group—the Jews. The panel in the *Keegstra* case[29] was unanimous "that the evil of hate propaganda is beyond doubt," but they divided 4-3 on the saving power of section 1. The majority opinion stressed the following: first, the "need to ensure that truth and the common good are attained" lies at the heart of freedom of expression, but it is unlikely that "statements intended to promote hatred against an identifiable group are true, or that their vision of society will lead to a better world"; second, freedom of expression must be tempered "insofar as it advocates with inordinate vitriol an intolerance and prejudice which views as execrable the process of individual self-development and human flourishing among all members of society"; third, and perhaps most important, while freedom of expression is undeniably vital to a liberal democracy,

> [it] can work to undermine our commitment to democracy where employed to propagate ideas anathemic to democratic values. Hate propaganda works in just such a way, arguing as it does for a society in which the democratic process is subverted and individuals are denied respect and dignity simply because of racial or religious characteristics. This brand of expressive activity is thus wholly inimical to the democratic aspirations of the free expression guaranteed.
>
> Indeed, one may quite plausibly contend that it is through rejecting hate propaganda that the state can best encourage the protection of values central to freedom of expression, while simultaneously demonstrating dislike for the vision forwarded by hate-mongers.

The dissenting judges accepted Parliament's objective as valid—to eliminate hate propaganda—but they maintained that the legislation failed all three components of the second *Oakes* criterion of "reasonableness" or proportionality (Charter section 1). In the first place they questioned whether there was a rational connection between the prohibition and the likelihood of reduced racism; instead, "theories of a grand conspiracy ... can become all too appealing if government dignifies them by completely suppressing their utterance." Second, they maintained that the Criminal Code did not infringe freedom of expression as little as possible; because the prohibition is expressed broadly, exempting only private conversations from scrutiny, it may have a "chilling effect on legitimate activities important to our society by subjecting innocent persons to constraints born out of fear of the criminal process." And it may actually fail to discourage the committed hate-monger. Therefore and third, the cure (even if the law produced one) was worse than the disease.

The Supreme Court has also dealt with other generally less spectacular freedom of expression issues. It has decided, for example, that government restrictions on picketing, media reporting, soliciting for the purpose of prostitution, certain types of advertising, and the use of languages other than French on commercial signs in Quebec, all violate section 2(b).

Picketing

In its first picketing case (*RWDSU v. Dolphin Delivery*, 1986)[30] the Court ruled that picketing was in principle a form of expression protected by the Charter, although in the case at hand the Charter was unavailable because the dispute was private litigation. (See the commentary on section 32.) In 1988 (*British Columbia Government Employees' Union*) the Court held that the picketing of court houses could not survive the application of section 1 because the picketing was bound to delay the administration of justice. Chief Justice Dickson delivered the Court's ruling:

> Of what value are the rights and freedoms guaranteed by the *Charter* if a person is denied or delayed access to a court of competent jurisdiction in order to vindicate them? How can the courts independently maintain the rule of law and effectively discharge the duties imposed by the *Charter* if court access is hindered, impeded or denied? The *Charter* protections would become merely illusory, the entire *Charter* undermined.[31]

Media Reporting

In two cases involving the media the Court agreed that banning publication of the identities of sexual assault victims, and restricting the reporting of matrimonial court proceedings, violated freedom of expression. In the first case (*Canadian Newspapers*, 1988), appeal to section 1 was successful on the grounds that the ban might encourage victims to come forward. The Court also noted that the media was not prevented from attending and reporting the trial, but only from reporting information likely to reveal the victim's identity.[32]

In the second case (*Edmonton Journal*, 1989), the Court stressed not only "the vital importance" of freedom of expression but, more specifically, that "the press must be free to comment upon court proceedings to ensure that the courts are, in fact, seen by all to operate openly in the penetrating light of public scrutiny." In other words justice must not only be done, but must also seem to be done. In this instance, and contrary to the previous case, appeal to section 1 was unsuccessful because the inconvenience to the people involved in judicial proceedings was deemed to be more than offset by the general public advantage provided by the media.[33]

Soliciting

In three cases decided the same day in 1990 the Supreme Court held that "every person who in a public place or in any place open to public view . . . communicates or attempts to communicate with any person for the purpose of engaging in prostitution or of obtaining the sexual services of a prostitute" is exercising freedom of expression as guaranteed by the Charter notwithstanding its proscription by the Criminal Code (s. 195.1). Nevertheless, this proscription is justified under Charter section 1. (The Court focused its attention on *Ref. re ss. 193 and 195.1 (1) (c) of the Criminal Code [Man.].*)[34] In terms of the *Oakes* criteria, the purpose of the legislation—to eliminate the "social nuisance arising from the public display of the sale of sex"—is a pressing and substantial concern. Second, there is a rational connection between the objective and the legislation, and the means does not unduly impair freedom of expression. Although the prohibition is very broad, applying to public places generally whether or not other people are present, Chief Justice Dickson noted that much soliciting occurs in areas where the nuisance results from the presence of several prostitutes and customers. It is this concentration that creates the nuisance the legislation seeks to discourage. "Parliament can only act by focusing on individual transactions. The notion of nuisance in connection with street soliciting extends beyond interference with the individual citizen to interference with the public at large, that is with the environment represented by streets, public places and neighbouring premises." Dickson acknowledged that the means might be excessive had the legislation been intended to control only street nuisance rather than the broader social nuisance. As to the final part of the *Oakes* test, the Court believed that the importance of the objective outweighed the impact of the proscription on the protected freedom.

In the same case the Court ruled that the prohibition (Criminal Code s. 193) of the keeping of a common bawdy-house did not violate freedom of expression.

Advertising

The Court has decided (*Irwin Toy*, 1989) that the prohibition of commercial advertising directed at children below age 13 could be justified under Charter section 1 by the "general goal of consumer protection legislation—to protect a group that is most vulnerable to commercial manipulation . . . The legislature reasonably concluded that advertisers should not be able to capitalize upon children's credulity."[35] The ban was minimal impairment of section 2(b) because it did not prevent the advertising of children's products. (This was a Quebec case, but that province's 1982 blanket override pursuant to section 33 of the Canadian Charter had expired.) The Court also ruled that the impugned legislation was *intra vires* the Quebec legislature because it served a valid provincial purpose, it applied to the advertiser, and only incidentally affected television broadcasting which falls within Federal jurisdiction.

In a second advertising case, *Rocket v. Royal College of Dental Surgeons of Ontario* (1990),[36] the Supreme Court declared that a general prohibition of advertising by dentists (other than basic information such as name, address, telephone number, academic degrees) contravened section 2(b). Justice McLachlin for the Court acknowledged that the case highlighted a conflict between two legitimate social values—free expression, and the need for some regulation of professional advertising to protect a lay public who are probably incapable of assessing many claims as to the quality of dental service. "The consuming public . . . [is] far more vulnerable to unregulated advertising from dental professionals than it would be to unregulated advertising from manufacturers or suppliers of many other, more standardized, goods or services." The Court concluded that the impugned regulation was too broad in its scope because it prohibited legitimate forms of expression. In terms of the *Oakes* criteria, the regulation did not limit the freedom as little as possible, and it was "disproportionate to its objectives." Rather than strike down the regulation under section 52 of the 1982 Constitution Act, and thereby remove all advertising restrictions, McLachlin concluded that regulations should be drafted to strike the proper balance between the competing social values.

Language

It must be noted that these "language" cases relate to freedom of expression and not to language rights *per se*. For discussion of language rights see the commentaries on Charter sections 16-23, but especially the commentary on section 133 of the 1867 Constitution Act (which also considers the parallel section 23 of the Manitoba Act and section 110 of the North-West Territories Act in relation to Saskatchewan and Alberta).

There is no general authority to enact legislation with respect to language:

> a law prescribing that a particular language or languages must or may be used in certain situations will be classified for constitutional purposes not as a law in relation to language, but as a law in relation to the institutions or activities that the provision covers. Language is not an independent matter of legislation but is rather "ancillary" to the exercise of jurisdiction with respect to some class of subject matter assigned to Parliament or the provincial legislatures.[37]

In *Devine*, for example, the Court upheld Quebec's Charter of the French Language (Bill 101) as an exercise of provincial jurisdiction because the challenged language sections were in relation to commerce within the province. The impugned sections required advertising publications, business forms, signs, and posters to be in the French language and, in some cases, only in the French language. Nevertheless, being *intra vires* the province did not immunize those sections from challenge under the Canadian Charter.

Devine and *Ford*[38] were decided on the same day in December 1988. In both instances the Court agreed that restricting the use of languages other than French in most commercial advertising violated freedom of expression. In *Devine* the Court accepted the argument that allowing a second language along with French made the restriction "reasonable" under section 1. In *Ford*, however, the Court decided that the French-only requirement for commercial signs and the names of firms could not be justified.

These cases can be understood only in the light of Bill 101 passed by the Lévesque Government in 1977. (Restriction of the English language on commercial signs was but one part of the Bill.) Following implementation of the

Canadian Charter of Rights and Freedoms in 1982, the Quebec government enacted a blanket override bill, under section 33 of the Canadian Charter, applicable to all previous Quebec legislation including Bill 101. (The controversy surrounding this use of the override is discussed in the commentary on section 33.) The government continued to apply the override to subsequent legislation until Premier Bourassa discontinued the practice following his 1985 election. Bourassa also allowed the original 1982 overrides to expire five years after their passage. These later actions were consistent with his election promise to relax the language restrictions on commercial signs, but he decided to delay the actual lifting of restrictions pending the outcome of the *Ford* and *Devine* cases.

When these cases reached the Supreme Court, the French-only commercial sign provision of Bill 101 was still protected by a 1984 use of the section 33 override, but the French-only name requirement had not been so protected. However, all of these provisions were subject to the freedom of expression guaranteed by Quebec's Charter of Human Rights and Freedoms (enacted by the Bourassa government in 1975) because they had not been protected by the override provision of that Charter.

By deciding that both the French-only and the French-along-with provisions of Bill 101 violated freedom of expression, the Supreme Court had given a broad interpretation—that the freedom included not only the expression of ideas but also the language of that expression. It referred to Chief Justice Dickson's concept of freedom enunciated in *Big M Drug Mart* (quoted in the commentary on section 2[a]) that freedom is "the absence of coercion or constraint," and that "one of the purposes of the Charter is to protect ... from compulsion or restraint." It also noted the preamble to Bill 101 itself which declares, speaking of the French language, that "language ... is the instrument by which that [the French-speaking] people has articulated its identity."[39] In other words, the medium is the message.

In striking down the French-only requirements of Bill 101 in *Ford*, the Court agreed that the legislation satisfied the first *Oakes* criterion (that the government's objective was valid) and the first part of the second criterion (that there was a rational connection between the objective and the legislation). However, Bill 101 failed the second part of that criterion in that it did not infringe freedom of expression as little as possible. By upholding the French-along-with parts of Bill 101 in *Devine*, the Court agreed that they were reasonable means to promote the valid goal of enhancing the status of the French language. The Court acknowledged that Quebec's *"visage linguistique"* was creating the impression that the English language was as important as the French. More immigrants were becoming assimilated into Quebec's English community than into the French, and the English language was dominant in the upper echelons of the Quebec economy. As a result, the Court concluded, "it strongly suggested to young and ambitious francophones that the language of success was almost exclusively English. It confirmed to anglophones that there was no great need to learn the majority language. And it suggested to immigrants that the prudent course lay in joining the anglophone community."[40] The fear that the French language might eventually disappear was real indeed.

Within days of these two decisions on December 15, 1988, Premier Bourassa announced his intention to override both Quebec's Charter of Human Rights and the Canadian Charter and to require French-only outdoor signs and French-dominant indoor signs. This became Bill 178. The political fallout in Canada was immediate. In Quebec, Bourassa was denounced by the English minority (as one would expect), but also by the French majority who demanded stronger action against the English language. Bourassa's move also had profound implications for the Meech Lake Accord. The Manitoba legislature, one of two legislatures yet to ratify the Accord, was ready to debate the Accord when Bourassa announced his intention. Manitoba Premier Filmon immediately withdrew the Meech Lake resolution thereby, in retrospect, probably ensuring the Accord's death.

Other Cases

Slaight Communications (1989) involved the wrongful dismissal of an employee. The Court upheld an earlier order that the employer provide a letter of recommendation containing specified factual information, and no other information, about the former employee. Although this order violated the employer's freedom of expression, the Court justified it on the grounds that the objective was "to counteract the effects of the unjust dismissal by enhancing the ability of the employee to seek new employment . . . To constitutionally protect freedom of expression in this case would be tantamount to condoning the continuation of an abuse of an already unequal relationship."[41]

A government does not have unfettered authority to limit expression on its property. The case (*Committee for the Commonwealth of Canada v. Canada*, 1991)[41a] involved the distribution of political pamphlets at Montreal's Dorval airport. Although the Supreme Court was unanimous that governments may not control activity on their property to the extent that private citizens may control private property, they differed as to the nature of public access which governments may reasonably deny. It seems that the creation of guidelines will have to await additional experience.

Does the Federal government's ban on partisan political activity by its employees, clearly an infringement of section 2(b), withstand the scrutiny of Charter section 1? Not according to the Supreme Court, the only exception being "deputy heads." The Public Service Employment Act prevented Federal employees from engaging in work either for or against a candidate or political party, upon punishment which could include dismissal. Although the objective of political neutrality was legitimate and rationally connected to its means, freedom of expression was not impaired "as little as reasonably possible." The restrictions applied too broadly and encompassed public servants who "in modern government are completely divorced from the exercise of any discretion that could be in any manner affected by political considerations."[41b]

Another case was settled at the provincial rather than the national level, but is interesting because it pertains to elections. In 1983 Parliament amended the Canada Elections Act to prevent a person who is not acting for a particular candidate or political party, from spending money on behalf of a particular candidate or party during an election campaign. The intent of the new legislation was to strengthen the enforcement of election spending limits, but the amendment also infringed freedom of expression—as do the spending limits themselves. When the amendment was successfully challenged in the Alberta Court of Queen's Bench the following year, the Federal government failed to persuade the Court that it was "demonstrably justified in a free and democratic society" under Charter section 1.[42] The Federal government neither appealed the Alberta court's decision nor invoked section 33.

Subsection (c): Freedom of peaceful assembly

It has already been noted that this freedom is closely related to freedom of expression for it involves the mobilizing and/or exchanging of ideas and beliefs. It may be especially important for minorities who lack easy access to the media and who wish to bring grievances to the attention of government for redress. Peaceful assembly is therefore an integral part of the political process in a liberal democracy. Indeed, without this freedom political parties (especially those in opposition to the Government of the day) could be proscribed.

When might action prohibiting an assembly be justified? This is a difficult question. Manning suggests that "it is the purpose of the meeting or the objective of the assembly that determines whether one can claim freedom of peaceful assembly not what ultimately occurs."[43] It may be difficult determining in advance that an assembly will be peaceful, and legislatures may not ban an assembly out of hand because it might become violent. The need constantly to balance the rights and freedoms of the individual and group with those of the community as a whole is an ever-present challenge. "If we really accept the fundamental importance of the political freedoms," says Lyon, "we should be prepared to go some distance to ensure their continuing viability, giving police protection if necessary, within reasonable limits of tolerance of disorder and of police manpower."[44]

Freedom of assembly may not preclude regulations governing time, place, nature, or noise level, in order to avoid interference with traffic and other legitimate activities, but such restrictions will not be upheld if the courts deem them to be unwarranted interference with the freedom guaranteed by the Charter. The Supreme Court has not been faced with a challenge based on this freedom.

Subsection (d): Freedom of association

Because this freedom includes freedom to form political parties it too is essential to liberal democracy; however, it goes far beyond political parties.

Laws against criminal conspiracy, the main limits on freedom of association in Canada, may well satisfy the requirements of Charter section 1 but they must be used carefully to avoid abuse. Would the Public Order Regulations made under the War Measures Act in 1970 have survived the Charter?[45] Among other things those Regulations outlawed the FLQ, but they were phrased so broadly that they encompassed "any group of persons or association that advocates the use of force or the commission of crime as a means of or as an aid in accomplishing governmental change within Canada." It would seem that even the advocacy of civil disobedience, such as the non-payment of income tax to pressure government into defence or foreign policy change, could have brought down the full force of the War Measures Act. In several instances, innocence rather than guilt of the accused had to be proved. (The commentary on section 11[d] discusses the constitutionality of "reverse onus" laws.) For example, regulation 8 stated that

> evidence that any person
> (a) attended any meeting of the unlawful association,
> (b) spoke publicly in advocacy for the unlawful association, or
> (c) communicated statements of the unlawful association as a representative or professed representative of the unlawful association
> is, in the absence of evidence to the contrary, proof that he is a member of the unlawful association.

Freedom of association should include the right not to divulge association membership. Nevertheless, conflict of interest situations may require both the divulging and the divesting of certain memberships, such as by cabinet ministers.

Association ties have sometimes been the basis for denying benefits. The following three situations illustrate the point. The case of *Roncarelli v. Duplessis* is a classic.[46] In 1946 Roncarelli, a Montreal restaurant owner, was denied renewal of his liquor licence "forever." The reason was that he was a member of the Jehovah's Witnesses and guaranteed bail money for other Witnesses charged under Quebec law for distributing their religious literature. The Supreme Court of Canada vindicated Roncarelli in 1959 on the grounds that his religious beliefs were irrelevant to the law governing the issuance of liquor licences.

As a second example, a University of British Columbia law graduate was denied entrance to the British Columbia Bar on the basis of his membership in the Labour Progressive (Communist) Party. It was assumed that he would be unable to take the oath required by the British Columbia Legal Professions Act to oppose "all traitorous conspiracies."[47] Third, the R.C.M.P. were instructed by a 1976 Federal cabinet decision to screen people who might be appointed to "sensitive positions" in the public service. Furthermore, the cabinet stated that "information that . . . [a person] is a separatist or a supporter of the Parti Québécois, is relevant to national security and is to be brought to the attention of the appropriate authorities."[48]

What effect will section 2(d) and (c) have on restrictions governing prisoners who are released from prison on probation? Will such restrictions be upheld on the basis of section 1? What effect will section 2(d) have on union membership as a condition of employment?

Regulations that control the financing of elections and political parties, including the requirement to publish names of those who contribute more than a specified sum, are criticized as unwarranted limitations on the freedom of association. They are also hailed as essential to the very preservation of political parties and the liberal democratic process. Governments argue that limitations are necessary to prevent major contributors from exercising inordinate influence over a party, especially the ruling party, and to enable less affluent parties to compete for the electorate's support on a more equitable basis with the wealthy.

In 1987 the Supreme Court ruled on three cases relating to freedom of association and a presumed constitutional right to strike. They were decided concurrently and, understandably, in the same way although the decisions were not unanimous.[49] In reaching its decision that section 2(d) contains no right to strike, the Court focused its attention on the *Alberta Labour Reference.* The impugned legislation prohibited strikes by Alberta's public service employees, firefighters, hospital employees, and police officers. So important was this case that the Alberta government was supported by six other provincial governments and the Government of Canada. Manitoba's N.D.P. Government supported the unions. The Saskatchewan government had invoked the Charter's notwithstanding clause (s. 33) pending this decision, and Alberta Premier Lougheed had threatened its use had the Supreme Court upheld a right to strike.

Apart from the group rights protected by sections 25 and 29, said McIntyre for the Court majority, the Charter is intended to protect the rights of individuals. "The group or organization is simply a device adopted by individuals to achieve a fuller realization of individual rights and aspirations. People, by merely combining together, cannot create an entity which has greater constitutional rights and freedoms than they, as individuals, possess. Freedom of association cannot therefore vest independent rights in the group." Charter protection will, therefore, extend only to those association activities that are constitutionally protected when exercised by an individual. According to McIntyre there are two reasons why the Charter does not contain a right to strike. In the first place, while an individual employee can cease work he or she may not, strictly speaking, lawfully do so during the currency—and therefore in breach of—an employment contract. (There is of course no question of the law ordering the employee back to work to fulfill the contract's terms.) Second, the secession of work by a single employee is not analogous to a strike conducted in accordance with modern labour legislation. "An employee who ceases work does not contemplate a return to work, while employees on strike always contemplate a return to work. In recognition of this fact, the law does not regard a strike as either a breach of contract or a termination of employment." Indeed, all eleven Canadian jurisdictions maintain the employer-employee relationship during a strike.

Neither Chief Justice Dickson nor Justice Wilson were impressed with the majority decision. The main reason for unions is to strengthen workers vis-à-vis their employers. It only makes sense, therefore, that freedom for workers to associate in a union must also protect the union's *raison d'être*—collective bargaining and, ultimately, the right to strike. Dickson and Wilson were nevertheless prepared to invoke section 1 to protect essential services, but in their view the Alberta government had not demonstrated that this applied to public servants, or to hospital employees other than nurses and medical doctors. The essential nature of police and firefighter services was obvious, they agreed, and did not have to be proven.

In 1990 the Supreme Court carried the *Alberta Labour Reference* reasoning a step further. Although section 2(d) protects the freedom to establish, belong to, and maintain an association, it does not create a right of that association to bargain for its members even if bargaining is a "foundational or essential purpose" of the association. The reason? The bargaining of working conditions is not a constitutional right of individuals.[50] Indeed, Justice Le Dain (as part of the Court majority) had made this explicit in the *Alberta Labour Reference* although the point was not then at issue.[51]

Does the Criminal Code's proscription of communicating in a public place for the purpose engaging the services of a prostitute violate freedom of association? (The Supreme Court ruled that it does infringe freedom of expression but is saved by section 1—see the commentary on section 2[b].) In *Skinner* (1990), Chief Justice Dickson for the majority distinguished between association and expression: "The target of the impugned legislation . . . is *expressive* conduct . . . of a commercial nature. It focuses on the prostitute or customer who stops or communicates . . . for the purpose of engaging in prostitution. In contrast, it does not attack conduct of an associational nature."[52] The expressive activity is of course intended to lead to an exchange of sex for money which "requires the involvement of another party, and contemplates as the final objective the 'association' of the individuals in some form of sexual activity." The impugned legislation prohibits neither the commercial agreement nor the prostitution itself, although Dickson left open the question whether section 2(d) would protect the exercise of either activity if it *were* to be proscribed. Justice Wilson disagreed with the Court's ruling: the legislation's intent notwithstanding, if a prostitute and customer can communicate only in a place that is neither public nor open to public view, its effect is to restrict freedom of association. This "effects" approach is consistent with Wilson's comments in *Big M Drug Mart* and noted in the commentary on section 15.

Democratic Rights

➤ **SECTION 3:** Every citizen of Canada has the right to vote in an election of members of the House of Commons or of a legislative assembly and to be qualified for membership therein.

In pre-Charter days the right to vote and to seek elective office in Canada was determined solely by statute. For a brief discussion of the changes in the

Federal franchise over the years see the commentary on section 41 of the 1867 Constitution Act.

Section 3 of the Charter now guarantees to all citizens the right to vote (although not the right to a secret ballot) in both Federal and provincial elections, and to seek elective office. There will continue to be restrictions but these will now have to withstand the scrutiny of Charter section 1. (Section 33's override does not apply to democratic rights.) The Canada Elections Act prohibits the following citizens from voting in Federal elections:

(1) Every person under the age of 18.
(2) The Chief Electoral Officer.
(3) The Assistant Chief Electoral Officer.
(4) The returning officer for each constituency, except to break a tied vote.
(5) Every judge appointed by the Federal government, except a judge of the Citizenship Court.
(6) Every person confined to a mental hospital.
(7) Every person confined to a penal institution.
(8) Every person disqualified under any law relating to the disqualification of electors for corrupt or illegal practices.

In addition the governor general does not vote in Federal elections nor do lieutenant governors vote in provincial elections, although they are not legally prohibited from voting.

In the fall of 1988 the Federal Court ruled that the restrictions against judges and mental patients could not be protected by section 1 of the Charter.[53] With respect to mental patients the Court held that the generality of the disqualification was arbitrary—both too broad and too narrow in scope. On the one hand, it caught anyone suffering from a personality disorder that might impair judgement in one area even though it might be unrelated to judgement needed for voting. On the other hand, because the disqualification applied only to the mentally handicapped who were "restrained of liberty of movement or deprived of the management of . . . property," it exempted those people who were cared for at home regardless of their mental capacity.

In February 1991 the Federal Court struck down the Canada Elections Act's denial of the franchise to inmates of Federal penitentiaries or provincial jails as a violation of section 3 that could not be justified as a reasonable limit under section 1. The government had argued that a democracy requires a "decent and responsible citizenry who respect and voluntarily abide by the laws of the state." In a statement analogous to its ruling respecting mental patients, the Court commented that "it is arbitrary in singling out one category of presumably indecent and irresponsible citizens to deny them a right which they otherwise clearly have. . . . It is self-apparent that there are many indecent and irresponsible persons outside prison who are entitled to vote." Perhaps the government should have argued that people who *are* convicted and imprisoned for disregarding the responsibilities of citizenship should be denied its privileges until their debts to society have been paid. The ruling is being appealed to the Appeal Division of the Federal Court.[54]

The Canada Elections Act provides for the voting abroad by members of the Canadian Forces, public servants, and their dependants, but not for other Canadians. Perhaps this *de facto* disqualification, at least of citizens who normally reside in Canada, may be challenged under section 3.

The following people are declared ineligible by the Canada Elections Act to seek election to the House of Commons:

- **(1)** Every person who is ineligible to vote.
- **(2)** Every person who has been convicted of a corrupt or an illegal election practice, such disqualification lasting for seven and five years respectively.
- **(3)** Every member of a provincial legislature or territorial council.
- **(4)** Every person, with minor exceptions, who holds a contract with the Dominion government.
- **(5)** Every employee of the Crown, except
  - **(a)** a cabinet minister,
  - **(b)** a part-time member of the Canadian Forces (and a full-time member during wartime),
  - **(c)** a public servant on leave without pay for the purpose of seeking election.

Furthermore, a Senator is prohibited by section 39 of the 1867 Constitution Act from election to the House. Whether these disqualifications will be more easily sustained under Charter section 1 than will some of the disqualifications from voting is yet to be determined. No case has reached the Supreme Court.

Because the Charter does not define the term "citizen" the meaning of citizenship remains, presumably, the prerogative of Parliament under the Citizenship Act—at least insofar as it does not "unreasonably" (in accordance with section 1) restrict democratic rights, mobility rights, or minority language educational rights. These are the only rights defined in terms of citizenship.

The Charter also guarantees (s. 30) the right to vote for councillors, and to seek election to the councils, of the Northwest Territories and the Yukon Territory. It does not, however, guarantee these rights with respect to municipal councils and school boards except, in the latter case, insofar as they may be part of the educational guarantee of section 93 of the 1867 Constitution Act (and confirmed by Charter section 29).

Another question pertains to the relative sizes of rural and urban constituencies and therefore to voting equality. This issue in relation to provincial elections was raised in the British Columbia Supreme Court which ruled in 1989 that Charter section 3 implies an equal right to vote. Although some inequality among constituency sizes is inevitable, the Court decided that the establishment of electoral boundaries must have greater population equality as its goal. The British Columbia government had sought to avoid the Charter challenge on the grounds that the electoral law was part of the "constitution of the province" (s. 45 of the present Act) and therefore within its exclusive jurisdiction.[55]

In March 1991 the Saskatchewan Court of Appeal ruled that the provincial government's proposed redistribution violated section 3 because its overrepresentation of the rural population violated the "one person-one vote" principle. The Saskatchewan government appealed the decision to the Supreme Court of Canada which upheld the redistribution in June 1991. The isue affects all provinces because the problem of rural-urban balance in legislatures is general, and so the Court's reasoning is especially relevant. The main point is that "the purpose of the right to vote enshrined in s. 3 of the Charter is not equality of voting power per se but the right to 'effective representation.' The right to vote therefore comprises many factors, of which equality is but one." Deviation from absolute equality "may be justified on the grounds of practical impossibility or the provision of more effective representation," so that governments may consider geography, community history and interests, and minority representation as well as arithmetic. The Court cautioned, nevertheless, that "beyond this, dilution of one citizen's vote as compared with another's should not be countenanced."[55a]

In a sense, the Court was reiterating arguments which have long supported deviation from the arithmetic mean both in redistributing Federal seats among the provinces and territories (such as by the "Senate floor"), and in adjusting the boundaries of those constituencies by use of the 25% rule. For consideration of these matters see the commentaries on sections 37, 51 and 52 of the 1867 Constitution Act, and section 42 of the present Act.

➤ **SECTION 4:** (1) No House of Commons and no legislative assembly shall continue for longer than five years from the date fixed for the return of the writs of a general election of its members.

(2) In time of real or apprehended war, invasion or insurrection, a House of Commons may be continued by Parliament and a legislative assembly may be continued by the legislature beyond five years if such continuation is not opposed by the votes of more than one-third of the members of the House of Commons or the legislative assembly, as the case may be.

The provisions of this section were covered with respect to the House of Commons in sections 50 and 91(1) of the 1867 Constitution Act. Section 50 remains (for no apparent reason) in that Act, but section 91(1) was repealed by item 1 of the Schedule to the 1982 Constitution Act. The application of this section 4 to the provinces (and by section 30 to the two territories) is new, although sections 85 and 88 of the 1867 Constitution Act are relevant.

➤ **SECTION 5:** There shall be a sitting of Parliament and of each legislature at least once every twelve months.

The essence of this requirement in relation to Parliament was contained in section 20 of the 1867 Constitution Act (repealed by item 1 of the Schedule to the 1982 Constitution Act). The wording of this section 5 accords more with recent practice whereby sessions, especially of Parliament, sometimes extend beyond one year. Furthermore, a literal rendition of section 20 of the 1867 Act could have allowed for the adjournment of a session of Parliament for more than a year without violating the letter of that section. If more than a year were to elapse between sittings the only recourse would be to the governor general (or lieutenant governor, for a province) who could dismiss the first minister and appoint another who would adhere to the terms of the Charter. The courts could not order a sitting. The shortest session of Parliament has been the Sixth of the 18th Parliament which opened and prorogued on January 25, 1940. The longest was the First of the 32nd Parliament which opened on April 14, 1980 and prorogued on November 30, 1983.

The application of this section 5 requirement to the provinces (and the territories) is new, although sections 86 and 88 of the 1867 Act are relevant. Furthermore, section 20 of the Manitoba Act imposed a similar restriction; it was repealed by item 2 of the Schedule to the 1982 Constitution Act.

Mobility Rights

➤ **SECTION 6:** (1) Every citizen of Canada has the right to enter, remain in and leave Canada.

(2) Every citizen of Canada and every person who has the status of a permanent resident of Canada has the right

(a) to move to and take up residence in any province; and

(b) to pursue the gaining of a livelihood in any province.

(3) The rights specified in subsection (2) are subject to

(a) any laws or practices of general application in force in a province other than those that discriminate among persons primarily on the basis of province of present or previous residence; and

(b) any laws providing for reasonable residency requirements as a qualification for the receipt of publicly provided social services.

(4) Subsections (2) and (3) do not preclude any law, program or activity that has as its object the amelioration in a province of conditions of individuals in that province who are socially or economically disadvantaged if the rate of employment in that province is below the rate of employment in Canada.

Subsection (1): The right to enter, remain in, and leave Canada

Even before the Charter, Canadians possessed the right to enter and remain in Canada. The Immigration Act acknowledged the right to enter, and its deportation provisions were inapplicable to Canadians. The right to leave the country was not assured, however, in the sense that there was no right to a passport which is often required to enter other countries.[56] The term "citizen" is defined by Parliament in the Citizenship Act.

This Charter right is, as are many others, expressed in absolute terms.

Nevertheless, in no case involving extradition under this section in any Canadian court through April 1989 was a litigant successful in attempting to avoid extradition.[57] In two later cases the Supreme Court used section 1 to uphold extradition of two Canadian citizens to the United States to face charges of conspiracy to import and distribute heroin in the United States. The situations were unusual in that the alleged offences had occurred in Canada and were punishable under Canadian law. While acknowledging this fact the Court (although not unanimous) argued that "it is often better that a crime be prosecuted where its harmful impact is felt and where witnesses and the persons most interested in bringing the criminal to justice reside."[58] In appeals against extradition heard under Charter section 7 the Supreme Court has acknowledged that there could be instances where section 1 would be inapplicable. See the commentary on section 7.

The courts may also at some time be called upon to decide "reasonableness" under section 1 to sustain laws that restrain from leaving Canada citizens who have been released on parole, released on bail, or who are witnesses involved in court cases.

Subsections (2) and (3): The right to move within Canada and to pursue the gaining of a livelihood, and limits upon these rights

The guarantee of internal mobility extends to permanent residents as well as to citizens. While movement to and taking up of residence in any province (and territory, under section 30) has not been restricted in the past, this cannot be said of the pursuit of a livelihood because provinces have sometimes sought to discriminate in favour of their own residents. Such discrimination is now unconstitutional unless it can be justified under subsections (3) or (4) or, of course, section 1. It should be noted that a right "to pursue" the gaining of a livelihood is not a right to gain a livelihood—that is, it is not a right to employment, however socially desirable such a right might be.

Provincial "laws or practices" limiting these rights must be "of general application" within that province and not directed "primarily" at non-residents of the province. There are, nevertheless, other factors that have tended in the past, and will doubtlessly continue into the future, to restrict mobility within Canada. For example, language is a barrier to movement to and from Quebec; health and pension benefits are not always fully portable from province to province; laws governing certification or licensing to engage in specific occupations are unique to each province. These factors will not be subject to section 6(2)(b) provided they are of general application within the province, do not discriminate on the basis of previous residence, and do not favour residents of the particular province unless they may be justified under subsection (4). Subsection (3) also allows "reasonable" residency requirements before people qualify for provincial social services.

In its first Charter case (*Law Society of Upper Canada v. Skapinker*, 1984)[59] the Supreme Court ruled that the requirement of Canadian citizenship for admission to the Ontario Bar was not a violation of section 6(2)(b). The claimant lived in Ontario and was a permanent resident of Canada although not a Canadian citizen. The Court decided that section 6(2)(b) deals with mobility—that is, that the right to pursue the gaining of a livelihood is not separate and distinct from the mobility right of 6(2)(a). Both paragraphs "relate to movement into another province, either to take up residence or to work without taking up residence." Because the claimant was already an Ontario resident there was no mobility involved and no Charter right for him to pursue the gaining of a livelihood. Even if that right had been relevant it seems likely that the Upper Canada Law Society's citizenship requirement would have survived subsection (3): although the requirement was indeed discrimination against non-citizens it was of "general application" and did not discriminate on the basis of "province of present or previous residence."

The only other section 6 case decided by the Supreme Court to mid-1991 was *Black v. Law Society of Alberta*, in 1989.[60] In that case the rules of the Law Society of Alberta prohibiting its members from forming partnerships with lawyers practising in other provinces were struck down because the right to pursue the gaining of a livelihood "does not require the movement of the individual to the province. A person can pursue a living in a province without being there personally." Clearly, a rule declaring that a lawyer who lives and practices in Alberta shall not form a partnership with "anyone who is not an active member ordinarily resident in Alberta" is discriminating on the basis of province of residence.

Subsection (4): Affirmative action

The right of a province or territory to discriminate in favour of its own residents when the rate of employment in that province or territory is below the national average was added, at Newfoundland Premier Peckford's request, during the final negotiations which produced the November 5, 1981 Constitutional Accord.[61] No doubt Peckford was anticipating development of off-shore oil fields.

Legal Rights

It has been reported that some 90% of all Charter cases in Canadian courts, and 74% of the Supreme Court's first 100 cases, have involved legal rights.[62] These rights are subject to the legislative override of section 33.

➤ SECTION 7: Everyone has the right to life, liberty and security of the person and the right not be be deprived thereof except in accordance with the principles of fundamental justice.

Justice McLachlin has provided a useful statement of the overall purpose of this section.

> The *Charter* through s. 7 seeks to impose limits on the power of the state over the detained person. It thus seeks to effect a balance between the interests of the detained individual and those of the state.

> On the one hand s. 7 seeks to provide to a person involved in the judicial process protection against the unfair use by the state of its superior resources. On the other, it maintains to the state the power to deprive the person of life, liberty or security of person provided that it respects fundamental principles of justice. The balance is critical. Too much emphasis on either of these purposes may bring the administration of justice into disrepute—in the first case because the state has improperly used its superior power against the individual, in the second because the state's legitimate interest in law enforcement has been frustrated without proper justification.[63]

The impact of this section depends upon the meanings of "life," "liberty," and "security of the person." Furthermore, and perhaps most especially, the strength of the section depends upon the meaning of "fundamental justice." Whether life, liberty, and security are three separate rights or a single right is another question, but it is not addressed in this commentary. Most cases involving alleged violation of section 7 rights refer either to the section generally or to two of the specific rights.

Operation Dismantle (1985) is a case in point.[64] It involved the relationship between section 7 and government foreign policy. Specifically, it was an attempt by several groups to strike down the Federal cabinet's decision to permit United States testing of cruise missiles in Canada. Such testing, it was argued, would increase the risk of nuclear war and thus pose a threat to life, liberty, and security of the person. The Court's unanimous judgement was based upon the failure of the claimants to "disclose facts which, if taken as true, would prove that the Canadian government's decision could cause a violation or a threat of violation of their rights under s. 7 of the *Charter*." Indeed, the Court acknowledged that proof would be virtually impossible inasmuch as "the foreign policy decisions of independent nations are not capable of prediction on the basis of evidence to any degree of certainty approaching probability." What is significant, however, is the Court's acknowledgement that cabinet decisions are subject to judicial review under Charter section 32(1)(a).

The meaning of the word "everyone" is also important. Justice Wilson stated in *Singh* (1985) that the term includes (for section 7 and, presumably, throughout the Charter) "every person physically present in Canada and by virtue of such presence amenable to Canadian law."[65] It therefore does not exclude even people who are in Canada illegally. For the purpose of section 7 "everyone" excludes "corporations and other artificial entities incapable of enjoying life, liberty or security of the person, and includes only human beings."[66] The commentary preceding section 1 considers the meaning of "everyone" and related terms.

The right to life:

Two basic questions immediately arise: When does life begin? When does life end? The first of these questions is the more emotional and turns on the question whether a fetus has a right to life under the Charter and, if so, at what stage. The social issue is, of course, abortion. Views on this issue differ markedly.

In 1989 the Supreme Court was asked (*Borowski*)[67] to decide whether the unborn child is included in "everyone" who has the right to life, liberty, and security of the person. In the wake of the *Morgentaler* decision the previous year (see below, "right to security of the person") which had struck down the abortion law that Borowski was challenging for the opposite reason—that the law violated the rights of the unborn—the Court decided not to rule on the issue which was now moot.

In *Tremblay v. Daigle*, six months after *Borowski*, the Supreme Court had another opportunity to address this question but chose not to do so.[68] Daigle, pregnant with Tremblay's child, appealed an injunction obtained by Tremblay preventing her from having an abortion. Quebec courts had held that a fetus is a "human being" within the Quebec Charter of Human Rights and Freedoms and thus enjoyed the right to life under that Charter. The Supreme Court, however, rejected this interpretation and ruled that the fetus had no such right—under the Quebec Charter. Having decided that issue, the Court declined to make an "unnecessary constitutional pronouncement" by addressing the question within the context of section 7 of the Canadian Charter. The reason was that the case, a civil action between two private individuals, did not involve the Canadian Charter, which is invoked only when some government action is challenged. In March 1991, however, the Court ruled that a fetus is not a human being under the Criminal Code, but it was not asked to decide the question in relation to the Canadian Charter.[69]

In recent years the question of what signifies the end of life has become increasingly important. Although judges and lawyers will now have to determine the answer, at least for the purpose of the Charter, useful input will come from biologists, philosophers, theologians, and others. Is a person to be judged legally dead whose brain has ceased to function and whose heartbeat can be maintained only by means of artificial support? The answer has obvious implications for organ donations when time is of the essence. The Supreme Court has not had to face the issue.

The right to liberty:

A balance must be struck between freedom and order for it is obvious that, in the absence of limitations on the right to liberty, one person's right soon conflicts with another's.

There are Charter provisions other than this which guarantee elements of liberty. They include the fundamental freedoms, democratic rights (especially section 3), mobility rights, equality rights, as well as many other legal rights. The courts will have to determine whether section 7 gives a unique meaning to "liberty." Whatever liberty may mean, it would seem from the *Edwards Books and Art* challenge to Ontario's Retail Business Holidays Act that it does not extend to "an unconstrained right to transact business whenever one wishes."[70]

This case is discussed in the commentary on section 2(a). Justice Wilson has commented that "all regulatory offences impose some restriction on liberty broadly construed. But I think it would trivialize the *Charter* to sweep all those offences into s. 7 as violations of the right to life, liberty and security of the person even if they can be sustained under s. 1."[71]

Liberty and security of the person have also been linked to extradition. The commentary on mobility rights (s. 6) noted that the Court has upheld the extradition of Canadian citizens as "reasonable" under section 1. Nevertheless, in a section 7 challenge to extradition the Court suggested that reasonableness may indeed have limits. "The [extradition] treaty, the extradition hearing in this country and the exercise of the executive discretion to surrender a fugitive must all conform to the requirements of the *Charter*, including the principles of fundamental justice." The Court clearly acknowledged, however, the essentially political nature of extradition. In deciding whether or not justice has been offended,

> the courts must begin with the notion that the executive must first have determined that the general system for the administration of justice in the foreign country sufficiently corresponds to our concepts of justice to warrant entering into the treaty in the first place, and must have recognized that it too has a duty to ensure that its actions comply with constitutional standards. Blind judicial deference to executive judgement cannot, of course, be expected. The courts have the duty to uphold the Constitution. Nonetheless, this is an area where the executive is likely to be far better informed than the courts, and where the courts must be extremely circumspect so as to avoid interfering unduly in decisions that involve the good faith and honour of this country in its relations with other states. In a word, judicial intervention must be limited to cases of real substance.[72]

The extradition of Charles Ng, charged with thirteen murders in the State of California where the death penalty exists, is now before the Canadian courts. The Supreme Court heard the case on February 21, 1991, but had not announced its decision by mid-year. The relationship between that decision and the above quotation will be most interesting.

The right to security of the person:
An important question is whether this right extends beyond physical security to include some aspects of economic, psychological, and social security. If so, how far does it go? Does it include one's reputation? Does it protect against government action that inhibits the ability of a person to satisfy basic needs because he or she has been removed from a welfare scheme, has had tools or other equipment essential to his or her work confiscated, or has had a professional or driver's licence suspended?[73] Security of the person could reach far indeed. It also raises the controversial question of preventive measures the

state may take to protect public health in the name of physical integrity, such as sterilization of the mentally handicapped, forced blood transfusions, and forced detoxication.

A broad conception of "security of the person," but one which our courts have not upheld, would include "not only protection of one's physical integrity, but the provision of necessaries for its support." Such necessaries could encompass, according to the Universal Declaration of Human Rights, "a standard of living adequate for the health and well-being of himself and of his family, including food, clothing, housing and medical care and necessary social services, and the right to security in the event of unemployment, sickness, disability, widowhood, old age, or other lack of livelihood in circumstances beyond his control."[74] As a minimum, security of the person includes freedom from physical punishment or suffering, or their threat. For example, to deny the right stated in the Immigration Act (1976) that a Convention refugee will not be "removed from Canada to a country where his life or freedom would be threatened" would be to deny the right to security of the person.

Morgentaler (1988) is no doubt one of the most controversial cases decided by the Supreme Court.[75] Convicted of performing abortions contrary to section 251 of the Criminal Code, Morgentaler and two other medical doctors appealed to the Supreme Court charging that Canada's abortion law violated section 7 of the Charter. Basically, section 251 sanctioned abortion only when the woman's life or health were endangered in the opinion of a hospital's therapeutic abortion committee, and when the operation was performed by a qualified medical practitioner in an approved hospital as designated by the provincial health minister. The impact of the legal requirements was that only about twenty percent of Canadian hospitals provided abortion services.[76]

Five of the seven judges who heard the case upheld the appeal and therefore struck down section 251, although the reasons for the decision differed significantly. All five agreed that section 251 violated the security of the person. Chief Justice Dickson, for example, stated that the section "clearly interferes with a woman's physical and bodily integrity. Forcing a woman, by threat of criminal sanction, to carry a foetus to term, unless she meets certain criteria unrelated to her own priorities and aspirations, is a profound interference with a woman's body and thus an infringement of security of the person."[77] Justice Wilson, who delivered the strongest condemnation of the abortion law, maintained that section 251 violated the right to liberty as well: This right "guarantees to every individual a degree of personal autonomy over important decisions intimately affecting his or her private life. Liberty in a free and democratic society does not require the state to approve such decisions but it does require the state to respect them. A woman's decision to terminate her pregnancy falls within this class of protected decisions."[78]

Contrary to some public opinion, however, the Court had not declared a right to abortion. It had ruled that the nature of the Criminal Code's restrictions violated the Charter, which is quite a different matter. The net result was that Canada was left without an abortion law until Parliament might enact a new one. In January 1991 the Senate rejected an abortion bill (C-43) which had been passed by the House of Commons.

Section 7 permits the violation of the right to life, liberty, and security of the person if the principles of fundamental justice are upheld. The five judges maintained that these principles had been denied.[79] According to Dickson and Lamer, "when Parliament creates a defence to a criminal charge, the defence should not be illusory or so difficult to attain as to be practically illusory"; the difficulties involved in satisfying the requirements of section 251 meant that access to abortion services was in fact denied at most hospitals, making the defence illusory. Beetz and Estey claimed that the multiplicity of procedural requirements itself was a denial of fundamental justice. Wilson believed that this violation of section 7 was also a denial of freedom of conscience (s. 2[a]) inasmuch as a decision whether or not to terminate a pregnancy is a moral decision. "A deprivation of the s. 7 right which has the effect of infringing a right guaranteed elsewhere in the *Charter* cannot be in accordance with the principles of fundamental justice."

These comments lead to the broader discussion of the meaning of fundamental justice.

Principles of fundamental justice:
"What is justice?" This question is as old as Socrates, and its answer seems as elusive today as it was when Socrates posed the question. The major question for Charter section 7 is whether fundamental justice pertains only to procedure or whether it has a substantive element—whether it pertains only to rules of procedure in applying the law or whether it includes the substance of the law. The former interpretation is consistent with a constitution based on legislative supremacy because the substance or merit of the law is placed beyond the reach of the courts. If the courts were to decide that this is the correct interpretation of the Charter, the scope of section 7 would be narrow indeed. Governments might then deprive us of life, liberty, and security so long as they did so by fair means! But if fundamental justice were to include the substance of the law, the scope of judicial review becomes much broader. The intent of the Department of Justice was clearly stated: "The words 'fundamental justice' would cover the same thing as what is called procedural due process. . . . However, it in our view does not cover the concept of what is called substantive due process. . . . Natural justice or fundamental justice in our view does not go beyond the procedural requirements of fairness."[80]

While acknowledging the government's view, a unanimous Supreme Court rejected the narrow interpretation in the 1985 *B.C. Motor Vehicle Act Reference*. Speaking for the Court, Justice (as he then was) Lamer commented that the Charter was the product of many actors, both federal and provincial; if the interpretation of section 7 were to be based on comments made before the Joint Committee on the Constitution, "rights, freedoms and values embodied in the *Charter* in effect become frozen in time to the moment of adoption with little or no possibility of growth, development and adjustment to changing societal needs." He added that to interpret "fundamental justice" as synonymous with natural justice "would strip the protected interests of much, if not most, of their content and leave the 'right' to life, liberty and security of the person in a sorely emaciated state. Such a result would be inconsistent with the broad, affirmative language in which those rights are expressed." Nevertheless, the concept of fundamental justice "cannot be given any exhaustive content or simple enumerative definition, but will take on concrete meaning as the courts address alleged violations of section 7."[81]

In the case then before the Court the judges ruled that section 94(2) of the British Columbia Motor Vehicle Act violated the principles of fundamental justice. That section enacted an absolute liability offence which carried mandatory imprisonment. Guilt was established by proof of driving while the defendant's licence was suspended, or while the driver was otherwise prohibited from driving, regardless of whether or not the defendant was aware of the suspension or prohibition. Therefore, no defence could be made even though the offence could have been committed unknowingly. It was not the absolute liability *per se* that offended the principles of fundamental justice; the violation resulted from the combination of absolute liability and the "potential of depriving of life, liberty, or security of the person" which obviously includes mandatory imprisonment. The Court acknowledged the desirability of keeping bad drivers off the road, so that the violation of fundamental justice might be saved by appeal to Charter Section 1. However, the British Columbia government had failed to demonstrate the necessary reasonableness.

Similar reasoning was applied in *Hess* and *Nguyen* (1990). Because there could be imprisonment (up to life) for a male who had sexual intercourse with a female under age fourteen, whether or not he believed her to be at least fourteen, no defence was possible. In the words of Justice McLachlin, under the Criminal Code "a person who is mentally innocent of the offence—who has no *mens rea* with respect to an essential element of the offence—may be convicted and sent to prision."[82] Furthermore, the impugned legislation could not be saved by Charter section 1. The objective of protecting young females from the harm of premature intercourse and possible pregnancy does address a pressing and substantial concern, and there is a rational connection between the objective and the legislation, but the section 7 right was not impaired as little as possible. This case is discussed in the commentary on section 15.

Justice Wilson dissenting in *Jones* (Alberta, 1986) believed that the principles of fundamental justice had been violated because, under the Alberta School Act, the only proof of proper instruction was the requisite certificate issued under the authority of the Department of Education. The person facing a charge of truancy who is unable to produce such a certificate is prevented from introducing relevant evidence and therefore from mounting a defence.[83] This case is briefly discussed in the commentary on section 2(a).

Within a broad concept of fundamental justice what might the necessary rocedural rules include? According to one interpretation:

> At the minimum we would expect . . . adequate notice of the hearing; the opportunity to be heard; a neutral decision-maker; an opportunity to make oral argument; an opportunity to present evidence or witnesses; a chance to meet the case put in by the other side and to cross-examine witnesses; the right to have a lawyer present; a decision based on a record with a statement of reasons for the desision; the right to pre-trial discovery of evidence; a public hearing; a transcript of the proceedings.[84]

In a 1990 case (*Hebert*)[85] a unanimous Court emphasized a pre-trial right to remain silent as an integral part of the section 7 guarantee. At stake was the accused's liberty; at issue was whether incriminating statements made by the accused to an undercover police officer who engaged him in conversation in the prison cell violated his right to silence. (After consulting counsel the accused had earlier declined to make a statement to the police.) Writing for a Court majority, Justice McLachlin suggested that the right to silence is supported also by sections 10(b), 11(c), and 13. The core of 10(b)—the right to retain and instruct counsel—"is to ensure that the accused understands his rights chief among which is his right to silence." Section 11(c) contains the right not to give evidence against oneself, and this is reinforced by section 13's guarantee that incriminating evidence cannot be used in any other proceedings. Clearly, the exercise of the accused's right to remain silent had been violated, through trickery, by the police. (The limitations clause [s. 1] was not available because the police violation was not "prescribed by law.")

Having come to the conclusion that the principles of fundamental justice had been violated, McLachlin then emphasized that the right to remain silent cannot be an absolute prohibition against the police obtaining confessions. If it were, no statements made by the accused after detention could be used unless the suspect waived the right to silence. (The "appreciation of the consequences" test of establishing voluntary waiver—noted briefly in the commentary on section 10[b]—implies that only those statements knowingly made to the authorities by the accused while in detention could be used.) The right to remain silent cannot be extended that far. According to McLachlin, the following five exceptions to that right strike the proper balance between the interest of the accused and the legitimate concern of society for the maintenance of law and order.

> First, there is nothing that prohibits the police from questioning an accused or a suspect in the absence of counsel after he has retained counsel. Police persuasion, short of denying the suspect the right to choose or of depriving him of an operating mind, does not breach the right to silence. Second, the right applies only after detention. Third, the right does not affect voluntary statements made to fellow cell mates. The violation of the suspect's rights occurs only when the

> Crown acts to subvert the suspect's constitutional right to choose not to make a statement to the authorities. Fourth, a distinction must be made between the use of undercover agents to observe the suspect, and the use of undercover agents to actively elicit information in violation of the suspect's choice to remain silent. Finally, even where a violation of the suspect's right is established, the evidence may, where appropriate, be admitted. Only if the court is satisfied that its reception would be likely to bring the administration of justice into disrepute can the evidence be rejected under s. 24(2) of the *Charter*. Where the police have acted with due care for the suspect's rights, it is unlikely that the statements they obtain will be held inadmissible.

In *Hebert*, however, the evidence was deemed inadmissible under section 24(2).

Several other Supreme Court decisions are noteworthy for their specific interpretations of fundamental justice.

Procedural fairness must include the right of a refugee claimant to state his or her case before the Immigration Appeal Board and to hear the case against that refugee—most specifically, to learn the advice that the Refugee Status Advisory Board has given the Minister. In effect, this means a right to an oral hearing. The "unintended consequences" of this decision included "a backlog of 124 000 refugee claimants; an amnesty for 15 000 claimants already in Canada; $179 million . . . in additional costs; and a new refugee law [effective January 1, 1989] that some critics say is more unfair than the original one."[86]

The sentencing of a "dangerous offender" (as defined by the Criminal Code) to an indeterminate prison term does not violate the principles of fundamental justice merely because the sentence is not based exclusively on the criterion of "just deserts." (See the commentary on section 9.) Justice La Forest held that punishment which contains an element of public protection accords "with the fundamental purpose of the criminal law generally, and of sentencing in particular, namely, the protection of society."[87] Justice Wilson maintained, however, that an accused should know the possible extent of the penalty before entering a plea. In the case at hand the accused had pleaded guilty and was convicted before being informed of the Crown's intention to apply for the "dangerous offender" designation.

The principles of fundamental justice imply the right of an accused person to control his or her own defence. These principles are violated, therefore, if the Crown is permitted to introduce evidence of insanity against the accused's wishes.

> The mere fact that the Crown is able to raise a defence which the accused does not wish to raise, and thereby to trigger a special verdict which the accused does not wish to trigger, means that the accused has lost a degree of control over the conduct of his or her defence. The Crown's ability to raise independently the issue of insanity could very well interfere with other defences being advanced by the accused and could irreversibly damage an accused's credibility.[87a]

Nevertheless, if the accused's evidence raises doubts as to his or her mental capacity the judge may then allow the Crown to introduce evidence of insanity.

Although section 7 might overlap other Charter rights it does not include equality before the law as a principle of fundamental justice. The attempt to invoke section 7 before equality rights (s. 15) became effective on April 17, 1985 was deemed an effort to circumvent the intended effective date of section 15. Furthermore, the right to equality before the law under the Bill of Rights was not infringed just because a section of the Criminal Code (providing for mandatory roadside breath testing) had not been proclaimed in all provinces. Specifically, the appellant had been charged in Ontario; the legislation had not been proclaimed in British Columbia or Quebec. "Parliament has the unquestioned legislative authority under the division of powers to limit the territorial application of the criminal law."[88] This statement would appear to settle the issue under section 15 of the Charter as well.

The fingerprinting of a person charged with an offence (but before conviction) does violate section 7 rights because the Criminal Code requires the accused "to appear at a [specified] time and place." Failure to comply is a punishable offence. However, this is not inconsistent with the principles of fundamental justice inasmuch as the rights of the accused are not "unduly invaded." Indeed, "a person who is charged on reasonable and probable grounds with having committed a serious crime must expect a significant loss of personal privacy incidental to his being taken into custody."[89]

Convicting a person of robbery, and also of using (as distinct from being armed with) a firearm, does not violate the principles of fundamental justice.[90]

Thomson Newspapers (1990) is particularly significant because of the sharply differing views of Justices La Forest and Wilson.[91] The issue was whether compelling officers of Thomson Newspapers to testify and produce documents at an investigation into possible predatory pricing by that newspaper chain violated the principles of fundamental justice. La Forest maintained that it did not, suggesting that the right to compel "strikes a just and proper balance between the interests of the individual and the state—an important factor that must be taken into account in defining the content of the principles of fundamental justice." Wilson vehemently disagreed and asserted that the right to compel could lead, in any subsequent proceedings against the witness, to the use of "derivative evidence" (evidence derived from the testimony though not the testimony itself), which use was not prohibited by Charter sections 11(c) or 13. Because of this, the principles of fundamental justice would be violated. Although La Forest acknowledged the absence of that protection he maintained that derivative evidence, which by definition exists independently of the compelled testimony, "*could* have been found by some other means, however low the probability of such discovery may have been." This issue is noted in the commentary on section 13. The Court's split decision was that compelling individuals to testify did not violate the principles of fundamental justice.

The prohibition of communication in a public place for the purpose of prostitution, or the keeping of a common bawdy-house, clearly violates the right to liberty because of the possibility of imprisonment upon conviction, but it does not violate the principles of fundamental justice. In *Ref. re ss. 193 and 195.1(1)(c) of the Criminal Code* (*Man.*) the Court decided, first, that while vagueness in legislation conflicts with those principles, the meanings of "prostitution," "keeps," "communicates," and "attempts to communicate," are sufficiently clear ("given the benefit of judicial interpretation") to be known in advance. Second, the criminalizing of solicitation but not prostitution "does not offend the basic tenets of our legal system. Unless or until this Court is faced with the direct question of Parliament's competence to criminalize prostitution, nothing prohibits Parliament from using the criminal law to express society's disapprobation of street solicitation."[92]

Section 7 does not include the right to property. This is significant because, as a result, there is no requirement either of fair procedures when property is expropriated or that compensation be paid in return for expropriated property. The Canadian Bill of Rights protects the "enjoyment of property," and because this statute is not repealed by the 1982 Constitution Act its rights remain protected (but are not entrenched) by section 26 of the Constitution Act. The Bill of Rights applies only to Federal legislation.

Before commenting on the remaining legal rights in sections 8-14, the Supreme Court's view should be noted that those sections are specific examples of rights to life, liberty and security of the person, so that their violation is contrary to the principles of fundamental justice and therefore a violation of section 7 as well.

> They are designed to protect, in a specific manner and setting, the right[s] . . . set forth in s. 7. . . . To put matters in a different way, ss. 7 to 14 could have been fused into one section, with inserted between the words of s. 7 and the rest of those sections the oft utilised provision in our statutes, "and, without limiting the generality of the foregoing (s. 7) the following shall be deemed to be in violation of a person's rights under this section." Clearly, some of those sections embody principles that are beyond what could be characterized as "procedural."
>
> . . .
>
> The principles of fundamental justice are to be found in the basic tenets of our legal system. They do not lie in the realm of general public policy but in the inherent domain of the judiciary as guardian of the justice system. Such an approach to the interpretation of "principles of fundamental justice" is consistent with the wording and structure of s. 7, the context of the section, i.e., ss. 8 to 14, and the character and larger objects of the *Charter* itself. It provides meaningful content for the s. 7 guarantee all the while avoiding adjudication of policy matters.[93]

➤ **SECTION 8:** Everyone has the right to be secure against unreasonable search or seizure.

The key to this section is the meaning of "unreasonable." Basically, according to Justice Lamer, "a search will be reasonable if it is authorized by law, if the law itself is reasonable and if the manner in which the search is carried out is reasonable."[93a] The Supreme Court faced the problem in its third Charter case (*Hunter v. Southam*, 1984).[94] In delivering the Court's unanimous judgement, Justice (as he was then) Dickson noted that "there is no specificity in the section beyond the bare guarantee of freedom from 'unreasonable' search and seizure; nor is there any particular historical, political or philosophic context capable of providing an obvious gloss on the meaning of the guarantee." Furthermore, "it is clear that the meaning . . . cannot be determined by recourse to a dictionary." In grappling with the problem the Court decided that the criterion of reasonableness is satisfied when search or seizure is authorized by a statute requiring:

(1) that there be "prior authorization, where feasible"; otherwise, "the party seeking to justify a warrantless search bears the onus of rebutting the presumption of unreasonableness";
(2) that the warrant be issued by a neutral person who can "assess the conflicting interests of the state and the individual," and be "capable of acting judicially"; and
(3) that there be "reasonable and probable grounds, established upon oath, to believe that an offence has been committed and that there is evidence to be found at the place of the search."

The Thomson and Southam newspaper chains each operated a daily paper in Ottawa and Winnipeg. An investigation of these companies had been undertaken upon the closure by each company of one of its papers, thus leaving the other company in a monopoly situation. The court case was a challenge to a section of the Combines Investigation Act which permitted the search of the office of the Edmonton *Journal* and other Southam offices in Canada. The Supreme Court found the search to be unreasonable for several reasons. First, the authorization was given by the Restrictive Trade Practices Commission, which also held investigatory powers and therefore was unable to make an impartial assessment of the conflicting interests of the state and the individual. Second, the Act did not require reasonable and probable grounds for believing that an offence had been committed and that evidence would be found during the search. Third, the place of search was broadly defined as the Edmonton *Journal* and Southam offices "elsewhere in Canada." In Dickson's words the authorization was "tantamount to a licence to roam at large on the premises of Southam Inc." anywhere in the country.

The Court has acknowledged that exceptions to the high standards established in *Hunter v. Southam* may be justified in certain circumstances. In

Thomson Newspapers (1990),[95] for example, it decided (through Justice La Forest) that application of those standards "would severely hamper and perhaps render impossible the effective investigation of anti-competitive offences." According to Justice L'Heureux-Dubé "public interest in the freedom and protection of citizens in the market-place prevails over the minimal infringement of the privacy interests of those required to disclose information of an economic nature." Justice Sopinka believed that the *Hunter v. Southam* standards should be reserved "for those state intrusions which are truly out of keeping with what individuals have come to expect as a routine fact of daily life in a modern state." The Thomson newspaper chain had been ordered to produce documents in the investigation of possible predatory pricing. The commentary on section 7 refers to this case.

In *Simmons* (1988)[96] the Court ruled that at Canadian ports of entry "the degree of personal privacy reasonably expected is lower than in most other situations." Because countries have the right to control the entry of persons and things, "travellers seeking to cross national boundaries fully expect to be subject to a screening process" including searches of luggage and the person when there are grounds to believe that prohibited goods are being transported. In such circumstances, the Court said, a strip search "is not so highly invasive of an individual's bodily integrity to be considered unreasonable" under section 8. Nevertheless, a person must be advised of his or her right to counsel before the search begins.

The other side of unreasonable search or seizure, therefore, is entitlement to a "reasonable" expectation of privacy. Hence the need to balance public and private interests: "whether in a particular situation the public's interest in being left alone by government must give way to the government's interest in intruding on the individual's privacy in order to advance its goals, notably those of law enforcement."[97] One of the most important matters relating to this delicate balance is police surveillance. The Supreme Court faced this issue in two cases (*Duarte* and *Wiggins*) decided the same day in early 1990. The following comments are from the *Duarte* ruling.[98]

The Criminal Code distinguishes between "electronic" and what is usually called "participant" surveillance, although both constitute "search or seizure." Electronic surveillance is defined by the Criminal Code as the interception of a private conversation by means of "an electromagnetic, acoustic, mechanical or other device." It is permitted (i.e., it is "reasonable" and therefore not a violation of section 8) only after an authorization has been granted by a superior court judge, and it must be performed precisely according to the terms of the authorization. The rationale of prior authorization is the protection of individual privacy. Participant surveillance, sometimes called (ironically) "consent" surveillance, is really electronic surveillance with a difference: one party to the conversation, generally a police informer or undercover officer, surreptitiously records the conversation. The more fundamental difference, however, is that participant surveillance is unrestricted, so that the police in their sole discretion decide upon whom, where, and for how long to conduct the surveillance.

The argument defending the constitutionality of participant surveillance was summarized (and rejected) by Justice La Forest for the Court:

> A person who has voluntarily chosen to confide his wrongdoing to another, and who, by happenstance, has had the misfortune (from his perspective) of doing so in the presence of a microphone, should not be able to invoke the *Charter* to prevent divulgation of the confidence in a court of law. Incriminating statements and confessions of wrongdoing are not *per se* constitutionally protected communications; provided the accused spoke of his own free will, there is no constitutional significance to be accorded the manner in which the evidence was gained.

La Forest noted that this defence is supported by the United States Supreme Court and many state appeal courts. However, our Supreme Court could see no logical difference between the two types of surveillance—the location of the hidden microphone is not relevant. There must, therefore, be a uniform standard in applying the Charter. Parliament has addressed the difficult issue of balancing individual privacy and the state's need to enforce the law by imposing the requirement of judicial authorization for electronic surveillance. The extension of this requirement to participant surveillance would not, in the Court's view, hamper efforts to combat crime. Without such authorization, search or seizure becomes "unreasonable" for the purpose of section 8.

A variation of electronic surveillance occurred in *R. v. Thompson* (1990), which involved the tapping of public pay telephones. This magnified the risk of monitoring conversations of innocent third parties especially when, as happened in this case, the tape recorders were set to run continuously throughout the night. Justice Sopinka for the Court majority ruled that this violated section 8 "in the absence of reasonable and probable grounds for believing that the telephone was in use by a target at the time the listening device was activated."[99] Nevertheless, and on the basis of Justice Lamer's *Collins* criteria (see the commentary on section 24), Sopinka concluded that the admission of evidence would not bring the administration of justice into disrepute.

Does video surveillance lie within the ambit of authorization envisaged by the Criminal Code? Not according to Justice La Forest for a Supreme Court majority. *Wong* (1990) involved the "unreasonable" video surveillance of a hotel room where illegal gaming was suspected. The Code contemplates the interception of private oral communications. La Forest said:

> it does not speak to the very different, and . . . more pernicious threat to privacy constituted by surreptitious video surveillance . . . The courts would be forgetting their role as guardians of our fundamental liberties if they were to usurp the role of Parliament and purport to give their sanction to video surveillance by adopting for that purpose a code of procedure dealing with an altogether different surveillance technology. It is for Parliament, and Parliament alone, to set out the

> conditions under which law enforcement agencies may employ video surveillance technology [or any other technology which may be developed in the future] in their fight against crime.[100]

Having come to this conclusion the Court ruled, again using the *Collins* criteria, that the evidence was admissible under section 24(2).

Several other Supreme Court section 8 decisions are noteworthy:

There is no unreasonable intrusion on privacy when police are making random check stops of motorists who are "required to produce a licence or permit or other documentary evidence of a status or compliance with some legal requirement that is a lawful condition of the exercise of a right or privilege."[101] The counter argument was that the search was unreasonable in the absence of guidelines for police officers in making these stops.

Section 8 is not violated by the Income Tax Act which authorizes the Minister of National Revenue to require the production of documents relevant to the filing of income tax returns "whether or not he has reasonable grounds for believing that a particular taxpayer has breached the Act . . . A spot check or a system of random monitoring may be the only way in which the integrity of the tax system can be maintained."[102]

Writs of assistance (general search warrants) are "constitutionally inadequate." A writ of assistance permits its holder to enter any place at any time to search for evidence of a specified type of crime. In two relevant cases the government did not defend the provision in the Narcotic Control Act which authorized the issuing of writs; indeed, the authorization had been repealed before the cases reached the Supreme Court.[103]

Taking a blood sample without consent or legal authority, or without justification based on urgency or other reason, violates section 8.[104]

While the guarantee against unreasonable search applies to both people and property, that against seizure relates only to property. Seizure of the person is prevented by the guarantee against arbitrary detention and imprisonment in section 9.

➤ **SECTION 9:** Everyone has the right not to be arbitrarily detained or imprisoned.

The meaning of this section hinges on the qualification "arbitrary." Cases involving the meanings of "detention" or "imprisonment" have been contested under section 10. Manning defines "arbitrary" as "unjust, illegal, unreasonable, cruel, or capricious. It includes conduct which is erratic, wilful, absolute, autocratic, overbearing and domineering . . . The concept of arbitrariness really consists of application of law or authority in an uneven and irregular fashion which fails to give the individual that same application as others."[105] Detention or imprisonment that lacks legal sanction is clearly "arbitrary." However, when does the element of discretion make detention or imprisonment arbitrary? Justice Le Dain (for the Supreme Court) has given a simple though broad answer: "A discretion is arbitrary if there are no criteria, express or implied, which govern its exercise."[106]

Several generalizations emerge from the cases decided by the Supreme Court.

Section 9 is not violated when an individual has been lawfully detained on reasonable and probable grounds that he or she has committed an offence.[107]

The random stopping of motor vehicles to check drivers' licences, proof of insurance, driver sobriety, and vehicle mechanical safety, is "arbitrary" because the determination of which vehicles are stopped is left to police discretion. Although violations of section 9, random check stops (whether or not they are part of an organized program) are reasonable under section 1, given the objective of improved highway safety and the important role played by check stops in increasing both the detection and the "perceived risk" of detection of vehicle offences.[108]

The imprisonment of "dangerous offenders" for indeterminate terms does not violate section 9.[109] The Criminal Code provides that an individual who has been found guilty of a "serious personal injury offence" may be declared by a court to be a dangerous offender if, for example, the offender has exhibited a pattern of repetitive aggressive behaviour or behaviour of a brutal nature such that normal standards of restraint will likely be ineffective. A serious personal injury offence is defined as an indictable offence (other than treason or murder) involving violence (including sexual assault) against another person, or conduct likely to endanger another's life or safety or to cause severe psychological damage. The Supreme Court ruled (*Lyons*, 1987) that imprisonment is not arbitrary, inasmuch as it is authorized by statute and applies only to a narrowly defined group of offenders. If these criteria themselves were to be found unconstitutional, Justice La Forest (for the Court) said, the constitutional issue would be the individual's liberty rather than arbitrary imprisonment. As to the element of discretion, La Forest maintained that its absence rather than its presence could make imprisonment arbitrary. In his view, the absence of discretion would require that the Crown seek to have an individual who has been found guilty of a serious personal injury offence declared dangerous "if there was the barest . . . case and the Court, upon making a finding that the offender is a dangerous offender would always be required to impose an indeterminate sentence."[110] Insofar as discretion leads to lack of geographic uniformity, La Forest added that "variation among provinces in this regard may be inevitable and, indeed, desirable in a country where a federal statute is administered by local authorities." (See also the commentary on section 12 for a relationship between indeterminate prison terms and "cruel and unusual punishment.")

In *Swain* (1991) it *was* the absence of discretion coupled with indeterminate detention that constituted a violation of section 9 and, with it, the principles of fundamental justice (s. 7). The Criminal Code required that a person found not guilty because of insanity be detained at the pleasure of the lieutenant governor. Because there was no assurance that the accused was dangerous, or even "insane" at the time of the trial (as distinct from the time of the offence), mandatory detention was clearly arbitrary and "based on no criteria or standards and before any kind of hearing can be conducted on the issue of present mental condition." Furthermore, although the objective of detention was "pressing and substantial" (to protect society from acquittees who are dangerous), and was rationally connected to the means, the section 9 right was not minimally impaired because of the indeterminate length of detention. Charter section 1 could not be invoked. Because of the important consequences of this landmark case and the potential danger to society of striking the law without an alternative in place, the Court allowed Parliament six months to redraft a law consistent with the Charter.[110a]

The imposition of a mandatory term of imprisonment does not of itself violate section 9. In *Luxton* (1990) the Court upheld the Criminal Code's mandatory 25-year minimum term without the possibility of parole for first degree murder. "The incarceration is statutorily authorized, it narrowly defines a class of offenders with respect to whom the punishment will be invoked and it prescribes quite specifically the conditions under which an offender may be found guilty of first degree murder."[111] Neither is the imposition of a mandatory term "cruel and unusual"—see the commentary on section 12.

➤ **SECTION 10:** Everyone has the right on arrest or detention
(a) to be informed promptly of the reasons therefor;
(b) to retain and instruct counsel without delay and to be informed of that right; and
(c) to have the validity of the detention determined by way of habeas corpus and to be released if the detention is not lawful.

While the meaning of "arrest" may be self-evident, the meaning of "detention" has been the subject of considerable litigation. The Supreme Court's definition of "detention" was stated in *Therens*.[112] It means

> restraint of liberty other than arrest in which a person may reasonably require the assistance of counsel but might be prevented from retaining and instructing counsel without delay but for the constitutional guarantee.
>
> In addition to the case of deprivation of liberty by physical constraint, there is . . . detention . . . when a police officer or other agent of the state assumes control over the movement of a person by a demand or direction which may have significant legal consequence and which prevents or impedes access to counsel.

The important element is compulsion but, Justice Le Dain added, this might be "of a psychological or mental nature":

> Most citizens are not aware of the precise legal limits of police authority. Rather than risk the application of physical force or prosecution for wilful obstruction, the reasonable person is likely to err on the side of caution, assume lawful authority and comply with the demand. The element of psychological compulsion, in the form of a reasonable perception of suspension of freedom of choice, is enough

> to make the restraint of liberty involuntary. Detention may be effected without the application or threat of application of physical restraint if the person concerned submits or acquiesces in the deprivation of liberty and reasonably believes that the choice to do otherwise does not exist.

At issue was whether a motorist who accompanies a police officer to the police station for a breathalyzer test is "detained" within the meaning of section 10 and therefore must be informed of his or her right to counsel without delay. The Court's answer was "yes."

Subsection (a): The right to be informed promptly of the reasons for arrest or detention

This right is intended to enable a person promptly to undertake any action that will best serve his or her interests, perhaps most immediately to retain counsel. The failure to inform "promptly" will, therefore, invalidate the detention or arrest. To become informed means that there has been communication meaningful to the person involved. The most obvious requirement is that the communication be in a language understood by the person detained or arrested, and this may require an interpreter. But what if communication is impossible because of intoxication or other temporary inability to understand what is being said? This became relevant in *Clarkson*. See the commentary on section 10(b) below.

Subsection (b): The right to retain and instruct counsel without delay and to be informed of that right

The right to counsel is not new; what has been added is the right to be informed of the right to counsel without delay. The decision to exercise this right is up to the person arrested or detained, but a voluntary waiver must, to be valid, "be premised on a true appreciation of the consequences of giving up that right." In *Clarkson* (1986) the Supreme Court ruled that a person accused of her husband's murder was too drunk to understand these consequences and that, in the absence of a compelling reason to proceed immediately with the interrogation, the police should have waited until she was sober before questioning her.[113]

The police have two responsibilities in addition to informing the detainee of the right to counsel: (1) they must provide a reasonable opportunity for that right to be exercised, including the use of a telephone if one is available even if there is no explicit request for its use; (2) they must delay questioning until the detainee has had a reasonable opportunity to retain and instruct counsel in order to seek advice as to the nature and use of the detainee's rights.[114] However, these two responsibilities "are suspended when the arrested or detained person is not reasonably diligent in the exercise of his rights" because, without such a limit, "it would be possible to delay needlessly and with impunity an investigation and even, in certain cases, to allow for an essential piece of evidence to be lost, destroyed or rendered impossible to obtain." The specific case (*Smith*, 1989)[115] involved a person who, having been charged early one evening, decided to wait until morning before attempting to contact his lawyer. The Court divided on the case, the majority ruling that the accused had not been diligent. The dissenting judges held that the case was not different from *Ross*.

In *Ross* (1989)[116] the two accused, having attempted without success to contact their lawyer in the middle of the night, decided to wait until morning rather than call a different lawyer. The Court unanimously agreed that section 10(b) rights had been violated when the police proceeded with a line-up before morning. Reasonable diligence, they said, "depends upon the context" facing the individual. The need for counsel is immediate upon arrest or detention; the search for the best counsel to conduct a trial is less immediate. "Nevertheless, accused or detained persons have a right to choose their counsel and it is only if the lawyer chosen cannot be available within a reasonable time that the detainee or the accused should be expected to exercise the right to counsel by calling another lawyer."

It would appear, then, that "the jury is still out" on specific applications of the obligation to give detainees "reasonable opportunity" to retain and instruct counsel.

Does the right to counsel imply, at least for the indigent, the right to counsel at public expense? Justice Minister Chrétien stated that such was not the intent. "It is a question of a private citizen dealing in society with his own problem. Legal aid is a social measure that exists in Canada and is available under the criteria that are established by the Attorneys General of the provinces."[117] In *Brydges* (1990),[118] however, the Supreme Court ruled that a person who has been detained or arrested must be made aware of the existence and availability of Legal Aid within the province. It is unclear how far this right to legal services, whether given freely or at public expense, may be carried.

Several other Supreme Court decisions are noteworthy for their specific interpretations of section 10(b):

A motorist who has been stopped by the police and subsequently required to take a breathalyzer test, whether at the side of the road (e.g., *Thomsen*, 1988)[119] or after accompanying a police officer to the police station (e.g., *Therens*, 1985),[120] has been detained and therefore has the right to counsel without delay. The Criminal Code section applicable to *Thomsen* requires the test to be made "forthwith." The relevant section in *Therens* requires the test to be made "forthwith or as soon as practicable." The Supreme Court decided in the former case that, while the motorist is indeed detained and therefore has the right to retain counsel without delay, that right could be limited by section 1. The reason? There is an "implied limitation" on the right to counsel in view of the "operational nature and purpose" of a roadside test. On the other hand, Charter section 1 was not relevant in *Therens* because the right to counsel without delay was subject to no limit, whether explicit or implicit, "prescribed by law."

A person required to undergo a strip search while going through customs has been detained, even though the right to be secure against unreasonable search and seizure (s. 8) has not been violated.[121]

The right to counsel applies to arrest or detention for a specific reason. Therefore, a person charged with one offence which is subsequently changed to another offence has the right to contact counsel following both the initial and the subsequent charge. "The individual . . . can only exercise his s. 10(b) rights in a meaningful way if he knows the extent of his jeopardy." The specific case involved a charge of attempted murder being changed to first degree murder.[122]

The obligation to inform a detainee of the right to counsel implies communication. One can generally tell when an accused understands what has been said. In *Evans* (1991), however, where "there is a positive indication [by the detainee, whose mental age was about 14] that . . . [he] does not understand his right to counsel, the police cannot rely on their mechanical recitation of the right to the accused; they must take steps to facilitate that understanding."[122a]

Subsection (c): The right of habeas corpus

The right of *habeas corpus* ensures that a person cannot be held indefinitely without having the validity of the detention reviewed by a judge. This historic right is traceable to the Habeas Corpus Act passed by the British Parliament in 1769. What is new for Canada is its entrenchment in the Charter. While the days of detention and arrest of political opponents on phoney charges are gone, the right of *habeas corpus* remains as valuable protection against the police who may wish to detain a person, whom they suspect of having committed a crime, pending sufficient evidence to lay a specific charge.

➤ **SECTION 11:** Any person charged with an offence has the right

(a) to be informed without unreasonable delay of the specific offence;
(b) to be tried within a reasonable time;
(c) not to be compelled to be a witness in proceedings against that person in respect of the offence;
(d) to be presumed innocent until proven guilty according to law in a fair and public hearing by an independent and impartial tribunal;
(e) not to be denied reasonable bail without just cause;
(f) except in the case of an offence under military law tried before a military tribunal, to the benefit of trial by jury where the maximum punishment for the offence is impris-onment for five years or a more severe punishment;
(g) not to be found guilty on account of any act or omission unless, at the time of the act or omission, it constituted an offence under Canadian or international law or was criminal according to the general principles of law recognized by the community of nations;
(h) if finally acquitted of the offence, not to be tried for it again and, if finally found guilty and punished for the offence, not to be tried or punished for it again; and

(i) if found guilty of the offence and if the punishment for the offence has been varied between the time of commission and the time of sentencing, to the benefit of the lesser punishment.

Subsection (a): The right to be informed without unreasonable delay of the specific offence

This right is important so that the accused knows for certain that a charge has been laid for breach of the law, and can therefore begin to prepare a defence. Specificity would, presumably, include the precise action, time, place, and victim. The original wording of 11(a) used the less flexible "promptly" rather than "without unreasonable delay." The latter term is sufficiently flexible to permit, for example, the postal service to be used for less serious charges (in spite of the frustrations the public has experienced with that service).

Subsection (b): The right to be tried within a reasonable time

The purpose of this provision, according to Justice (as he then was) Lamer, is "to secure, within a specific framework, the more extensive rights to liberty and security of the person" in section 7. In his view, security of the person means not only physical integrity; it also relates to the "vexations and vicissitudes" while awaiting trial, including "stigmatization of the accused, loss of privacy, stress and anxiety resulting from a multitude of factors, including possible disruption of family, social life and work, legal costs, and uncertainty as to outcome and sanction."[123] Furthermore, the avoidance of delay reduces the possibility of witnesses moving away, dying, or forgetting important facts. There are societal considerations as well as the protection of individual rights for, as Justice Cory has observed, "the failure of the justice system to deal fairly, quickly and efficiently with criminal trials inevitably leads to the community's frustration with the judicial system and eventually to a feeling of contempt for court procedures."[124]

But what is "reasonable time"? Although the Supreme Court had earlier encountered section 11(b) cases, it was in *Askov* (1990) that a majority established guidelines to determine when the section's rights are violated. Justice Cory, who delivered the majority decision, enumerated the factors to be considered:[125]

(1) The length of the delay: After noting the time required in several Canadian jurisdictions to bring accused persons to trial, Cory suggested that a delay "in a range of some six to eight months . . . might be deemed to be the outside limit of what is reasonable." The delay in *Askov* had been almost two years.

(2) Explanation for the delay:

 (a) Conduct of, or delay attributable to, the Crown. This includes delay related to the complexity of cases that may take longer to prepare and prosecute—conspiracy as compared with simple break and enter, for example.

(b) Systemic or institutional delays. While Cory recognized the inevitability of regional variations based on geography, population, and material resources, he emphasized the need for comparison among like regions. The Peel District of Ontario, where *Askov* was heard, was (according to studies) the slowest in the province, in the country, and indeed north of Mexico! "Some solution must be found," Cory declared, "to eradicate this malignant growth of unreasonable trial delay that constitutes such an unacceptable blight upon the administration of justice. . . ."

(c) Conduct of, or delay attributable to, the accused. It is incumbent upon the Crown to prove this factor.

(3) Waiver (although this could be considered delay attributable to the accused): According to Justice Lamer (*Rahey*, 1987) a waiver must be "clear, unequivocal, and informed." In *Rahey* the nineteen trial adjournments requested by the judge (resulting in an eleven-month delay) did not constitute waiver:

> Acquiescence to a delay that is requested by the judge in whose hands the fate of a motion for a directed verdict [judge's instructions for the jury to find the accused not guilty] lies must be assessed differently than acquiescence to those delays in proceedings that are at the request of the Crown . . . That judge is in a position of authority and the accused would be well advised by counsel to extend to the judge every courtesy.[126]

(4) Prejudice to the accused, including bail restrictions such as (in *Askov*) curfew, denial of contact with co-accused, and regular reporting to police: The Crown must demonstrate the absence of prejudice.

It is clear that consideration of institutional resources must not be used to rationalize and legitimize the *status quo*: the administration of justice must be made to conform to the Charter, not the other way around. The fallout from *Askov* is bound to be significant. For example, five months after *Askov* it was reported that some 27,000 Ontario cases had been withdrawn or stayed, and that about 3,000 youth-court cases in Alberta were endangered.[127]

Subsection (c): The right not to be compelled to be a witness in proceedings against oneself in respect of the offence

Although a person cannot be compelled to be a witness for the Crown at one's own trial, such a person may be a witness in his or her own defence. However, once on the stand the witness is subject to cross-examination by the Crown as is any other witness, and must answer questions even if it involves self-incrimination. This may be regarded as an element of compromise between the view that the Crown's responsibility is to prove guilt without any assistance from the accused, and the view that all evidence that can be elicited from whatever source is important to the establishment of innocence or guilt. Whatever the "cost" to the defendant in terms of a jury's interpretation of a refusal to testify, it must be weighed against the "cost" of testifying and thereby having to answer questions of the prosecution.

Note that this protection against self-incrimination exists only at a person's own trial. There are several interesting implications.[128] In the first place a person charged with murder, for example, could be compelled to testify at the inquest into the death because the inquest would not be "proceedings against that person in respect of the offence." Second, a person accused as an accessory to a crime may be compelled to testify against the person accused of the crime, although in the subsequent trial of the accessory the evidence he or she gave at the earlier trial would (under section 13) be inadmissible. Third, if two persons are charged with the same offence but tried separately, each could be required to testify against the other although, by virtue of section 13, the evidence of neither would be admissible at his or her own trial. See the commentary on section 13.

There has been no section 11(c) litigation before the Supreme Court. The closest was *Amway* (1989)[129] which made explicit that although a corporation employee can be a witness, a corporation itself cannot.

Subsection (d): The right to be presumed innocent until proven guilty according to law in a fair and public hearing by an independent and impartial tribunal

Chief Justice Dickson has pointed out that "the presumption of innocence is a hallowed principle lying at the very heart of criminal law . . . This is essential in a society committed to fairness and social justice. The presumption of innocence confirms our faith in humankind; it reflects our belief that individuals are decent and law-abiding members of the community until proven otherwise."[130] An accused is presumed innocent until proven guilty by the application of the standards enunciated in this subsection.

The burden of proof rests with the Crown, and the proof must be beyond a reasonable doubt. An immediate issue that arises in connection with the presumption of innocence is what is called the "reverse onus" provision of some statutes including the Criminal Code, the Narcotic Control Act, and the Customs Act. A reverse onus clause presumes guilt under certain conditions until the innocence of the accused has been proved. For example, the Criminal Code provides that a person who was in the driver's seat of a vehicle, and who is charged with being in control of the vehicle while under the influence of drugs or alcohol, is deemed to have been in control "unless he establishes that he did not enter or mount the vehicle for the purpose of setting it in motion." Until the *Oakes* (1986) decision, the Narcotic Control Act presumed that possession of an illegal drug is intended for trafficking unless the accused can prove otherwise. Under the Customs Act, proof that a person is in possession of imported goods places the onus on that person to prove that the goods were lawfully imported.

Pre-Charter case law dealing with challenges to reverse onus provisions under the presumption-of-innocence clause of the Canadian Bill of Rights tended to uphold reverse onus legislation under narrowly defined conditions.[131] Under the Charter, however, the Supreme Court stated that "ordinary legislation must conform to the constitutional requirements. An interpretation of s. 11(d) that would make the presumption of innocence subject to legislative exceptions would run directly contrary to the overall purpose of an entrenched constitutional document."[132] This contrast illustrates the decline of legislative supremacy when the Charter was adopted.

In several reverse onus cases under the Charter, the Supreme Court ruled that section 11(d) had been violated. The following statement is perfectly clear: "If an accused is required to prove some fact on the balance of probabilities to avoid conviction, the provision violates the presumption of innocence because it permits a conviction in spite of a reasonable doubt in the mind of the trier of fact as to the guilt of the accused . . . Only if the existence of the substituted fact leads inexorably to the conclusion that the essential element exists, with no other reasonable possibilities, will the statutory presumption be constitutionally valid."[133]

In the first case (*Oakes*, 1986),[134] the impugned section of the Narcotic Control Act did not survive the scrutiny of Charter section 1. The Court acknowledged the legitimacy of Parliament's desire to decrease drug trafficking; but in the absence of a rational connection between the fact of drug possession and the presumed fact of possession for the purpose of trafficking, it ruled that the means (the legislation) was disproportionate to the objective. In *Whyte* (1988),[135] however, the reverse onus section of the Criminal Code survived the *Oakes* test—both the objective (protecting the public against drunk drivers) and the proportionality test for balancing individual and societal interests.

Penno (1990) presented the interesting situation of an accused trying to use his state of intoxication to prove an absence of intent, and therefore as a defence against the charge of having care or control of a motor vehicle while impaired![136] Justice Wilson was emphatic (and other members of the Court agreed) that "impairment cannot be at one and the same time an essential element of the offence and a defence to the offence." The rights in sections 11(d) or 7 were not infringed because, according to Justice McLachlin, the intent to commit the offence "lies not in the intention to assume care or control of a motor vehicle, but in voluntarily becoming intoxicated."

The section of the Criminal Code (s. 319) under which James Keegstra was tried (see the commentary on Charter section 2[b]) provided that "no person shall be convicted of an offence . . . if he establishes that the statements communicated were true." Clearly, this is reverse onus; however, given the gravity of the offence, the Court majority had no difficulty preserving the impugned section by application of the *Oakes* criteria. Parliament's objective in using reverse onus was pressing and substantial—to prevent harm caused by hate-mongering. There was a rational connection between the legislation and the objective. The legislation impaired the guaranteed right as little as possible if one accepts that Parliament intended to strike a balance between the legitimate concerns of preventing harm and acknowledging the importance of truth. This balance would be severely skewed, said Chief Justice Dickson, if all that were required to acquit was reasonable doubt as to the falsity of the accused's statements. "To accept such a result it would have to be agreed that this relatively small possibility of truthfulness outweighs the harm caused through the willful promotion of hatred . . . Having the accused prove truthfulness on the balance of probabilities is an understandable and valid precaution against too easily justifying . . . harm."[137] Finally, therefore, infringement of the section 11(d) guarantee was outweighed by the importance of preventing harm caused by hate-mongering.

In 1987 and 1990 the Supreme Court struck down two provisions of the Criminal Code as violations of the presumption of innocence (s. 11[d]) and therefore of the principles of fundamental justice (s. 7). According to (then) section 213 of the Code:

> Culpable homicide is murder where a person causes the death of a human being while committing or attempting to commit . . . robbery, breaking and entering . . . whether or not the person means to cause death . . . and whether or not he knows that death is likely to be caused . . ., if (a) he means to cause bodily harm for the purpose of facilitating the commission of the offence, or . . . (d) he uses a weapon or has it upon his person during or at the time he commits or attempts to commit the offence, . . . and the death ensues as a consequence.

The problem lay with the fact that, because this section makes the foresight of death unnecessary, all that was required for conviction was proof of intent to harm, or of possession or use of a weapon, while committing one of several enumerated offences when death ensued. In other words, conviction could result even when there was reasonable doubt that the accused meant to cause death (called "subjective foresight") or should have known that death was a likely result (called "objective foresight"). In *Vaillancourt* (1987) which brought down section 213(d), the accused's accomplice shot and killed a person, although the accused believed the accomplice had emptied his gun beforehand. In *Martineau* (1990) which struck down section 213(a), the accused's accomplice shot and killed two people from fear of later being identified. In neither case did the legislation survive the Charter's limitations clause (s. 1): While the government's objective was valid (to deter the carrying or use of a weapon [*Vaillancourt*] and to deter the infliction of bodily harm [*Martineau*]), and while the means was rationally connected to the objective, the means "unduly impair the rights and freedoms in question. Indeed, it is not necessary to convict of murder persons who did not intend or foresee the death and who could not even have foreseen the death [,] in order to deter others from using or carrying weapons [or from causing bodily harm]. If Parliament wishes to deter the use or carrying of weapons [or 'deter persons from causing bodily harm during certain offences'], it should . . . punish the use or carrying of weapons [or 'punish persons for causing the bodily harm']."[138]

In 1990 (*Chaulk*)[138a] the Court used Charter section 1 to uphold the Criminal Code's presumption of sanity "until the contrary is proved." This provision illustrates reverse onus because the accused must disprove sanity—i.e., prove insanity—on a balance of probabilities rather than merely raise a reasonable doubt. This violates the presumption of innocence in that conviction is possible in spite of reasonable doubt as to the accused's guilt. (When an "insane" accused is judged to have committed a crime, the verdict is "not guilty by reason of insanity" rather than acquittal.)

Another case (*Schwartz*, 1988)[139] is noteworthy for what the Court ruled was not reverse onus in a different section of the Criminal Code. That section (106.7) stated that "the onus is on the accused" possessor of a restricted weapon to prove that he or she has the required firearm registration certificate. (According to section 89[1], a person who had a restricted firearm but no certificate was guilty of an offence.) The Court majority ruled that a person who had the necessary certificate could not be convicted under section 89(1) which applied only to a person without the certificate. "The holder of a registration certificate . . . is not required to prove or disprove . . . anything related to the offence. At most, he may be required to show by the production of the certificate that . . . [the section] does not apply to him." Chief Justice Dickson and Justice Lamer dissented, claiming that the accused had to do more than raise a reasonable doubt; he or she had to establish the fact of possession on a balance of probabilities, thus denying the presumption of innocence.

The hearing must be fair. Might the right to a fair hearing include a right to legal aid at public expense if the accused cannot afford counsel? (This was noted in the commentary on section 10.) Might even the question of counsel competency arise in relation to this right?

Fairness may also be related to the use of military tribunals. Section 2 of the National Defence Act provides for the trial of "service offences" by a military tribunal and without a jury. Service offences are not limited to service-related offences, but are defined as any offences under Federal law committed by persons who are subject to the Code of Service Discipline. See the commentary on section 11(f) for consideration of the issue.

The Canada Evidence Act permits a witness to be asked whether or not he or she has been convicted of a previous offence. In *Corbett* (1988) the witness was the accused who had agreed to testify. Does such evidence deprive the accused of a fair trial? The Court answered "no." Chief Justice Dickson reasoned that the purpose of such evidence is "simply . . . for the jury to consider along with everything else, in assessing the credibility of the accused." The introduction of the evidence does not create a presumption of guilt or incredibility, Dickson asserted, although he acknowledged the potential danger. However, "to conceal the prior criminal record of an accused who testifies would deprive the jury of information relevant to credibility, and create a much more serious risk that the jury will be presented with a misleading picture. The best way to balance and alleviate these risks is . . . to give the jury all the information."[140] The judge does have discretion to exclude evidence in cases where its admission would infringe the right to a fair trial.

The question in *Vermette* (1988) was whether the widespread publicity given to statements made by Quebec Premier Lévesque in the National Assembly, attacking the credibility of a defence witness and the actions of defence lawyers, compromised the right to a fair trial. Vermette was an R.C.M.P. inspector accused of breaking and entering and the theft of Parti Québécois membership lists. The Supreme Court ruled that the stay of proceedings granted by a lower court had been premature. Whether or not a person can be tried by an impartial jury is determinable only when the jury is selected. "Although publicity should lead to challenge for cause at trial in an extreme case, it need not be assumed that a person subjected to such publicity will necessarily be biased. A jury is quite capable of disabusing itself of information that it is not entitled to consider."[141]

The hearing must be public. It is important not only that justice be done but also that it appear to the public to be done. Nevertheless, section 1 would probably sustain a closed trial in exceptional circumstances, such as in the interest of national security, public order, or where publicity might jeopardize the assurance of a fair trial. In other words, a "fair" hearing and a "public" hearing may sometimes be mutually exclusive. The Criminal Code, Young Offenders (formerly Juvenile Delinquents) Act, and Official Secrets Act are examples of legislation providing for *in camera* hearings.[142] They will now have to be justified under section 1, or explicitly validated under the "notwithstanding" clause of section 33, to survive the Charter.

The right to a public hearing is consistent with a ban on media publication of trial proceedings, although such a ban may violate freedom of the press.[143] See the commentary on section 2(b).

The hearing must be by an independent and impartial tribunal. The Supreme Court addressed the meaning of this right in *Valente* (1985).[144] The question was whether courts staffed by provincially appointed judges (the case related specifically to Ontario) are independent and impartial. It should be noted that about 90% of all cases in Canada are heard by these courts.[145] The challenge was based on a large number of specific reasons, all relating to cabinet control of the judiciary. For example, salaries were determined by order-in-council rather than by statute and were subject to annual appropriation; pensions were part of the public service pension plan; judicial tenure might be "during pleasure" rather than "good behaviour"; "senior" judges might be appointed at higher salaries than "ordinary" judges; judges might be authorized to "engage in any business, trade or occupation." The Supreme Court held that while some of these provisions, especially that regarding tenure, may fall short of the ideal, none of them violated the three essential conditions of judicial independence. Those conditions are security of tenure, financial security, and institutional independence in administrative matters "that bear directly and immediately on the exercise of the judicial function." The test of independence is whether the tribunal is perceived to be independent. This does not require uniformity among all jurisdictions in the country, for "that construction would . . . amend the judicature provisions of the Constitution." The Court did not deal with the concept of "impartiality" other than to refer to it as "a state of mind or attitude of the tribunal in relation to the issues and the parties in a particular case."

Lippe (1990) raised a somewhat different question.[145a] Is a part-time municipal court judge who is also allowed to practice law an "independent and impartial tribunal"? Because the issue is not one of the relationship between courts and the state, the three *Valente* criteria do not arise. According to Chief Justice Lamer, "whether or not any particular judge harboured pre-conceived ideas or biases, if the system is structured in such a way as to create a reasonable apprehension of bias on an institutional level, the requirement of impartiality is not met." Any apprehension of bias is related not to the part-time nature of judges but to the nature of the additional activity in which they engage. There is an inherent incompatibility between judging and practicing law because this combination "gives rise to a reasonable apprehension of bias in the mind of a fully informed person in a substantial number of cases." However, the combination of judicial immunity, judicial oath, code of ethics regulating judicial behaviour, and restrictions within the Cities and Towns Act (of Quebec), suggests that a "reasonably informed person should not have an apprehension of bias in a substantial number of cases." Part-time municipal court judges are therefore "independent and impartial."

Are military tribunals "independent and impartial"? Inasmuch as section 11(f) anticipates the use of these tribunals, it seems likely that they would be sustained against an 11(d) challenge. The commentary on section 11(f) includes a discussion of military tribunals within the judicial system.

Subsection (e): The right to reasonable bail

Bail is the release of an accused from custody before the trial. The Criminal Code permits the denial of bail if there is doubt that the accused would return for the trial or if it seems likely that the accused might commit more crimes before the trial. Both grounds for denial have been upheld as "just cause" under the Charter, although no case has been heard by the Supreme Court.[146] The concept of reasonableness is important because an inability of the accused to meet bail conditions makes those conditions tantamount to an order of detention.

There may be conflict between the right to reasonable bail and mobility rights under section 6(2) when a condition of bail requires the accused to remain in a certain part of the country. It is possible that section 1 could be successfully invoked if the mobility restriction were challenged. Section 6(2) would apply only if the accused were a citizen or permanent resident of Canada.

Subsection (f): The right to a jury trial (except in the case of an offence under military law tried before a military tribunal) where maximum punishment is five years or a more severe punishment

We are accustomed to viewing the right to a jury trial—a trial before one's peers—primarily as a protection of individual interests. However, the Supreme Court has emphasized that the jury also serves societal interests "by acting as a vehicle of public education and lending the weight of community standards to trial verdicts." This gives to society an important sense of ownership which might otherwise be unattainable in the administration of justice.[147]

A comparison of severity for the purpose of this section need not be a major problem. Incarceration is presumably more severe than a fine. However, how might corporal punishment compare were that form of penalty restored in Canada? (The whip was abolished in 1972.) Capital punishment, if restored, could be more easily assessed! Would the possibility of indeterminate imprisonment be interpreted as "more severe" than five years? This relationship between the right to a jury trial and the sentencing of "dangerous offenders" is considered in the following paragraph as one of three section 11(f) issues faced by the Supreme Court.

Does a person already convicted of an offence have the right to a jury when a court is deciding whether, upon application by the Crown, that person is a "dangerous offender" to be sentenced to an indeterminate prison term under the Criminal Code? (The dangerous offender designation is made only after a person has been found guilty of an offence.) Because the proceedings have therefore been completed except for the sentencing, any decision whether the trial itself is to be held before a judge and jury is no longer relevant. In *Lyons* (1987)[148] the Supreme Court held that a Crown application to declare the offender dangerous does not fall within section 11(f), and therefore needs not be determined by judge and jury, because "it is not equivalent to 'charging' the offender with an 'offence.'" Rather, it is part of sentencing. (The Criminal Code specifies that the application is to be determined by a court without a jury.) But might a jury hearing be required to meet section 7's standard of fairness? The Court reminded itself that section 11 does not limit section 7 but merely illustrates some of the applications of that section. Nevertheless, the answer to the question was "no": while section 7 does entitle a person to a fair hearing "it does not entitle him to the most favourable procedures that could possibly be imagined."

As to the second issue, the Criminal Code requires that an accused charged with murder be tried by judge and jury (except in Alberta where trial by judge alone is permitted). Does this prevent the accused from using section 11(f) to waive the right to a jury? The Court ruled in *Turpin* (1989) that "the purpose of s. 11(f) is to ensure that the interests of the accused are respected. It gives the accused the right to the benefit of a jury trial but does not force a jury trial on an accused if it is not to his benefit."[149] The right to waive this "benefit" is implied in section 11(f). To deny such a right would be akin to "imprison a man in his privileges and call it the constitution."[150] Furthermore, it is the accused who will determine what is in his or her best interests. In view of these 1989 statements by the Court it is interesting to note a 1985 amendment to the Criminal Code requiring the consent of the attorney general for an Alberta resident to waive the right to a jury trial or, once waived, to change his or her mind and elect a jury trial. Justice Wilson, who delivered the Court's unanimous decision, declined to comment upon the validity of this amendment. (The *Turpin* case in relation to equality rights is noted in the commentary on section 15.)

Third, the Criminal Code states that an accused who fails to appear, without a legitimate excuse, for the beginning of the trial forfeits the right to a jury. In *Lee* (1989) the Court ruled that failure to appear is not an effective waiver and therefore that the Criminal Code in this respect violates section 11(f). It decided, nevertheless, that the legislation survived the scrutiny of the *Oakes* test as applied to section 1, on the grounds that its purpose justified overriding the accused's right to a jury trial, that the legislation was rationally connected to the purpose, and that it infringed the accused's rights as little as possible. The purpose of the legislation, the Court suggested, was "to protect the administration of justice from delay, inconvenience, expense and abuse, and to secure the respect of the public for the criminal trial process."[151]

In 1983, the British Columbia Court of Appeal ruled that a person accused under the Juvenile Delinquents Act of an offence punishable by a sentence exceeding five years in an "industrial school" could be denied a jury trial, because the purpose of confinement was treatment rather than punishment. Therefore, section 11(f) did not apply. In commenting on the decision, Hogg suggests that "the Court was unduly influenced by the euphemisms in which Parliament had couched the provisions" of the Act, that compulsory confinement whether in a prison or an industrial school was surely "punishment," and that any justification of the legislation should be tested by the application of Charter section 1.[152] The case did not reach the Supreme Court.

Inasmuch as the term "jury" is not defined by the Charter, one might only speculate whether governments are unrestrained in determining jury size, composition, method of selection, or even decision-making such as changing the rule of unanimity to some form of majority.

The exception of "an offence under military law" from the right to a jury trial needs comment, for it also relates to the right to a "fair and public hearing by an independent and impartial tribunal" under section 11(d). The National Defence Act provides (s. 2) for the trial of "service offences" by a military tribunal and without a jury. Furthermore, a "service offence" is defined as "an offence under this Act, the *Criminal Code*, or any other Act of the Parliament of Canada, committed by a person while subject to the Code of Service Discipline." However, section 11(f) of the Charter refers to "an offence under military law," and not to a "service offence." The interpretation of this section (and therefore the denial of the right to a jury trial) could be restricted to service-related offences. Alternatively, as Justice McIntyre noted in a 1980 pre-Charter case (*MacKay*),[153] "if we are to apply the definition of service offence literally, then all prosecutions of servicemen for any offences under any penal statute of

Canada could be conducted in military courts." Such an interpretation would significantly broaden the scope for denying the right to a jury trial under section 11(f). Chief Justice Laskin suggested in the same case that:

> The fact that "service offences" are so broadly defined as to include breaches of the ordinary law does not, in my opinion, make a Standing Court Martial the equivalent of an independently appointed judicial officer or other than an *ad hoc* appointee, having no tenure and coming from the very special society of which both the accused, his prosecutor and his "Judge" are members.
>
> In my opinion, it is fundamental that when a person, any person, whatever his or her status or occupation, is charged with an offence under the ordinary criminal law and is to be tried under that law and in accordance with its prescriptions, he or she is entitled to be tried before a court of justice, separate from the prosecution and free from any suspicion of influence of or dependency on others. There is nothing in such a case, where the person charged is in the armed forces, that calls for any special knowledge or special skill of a superior officer, as would be the case if a strictly service or discipline offence, relating to military activity, was involved.

Laskin's line of reasoning may well prevail under the Charter. Indeed, the narrower jurisdiction of military tribunals was upheld by a 1983 Court Martial Appeal Court decision: for section 11(f) to apply, the offence had to fall within the National Defence Act's definition and have "a military nexus."[154] The issue has not yet faced a post-Charter Supreme Court.

Subsection (g): Protection against laws having retroactive effect, with two exceptions

For a person to be convicted, the act or omission must have been a crime at the time of commission or omission. In other words, this section 11(g) prohibits *ex post facto* laws. The justification of such a general prohibition needs no explanation. Nevertheless, even if Canadian law at the time did not consider an event to be an offence, the person may be convicted if the act or omission (a) was at the time an offence under "international law" or (b) "was criminal according to the general principles of law recognized by the community of nations." These two exceptions were not in the original version of 11(g) as submitted to the joint Senate-House of Commons committee in the fall of 1980. They were added to enable Canada to prosecute people for Nazi war crimes committed at a time when no Canadian law addressed the issue. Without these exceptions it is doubtful that our War Crimes Act, passed in 1946 and obviously retroactive, would have stood against section 11(g), unless section 1 were successfully invoked or section 33's legislative override used.

The retroactivity of regulations made pursuant to the 1970 proclamation of the War Measures Act, making it an offence to have belonged to the FLQ even before the regulations were made, would have violated this provision of the

Charter and could have been applied only by appealing to section 1 or invoking section 33.

Fortunately for governments, this section does not prohibit retroactive taxation, a practice made necessary by the inevitable delay between the announcement of the Budget and the introduction and passage of legislation to implement the Budget's provisions. Announced taxes are frequently effective immediately in order to prevent people from benefiting from foreknowledge of tax changes. The reason section 11(g) is inapplicable to retroactive taxation is that no offence is involved.

Subsection (h): Protection against double jeopardy

This protection against double jeopardy prevents a person who has been either acquitted, or found guilty and punished, from being tried again for the same offence. This subsection does not preclude a second trial for the same offence in the event of a mistrial, a stay of proceedings, or the granting of an appeal.

Criteria for deciding whether double jeopardy exists for the purpose of section 11(h) were formulated in *Wigglesworth* (1987).[155] According to Justice Wilson who delivered the majority ruling, section 11 applies if in both instances the proceedings are criminal in nature or if the punishments involve the imposition of "true penal consequences." True penal consequences, she suggested, would include imprisonment or a fine "which by its magnitude would appear to be imposed for the purpose of redressing the wrong to society at large rather than to be the maintenance of internal discipline within the limited sphere of activity." In the case at hand an R.C.M.P. officer had been convicted under both the Royal Canadian Mounted Police Act and the Criminal Code for what was ostensibly the same offence—unnecessary violence toward a prisoner (a "major service offence") under the R.C.M.P. Act, and common assault under the Criminal Code. The first charge was not criminal; the second was. However, both charges involved true penal consequences—the possibility of imprisonment. The Court ruled nevertheless that while there was but one assault there were two quite different offences. One involved internal discipline for which the individual was accountable to his profession; the other involved a criminal offence for which the individual was accountable to society. Therefore, the protection of section 11(h) was not available.

This conclusion also implies that a person may be convicted in both another country and Canada for the "same" offence. In *Van Rassel* (1990) the appellant was an R.C.M.P. officer and also part of an international drug enforcement team operating at the time in the United States. He was tried and acquitted in the United States on a charge of soliciting and accepting bribes, and was subsequently charged in Canada with breach of trust under the Criminal Code. The Supreme Court ruled that section 11(h) did not apply inasmuch as

> the alleged conduct of the accused has a double aspect: first, wrongdoing as a Canadian official with a special duty to the Canadian public . . . and second, wrongdoing as an American official or member of

> the American public, temporarily subject to American law. The accused must now account for his conduct to the Canadian public as well as to the American public, as the offences relate to different duties.[156]

In *Shubley* (1990)[157] a prison inmate was placed in solitary confinement for five days on a restricted diet following his assault of another prisoner. The inmate was later charged under the Criminal Code with assault causing bodily harm. The Court agreed that the disciplinary action was not a criminal proceeding—its purpose being to maintain prison discipline—so that the first test established in *Wigglesworth* did not apply. However, the Court divided as to whether the prison's disciplinary action was a "true penal consequence." The majority decided that it was not and, therefore, that section 11(h) was inapplicable. (Disciplinary action under the Criminal Code *would* be a "true penal consequence.") The prisoner was answerable, therefore, to the state for his assault, to the victim for injury sustained, and to prison officials for breach of discipline.

But what if the Court rules that section 11(h) applies and that the two trials are for the same offence? How does it decide when a person has been "finally" acquitted or "finally" found guilty? This question was addressed in *Corporation professionnelle des médecins du Québec v. Thibault* (1988).[158] Thibault had been acquitted of a charge of practicing medicine contrary to the Quebec Medical Act, and the Quebec medical association was appealing the acquittal under Quebec's Summary Convictions Act. It is true that a person has not been "finally" acquitted or found guilty until the completion of appeal procedures. However, care must be taken to avoid contradicting the intention of section 11(h). Justice (as he then was) Lamer for a unanimous Court stated that the case was not a true appeal but rather "a new trial disguised as an appeal." A person who has been acquitted cannot avoid an appeal if the trial judge has erred, for there would have been no true acquittal. However, Quebec's Summary Convictions Act would permit a second trial even if all the proper rules had been followed. In fact, Lamer declared, "it is just as if once the accused was acquitted the prosecutor filed a new information alleging the same offence based on the same facts. This is precisely the type of abuse that s. 11(h) seeks to prevent." The conclusion? "An accused who is acquitted by a judgement containing no error is 'finally acquitted.'"

Subsection (i): The right, if found guilty of the offence and if the punishment for the offence has been varied between the time of commission and the time of sentencing, to the benefit of the lesser punishment

The penalty to be applied upon conviction is to be that existing at the time the crime was committed unless, before sentencing, the penalty has subsequently been reduced, in which case the lesser penalty must be imposed. In the event of an increased penalty during the interval between the offence and sentencing, an attempt to impose the increased penalty would violate not only this subsection but also the prohibition against *ex post facto* laws (s. 11[g]).

No protection is afforded once the sentence has been pronounced. Neither does this subsection explicitly address the situation of a reduction of the penalty under the law after sentencing but before a final disposition of the case upon appeal. The wording of the subsection does not preclude the lesser penalty, and its spirit would seem to demand it.

➤ **SECTION 12:** Everyone has the right not to be subjected to any cruel and unusual treatment or punishment.

In 1977 Chief Justice Laskin described the phrase "cruel and unusual" (for the purpose of the Bill of Rights) as a "compendious expression of a norm." The criterion for determining if a punishment is cruel and unusual, he said, was whether it is "so excessive as to outrage standards of decency. This is not a precise formula . . . but I doubt whether a more precise one can be found."[159] Justice Lamer, writing ten years later for a Court majority in *Smith (Edward Dewey)*, added that "the test for review under s. 12 of the *Charter* is one of gross disproportionality, because it is aimed at punishments that are more than merely excessive."[160] What are the relevant factors for consideration?

> The court must first consider the gravity of the offence, the personal characteristics of the offender and the particular circumstances of the case in order to determine what range of sentence would have been appropriate to punish, rehabilitate or deter this particular offender or to protect the public from this particular offender. The other purposes which may be pursued by the imposition, in particular the deterrence of other potential offenders, are thus not relevant at this stage of the inquiry. This does not mean that the judge or the legislator can no longer consider general deterrence or other penological purposes that go beyond the particular offender in determining a sentence, but only that the resulting sentence must not be grossly disproportionate to what the offender deserves,

unless of course it is prescribed by law and can be justified by some overriding societal objective and therefore sustained under section 1. He also noted that the effect of the actual sentence must be measured. For example, a 20-year sentence for a first offence against property would be grossly disproportionate and therefore cruel and unusual, as would a 3-month sentence to be served in solitary confinement. Some sentences or treatments would always outrage common decency, he suggested. These would include "the lash, . . . the lobotomization of certain dangerous offenders or the castration of sexual offenders."[161] One might only speculate as to the Court's reaction to forced detoxication, forced treatment for drug addiction, shock treatment administered to mental patients, or forced sterilization of the mentally handicapped.

The Supreme Court has considered section 12 in relation to the minimum sentence prescribed by the Narcotic Control Act for importing or exporting a narcotic, and the minimum required by the Criminal Code for first degree murder. In *Smith (Edward Dewey)* (1987) the Court ruled that a minimum mandatory prison term is not necessarily cruel and unusual, but that the seven-year minimum was "grossly disproportionate" inasmuch as the Narcotic Control Act made no allowance for the degree of danger presented by the narcotic, the quantity of the substance imported, or the possible existence of previous convictions.

In *Luxton* (1990), on the other hand, the court decided that a minimum 25-year sentence with no eligibility for parole for first degree murder did not violate section 12 because it "reflects society's condemnation of a person who has exploited a position of power and dominance to the greatest extent possible. . . . The punishment is not excessive and clearly does not outrage our standards of decency."[161a] Indeed, some people may consider the punishment insufficient. (Neither does the sentence violate section 9; see that commentary.)

The Court has also ruled (*Lyons*, 1987) that an indeterminate prison sentence imposed on a dangerous offender is not cruel and unusual.[162]

> The legislative objectives . . . are of sufficient importance to warrant limiting the rights and freedoms of dangerous offenders and the legislative classification of the target group of offenders meets the highest standard of rationality and proportionality that society can reasonably expect of Parliament. Preventive detention is not cruel and unusual treatment in the case of dangerous offenders, for the group to whom the legislation applies has been functionally defined so as to ensure that persons within the group evince the characteristics that render such detention necessary.

In November 1990 the Supreme Court upheld the release, by the British Columbia Court of Appeal, of a prisoner sentenced thrity-seven years earlier to an indeterminate prison term as a dangerous offender—specifically, as a "criminal sexual psychopath." Justice Cory (for a unanimous Court) noted that the prisoner had already served a term "longer than the vast majority of the most cruel and callous murderers," and that evidence suggested the unlikelihood of his being "an undue risk to society." The Court nevertheless upheld the Appeal Court's condition that the individual be returned to prison if his conduct following release created a danger of serious harm. Cory added that

> the inordinate length of his incarceration has long since become grossly disproportionate to the circumstances of this case. It will only be on rare and unique occasions that a court will find a sentence so grossly disproportionate that it violates the provisions of s. 12 of the Charter. The test for determining whether a sentence is disproportionately long is very properly stringent and demanding. A lesser test would tend to trivialize the Charter.[163]

A change in the law, such that an offence no longer qualifies for an indeterminate prison sentence, does not make the continuation of such a sentence cruel and unusual for an individual sentenced before the law was changed.[164]

Finally, how might the courts deal with a reinstatement of the death penalty for murder, treason or piracy crimes under the Criminal Code that were abolished in the 1970s? In 1977, shortly after the penalty was abolished, the Supreme Court ruled unanimously that the death penalty for murder was not cruel and unusual under the Bill of Rights.[165] The Supreme Court's disposition (expected in 1991) of the case involving the extradition of Charles Ng to the United States, possibly to face the death penalty, may be instructive on this point.

➤ **SECTION 13:** A witness who testifies in any proceedings has the right not to have any incriminating evidence so given used to incriminate that witness in any other proceedings, except in a prosecution for perjury or for the giving of contradictory evidence.

The commentary on section 11(c) noted that a person cannot be compelled to testify at one's own trial, but that if he or she does testify, the prosecution's cross-examination may produce self-incriminating evidence which becomes admissible. It was noted further that the protection of 11(c) does not immunize the person, during other proceedings which are not against him or her, from a requirement to testify or to give evidence that might be self-incriminating. What section 13 does is to exclude that incriminating evidence from any later proceedings against that person ("except in a prosecution for perjury or for the giving of contradictory evidence").

However, there remains a significant gap in the protection afforded such a person because derivative evidence may be used in later proceedings. Bluntly stated:

> The police may feel that a particular individual ought to be charged with an offence but they do not have sufficient evidence. The procedure that could be followed points out the problem; call the individual as a witness at another proceeding, subject him to examination with a view toward uncovering his participation in criminal acts and then lay a charge against him based on the evidence. It will not be necessary in that case to use the evidence as the damage has been done. The derivative evidence could reveal names of potential defence witnesses, possible defences and one could involve the individual in sufficient publicity to destroy the individual's chance for a fair trial. The witness is not given any of the protections guaranteed to an accused as there is no accusation and he will not be allowed to have his day in court until such time as the prosecuting authorities are ready. At that time he is completely exposed.[166]

A major disagreement between Justices La Forest and Wilson as to whether the admission of derivative evidence violates the principles of fundamental justice was noted in the commentary on section 7. One way to close this gap is to interpret section 13 as prohibiting the later use of incriminating derivative evidence. Alternatively, the right of non-compellability under section 11(c) could be extended to include a person likely to be charged, and "proceedings against that person" in 11(c) could be broadened to include proceedings that could prejudice the person's standing as an accused in later proceedings. This might be accomplished through judicial interpretation on the grounds that the right not to testify at one's own trial may be virtually negated by being compelled to testify at other proceedings.[167]

Before the *Dubois*[168] case was decided by the Supreme Court in 1985 a second trial, resulting from mistrial or appeal, on the same charge was not "other proceedings" for the purpose of section 13, and so evidence given at the first trial was admissible at the second. In *Dubois* the Court decided that such a second trial *was* "other proceedings": "To allow the Crown to use, as part of its case, the accused's previous testimony would in effect allow the Crown to do indirectly what it is estopped from doing directly by s. 11(c), *i.e.*, to compel the accused to testify. It would also permit an indirect violation" of section 11(d)'s presumption of innocence. However (*Kuldip*, 1990), cross-examining an accused at his or her second trial for the purpose of "incriminating" the accused—that is, for establishing guilt—must be distinguished from cross-examining "for the purpose of impeaching credibility." The latter is permissible: "An interpretation of s. 13 which insulates an accused from having previous inconsistent statements put to him or her on cross-examination for the sole purpose of challenging credibility would 'stack the deck' too highly in favour of the accused."[168a]

➤ **SECTION 14:** A party or witness in any proceedings who does not understand or speak the language in which the proceedings are conducted or who is deaf has the right to the assistance of an interpreter.

This right extends beyond the accused to include other participants in a trial. Although this section is silent as to the credentials of an interpreter it is essential that such a person be impartial as well as competent in the language of the person to be interpreted. The section does not specify who is to pay for the interpreter, but the reasonable answer is the government, especially if the person requiring the service is unable to pay.

Equality Rights

➤ **SECTION 15:** (1) Every individual is equal before and under the law and has the right to the equal protection and equal benefit of the law without discrimination and, in particular, without discrimination based on race, national or ethnic origin, colour, religion, sex, age or mental or physical disability.

(2) Subsection (1) does not preclude any law, program or activity that has as its object the amelioration of conditions of disadvantaged indviduals or groups including those that are disadvantaged because of race, national or ethnic origin, colour, religion, sex, age or mental or physical disability.

By virtue of section 32(2) this section did not come into effect until April

17, 1985, three years after the Constitution Act was proclaimed. The reason for the delay was to allow time for all governments to make necessary changes to their legislation.

Tarnopolsky suggests that the inclusion of four equality provisions—equality before the law, equality under the law, equal protection of the law, and equal benefit of the law—"made it abundantly evident that the drafters intended to cover every conceivable operation of the law and to require that, in its operation, 'every individual' be treated 'without discrimination', particularly with respect to a number of specifically recognized categories."[169] This view is supported by amendments submitted by Justice Minister Chrétien to the 1980-1981 joint Senate-House of Commons Committee on the Constitution. Intended to overcome narrow judicial interpretation of the Bill of Rights' "equality before the law," the amendments added equality "under" the law to "ensure that the right to equality would apply in respect of the substance as well as the administration of the law"; as well as "equal benefit" of the law "to ensure that people enjoy equality of benefits as well as the protection of the law."[170]

The Supreme Court's first Charter section 15 decision confirmed the need for a broader interpretation of "equality." In that case (*Andrews v. Law Society of British Columbia* 1989),[171] the respondent who was a permanent resident of Canada challenged the requirement of Canadian citizenship for admission to the British Columbia Bar. The importance of the case, however, is the fact that the Court established principles to guide its future rulings. Justice McIntyre (for the Court) rejected a "similarly situated" test of equality which would permit "inequality" if everyone in the particular group were treated alike.

Lavell and Bedard (1973)[172] was a good illustration of this restrictive Bill of Rights interpretation. The case involved discrimination within the Indian Act which then provided that an Indian woman lost her Indian status when she married a white man, but that an Indian man retained his status when he married a white woman. In upholding the Act the Supreme Court ruled that the Bill of Rights referred only to "equality of treatment in the enforcement and application of the laws"—that is, equality in the administration and not the substance of the law. The only requirement was that all Indian women be treated alike. Similarly in *Bliss* (1979),[173] the denial of unemployment insurance benefits to a pregnant woman was deemed not a violation of equality rights because those "similarly situated" were pregnant women, all of whom were treated alike by the legislation. Discrimination based on pregnancy was not discrimination based on sex! *Bliss* was overruled by the Supreme Court in 1989 when, in a non-Charter case (*Brooks*) under the Manitoba Human Rights Act, it ruled that "discrimination on the basis of pregnancy is discrimination on the basis of sex . . . simply because of the basic biological fact that only women have the capacity to become pregnant." It is irrelevant, said the Court, that not all women become pregnant. "The fact, therefore, that the [benefit] plan did not discriminate against all women, but only against pregnant women, did not make the impugned distinction any less discriminatory."[174]

In commenting on the *Lavell* and *Bliss* reasoning Justice McIntyre in

Andrews asserted that it

> is seriously deficient in that it excludes any consideration of the nature of the law. If it were to be applied literally, it could be used to justify the Nuremberg laws of Adolf Hitler. Similar treatment was contemplated for all Jews. The similarity test would have justified the formalistic separate but equal doctrine of *Plessy v. Ferguson*.[175]

The "separate but equal" concept, enunciated by the United States Supreme Court in 1896, remained part of that country's constitution until the doctrine was reversed in *Brown v. Board of Education of Topeka* in 1954, when the Court ruled that separate can never be equal. It is ironic that the Canadian Supreme Court in *Drybones* (1970)[176] had rejected the "similarly situated" test even before the *Lavell* and *Bliss* rulings. Drybones, an Indian convicted of drunkenness off an Indian Reserve, was subject to a penalty under the Indian Act which differed from that applicable to a non-Indian.

But, said McIntyre, section 15 is not intended to eliminate all distinctions; that would deny a place for other Charter sections which promote diversity, such as 27 (multicultural heritage), 2(a) (conscience and religion), and 25 (aboriginal rights and freedoms). Indeed, the provision for affirmative action programs under 15(2) is an explicit acknowledgement that equal treatment may create serious inequality.

If section 15 is intended to preserve equality and to prevent discrimination what, then, is "discrimination"? According to McIntyre,

> discrimination may be described as a distinction, whether intentional or not but based on grounds relating to personality characteristics of the individual or group, which has the effect of imposing burdens, obligations, or disadvantages on such individual or group not imposed upon others, or which withholds or limits access to opportunities, benefits, and advantages available to other members of society. Distinctions based on personal characteristics attributed to an individual solely on the basis of association with a group will rarely escape the charge of discrimination, while those based on an individual's merits and capacities will rarely be so classed.[177]

Section 15 specifies some of these "personal characteristics": race, national or ethnic origin, colour, religion, sex, age, mental disability, physical disability. But what about other bases of discrimination? Citizenship, for example. Clearly, the wording of section 15 does contemplate other possibilities. According to McIntyre the section applies to other bases "analogous" to those enumerated, and the Court agreed that citizenship was one of these. If the Court follows the *Brooks* ruling for section 15 cases, pregnancy will either be an "analogous" basis or it will be explicitly subsumed under sex.

McIntyre then enunciated a two-step test for discrimination.[178] First, the complainant must demonstrate that one of the four aspects of equality in section 15 has been violated. Second, he or she must demonstrate that the impact of the disputed law is discriminatory. This test relates to the position adopted by Justice Wilson in *Big M Drug Mart.* (In that case the Court ruled the Lord's Day Act unconstitutional because its purpose was religious. See the commentary on section 2[a].) Wilson argued that the Charter is effects-oriented and not purpose-oriented: the Charter asks not "whether the legislature has acted for a purpose that is within the scope of the authority of that government, but rather in so acting it has had the effect of violating an entrenched individual right."[179]

A unanimous Court in *Andrews* ruled that the citizenship requirement of the British Columbia Law Society was discriminatory and therefore violated section 15. It divided, however, on the saving power of section 1, the majority agreeing that the proportionality requirement of the *Oakes* test was not met. While it is desirable that lawyers be familiar with Canadian institutions and customs and be committed to Canadian society, citizenship neither ensures nor is necessary to ensure this familiarity and commitment.

Although *Andrews* is the key decision for defining the meaning of section 15, the *Turpin* (1989)[180] ruling is important for its application of the two-part discrimination test enunciated in *Andrews.* (The *Turpin* ruling was noted also in the commentary on section 11[f].) Does the fact that Alberta residents have an opportunity to elect trial by judge rather than judge and jury discriminate against residents in the rest of Canada? The first part of the test asks whether any of the four equality rights in section 15 are denied. Justice Wilson for a unanimous Court suggested that "in these early days of interpreting s. 15 it would be unwise, if not foolhardy, to attempt to provide exhaustive definitions of phrases which are not susceptible of easy definition." She maintained, nevertheless, that equality before the law had been denied, inasmuch as the Criminal Code treats those charged under one section of the Code more harshly than those charged with the same offence under another section (which applies to Alberta).

This distinction was not "discriminatory," however. Extending the *Andrews* reasoning, Wilson stated that in deciding whether a group falls into a category "analogous" to those enumerated in section 15 it is necessary to note "the context of the place of the group in the entire social, political and legal fabric of our society. If the larger context is not examined, the s. 15 analysis may become a mechanical and sterile categorization process conducted entirely within the four corners of the impugned legislation." She concluded that although a person's province of residence might in some circumstances constitute discrimination, "it would be stretching the imagination to characterize persons accused of one of the crimes listed in s. 427 of the *Criminal Code* in all provinces except Alberta" as constituting an analogous category. To call this discrimination under section 15 would do nothing to "advance the purposes of s. 15 in remedying or preventing discrimination against groups suffering social, political and legal disadvantage in our society."

The Criminal Code (s. 146, as of May 1985) provides that "every male person who has sexual intercourse with a female person who (a) is not his wife, and (b) is under the age of fourteen years, whether or not he believes that she is fourteen years of age or more, is guilty of an indictable offence and is liable to imprisonment for life." (Section 147 of the Code adds that "no male shall be deemed to commit an offence . . . while he is under the age of fourteen years.") The Court majority through Justice Wilson ruled in *Hess* and *Nguyen* (1990)[181] that this does not violate equality rights. Wilson noted the Court's *Andrews* ruling that discrimination is not the inevitable result of differential treatment, and her own emphasis (above) in *Turpin* of the need to look to the "larger context." But she acknowledged "the dangers inherent in arguments that seek to justify particular distinctions on the basis of alleged sex-related factors. All too often arguments of this kind have been used to justify subtle and sometimes not so subtle forms of discrimination. They are tied up with popular yet ill-conceived notions about a given sex's strengths and weaknesses or abilities and disabilities." However, she maintained, the impugned legislation created an offence which, as a biological fact, only one sex could commit and which therefore did not violate the right of equality before the law. Just as a proscription of self-induced abortions could not apply to males, so sexual intercourse, which is defined by the Criminal Code in terms of penetration, cannot apply to females with males under age fourteen. Section 147 (quoted above) "reflects the common law's rather artificial assumption than boys under 14 are not physically capable of sexual intercourse . . . [It is] clear that the legislature was of the opinion that, because only males over a certain age were physically capable of penetrating another person, only they needed to be listed as potential accused." It is not up to the courts under section 15, Wilson added, "to decide whether a female who chooses to have intercourse with a boy under fourteen merits the same societal disapprobation as a male who has intercourse with a girl under fourteen. These issues go to the heart of a society's code of sexual morality and are . . . properly left for resolution to Parliament."

Justice McLachlin disagreed: The impugned section "makes distinctions on the enumerated ground of sex. It burdens men as it does not burden women. It offers protection to young females which it does not offer to young males. It is discriminatory" and therefore a violation of section 15(1). Furthermore, because females do not benefit from the discrimination, the law cannot be defended as affirmative action under section 15(2).

Several other section 15 rulings are noteworthy:

One part of the "Constitution of Canada" (as enumerated pursuant to section 52 of the 1982 Constitution Act) cannot invalidate another part. In *Ref. re Bill 30, an Act to Amend the Education Act (Ont.)* (1987),[182] the Court upheld Ontario's Bill 30 under section 93 of the 1867 Constitution Act. The Bill would extend funding to Roman Catholic schools through grade 13 on the same basis as public schools. The section 15 challenge was based on the claim that the Bill created unequal benefits for people in non-Catholic denominational schools, or indeed in nondenominational private schools. (This case is also relevant to Charter section 29 and is noted in the commentary on that section.)

In her delivery of the Court's unanimous decision, Justice Wilson noted that the purpose of section 93 of the 1867 Constitution Act was to allow provinces to legislate "in a *prima facie* selective and distinguishing manner with respect to education whether or not some segments of the community might consider the result to be discriminatory." This means that Bill 30, enacted pursuant to section 93 of the 1867 Act, violates Charter section 15 if the Charter applies to the Bill. The "real contest," then, is between "the operation of the *Charter* in its entirety and the integrity of s. 93," both of which are components of the Constitution of Canada. The Court's conclusion was that the Charter is not intended to repeal other parts of the Constitution. Wilson added that "action taken under the *Constitution Act, 1867* is of course subject to *Charter* review. That is a far different thing from saying that a specific power to legislate as existing prior to April 1982 has been entirely removed by the simple advent of the *Charter*." The only way to eliminate alleged discrimination of this sort would be by formal amendment of the Constitution.

The Crown is not an "individual" for the purpose of section 15. Two 1990 cases decided the same day involved challenges to provisions of the Federal Court Act giving that Court exclusive jurisdiction to hear cases against the Crown (subject, of course, to the possibility of appeal to the Supreme Court).[183] Provincial superior courts are thus denied jurisdiction. The appellants brought action against the Crown in an Ontario court, but the Crown had the charge dismissed on the grounds that the Ontario court lacked jurisdiction. In ruling that the legislation did not infringe section 15, the Supreme Court stated that "the Crown represents the State, and . . . must represent the interests of all members of Canadian society in court claims brought against the Crown in the right of Canada. The interests and obligations of the Crown are vastly different from those of private litigants making claims against the Federal Government." The Court noted further that only Parliament could give private individuals the right to bring actions against the Crown, and that Parliament had the undoubted authority to determine which court would hear cases that might arise. Before this case reached the Supreme Court a bill giving concurrent jurisdiction to the Federal Court and provincial superior courts had received second reading in the House of Commons.

In *Borowski* (1989)[184] the Supreme Court had, but did not seize, the opportunity to decide whether a fetus is an "individual" under section 15 and therefore has the right to equality and, indeed, to life itself. In view of its earlier *Morgentaler* decision which struck down the Criminal Code's abortion section challenged by Borowski, the Court decided the case was moot and declined to rule on this highly controversial issue.

In 1990 the Supreme Court was called upon to decide whether mandatory retirement policies of Ontario public universities violated equality rights based on age (*McKinney*).[185] The Court ruled, first, that universities are not caught by the Charter because their policies are not "law" and are not government activity within the meaning of Charter section 32. (See the commentary on that section.) The Court added that, had the Charter applied, a mandatory retirement policy would be in violation of equality rights because the "similarly situated" test had been repudiated by the *Andrews* ruling (see above). However, mandatory retirement would be sustained (using the *Oakes* test) as a reasonable limitation under section 1 because it is "rationally connected to the objectives" which were identified as academic freedom and excellence. "It is intimately tied to the tenure system which undergirds the specific and necessary ambience of university life and ensures continuing faculty renewal, a necessary process in enabling universities to be centres of excellence on the cutting edge of new discoveries and ideas. It ensures a continuing, and necessary, infusion of new people" especially when a university is not expanding. Finally, and acknowledging the conflicting claims of legitimate social values, the Court concluded that the equality right was minimally impaired.

The Court also ruled that the Ontario Human Rights Code, which protects against age discrimination only to age 65 and is of course government activity, violated section 15, but that it too was saved by section 1. In applying the *Oakes* test the Court accepted the rationale that the legislature had "balanced its concern for not according protection beyond 65 against the fear that . . . a change might result in delayed retirement and delayed benefits for older workers, as well as for the labour market and pension ramifications." In addition, the equality right was impaired as little as possible. In making this assessment the Court deemed as "very relevant" the "historical origins of mandatory retirement at age 65 and its evolution as one of the important structural elements in the organization of the workplace." Furthermore, "the repercussions of abolishing mandatory retirement would be felt in all dimensions of the personnel function with which it is closely entwined: hiring, training, dismissals, monitoring and evaluation, and compensation. The Legislature was faced with competing socio-economic theories and was entitled to choose between them."

The denial of unemployment insurance benefits to individuals over age 65 is a violation of equality rights, and it cannot be upheld by appeal to section 1. The *Oakes* "objectives test" is met: to prevent people (who intend to retire) from abusing the system by receiving both pension and unemployment benefits, to integrate unemployment benefits with other social programs, and at the same time to provide some economic security to the temporarily unemployed. However, "the law has not been carefully designed to achieve . . . the objectives," and may even lack rational connection with them. Finally, the law fails the minimum impairment test. For example, double benefits could be prevented by deducting amounts of pension from the unemployment benefit; and no allowance is made for individuals over 65 who must work.[186]

Does the permissive "may" impose an obligation upon government? According to Parliament's Young Offenders Act (ss. 2-4) "alternative measures may be used" to deal with young offenders. These are measures other than judicial proceedings which will satisfy society's need that there be "supervision, discipline and control," but will also recognize that because of young offenders' "state of dependency and level of development and maturity, [young people] . . . also have special needs and require guidance and assistance." The issue in *R. v.*

S. (S.) (1990) was whether Ontario's then failure to create alternative measures programs violated the accused's right to equality before the law, especially in view of the fact that all other provinces had made such provision. The Supreme Court ruled that the Young Offenders Act "does not impose a mandatory duty," and so the absence of such a program cannot contravene section 15. "To find otherwise would potentially open to *Charter* scrutiny every jurisdictionally permissible exercise of power by a province, solely on the basis that it creates a distinction in how individuals are treated in different provinces."[187]

Notwithstanding the prohibitions in section 15(1), subsection (2) permits the establishment of affirmative action—that is, reverse discrimination—programs intended to benefit disadvantaged individuals or groups. Although section 28 is considered below it seems appropriate to speculate here, in the light of that section, as to the status of affirmative action programs designed to benefit women. Section 28 states that the rights and freedoms "referred to" in the Charter apply equally to male and female persons "notwithstanding anything in this Charter." Would affirmative action programs favouring women withstand challenge based on section 28? (Section 28 is not subject to section 33's legislative override.) Tarnopolsky's response is unequivocal:

> The answer unquestionably must be that such programs must be valid. In the first place, it would be impossible to ignore the clear historical fact that s. 28 was enacted in order to escape the possibility of applying s. 1 so as to "justify" discrimination against women, or s. 33 so as to totally exempt discriminatory statutes. Second, subs. 15(2) is evidently only an explanation of the substantive provision . . . 15(1) which provides for the right of equality and which is reaffirmed in s. 28 as having always to be applied equally to men and women. Subsection (2) merely defines that "affirmative action programs" do not constitute infringement of subs. (1).[188]

The Supreme Court has yet to rule on a section 15(2) issue.

Official Languages of Canada

➤ **SECTION 16:** (1) English and French are the official languages of Canada and have equality of status and equal rights and privileges as to their use in all institutions of the Parliament and government of Canada.

(2) English and French are the official languages of New Brunswick and have equality of status and equal rights and privileges as to their use in all institutions of the legislature and government of New Brunswick.

(3) Nothing in this Charter limits the authority of Parliament or a legislature to advance the equality of status or use of English and French.

The language sections of the Charter, specifically 16-20, may not be interpreted as reducing existing language guarantees. Because of section 21, the guarantees of section 133 of the 1867 Constitution Act and the analogous guarantees of section 23 of the Manitoba Act remain intact, even though the Charter refers only to the Federal and New Brunswick governments. As a consequence, Ottawa and New Brunswick provide the most comprehensive guarantees, Quebec and Manitoba are next, and the other seven provinces have the least. Those seven are bound only by the Charter's section 23—minority language educational rights—which applies throughout the country (except for 23(1)(a) in relation to Quebec). Saskatchewan and Alberta were also bound by section 110 of the North-West Territories Act (analogous to the 1867 Constitution Act's section 133) until they repealed that section in 1988 in response to the Supreme Court's *Mercure* decision. See the commentary on section 133 of the 1867 Constitution Act.

Section 16 entrenches for Ottawa the provision of the 1969 Official Languages Act which declares that "the English and French languages are the official languages of Canada for all purposes of the Parliament and Government of Canada, and possess and enjoy equality of status and equal rights and privileges as to their use in all the institutions of the Parliament and Government of Canada." The phrase "official languages of Canada" means official languages within the jurisdiction of the Federal government. Section 16 also entrenches for New Brunswick the analogous declaration in the 1969 Official Languages of New Brunswick Act. Both statutes were upheld by the Supreme Court in *Jones v. A.G. New Brunswick* in 1975.[189] In those statutes, and now in the present section of the Charter, reference to "government" as well as to "Parliament" or "legislature" suggests that the guarantees extend both languages to the workplace within government institutions including, for example, departments, agencies, Crown corporations, and armed forces.

Subsection (3) permits Ottawa or any province to move beyond the requirements of the Charter. This principle was established in 1975 when the Supreme Court declared (in upholding the constitutionality of Ottawa's Official Languages Act) that section 133 of the Constitution Act did not preclude "the conferring of additional rights or privileges or the imposing of additional obligations respecting the use of English and French, if done in relation to matters within the competence of the enacting Legislature."[190]

Section 16 does not require that government employees be bilingual; indeed, it supports a position that employees should be permitted to work in their chosen language. Tremblay comments, nevertheless, that the section "would not exempt all federal employees to work 'at times' in their second language. But if in reality it is mainly Francophones who must work 'at times' in English, there is not equality under section 16(1) of the Charter, especially if 'at times' means all the time."[191]

Although section 16 has not been the subject of litigation before the Supreme Court it was referred to by members of that Court in *Société des Acadiens du Nouveau-Brunswick v. Association of Parents for Fairness in Education* (1986).[192] The Court ruled that while section 19(2) guarantees the right to use either official language in New Brunswick courts it does not guarantee the right to be understood. Chief Justice Dickson and Justice Wilson maintained, however, that the right to use implied the right to be understood. They used section 16 to support their view. According to Dickson:

> In my opinion, "all institutions of . . . government" includes judicial bodies or courts . . . Despite academic debate about the precise significance of s. 16, at the very least it provides a strong indicator of the purpose of the language guarantees in the *Charter*. By adopting the special constitutional language protections in the *Charter*, the federal government of Canada and New Brunswick have demonstrated their commitment to official bilingualism within their respective jurisdictions. Whether s. 16 is visionary, declaratory or substantive in nature, it is an important interpretive aid in construing the other language provisions of the *Charter*, including s. 19(2).

In explaining the Court's narrow interpretation of the language guarantee, Justice Beetz stressed that language rights were based upon political compromise. Courts should be cautious, therefore, and approach the language rights provisions "with more restraint than they would in construing legal rights." If language rights are to be advanced, the instrument should be political (i.e., legislative), not judicial. This is especially so, he maintained, if other provinces are expected to opt into the Charter's "Official Languages" provisions:

> If . . . the provinces were told that the scheme provided by ss. 16 to 22 of the *Charter* was inherently dynamic and progressive, apart from legislation and constitutional amendment, and that the speed of progress of this scheme was to be controlled mainly by the courts, they would have no means to know with relative precision what it was that they were opting into. This would certainly increase their hesitation in so doing and would run contrary to the principle of advancement contained in s. 16(3).

As additional rationale Beetz noted that section 17 allows individuals to "use" the official language of their choice in the legislature. This could not be construed as a right to be understood for that would require all members to be bilingual. Section 20, on the other hand, gives the public the right to "communicate" in the official language of their choice. Communication must imply understanding. Therefore, he concluded, if the right to be understood had been intended in section 19, "communicate" would have been the obvious word to use. Beetz also commented that if section 16 were held to guarantee the right to be understood in court, this would require a bilingual judiciary—"a surprisingly roundabout and implicit way of amending the judicature provisions of the Constitution of Canada."

The commentary on section 32 notes the meaning that the Supreme Court has given to the phrase "Parliament and Government" or "Legislature and Government."

➤ **SECTION 17:** (1) Everyone has the right to use English or French in any debates and other proceedings of Parliament.

(2) Everyone has the right to use English or French in any debates and other proceedings of the legislature of New Brunswick.

Except for the minor qualification noted in the next paragraph, sections 17(1), 18(1), and 19(1) reproduce the content of section 133 of the 1867 Constitution Act, insofar as that section applies to the Federal government. They do not, therefore, add to the existing constitutional guarantee. Sections 17(2), 18(2), and 19(2) establish similar guarantees for New Brunswick.

The extension of section 17 to "other proceedings" (such as committee proceedings) is an addition to the section 133 guarantee, but it does not represent a change in practice.

For a brief note on the possible significance of the word "use" in this section and in section 19, as contrasted with "communicate" in section 20, see the remarks of Justice Beetz (for the Court) in the commentary on section 16.

➤ **SECTION 18:** (1) The statutes, records and journals of Parliament shall be printed and published in English and French and both language versions are equally authoritative.

(2) The statutes, records and journals of the legislature of New Brunswick shall be printed and published in English and French and both language versions are equally authoritative.

This section needs no comment beyond that for section 17 above and section 133 of the 1867 Constitution Act.

➤ **SECTION 19:** (1) Either English or French may be used by any person in, or in any pleading in or process issuing from, any court established by Parliament.

(2) Either English or French may be used by any person in, or in any pleading in or process issuing from, any court of New Brunswick.

On May 1, 1986, the Supreme Court delivered three judgements relating to language.[193] *MacDonald v. City of Montreal* involved section 133 of the 1867 Constitution Act; *Bilodeau* pertained to the analogous section 23 of the Manitoba Act; and *Société des Acadiens du Nouveau-Brunswick v. Association of Parents for Fairness in Education* referred to the present section 19(2). Because all three involve similar rights they are considered in the commentary on section 133 of the 1867 Act. See also the commentary on section 16 of the present Act, especially for reference to *Société des Acadiens du Nouveau-Brunswick*. Although the right to use either official language in court does not imply the right to be understood, the latter right does nevertheless exist. Its basis is the right to a fair trial (s. 11[d]), the right to understand the language of proceedings (s. 14), and the right to fundamental justice (s. 7).

For New Brunswick as for the Federal government, a "court" includes an administrative tribunal that exercises judicial authority.

➤ **SECTION 20:** (1) Any member of the public in Canada has the right to communicate with, and to receive available services from, any head or central office of an institution of the Parliament or government of Canada in English or French, and has the same right with respect to any other office of any such institution where

(a) there is a significant demand for communications with and services from that office in such language; or

(b) due to the nature of the office, it is reasonable that communications with and services from that office be available in both English and French.

(2) Any member of the public in New Brunswick has the right to communicate with, and to receive available services from, any office of an institution of the legislature or government of New Brunswick in English or French.

The courts will have to interpret "significant demand," "nature of the office," and "reasonable" in subsection (1)(a) and (b). Ottawa's Official Languages Act provided for services in both languages within "federal bilingual districts" established under that Act. The Official Languages of New Brunswick Act included the content of the present section 20(2).

This section will not require bilingualism throughout the Federal public service. Except for head or central offices, with which any person may communicate in either language, the Federal government must ensure only that documents in both languages and employees proficient in both languages are available in those parts of Canada where the demand is "significant." Because New Brunswick residents may communicate with "any [provincial] office" in either language, it seems that bilingualism in the province's public service exceeds that in the Federal service.

For a brief note on the possible significance of the word "communicate" in this section, as contrasted with "use" in sections 17 and 19, see the remarks of Justice Beetz (for the Court) in the commentary on section 16. The commentary on section 32 notes the meaning that the Supreme Court has given to the phrase "Parliament and Government" or "Legislature and Government."

➤ **SECTION 21:** Nothing in sections 16 to 20 abrogates or derogates from any right, privilege or obligation with respect to the English and French languages, or either of them, that exists or is continued by virtue of any other provision of the Constitution of Canada.

The "other" provisions referred to are section 133 of the 1867 Constitution Act (which applies to the Quebec and Federal governments), and section 23 of the Manitoba Act which is analogous to 133.

➤ **SECTION 22:** Nothing in sections 16 to 20 abrogates or derogates from any legal or customary right or privilege acquired or enjoyed either before or after the coming into force of this Charter with respect to any language that is not English or French.

This section grants no right or privilege, but only acknowledges that sections 16-20 of the Charter alter none of the legal or customary rights or privileges that may exist for languages other than English and French. This section does not stand in the way of a government increasing or decreasing any such legal or customary right.

Minority Language Educational Rights

➤ **SECTION 23:** (1) Citizens of Canada

(a) whose first language learned and still understood is that of the English or French linguistic minority population of the province in which they reside, or

(b) who have received their primary school instruction in Canada in English or French and reside in a province where the language in which they received that instruction is the language of the English or French linguistic minority population of the province,

have the right to have their children receive primary and secondary school instruction in that language in that province.

(2) Citizens of Canada of whom any child has received or is receiving primary or secondary school instruction in English or French in Canada, have the right to have all their children receive primary and secondary school instruction in the same language.

(3) The right of citizens of Canada under subsections (1) and (2) to have their children receive primary and secondary school instruction in the language of the English or French linguistic minority population of a province

(a) applies wherever in the province the number of children of citizens who have such a right is sufficient to warrant the provision to them out of public funds of minority language instruction; and

(b) includes, where the number of those children so warrants, the right to have them receive that instruction in minority language educational facilities provided out of public funds.

Whereas the language rights in the previous sections exist without regard to citizenship, minority language educational rights apply only to Canadian citizens. Furthermore, except for section 23(1)(a) which does not apply to Quebec until that province opts in (see section 59), the entire section is applicable throughout Canada including (by virtue of section 30) the Yukon Territory and the Northwest Territories. For practical purposes this section refers to the English minority in Quebec and to the French minority elsewhere. Three groups of citizens are eligible under subsections (1) and (2) to have their children receive primary and secondary school instruction in a province's minority language.

Citizens whose first language learned and still understood—that is, whose mother tongue—is the minority language of the province where they live may have their children educated in that language (subsection [1][a]).

As noted above, the English minority in Quebec does not yet possess this right. This exemption for Quebec was a last-ditch effort to secure Premier Lévesque's support for the November 5, 1981 Constitutional Accord. Because Quebec's 1977 Charter of the French Language (Bill 101) was, and still is, much more restrictive than 23(1)(a) with respect to English-language education, it was deemed prudent to exempt that province. Quebec had no objection to English-language education for its own anglophone population but it wanted all newcomers to be educated in French.

Citizens whose primary school instruction was in Canada and in the minority language of the province where they now live may have their children educated in that language (subsection [1][b]).

This provision, sometimes called the "Canada clause," applies across the country. Although this principle was accepted by all premiers in 1978, the "Quebec clause" of Bill 101 restricted English-language education to children whose parents or older siblings had been educated in English within Quebec. Because this subsection applies to Quebec as well as to the other provinces, the Quebec government sought to have its Quebec clause upheld in the courts by claiming exemption under Charter section 1 in order to protect French language and culture. The Quebec courts rejected the argument on the grounds that the number of children involved would not be significant. They also pointed out that if language and culture were not threatened when Premier Lévesque agreed to the Canada clause in 1978 they were probably not threatened in 1982 when the issue was before the court.[194] A unanimous Supreme Court of Canada dismissed Quebec's appeal (*Quebec Association of Protestant School Boards*)[195] but not on the basis of section 1. The Court ruled that Quebec's legislation was in effect a redefinition of the class of eligible parents and was therefore an amendment to the Charter which could be made only in accordance with the amending procedures of Part V of the Constitution Act. Bill 101 had to yield. This decision is noted in the commentary on section 1.

Citizens who have a child who has received or who is receiving primary or secondary education in Canada, in English or French, may have all of their children receive their primary and secondary education in the same language (subsection [2]).

Although this provision does not specify the right to an education in a province's minority language, it has little practical application except in such a situation, for it is unlikely there would be a problem receiving education in the province's majority language. For example, a person living in a predominantly English-speaking province, and who had a child educated in French in the same or a different province, may have all his or her children educated in French. Nevertheless, without this guarantee there could be a problem for an anglophone living in a predominantly French area within an English-speaking province.

The extent to which citizens may actually claim the rights stated in subsections (1) and (2) is outlined in subsection (3). In the first place these rights apply only where numbers warrant; second, they include (where numbers warrant) the delivery of education in minority-language facilities. The Supreme Court had to address the meanings of subsection (3)'s key phrases in its first case under section 23—*Mahe v. Alberta* (1990).[196] The issue was whether, and to what extent, francophone parents in Edmonton had the right to publicly funded French-language instruction for their children, and the right to manage and control the facilities in which that education was delivered.

Chief Justice Dickson delivered the Court's unanimous decision. When the number of students involved warrants positive action, section 23 provides a sliding scale of institutional requirements. At the lower end of the scale is subsection 3(a) which requires minority language instruction but without special facilities. At the upper end is 3(b) which requires that the instruction be delivered in minority-language educational facilities. These facilities can range, again depending upon the number of students, from an independent school board to representation of the minority group on the existing board, to some lesser degree of management and control such as (perhaps) a classroom within an otherwise majority-language school and system. This sliding scale approach ensures, Dickson maintained, that a minority group will receive all the protection warranted by its numbers. The Court declined to suggest the numbers which might require the several levels of instruction or facilities; rather, it suggested that a standard will have to evolve over time as cases arise. Nevertheless, numbers cannot be the sole criterion. For example, the criteria could vary between rural and urban areas; the bussing or boarding of students may be relevant considerations. Dickson noted that 3(a) refers to numbers "in the province," so that even the alteration of existing school district boundaries might be contemplated under certain circumstances.

Does section 23 require that a measure of "management and control" be placed in the hands of the minority group? The Court's answer was an unequivocal "yes." Why else, Dickson asked rhetorically, was there provision for facilities beyond mere instruction? Although the wording of the English version of 3(b) is ambiguous—does the phrase "minority language educational facilities" refer to facilities "of" or "for" the minority?—the French version seems to support the Court's view. That version reads "*Le droit . . . (b) comprend, lorsque le nombre de ces enfants le justifie, le droit de les faire instruire dans des établissements d'enseignement de la minorité linguistique finances sur les fonds publics.*" The phrase "facilities of the—*de la*—minority language" suggests that the facilities belong to the minority group. The Court has stated that where a Charter provision contains greater ambiguity in one official language than in the other, the less ambiguous language will be used—in this case, the French.

Furthermore, management and control is essential to ensure that issues such as curricula, hiring, and expenditures are decided in a manner satisfactory to the minority culture. Majorities may be unaware of the subtle impact that these decisions may have on culture. What, then, might constitute appropriate management and control in a situation that warrants something just short of an independent school board? The Court established the following principles:

> (1) The representation of the linguistic minority on local boards or other public authorities which administer minority language instruction or facilities should be guaranteed;
> (2) The number of minority language representatives on the board should be, at a minimum, proportional to the number of minority language students in the school district, i.e. the number of minority language students for whom the board is responsible;
> (3) The minority language representatives should have exclusive authority to make decisions relating to the minority language instruction and facilities, including:
> (a) expenditures of funds provided for such instruction and facilities;
> (b) appointment and direction of those responsible for the administration of such instruction and facilities;
> (c) establishment of programs of instruction;
> (d) recruitment and assignment of teachers and other personnel; and
> (e) making of agreements for education and services for minority language pupils.
>
> [Furthermore,] the quality of education provided to the minority language group . . . should be on a basis of reasonable equality with the majority, although it need not be identical, and public funding adequate for this purpose must be provided.[197]

The Chief Justice suggested that reference to the Charter's equality and multicultural provisions (ss. 15, 27) was unnecessary because section 23 contains its own element of equality between the French and English languages. He acknowledged, nevertheless, that section 23's preferred treatment of French and English peoples constituted an exception to sections 15 and 27.

In the case at hand the Court ruled that the number of francophone children in Edmonton warranted "in both pedagogical and financial terms" the creation of a francophone school such as the one then existing. The potential number of francophone students did not, in the Court's opinion, require an independent francophone school board but it did justify the application of the principles enumerated above.

In view of the right granted by section 23 that all instruction be in the French language, the Court also had to rule on an Alberta School Act regulation requiring at least 20% (300 minutes per week) instruction time to be in the English language. Was the requirement a reasonable limit which could be saved by section 1? The Court acknowledged the necessity of some English instruction for all Alberta students, and that 20% may indeed be appropriate for francophone schools. However, the Alberta government had not demonstrated that the 20% requirement infringed section 23 rights as little as possible, and so the regulation was not saved. Dickson added that the Court's ruling did not preclude a future attempt by the Alberta government to demonstrate the reasonableness (under section 1) of some mandatory English-language instruction.

Enforcement

➤ **SECTION 24:** (1) Anyone whose rights or freedoms, as guaranteed by this Charter, have been infringed or denied may apply to a court of competent jurisdiction to obtain such remedy as the court considers appropriate and just in the circumstances.

(2) Where, in proceedings under subsection (1), a court concludes that evidence was obtained in a manner that infringed or denied any rights or freedoms guaranteed by this Charter, the evidence shall be excluded if it is established that, having regard to all the circumstances, the admission of it in the proceedings would bring the administration of justice into disrepute.

This enforcement provision applies only to the Charter. Section 52 contemplates the invalidation of laws that violate the "Constitution of Canada" generally. See the commentary on that section.

Subsection (1): This subsection raises a number of questions.

May only the aggrieved person apply to the courts, or may application be made on behalf of the aggrieved by someone else? The wording of the section seems clear—only the aggrieved may apply—and this interpretation has been made explicit in at least two cases. Speaking for the Supreme Court, Justice Sopinka in *Borowski* (1989)[198] denied the applicability of section 24(1) because Borowski alleged "that the rights of a foetus, not his own rights, have been violated." And according to Justice Wilson, speaking for herself and Chief Justice Dickson, "I want to stress [that] an application for relief under s. 24(1) can only be made by a person whose right under s. 11(b) [in that particular case, *Rahey* (1987)] has been infringed. This is clear from the opening words of s. 24(1)."[199]

Must the alleged infringement already have occurred at the time of application, or may application be made on the basis of apprehended infringement? According to Justice (as he then was) Dickson for the Court in *Operation Dismantle* (1985) the appellants "must at least be able to establish a threat of violation, if not an actual violation, of their rights under the Charter" for section 24(1) to apply.[200]

What is a "court of competent jurisdiction"? As a general rule it is the trial court inasmuch as the judge has jurisdiction over the person and the subject matter. A provincial superior court, also, has original jurisdiction to hear section 24(1) applications; however, such a court "should usually decline to exercise its jurisdiction unless the trial court is an inappropriate forum to seek a remedy because, for example, it is itself allegedly in violation of the *Charter's* guarantees."[201] In the case at hand (*Rahey*, 1987) the trial judge delayed proceedings beyond a "reasonable time" through repeated adjournments—nineteen in all.

The Court has also ruled that neither a preliminary hearing magistrate (as empowered by the Criminal Code)[202] nor an extradition judge (under the Extradition Act)[203] constitutes a court of competent jurisdiction for the purpose of 24(1). In the latter instance, Justices Wilson and Lamer disagreed if the extradition judge is also a superior court judge.

What remedies are available under 24(1)? Justice McIntyre has noted that "it is difficult to imagine language which could give the court a wider and less fettered discretion. It is impossible to reduce this wide discretion to some sort of binding formula for general application in all cases."[204] Each case must, therefore, be decided on its own merits. For example, if an accused has not been tried within a "reasonable time" (s. 11[b]), a stay of proceedings must be the minimum remedy. By that time "no trial, not even the fairest possible trial, is permissible" for this "would be to participate in a further violation of the *Charter*."[205] This is not to deny the propriety of additional remedies such as damages when circumstances warrant. Justice (as he then was) Lamer suggested that cases might arise when the appropriate remedy is not merely a stay but an acquittal, although this point had not at the time been raised in the Supreme Court or any lower court.

Given the breadth of possible remedies available under 24(1), might one of the remedies be the exclusion of evidence whose inclusion "would bring the administration of justice into disrepute"? The Supreme Court's answer is "no." As explained by Justice Le Dain, provision in 24(2) for the remedy of exclusion, following the generality of 24(1), must imply that exclusion was to be governed solely by 24(2):

> It is not reasonable to ascribe to the framers of the Charter an intention that the courts should address two tests or standards on an application for the exclusion of evidence—first, whether the admission of the evidence would bring the administration of justice into disrepute, and if not, secondly, whether its exclusion would nevertheless be appropriate and just in the circumstances. The inevitable result of this alternative test or remedy would be that s. 24(2) would become a dead letter.[206]

Subsection (2): The treatment of "tainted" evidence under the Charter lies between that in pre-Charter Canada and that in the United States. In Canada, evidence obtained illegally or in violation of the Canadian Bill of Rights was admissible if it was relevant, whereas in the United States the admissibility of such evidence is forbidden no matter how relevant it may be.[207] Under the Charter, evidence gained in violation of the Charter is not admissible if, "having regard to all the circumstances," it "would bring the administration of justice into disrepute."

Chief Justice Dickson has noted that "the decision to exclude evidence always represents a balance between the interests of truth on one side and the integrity of the judicial system on the other. In some cases the harm to the integrity of the judicial system resulting from excluding the evidence will be so great that exclusion and not admission will bring the administration of justice into disrepute."[208] This indeed is the dilemma, and the Supreme Court attempted to address it in the twenty-six cases that had come before it by mid-1991. Perhaps the most fundamental question is to determine in whose eyes there must be a perception of disrepute.

Although the Supreme Court had been faced with section 24(2) on two previous occasions, it was in *Collins* (1987) that it established the principles to guide the Court's later rulings.[209] In delivering the Court's ruling Justice Lamer began with the "reasonable person" test proposed by Yves-Marie Morissette.[210] That test asks if the admission of evidence would bring disrepute "in the eyes of the reasonable man, dispassionate and fully apprised of the circumstances of the case." The difficulty of grappling in a meaningful way with the concept of reasonableness is illustrated by Lamer's added comments:

> The reasonable person is usually the average person in the community, but only when that community's current mood is reasonable.
>
> The decision is thus not left to the untrammelled discretion of the judge. In practice, as Professor Morissette wrote, the reasonable person test is there to require of judges that they "concentrate on what they do best: finding within themselves, with cautiousness and impartiality, a basis for their own decisions, articulating their reasons carefully and accepting review by a higher court where it occurs." It serves as a reminder to each individual judge that his discretion is grounded in community values, and, in particular, long term community values. He should not render a decision that would be unacceptable to the community when that community is not being wrought with passion or otherwise passing stress due to current events.[211]

Canadian courts have considered many factors in deciding the issue of repute. Lamer groups these into three broad categories.

What effect would the admission of evidence have on the fairness of the trial? If it is adverse then, depending upon the two other broad categories, the evidence should be excluded. The factors in this category are the nature of the evidence and the nature of the Charter right that has been violated. "Real" evidence—evidence such as the possession of drugs or a murder weapon which exists independently of the Charter violation—will seldom affect the trial's fairness. However, self-incriminating evidence such as a statement given following a violation of the Charter (such as the denial of the right to counsel—the most common violation of this nature) may well make the trial unfair. When an individual is thus conscripted against himself or herself, being used to build the case against him or her, the evidence should normally be excluded.

How serious is the Charter violation, and what were the reasons for it? Was the violation committed in good faith, inadvertent, or merely of a technical nature? Was it deliberate and flagrant? Was it motivated by urgency or necessity to preserve evidence from loss or destruction? Lamer suggested that a Charter violation is more serious when the police could have gained the evidence by acting properly. The case at hand involved the unreasonable search, without a warrant, of an individual for drug possession. The police officer had seized the person in a pub, wrestled her to the floor, and secured a bag of heroin clenched in her hand. According to Lamer (for the Court) the officer lacked reasonable and proper grounds for the search. Lamer acknowledged that the evidence would be unlikely to affect the trial's fairness, and he admitted that its exclusion might bring the administration of justice into disrepute because someone guilty of a serious offence would go free. However, he believed that the disrepute would be greater if the Court admitted the evidence and thereby condoned the "flagrant and serious" violation of section 8's protection against unreasonable search. "We cannot accept that police officers take flying tackles at people and seize them by the throat when they do not have reasonable and probable grounds to believe that those people are either dangerous or handlers of drugs."[212] (The throat hold is common to prevent the swallowing of drugs contained in a balloon or condom.)

Would the administration of justice be brought into greater disrepute by excluding or by admitting the evidence gained through a Charter violation? That, of course, is the fundamental question. Lamer suggested that the more serious the offence, the more likely the exclusion of evidence would bring disrepute. Nevertheless, the seriousness of an offence could not make evidence admissible if the trial would thereby be unfair. Indeed, "the more serious the offence, the more damaging to the system's repute would be an unfair trial."[213]

The Supreme Court had ruled on the admissibility of evidence under section 24(2) in about twenty-six cases through mid-1991. Fifteen of these cases involved violations of the right to counsel (s. 10[b]); evidence was excluded in eight of these, and partially in a ninth. Ten (including one of the fifteen above) concerned violations of the right against unreasonable search or seizure (s. 8); evidence was excluded in four of them. In the one case of arbitrary detention (s. 9), and the one involving the violation of the principles of fundamental justice (s. 7), the evidence was excluded. In total, therefore, evidence was excluded in slightly more than half of the cases. There were nine split decisions, six of them occurring when the Court majority had ruled against the admissibility of evidence.

It is probably inevitable that, in spite of the Court's best efforts to determine whether evidence should be admitted, some people will question the "justice" of allowing criminals to go free on grounds that many people may consider to be technicalities. It is debatable whether the public is as concerned with some of the niceties of law and the constitution as they are with punishment of the guilty. Does the community at large really believe that an accused who voluntarily confesses to the crime of armed robbery, for example, should have the confession declared inadmissible because the police officer who did the questioning continued to do so when the accused asked to see a lawyer?

Would the administration of justice be brought into disrepute by the admission of such a confession? This is what the Supreme Court decided in *Manninen* (1987),[214] notwithstanding the Court's acknowledgement that the accused's guilt had been clearly established by the confession. Or did the administration of justice fall into disrepute in the eyes of the community by the declaration of inadmissibility?

In *Greffe* (1990),[215] the Court excluded evidence secured in violation of both the right to counsel and the right to be secure against unreasonable search and seizure. Greffe was subjected to a body search, during which some heroin was found in a condom in his anal cavity. Although the Court acknowledged that this "real" evidence would not likely affect the trial's fairness, the Charter violations were so serious as to require the exclusion of the evidence. The seriousness was increased by the Crown's failure to elicit from the police, information which would support the claim that there were reasonable and probable grounds to believe Greffe was in possession of heroin, and which would therefore justify a warrantless search. Although the R.C.M.P. had alerted Canada Customs that Greffe was arriving from abroad with a quantity of heroin, there was conflicting police testimony as to whether the actual charge was for outstanding traffic warrants or for importing heroin. Justice Lamer (for the Court majority) felt that he was "unfortunately given to no other choice but to proceed on the premise that the [rectal] search proceeded as incident to an arrest for outstanding traffic warrants." Chief Justice Dickson did not share Lamer's concern. He believed that the "reasonable person would be shocked and appalled to learn that an accused, unquestionably guilty of importing a sizable amount of heroin, was acquitted of all charges because of a slip of the tongue by a police officer when the accused was arrested and read his s. 10 counsel rights."

Lamer added that, especially when a person may be acquitted of a serious crime when evidence is excluded, the Court must consider the long-term effects of "regular admission or exclusion of evidence on the repute of the administration of justice." While he supported the conviction and punishment of those guilty of serious crimes, he feared that the long-run effect of admitting evidence obtained in violation of the Charter would be that "s. 24(2) will only be used to exclude evidence when less serious crimes are involved." Many people might applaud such an effect!

It is paradoxical that evidence gained illegally, but which does not infringe or deny rights under the Charter, is not subject to this admissibility test. Such evidence is not, therefore, inadmissible by virtue of its having been secured illegally unless its inadmissibility is declared by a particular statute. For example, section 189 of the Criminal Code declares that "a private communication that has been intercepted is inadmissible as evidence . . . unless . . . the interception was lawfully made."[215a] Consider this hypothetical situation:

> Suppose that police extract a confession from an accused person by falsely telling him that his aged mother is at death's door, and showing him a forged letter, purportedly from the mother, urging him, as her last wish, to confess. Although the conduct of the police would

> be both criminal and likely to bring the administration of justice into disrepute, the confession would probably be admissible, because no violation of Charter rights would likely be involved.[216]

The entire controversy over the admission of evidence and the repute of the justice system gives some credence to the following assertion (made in reference to the United States): "Our way of upholding the Constitution is not to strike at the man who breaks it, but to let off somebody else who broke something else."[217]

General

➤ **SECTION 25:** The guarantee in this Charter of certain rights and freedoms shall not be construed so as to abrogate or derogate from any aboriginal, treaty or other rights or freedoms that pertain to the aboriginal peoples of Canada including

(a) any rights or freedoms that have been recognized by the Royal Proclamation of October 7, 1763; and

(b) any rights or freedoms that now exist by way of land claims agreements or may be so acquired.

This section creates no new rights, and perhaps does little else than protect "aboriginal, treaty or other" rights and freedoms from the equality provision of section 15. Aboriginal and treaty rights have been described as follows:

> "Aboriginal rights" would refer to rights that originated in the fact that the native peoples were in possession of most of the lands now making up Canada, and the phrase "aboriginal rights" recognizes that some of these rights have survived the process of European settlement. "Treaty rights" would refer to rights based on promises [such as the allocation of specific lands as Indian reserves, the making of annual payments, and the granting of hunting and fishing rights in the ceded lands] made to the native peoples, often in return for the surrender of land rights, in agreements usually styled "treaties." In addition, s. 35(3) [of the 1982 Constitution Act] provides that "treaty rights" includes "rights that now exist by way of land claims agreements or may be so acquired." This makes clear that modern "land claims agreements" possess the same constitutional status as the old treaties with the Indians.[218]

Specific reference to the aboriginal peoples of Canada is made in sections 35, 35.1, and 37.1, as well as 25. Section 37 was repealed on April 17, 1983, in accordance with section 54. Section 25 is broader than section 35 which is not part of the Charter and which is restricted to "existing" and to "aboriginal and treaty" rights. The term "aboriginal peoples" includes (s. 35[2]) Indians, Inuit, and Métis.

Subsection (b) was replaced by the 1983 Constitution Amendment Proclamation with the agreement of representatives of the aboriginal peoples reached at the March 1982 constitutional conference held pursuant to section 37. The altered wording is probably for clarification only. As originally enacted subsection (b) read as follows:

> (b) any rights or freedoms that may be acquired by the aboriginal peoples of Canada by way of land claims settlement.

The extent of rights protected by the 1763 Royal Proclamation is vague. Although lands reserved for Indians were west of Quebec, their western boundary was undefined. Not surprisingly, the extent of reserved lands within present-day Canada has been disputed. Some native leaders consider the Proclamation as the basis of their claims to "sovereignty" (or "self-government"—the terms have not been defined or used consistently), but so far as the courts are concerned "there was from the outset never any doubt that sovereignty and legislative power, and indeed the underlying title, to such lands vested in the Crown."[219] The section 25 guarantee of rights or freedoms "that have been recognized" by the Proclamation or "that now exist" in land claims agreements might therefore mean, Greene adds, "only that the Charter cannot be interpreted so as to *further* erode the rights that the native peoples . . . thought they had" in the Proclamation and treaties. The fact that natives lost all nineteen section 25 court cases between 1982 and 1985 seems to confirm that a narrow interpretation of this section prevails.[220]

The Royal Proclamation is not part of the "Constitution of Canada" as included in the Schedule to this Act.

➤ **SECTION 26:** The guarantee in this Charter of certain rights and freedoms shall not be construed as denying the existence of any other rights or freedoms that exist in Canada.

This section makes explicit that the rights and freedoms within the Charter are not meant to be exhaustive, and that they are not to be construed as limiting any non-Charter rights existing by statute or common law. Non-Charter rights are subject to change, including elimination, by legislative action. They include the Saskatchewan, Alberta, and Quebec bills of rights insofar as their provisions are not included in the Charter. They also include the following provisions of the Canadian Bill of Rights which are not duplicated by the Charter:[221]

(1) Section 1(a), "the right of the individual to . . . enjoyment of property, and the right not to be deprived thereof except by due process of law."

(2) Section 1(b), "the right of the individual to equality before the law." This exception ended on April 17, 1985, when the Charter's section 15 came into force.

(3) Section 2(e), the right of a person "to a fair hearing in accordance with the principles of fundamental justice for the determination of his rights and obligations."

(4) Section 3, requiring the Minister of Justice to examine subordinate legislation and all bills introduced in the House of Commons, to determine whether there is any inconsistency with the Bill of Rights, and to report any inconsistency to the House.

➤ **SECTION 27:** This Charter shall be interpreted in a manner consistent with the preservation and enhancement of the multicultural heritage of Canadians.

This section, which creates no rights, seems to be basically "an interpretive guideline for the *Charter*."[222] It could also be valuable politically, especially for cultural minorities who seek inclusion in affirmative action programs. One should note, however, the seeming inconsistency between this section and section 23's minority language educational rights which apply only to English and French minorities.

While section 27 has not been raised in the Supreme Court as a constitutional issue, members of the Court have referred to it in several cases. For example, Chief Justice Dickson in *Big M Drug Mart* (1985)[223] acknowledged the inconsistency between the preservation and enhancement of our multicultural heritage and a view that Parliament may compel universal observance of a particular religion's day of rest. Justice Wilson suggested in *Société des Acadiens du Nouveau-Brunswick*[224] that section 27 was not to be interpreted so as to "deter the movement towards the equality of status of English and French until such time as a similar status could be attained for all the other languages spoken in Canada." And Chief Justice Dickson in *Keegstra* stressed the principle of non-discrimination as integral to the meaning of section 27.[225]

Section 27 was the basis for part of Wilson's dissenting opinion in *Edwards Books and Art* (1986).[226] Ontario's Retail Business Holidays Act permitted some (but not all) retail store owners who close on Saturdays for religious observance to remain open on Sundays in recognition of their section 2(a) religious freedom. Only those businesses with fewer than eight employees and having less than 5,000 square feet had this option (s. 3[4] of the Act). This meant that the violation of the religious freedom of other Saturday observers was sanctioned by law. According to Wilson:

> It seems to me that when the *Charter* protects group rights such as freedom of religion, it protects the rights of all members of the group. It does not make fish of some and fowl of the others. For, quite apart from considerations of equality, to do so is to introduce an invidious distinction into the group and sever the religious and cultural tie that binds them together. It is, in my opinion, an interpretation of the *Charter* expressly precluded by s. 27 which requires the *Charter* to be interpreted "in a manner consistent with the preservation and enhancement of the multicultural heritage of Canadians."

The inconsistency created by the Act cannot, Wilson concluded, be a reasonable limit under section 1.

➤ **Section 28:** Notwithstanding anything in this Charter, the rights and freedoms referred to in it are guaranteed equally to male and female persons.

This section, which is to operate "notwithstanding anything in this Charter," has the merit of preventing sex discrimination that might otherwise be attempted by means of appeal to section 1 or use of the "notwithstanding" provision of section 33. The potential significance of this section was greater during the first three years of the Charter before section 15 became operative. When section 33 was added on November 5, 1981, during the final effort to reach a consensus it seemed logical to make section 28 subject to the override inasmuch as section 15 was also subject to it. However, in response to the lobbying of women's groups section 28 was removed from the override (and agreed to by all signatories to the Accord) before the end of November.

The unlikelihood of section 28 being upheld by the courts to prevent affirmative action programs to benefit females was noted in the commentary on section 15(2). Nevertheless, it was concern that this could in fact happen that delayed Saskatchewan's agreement for a free-standing section 28.[227]

➤ **Section 29:** Nothing in this Charter abrogates or derogates from any rights or privileges guaranteed by or under the Constitution of Canada in respect of denominational, separate or dissentient schools.

The purpose of this section is to ensure that the Charter cannot be interpreted so as to endanger the security of the obviously unequal education rights in section 93 of the 1867 Constitution Act (and, through extension by British order-in-council, to British Columbia and Prince Edward Island), as well as education rights in the corresponding provisions of the Manitoba Act, Alberta Act, Saskatchewan Act, and Terms of Union of Newfoundland with Canada Act. The reason is that these rights (at least in the original section 93) were an essential part of the Confederation bargain, and the framers of the Charter were not about to permit their demise.

By mid-1991 the Supreme Court had twice been called upon to interpret this section. In 1985 the Government of Ontario wanted to know if its Bill 30 was constitutional. The Bill would extend full funding through high school to Roman Catholic schools on the same basis as public schools. Ontario's Court of Appeal ruled that the Bill was constitutional, and an appeal went to the Supreme Court of Canada which confirmed that decision. The Supreme Court decided that Bill 30 essentially returned to Roman Catholic separate school supporters the rights guaranteed by section 93(1) of the 1867 Constitution Act. It was, in other words, a right or privilege guaranteed by or under the Constitution of Canada and therefore protected by section 29 from Charter review. (Justice Wilson for the Court suggested, nevertheless, that section 29 was unnecessary to justify Bill 30. See the commentary on section 15.)

Wilson then speculated what the situation would be if the rights granted by Bill 30 were deemed to have been provided as post-Confederation legislation under section 93(3) rather than as a return of the rights guaranteed by section 93(1).[228] "The question then becomes: does s. 29 protect rights or privileges conferred by legislation passed under the province's plenary power in relation to education under the opening words of s. 93?" Wilson believed it does although, as for rights under 93(1), she suggests it is not necessary. The protection is not the same as that afforded section 93(1) rights through the possibility of legal challenge to legislation that prejudicially affects them. "Their protection from *Charter* review lies not in the guaranteed nature of the rights and privileges conferred by the legislation but in the guaranteed nature of the province's plenary power to enact that legislation." Rights and privileges under 93(1) can be protected either by legal challenge or (under 93[3]) by a political appeal to the governor general in council. Rights and privileges under 93(3) can be protected only by the political challenge. There is no question of the legal competence of a province to pass legislation after Confederation under 93(3) affecting denominational schools.

The second case involving section 29 was *Mahe* (1990).[229] This case is discussed in the commentary on section 23. Chief Justice Dickson for a unanimous Court ruled that conferring upon minority language parents the right to manage and control minority language educational facilities does not infringe any rights or privileges guaranteed to separate schools under section 93 of the 1867 Constitution Act or the corresponding section 17 of the Alberta Act. (The Court decided that the two provisions are similar enough to warrant identical interpretation.) Dickson noted the Court's 1989 *Greater Montreal Protestant School Board* ruling that "section 93(1) protects . . . the denominational aspects of denominational schools . . . [and] the non-denominational aspects which are necessary to give effect to denominational guarantees."[230] The right to manage and control relates to a non-denominational aspect of education—namely, the language of instruction. In *Mahe*, the trustees who manage and control will be part of the denominational school board and so that board's power to operate its entire system remains intact. Because section 29 protects the rights or privileges of denominational schools, and because those rights are not infringed by conferring the right to manage and control, section 29 is inapplicable to the case at hand.

➤ **SECTION 30:** A reference in this Charter to a province or to the legislative assembly or legislature of a province shall be deemed to include a reference to the Yukon Territory and the Northwest Territories, or to the appropriate legislative authority thereof, as the case may be.

The intent of this section is clear. Indeed, section 32(1)(a) would appear to cover almost the same purpose because the governments of the Yukon Territory and the Northwest Territories are under the direct control of Parliament. However, because sections 3, 4, and 5, of the Charter refer explicitly to the "House of Commons," "Parliament," or "legislative assembly," they would not necessarily apply to territorial councils without section 30. Furthermore, reference to "province" in sections 6 (mobility rights) and 23 (minority language educational rights) would not automatically include the territories.

➤ **SECTION 31:** Nothing in this Charter extends the legislative powers of any body or authority.

This cautionary provision may be partly the result of provincial apprehension that the reduction in their legislative authority, which accompanies the entrenchment of Charter rights, could somehow increase the power of Parliament. While it is true that the Charter does not extend legislative authority, it may well have a centralizing or at least a homogenizing impact. This was noted in Chapter 4 under "Federalism."

Application of Charter

➤ **SECTION 32:** (1) This Charter applies

(a) to the Parliament and government of Canada in respect of all matters within the authority of Parliament including all matters relating to the Yukon Territory and Northwest Territories; and

(b) to the legislature and government of each province in respect of all matters within the authority of the legislature of each province.

(2) Notwithstanding subsection (1), section 15 shall not have effect until three years after this section comes into force.

There has been disagreement whether subsection (1) makes the Charter applicable only to governments, or whether it applies also to relationships between private individuals. In *RWDSU v. Dolphin Delivery* (1986) the Supreme Court ruled that the Charter "does not apply to private litigation completely divorced from any connection with government."[231] In other words, notes Hogg, "such actions as an employer restricting an employee's freedom of speech or assembly, a parent restricting the mobility of a child, or a landlord discriminating on the basis of race in his selection of tenants, cannot be breaches of the Charter" because no legislative or governmental action has been involved. Redress must be found elsewhere such as, for example, in laws pertaining to human rights, labour, families, and property.[232] The Court's view also accords with the intention of the Department of Justice that the Charter "addresses itself only to laws and relationships between the state and individuals, it does not attempt to deal with private relationships."[233]

Do decisions of the cabinet based upon the royal prerogative, a source of authority which in a historical sense exists independently of Parliament, fall within the scope of "matters within the authority of Parliament"? In *Operation Dismantle* (1985) the Supreme Court unanimously said "yes." The argument of the Court was stated by Justice Wilson:

> The royal prerogative [in this case, the authority for making international agreements] is "within the authority of Parliament" in the

> sense that Parliament is competent to legislate with respect to matters falling within its scope. Since there is no reason in principle to distinguish between cabinet decisions made pursuant to statutory authority and those made in the exercise of the royal prerogative, and since the former clearly fall within the ambit of the *Charter*, I conclude that the latter do so also.[234]

Justice McIntyre for the Court in *Dolphin Delivery*[235] suggested that the words "Parliament and government of Canada" are intended to distinguish between the legislative and executive (including the administrative) branches of government: "where the word 'government' is used . . . it refers not to government in its generic sense—meaning the whole of the governmental apparatus of the state—but to a branch of government. The word 'government,' following as it does the words 'Parliament' and 'Legislature,' must then . . . refer to the executive or administrative branch of government."

But how far beyond the Acts of Parliament or provincial legislatures, and cabinet decisions, does the Charter extend before the area of "private litigation completely divorced from government" is reached? The Charter will apply wherever "one party invokes or relies upon . . . [governmental action] to produce an infringement of the *Charter* rights of another," and this will include rules and regulations made pursuant to statutes, "possibly municipal by-laws, and by-laws and regulations of other creatures of Parliament and the Legislatures."

In *Dolphin Delivery*, however, the Canada Labour Code did not refer to secondary picketing, and so no government action was involved. The litigation was strictly between private parties. (Federal jurisdiction was involved because interprovincial transportation and communication were affected.) The case involved the threatened picketing of Dolphin Delivery, a courier company which made deliveries for Purolator. Purolator had locked out its employees in a labour dispute and Dolphin Delivery continued to do business indirectly through a third company. As a result, the Purolator employees' union threatened to picket Dolphin Delivery.

Is the Charter applicable to the personnel policies of public universities? In December 1990 the Supreme Court in a split decision (*McKinney v. University of Guelph*)[236] ruled that it was not. The fact that universities are created by statute does not of itself make their actions subject to Charter review. "Although the Charter is not limited to activities discharging inherently governmental functions, more would have to be shown to make them [the universities] subject to Charter review than that they engaged in activities or the provision of services that are subject to the legislative jurisdiction of either the federal or provincial governments." Therefore, each university is its "own master with respect to the employment of professors." Its policies (mandatory retirement in this case—see the commentary on section 15) are not "law" as would make them subject to the Charter.

Justices Wilson and Cory disagreed with this part of the ruling. According to Wilson, governments perform many roles in relation to the people and some of these "cannot be best effected directly by the apparatus of government itself. Form therefore should not be placed ahead of substance. . . . The nature of the relationship between . . . [a separate entity, such as the university] and government must be examined in order to decide whether when it [the entity] acts it truly is 'government' which is acting." Upon further analysis Wilson concluded that "government" was indeed acting. Her reasoning is analogous to her position in *Big M Drug Mart* that the Charter is effects-oriented rather than purpose-oriented.

Section 32(2) is now spent inasmuch as section 15 came into force on April 17, 1985. The reason for the delay was to enable all governments to make the necessary adjustments to their laws.

➤ **SECTION 33:** (1) Parliament or the legislature of a province may expressly declare in an Act of Parliament or of the legislature, as the case may be, that the Act or a provision thereof shall operate notwithstanding a provision included in section 2 or sections 7 to 15 of this Charter.

(2) An Act or a provision of an Act in respect of which a declaration made under this section is in effect shall have such operation as it would have but for the provision of this Charter referred to in the declaration.

(3) A declaration made under subsection (1) shall cease to have effect five years after it comes into force or on such earlier date as may be specified in the declaration.

(4) Parliament or the legislature of a province may re-enact a declaration made under subsection (1).

(5) Subsection (3) applies in respect of a re-enactment made under subsection (4).

This is the "notwithstanding" or "legislative override" provision. These provisions are not new in Canada. The Canadian Bill of Rights, for example, states in section 2 that "every law of Canada shall, unless it is expressly declared by an Act of the Parliament of Canada that it shall operate notwithstanding the Canadian Bill of Rights, be so construed and applied as not to abrogate, abridge or infringe ... any of the rights and freedoms herein recognized and declared." When the Bill of Rights was enacted it also contained an amendment to the War Measures Act providing a blanket exemption of that Act from the provisions of the Bill of Rights. When the War Measures Act was proclaimed on October 16, 1970, it therefore operated "notwithstanding" the Bill of Rights. The proclamation and the Public Order Regulations made pursuant to the War Measures Act were revoked by the Public Order (Temporary Measures) Act on December 2, 1970. This Act, the only other Federal statute to invoke the notwithstanding provision of the Bill of Rights, expired on April 30, 1971, although its life could have been extended by a joint resolution of the Senate and the House of Commons. The Emergencies Act replaced the War Measures Act in 1988, but it has no notwithstanding clause. This means that any action taken pursuant to it which infringes Charter rights could be sustained only by successful appeal to Charter section 1. The Quebec Charter of Human Rights and

Freedoms as well as the Alberta and Saskatchewan bills of rights contain "notwithstanding" provisions. Quebec's was used nine times between 1975 and 1982.[237]

Before 1982, Canada's legislatures collectively enjoyed virtual supremacy in that, with few exceptions, the distribution of legislative powers between the two orders of government was exhaustive. Section 33 was the major compromise at the eleventh hour on November 5, 1981, between those (especially Prime Minister Trudeau) who desired a strongly entrenched Charter, and those (most notably Manitoba Premier Lyon) who objected in principle to entrenchment. Without the compromise the Constitutional Accord would have been impossible.

Subsection (1) authorizes Parliament, provincial legislatures, and (through section 30) territorial councils to enact legislation in direct contravention of the Charter's fundamental freedoms (s. 2), legal rights (ss. 7-14), and equality rights (s. 15). The remaining rights and freedoms are inviolable unless appeal to section 1 is successful. An Act containing the override must "expressly declare" that the legislation "shall operate notwithstanding" the Charter's guarantee. In light of the *Ford* decision (noted below) upholding Quebec's omnibus override, it is reasonable to conclude that use of section 33 is not itself reviewable under Charter section 1. Before *Ford*, differing opinions on this point had been expressed.[238] The framers of section 33 certainly did not anticipate a section 1 override of the override.

Subsection (3) places a five-year time limit on any override, but the declaration may be repeated, presumably indefinitely, under subsections (4) and (5). The purpose of the time limit is, therefore, to force periodic review. The five-year maximum time between reviews ensures an intervening election with the possibility of a new government. A government may, of course, terminate the override at any time within the five years.

On June 23, 1982, as a political expression of Quebec's displeasure with the process which led to the November Accord without Quebec's consent, Quebec's National Assembly passed Bill 62, an Act Respecting the Constitution Act, 1982. By this Act a standard clause was added to every Act (excluding some private Acts) on the statute books, thus taking full advantage of section 33. The clause states that "this Act shall operate notwithstanding the provisions of sections 2 and 7 to 15 of the Constitution Act, 1982." This blanket use of the override was challenged, but the Supreme Court upheld it in *Ford* as a valid use of section 33. The override could not, however, be applied retroactively to a date before the override legislation was proclaimed. Quebec legislation passed after June 23, 1982, also included the standard "notwithstanding" provision. However, this practice was discontinued on March 6, 1986, following Premier Bourassa's defeat of the Parti Québécois the previous December. According to Quebec's Minister of Intergovernmental Affairs (Gil Rémillard), "we want Quebecers to have the same protection of their fundamental rights as other Canadians."[239] This attitude was also reinforced by the fact that Quebec did not use the override in its own Charter of Human Rights and Freedoms. Quebec also allowed earlier uses of the override to expire at the end of their five-year time limits. However, on December 18, 1988, only three days after the Supreme Court's *Ford* ruling that Quebec's French-only sign law was unconstitutional—ironically, the same ruling which upheld the omnibus override legislation—Bourassa used the override to sidestep that part of the decision.

Those opposed to the standard override insisted that any override should be required to specify the section of the particular law which might infringe a Charter right or freedom, as well as to identify—in words, not by section number—the precise right or freedom which might be infringed. The Court could find no legal justification for this interpretation of section 33. Indeed, because a legislature may be unable to anticipate with certainty whether or not a piece of legislation might successfully be challenged, "it must be permitted in a particular case to override more than one provision of the *Charter* and indeed all of the provisions which it is permitted to override by the terms of s. 33."[240]

The only other use of the override by mid-1991 was made by the Saskatchewan government to end a strike of its public servants following the 1985 ruling of that province's Court of Appeal that Charter section 2(d) contained an implicit right to strike. In 1987, however, the Supreme Court reversed that decision and ruled that "freedom of expression" does not include this right. Indeed, the Court's message was contained in three rulings delivered the same day—two of them in relation to provincial laws, one a Federal law.[241] Alberta Premier Lougheed had stated his government's intention to use section 33 if the Supreme Court were to find a Charter right to strike in the *Alberta Labour Reference* when it considered the challenge to three Alberta laws prohibiting certain public employees from striking. See the commentary on section 2(d).

Critics of section 33 believe that legislatures should pay a political price for using the override by being forced to debate the merits of individual overrides so as to increase public awareness of the potential threat to their "guaranteed" rights and freedoms. In view of the *Ford* decision these critics may well argue that section 33 allows governments to circumvent the very purpose of the Charter. Defenders of section 33 probably hope so! At least it is a potentially important federalizing tool in the hands of the provinces. Furthermore, any "abuse" of the override can be punished by a vigilant electorate.

Knopff and Morton suggest that the override is defensible on principle. The equality which is central to liberal democracy requires both the protection of rights and freedoms as the "end of government" and popular consent as the "procedure of government." In performing its role as a protector of rights and freedoms the courts must realize that "the capacity of appointed judges to stand against the public will depends upon a general perception that they are not speaking merely in their own name—i.e., imposing on the nation their particular policy preferences—but in the name of long-range principles enshrined in the constitution." Section 33 establishes public opinion as enunciated by legislative bodies as a formal limitation on judicial power.[242]

Citation

➤ **SECTION 34:** This Part may be cited as the Canadian Charter of Rights and Freedoms.

This section needs no comment.

Part II: Rights of the Aboriginal Peoples of Canada

➤ **SECTION 35:** (1) The existing aboriginal and treaty rights of the aboriginal peoples of Canada are hereby recognized and affirmed.

(2) In this Act, "aboriginal peoples of Canada" includes the Indian, Inuit and Métis peoples of Canada.

(3) For greater certainty, in subsection (1) "treaty rights" includes rights that now exist by way of land claims agreements or may be so acquired.

(4) Notwithstanding any other provision of this Act, the aboriginal and treaty rights referred to in subsection (1) are guaranteed equally to male and female persons.

Much has been written on the subject of native rights, including attempts to determine their precise nature. The 1982 Constitution Act does not resolve that issue. The legal status of aboriginal and treaty rights is entrenched by sections 25 and 35 of this Act. As already noted section 25 (which is part of the Charter) creates no rights. What it does is ensure that the equality provisions of section 15 do not jeopardize whatever "aboriginal, treaty or other rights or freedoms" may exist.

It is necessary, therefore, to look to section 35 to try to find out what those protected rights are. But while this section recognizes and affirms, it does not define, "existing" rights. Nevertheless, these rights (whatever they may be) are not subject to limitation by section 1 because section 35 is outside the Charter. Neither are aboriginal rights subject to the section 33 override. On the other hand, because section 35 is beyond the Charter the violation of rights cannot trigger remedies under section 24. Total reliance must be on section 52 declarations that offending statutes or parts thereof (or regulations) are of no force or effect.

Section 35 had an on-again-off-again history before it became part of the new Constitution Act. It was not part of the original Resolution, but was added (without the qualifying "existing") during the joint Senate-House of Commons committee hearings. (At that time it included only subsections [1] and [2].) The section was deleted at the last moment during negotiation of the November 5 Accord. According to Romanow, the ministers and officials had not carefully considered, and therefore did not really understand, the demands of native organizations. The result was government uncertainty (and probably uneasiness) of what these rights might entail and what impact they might have on provincial legislative authority. Furthermore, "the first ministers, ministers, and officials were mesmerized by the tantalizing prospect of achieving a constitutional accord, at long last. The nature of the last minute negotiations—complex, occasionally bitter and hurried—militated against any careful consideration of the entrenchment of aboriginal rights."[243]

When the Accord was reopened to remove section 28 from the section 33 override, Saskatchewan (which had supported the aboriginal peoples' constitutional demands) insisted upon the revival of what is now section 35(1) and (2). The other parties to the Accord agreed but, primarily at Alberta's insistence, only if the qualifying "existing" were added.[244]

Section 35 now has four subsections. Subsection (1), as discussed above, recognizes and affirms but does not define aboriginal and treaty rights. Subsection (2) defines the term "aboriginal peoples" but does not state who is included within each of these three groups. Presumably, the courts will accept any reasonable definition enacted by Parliament. Subsection (3) places land claims on the same constitutional footing as treaty rights. It also guarantees that any new land claim agreements will be entrenched even though they were not "existing" on April 17, 1982. Subsection (4) was made necessary because the similar guarantee in section 25 applies only to Charter rights. These last two subsections were added by the 1983 Constitution Amendment Proclamation, and with the agreement of representatives of the aboriginal peoples reached at the March 1983 constitutional conference called pursuant to section 37.

By mid-1991 the only Supreme Court case involving aboriginal rights was *Sparrow*.[245] The importance of this case lies in the Court's grappling with the meaning of "existing rights" and of the commitment that these rights are "recognized and affirmed." The native appellant, Sparrow, had been charged under Federal Fisheries Act regulations with fishing using a drift net longer than allowed by the Band's licence. Sparrow admitted the "offence" but claimed he was exercising an existing aboriginal right under this section 35(1) and consequently that the licence restriction was unconstitutional. Chief Justice Dickson and Justice La Forest co-authored the Court's unanimous decision.

What is the meaning of "existing"? In the first place, because the Constitution Act does not revive pre-existing rights, rights are those existing on April 17, 1982. Second, the word "existing" cannot be defined in terms of detailed regulations as of 1982. "The notion of freezing existing rights would incorporate into the Constitution a crazy patchwork of regulations"[246] as to seasons, types of fish that may be caught, and catch limits, for example, which vary across a province and among provinces. As Slattery points out, the concept of frozen rights "might require that a constitutional amendment be enacted to implement regulations more stringent than those in existence on April 17, 1982"—an obviously unsatisfactory situation.[247] The Court ruled, therefore, that "existing" rights are rights which have not been "extinguished," and this permits their evolution over time.

The Court agreed that Sparrow was exercising an aboriginal right by fishing for salmon "in ancient tribal territory where his ancestors had fished from time immemorial in that part of the mouth of the Fraser River."[248] The scope of this right included fishing for food and for consumption for social and ceremonial activities, but not commercial or sport fishing. But did this right exist in 1982 or had it been extinguished piecemeal through regulation over the years? Regulations affecting Indian food fishing (though not commercial or sport fishing) had remained virtually unchanged for years after 1917, but in 1977 a licence (specifying method, locale, and times of fishing) was required. The Crown argued that the aboriginal right to fish had become extinguished by "progressive restriction and detailed regulation of the fisheries," and that extinguishment need not be made explicit. According to the Court, however, the Crown "confuses regulation with extinguishment," and "the Sovereign's intention [to extinguish] must be clear and plain."

What does it mean to "recognize and affirm"? What is the impact of this commitment on the power to regulate? The Court acknowledged that "British policy towards the native population was based on respect for their right to occupy their traditional lands, a proposition to which the Royal Proclamation of 1763 bears witness," but insisted that "there was from the outset never any doubt that sovereignty and legislative power, and indeed, the underlying title, to such lands vested in the Crown." Dickson added that the observance of these native rights over the years was not impressive. Whatever else section 35(1) may do it at least provides "a solid constitutional base upon which subsequent negotiations can take place."[249] Dickson quoted Lyon with approval: This section must be more than "just a codification of the case law on aboriginal rights" existent in 1982. Rather, it requires "a just settlement for aboriginal peoples. It renounces the old rules of the game under which the Crown established courts of law and denied those courts the authority to question sovereign claims made by the Crown."[250]

Having said all this, what was the Court's view of the constitutional impact of the "solemn commitment" to recognize and affirm? In the first place it does not mean that section 52(1) of the 1982 Constitution Act will automatically be used to strike down a law or regulation restricting aboriginal rights. Such law or regulation will be valid "if it meets the test for justifying an interference" with these rights. Federal power under section 91(24) of the 1867 Constitution Act continues, but must now be "reconciled with federal duty [under this section 35(1)] and the best way to achieve that reconciliation is to demand the justification of any government regulation that infringes upon or denies aboriginal rights."[251] This implies a compromise between the "patchwork" noted above and a guarantee of rights "in their original form unrestricted by subsequent regulation." Governments must accept the legitimacy of challenge to their social and economic policy objectives affecting aboriginal rights.

Dickson outlined a test for determining "justifiable" government interference with aboriginal rights. First, does the impugned legislation or regulation interfere with an existing right? If so, and second, when is such interference justified, given the special trust relationship which the Court declares to exist between the government and the aboriginal peoples? Several issues are involved here. For example, is there a valid legislative objective? This would include the conservation and management of a natural resource, an objective consistent with aboriginal beliefs and practices; or the prevention of activity harmful to the general population or the aboriginal peoples themselves. But a restriction "in the public interest" would, said Dickson, be too vague. If the objective is conservation and management, then priorities must be established once the measures are in place. The first priority must be aboriginal food requirements. Only then may commercial and sport activities be considered; otherwise, the effect of conservation measures will be borne by aboriginals in pursuit of food rather than by people engaged in commercial and sport activities. Because government policy regarding the British Columbia fishery already gives aboriginal food fishing top priority, the Crown must now ensure that its regulations are in fact consistent with that priority. Once the priorities are established, has the infringement on rights been as slight as possible? If there are conservation measures, were aboriginal peoples consulted or at least informed? If there has been expropriation was there fair compensation? Dickson added that other questions as well would have to be asked in assessing justification. The bottom line is this: "Recognition and affirmation requires sensitivity to and respect for the rights of aboriginal peoples on behalf of the government, courts and indeed all Canadians."

The Supreme Court called for a new trial to determine whether or not there had been infringement of aboriginal rights (the onus resting upon the appellant) and, if there was an infringement, whether it was consistent with section 35(1) (the onus resting upon the Crown). The entire determination must be "in accordance with the [Court's] analysis set out here."

What are we to make of this case? Aboriginal peoples may be excused if to them it seems like *déjà vu*. However, this is the first attention paid to aboriginal rights under the 1982 Constitution Act, and the Supreme Court is making perfectly clear its intention to ensure that the system does change. We must wait and see.

➤ **SECTION 35.1:** The government of Canada and the provincial governments are committed to the principle that, before any amendment is made to Class 24 of section 91 of the "Constitution Act, 1867," to section 25 of this Act or to this Part,

(a) a constitutional conference that includes in its agenda an item relating to the proposed amendment, composed of the Prime Minister of Canada and the first ministers of the provinces, will be convened by the Prime Minister of Canada; and

(b) the Prime Minister of Canada will invite representatives of the aboriginal peoples of Canada to participate in the discussions on that item.

This section was added by the 1983 Constitution Amendment Proclamation. It ensures that native groups will be invited to participate at any constitutional conference which considers a constitutional amendment affecting section

91(24) of the 1867 Constitution Act, or sections 25, 35, or 35.1 of the 1982 Constitution Act. There is, of course, no assurance that native input at such a conference will be heeded, but the fact that native peoples now have a guaranteed right to participate, a right extended to no other group, is indicative of their special status.

This section was itself the result of agreement with representatives of the aboriginal peoples reached at the March 1983 constitutional conference called pursuant to section 37.

Part III: Equalization and Regional Disparities

➤ **SECTION 36:** (1) Without altering the legislative authority of Parliament or of the provincial legislatures, or the rights of any of them with respect to the exercise of their legislative authority, Parliament and the legislatures, together with the government of Canada and the provincial governments, are committed to

(a) promoting equal opportunities for the well-being of Canadians;
(b) furthering economic development to reduce disparity in opportunities; and
(c) providing essential public services of reasonable quality to all Canadians.

(2) Parliament and the government of Canada are committed to the principle of making equalization payments to ensure that provincial governments have sufficient revenues to provide reasonably comparable levels of public services at reasonably comparable levels of taxation.

One implication of this section is that it strengthens arguments favouring the continued use of Ottawa's spending power in order further to promote the goals which this section enunciates. Whatever the effects of these rather vaguely worded, but nonetheless worthy, commitments they will probably be the result of political and not judicial pressure.

Part IV: Constitutional Conference

➤ **SECTION 37:** (1) A constitutional conference composed of the Prime Minister of Canada and the first ministers of the provinces shall be convened by the Prime Minister of Canada within one year after this Part comes into force.

(2) The conference convened under subsection (1) shall have included in its agenda an item respecting constitutional matters that directly affect the aboriginal peoples of Canada, including the identification and definition of the rights of those peoples to be included in the Constitution of Canada, and the Prime Minister of Canada shall invite representatives of

those peoples to participate in the discussions on that item.

(3) The Prime Minister of Canada shall invite elected representatives of the governments of the Yukon Territory and the Northwest Territories to participate in the discussions on any item on the agenda of the conference convened under subsection (1) that, in the opinion of the Prime Minister, directly affects the Yukon Territory and the Northwest Territories.

This section was repealed on April 17, 1983, pursuant to section 54. The required constitutional conference was held in March 1983. It led to the amendments which produced a new section 25(b), added subsections (3) and (4) to section 35, and added sections 35.1 and 37.1. Two consequential amendments were the addition of section 54.1 providing for the automatic repeal of section 37.1 on April 18, 1987, and the addition of section 61 adding the amending document itself to the term "Constitution Acts, 1867-1982."

Perhaps predictably, the March 1983 constitutional conference failed to achieve its high goals as stated in subsection (2)—"the identification and definition of the rights" of aboriginal peoples. The process may continue during forthcoming constitutional conferences, although the required agenda of the two conferences specified in section 37.1 does not include that item.

Subsection (3) required that representatives of the two territorial governments be invited to participate in discussions of any matters to be considered at the conference which directly affected the territories.

Part IV.1: Constitutional Conferences

➤ SECTION 37.1: (1) In addition to the conference convened in March 1983, at least two constitutional conferences composed of the Prime Minister of Canada and the first ministers of the provinces shall be convened by the Prime Minister of Canada, the first within three years after April 17, 1982 and the second within five years after that date.

(2) Each conference convened under subsection (1) shall have included in its agenda constitutional matters that directly affect the aboriginal peoples of Canada, and the Prime Minister of Canada shall invite representatives of those peoples to participate in the discussions on those matters.

(3) The Prime Minister of Canada shall invite elected representatives of the governments of the Yukon Territory and the Northwest Territories to participate in the discussions on any item on the agenda of a conference convened under subsection (1) that, in the opinion of the Prime Minister, directly affects the Yukon Territory and the Northwest Territories.

(4) Nothing in this section shall be construed so as to derogate from subsection 35(1).

Part IV.1 was added by the 1983 Constitution Amendment Proclamation. The Proclamation also added section 54.1 providing for the automatic repeal of this Part (and s. 54.1) upon the expiry of its life on April 18, 1987.

Section 37.1 required that at least two constitutional conferences (in addition to that of 1983) be convened by April 17, 1987. In fact, three conferences were held: in 1984, 1985, and 1987. However, one of the goals stated (s. 37) for the 1983 conference—"the identification and definition of the rights of" aboriginal peoples to be included in the Constitution of Canada—was not included in section 37.1. The last of the conferences was held in March 1987 and ended with the "irreconcilability of the respective positions . . . finally admitted."[252] Before this conference was held, Prime Minister Mulroney secured provincial agreement that the Quebec question had to be resolved before serious consideration could be given to the issue of aboriginal self-government.[253] This would also ensure Quebec's return to the constitutional table.

In his March 26 opening remarks to the 1987 First Ministers Conference on Aboriginal Constitutional Affairs, George Erasmus declared the minimum demand of the Assembly of First Nations to be "explicit constitutional recognition of the right to self-government," including "lands and resources, an historic right inherent in our unsurrendered sovereignty."[254] Any constitutional amendment, he asserted, must contain the right of bands to negotiate self-government agreements with Ottawa or with Ottawa and provincial governments. The Conference rejected the proposal as being too vague.

Three months later the Meech Lake Accord was on the national agenda. Its sole reference to aboriginal peoples was the statement in section 16 that the new "distinct society" provision for Quebec was to affect neither the aboriginal rights referred to in sections 25 or 35 or the multicultural heritage section 26 (of the 1982 Constitution Act), nor Parliament's authority to legislate in relation to Indians and reserves (s. 91[24]) under the 1867 Constitution Act. The Accord's insult, so far as Erasmus was concerned, was that the distinct society clause "perpetuates the idea of a duality in Canada, and strengthens the myth that the French and the English peoples are the foundation of Canada. It neglects the original inhabitants and distorts history . . . [and suggests that] the French peoples in Quebec form the *only* distinct society." He added that for five years governments had been unwilling to entrench in the Constitution "undefined self-government of aboriginal peoples," but they willingly accepted the "equally vague" distinct society whose interpretation will be left to the courts.[255] There is, however, a significant difference between the two situations. Quebec already exists with its legislative authority determined mainly by the 1867 Constitution Act, whereas the demand of aboriginal peoples for self-government is tantamount to a call for a third order of government between Ottawa and the provinces. It seems ironic that it was an Indian (M.L.A. Elijah Harper) who orchestrated Manitoba's failure to ratify the Meech Lake Accord and therefore (with Newfoundland's inaction) relegated the Accord to the history books.

This section 37.1 also repeated the section 37 assurance that representatives of the two territorial governments would be invited to participate in discussions of any matters to be discussed at these conferences which directly affected the territories. Territorial representatives attended these conferences.

Part V: Procedure for Amending Constitution of Canada

Chapter 6, it will be recalled, traced the efforts of more than half a century to reach agreement on an amending formula for the 1867 Constitution Act. One of the principles established in the mid-1930s was that different amending procedures were needed for different situations. This principle, although with changes in detail, endured and is reflected in this Part V as follows:

(1) Amendment by a "general" formula—basically, section 38(1). Also relevant to this formula are sections 38(2)(3)(4), 39, 40, and 42.
(2) Amendment with the concurrence of Ottawa and all provinces (the unanimity rule)—section 41.
(3) Amendment with the concurrence of Ottawa and provinces affected by the provision amended—section 43.
(4) Amendment by Ottawa alone—section 44, as qualified by sections 41 and 42.
(5) Amendment by individual provinces—section 45, as qualified by section 41.

The remainder of Part V, sections 46-49, is a miscellany of provisions.

Part V is entitled "Procedure for Amending Constitution of Canada," and most of the provisions of Part V refer to amendments to that "Constitution." The notable exception is section 45; see the commentary on that section for possible implications. For the purpose of the amending procedures in Part V, the meaning of "Constitution" is that stated in section 52(2). Basically, then, the Constitution includes the 1867 B.N.A. Act and its amendments over the years (each of these Acts being renamed "Constitution Act"), the 1982 Constitution Act (with amendments), the instruments admitting territories or provinces or creating new provinces, and the Statute of Westminster. See the Schedule to the present Act in Appendix B.

By mid-1991 only one constitutional amendment had been proclaimed—that of 1983.[256] The specific changes made by that amendment are noted in the commentary on section 37. Another amendment, establishing a new formula for distributing House of Commons seats under section 51 of the 1867 Constitution Act, was made by Parliament in 1985 under the authority of section 44 of this Part V. Amendments such as this, or those by a province under section 45, are made by ordinary statute rather than by resolution. In these cases, proclamations prescribed for amendments requiring the concurrence of both orders of government are not part of the amendment procedure.

It seems likely, given the degree of consensus needed for amendments, that little if any significant change to our government machinery can be expected. The reason is not only the number of governments which must agree; it is also that first ministers have no incentive to accept change that is not to their individual province's advantage. Furthermore, the provision (s. 38[3]) allowing a province to opt out of certain types of amendment creates the possibility of a crazy quilt Constitution, if meaningful amendments are in fact made.

While it is true that Part V specifies the consent of legislatures rather than first ministers, the control which those ministers exert over their legislatures renders legislative consent of little practical consequence.

➤ **SECTION 38:** (1) An amendment to the Constitution of Canada may be made by proclamation issued by the Governor General under the Great Seal of Canada where so authorized by

(a) resolutions of the Senate and House of Commons; and

(b) resolutions of the legislative assemblies of at least two-thirds of the provinces that have, in the aggregate, according to the then latest general census, at least fifty per cent of the population of all the provinces.

(2) An amendment made under subsection (1) that derogates from the legislative powers, the proprietary rights or any other rights or privileges of the legislature or government of a province shall require a resolution supported by a majority of the members of each of the Senate, the House of Commons and the legislative assemblies required under subsection (1).

(3) An amendment referred to in subsection (2) shall not have effect in a province the legislative assembly of which has expressed its dissent thereto by resolution supported by a majority of its members prior to the issue of the proclamation to which the amendment relates unless that legislative assembly, subsequently, by resolution supported by a majority of its members, revokes its dissent and authorizes the amendment.

(4) A resolution of dissent made for the purposes of subsection (3) may be revoked at any time before or after the issue of the proclamation to which it relates.

Section 38 may be regarded as the "general" formula, in that it is used for all Constitutional amendments to which no other section of Part V applies.

Subsection (1): This is the core of the general formula. It requires the consent of both Houses of Parliament and at least two-thirds (in effect, seven) of the provinces containing a minimum of 50% of the population of all the provinces. Based on the 1981 census this means that an amendment is impossible without the support of at least one of the four Atlantic provinces, one of the two central provinces, and one of the four western provinces. Viewed in another way:[257]

(1) No province acting alone will block an amendment.
(2) Ontario and Quebec acting together will block an amendment.
(3) Ontario and British Columbia together with one of Alberta, Saskatchewan, Manitoba, Nova Scotia, will block an amendment.
(4) Any four provinces acting together will block an amendment because the two-thirds requirement will not have been met.

The blocking power of the provinces may therefore be ranked in decreasing order as follows: (1) Ontario, (2) Quebec, (3) British Columbia, (4) Alberta, Saskatchewan, Manitoba, Nova Scotia, (5) New Brunswick, Prince Edward Island, Newfoundland. Once the required consent has been obtained, the governor general will issue a proclamation making the amendment effective. Section 39 establishes a minimum and a maximum time limit for the amending process.

The only amendment made under this section was approved by all provinces except Quebec. As a gesture of its opposition to the 1982 Accord, Quebec has not participated in post-1982 constitutional conferences other than those relating to Meech Lake.

Subsection (2): This refers to any amendment under subsection (1) that "derogates from the legislative powers, the proprietary rights or any other rights or privileges" of a province. The only difference from the requirement in (1) is that the resolution must be supported by a "majority of the members of" the legislative bodies—that is, a majority of the total membership rather than, as in (1), a majority of those present and voting. The reason for the more stringent requirement is doubtlessly to ensure full discussion within the legislature and to avoid a hasty decision.

Subsection (3): A province may opt out of certain amendments, but only those to which subsection (2) refers—that is, those which reduce provincial authority. To opt out, the proposed amendment must be opposed by a majority of the legislature's membership, and before the proclamation is issued. See the commentary on section 39. If more than three provinces opt out of an amendment, the amendment fails for want of seven supporting provinces. An amendment approved by Ottawa and seven provinces (with 50% of the population) applies to all provinces that do not opt out. As noted in Chapter 6, the concept of opting out was first proposed in 1936, but it lay dormant until its revival by Alberta in the 1970s. A province opting out of an amendment may, according to subsections (3) and (4), change its mind at any time and opt in by a majority vote of the legislature's membership.

The impact of opting out may be described as follows. Suppose that Ottawa and seven provinces (containing the required population) approve an amendment transferring some provincial authority to the Federal government. If Alberta (for example) opts out, subsequent Federal legislation in that subject area will be effective in all provinces except Alberta, including the two other provinces which did not assent to the resolution but did not opt out. Alberta's members of the House of Commons and the Senate will, nevertheless, participate fully in the making of such legislation, notwithstanding its inapplicability to their province. It would be inappropriate to deny such members the opportunity of full participation inasmuch as they have been duly elected to the House of Commons (or appointed to the Senate). Furthermore, a Government's majority in the Commons could be reduced or eliminated by denying participation.

During the 1960s debates on Canadian federalism, one of the suggested options for satisfying Quebec's aspirations within Confederation was "special status." One of the perceived difficulties with this option was that Quebec

M.P.'s would be participating in legislation which did not affect their province. That scenario could now become a reality for any province. Extensive use of the opting out provision might indeed create a crazy quilt constitution.

➤ **SECTION 39:** (1) A proclamation shall not be issued under subsection 38(1) before the expiration of one year from the adoption of the resolution initiating the amendment procedure thereunder, unless the legislative assembly of each province has previously adopted a resolution of assent or dissent.

(2) A proclamation shall not be issued under subsection 38(1) after the expiration of three years from the adoption of the resolution initiating the amendment procedure thereunder.

The proclamation to enact an amendment under section 38 cannot be issued for at least one year following the adoption of a resolution initiating the amendment process. The only exception is that a proclamation may be issued within the year if each of the ten provinces has made a decision either to approve or to reject the proposed amendment. The full year is required even if Parliament and the required seven provinces favour the amendment, in order to give the remaining provinces sufficient time to opt out if they wish—assuming that opting out is permitted for that amendment. The entire procedure is initiated when the first legislature, provincial or Parliament, adopts the resolution.

In order to prevent an amendment proposal from dragging on indefinitely in search of the required support, subsection (2) provides a maximum period of three years, again from the time the resolution is adopted by the first legislature. At the end of the three years the proposal lapses. Given the experience of the ill-fated Meech Lake amendments, consideration is being given to shortening the three-year period. This would lessen the possibility that legislative approval of proposed amendments (which may have been accepted by all First Ministers) might be rescinded, rejected, or delayed beyond the time limit, following a change of government.

It seems appropriate to comment here upon the Meech Lake Accord's peculiar combination of two distinct amending procedures—the three-year ratification time limit and the unanimity requirement. The time limit applies to amendments made under the general formula (s. 38[1]) but not under the unanimity rule (s. 41); the unanimity requirement carries no time limit. Why this combination for Meech Lake? The rationale for unanimity was that two of the proposed changes required unanimity: one was in relation to "the composition of the Supreme Court" (s. 41[d]) (to entrench the current legislative provision for three Quebec judges); the other was the change in the amending formula (to shift the contents of section 42, currently amendable under the general formula, to section 41's unanimity rule). The other parts of the Accord, not subject to unanimity, fell automatically under the general formula and this triggered the three-year time limit. The change in the method of selecting senators (to be but temporary until agreement was reached on Senate reform), as well perhaps as some of the changes to the Supreme Court, explicitly required (by section

42[1][b][d]) the general formula. Thus Canadians were presented with the most stringent amending requirement possible. Was this really necessary? Gordon Robertson does not think so,[258] but his reasoning was not picked up by any of the players in the Meech Lake drama unless the eleventh-hour suggestion that the Supreme Court be asked to rule on the time limit is considered. By then, however, the emotionally-charged atmosphere, but perhaps especially Bourassa, made a change in what had become the conventional wisdom politically unfeasible.

There is no time limit for amendments that require the consent of all provinces (s. 41) or all provinces to which an amended section applies (s. 43). A minimum time limit is inappropriate because there is no such thing as opting out. Without a maximum time limit, proposals could drag on indefinitely.

➤ **SECTION 40:** Where an amendment is made under subsection 38(1) that transfers provincial legislative powers relating to education or other cultural matters from provincial legislatures to Parliament, Canada shall provide reasonable compensation to any province to which the amendment does not apply.

This section provides for "reasonable" compensation to be paid by the Federal government to provinces opting out of amendments which transfer "provincial legislative powers relating to education or other cultural matters from provincial legislatures to Parliament." The terms "reasonable," "education," and "other cultural matters," are undefined.

Quebec had sought compensation in respect of all amendments from which a province might exempt itself. Otherwise, Premier Lévesque argued, a province would be penalized if it opted out of an amendment which, for example, transferred jurisdiction to Parliament. The province would continue to finance its own program(s) in the transferred area, and yet its residents would pay Federal taxes to finance the program(s) in other provinces. Lévesque's proposal was unacceptable to Prime Minister Trudeau. The partial restoration represented by this section was one of two compromises offered by Trudeau in an unsuccessful effort to secure Lévesque's support for the November 1981 Accord. (See the commentary on section 59 for the other change.) Culture, including education, is of great importance to Quebec.

While at first glance the notion of compensation may seem unreasonable—payment for non-cooperation—it may also be viewed from a different perspective. Legislative control in cultural areas may be important to a province. Nevertheless, because of financial cost the province may be tempted to accept, rather than reject, an amendment that transfers legislative authority with its attendant expenses to Ottawa. The provision of financial compensation encourages the province to base its decision on principle rather than financial expediency.

If the Meech Lake amendments had been approved, the words "relating to education or other cultural matters" would have been deleted from section 40. Fiscal compensation would therefore have become available to opting-out provinces regardless of the nature of the Constitutional amendment under section 38(1).

➤ **SECTION 41:** An amendment to the Constitution of Canada in relation to the following matters may be made by proclamation issued by the Governor General under the Great Seal of Canada only where authorized by resolutions of the Senate and House of Commons and of the legislative assembly of each province:

(a) the office of the Queen, the Governor General and the Lieutenant Governor of a province;

(b) the right of a province to a number of members in the House of Commons not less than the number of Senators by which the province is entitled to be represented at the time this Part comes into force;

(c) subject to section 43, the use of the English or the French language;

(d) the composition of the Supreme Court of Canada; and

(e) an amendment to this Part.

This is the unanimity rule which, as noted in Chapter 6, was included (with variations as to detail) in all amendment proposals except the 1971 Victoria Charter. The pre-1982 status of each item in this section is described below. The probable post-1982 status of the items in the absence of a unanimity requirement is also noted. The commentary on section 39 considers the rather strange procedure adopted for the Meech Lake proposed constitutional amendments.

Subsection (a): Section 91(1) of the 1867 Constitution Act authorized the Canadian Parliament to amend the Constitution of Canada (which at that time was completely undefined). Although there were certain exclusions from this generalization the Crown was not one of them. It may be argued, therefore, that the office of the Queen and governor general could have been altered by Parliament. The alternative was that authority resided in Britain. Under section 92(1) of the 1867 Act, the amendment of provincial constitutions "as regards" the office of lieutenant governor was explicitly placed beyond provincial jurisdiction; it therefore rested with the British Parliament.

In the absence of this section 41(a) it would appear that amendments in relation to these offices could have been made under sections 44 (for Canada as a whole) and 45 (for the provinces).

Subsection (b): This is the "Senate floor" guarantee which itself was added to the 1867 Constitution Act (s. 51A, retained in 1982 for no apparent reason) by the British Parliament in 1915. Following the creation of the renumbered section 91(1) in 1949, this matter probably fell within the competence of the Canadian Parliament. The Senate floor for each province as of April 17, 1982 (the date Part V came into force) is as follows:

Alberta	6	Nova Scotia	10
British Columbia	6	Ontario	24
Manitoba	6	Prince Edward Island	4
New Brunswick	10	Quebec	24
Newfoundland	6	Saskatchewan	6

This provision does not preserve Commons representation by the Northwest Territories or the Yukon Territory. Without this subsection (b) the Senate floor would likely have come within Parliament's jurisdiction under section 44.

The commentary on section 26 of the 1867 Constitution Act discusses the Senate floor in relation to Prime Minister Mulroney's appointment of eight additional senators in September 1990.

Subsection (c): The only reference to language rights in the 1867 Constitution Act is section 133, and this matter was excluded by section 91(1) from the jurisdiction of the Canadian Parliament. Amendment was possible, therefore, only by the British Parliament. In the absence of subsection (c), amendments in relation to language would probably have been subject to the general formula of section 38, although the subordination of section 41(c) to section 43 should be noted.

As it stands, section 41(c) will govern possible amendment of Constitution Act section 133, but only with respect to Ottawa. It will also govern the amendment of the following sections of the present Act: 16(1)(3), 17(1), 18(1), 19(1), 20(1), 21, 23 (except [1][a]), 55, 56, and 57.

Amendments of the following provisions are governed by section 43(b) because they apply to "one or more, but not all, provinces": 1867 Constitution Act section 133 with respect to Quebec; the present Act's sections 16-20 with respect to New Brunswick, and section 23(1)(a) which currently is inapplicable to Quebec; and Manitoba Act section 23 which, of course, applies only to Manitoba.

Ottawa's Official Languages Act illustrates the point that this subsection does not govern amendments to all legislation in relation to the use of the English and French languages. Because that Act is not part of the Constitution of Canada (although see the commentary on section 52[2]), Ottawa may amend it unilaterally provided that in so doing it does not impinge upon a provision of the Constitution of Canada.

Subsection (d): This was amendable by the Canadian Parliament and would have continued under Parliament's control because the Supreme Court was created by Parliament. The inclusion of the Supreme Court in this section and again in section 42, is interesting because the Supreme Court Act is not part of the Schedule which "includes" the components of the Constitution of Canada. The possible status of that Act as part of our "Constitution" is considered in the commentary on section 52(2). For the moment, suffice it to say that the "composition" of the Court probably refers most importantly to the sections which fix the complement at nine and require a minimum of three judges to be appointed from Quebec, although it might also include the qualifications and tenure of judges.

Subsection (e): Because there was no amending formula under the 1867 Constitution Act this item had no pre-1982 equivalent. Note that section 49 requires a review of Part V within fifteen years—that is, by April 17, 1997. Given the problem of finding agreement in the first place, which agreement still excludes Quebec, the achievement of unanimity (which would have to include Quebec) for any substantial change seems unlikely.

Without a requirement of unanimity, alterations to Part V would have been made under section 38.

➤ **SECTION 42:** (1) An amendment to the Constitution of Canada in relation to the following matters may be made only in accordance with subsection 38(1):

(a) the principle of proportionate representation of the provinces in the House of Commons prescribed by the Constitution of Canada;
(b) the powers of the Senate and the method of selecting Senators;
(c) the number of members by which a province is entitled to be represented in the Senate and the residence qualifications of Senators;
(d) subject to paragraph 41(d), the Supreme Court of Canada;
(e) the extension of existing provinces into the territories; and
(f) notwithstanding any other law or practice, the establishment of new provinces.

(2) Subsections 38(2) to (4) do not apply in respect of amendments in relation to matters referred to in subsection (1).

This section makes explicit that amendments in relation to these particular matters must be made according to the general formula of section 38(1). Because some of these matters were part of the proposed Meech Lake amendments, the commentary on section 39 considers the rather strange procedure adopted for Meech Lake. Subsection (2) denies the right of a province to opt out of amendments made under section 42(1).

Except for subsection (1)(e) it seems likely that the items would, in the absence of instructions to the contrary, have been amendable by Parliament under section 44. The following paragraphs explore this possibility. Although the items do not (except for [e]) affect provincial powers they are obviously of provincial interest, and that is probably the reason for section 42.

Subsection (1)(a): Would the "principle of proportionate representation of the provinces . . . prescribed by" the Constitution of Canada otherwise have been amendable by Parliament alone under section 44? The answer would seem to depend upon whether section 52 of the 1867 Constitution Act (which contains identical wording) was amendable by Parliament under the authority of section 91(1). See the commentary on that section 52. In any event it is clear that Parliament may continue unilaterally to alter the details of section 51 of the 1867 Act (except for the "Senate floor" which is now protected by section

41[b] of the present Act) provided that the "principle of proportionate representation" is not disturbed.

Parliament has already altered section 51 since the 1982 Constitution Act became effective, but that redistribution formula effected by the 1985 Representation Act (see the commentary on section 51) was challenged in the British Columbia courts (*Campbell v. A.G. Canada*).[259] It was claimed that the Representation Act was in relation to proportionate representation within the meaning of section 42 and therefore could be enacted only in accordance with the general amending formula of section 38. Specifically, it was claimed that the principle of proportionate representation was violated by the provision that no province would lose House of Commons seats under the new system. As a result, some provinces received "too many" seats and some "too few." The Federal response was essentially a defence of the situation as it had developed over the years: the Constitution never intended to guarantee absolute proportionate representation because of the importance of other, competing, factors including a concept of "meaningful" representation. These exceptions to absolute proportionality have included the so-called "one-twentieth" (1867) and "fifteen per cent" (1952) rules, as well as the Senate floor established in 1915. In upholding the Federal position the British Columbia Supreme Court ruled that the Representation Act was not a law in relation to proportionate representation prescribed by the Constitution of Canada (which would have applied to both this section and section 52 of the 1867 Constitution Act). That principle was not intended to imply "perfect mathematical representation"; rather, the Constitution required "representation based primarily, but not entirely, upon population." The Court also noted that the 1952 and 1974 changes in the method of allocating seats had been declared by the Supreme Court of Canada in the *Senate Reference* to be consistent with the representation by population principle. The British Columbia Court of Appeal also upheld the 1985 Representation Act. In 1988 the Supreme Court of Canada refused to hear an appeal but it stated no reason.

Sancton argues that the courts may have decided differently had a case been made that the 1985 Act was unique in its guarantee that no province would lose seats in the House. This guarantee is only superficially similar to that of 1974. Under the earlier formula Quebec would be given four additional seats at each redistribution and the remaining seats would be distributed amongst the provinces proportionately. It would be highly unlikely, Sancton believes, that another province would actually be in line to lose seats (were it not for the no-loss guarantee) under a rule of proportionality. In other words the guarantee was probably of no practical significance. The fact that the 1974 formula was used only once makes that question somewhat academic.

Subsection (1)(b): The Senate is specifically included within Parliament's jurisdiction under section 44, except for the powers of the Senate and the selection of senators as stated in the present subsection. It seems likely, therefore, that in the absence of this restriction the entire jurisdiction over the Senate would have rested with Parliament. In the 1980 *Senate Reference* the Supreme

Court decided that Parliament did not have the authority under section 91(1) to amend the Constitution regarding the Senate. At that time, therefore, the British Parliament was the amending authority.

Subsection (1)(c): The comments on subsection (b) apply here as well, except that this subsection refers to "provincial" representation and residence qualifications. Note that qualifications other than residency are not included.

Subsection (1)(d): In the absence of this item the Supreme Court Act would have come within Parliament's jurisdiction, but not under section 44 unless that Act is found by the courts to be part of the "Constitution of Canada." Note that the "composition" of the Court falls under the unanimity rule of section 41 only if the Supreme Court Act is part of the "Constitution of Canada." If the entire balance of the Supreme Court Act is amendable only by the general formula (s. 38), many provisions which are but administrative detail will be caught. See the commentary on section 41(d), and especially on section 52(2).

Subsection (1)(e): Although the extension of provinces into the territories directly affects only the extended provinces and, of course, the Federal government which has jurisdiction over the territories, other provinces would be affected indirectly. Hence this inclusion in section 42 rather than 43. Note, however, that boundary adjustments between provinces are subject to section 43.

Subsection (1)(f): The same reasoning applies here as to item (e) except that, in the absence of this provision, the creation of new provinces wholly from territories would have fallen under section 44 by virtue of the following section 2 of the 1871 Constitution Act:

> The Parliament of Canada may from time to time establish new Provinces in any territories forming for the time being part of the Dominion of Canada, but not included in any Province thereof, and may, at the time of such establishment, make provision for the constitution and administration of any such Province, and for the passing of laws for the peace, order, and good government of such Province, and for its representation in the said Parliament.

Manitoba, Saskatchewan, and Alberta, were created in this fashion. Although the above-quoted section 2 was not repealed by the 1982 Constitution Act, it was made inoperative by the statement in this 42 (1)(f) that section 38 applies "notwithstanding any other law or practice."

If the Meech Lake amendments had been approved, the contents of this section would have become subject to section 41's unanimity rule.

➤ **SECTION 43:** An amendment to the Constitution of Canada in relation to any provision that applies to one or more, but not all, provinces, including

(a) any alteration to boundaries between provinces, and
(b) any amendment to any provision that relates to the use of the English or the French language within a province,

> may be made by proclamation issued by the Governor General under the Great Seal of Canada only where so authorized by resolutions of the Senate and House of Commons and of the legislative assembly of each province to which the amendment applies.

The most important fact to be noted here is that this section refers to provisions, not amendments, which apply to one or more but not all provinces. The provisions to which this section applies include the following:[260]

(1) **From the 1867 Constitution Act:**

- (a) Section 93—education—which does not apply to Manitoba, Saskatchewan, Alberta, or Newfoundland, although similar provisions (to which this section 43 applies) are included in the instruments creating those provinces. (Term 17 of the Union of Newfoundland with Canada is somewhat different, and does not contain the right of appeal to Ottawa by an aggrieved group.) The 1867 Constitution Act was made generally applicable to British Columbia and Prince Edward Island upon their admission (by British order-in-council) "as if the Colony . . . had been one of the Provinces originally united by the said Act"; therefore, section 93 applies.
- (b) Section 94—uniformity of laws—which excludes Quebec.
- (c) Section 97—selection of judges—which excludes Quebec.
- (d) Section 98—selection of judges—which includes only Quebec.
- (e) Section 133—language law—which includes only Quebec (as well, of course, as Ottawa).

(2) **From the 1982 Constitution Act:**

- (a) Sections 16(2), 17(2), 18(2), 19(2), 20(2)—language law—which apply only to New Brunswick.
- (b) Section 23(1)(a)—minority education language law—which does not apply to Quebec until such time as that province consents to its application. At some time in the future, therefore, this section may become subject to the unanimity rule of section 41(c).

(3) **From the Manitoba Act:** Section 23 language law which applies only to Manitoba.

Because the North-West Territories Act is not included in the Schedule as part of the Constitution of Canada, the language requirement imposed on Alberta and Saskatchewan by section 110 would presumably not have been caught by this section 43 even if that Act had denied those provinces authority to repeal the requirement unilaterally. The language provision of the North-West Territories Act is discussed in the commentary on section 133 of the 1867 Constitution Act.

The purpose of section 43 is to establish an amending procedure which is easier to satisfy than the "general" formula of section 38. In fact, greater difficulty is created for provisions which apply to eight or nine provinces—that is, to more than the seven required by section 38. In the above list this would be true for sections 94 and 97 of the 1867, and section 23(1)(a) of the 1982, Constitution Act.

The phrasing of section 43 presents an interesting question of interpretation.[261] The section refers to amendments to the "Constitution of Canada." The instruments admitting or creating the six provinces which joined Confederation after 1867, which instruments form the bulk of those provinces' constitutions, are also part of the Constitution of Canada as declared by section 52(2). And because the 1867 Constitution Act is part of the Constitution of Canada, so too are its sections 69-87 establishing the separate provinces of Quebec and Ontario. The same applies to section 88 in relation to Nova Scotia and New Brunswick.

Does all this mean that section 43 rather than 45 must be used whenever an individual province wishes to change part of its constitution which happens also to be part of the "Constitution of Canada"? Surely not! If such were the meaning, Parliament also would have to approve. This would be untenable for it would represent a significant diminution of provincial authority from pre-1982 years when the provinces could, by virtue of section 92(1) of the 1867 Constitution Act, amend their own constitutions without the benefit of Parliament's consent. A more reasonable interpretation would be that section 43 is to be used only when the provision being amended is not part of the "constitution of the province" (s. 45). Otherwise, section 45 would be largely superfluous.

Finally, section 43 explicitly includes boundary changes affecting more than one province, and amendments to provisions relating to the use of the English or French language within the province.

➤ **Section 44:** Subject to sections 41 and 42, Parliament may exclusively make laws amending the Constitution of Canada in relation to the executive government of Canada or the Senate and House of Commons.

This section replaces the essence of 1867 Constitution Act section 91(1) which is repealed by the 1982 Constitution Act. Of the several amending procedures provided by Part V only this one and that of section 45 permit amendment by the ordinary law-making process of a single legislature. The 1985 amendment to section 51 of the 1867 Constitution Act was made pursuant to section 44, although it was challenged in the British Columbia courts. (See the commentary on section 42 of the present Act.) This section is subject to the limitations enumerated in sections 41 and 42.

The restrictions of the former section 91(1) upon Parliament are amendable within Part V as follows:

(1) Matters under provincial jurisdiction—section 45.
(2) Education—section 43. See the commentary on that section.
(3) Language—sections 41 and 43.
(4) Annual session of Parliament—required by section 5 of the Charter which may be amended under section 38 inasmuch as no other procedure is specified within Part V.
(5) Five-year maximum duration of a Parliament between elections—required by section 4 of the Charter which may be amended under section 38 inasmuch as no other procedure is specified within Part V. Note that the exception to this maximum as contained in section 91(1) is reproduced in section 4 of the Charter.

Limitations on Parliament's authority in relation to the Senate (s. 42) were deemed by the Supreme Court in the *Senate Reference* to be limitations under 91(1) as well.

➤ **SECTION 45:** Subject to section 41, the legislature of each province may exclusively make laws amending the constitution of the province.

This section is analogous to 1867 Constitution Act section 92(1) which is repealed by the 1982 Constitution Act. As mentioned in the commentary on section 44, of the several amending procedures only those of sections 44 and 45 involve nothing more than the ordinary law-making process of a single legislature. The restriction in 92(1) pertaining to the office of lieutenant governor is now contained in section 41 (the unanimity rule) of the present Act.

This section refers to the "constitution of a province" (as did 92[1]), a term that is not defined in either the 1867 Constitution Act or the present Act. See the commentaries on section 133 of the 1867 Act in relation to Quebec, and section 3 of the present Act, for references to court cases which hinged on the meaning of "constitution of a province." The commentary on section 92(1) of the 1867 Act is also relevant. The paradoxical relationship between this section 45 and section 43 is noted in the commentary on 43; so is the reasonable conclusion that section 45 should apply to provisions of the Constitution of Canada which are also part of a province's constitution.

➤ **SECTION 46:** (1) The procedures for amendment under sections 38, 41, 42 and 43 may be initiated either by the Senate or the House of Commons or by the legislative assembly of a province.

(2) A resolution of assent made for the purposes of this Part may be revoked at any time before the issue of a proclamation authorized by it.

Any of the legislative bodies in Canada which may be involved in the amendment process under sections 38, 41, 42, or 43, may initiate an amendment resolution. A resolution of assent may be revoked only before an amendment proclamation is issued. The normal one-year minimum period (s. 39[1]) before a proclamation may be issued for amendments made under the general formula (s. 38[1]) is eliminated if all provinces register their assent or dissent within the year. In such a situation the time available to a province wishing to revoke its assenting resolution could be rather short.

Resolutions of dissent are relevant only in relation to amendments under the general formula of section 38, but not with respect to subjects listed in section 42 even though the general formula applies. Amendments under sections 41 and 43 require the consent of all provinces (s. 41), or of those provinces to which the provision applies (s. 43).

➤ **SECTION 47:** (1) An amendment to the Constitution of Canada made by proclamation under section 38, 41, 42, or 43 may be made without a resolution of the Senate authorizing the issue of the proclamation if, within one hundred and eighty days after the adoption by the House of Commons of a resolution authorizing its issue, the Senate has not adopted such a resolution and if, at any time after the expiration of that period, the House of Commons again adopts the resolution.

(2) Any period when Parliament is prorogued or dissolved shall not be counted in computing the one hundred and eighty day period referred to in subsection (1).

The Senate has only a 180-day suspensive veto over amendments made pursuant to sections 38, 41, 42, and 43. To bypass the Senate, the House of Commons must pass an amendment resolution a second time "at any time" after the 180-day period has elapsed. This was done for the Meech Lake resolution. Note, however, that the Senate's veto is absolute in relation to amendments made by Parliament alone (s. 44).

Because section 42(b) and (c) has made significant Senate reform subject to the general formula (s. 38), the Senate can only delay such reform. If jurisdiction over the Senate as stated in section 44 had not been qualified in section 42 the Senate would have possessed an absolute veto over its own reform.

➤ **SECTION 48:** The Queen's Privy Council for Canada shall advise the Governor General to issue a proclamation under this Part forthwith on the adoption of the resolutions required for an amendment made by proclamation under this Part.

The Canadian privy council (that is, the cabinet) will "advise" (that is, instruct) the governor general to issue an amendment proclamation "forthwith" upon the adoption of a resolution as required for the amendment. "Forthwith" must not, presumably, be within one year for amendments under sections 38 and 42 unless every province has made its decision of assent or (excluding 42) dissent. See the commentary on section 39.

➤ **SECTION 49:** A constitutional conference composed of the Prime Minister of Canada and the first ministers of the provinces shall be convened by the Prime Minister of Canada within fifteen years after this Part comes into force to review the provisions of this Part.

Given the difficulty reaching the present agreement, and then without Quebec's participation, the likelihood of unanimity (as required by section 41) to alter the amending formula seems remote. The fifteen years specified in this section will expire on April 17, 1997.

Part VI: Amendment to the Constitution Act, 1867

- **SECTION 50:** This section becomes section 92A of the 1867 Constitution Act and is discussed under that number in Chapter 7.

- **SECTION 51:** This section becomes the Sixth Schedule to the 1867 Constitution Act and appended to section 92A. It is included and discussed with section 92A of that Act in Chapter 7.

If the Meech Lake amendments had been approved, a new Part VI entitled "Constitutional Conferences" would have required annual constitutional conferences of first ministers. The agenda of these conferences would have included:

(a) Senate reform, including the role and functions of the Senate, its powers, the method of selecting Senators and representation in the Senate;
(b) roles and responsibilities in relation to fisheries; and
(c) such other matters as are agreed upon.

Part VII: General

- **SECTION 52:** (1) The Constitution of Canada is the supreme law of Canada, and any law that is inconsistent with the provisions of the Constitution is, to the extent of the inconsistency, of no force or effect.

  (2) The Constitution of Canda includes
  (a) the *Canada Act 1982*, including this Act;
  (b) the Acts and orders referred to in the schedule; and
  (c) any amendment to any Act or order referred to in paragraph (a) or (b).

  (3) Amendments to the Constitution of Canada shall be made only in accordance with the authority contained in the Constitution of Canada.

Subsection (1): Because the Constitution of Canada is the "supreme law," all laws inconsistent with it may be struck down by the courts. While this assertion is not made explicit, such is clearly the intent and the Supreme Court has acted accordingly since 1982. (Canada has not had an equivalent of the United States *Marbury v. Madison* declaring the right of courts to strike down legislation that is inconsistent with the Constitution.) Several comments are relevant.

This marks a significant departure for the role of the courts from the pre-1982 era. In those years the courts were involved primarily with the constitutionality of laws in terms of the Federal-provincial distribution of legislative authority. The reason was that with few exceptions the principle of legislative supremacy prevailed in Canada.

In addition to this judicial role (undiminished under the 1982 Constitution Act) the courts are now responsible for determining the constitutionality of laws in relation to the absolute standard of the Constitution of Canada. The main component of this new standard is the Charter of Rights and Freedoms. If United States experience is an indication of things to come in Canada, judicial activity in relation to the Charter will over the years become the bulk of judicial action. In making this comparison, however, it must be recognized that Canada's federal system is much more decentralized than the United States', and for this reason the adjudication of Federal-provincial disputes will remain significant.

Individuals who allege violations of the Charter have recourse to both this section 52 and the Charter's enforcement provision (s. 24). All other alleged violations of the Constitution of Canada may be adjudicated only under section 52.

For a law or potential law to be declared inconsistent with the Constitution it must be brought to the attention of the courts—either by means of an actual challenge, or by the Federal or a provincial government in the form of a reference seeking the court's opinion on the law's constitutionality. In other words, the courts will not as a matter of course review legislation to determine constitutionality.

The judicial body determining the constitutionality of a law need not be a "court of competent jurisdiction" within the meaning of section 24(1). According to the Supreme Court, an administrative tribunal in carrying out its functions as prescribed by law "is entitled not only to construe the relevant legislation but also to determine whether that legislation was validly enacted . . . A tribunal, if it finds a law it is applying to be constitutionally invalid, must treat it as having no force or effect."[261a]

Because the Constitution of Canada includes sections 1 and 33 of this Act, laws conflicting with certain Charter rights and freedoms may nevertheless be upheld on the grounds that they are "reasonable limits prescribed by law as can be demonstrably justified in a free and democratic society," or that they are a legitimate use of the legislative override. The principle of legislative supremacy remains, therefore, with respect to fundamental rights, legal rights, and equality rights, provided that the conditions of section 33 are met.

The term "any law" includes all Federal and provincial statutes as well as subordinate legislation authorized by them. It also includes common law,[262] and British statutes that may apply to Canada (such as any relevant portions of our pre-Confederation constitutional documents). Justice Wilson in *Operation Dismantle* (1985)[263] was also "prepared to assume, without deciding," that the decision to permit the testing of cruise missiles in Canada, which was not a "law" in any conventional sense, is also caught by this subsection. The issue did not have to be decided in the case. Nevertheless, the ruling in the same case that cabinet decisions are caught by section 32(1)(a) and therefore subject to the Charter, would seem to make the question academic.

Subsection (2): The major question here is whether the Constitution of Canada only "includes" the documents referred to in this subsection, or "means" or "is defined as" those documents. This question is immediately relevant because of the purported entrenchment of the Supreme Court Act by sections 41(d) and 42(d). If the Constitution is "defined" by section 52(2), then references to the Supreme Court Act in sections 41 and 42 are presumably of no effect until such time as that Act is added, through constitutional amendment, to the Schedule. If the other interpretation is correct, then the Constitution in fact "includes" the enumerated documents plus at least the Supreme Court Act which has been an ordinary statute of Parliament. In this event the courts must determine how much (if not all) of that Act's 106 sections, many of which consist of administrative detail, is "Constitution."

The question raised by subsection (2) is also more generally relevant. There is the frightening prospect of the courts entrenching, through their interpretation of 52(2), many statutes which, while of "c"onstitutional importance, were never intended to be entrenched. It is mind-boggling to contemplate the uncertainty which this potentially overwhelming judicial activism would create.

The documents referred to in section 52(2) and listed in the Schedule entitled "Modernization of the Constitution" may be summarized as follows. (In the modernizing process several statutes are repealed.)

(1) The Canada Act, including the 1982 Constitution Act (with amendments). This is noted individually in 52(2) and is not, therefore, contained in the Schedule.

(2) The Constitution Act, 1867, and all amendments originally entitled "B.N.A. Act." These are Schedule items 1, 5, 9, 14-16, 18, 21, 25-30. (The 1916 amendment extending the life of Parliament by one year was repealed by Britain's 1927 Statute Law Revision Act, and so it is not included in the Schedule.)

(3) Other *de facto* amendments to the 1867 Constitution Act. These are Schedule items 7 and 10. See Chapter 5 under "Amendment by the Federal Parliament" and "Amendment by the British Parliament" for a discussion of the concept of Constitution Act amendment.

(4) Instruments (statutes or orders-in-council) adding territories or provinces to Canada, or creating provinces from existing Canadian territory. These are Schedule items 2-4, 6, 8, 12, 13. (Item 21, admitting Newfoundland, is included in [2] above as it was originally entitled "B.N.A. Act.")

(5) Statute of Westminster. This is Schedule item 17.

By virtue of subsection 2(c), the Constitution of Canada includes the 1983 amendment to the 1982 Constitution Act (see section 61) and the 1985 amendment (replacing section 51) to the 1867 Constitution Act.

Subsection (3): This subsection places changes to the "Constitution of Canada" beyond the ordinary reach of Canadian legislatures. It is this characteristic which makes the Constitution "rigid," a term that applies to a Constitution which legally can be altered only by a procedure more restrictive than the ordinary law-making process. It is the provisions of Part V of the Act which provide the rigidity. As pointed out in the commentaries, sections 44 and 45 are not "rigid" because amendments authorized by them may be made by the normal law-making process.

➤ **SECTION 53:** (1) The enactments referred to in Column I of the schedule are hereby repealed or amended to the extent indicated in Column II thereof and, unless repealed, shall continue as law in Canada under the names set out in Column III thereof.

(2) Every enactment, except the *Canada Act 1982*, that refers to an enactment referred to in the schedule by the name in Column I thereof is hereby amended by substituting for that name the corresponding name in Column III thereof, and any British North America Act not referred to in the schedule may be cited as the *Constitution Act* followed by the year and number, if any, of its enactment.

This section confirms the repeals, amendments and renaming, of documents to the extent contained in the Schedule. The most significant name change is that of every B.N.A. Act to "Constitution Act" followed by the year of enactment. The section also makes the consequential name changes within other documents that refer to those listed in the Schedule.

Perhaps the most important amendment is the repeal of sections 4 and 7(1) of the Statute of Westminster insofar as those provisions applied to Canada. These sections read as follows:

> 4. No Act of Parliament of the United Kingdom passed after the commencement of this Act shall extend or be deemed to extend, to a Dominion as part of the law of that Dominion, unless it is expressly declared in that Act that the Dominion has requested, and consented to, the enactment thereof.
>
> . . .
>
> 7(1) Nothing in this Act shall be deemed to apply to the repeal, amendment or alteration of the British North America Acts, 1867 to 1930, or any order, rule or regulation made thereunder.

This repeal is the result of the "sign off" or patriation section 2 of the Canada Act.

➤ **SECTION 54:** Part IV is repealed on the day that is one year after this Part comes into force and this section may be repealed and this Act renumbered, consequentially upon the repeal of Part IV and this section, by proclamation issued by the Governor General under the Great Seal of Canada.

This Part VII came into force on April 17, 1982, as did the rest of the Constitution Act (except for the equality rights of section 15 which was delayed three years). Part IV was repealed, therefore, on April 17, 1983. It consisted of section 37 which required the calling of a constitutional conference within the first year.

Section 54 authorizes its own repeal by proclamation.

➤ **SECTION 54.1:** Part IV.1 and this section are repealed on April 18, 1987.

This section was added by the 1983 Constitution Amendment Proclamation. Part IV.1 consists of section 37.1 which requires that two additional constitutional conferences be called by April 17, 1987. Part IV.1 and section 54.1 were automatically repealed on April 18, 1987.

➤ **SECTION 55:** A French version of the portions of the Constitution of Canada referred to in the schedule shall be prepared by the Minister of Justice of Canada as expeditiously as possible and, when any portion thereof sufficient to warrant action being taken has been so prepared, it shall be put forward for enactment by proclamation issued by the Governor General under the Great Seal of Canada pursuant to the procedure then applicable to an amendment of the same provisions of the Constitution of Canada.

Because most of the documents included in the Constitution of Canada were enacted by the British Parliament they were enacted only in English. The sole exception among those British documents is the Canada Act (including, therefore, the 1982 Constitution Act) which was enacted in both official languages. Section 3 of the Canada Act states that the French version of that Act as set out in Schedule A "has the same authority" as the English version. Schedule B to the Canada Act contains the 1982 Constitution Act in both languages so that they, too, are equally authoritative.

All of the documents enacted by the British Parliament have been translated into French, but before 1982 only the English versions were authoritative. In the event of discrepancy between the two languages the English prevailed. Now, according to section 55, official French versions of all constitutional documents which lack them must be prepared and then enacted according to the relevant amending procedures of Part V.

Section 133 of the 1867 Constitution Act as well as section 18(1) of the 1982 Constitution Act require all Federal statutes to be "printed and published" in both official languages. The seven Canadian statutes in the Schedule will not, therefore, require the preparation of French versions. These seven (2, 12, 13, 27-30) are the Manitoba Act, Saskatchewan Act, Alberta Act, and the four Constitution Act amendments made under the authority of section 91(1): 1965, 1974, 1975 (No. 1), and 1975 (No. 2). The 1952 amendment, also a Canadian statute, is repealed. (The 1985 amendment to section 51 of the 1867 Constitution Act was made under the authority of section 44 of the 1982 Constitution Act.)

➤ **SECTION 56:** Where any portion of the Constitution of Canada has been or is enacted in English and French or where a French version of any portion of the Constitution is enacted pursuant to section 55, the English and French versions of that portion of the Constitution are equally authoritative.

Now that the entire Constitution of Canada will have two equally authoritative versions the problem of reconciling linguistic differences which go beyond mere semantics is aggravated. The problem has existed in the past but it is potentially more serious now that the 1867 and 1982 Constitution Acts are included. The issue goes beyond the scope of this book but is alluded to in the commentaries on section 3 of the Canada Act and Charter section 23(3)(b).

The problem has existed for Quebec as well, in that section 133 requires Quebec statutes to be "printed and published" in both French and English. However, Quebec's courts have tended to favour the former. This should have been an issue also for Manitoba since 1870, but in fact the preparation of two versions as required by section 23 of the Manitoba Act was begun only in 1979. New Brunswick began to face the problem in 1982 by virtue of section 18(2) of the Constitution Act. If other provinces opt into this part of the Charter they too will be confronted with the problem; until then, they will continue to use English, at least as the official version.

➤ **SECTION 57:** The English and French versions of this Act are equally authoritative.

Given that this Act was enacted by the British Parliament in both languages, and given the statement of section 56, this section seems to be redundant.

➤ **SECTION 58:** Subject to section 59, this Act shall come into force on a day to be fixed by proclamation issued by the Queen or the Governor General under the Great Seal of Canada.

The proclamation was issued by the Queen in Ottawa on April 17, 1982, and the Act became effective on that date. See the commentary on section 59 for the significance of the exception noted in section 58. Although the Act is effective only since the date of proclamation, events occurring before 1982 have been relevant to the Act's application. For example, time before April 17, 1982 has been included in determining "reasonable time" (s. 11[b]) within which a trial is to be held. Also, some punishment begun before, but continuing after, the Act's effective date has been deemed "cruel and unusual" and therefore in violation of section 12.[264] These examples merely illustrate a process of transition.

➤ **SECTION 59:** (1) Paragraph 23(1)(a) shall come into force in respect of Quebec on a day to be fixed by proclamation issued by the Queen or the Governor General under the Great Seal of Canada.

(2) A proclamation under subsection (1) shall be issued only where authorized by the legislative assembly or government of Quebec.

(3) This section may be repealed on the day paragraph 23(1)(a) comes into force in respect of Quebec and this Act amended and renumbered, consequentially upon the repeal of this section, by proclamation issued by the Queen or the Governor General under the Great Seal of Canada.

This is the provision exempting Quebec from the minority language educational requirements of section 23(1)(a)—the "mother-tongue" clause. It is one of the two concessions offered by Prime Minister Trudeau (with the agreement of the provincial premiers) immediately following the November 1981 conference, in an effort to secure Lévesque's acceptance of the Constitutional Accord. The provision for financial compensation under section 40 was the other concession.

Subsection (2) permits either the legislature or the Government of Quebec to authorize Quebec's acceptance of 23(1)(a). However, a Quebec Government bill passed in June 1982 provides that "the Government shall not authorize a proclamation under subsection 1 of section 59 of the Constitution Act, 1982, without obtaining the prior consent of the National Assembly of Quebec." This is the same bill which invoked the "notwithstanding" clause for all Quebec legislation.

By mid-1991 Quebec remained exempt from 23(1)(a).

➤ **SECTION 60:** This Act may be cited as the *Constitution Act,* 1982, and the Constitution Acts 1867 to 1975 (No. 2) and this Act may be cited together as the *Constitution Acts, 1867 to 1982.*

This section needs no comment.

➤ **SECTION 61:** A reference to the *"Constitution Acts, 1867 to 1982"* shall be deemed to include a reference to the *"Constitution Amendment Proclamation, 1983"*.

This section was added by the 1983 Constitution Amendment Proclamation. It adds that proclamation to the "Constitution Acts, 1867 to 1982." In view of section 52(2)(c) which seems to accomplish the same thing, this section may be redundant.

A constitution is never static. In Canada, this is true of both the codified and the uncodified parts. The "C"onstitution may change through the replacement of one codified document by another, as happened several times between the 1763 Royal Proclamation and the 1867 Constitution Act. An existing Constitution may be formally amended, as has happened two dozen times to the 1867 Act and once to the 1982 Act. Or a major component (such as the 1982 Canada and Constitution Acts) which is too important to be called an amendment may be added to the Constitution. These kinds of changes are easily documented, although the reader may recall the possible ambiguities noted in Chapter 5 relating to 1867 Constitution Act "amendments."

Of somewhat greater difficulty is knowing what else merits the status of "constitution." Here again, some things are obvious such as statutes whose "constitutional" importance cannot be denied—such as the Statute of Westminster, the Canada Elections Act, the Citizenship Act, and the Manitoba, Saskatchewan, and Alberta Acts. But two other major components of our constitution create greater uncertainty. These are convention and judicial decisions.

The problem with convention lies both in recognizing it, and coping with the realization that it cannot be enforced in a court of law (although views on the latter are not unanimous). Part of the difficulty may be traced to the misleading nature of the 1867 Constitution Act. To a large extent this was a reflection of the fact that much of Britain's constitution—recall that ours was to be "similar in principle"—is convention. The misleading nature of the 1867 Act continues today and is "corrected" through convention. This is not to say convention lacks authority, for in a sense that would be a contradiction of terms. By its very meaning, a conventional rule is effective partly because the actors consider themselves "bound" by it.

What, then, is the problem? The answer takes us back to the meaning of a constitution as the body of fundamental rules according to which a country (for example) is governed. Surely, rules which are fundamental should at least be knowable! Was convention violated by Prime Minister Pearson's response to the February 1968 third reading defeat of the taxation bill? Probably not, although views differed at the time. Would convention have been violated if Prime Minister Trudeau in 1981 had proceeded unilaterally to London with the Patriation package? The Supreme Court said "yes." Was convention violated by the 1981 Accord which produced the 1982 Constitution Act without the agreement of Quebec—i.e., did Quebec possess a conventional veto? The Supreme Court said "no." Was convention violated when Prime Minister King decided to retain power following the 1925 election which gave the plurality of

Commons seats to the opposition Conservative Party, defeated King in his own riding and decimated his cabinet? The answer clearly is "no." Or was convention violated during the events surrounding the 1926 "King-Byng Thing"? Opinion probably remains divided. And on it goes. Whether for good or ill, conventions may not always be recognized, but the problem seems to create no permanent damage. Indeed, the uncertainty and controversy surrounding the identification of conventions form part of the fascination of politics. Incidentally, it is important to distinguish between convention and ethics. For example, one may question the ethics though not the constitutionality of King's retention of power in 1925.

Although convention is not justiciable (according to the Supreme Court), courts have been asked to enforce claims of convention violation. The most spectacular efforts were doubtlessly at the time of the 1981 Constitutional Accord. During the *Patriation Reference* the Supreme Court acknowledged the existence of a convention, but denied that it had legal status, that the Federal government will secure provincial consent before asking the British Parliament to amend the 1867 Constitution Act in a manner that affects provincial powers. In the *Quebec Veto Reference*, the Supreme Court was not even persuaded that Quebec held a conventional veto over Constitutional amendments affecting Quebec's legislative authority. More recently, one of the unsuccessful challenges to the 1990 appointment of additional senators was based on the presumption that the hitherto non-use of section 26 had created a legally binding convention.

In June 1991 the Court reinforced its view that conventions are not justiciable "unless they are incorporated into legislation": Furthermore, "statutes embodying constitutional conventions do not automatically become entrenched to form part of the constitutional law, but retain their status as ordinary statutes. Being a provision in an ordinary statute, s. 33 [of the Public Service Employment Act which prohibited political activity by Federal employees] is subject to review under the Charter as any ordinary legislation."[1]

The uncertainty created by judicial decision-making as a constitutional component differs from that caused by convention. There is, of course, no uncertainty about the legal impact of court rulings, for they become part of the common law. Decisions by upper courts are binding on courts below, so rulings of the Supreme Court of Canada are binding throughout the country. It is possible, of course, for the Supreme Court to overturn one of its earlier rulings but this is rare. Even the major shifts of Privy Council decisions in relation to p.o.g.g. and property and civil rights, for example, were not announced within the context of changed opinions. The uncertainty associated with court decisions arises from not knowing how a particular case will be decided, and whether the courts will view that decision as a precedent in a later, seemingly similar, case.

This becomes critical when (as is still true for much of the Charter) the courts are virtually defining important segments of the codified Constitution.

For example, can stores be required to close on Sundays? That seems to depend upon the purpose of the legislation rather than its effect (*Big M Drug Mart, Edwards Books and Art*). Does freedom of association include the right to strike? No (*Alberta Labour Reference*). When has an accused really waived the right to counsel? Only when he or she fully recognizes the consequences (*Clarkson*). How that recognition is determined is not so easily answered. When has a government whose legislation has been impugned demonstrated that the limitation of a Charter right or freedom is "reasonable" in a free and democratic society? Or when might it truly be said that evidence obtained in violation of a Charter right would, if admitted, bring the administration of justice into disrepute? And in whose eyes? Does a fetus have a right to life? Not under the Quebec Charter (*Tremblay v. Daigle*) or the Criminal Code (*R. v. Sullivan*), but we do not yet know for the Canadian Charter.

These and many other questions are now decided by the courts, and in the early years of the new Constitution Act the Supreme Court has endeavoured to establish guidelines for its own and therefore lower court future decisions. Some of the issues, and the cases which produced guiding criteria, are noted below.

(1) What is a "reasonable" limit to Charter rights and freedoms (s. 1)?—*Oakes.*

(2) When does search or seizure become "reasonable" (s. 8)?—*Hunter v. Southam.*

(3) What length of delay before trial is "reasonable" (s. 11[b])?—*Askov.*

(4) When does double jeopardy exist (s. 11[h])?—*Wigglesworth.*

(5) When is treatment or punishment "cruel and unusual" (s. 12)? —*Smith (Edward Dewey).*

(6) What is "discrimination" within the context of equality rights (s. 15)?—*Andrews v. Law Society of British Columbia.*

(7) What might "minority language educational facilities" entail and, short of the establishment of an independent school board, what might constitute appropriate management and control of those facilities by the linguistic minority (s. 23[3])?—*Mahe.*

(8) When might the admission of evidence gained in violation of a Charter right or freedom "bring the administration of justice into disrepute" (s. 24[2])?—*Collins.*

(9) When might government interference with "existing" aboriginal rights, which are "recognized and affirmed," be justified (s. 35)?—*Sparrow.*

What generalizations may be made about judicial review of the 1867 and 1982 Constitution Acts? A major part of Chapter 5 summarized judicial activity in relation to some of the more contentious sections of the 1867 Act. Some tentative conclusions are possible about the Supreme Court's treatment of the Charter (which has been the source of the overwhelming bulk of the litigation relating to the 1982 Act), a few of which impinge upon Canadian federalism as well.

The year 1982 marked a fundamental shift in the role of the courts and therefore in the focus of much thinking about our constitution. This role change was described in Chapter 4 as a movement from legislative supremacy or "unlimited" government to "semi-limited" government. The advent of the Charter has led some people to view the 1982 Constitution Act as a new Constitution. So far as the ordinary citizen is concerned, there is probably justification of that view because of the new emphasis of the judicial system on individual rights and freedoms. Indeed, there is now much greater and more prominent media coverage of Supreme Court rulings because of their potential impact on our personal lives. The adjudication of inter-governmental jurisdiction disputes seldom has the same personal impact.

The task of the courts in interpreting the Charter is complicated by the fact that courts face virtually a clean slate. (This is in sharp contrast with the precedents, sometimes contradictory, available when the Supreme Court took over interpretation of the Constitution Act from the Privy Council in 1949.) This means that the judicial system as final decision-maker must earn public respect. Even if popular opinion is not excited about something called "legislative supremacy," it may well question whether judges have a unique competence to decide social or moral issues such as Sunday closing or abortion. And the public certainly expects "fairness" (or justice) in court rulings, doubtlessly including decisions as to when the administration of justice might *really* be brought into disrepute. We must not forget, however, that it was our representatives who bestowed this awesome responsibility upon the courts.

The success rate of Charter claimants fell from 67% in the first two years of Supreme Court decisions (1984 and 1985) to about 30% during the next four years. The reason for this change is more likely a philosophical shift on the part of continuing justices rather than the fact that the Mulroney government filled all six vacancies during those six years. During the "honeymoon" of the first two years, all but two (about 85%) of the Court's rulings were unanimous; subsequently, the frequency of unanimity has fallen to about 60%. These developments "reflect the same hard reality—the inescapably contentious character of modern judicial review" vis-à-vis the former system of legislative supremacy.[2] The *Morgentaler* decision, in which five judges wrote three separate opinions supporting the Court's ruling, and from which two judges dissented, illustrates the diversity of judicial thinking. Furthermore, the ruling provides no real guidance as to what abortion legislation might be judicially acceptable.

The increasing judicial self-restraint is evident in the Court's attitude toward section 1 as well. As noted in the commentary on this limitations clause, the rate of successful government appeal rose from one in about a dozen through 1987, to more than half since then. Morton, Russell and Withey suggest that this shift "simply confirm[s] what was already an open secret: that the Court has been badly divided on how to handle the section 1 issue."[3]

Legal rights cases have dominated Supreme Court decisions. (It is recognized that these rights constitute a large part of the Charter.) Of those rights, alleged violations of sections 7 (especially the principles of fundamental justice) and 11 (especially trial within reasonable time [b], and the presumption of innocence [d]) have been the most frequent. These cases, which relate primarily to criminal law and therefore to Federal jurisdiction, have led to "a new constitutional code of conduct for Canadian police officers in dealing with suspects and accused persons, and in the process has pushed the Canadian criminal process away from the 'crime control' toward the 'due process' side of the ledger."[4] This emphasis on due process was noted in the commentaries on several Charter sections, including the fact that section 1 is not available to sustain Charter violations by the police because these violations are not "prescribed by law."

There is no doubt of the Charter's centralizing tendency as the Supreme Court applies uniform standards across the country. Swinton suggests that Prime Minister Trudeau's intention with the entire patriation package, including the Charter, was to "strengthen ties to the national community and weaken the centrifugal forces." The package, she goes on, was part of his broader intention to strengthen the Federal government vis-à-vis the provinces.[5] Offsetting this centralizing tendency is the following recognition of diversity within the Charter. (The final item relates to the amending formula.)

(1) The possibility that "reasonable limits . . . demonstrably justified in a free and democratic society" may be placed on Charter rights or freedoms, and therefore that legislation (provincial or Federal) which violates the Charter may be sustained (s. 1).

(2) The ability of a province to discriminate in favour of its residents, and in so doing to restrict mobility rights, when its rate of unemployment exceeds the national average (s. 6).

(3) The ability of a province (or the Federal government) to establish affirmative action programs beneficial to disadvantaged individuals or groups, and in so doing to restrict equality rights (s. 15).

(4) The fact that the official languages sections (16-22) have specific application only (with certain exceptions discussed in the appropriate commentaries) to the Federal government and New Brunswick.

(5) For Quebec, the exemption (until that province decides otherwise pursuant to section 59) from the so-called "mother-tongue" clause of section 23's minority language educational rights.

(6) The application of minority language educational rights within a province only where numbers warrant (s. 23[3]).

(7) The ability of a province (and the Federal government) to legislate notwithstanding some of the Charter rights and freedoms (s. 33).

(8) The ability of a province to opt out of certain constitutional amendments, and in some cases to receive financial compensation (ss. 38[3], 40).

While several Supreme Court decisions acknowledge the existence of diversity it is too soon to know the long term impact that federalism or, more broadly, diversity will have on Court rulings.[6] For reference to several cases where federalism or the element of diversity have been made explicit, see the commentaries on the following sections:

Section 1: As noted in the commentary on this section, and commentaries on other sections in which the "limitations" clause emerged, the Supreme Court invariably acknowledged the importance of the government's objective, and almost invariably agreed there was a rational connection between the objective and the impugned legislation. Unsuccessful appeals related to proportionality—the Charter right or freedom was not infringed as little as possible. Swinton comments that of the Supreme Court judges, it is La Forest who has been the most receptive to arguments stressing the value of diversity and of deference to legislatures. She notes his judgements (which are not considered in the present volume) in *Edwards Books and Art, Jones* (Alberta)—section 2(a)—and in *Andrews* (section 15). In the last of these cases, for example, La Forest states that he prefers "to think in terms of a single test for s. 1, but one that is to be applied to vastly differing situations with the flexibility and realism inherent in the word 'reasonable' mandated by the Constitution."[7]

Section 2(a): *Edwards Books and Art*, in relation to Sunday closing and the purpose of the legislation—noting the difference between the Lord's Day Act and Ontario's Retail Business Holidays Act.

Section 9: *Lyons*, in relation to the discretionary application, and hence the absence of geographical uniformity, of the Criminal Code's provisions for imprisoning "dangerous offenders."

Section 15: *Turpin* (applying criteria established in *Andrews* for identifying "discrimination"), in relation to the fact that residents of Alberta, but not of the rest of Canada, may elect trial by judge alone rather than by judge and jury.

When this project began, Meech Lake was a virtually unknown body of water in the Gatineau Hills north of Ottawa. When the manuscript was being prepared for publication, a major question was how much of Meech Lake—by then associated with the Constitutional Accord—should be included. The Accord was intended to "bring Quebec into the Constitution"—a misleading statement given the fact that Quebec had been "in" (albeit unwillingly) since April 17, 1982.

The death of Meech Lake on June 23, 1990 resolved that dilemma but almost immediately created another. What should be said about the studies launched by the governments in Ottawa, Quebec and other provincial capitals to decide Canada's future? The Constitutional significance of these post-Meech developments is obvious for it seems clear that, regardless of Quebec's future within Canada, the Constitution is about to undergo major change. Indeed every aspect of our Constitution, not just the "Quebec question," is now open for discussion. The initiative taken by the Alberta government in August 1990 illustrates the point. The discussion paper of Alberta's Constitutional Reform Task Force is titled "Alberta in a New Canada."[8] The Paper continues: The failure of the Meech Lake Accord

> has caused many Canadians to begin a broader and more fundamental examination of our national community. Alberta must be prepared not only to respond to suggestions for change coming from other parts of the country, but also be ready to advance Alberta's views on the future course for Canada.
>
> ALBERTA IN A NEW CANADA raises issues on various systems of government, federal institutions, the division of responsibilities between the federal and provincial governments, fundamental rights and freedom, bilingualism, aboriginal constitutional matters, and the amending formula.

Intergovernmental Affairs Minister Jim Horsman, Task Force chairman, stated the government's intention that this study be "the most comprehensive review of the Constitution ever undertaken in Alberta." Three phases were envisaged. During the fall and early winter of 1990 the Task Force held roundtable discussions of thirteen topics within the following four general areas. Each topic was chaired by a person having relevant expertise.

(1) "An overview of federalism," including the evolution of Alberta's position on the Constitution.

(2) "Dynamics of federalism," including aboriginal constitutional issues, the Charter of Rights and Freedoms, and institutional reform.

(3) "Restructuring federalism," including perspectives from Atlantic Canada, Quebec, and the West.

(4) "The amending process and the economics of federalism," including a discussion of the amending formula, public participation in the amendment process, federalism and the economy, and the economics of the Constitution.

These meetings were followed by public hearings throughout the province. Finally (the third phase) the legislature would formulate its position on Constitutional reform.

The best known post-Meech initiatives, however, have been taken by the Federal and Quebec governments. They are briefly described below.

Ottawa:

November 1990: Creation of the Citizens' Forum on Canada's Future—the Spicer Commission—which crisscrossed the country seeking the opinions of ordinary citizens on Canadian unity. The Commission reported on June 27, 1991. What it found, and seemed predictable, was that "Canada is in a crisis of identity, understanding, and leadership." Its major recommendations included the following:[9]

Quebec: "Quebec should have the freedom and means to be itself—a unique society with its own distinctive place in a renewed" federalism. This apparent call for Quebec special status was at marked variance with the overwhelming sentiment expressed during the course of the Commission's hearings, that "Quebec's continued presence in Confederation cannot be bought . . . by sacrificing individual or provincial equality." This popular sentiment does not bode well for achievement of the national consensus necessary to keep the country together. The Commission framed its recommendation more generally: that "the provinces . . . entered confederation on different terms and operate under different provisions," that "special arrangements in provinces based on special needs are a fundamental principle of Canadian federalism," and so "this principle would apply where needed to all provinces." The question of asymmetrical federalism is noted below.

Aboriginal peoples: There should be "prompt, fair settlement of the territorial and treaty claims" in order to facilitate the achievement of native self-government; and the Indian Act and the department which administers Indian affairs should be "phased out as self-government becomes a reality."

Official languages: The Commission accepted the concept of official languages. However, application of the principle should be reviewed "to clear the air—with a view to ensuring that it is fair and sensible"—to explain its purpose, and to make clear its costs and benefits. Otherwise, the Commission feared, "rising public dissatisfaction and misunderstanding" might cause rejection of the principle itself.

Cultural diversity: Federal funding of multicultural activities should be eliminated except for "those serving immigrant orientation, reduction of racial discrimination and promotion of equality." Ottawa should "devise far clearer, bolder and more imaginative public information programs on the value and benefits of cultural diversity."

Leadership and democracy: The Commission deplored "the mindless, and sometimes disgraceful, behaviour of members of both Houses in bringing the parliamentary system into disrepute." The Senate should be either fundamentally reformed or abolished. Party discipline in the House of Commons should be substantially relaxed, with more free votes, so that the peoples' representatives may more adequately represent their constituents. Prime Minister Mulroney had anticipated this criticism in his May 1991 Throne Speech promise to change Commons procedure. The Commission did not, however, support the adoption of machinery for impeaching or recalling members of Parliament. These features do not square easily with the parliamentary system.

As for the process of constitutional amendment, the chairman urged, but the Commission did not recommend, that Ottawa reconsider its oft-repeated rejection of a constituent assembly.

December 1990: Establishment of the Special Joint Committee on the Process for Amending the Constitution of Canada (the Beaudoin-Edwards Committee). The Committee reported on June 20, 1991. It recommended replacement of the present general amending formula (seven provinces containing 50% of provincial populations) with a resurrected 1971 Victoria Charter general formula. Amendments under that formula required approval by all four regions—Quebec, Ontario, two of the four Atlantic provinces, and two or three of the four western provinces as needed to include 50% of the population of those provinces. The Committee also proposed a veto for aboriginal peoples over any amendments affecting aboriginal rights. The inherent provincial inequality created by the Victoria formula led Alberta's Minister of Intergovernmental Affairs Jim Horsman immediately to reject the Beaudoin-Edwards recommendation. Not only would both central provinces possess vetoes; the present populations of the western provinces would give British Columbia a de facto veto of any proposed amendment not supported by all three remaining provinces. Whereas the Victoria formula had no unanimity rule, the Committee proposed unanimity for amendments affecting the status of official languages, Canada's relationship to the monarchy, and provincial control of natural resources. The time permitted for necessary approvals would be reduced from the current three years to two. Given the fact that any change to the present amending formula requires approval by all eleven legislatures, prospects for the Committee's "new" formula are bleak.

Rather than propose a constituent assembly the Committee recommended that public hearings become part of the amending process, and that they be held early during that process. However, hearings would be only consultative. It also recommended national referenda on proposed amendments, with approval requiring both an overall majority and a majority within each of the four regions. Referenda would be held at the option of the Federal government and, as for public hearings, would not bind Parliament. This represents no change from what is currently possible.

April 1991: Creation of an 18-member cabinet committee on national unity, chaired by Joe Clark who moved from External Affairs to head the new portfolio of Constitutional Affairs. The committee travelled the country, meeting with provincial and Territorial leaders, as well as other groups, and was to submit its recommendations for consideration by the Government in the fall.

May 1991: The prime minister announced in the Throne Speech that once the Government had considered the recommendations of the various Federal and provincial studies—itself an overwhelming task, given the great diversity of those recommendations—it would submit its own proposals to a new joint Senate-House of Commons committee. Beginning in September this committee would meet with provincial and Territorial legislative committees, as well as aboriginal and perhaps other special interest groups, and report to Parliament by the end of February 1992. At that point, according to the Throne Speech, the Government would "propose a plan for a renewed Canada for consideration by the people of Canada," and ask Parliament to pass legislation giving Canadians "greater participation . . . in constitutional change."[10] The nature of this "greater participation" is unclear, but Constitutional Affairs Minister Clark all but rejected the notion of a constituent assembly as part of the amending process so long as Quebec refuses to participate. Only "at some later stage in the process, if things break down," would he be "prepared to look at a constituent assembly."[11] Establishment of the new committee, consisting of ten senators and fifteen members of the Commons, was approved by Parliament in June.

Quebec:

July 1990: Establishment of the Bélanger-Campeau Commission by the National Assembly to study Quebec's political future. The Commission reported in March 1991. Because of the divergence of opinions between separatist and federalist elements, agreement within the Commission was difficult. As a result, a compromise recommendation called for a referendum no later than October 1992 either on sovereignty, or on a proposal for renewed federalism which might come from the rest of the country (if such a proposal were acceptable to the Quebec government).

January 1991: Report prepared for the Quebec Liberal Party (Allaire Report, "A Quebec Free to Choose") and adopted by the Party in March. If implemented, its recommendations would emasculate the federal system and create virtual "sovereignty-association" because of the major shift in legislative jurisdiction from Ottawa to Quebec.[12] Quebec would gain jurisdiction in the following areas currently shared with Ottawa or under Ottawa's exclusive control:

recreation and sports
natural resources
unemployment insurance
regional development
industry and commerce
research and development
income security
municipal affairs
social affairs
culture
health
tourism
agriculture
education
public security
energy
environment
housing
family policy
manpower
language
communications

Quebec and Ottawa would share jurisdiction in the following areas:

post office and telecommunications
taxation and revenue
financial institutions
immigration
fisheries
foreign policy
transport
native affairs
justice (appeal to the Supreme Court of Canada in Quebec civil cases to be eliminated)

Ottawa would retain exclusive jurisdiction in the following areas:

defence and territorial security
currency and common debt
customs and tariffs
equalization

The Report also called for a fall 1992 Quebec referendum, either on Quebec sovereignty or on any proposal from the rest of the country on renewed federalism.

Reaction beyond Quebec clearly indicated that the Report was unacceptable to the rest of the country. When the Quebec Liberal Party adopted the Report in March, Premier Bourassa chose to characterize it as a bargaining position.

Referendum legislation (Bill 150) was passed in June 1991. It provided for two legislative committees, one to study the economic implications of Quebec sovereignty and the other to consider any proposals for renewed federalism from the rest of the country. The Parti Québécois opposed the Bill which guaranteed neither a referendum on sovereignty nor, indeed, a referendum at all.

The Quebec government has stated that it will not take the initiative in negotiating renewed federalism, but will await proposals from the rest of Canada. Furthermore, the province intends to bargain only with Ottawa. Although the practicality of one-on-one negotiation seems dubious, such bargaining would require that Ottawa forge an agreement among Parliament and the nine remaining provincial legislatures in advance, and then establish some sort of ongoing consultative machinery during the bargaining with Quebec.

Quebec's position was stated by Intergovernmental Affairs Minister Gil Rémillard: Quebec's Meech Lake proposals having been rejected, the next move should be up to the rest of the country. "Ottawa and the other provinces know what we want. So we will wait for some proposals. And if they propose something interesting, we can study the proposals and see if we can hold a referendum on that. Or, if we don't get any proposals, or if those proposals are not good enough, we will have to go for a referendum on sovereignty."[13] In spite of Prime Minister Mulroney's insistence that he will not be driven by Quebec's October 1992 referendum deadline, the political reality of that deadline cannot be ignored.

What is the likelihood of an agreement with Quebec? Considering what the Spicer Commission was told, as distinct from the Commission's recommendation of special status, the prospect is not encouraging. The apparent popular rejection of asymmetrical federalism flies in the face of one of the presumed advantages of a federal structure—to allow (within limits) component units to tailor political, economic and social systems to fit their needs. It also ignores significant asymmetrical elements already within our system. Those within the 1982 Constitution Act were noted earlier in this Conclusion/Epilogue. Others, from the 1867 Act, include the various special arrangements over the years for representation in the House of Commons (ss. 51, 51A); acknowledgement of Quebec's civil law (s. 94, as well as statutory provision for three Quebec judges on the Supreme Court); special protection of the minority "official" language in Quebec and, since 1870, Manitoba (s. 133, and s. 23 of the Manitoba Act). Furthermore, Federal-provincial financial agreements have for years acknowledged differences among provinces through equalization payments and opting out arrangements for many joint-cost programs. Admittedly, none of these asymmetrical features seem to approach Quebec's current needs, especially if the Allaire Report becomes the basis of negotiation, but they do debunk the myth of provincial equality as the historic norm.

The alternative to special status seems to be an even more decentralized federal system than that envisaged by Meech Lake. But if Meech Lake called for too much decentralization to suit many people outside Quebec, how could an even weaker Federal government be acceptable? And yet that seems to be the inevitable conclusion if Quebec is to stay within Canada and the federal system is to retain its existing degree of symmetry.

If there is to be a new constitutional arrangement, through what mechanism might it be achieved? One of the lessons of Meech Lake is that greater public involvement is essential. The people are not prepared to have their political leaders wheeling and dealing behind closed doors to strike some agreement which may or may not be acceptable to the country. The executive federalism approach to Meech Lake, and indeed to the 1982 Accord, is unacceptable.

But what sort of involvement is needed? One popular suggestion is the creation of a constituent assembly. This would be consistent with the current mistrust of our politicians, and might add the legitimacy which the Meech Lake Accord lacked, but it raises a host of questions even if our politicians were prepared to risk an assembly. Furthermore, any decisions made by an assembly would also require approval by the country's eleven legislatures pursuant to the present amending formula.

The thorny questions relate to (among other things) an assembly's mandate, size, method of delegate selection, distribution of delegates across the country, delegate qualification, representation of special interest groups, voting procedure (by individuals or blocks), and nature of the required majority (numerical as well as geographic). If a referendum were subsequently held what majority would it require? An overall majority? A majority in every province? A majority in seven provinces having at least half of all provincial populations? A majority in each of the four proposed regions? Following this public input would the legislatures by bound to ratify the result? Of more immediate importance, is an assembly practical if Quebec still refuses to participate? Even if the answer is "yes," would there be time to meet Quebec's referendum deadline—unless Premier Bourassa were to delay it—given the absence of assurance that the experiment would be successful?

All this and much more is now the subject of intense discussion, but beyond the scope of the present volume. The bottom line for accommodation between Quebec and the rest of the country, the core of the present controversy, is doubtlessly the strength of the loyalty which all of us, both within and without Quebec, have to our country. In practical terms this means the extent to which all Canadians are willing to compromise for the sake of that accommodation.

Perhaps the following statement, which has a contemporary ring but was written five centuries ago, is an appropriate concluding comment: "There is nothing more difficult to handle, more doubtful of success, and more dangerous to carry through than initiating changes in a state's constitution"—Niccolo Machiavelli.

APPENDIX A

1867 Constitution Act as Amended (to 1991)

Preamble

An Act for the Union of Canada, Nova Scotia, and New Brunswick, and the Government thereof; and for Purposes connected therewith.

Whereas the Provinces of Canada, Nova Scotia and New Brunswick have expressed their Desire to be federally united into One Dominion under the Crown of the United Kingdom of Great Britain and Ireland, with a Constitution similar in Principle to that of the United Kingdom:

And whereas such a Union would conduce to the Welfare of the Provinces and promote the Interests of the British Empire:

And whereas on the Establishment of the Union by Authority of Parliament it is expedient, not only that the Constitution of the Legislative Authority in the Dominion be provided for, but also that the Nature of the Executive Government therein be declared:

And whereas it is expedient that Provision be made for the eventual Admission into the Union of other Parts of British North America:

Be it therefore enacted and declared by the Queen's Most Excellent Majesty, by and with the Advice and Consent of the Lords Spiritual and Temporal, and Commons, in this present Parliament assembled, and by the Authority of the same, as follows:

I. Preliminary

SECTION 1: This Act may be cited as the *Constitution Act, 1867.*

SECTION 2: The Provisions of this Act referring to Her Majesty the Queen extend also to the Heirs and Successors of Her Majesty, Kings and Queens of the United Kingdom of Great Britain and Ireland.

II. Union

SECTION 3: It shall be lawful for the Queen, by and with the Advice of Her Majesty's Most Honourable Privy Council, to declare by Proclamation that, on and after a Day therein appointed, not being more than Six Months after the passing of this Act, the Provinces of Canada, Nova Scotia, and New Brunswick shall form and be One Dominion under the Name of Canada; and on and after that Day those Three Provinces shall form and be One Dominion under that Name accordingly.

SECTION 4: The subsequent Provisions of this Act, shall, unless it is otherwise expressed or implied, commence and have effect on and after the Union, that is to say, on and after the Day appointed for the Union taking effect in the Queen's Proclamation; and in the same Provisions, [U]nless it is otherwise expressed or implied, the Name Canada shall be taken to mean Canada as constituted under this Act.

SECTION 5: Canada shall be divided into Four Provinces, named Ontario, Quebec, Nova Scotia, and New Brunswick.

SECTION 6: The Parts of the Province of Canada (as it exists at the passing of this Act) which formerly constituted respectively the Provinces of Upper Canada and Lower Canada shall be deemed to be severed, and shall form Two separate Provinces. The Part which formerly constituted the

(Repealed sections are underlined)
Department of Justice Canada

Province of Upper Canada shall constitute the Province of Ontario; and the Part which formerly constituted the Province of Lower Canada shall constitute the Province of Quebec.

SECTION 7: The Provinces of Nova Scotia and New Brunswick shall have the same Limits as at the passing of this Act.

SECTION 8: In the general Census of the Population of Canada which is hereby required to be taken in the Year One thousand eight hundred and seventy-one, and in every Tenth Year thereafter, the respective Populations of the Four Provinces shall be distinguished.

III. Executive Power

SECTION 9: The Executive Government and Authority of and over Canada is hereby declared to continue and be vested in the Queen.

SECTION 10: The Provisions of this Act referring to the Governor General extend and apply to the Governor General for the Time being of Canada, or other the Chief Executive Officer or Administrator for the Time being carrying on the Government of Canada on behalf and in the Name of the Queen, by whatever Title he is designated.

SECTION 11: There shall be a Council to aid and advise in the Government of Canada, to be styled the Queen's Privy Council for Canada; and the Persons who are to be Members of that Council shall be from Time to Time chosen and summoned by the Governor General and sworn in as Privy Councillors, and Members thereof may be from Time to Time removed by the Governor General.

SECTION 12: All Powers, Authorities, and Functions which under any Act of the Parliament of Great Britain, or of the Parliament of the United Kingdom of Great Britain and Ireland, or of the Legislature of Upper Canada, Lower Canada, Canada, Nova Scotia, or New Brunswick, are at the Union vested in or exerciseable by the respective Governors or Lieutenant Governors of those Provinces, with the Advice, or with the Advice and Consent, of the respective Executive Councils thereof, or in conjunction with those Councils, or with any Number of Members thereof, or by those Governors or Lieutenant Governors individually, shall, as far as the same continue in existence and capable of being exercised after the Union in relation to the Government of Canada, be vested in and exerciseable by the Governor General, with the Advice or with the Advice and Consent of or in conjunction with the Queen's Privy Council for Canada, or any Member thereof, or by the Governor General individually, as the Case requires, subject nevertheless (except with respect to such as exist under Acts of the Parliament of Great Britain or of the Parliament of the United Kingdom of Great Britain and Ireland) to be abolished or altered by the Parliament of Canada.

SECTION 13: The Provisions of this Act referring to the Governor General in Council shall be construed as referring to the Governor General acting by and with the Advice of the Queen's Privy Council for Canada.

SECTION 14: It shall be lawful for the Queen, if Her Majesty thinks fit, to authorize the Governor General from Time to Time to appoint any Person or any Persons jointly or severally to be his Deputy or Deputies within any Part or Parts of Canada, and in that Capacity to exercise during the Pleasure of the Governor General such of the Powers, Authorities, and Functions of the Governor General as the Governor General deems it necessary or expedient to assign to him or them, subject to any Limitations or Directions expressed or given by the Queen; but the Appointment of such a Deputy or Deputies shall not affect the Exercise by the Governor General himself of any Power, Authority or Function.

SECTION 15: The Command-in-Chief of the Land and Naval Militia, and of all Naval and Military Forces, of and in Canada, is hereby declared to continue and be vested in the Queen.

SECTION 16: Until the Queen otherwise directs, the Seat of Government of Canada shall be Ottawa.

IV. Legislative Power

SECTION 17: There shall be One Parliament for Canada, consisting of the Queen, an Upper House styled the Senate, and the House of Commons.

SECTION 18: The privileges, immunities, and powers to be held, enjoyed, and exercised by the Senate and by the House of Commons, and by the Members thereof respectively, shall be such as are from time to time defined by Act of the Parliament of Canada, but so that any Act of the Parliament of Canada defining such privileges, immunities, and powers shall not confer any privileges, immunities, or powers exceeding those at the passing of such Act held, enjoyed, and exercised by the Commons House of Parliament of the United Kingdom of Great Britain and Ireland, and by the Members thereof.

SECTION 19: The Parliament of Canada shall be called together not later than Six Months after the Union.

SECTION 20: <u>There shall be a Session of the Parliament of Canada once at least in every Year, so that Twelve Months shall not intervene between the last Sitting of the Parliament in one Session and its first Sitting in the next Session.</u>

The Senate

SECTION 21: The Senate shall, subject to the Provisions of this Act, consist of One Hundred and four Members, who shall be styled Senators.

SECTION 22: In relation to the Constitution of the Senate Canada shall be deemed to consist of Four Divisions:-

1. Ontario;
2. Quebec;
3. The Maritime Provinces, Nova Scotia and New Brunswick, and Prince Edward Island;
4. The Western Provinces of Manitoba, British Columbia, Saskatchewan, and Alberta;

which Four Divisions shall (subject to the Provisions of this Act) be equally represented in the Senate as follows: Ontario by twenty-four senators; Quebec by twenty-four senators; the Maritime Provinces and Prince Edward Island by twenty-four senators, ten thereof representing Nova Scotia, ten thereof representing New Brunswick, and four thereof representing Prince Edward Island; the Western Provinces by twenty-four senators, six thereof representing Manitoba, six thereof representing British Columbia, six thereof representing Saskatchewan, and six thereof representing Alberta; Newfoundland shall be entitled to be represented in the Senate by six members; the Yukon Territory and the Northwest Territories shall be entitled to be represented in the Senate by one member each.

In the Case of Quebec each of the Twenty-four Senators representing that Province shall be appointed for One of the Twenty-four Electoral Divisions of Lower Canada specified in Schedule A. to Chapter One of the Consolidated Statutes of Canada.

SECTION 23: The Qualification of a Senator shall be as follows:

(1) He shall be of the full age of Thirty Years:

(2) He shall be either a natural-born Subject of the Queen, or a Subject of the Queen naturalized by an Act of the Parliament of Great Britain, or of the Parliament of the United Kingdom of Great Britain and Ireland, or of the Legislature of One of the Provinces of Upper Canada, Lower Canada, Canada, Nova Scotia, or New Brunswick, before the Union, or of the Parliament of Canada, after the Union:

(3) He shall be legally or equitably seised as of Freehold for his own Use and Benefit of Lands or Tenements held in Free and Common Socage, or seised or possessed for his own. Use and Benefit of Lands or Tenements held in Franc-alleu or in Roture, within the. Province for which he is appointed, of the Value of Four thousand Dollars, over and above all Rents, Dues, Debts, Charges, Mortgages, and Incumbrances due or payable out of or charged on or affecting the same:

(4) His Real and Personal Property shall be together worth Four thousand Dollars over and above his Debts and Liabilities:

(5) He shall be resident in the Province for which he is appointed:

(6) In the Case of Quebec he shall have his Real Property Qualification in the Electoral Division for which he is appointed, or shall be resident in that Division.

SECTION 24: The Governor General shall from Time to Time, in the Queen's Name, by Instrument under the Great Seal of Canada, summon qualified Persons to the Senate; and, subject to the Provisions of this Act, every Person so summoned shall become and be a Member of the Senate and a Senator.

SECTION 25: <u>Such Persons shall be first summoned to the Senate as the Queen by Warrant under Her Majesty's Royal Sign Manual thinks fit to approve, and their Names shall be inserted in the Queen's Proclamation of Union.</u>

SECTION 26: If at any Time on the Recommendation of the Governor General the Queen thinks fit to direct that Four or Eight Members be added to the Senate, the Governor General may by Summons to Four or Eight qualified Persons (as the Case may be), representing equally the Four Divisions of Canada, add to the Senate accordingly.

SECTION 27: In case of such Addition being at any Time made, the Governor General shall not summon any Person to the Senate, except upon a further like Direction by the Queen on the like Recommendation, to represent one of the Four Divisions until such Division is represented by Twenty-four Senators and no more.

SECTION 28: The Number of Senators shall not at any Time exceed One Hundred and twelve.

SECTION 29: (1) Subject to subsection (2), a Senator shall, subject to the provisions of this Act, hold his place in the Senate for life.

(2) A Senator who is summoned to the Senate after the coming into force of this subsection shall, subject to this Act, hold his place in the Senate until he attains the age of seventy-five years.

SECTION 30: A Senator may by Writing under his Hand addressed to the Governor General resign his Place in the Senate, and thereupon the same shall be vacant.

SECTION 31: The Place of a Senator shall become vacant in any of the following Cases:

(1) If for Two consecutive Sessions of the Parliament he fails to give his Attendance in the Senate:

(2) If he takes an Oath or makes a Declaration or Acknowledgement of Allegiance, Obedience, or Adherence to a Foreign Power, or does an Act whereby he becomes a Subject or Citizen, or entitled to the Rights or Privileges of a Subject or Citizen, of a Foreign Power:

(3) If he is adjudged Bankrupt or Insolvent, or applies for the Benefit of any Law relating to Insolvent Debtors, or becomes a public Defaulter:

(4) If he is attainted of Treason or convicted of

Felony or of any infamous Crime:

(5) If he ceases to be qualified in respect of Property or of Residence; provided, that a Senator shall not be deemed to have ceased to be qualified in respect of Residence by reason only of his residing at the Seat of the Government of Canada while holding an Office under that Government requiring his Presence there.

SECTION 32: When a Vacancy happens in the Senate by Resignation, Death or otherwise, the Governor General shall by Summons to a fit and qualified Person fill the Vacancy.

SECTION 33: If any Question arises respecting the Qualification of a Senator or a Vacancy in the Senate the same shall be heard and determined by the Senate.

SECTION 34: The Governor General may from Time to Time, by Instrument under the Great Seal of Canada, appoint a Senator to be Speaker of the Senate, and may remove him and appoint another in his Stead.

SECTION 35: Until the Parliament of Canada otherwise provides, the Presence of at least Fifteen Senators, including the Speaker, shall be necessary to constitute a Meeting of the Senate for the Exercise of its Powers.

SECTION 36: Questions arising in the Senate shall be decided by a Majority of Voices, and the Speaker shall in all Cases have a Vote, and when the Voices are equal the Decision shall be deemed to be in the Negative.

The House of Commons

SECTION 37: The House of Commons shall, subject to the Provisions of this Act, consist of two hundred and ninety-five members of whom ninety-nine shall be elected for Ontario, seventy-five for Quebec, eleven for Nova Scotia, ten for New Brunswick, fourteen for Manitoba, thirty-two for British Columbia, four for Prince Edward Island, twenty-six for Alberta, fourteen for Saskatchewan, seven for Newfoundland, one for the Yukon Territory and two for the Northwest Territories.

SECTION 38: The Governor General shall from Time to Time, in the Queen's Name, by Instrument under the Great Seal of Canada, summon and call together the House of Commons.

SECTION 39: A Senator shall not be capable of being elected or of sitting or voting as a Member of the House of Commons.

SECTION 40: Until the Parliament of Canada otherwise provides, Ontario, Quebec, Nova Scotia and New Brunswick shall, for the Purposes of the Election of Members to serve in the House of Commons, be divided into Electoral districts as follows:

1.—ONTARIO.

Ontario shall be divided into the Counties, Ridings of Counties, Cities, Parts of Cities, and Towns enumerated in the First Schedule to this Act, each whereof shall be an Electoral District, each such District as numbered in that Schedule being entitled to return One Member.

2.—QUEBEC.

Quebec shall be divided into Sixty-five Electoral Districts, composed of the Sixty-five Electoral Divisions into which Lower Canada is at the passing of this Act divided under Chapter Two of the Consolidated Statutes of Canada, Chapter Seventy-five of the Consolidated Statutes for Lower Canada, and the Act of the Province of Canada of the Twenty-third Year of the Queen, Chapter One, or any other Act amending the same in force at the Union, so that each such Electoral Division shall be for the Purposes of this Act an Electoral District entitled to return One Member.

3.—NOVA SCOTIA.

Each of the Eighteen Counties of Nova Scotia shall be an Electoral District. The County of Halifax shall be entitled to return Two Members, and each of the other Counties One Member.

4.—NEW BRUNSWICK.

Each of the Fourteen Counties into which New Brunswick is divided, including the City and County of St. John, shall be an Electoral District. The City of St. John shall also be a separate Electoral District. Each of those Fifteen Electoral Districts shall be entitled to return One Member.

SECTION 41: Until the Parliament of Canada otherwise provides, all Laws in force in the several Provinces at the Union relative to the following Matters or any of them, namely,—the Qualifications and Disqualifications of Persons to be elected or to sit or vote as Members of the House of Assembly or Legislative Assembly in the several Provinces, the Voters at Elections of such Members, the Oaths to be taken by Voters, the Returning Officers, their Powers and Duties, the Proceedings at Elections, the Periods during which Elections may be continued, the Trial of controverted Elections, and Proceedings incident thereto, the vacating of Seats of Members, and the Execution of new Writs in case of Seats vacated otherwise than by Dissolution,—shall respectively apply to Elections of Members to serve in the House of Commons for the same several Provinces.

Provided that, until the Parliament of Canada otherwise provides, at any Election for a Member of the House of Commons for the District of Algoma, in addition to Persons qualified by the Law of the Province of Canada to vote, every Male British Subject, aged Twenty-one Years or upwards, being a Householder, shall have a Vote.

SECTION 42: For the First Election of Members to serve in the House of Commons the Governor

General shall cause Writs to be issued by such Person, in such Form, and addressed to such Returning Officers as he thinks fit.

The Person issuing Writs under this Section shall have the like Powers as are possessed at the Union by the Officers charged with the issuing of Writs for the Election of Members to serve in the respective House of Assembly or Legislative Assembly of the Province of Canada, Nova Scotia, or New Brunswick; and the Returning Officers to whom Writs are directed under this Section shall have the like Powers as are possessed at the Union by the Officers charged with the returning of Writs for the Election of Members to serve in the same respective House of Assembly or Legislative Assembly.

SECTION 43: In case a Vacancy in the Representation in the House of Commons of any Electoral District happens before the Meeting of the Parliament, or after the Meeting of the Parliament before Provision is made by the Parliament in this Behalf, the Provisions of the last foregoing Section of this Act shall extend and apply to the issuing and returning of a Writ in respect of such vacant District.

SECTION 44: The House of Commons on its first assembling after a General Election shall proceed with all practicable Speed to elect One of its Members to be Speaker.

SECTION 45: In case of a Vacancy happening in the Office of Speaker by Death, Resignation, or otherwise, the House of Commons shall with all practicable Speed proceed to elect another of its Members to be Speaker.

SECTION 46: The Speaker shall preside at all Meetings of the House of Commons.

SECTION 47: Until the Parliament of Canada otherwise provides, in case of the Absence for any Reason of the Speaker from the Chair of the House of Commons for a Period of Forty-eight consecutive Hours, the House may elect another of its Members to act as Speaker, and the Member so elected shall during the Continuance of such Absence of the Speaker have and execute all the Powers, Privileges, and Duties of Speaker.

SECTION 48: The Presence of at least Twenty Members of the House of Commons shall be necessary to constitute a Meeting of the House for the Exercise of its Powers, and for that Purpose the Speaker shall be reckoned as a Member.

SECTION 49: Questions arising in the House of Commons shall be decided by a Majority of Voices other than that of the Speaker, and when the Voices are equal, but not otherwise, the Speaker shall have a Vote.

SECTION 50: Every House of Commons shall continue for Five Years from the Day of the Return of the Writs for choosing the House (subject to be sooner dissolved by the Governor General), and no longer.

SECTION 51: (1) The number of members of the House of Commons and the representation of the provinces therein shall, on the coming into force of this subsection and thereafter on the completion of each decennial census, be readjusted by such authority, in such manner, and from such time as the Parliament of Canada from time to time provides, subject and according to the following rules:

1. There shall be assigned to each of the provinces a number of members equal to the number obtained by dividing the total population of the provinces by two hundred and seventy-nine and by dividing the population of each province by the quotient so obtained, counting any remainder in excess of 0.50 as one after the said process of division.
2. If the total number of members that would be assigned to a province by the application of rule 1 is less than the total number assigned to that province on the date of coming into force of this subsection, there shall be added to the number of members so assigned such number of members as will result in the province having the same number of members as were assigned on that date.

(2) The Yukon Territory as bounded and described in the schedule to chapter Y-2 of the Revised Statutes of Canada, 1970, shall be entitled to one member, and the Northwest Territories as bounded and described in section 2 of chapter N-22 of the Revised Statutes of Canada, 1970, shall be entitled to two members.

SECTION 51A: Notwithstanding anything in this Act a province shall always be entitled to a number of members in the House of Commons not less than the number of senators representing such province.

SECTION 52: The Number of Members of the House of Commons may be from Time to Time increased by the Parliament of Canada, provided the proportionate Representation of the Provinces prescribed by this Act is not thereby disturbed.

Money Votes; Royal Assent

SECTION 53: Bills for appropriating any Part of the Public Revenue, or for imposing any Tax or Impost, shall originate in the House of Commons.

SECTION 54: It shall not be lawful for the House of Commons to adopt or pass any Vote, Resolution, Address, or Bill for the Appropriation of any Part of the Public Revenue, or of any Tax or Impost, to any Purpose that has not been first recommended to that House by Message of the Governor General in the Session in which such Vote, Resolution, Address, or Bill is proposed.

SECTION 55: Where a Bill passed by the Houses of the Parliament is presented to the Governor General for the Queen's Assent, he shall declare, according to his Discretion, but subject to the Provisions of this Act and to Her Majesty's Instructions, either that he assents thereto in the Queen's Name, or that he withholds the Queen's Assent, or that he reserves the Bill for the Signification of the Queen's Pleasure.

SECTION 56: Where the Governor General assents to a Bill in the Queen's Name, he shall by the first convenient Opportunity send an authentic Copy of the Act to one of Her Majesty's Principal Secretaries of State, and if the Queen in Council within Two Years after Receipt thereof by the Secretary of State thinks fit to disallow the Act, such Disallowance (with a Certificate of the Secretary of State of the Day on which the Act was received by him) being signified by the Governor General, by Speech or Message to each of the Houses of the Parliament or by Proclamation, shall annul the Act from and after the Day of such Signification.

SECTION 57: A Bill reserved for the Signification of the Queen's Pleasure shall not have any Force unless and until, within Two Years from the Day on which it was presented to the Governor General for the Queen's Assent, the Governor General signifies, by Speech or Message to each of the Houses of the Parliament or by Proclamation, that it has received the Assent of the Queen in Council.

An Entry of every such Speech, Message, or Proclamation shall be made in the Journal of each House, and a Duplicate thereof duly attested shall be delivered to the proper Officer to be kept among the Records of Canada.

V. Provincial Constitutions

Executive Power

SECTION 58: For each Province there shall be an Officer, styled the Lieutenant Governor, appointed by the Governor General in Council by Instrument under the Great Seal of Canada.

SECTION 59: A Lieutenant Governor shall hold Office during the Pleasure of the Governor General; but any Lieutenant Governor appointed after the Commencement of the First Session of the Parliament of Canada shall not be removeable within Five Years from his Appointment, except for Cause assigned, which shall be communicated to him in Writing within One Month after the Order for his Removal is made, and shall be communicated by Message to the Senate and to the House of Commons within One Week thereafter if the Parliament is then sitting, and if not then within One Week after the Commencement of the next Session of the Parliament.

SECTION 60: The Salaries of the Lieutenant Governors shall be fixed and provided by the Parliament of Canada.

SECTION 61: Every Lieutenant Governor shall, before assuming the Duties of his Office, make and subscribe before the Governor General or some Person authorized by him Oaths of Allegiance and Office similar to those taken by the Governor General.

SECTION 62: The Provisions of this Act referring to the Lieutenant Governor extend and apply to the Lieutenant Governor for the Time being of each Province, or other the Chief Executive Officer or Administrator for the Time being carrying on the Government of the Province, by whatever Title he is designated.

SECTION 63: The Executive Council of Ontario and of Quebec shall be composed of such Persons as the Lieutenant Governor from Time to Time thinks fit, and in the first instance of the following Officers, namely,—the Attorney General, the Secretary and Registrar of the Province, the Treasurer of the Province, the Commissioner of Crown Lands, and the Commissioner of Agriculture and Public Works, within Quebec, the Speaker of the Legislative Council and the Solicitor General.

SECTION 64: The Constitution of the Executive Authority in each of the Provinces of Nova Scotia and New Brunswick shall, subject to the Provisions of this Act, continue as it exists at the Union until altered under the Authority of this Act.

SECTION 65: All Powers, Authorities, and Functions which under any Act of the Parliament of Great Britain, or of the Parliament of the United Kingdom of Great Britain and Ireland, or of the Legislature of Upper Canada, Lower Canada, or Canada, were or are before or at the Union vested in or exerciseable by the respective Governors or Lieutenant Governors of those Provinces, with the Advice or with the Advice and Consent of the respective Executive Councils thereof, or in conjunction with those Councils, or with any Number of Members thereof, or by those Governors or Lieutenant Governors individually, shall, as far as the same are capable of being exercised after the Union in relation to the Government of Ontario and Quebec respectively, be vested in and shall or may be exercised by the Lieutenant Governor of Ontario and Quebec respectively, with the Advice or with the Advice and Consent of or in conjunction with the respective Executive Councils, or any Members thereof, or by the Lieutenant Governor individually, as the Case requires, subject nevertheless (except with respect to such as exist under Acts of the Parliament of Great Britain, or of the Parliament of the United Kingdom of Great Britain and Ireland,) to be abolished or altered by the respective Legislatures of Ontario and Quebec.

SECTION 66: The Provisions of this Act referring to the Lieutenant Governor in Council shall be construed as referring to the Lieutenant Governor of the Province acting by and with the Advice of the Executive Council thereof.

SECTION 67: The Governor General in Council may from Time to Time appoint an Administrator to execute the office and Functions of Lieutenant Governor during his Absence, Illness, or other Inability.

SECTION 68: Unless and until the Executive Government of any Province otherwise directs with respect to that Province, the Seats of Government of the Provinces shall be as follows, namely,—of Ontario, the City of Toronto; of Quebec, the City of Quebec; of Nova Scotia, the City of Halifax; and of New Brunswick, the City of Fredericton.

Legislative Power

1. ONTARIO

SECTION 69: There shall be a Legislature for Ontario consisting of the Lieutenant Governor and of One House, styled the Legislative Assembly of Ontario.

SECTION 70: The Legislative Assembly of Ontario shall be composed of Eighty-two Members, to be elected to represent the Eighty-two Electoral Districts set forth in the First Schedule to this Act.

2. QUEBEC

SECTION 71: There shall be a Legislature for Quebec consisting of the Lieutenant Governor and of Two Houses, styled the Legislative Council of Quebec and the Legislative Assembly of Quebec.

SECTION 72: The Legislative Council of Quebec shall be composed of Twenty-four Members, to be appointed by the Lieutenant Governor, in the Queen's Name, by Instrument under the Great Seal of Quebec, One being appointed to represent each of the Twenty-four Electoral Divisions of Lower Canada in this Act referred to, and each holding Office for the Term of his Life, unless the Legislature of Quebec otherwise provides under the Provisions of this Act.

SECTION 73: The Qualifications of the Legislative Councillors of Quebec shall be the same as those of the Senators for Quebec.

SECTION 74: The Place of a Legislative Councillor of Quebec shall become vacant in the Cases, *mutatis mutandis,* in which the Place of Senator becomes vacant.

SECTION 75: When a Vacancy happens in the Legislative Council of Quebec by Resignation, Death, or otherwise, the Lieutenant Governor, in the Queen's Name, by Instrument under the Great Seal of Quebec, shall appoint a fit and qualified Person to fill the Vacancy.

SECTION 76: If any Question arises respecting the Qualification of a Legislative Councillor of Quebec, or a Vacancy in the Legislative Council of Quebec, the same shall be heard and determined by the Legislative Council.

SECTION 77: The Lieutenant Governor may from Time to Time, by Instrument under the Great Seal of Quebec, appoint a Member of the Legislative Council of Quebec to be Speaker thereof, and may remove him and appoint another in his Stead.

SECTION 78: Until the Legislature of Quebec otherwise provides, the Presence of at least Ten Members of the Legislative Council, including the Speaker, shall be necessary to constitute a Meeting for the Exercise of its Powers.

SECTION 79: Questions arising in the Legislative Council of Quebec shall be decided by a Majority of Voices, and the Speaker shall in all Cases have a Vote, and when the Voices are equal the Decision shall be deemed to be in the Negative.

SECTION 80: The Legislative Assembly of Quebec shall be composed of Sixty-five Members, to be elected to represent the Sixty-five Electoral Divisions or Districts of Lower Canada in this Act referred to, subject to Alteration thereof by the Legislature of Quebec: Provided that it shall not be lawful to present to the Lieutenant Governor of Quebec for Assent any Bill for altering the Limits of any of the Electoral Divisions or Districts mentioned in the Second Schedule to this Act, unless the Second and Third Readings of such Bill have been passed in the Legislative Assembly with the Concurrence of the Majority of the Members representing all those Electoral Divisions or Districts, and the Assent shall not be given to such Bill unless an Address has been presented by the Legislative Assembly to the Lieutenant Governor stating that it has been so passed.

3. ONTARIO AND QUEBEC

SECTION 81: The Legislatures of Ontario and Quebec respectively shall be called together not later than Six Months after the Union.

SECTION 82: The Lieutenant Governor of Ontario and of Quebec shall from Time to Time, in the Queen's Name, by Instrument under the Great Seal of the Province, summon and call together the Legislative Assembly of the Province.

SECTION 83: Until the Legislature of Ontario or of Quebec otherwise provides, a Person accepting or holding in Ontario or in Quebec any Office, Commission, or Employment, permanent or temporary, at the Nomination of the Lieutenant Governor, to which an annual Salary, or any Fee, Allowance, Emolument, or Profit of any Kind or Amount whatever from the Province is attached, shall not be eligible as a Member of the Legislative Assembly of the respective Province, nor shall he sit or vote as such; but nothing in this Section shall make ineligible any Person being a member of the Executive Council of the respective Province, or holding any of the following Offices, that is to say, the Offices of Attorney General, Secretary and Registrar of the Province, Treasurer of the Province, Commissioner of Crown Lands, and Commissioner of Agriculture and Public Works, and in

Quebec Solicitor General, or shall disqualify him to sit or vote in the House for which he is elected, provided he is elected while holding such Office.

SECTION 84: Until the legislatures of Ontario and Quebec respectively otherwise provide, all Laws which at the Union are in force in those Provinces respectively, relative to the following Matters, or any of them, namely,—the Qualifications and Disqualifications of Persons to be elected or to sit or vote as Members of the Assembly of Canada, the Qualifications or Disqualifications of Voters, the Oaths to be taken by Voters, the Returning Officers, their Powers and Duties, the Proceedings at Elections, the Periods during which such Elections may be continued, and the Trial of controverted Elections and the Proceedings incident thereto, the vacating of the Seats of Members and the issuing and execution of new Writs in case of Seats vacated otherwise than by Dissolution,—shall respectively apply to Elections of Members to serve in the respective Legislative Assemblies of Ontario and Quebec.

Provided that, until the Legislature of Ontario otherwise provides, at any Election for a Member of the Legislative Assembly of Ontario for the District of Algoma, in addition to Persons qualified by the Law of the Province of Canada to vote, every male British Subject, aged Twenty-one Years or upwards, being a Householder, shall have a vote.

SECTION 85: Every Legislative Assembly of Ontario and every Legislative Assembly of Quebec shall continue for Four Years from the Day of the Return of the Writs for choosing the same (subject nevertheless to either the Legislative Assembly of Ontario or the Legislative Assembly of Quebec being sooner dissolved by the Lieutenant Governor of the Province), and no longer.

SECTION 86: There shall be a Session of the Legislature of Ontario and of that of Quebec once at least in every Year, so that Twelve Months shall not intervene between the last Sitting of the Legislature in each Province in one Session and its first Sitting in the next Session.

SECTION 87: The following Provisions of this Act respecting the House of Commons of Canada shall extend and apply to the Legislative Assemblies of Ontario and Quebec, that is to say,—the Provisions relating to the Election of a Speaker originally and on Vacancies, the Duties of the Speaker, the Absence of the Speaker, the Quorum, and the Mode of voting, as if those Provisions were here re-enacted and made applicable in Terms to each such Legislative Assembly.

4. NOVA SCOTIA AND NEW BRUNSWICK

SECTION 88: The Constitution of the Legislature of each of the Provinces of Nova Scotia and New Brunswick shall, subject to the Provisions of this Act, continue as it exists at the Union until altered under the Authority of this Act.

5. ONTARIO, QUEBEC, AND NOVA SCOTIA

SECTION 89: Each of the Lieutenant Governors of Ontario, Quebec and Nova Scotia shall cause Writs to be issued for the First Election of Members of the Legislative Assembly thereof in such Form and by such Person as he thinks fit, and at such Time and addressed to such Returning Officer as the Governor General directs, and so that the First Election of Member of Assembly for any Electoral District or any Subdivision thereof shall be held at the same Time and at the same Places as the Election for a Member to serve in the House of Commons of Canada for the Electoral District.

6. THE FOUR PROVINCES

SECTION 90: The following Provisions of this Act respecting the Parliament of Canada, namely,—the Provisions relating to Appropriation and Tax Bills, the Recommendation of Money Votes, the Assent to Bills, the Disallowance of Acts, and the Signification of Pleasure on Bills reserved,—shall extend and apply to the Legislatures of the several Provinces as if those Provisions were here re-enacted and made applicable in Terms to the respective Provinces and the Legislatures thereof, with the Substitution of the Lieutenant Governor of the Province for the Governor General, of the Governor General for the Queen and for a Secretary of State, of One Year for Two Years, and of the Province for Canada.

VI. Distribution of Legislative Powers

Powers of the Parliament

SECTION 91: It shall be lawful for the Queen, by and with the Advice and Consent of the Senate and House of Commons, to make Laws for the Peace, Order, and good Government of Canada, in relation to all Matters not coming within the Classes of Subjects by this Act assigned exclusively to the Legislatures of the Provinces; and for greater Certainty, but not so as to restrict the Generality of the foregoing Terms of this Section, it is hereby declared that (notwithstanding anything in this Act) the exclusive Legislative Authority of the Parliament of Canada extends to all Matters coming within the Classes of Subjects next hereinafter enumerated; that is to say,—

1. The amendment from time to time of the Constitution of Canada, except as regards matters coming within the classes of subjects by this Act assigned exclusively to the Legislatures of the provinces, or as regards rights or privileges by this or any other Constitutional Act granted or secured to the Legislature or the Government of a province, or to any class of persons with respect to schools or as regards the use of the English or the French language or as regards the requirement that there shall be a session of

the Parliament of Canada at least once each year, and that no House of Commons shall continue for more than five years from the day of the return of the Writs for choosing the House: provided, however, that a House of Commons may in time of real or apprehended war, invasion or insurrection be continued by the Parliament of Canada if such continuation is not opposed by the votes of more than one-third of the members of such House.

1A. The Public Debt and Property.
2. The Regulation of Trade and Commerce.
2A. Unemployment insurance.
3. The raising of Money by any Mode or System of Taxation.
4. The borrowing of Money on the Public Credit.
5. Postal Service.
6. The Census and Statistics.
7. Militia, Military and Naval Service, and Defence.
8. The fixing of and providing for the Salaries and Allowances of Civil and other Officers of the Government of Canada.
9. Beacons, Buoys, Lighthouses, and Sable Island.
10. Navigation and Shipping.
11. Quarantine and the Establishment and Maintenance of Marine Hospitals.
12. Sea Coast and Inland Fisheries.
13. Ferries between a Province and any British or Foreign Country or between Two Provinces.
14. Currency and Coinage.
15. Banking, Incorporation of Banks, and the Issue of Paper Money.
16. Savings Banks.
17. Weights and Measures.
18. Bills of Exchange and Promissory Notes.
19. Interest.
20. Legal Tender.
21. Bankruptcy and Insolvency
22. Patents of Invention and Discovery.
23. Copyrights.
24. Indians, and Lands reserved for the Indians.
25. Naturalization and Aliens.
26. Marriage and Divorce.
27. The Criminal Law, except the Constitution of Courts of Criminal Jurisdiction, but including the Procedure in Criminal Matters.
28. The Establishment, Maintenance, and Management of Penitentiaries.
29. Such Classes of Subjects as are expressly excepted in the Enumeration of the Classes of Subjects by this Act assigned exclusively to the Legislatures of the Provinces.

And any Matter coming within any of the Classes of Subjects enumerated in this Section shall not be deemed to come within the Class of Matters of a local or private Nature comprised in the Enumeration of the Classes of Subjects by this Act assigned exclusively to the Legislatures of the Provinces.

Exclusive Powers of Provincial Legislatures

SECTION 92: In each Province the Legislature may exclusively make Laws in relation to Matters coming within the Classes of Subjects next hereinafter enumerated; that is to say,—

1. The Amendment from Time to Time, notwithstanding anything in this Act, of the Constitution of the Province, except as regards the Office of Lieutenant Governor.
2. Direct Taxation within the Province in order to the raising of a Revenue for Provincial Purposes.
3. The borrowing of Money on the sole Credit of the Province.
4. The Establishment and Tenure of Provincial Offices and the Appointment and Payment of Provincial Officers.
5. The Management and Sale of the Public Lands belonging to the Province and of the Timber and Wood thereon.
6. The Establishment, Maintenance, and Management of Public and Reformatory Prisons in and for the Province.
7. The Establishment, Maintenance, and Management of Hospitals, Asylums, Charities, and Eleemosynary Institutions in and for the Province, other than Marine Hospitals.
8. Municipal Institutions in the Province.
9. Shop, Saloon, Tavern, Auctioneer, and other Licences in order to the raising of a Revenue for Provincial, Local, or Municipal Purposes.
10. Local Works and Undertakings other than such as are of the following Classes:—
    (a) Lines of Steam or other Ships, Railways, Canals, Telegraphs, and other Works and Undertakings connecting the Province with any other or others of the Provinces, or extending beyond the Limits of the Province;
    (b) Lines of Steam Ships between the Province and any British or Foreign Country;
    (c) Such Works as, although wholly situate within the Province, are before or after their Execution declared by the Parliament of Canada to be for the general Advantage of Canada or for the Advantage of Two or more of the Provinces.
11. The Incorporation of Companies with Provincial Objects.
12. The Solemnization of Marriage in the Province.
13. Property and Civil Rights in the Province.
14. The Administration of Justice in the Province, including the Constitution, Maintenance, and Organization of Provincial Courts, both of Civil and of Criminal Jurisdiction, and includ-

ing Procedure in Civil Matters in those Courts.

15. The Imposition of Punishment by Fine, Penalty, or Imprisonment for enforcing any Law of the Province made in relation to any Matter coming within any of the Classes of Subjects enumerated in this Section.
16. Generally all Matters of a merely local or private Nature in the Province.

Non-Renewable Natural Resources, Forestry Resources and Electrical Energy

SECTION 92A: (1) In each province, the legislature may exclusively make laws in relation to

- (a) exploration for non-renewable natural resources in the province;
- (b) development, conservation and management of non-renewable natural resources and forestry resources in the province, including laws in relation to the rate of primary production therefrom; and
- (c) development, conservation and management of sites and facilities in the province for the generation and production of electrical energy.

(2) In each province, the legislature may make laws in relation to the export from the province to another part of Canada of the primary production from non-renewable natural resources and forestry resources in the province and the production from facilities in the province for the generation of electrical energy, but such laws may not authorize or provide for discrimination in prices or in supplies exported to another part of Canada.

(3) Nothing in subsection (2) derogates from the authority of Parliament to enact laws in relation to the matters referred to in that subsection and, where such a law of Parliament and a law of a province conflict, the law of Parliament prevails to the extent of the conflict.

(4) In each province, the legislature may make laws in relation to the raising of money by any mode or system of taxation in respect of

- (a) non-renewable natural resources and forestry resources in the province and the primary production therefrom, and
- (b) sites and facilities in the province for the generation of electrical energy and the production therefrom,

whether or not such production is exported in whole or in part from the province, but such laws may not authorize or provide for taxation that differentiates between production exported to another part of Canada and production not exported from the province.

(5) The expression "primary production" has the meaning assigned by the Sixth Schedule.

(6) Nothing in subsections (1) to (5) derogates from any powers or rights that a legislature or government of a province had immediately before the coming into force of this section.

THE SIXTH SCHEDULE

Primary Production from Non-Renewable Natural Resources and Forestry Resources

1. For the purposes of section 92A of this Act,
   - (a) production from a non-renewable natural resource is primary production therefrom if
     - (i) it is in the form in which it exists upon its recovery or severance from its natural state, or
     - (ii) it is a product resulting from processing or refining the resource, and is not a manufactured product or a product resulting from refining crude oil, refining upgraded heavy crude oil, refining gases or liquids derived from coal or refining a synthetic equivalent or crude oil; and
   - (b) production from a forestry resource is primary production therefrom if it consists of sawlogs, poles, lumber, wood chips, sawdust or any other primary wood product, or wood pulp, and is not a product manufactured from wood.

Education

SECTION 93: In and for each Province the Legislature may exclusively make Laws in relation to Education, subject and according to the following Provisions:-

(1) Nothing in any such Law shall prejudicially affect any Right or Privilege with respect to Denominational Schools which any Class of Persons have by Law in the Province at the Union:

(2) All the Powers, Privileges, and Duties at the Union by Law conferred and imposed in Upper Canada on the Separate Schools and School Trustees of the Queen's Roman Catholic Subjects shall be and the same are hereby extended to the Dissentient Schools of the Queen's Protestant and Roman Catholic Subjects in Quebec:

(3) Where in any Province a System of Separate or Dissentient Schools exists by Law at the Union or is thereafter established by the Legislature of the Province, an Appeal shall lie to the Governor General in Council from any Act or Decision of any Provincial Authority affecting any Right or Privilege of the Protestant or Roman Catholic Minority of the Queen's Subjects in relation to Education:

(4) In case any such Provincial Law as from Time to Time seems to the Governor General in Council requisite for the due Execution of the Provisions of this Section is not made, or in case any Decision of the Governor General in Council on any Appeal under this Section is not duly executed by the proper Provincial Authority in that Behalf, then and in every

such Case, and as far only as the Circumstances of each Case require, the Parliament of Canada may make remedial Laws for the due Execution of the Provisions of this Section and of any Decision of the Governor General in Council under this Section.

Uniformity of Laws in Ontario, Nova Scotia and New Brunswick

SECTION 94: Notwithstanding anything in this Act, the Parliament of Canada may make Provision for the Uniformity of all or any of the Laws relative to Property and Civil Rights in Ontario, Nova Scotia, and New Brunswick, and of the Procedure of all or any of the Courts in Those Three Provinces, and from and after the passing of any Act in that Behalf the Power of the Parliament of Canada to make Laws in relation to any Matter comprised in any such Act shall, notwithstanding anything in this Act, be unrestricted; but any Act of the Parliament of Canada making Provision for such Uniformity shall not have effect in any Province unless and until it is adopted and enacted as Law by the Legislature thereof.

Old Age Pensions

SECTION 94A: The Parliament of Canada may make laws in relation to old age pensions and supplementary benefits, including survivors, and disability benefits irrespective of age, but no such law shall affect the operation of any law present or future of a provincial legislature in relation to any such matter.

Agriculture and Immigration

SECTION 95: In each Province the Legislature may make Laws in relation to Agriculture in the Province, and to Immigration into the Province; and it is hereby declared that the Parliament of Canada may from Time to Time make Laws in relation to Agriculture in all or any of the Provinces, and to Immigration into all or any of the Provinces; and any Law of the Legislature of a Province relative to Agriculture or to Immigration shall have effect in and for the Province as long and as far only as it is not repugnant to any Act of the Parliament of Canada.

VII. Judicature

SECTION 96: The Governor General shall appoint the Judges of the Superior, District, and County Courts in each Province, except those of the Courts of Probate in Nova Scotia and New Brunswick.

SECTION 97: Until the laws relative to Property and Civil Rights in Ontario, Nova Scotia, and New Brunswick, and the Procedure of the Courts in those Provinces, are made uniform, the Judges of the Courts of those Provinces appointed by the Governor General shall be selected from the respective Bars of those Provinces.

SECTION 98: The Judges of the Courts of Quebec shall be selected from the Bar of that Province.

SECTION 99: (1) Subject to subsection two of this section, the Judges of the Superior Courts shall hold office during good behaviour, but shall be removable by the Governor General on Address of the Senate and House of Commons.

(2) A Judge of a Superior Court, whether appointed before or after the coming into force of this section, shall cease to hold office upon attaining the age of seventy-five years, or upon the coming into force of this section if at that time he has already attained that age.

SECTION 100: The Salaries, Allowances, and Pensions of the Judges of the Superior, District, and County Courts (except the Courts of Probate in Nova Scotia and New Brunswick), and of the Admiralty Courts in Cases where the Judges thereof are for the Time being paid by Salary, shall be fixed and provided by the Parliament of Canada.

SECTION 101: The Parliament of Canada may, notwithstanding anything in this Act, from Time to Time provide for the Constitution, Maintenance, and Organization of a General Court of Appeal for Canada, and for the Establishment of any additional Courts for the better Administration of the Laws of Canada.

VIII. Revenues; Debts; Assets; Taxation

SECTION 102: All Duties and Revenues over which the respective Legislatures of Canada, Nova Scotia, and New Brunswick before and at the Union had and have Power of Appropriation, except such Portions thereof as are by this Act reserved to the respective Legislatures of the Provinces, or are raised by them in accordance with the special Powers conferred on them by this Act, shall form One Consolidated Revenue Fund, to be appropriated for the Public Service of Canada in the Manner and subject to the Charges of this Act provided.

SECTION 103: The Consolidated Revenue Fund of Canada shall be permanently charged with the Costs, Charges, and Expenses incident to the Collection, Management, and Receipt thereof, and the same shall form the First Charge thereon, subject to be reviewed and audited in such Manner as shall be ordered by the Governor General in Council until the Parliament otherwise provides.

SECTION 104: The annual Interest of the Public Debts of the several Provinces of Canada, Nova Scotia, and New Brunswick at the Union shall form the Second Charge on the Consolidated Revenue Fund of Canada.

SECTION 105: Unless altered by the Parliament of Canada, the Salary of the Governor General shall be Ten thousand Pounds Sterling Money of the United Kingdom of Great Britain and Ireland, payable out of the Consolidated Revenue Fund of Canada, and the same shall form the Third Charge thereon.

SECTION 106: Subject to the several Payments by this Act charged on the Consolidated Revenue Fund of Canada, the same shall be appropriated by the Parliament of Canada for the Public Service.

SECTION 107: All Stocks, Cash, Bankers' Balances, and Securities for Money belonging to each Province at the Time of the Union, except as in this Act mentioned, shall be the Property of Canada, and shall be taken in Reduction of the Amount of the respective Debts of the Provinces at the Union.

SECTION 108: The Public Works and Property of each Province, enumerated in the Third Schedule to this Act, shall be the Property of Canada.

SECTION 109: All Lands, Mines, Minerals, and Royalties belonging to the several Provinces of Canada, Nova Scotia, and New Brunswick at the Union, and all Sums then due or payable for such Lands, Mines, Minerals, or Royalties, shall belong to the several Provinces of Ontario, Quebec, Nova Scotia, and New Brunswick in which the same are situate or arise, subject to any Trusts existing in respect thereof, and to any Interest other than that of the Province in the same.

SECTION 110: All Assets connected with such Portions of the Public Debt of each Province as are assumed by that Province shall belong to that Province.

SECTION 111: Canada shall be liable for the Debts and Liabilities of each Province existing at the Union.

SECTION 112: Ontario and Quebec conjointly shall be liable to Canada for the Amount (if any) by which the Debt of the Province of Canada exceeds at the Union Sixty-two million five hundred thousand Dollars, and shall be charged with Interest at the Rate of Five per Centum per Annum thereon.

SECTION 113: The Assets enumerated in the Fourth Schedule to this Act belonging at the Union to the Province of Canada shall be the Property of Ontario and Quebec conjointly.

SECTION 114: Nova Scotia shall be liable to Canada for the Amount (if any) by which its Public Debt exceeds at the Union Eight million Dollars, and shall be charged with Interest at the Rate of Five per Centum per Annum thereon.

SECTION 115: New Brunswick shall be liable to Canada for the Amount (if any) by which its Public Debt exceeds at the Union Seven million Dollars, and shall be charged with Interest at the Rate of Five per Centum per Annum thereon.

SECTION 116: In case the Public Debts of Nova Scotia and New Brunswick do not at the Union amount to Eight million and Seven million Dollars respectively, they shall respectively receive by half-yearly Payments in advance from the Government of Canada Interest at Five per Centum per Annum on the Difference between the actual Amounts of their respective Debts and such stipulated Amounts.

SECTION 117: The several Provinces shall retain all their respective Public Property not otherwise disposed of in this Act, subject to the Right of Canada to assume any Lands or Public Property required for Fortifications or for the Defence of the Country.

SECTION 118: The following Sums shall be paid yearly by Canada to the several Provinces for the Support of their Governments and Legislatures:

	Dollars
Ontario	Eighty thousand.
Quebec	Seventy thousand.
Nova Scotia	Sixty thousand.
New Brunswick	Fifty thousand.
	Two hundred and sixty thousand;

and an annual Grant in aid of each Province shall be made, equal to Eighty Cents per Head of the Population as ascertained by the Census of One thousand eight hundred and sixty-one, and in the Case of Nova Scotia and New Brunswick, by each subsequent Decennial Census until the Population of each of those two Provinces amounts to Four hundred thousand Souls, at which Rate such Grant shall thereafter remain. Such Grants shall be in full Settlement of all future Demands on Canada, and shall be paid half-yearly in advance to each Province; but the Government of Canada shall deduct from such Grants, as against any Province, all Sums chargeable as Interest on the Public Debt of that Province in excess of the several Amounts stipulated in this Act.

SECTION 119: New Brunswick shall receive by half-yearly Payments in advance from Canada for the period of Ten years from the Union an additional Allowance of Sixty-three thousand Dollars per Annum; but as long as the Public Debt of that Province remains under Seven million Dollars, a Deduction equal to the Interest at Five per Centum per Annum on such Deficiency shall be made from that Allowance of Sixty-three thousand Dollars.

SECTION 120: All Payments to be made under this Act, or in discharge of Liabilities created under any Act of the Provinces of Canada, Nova Scotia, and New Brunswick respectively, and assumed by Canada, shall, until the Parliament of Canada otherwise directs, be made in such Form and Manner as may from Time to Time be ordered by the Governor General in Council.

SECTION 121: All Articles of the Growth, Produce, or Manufacture of any one of the Provinces shall, from and after the Union, be admitted free into each of the other Provinces.

Section 122: The Customs and Excise Laws of each Province shall, subject to the Provisions of this Act, continue in force until altered by the Parliament of Canada.

Section 123: Where Customs Duties are, at the Union, leviable on any Goods, Wares, or Merchandises in any Two Provinces, those Goods, Wares, and Merchandises may, from and after the Union, be imported from one of those Provinces into the other of them on Proof of Payment of the Customs Duty leviable thereon in the Province of Exportation, and on Payment of such further Amount (if any) of Customs Duty as is leviable thereon in the Province of Importation.

Section 124: Nothing in this Act shall affect the Right of New Brunswick to levy the Lumber dues provided in Chapter Fifteen of Title Three of the Revised Statutes of New Brunswick, or in any Act amending that Act before or after the Union, and not increasing the Amount of such Dues; but the Lumber of any of the Provinces other than New Brunswick shall not be subject to such Dues.

Section 125: No Lands or Property belonging to Canada or any Province shall be liable to Taxation.

Section 126: Such Portions of the Duties and Revenues over which the respective Legislatures of Canada, Nova Scotia, and New Brunswick had before the Union Power of Appropriation as are by this Act reserved to the respective Governments or Legislatures of the Provinces, and all Duties and Revenues raised by them in accordance with the special Powers conferred upon them by this Act, shall in each Province form One Consolidated Revenue Fund to be appropriated for the Public Service of the Province.

IX. Miscellaneous Provisions

General

Section 127: If any Person being at the passing of this Act a Member of the Legislative Council of Canada, Nova Scotia, or New Brunswick to whom a Place in the Senate is offered, does not within Thirty Days thereafter, by Writing under his Hand addressed to the Governor General of the Province of Canada or to the Lieutenant Governor of Nova Scotia or New Brunswick (as the Case may be), accept the same, he shall be deemed to have declined the same; and any Person who, being at the passing of this Act a Member of the Legislative Council of Nova Scotia or New Brunswick, accepts a Place in the Senate, shall thereby vacate his Seat in such Legislative Council.

Section 128: Every Member of the Senate or House of Commons of Canada shall before taking his Seat therein take and subscribe before the Governor General or some Person authorized by him, and every Member of a Legislative Council or Legislative Assembly of any Province shall before taking his Seat therein take and subscribe before the Lieutenant Governor of the Province or some Person authorized by him, the Oath of Allegiance contained in the Fifth Schedule to this Act; and every Member of the Senate of Canada and every Member of the Legislative Council of Quebec shall also, before taking his Seat therein, take and subscribe before the Governor General, or some Person authorized by him, the Declaration of Qualification contained in the same Schedule.

Section 129: Except as otherwise provided by this Act, all Laws in force in Canada, Nova Scotia, or New Brunswick at the Union, and all Courts of Civil and Criminal Jurisdiction, and all legal Commissions, Powers, and Authorities, and all Officers, Judicial, Administrative, and Ministerial, existing therein at the Union, shall continue in Ontario, Quebec, Nova Scotia, and New Brunswick respectively, as if the Union had not been made; subject nevertheless (except with respect to such as are enacted by or exist under Acts of the Parliament of Great Britain or of the Parliament of the United Kingdom of Great Britain and Ireland), to be repealed, abolished, or altered by the Parliament of Canada, or by the Legislature of the respective Province, according to the Authority of the Parliament or of that Legislature under this Act.

Section 130: Until the Parliament of Canada otherwise provides, all Officers of the several Provinces having Duties to discharge in relation to Matters other than those coming within the Classes of Subjects by this Act assigned exclusively to the Legislatures of the Provinces shall be Officers of Canada, and shall continue to discharge the Duties of their respective Offices under the same Liabilities, Responsibilities, and Penalties as if the Union had not been made.

Section 131: Until the Parliament of Canada otherwise provides, the Governor General in Council may from Time to Time appoint such Officers as the Governor General in Council deems necessary or proper for the effectual Execution of this Act.

Section 132: The Parliament and Government of Canada shall have all Powers necessary or proper for performing the Obligations of Canada or of any Province thereof, as Part of the British Empire, towards Foreign Countries, arising under Treaties between the Empire and such Foreign Countries.

Section 133: Either the English or the French Language may be used by any Person in the Debates of the Houses of the Parliament of Canada and of the Houses of the Legislature of Quebec; and both those Languages shall be used in the respective Records and Journals of those Houses; and either of those Languages may be used by any Person or in any Pleading or Process in or issuing from any Court of Canada established under this Act, and in or from all or any of the Courts of Quebec.

The Acts of the Parliament of Canada and of the Legislature of Quebec shall be printed and published in both those Languages.

Ontario and Quebec

SECTION 134: Until the Legislature of Ontario or of Quebec otherwise provides, the Lieutenant Governors of Ontario and Quebec may each appoint under the Great Seal of the Province the following Officers, to hold Office during Pleasure, that is to say,— the Attorney General, the Secretary and Registrar of the Province, the Treasurer of the Province, the Commissioner of Crown Lands, and the Commissioner of Agriculture and Public Works, and in the Case of Quebec the Solicitor General, and may, by Order of the Lieutenant Governor in Council, from Time to Time prescribe the Duties of those Officers, and of the several Departments over which they shall preside or to which they shall belong, and of the Officers and Clerks thereof, and may also appoint other and additional Officers to hold Office during Pleasure, and may from Time to Time prescribe the Duties of those Officers, and of the several Departments over which they shall preside or to which they shall belong, and of the Officers and Clerks thereof.

SECTION 135: Until the Legislature of Ontario or Quebec otherwise provides, all Rights, Powers, Duties, Functions, Responsibilities, or Authorities at the passing of this Act vested in or imposed on the Attorney General, Solicitor General, Secretary and Registrar of the Province of Canada, Minister of Finance, Commissioner of Crown Lands, Commissioner of Public Works, and Minister of Agriculture and Receiver General, by any Law, Statute, or Ordinance of Upper Canada, Lower Canada, or Canada, and not repugnant to this Act, shall be vested in or imposed on any Officer to be appointed by the Lieutenant Governor for the discharge of the same or any of them; and the Commissioner of Agriculture and Public Works shall perform the Duties and Functions of the Office of Minister of Agriculture at the passing of this Act imposed by the Law of the Province of Canada, as well as those of the Commissioner of Public Works.

SECTION 136: Until altered by the Lieutenant Governor in Council, the Great Seals of Ontario and Quebec respectively shall be the same, or of the same Design, as those used in the Provinces of Upper Canada and Lower Canada respectively before their Union as the Province of Canada.

SECTION 137: The words "and from thence to the End of the then next ensuing Session of the Legislature," or Words to the same Effect, used in any temporary Act of the Province of Canada not expired before the Union, shall be construed to extend and apply to the next Session of the Parliament of Canada if the Subject Matter of the Act is within the Powers of the same as defined by this Act, or to the next Sessions of the Legislatures of Ontario and Quebec respectively if the Subject Matter of the Act is within the Powers of the same as defined by this Act.

SECTION 138: From and after the Union the Use of the Words "Upper Canada," instead of "Ontario," or "Lower Canada" instead of "Quebec," in any Deed, Writ, Process, Pleading, Document, Matter, or Thing shall not invalidate the same.

SECTION 139: Any Proclamation under the Great Seal of the Province of Canada issued before the Union to take effect at a Time which is subsequent to the Union, whether relating to that Province, or to Upper Canada, or to Lower Canada, and the several Matters and Things therein proclaimed, shall be and continue of like Force and Effect as if the Union had not been made.

SECTION 140: Any Proclamation which is authorized by any Act of the Legislature of the Province of Canada to be issued under the Great Seal of the Province of Canada, whether relating to that Province, or to Upper Canada, or to Lower Canada, and which is not issued before the Union, may be issued by the Lieutenant Governor of Ontario or Quebec, as its Subject Matter requires, under the Great Seal thereof; and from and after the Issue of such Proclamation the same and the several Matters and Things therein proclaimed shall be and continue of the like Force and Effect in Ontario or Quebec as if the Union had not been made.

SECTION 141: The Penitentiary of the Province of Canada shall, until the Parliament of Canada otherwise provides, be and continue the Penitentiary of Ontario and of Quebec.

SECTION 142: The Division and Adjustment of the Debts, Credits, Liabilities, Properties, and Assets of Upper Canada and Lower Canada shall be referred to the Arbitrament of Three Arbitrators, One chosen by the Government of Ontario, One by the Government of Quebec, and One by the Government of Canada; and the Selection of the Arbitrators shall not be made until the Parliament of Canada and the Legislatures of Ontario and Quebec have met; and the Arbitrator chosen by the Government of Canada shall not be a Resident either in Ontario or in Quebec.

SECTION 143: The Governor General in Council may from Time to Time order that such and so many of the Records, Books, and Documents of the Province of Canada as he thinks fit shall be appropriated and delivered either to Ontario or to Quebec, and the same shall thenceforth be the Property of that Province; and any Copy thereof or Extract therefrom, duly certified by the Officer having charge of the Original thereof, shall be admitted as Evidence.

Section 144: The Lieutenant Governor of Quebec may from Time to Time, by Proclamation under the Great Seal of the Province, to take effect from a Day to be appointed therein, constitute Townships in those Parts of the Province of Quebec in which Townships are not then already constituted, and fix the Metes and Bounds thereof.

X. Intercolonial Railway

Section 145: Inasmuch as the Provinces of Canada, Nova Scotia, and New Brunswick have joined in a Declaration that the Construction of the Intercolonial Railway is essential to the Consolidation of the Union of British North America, and to the Assent thereto of Nova Scotia and New Brunswick, and have consequently agreed that Provision should be made for its immediate Construction by the Government of Canada; Therefore, in order to give effect to that Agreement, it shall be the Duty of the Government and Parliament of Canada to provide for the Commencement, within Six Months after the Union, of a Railway connecting the River St. Lawrence with the City of Halifax in Nova Scotia, and for the Construction thereof without Intermission, and the Completion thereof with all practicable Speed.

XI. Admission of Other Colonies

Section 146: It shall be lawful for the Queen, by and with the Advice of Her Majesty's Most Honourable Privy Council, on Addresses from the Houses of the Parliament of Canada, and from the Houses of the respective Legislatures of the Colonies or Provinces of Newfoundland, Prince Edward Island, and British Columbia, to admit those Colonies or Provinces, or any of them, into the Union, and on Address from the Houses of the Parliament of Canada to admit Rupert's Land and the North-western Territory, or either of them, into the Union, on such Terms and Conditions in each Case as are in the Addresses expressed and as the Queen thinks fit to approve, subject to the Provisions of this Act; and the Provisions of any Order in Council in that Behalf shall have effect as if they had been enacted by the Parliament of the United Kingdom of Great Britain and Ireland.

Section 147: In case of the Admission of Newfoundland and Prince Edward Island, or either of them, each shall be entitled to a Representation in the Senate of Canada of Four Members, and (notwithstanding anything in this Act) in case of the Admission of Newfoundland the normal Number of Senators shall be Seventy-six and their maximum Number shall be Eighty-two; but Prince Edward Island when admitted shall be deemed to be comprised in the Third of Three Divisions into which Canada is, in relation to the Constitution of the Senate, divided by this Act, and accordingly, after the Admission of Prince Edward Island, whether Newfoundland is admitted or not, the Representation of Nova Scotia and New Brunswick in the Senate shall, as Vacancies occur, be reduced from Twelve to Ten Members respectively, and the Representation of each of those Provinces shall not be increased at any Time beyond Ten, except under the Provisions of this Act for the Appointment of Three or Six additional Senators under the Direction of the Queen.

APPENDIX B

Canada Act and 1982 Constitution Act as Amended (to 1991)

CANADA ACT, 1982

An Act to give effect to a request by the Senate and House of Commons of Canada.

Whereas Canada has requested and consented to the enactment of an Act of the Parliament of the United Kingdom to give effect to the provisions hereinafter set forth and the Senate and the House of Commons of Canada in Parliament assembled have submitted an address to Her Majesty requesting that Her Majesty may graciously be pleased to cause a Bill to be laid before the Parliament of the United Kingdom for that purpose.

Be it therefore enacted by the Queen's Most Excellent Majesty, by and with the advice and consent of the Lords Spiritual and Temporal, and Commons, in this present Parliament assembled, and by the authority of the same, as follows:

Section 1: *The Constitution Act, 1982* set out in Schedule B to this Act is hereby enacted for and shall have the force of law in Canada and shall come into force as provided in that Act.

Section 2: No Act of the Parliament of the United Kingdom passed after the *Constitution Act, 1982* comes into force shall extend to Canada as part of its law.

Section 3: So far as it is not contained in Schedule B, the French version of this Act is set out in Schedule A to this Act and has the same authority in Canada as the English version thereof.

Section 4: This Act may be cited as the *Canada Act 1982.*

1982 CONSTITUTION ACT AS AMENDED TO 1991

Part I: Canadian Charter of Rights and Freedoms

Whereas Canada is founded upon principles that recognize the supremacy of God and the rule of law:

Guarantee of Rights and Freedoms

Section 1: The *Canadian Charter of Rights and Freedoms* guarantees the rights and freedoms set out in it subject only to such reasonable limits prescribed by law as can be demonstrably justified in a free and democratic society.

Fundamental Freedoms

Section 2: Everyone has the following fundamental freedoms:

(a) freedom of conscience and religion;
(b) freedom of thought, belief, opinion and expression, including freedom of the press and other media of communication;
(c) freedom of peaceful assembly; and
(d) freedom of association.

Democratic Rights

Section 3: Every citizen of Canada has the right to vote in an election of members of the House of Commons or of a legislative assembly and to be qualified for membership therein.

(Repealed sections are underlined)
Department of Justice Canada

Section 4: (1) No House of Commons and no legislative assembly shall continue for longer than five years from the date fixed for the return of the writs of a general election of its members.
(2) In time of real or apprehended war, invasion or insurrection, a House of Commons may be continued by Parliament and a legislative assembly may be continued by the legislature beyond five years if such continuation is not opposed by the votes of more than one-third of the members of the House of Commons or the legislative assembly, as the case may be.
Section 5: There shall be a sitting of Parliament and of each legislature at least once every twelve months.

Mobility Rights

Section 6: (1) Every citizen of Canada has the right to enter, remain in and leave Canada.
(2) Every citizen of Canada and every person who has the status of a permanent resident of Canada has the right

- (a) to move to and take up residence in any province; and
- (b) to pursue the gaining of a livelihood in any province.

(3) The rights specified in subsection (2) are subject to

- (a) any laws or practices of general application in force in a province other than those that discriminate among persons primarily on the basis of province of present or previous residence; and
- (b) any laws providing for reasonable residence requirements as a qualification for the receipt of publicly provided social services.

(4) Subsections (2) and (3) do not preclude any law, program or activity that has as its object the amelioration in a province of conditions of individuals in that province who are socially or economically disadvantaged if the rate of employment in that province is below the rate of employment in Canada.

Legal Rights

Section 7: Everyone has the right to life, liberty and security of the person and the right not to be deprived thereof except in accordance with the principles of fundamental justice.
Section 8: Everyone has the right to be secure against unreasonable search or seizure.
Section 9: Everyone has the right not to be arbitrarily detained or imprisoned.
Section 10: Everyone has the right on arrest or detention

- (a) to be informed promptly of the reasons therefor;
- (b) to retain and instruct counsel without delay and to be informed of that right; and
- (c) to have the validity of the detention determined by way of *habeas corpus* and to be released if the detention is not lawful.

Section 11: Any person charged with an offence has the right

- (a) to be informed without unreasonable delay of the specific offence;
- (b) to be tried within a reasonable time;
- (c) not to be compelled to be a witness in proceedings against that person in respect of the offence;
- (d) to be presumed innocent until proven guilty according to law in a fair and public hearing by an independent and impartial tribunal;
- (e) not to be denied reasonable bail without just cause;
- (f) except in the case of an offence under military law tried before a military tribunal, to the benefit of trial by jury where the maximum punishment for the offence is imprisonment for five years or a more severe punishment;
- (g) not to be found guilty on account of any act or omission unless, at the time of the act or omission, it constituted an offence under Canadian or international law or was criminal according to the general principles of law recognized by the community of nations;
- (h) if finally acquitted of the offence, not to be tried for it again and, if finally found guilty and punished for the offence, not to be tried or punished for it again; and
- (i) if found guilty of the offence and if the punishment for the offence has been varied between the time of commission and the time of sentencing, to the benefit of the lesser punishment.

Section 12: Everyone has the right not to be subjected to any cruel and unusual treatment or punishment.
Section 13: A witness who testifies in any proceedings has the right not to have any incriminating evidence so given used to incriminate that witness in any other proceedings, except in a prosecution for perjury or for the giving of contradictory evidence.
Section 14: A party or witness in any proceedings who does not understand or speak the language in which the proceedings are conducted or who is deaf has the right to the assistance of an interpreter.

Equality Rights

Section 15: (1) Every individual is equal before and under the law and has the right to the equal protection and equal benefit of the law without discrimination and, in particular, without

discrimination based on race, national or ethnic origin, colour, religion, sex, age or mental or physical disability.
(2) Subsection (1) does not preclude any law, program or activity that has as its object the amelioration of conditions of disadvantaged individuals or groups including those that are disadvantaged because of race, national or ethnic origin, colour, religion, sex, age or mental or physical disability.

Official Languages of Canada

SECTION 16: (1) English and French are the official languages of Canada and have equality of status and equal rights and privileges as to their use in all institutions of the Parliament and government of Canada.
(2) English and French are the official languages of New Brunswick and have equality of status and equal rights and privileges as to their use in all institutions of the legislature and government of New Brunswick.
(3) Nothing in this Charter limits the authority of Parliament or a legislature to advance the equality of status or use of English and French.

SECTION 17: (1) Everyone has the right to use English or French in any debates and other proceedings of Parliament.
(2) Everyone has the right to use English or French in any debates and other proceedings of the legislature of New Brunswick.

SECTION 18: (1) The statutes, records and journals of Parliament shall be printed and published in English and French and both language versions are equally authoritative.
(2) The statutes, records and journals of the legislature of New Brunswick shall be printed and published in English and French and both language versions are equally authoritative.

SECTION 19: (1) Either English or French may be used by any person in, or in any pleading in or process issuing from, any court established by Parliament.
(2) Either English or French may be used by any person in, or in any pleading in or process issuing from, any court of New Brunswick.

SECTION 20: (1) Any member of the public in Canada has the right to communicate with, and to receive available services from, any head or central office of an institution of the Parliament or government of Canada in English or French, and has the same right with respect to any other office of any such institution where

(a) there is a significant demand for communications with and services from that office in such language; or
(b) due to the nature of the office, it is reasonable that communications with and services from that office be available in both English and French.

(2) Any member of the public in New Brunswick has the right to communicate with, and to receive available services from, any office of an institution of the legislature or government of New Brunswick in English or French.

SECTION 21: Nothing in sections 16 to 20 abrogates or derogates from any right, privilege or obligation with respect to the English and French languages, or either or them, that exists or is continued by virtue of any other provision of the Constitution of Canada.

SECTION 22: Nothing in sections 16 to 20 abrogates or derogates from any legal or customary right or privilege acquired or enjoyed either before or after the coming into force of this Charter with respect to any language that is not English or French.

Minority Language Educational Rights

SECTION 23: (1) Citizens of Canada

(a) whose first language learned and still understood is that of the English or French linguistic minority population of the province in which they reside, or
(b) who have received their primary school instruction in Canada in English or French and reside in a province where the language in which they received that instruction is the language of the English or French linguistic

minority population of the province, have the right to have their children receive primary and secondary school instruction in that language in that province.
(2) Citizens of Canada of whom any child has received or is receiving primary or secondary school instruction in English or French in Canada, have the right to have all their children receive primary and secondary school instruction in the same language.
(3) The right of citizens of Canada under subsections (1) and (2) to have their children receive primary and secondary school instruction in the language of the English or French linguistic minority population of a province

(a) applies wherever in the province the number of children of citizens who have such a right is sufficient to warrant the provision to them out of public funds of minority language instruction; and
(b) includes, where the number of those children so warrants, the right to have them receive that instruction in minority language educational facilities provided out of public funds.

Enforcement

SECTION 24: (1) Anyone whose rights or freedoms, as guaranteed by this Charter, have been infringed or denied may apply to a court of competent jurisdiction to obtain such remedy as the

court considers appropriate and just in the circumstances.
(2) Where, in proceedings under subsection (1), a court concludes that evidence was obtained in a manner that infringed or denied any rights or freedoms guaranteed by this Charter, the evidence shall be excluded if it is established that, having regard to all the circumstances, the admission of it in the proceedings would bring the administration of justice into disrepute.

General

SECTION 25: The guarantee in this Charter of certain rights and freedoms shall not be construed so as to abrogate or derogate from any aboriginal, treaty or other rights or freedoms that pertain to the aboriginal peoples of Canada including

(a) any rights or freedoms that have been recognized by the Royal Proclamation of October 7, 1763; and
(b) any rights or freedoms that now exist by way of land claims agreements or may be so acquired.

SECTION 26: The guarantee in this Charter of certain rights and freedoms shall not be construed as denying the existence of any other rights or freedoms that exist in Canada.

SECTION 27: This Charter shall be interpreted in a manner consistent with the preservation and enhancement of the multicultural heritage of Canadians.

SECTION 28: Notwithstanding anything in this Charter, the rights and freedoms referred to in it are guaranteed equally to male and female persons.

SECTION 29: Nothing in this Charter abrogates or derogates from any rights or privileges guaranteed by or under the Constitution of Canada in respect of denominational, separate or dissentient schools.

SECTION 30: A reference in this Charter to a province or to the legislative assembly or legislature of a province shall be deemed to include a reference to the Yukon Territory and the Northwest Territories, or to the appropriate legislative authority thereof, as the case may be.

SECTION 31: Nothing in this Charter extends the legislative powers of any body or authority.

Application of Charter

SECTION 32: (1) This Charter applies

(a) to the Parliament and government of Canada in respect of all matters within the authority of Parliament including all matters relating to the Yukon Territory and Northwest Territories; and
(b) to the legislature and government of each province in respect of all matters within the authority of the legislature of each province.

(2) Notwithstanding subsection (1), section 15 shall not have effect until three years after this section comes into force.

SECTION 33: (1) Parliament or the legislature of a province may expressly declare in an Act of Parliament or of the legislature, as the case may be, that the Act or a provision thereof shall operate notwithstanding a provision included in section 2 or sections 7 to 15 of this Charter.
(2) An Act or a provision of an Act in respect of which a declaration made under this section is in effect shall have such operation as it would have but for the provision of this Charter referred to in the declaration.
(3) A declaration made under subsection (1) shall cease to have effect five years after it comes into force or on such earlier date as may be specified in the declaration.
(4) Parliament or the legislature of a province may re-enact a declaration made under subsection (1).
(5) Subsection (3) applies in respect of a re-enactment made under subsection (4).

Citation

SECTION 34: This Part may be cited as the *Canadian Charter of Rights and Freedoms.*

Part II: Rights of the Aboriginal Peoples of Canada

SECTION 35: (1) The existing aboriginal and treaty rights of the aboriginal peoples of Canada are hereby recognized and affirmed.
(2) In this Act, "aboriginal peoples of Canada" includes the Indian, Inuit and Métis peoples of Canada.
(3) For greater certainty, in subsection (1) "treaty rights" includes rights that now exist by way of land claims agreements or may be so acquired.
(4) Notwithstanding any other provision of this Act, the aboriginal and treaty rights referred to in subsection (1) are guaranteed equally to male and female persons.

SECTION 35.1: The government of Canada and the provincial governments are committed to the principle that, before any amendment is made to Class 24 of section 91 of the "*Constitution Act, 1867,*" to section 25 of this Act or to this Part,

(a) a constitutional conference that includes in its agenda an item relating to the proposed amendment, composed of the Prime Minister of Canada and the first ministers of the provinces, will be convened by the Prime Minister of Canada; and
(b) the Prime Minister of Canada will invite representatives of the aboriginal peoples of Canada to participate in the discussions on that item.

Part III: Equalization and Regional Disparities

SECTION 36: (1) Without altering the legislative authority of Parliament or of the provincial legislatures, or the rights of any of them with respect to the exercise of their legislative authority, Parliament and the legislatures, together with the government of Canada and the provincial governments, are committed to

(a) promoting equal opportunities for the well-being of Canadians;
(b) furthering economic development to reduce disparity in opportunities; and
(c) providing essential public services of reasonable quality to all Canadians.

(2) Parliament and the government of Canada are committed to the principle of making equalization payments to ensure that provincial governments have sufficient revenues to provide reasonably comparable levels of public services at reasonably comparable levels of taxation.

Part IV: Constitutional Conference

SECTION 37: (1) A constitutional conference composed of the Prime Minister of Canada and the first ministers of the provinces shall be convened by the Prime Minister of Canada within one year after this Part comes into force.

(2) The conference convened under subsection (1) shall have included in its agenda an item respecting constitutional matters that directly affect the aboriginal peoples of Canada, including the identification and definition of the rights of those peoples to be included in the Constitution of Canada, and the Prime Minister of Canada shall invite representatives of those peoples to participate in the discussions on that item.

(3) The Prime Minister of Canada shall invite elected representatives of the governments of the Yukon Territory and the Northwest Territories to participate in the discussions on any item on the agenda of the conference convened under subsection (1) that, in the opinion of the Prime Minister, directly affects the Yukon Territory and the Northwest Territories.

Part IV.1: Constitutional Conferences

SECTION 37.1: (1) In addition to the conference convened in March 1983, at least two constitutional conferences composed of the Prime Minister of Canada and the first ministers of the provinces shall be convened by the Prime Minister of Canada, the first within three years after April 17, 1982 and the second within five years after that date.

(2) Each conference convened under subsection (1) shall have included in its agenda constitutional matters that directly affect the aboriginal peoples of Canada, and the Prime Minister of Canada shall invite representatives of those peoples to participate in the discussions on those matters.

(3) The Prime Minister of Canada shall invite elected representatives of the governments of the Yukon Territory and the Northwest Territories to participate in the discussions on any item on the agenda of a conference convened under subsection (1) that, in the opinion of the Prime Minister, directly affects the Yukon Territory and the Northwest Territories.

(4) Nothing in this section shall be construed so as to derogate from subsection 35(1).

Part V: Procedure for Amending Constitution of Canada

SECTION 38: (1) An amendment to the Constitution of Canada may be made by proclamation issued by the Governor General under the Great Seal of Canada where so authorized by

(a) resolutions of the Senate and House of Commons; and
(b) resolutions of the legislative assemblies of at least two-thirds of the provinces that have, in the aggregate, according to the then latest general census, at least fifty per cent of the population of all the provinces.

(2) An amendment made under subsection (1) that derogates from the legislative powers, the proprietary rights or any other rights or privileges of the legislature or government of a province shall require a resolution supported by a majority of the members of each of the Senate, the House of Commons and the legislative assemblies required under subsection (1).

(3) An amendment referred to in subsection (2) shall not have effect in a province the legislative assembly of which has expressed its dissent thereto by resolution supported by a majority of its members prior to the issue of the proclamation to which the amendment relates unless that legislative assembly, subsequently, by resolution supported by a majority of its members, revokes its dissent and authorizes the amendment.

(4) A resolution of dissent made for the purposes of subsection (3) may be revoked at any time before or after the issue of the proclamation to which it relates.

SECTION 39: (1) A proclamation shall not be issued under subsection 38(1) before the expiration of one year from the adoption of the resolution initiating the amendment procedure thereunder, unless the legislative assembly of each province has previously adopted a resolution of assent or dissent.

(2) A proclamation shall not be issued under subsection 38(1) after the expiration of three years from the adoption of the resolution initiating the amendment procedure thereunder.

SECTION 40: Where an amendment is made

under subsection 38(1) that transfers provincial legislative powers relating to education or other cultural matters from provincial legislatures to Parliament, Canada shall provide reasonable compensation to any province to which the amendment does not apply.

Section 41: An amendment to the Constitution of Canada in relation to the following matters may be made by proclamation issued by the Governor General under the Great Seal of Canada only where authorized by resolutions of the Senate and House of Commons and of the legislative assembly of each province:

(a) the office of the Queen, the Governor General and the Lieutenant Governor of a province;
(b) the right of a province to a number of members in the House of Commons not less than the number of Senators by which the province is entitled to be represented at the time this Part comes into force;
(c) subject to section 43, the use of the English or the French language;
(d) the composition of the Supreme Court of Canada; and
(e) an amendment to this Part.

Section 42: (1) An amendment to the Constitution of Canada in relation to the following matters may be made only in accordance with subsection 38(1):

(a) the principle of proportionate representation of the provinces in the House of Commons prescribed by the Constitution of Canada;
(b) the powers of the Senate and the method of selecting Senators;
(c) the number of members by which a province is entitled to be represented in the Senate and the residence qualifications of Senators;
(d) subject to paragraph 41(d), the Supreme Court of Canada;
(e) the extension of existing provinces into the territories; and
(f) notwithstanding any other law or practice, the establishment of new provinces.

(2) Subsections 38(2) to (4) do not apply in respect of amendments in relation to matters referred to in subsection (1).

Section 43: An amendment to the Constitution of Canada in relation to any provision that applies to one or more, but not all, provinces, including

(a) any alteration to boundaries between provinces, and
(b) any amendment to any provision that relates to the use of the English or the French language within a province,

may be made by proclamation issued by the Governor General under the Great Seal of Canada only where so authorized by resolutions of the Senate and House of Commons and of the legislative assembly of each province to which the amendment applies.

Section 44: Subject to sections 41 and 42, Parliament may exclusively make laws amending the Constitution of Canada in relation to the executive government of Canada or the Senate and House of Commons.

Section 45: Subject to section 41, the legislature of each province may exclusively make laws amending the constitution of the province.

Section 46: (1) The procedures for amendment under sections 38, 41, 42 and 43 may be initiated either by the Senate or the House of Commons or by the legislative assembly of a province.
(2) A resolution of assent made for the purposes of this Part may be revoked at any time before the issue of a proclamation authorized by it.

Section 47: (1) An amendment to the Constitution of Canada made by proclamation under section 38, 41, 42 or 43 may be made without a resolution of the Senate authorizing the issue of the proclamation if, within one hundred and eighty days after the adoption by the House of Commons of a resolution authorizing its issue, the Senate has not adopted such a resolution and if, at any time after the expiration of that period, the House of Commons again adopts the resolution.
(2) Any period when Parliament is prorogued or dissolved shall not be counted in computing the one hundred and eighty day period referred to in subsection (1).

Section 48: The Queen's Privy Council for Canada shall advise the Governor General to issue a proclamation under this Part forthwith on the adoption of the resolutions required for an amendment made by proclamation under this Part.

Section 49: A constitutional conference composed of the Prime Minister of Canada and the first ministers of the provinces shall be convened by the Prime Minister of Canada within fifteen years after this Part comes into force to review the provisions of this Part.

Part VI: Amendment to the Constitution Act, 1867

Section 50: [This is section 92A of the Constitution Act, 1867.]

Section 51: [This is the Sixth Schedule to the Constitution Act, 1867. See section 92A of that Act.]

Part VII: General

Section 52: (1) The Constitution of Canada is the supreme law of Canada, and any law that is inconsistent with the provisions of the Constitution is, to the extent of the inconsistency, of no force or effect.

(2) The Constitution of Canada includes

(a) the *Canada Act 1982*, including this Act;

(b) the Acts and orders referred to in the schedule; and

(c) any amendment to any Act or order referred to in paragraph (a) or (b).

(3) Amendments to the Constitution of Canada shall be made only in accordance with the authority contained in the Constitution of Canada.

SECTION 53: (1) The enactments referred to in Column I of the schedule are hereby repealed or amended to the extent indicated in Column II thereof and, unless repealed, shall continue as law in Canada under the names set out in Column III thereof.

(2) Every enactment, except the *Canada Act 1982*, that refers to an enactment referred to in the schedule by the name in Column I thereof is hereby amended by substituting for that name the corresponding name in Column III thereof, and any British North America Act not referred to in the schedule may be cited as the *Constitution Act* followed by the year and number, if any, of its enactment.

SECTION 54: Part IV is repealed on the day that is one year after this Part comes into force and this section may be repealed and this Act renumbered, consequentially upon the repeal of Part IV and this section, by proclamation issued by the Governor General under the Great Seal of Canada.

SECTION 54.1: Part IV.1 and this section are repealed on April 18, 1987.

SECTION 55: A French version of the portions of the Constitution of Canada referred to in the schedule shall be prepared by the Minister of Justice of Canada as expeditiously as possible and, when any portion thereof sufficient to warrant action being taken has been so prepared, it shall be put forward for enactment by proclamation issued by the Governor General under the Great Seal of Canada pursuant to the procedure then applicable to an amendment of the same provisions of the Constitution of Canada.

SECTION 56: Where any portion of the Constitution of Canada has been or is enacted in English and French or where a French version of any portion of the Constitution is enacted pursuant to section 55, the English and French versions of that portion of the Constitution are equally authoritative.

SECTION 57: The English and French versions of this Act are equally authoritative.

SECTION 58: Subject to section 59, this Act shall come into force on a day to be fixed by proclamation issued by the Queen or the Governor General under the Great Seal of Canada.

SECTION 59: (1) Paragraph 23(1)(a) shall come into force in respect of Quebec on a day to be fixed by proclamation issued by the Queen or the Governor General under the Great Seal of Canada.

(2) A proclamation under subsection (1) shall be issued only where authorized by the legislative assembly or government of Quebec.

(3) This section may be repealed on the day paragraph 23(1)(a) comes into force in respect of Quebec and this Act amended and renumbered, consequentially upon the repeal of this section, by proclamation issued by the Queen or the Governor General under the Great Seal of Canada.

SECTION 60: This Act may be cited as the *Constitution Act, 1982*, and the Constitution Acts 1867 to 1975 (No. 2) and this Act may be cited together as the *Constitution Acts, 1867 to 1982*.

SECTION 61: A reference to the "*Constitution Acts, 1867 to 1982*" shall be deemed to include a reference to the "*Constitution Amendment Proclamation, 1983*".

Schedule to the Constitution Act, 1982: Modernization of the Constitution

Item	Column I Act Affected	Column II Amendment	Column III New Name
1.	British North America Act, 1867, 30-31 Vict., c. 3 (U.K.)	(1) Section 1 is repealed and the following substituted therefor: "1. This Act may be cited as the *Constitution Act, 1867.*" (2) Section 20 is repealed. (3) Class 1 of section 91 is repealed. (4) Class 1 of section 92 is repealed.	Constitution Act, 1867
2.	An Act to amend and continue the Act 32-33 Victoria chapter 3; and to establish and provide for the Government of the Province of Manitoba, 1870, 33 Vict., c. 3 (Can.)	(1) The long title is repealed and the following substituted therefor: "*Manitoba Act, 1870.*" (2) Section 20 is repealed.	Manitoba Act, 1870
3.	Order of Her Majesty in Council admitting Rupert's Land and the North-Western Territory into the Union, dated the 23rd day of June, 1870.		Rupert's Land and North-Western Territory Order
4.	Order of Her Majesty in Council admitting British Columbia into the Union, dated the 16th day of May, 1871.		British Columbia Terms of Union
5.	British North America Act, 1871, 34-35 Vict., c. 28 (U.K.)	Section 1 is repealed and the following substituted therefor: "1. This Act may be cited as the *Constitution Act, 1871.*"	Constitution Act, 1871
6.	Order of Her Majesty in Council admitting Prince Edward Island into the Union, dated the 26th day of June, 1873.		Prince Edward Island Terms of Union
7.	Parliament of Canada Act, 1875, 38-39 Vict., c. 38 (U.K.)		Parliament of Canada Act, 1875
8.	Order of Her Majesty in council admitting all British possessions and Territories in North America and islands adjacent thereto into the Union, dated the 31st day of July, 1880.		Adjacent Territories Order
9.	British North America Act, 1871, 49-50 Vict., c. 35 (U.K.)	Section 3 is repealed and the following substituted therefor: "3. This Act may be cited as the *Constitution Act, 1886.*"	Constitution Act, 1886

Item	Column I Act Affected	Column II Amendment	Column III New Name
10.	Canada (Ontario Boundary) Act, 1889, 52-53 Vict., c. 28 (U.K.)		Canada (Ontario Boundary) Act, 1889
11.	Canadian Speaker (Appointment of Deputy) Act, 1895, 2nd Sess., 59 Vict., c. 3 (U.K.)	The Act is repealed.	
12.	The Alberta Act, 1905, 4-5 Edw. VII, c. 3 (Can.)		Alberta Act
13.	The Saskatchewan Act, 1905, Edw. VII, c. 42 (Can.)		Saskatchewan Act
14.	British North America Act, 1907, 7 Edw. VII, c. 11 (U.K.)	Section 2 is repealed and the following substituted therefor: "2. This Act may be cited as the *Constitution Act, 1907*."	Constitution Act, 1907
15.	British North America Act, 1915, 5-6 Geo. V, c. 45 (U.K.)	Section 3 is repealed and the following substituted therefor: "3. This Act may be cited as the *Constitution Act, 1915*."	Constitution Act, 1915
16.	British North America Act, 1930, 20-21 Geo. V, c. 26 (U.K.)	Section 3 is repealed and the following substituted therefor: "3. This Act may be cited as the *Constitution Act, 1930*."	Constitution Act, 1930
17.	Statute of Westminster, 1931, 22 Geo. V, c. 4 (U.K.)	In so far as they apply to Canada, (a) section 4 is repealed; and (b) subsection 7(1) is repealed.	Statute of Westminster, 1931
18.	British North America Act, 1940, 3-4 Geo. VI, c. 36 (U.K.)	Section 2 is repealed and the following substituted therefor: "2. This Act may be cited as the *Constitution Act, 1940*."	Constitution Act, 1940
19.	British North America Act, 1943, 6-7 Geo. VI, c. 30 (U.K.)	The Act is repealed.	
20.	British North America Act, 1946, 9-10 Geo. VI, c. 63 (U.K.)	The Act is repealed.	
21.	British North America (No. 1) Act, 1949, 12-13 Geo. VI, c. 22 (U.K.)	Section 3 is repealed and the following substituted therefor: "3. This Act may be cited as the *Newfoundland Act, 1949*."	Newfoundland Act
22.	British North America (No. 2) Act, 1949, 13 Geo. VI, c. 81 (U.K.)	The Act is repealed.	
23.	British North America Act, 1951, 14-15 Geo. VI, c. 32 (U.K.)	The Act is repealed.	

Item	Column I Act Affected	Column II Amendment	Column III New Name
24.	British North America Act, 1952, 1 Eliz. II, c. 15 (Can.)	The Act is repealed.	
25.	British North America Act, 1960, 9 Eliz. II, c. 2 (U.K.)	Section 2 is repealed and the following substituted therefor: "2. This Act may be cited as the *Constitution Act, 1960.*"	Constitution Act, 1960
26.	British North America Act, 1964, 12-13 Eliz. II, c. 73 (U.K.)	Section 2 is repealed and the following substituted therefor: "2. This Part may be cited as the *Constitution Act, 1964.*"	Constitution Act, 1964
27.	British North America Act, 1965, 14 Eliz. II, c. 4, Part I (Can.)	Section 2 is repealed and the following substituted therefor: "2. This Act may be cited as the *Constitution Act, 1965.*"	Constitution Act, 1965
28.	British North America Act, 1974, 23 Eliz. II, c. 13, Part I (Can.)	Section 3, as amended by 25-26 Eliz. II, c. 28, s. 38(1) (Can.), is repealed and the following substituted therefor: "3. This Part may be cited as the *Constitution Act, 1974.*"	Constitution Act, 1974
29.	British North America Act, 1975, 23-24 Eliz. II, c. 28, Part I (Can.)	Section 3, as amended by 25-26 Eliz. II, c. 28, s. 31 (Can.), is repealed and the following substituted therefor: "3. This Act may be cited as the *Constitution Act (No. 1), 1975.*"	Constitution Act (No. 1), 1975
30.	British North America Act (No. 2), 1975, 23-24 Eliz. II, c. 53, (Can.)	Section 3 is repealed and the following substituted therefor: "3. This Act may be cited as the *Constitution Act (No. 2), 1975.*"	Constitution Act (No. 2), 1975

INTRODUCTION

1. Austin Ranney, *The Governing of Men*, 4th ed. (Hinsdale, Illinois: Dryden Press, 1975), p. 263.

CHAPTER 1

1. W.P.M. Kennedy, ed., *Documents of the Canadian Constitution, 1759-1915* (Toronto: Oxford University Press, 1918), pp. 6-14. (Hereinafter referred to as *Documents*.)
2. *Ibid.*, pp. 18-21, 27-37.
3. Governor Murray, quoted in Edgar McInnis, *Canada: A Political and Social History*, 1st ed., rev. (New York: Holt, Rinehart and Winston, 1959), p. 137. (Hereinafter referred to as *Canada*.)
4. J.H. Stewart Reid, Kenneth McNaught and Harry S. Crowe, eds., *A Source-Book of Canadian History: Selected Documents and Personal Papers*, 1st ed., rev. (Toronto: Longmans Canada Limited, 1964), p. 52. (Hereinafter referred to as *Source-Book*.)
5. Reid, *Source-Book*, p. 54.
6. Kennedy, *Documents*, pp. 132-36.
7. See, for example, R. MacGregor Dawson, *The Government of Canada*, 5th ed., rev. by Norman Ward (Toronto: University of Toronto Press, 1970), p. 7; McInnis, *Canada*, pp. 143-44; Hilda Neatby, *The Quebec Act: Protest and Policy* (Scarborough, Ontario: Prentice-Hall of Canada, Ltd., 1972), pp. 3-4. (All later references to Dawson's *The Government of Canada* are to the 5th ed. unless otherwise stated.)
8. Quoted in McInnis, *Canada*, p. 153.
9. Reid, *Source-Book*, p. 60.
10. *Ibid.*, pp. 63-64.
11. *Ibid.*, p. 64.
12. Kennedy, *Documents*, pp. 207-20.
13. Lord Durham, *Report on the Affairs of British North America*, ed. Gerald M. Craig (Toronto: McClelland and Stewart Limited, 1963), p. 56.
14. Arthur R.M. Lower, *Colony to Nation: A History of Canada*, 3rd. ed. (Toronto: Longmans, Green & Company, 1957), p. 215.
15. Governor Head, in J.M. Bliss, ed., *Canadian History in Documents, 1763-1966*, (Toronto: Ryerson Press, 1966), pp. 43-44.

16. W.P.M. Kennedy, quoted in Carl Wittke, *A History of Canada*, 3rd ed. (Toronto: McClelland & Stewart, Limited, 1941), p. 108.
17. John Neilson, quoted in George F.G. Stanley, *A Short History of the Canadian Constitution* (Toronto: Ryerson Press, 1969), p. 40. (This volume is hereinafter referred to as *Short History*.)
18. Quoted in Stanley B. Ryerson, *Unequal Union: Confederation and the Roots of Conflict in the Canadas, 1815-1873*, 2nd ed. (Toronto: Progress Books, 1973), p. 282.
19. William Lyon Mackenzie, "Sketches of Canada and the United States," quoted *ibid.*, p. 93.

CHAPTER 2

1. A.R.M. Lower and J.W. Chafe, *Canada—A Nation*, 2nd ed., rev. (Toronto: Longmans, Green & Company, 1948), p. 258.
2. Durham, *Report on the Affairs of British North America*, pp. 22-23, 33.
3. *Ibid.*, p. 147.
4. *Ibid.*, p. 28.
5. *Ibid.*, p. 150.
6. *Ibid.*, p. 45.
7. *Ibid.*, p. 146.
8. *Ibid.*, p. 119.
9. *Ibid.*, p. 159.
10. *Ibid.*, pp. 140-41.
11. Letters from Lord Russell to Governor Thomson dated September 7, October 14 and 16, 1839, in Kennedy, *Documents*, pp. 517-18, 524.
12. Russell speaking in the British Parliament on June 3, 1839, in Kennedy, *Documents*, p. 480; letter from Russell to Thomson dated October 14, 1839, in Kennedy, *Documents*, p. 522.
13. Kennedy, *Documents*, pp. 536-50.
14. W.L. Morton, *The Kingdom of Canada: A General History from Earliest Times*, 2nd ed. (Toronto: McClelland and Stewart Limited, 1969), p. 258.
15. Stanley, *Short History*, p. 53.
16. Morton, *The Kingdom of Canada: A General History from Earliest Times*, p. 262.
17. Resolutions of the Legislative Assembly of Canada (as amended by Lord Sydenham and accepted by the Assembly), 1841, in Kennedy, *Documents*, pp. 564-65.

18. Lord Sydenham, quoted in H.E. Egerton and W.L. Grant, *Canadian Constitutional Development* (Toronto: Musson Book Co. Limited, 1907), pp. 254, 255.
19. J.R. Mallory, *The Structure of Canadian Government*, rev. ed. (Toronto: Gage Publishing Limited, 1984), p. 12.
20. Lower and Chafe, *Canada —A Nation*, p. 265.
21. Governor Metcalfe, quoted in Stanley, *Short History*, p. 59.
22. Metcalfe to Lord Stanley, in Kennedy, *Documents*, p. 570.
23. Lord Grey to Lieutenant Governor Harvey, in Kennedy, *Documents*, pp. 572, 573.
24. *Ibid.*, p. 577.
25. Kennedy, *Documents*, pp. 480-514.
26. Quoted in Stanley, *Short History*, p. 47.

CHAPTER 3

1. Stanley, *Short History*, p. 73.
2. William Ormsby, *The Emergence of the Federal Concept in Canada, 1839-1845* (Toronto: University of Toronto Press, 1969), p. 25.
3. Reid, *Source-Book*, p. 144.
4. The Grit program is reproduced *ibid.*, pp. 143-44.
5. McInnis, *Canada*, p. 283.
6. *Ibid.*, p. 280.
7. *Ibid.*
8. Stanley, *Short History*, p. 73.
9. Dawson, *The Government of Canada*, p. 329 (n. 9).
10. Reid, *Source-Book*, pp. 200-201.
11. J.M.S. Careless, *Brown of the Globe, Volume II: Statesman of Confederation, 1860-1880* (Toronto: Macmillan Company of Canada Limited, 1963), pp. 145-46.
12. McInnis, *Canada*, p. 290.
13. P.B. Waite, ed., *The Confederation Debates in the Province of Canada/1865* (Toronto: McClelland and Stewart Limited, 1963), p. 40.
14. Senate of Canada, *Report on the British North America Act, 1939* (Ottawa: Queen's Printer, 1961), Annex 4, p. 32.
15. Waite, *The Confederation Debates in the Province of Canada/1865*, p. iii.
16. Stanley, *Short History*, p. 79.
17. Waite, *The Confederation Debates in the Province of Canada/1865*, p. 118.

18. Quoted in P.B. Waite, *The Life and Times of Confederation, 1864-1867*, 2nd ed. (Toronto: University of Toronto Press, 1962), p. 123.
19. Dawson, *The Government of Canada*, p. 35.
20. *Ibid.*
21. All statutes and orders-in-council, except the 1898 Yukon Territory Act, are in Maurice Ollivier, *British North America Acts and Selected Statutes*, 1867-1962 (Ottawa: Queen's Printer, 1962). (Hereinafter referred to as *B.N.A. Acts.*)
22. Durham, *Report on the Affairs of British North America*, pp. 141-42.
23. Reid, *Source-Book*, p. 199.
24. Stanley, *Short History*, p. 174.
25. Dawson, *The Government of Canada*, p. 46.
26. Quoted in Stanley, *Short History*, p. 182.
27. Quoted in McInnis, *Canada*, p. 468.
28. Peter W. Hogg, *Constitutional Law of Canada* (Toronto: Carswell Company Limited, 1977), p. 3 (n. 5). (All later references to this book are to the 2nd ed., 1985, unless otherwise stated.)

CHAPTER 4

1. Alan C. Cairns, "The Living Canadian Constitution," in *Canadian Federalism: Myth or Reality*, 2nd ed., ed. J. Peter Meekison, (Toronto: Methuen, 1971), p. 143.
2. Frank MacKinnon, *The Crown in Canada* (Calgary, Alberta: Glenbow-Alberta Institute, McClelland and Stewart West, 1976), p. 13.
3. Herman Finer, *Governments of Greater European Powers* (New York: Holt, Rinehart and Winston, Inc., 1956), pp. 189-90, quoted in Ranney, *The Governing of Men*, p. 387.
4. Quoted in MacKinnon, *The Crown in Canada*, p. 27.
5. Section II of 1947 Letters Patent. The 1947 Letters Patent are in Ollivier, *B.N.A. Acts*, pp. 653-57.
6. Mallory, *The Structure of Canadian Government*, p. 38.
7. A.V. Dicey, *Introduction to the Study of the Law of the Constitution*, 10th ed. (London: MacMillan & Co. Ltd., 1959), p. 424. (Hereinafter referred to as *Law of the Constitution.*)
8. Walter Bagehot, *The English Constitution* (London: Kegan Paul, Trench, Trubner & Co., Ltd., 1921), p. 75.
9. Dawson, *The Government of Canada*, p. 162.
10. John T. Saywell, *The Office of Lieutenant-Governor: A Study in Canadian Government and Politics* (Toronto: University of Toronto Press, 1957), pp. 112-44.

11. Eugene A. Forsey, *The Royal Power of Dissolution of Parliament in the British Commonwealth* (Toronto: Oxford University Press, 1968), pp. 139-40.
12. Quoted in Eugene Forsey, "The Role and Position of the Monarch in Canada," in *Canadian Politics: A Comparative Reader*, ed. Ronald G. Landes (Scarborough, Ontario: Prentice-Hall Canada Inc., 1985), p. 56.
13. Mallory, *The Structure of Canadian Government*, p. 52.
14. Dawson, *The Government of Canada*, p. 161.
15. Quoted in Geoffrey Marshall, *Constitutional Conventions: The Roles and Forms of Political Accountability* (New York: Oxford University Press, 1984), p. 26. (Hereinafter referred to as *Constitutional Conventions.*)
16. Aristotle, *Politics*, trans. Benjamin Jowett (New York: Random House, 1943), ii, 16, p. 163, by permission of Oxford University Press.
17. Magna Carta, quoted in F.L. Morton, Introduction to Chapter 1, "The Rule of Law in the Canadian Constitution," in *Law, Politics and the Judicial Process in Canada*, ed. F.L. Morton (Calgary, Alberta: University of Calgary Press, 1984), p. 2 (n. 1).
18. Allan C. Hutchinson and Patrick Monahan, "Democracy and the Rule of Law," in *Rule of Law: Ideal or Ideology*, ed. Allan C. Hutchinson and Patrick Monahan (Toronto: Carswell, 1987), pp. 102-3.
19. Dicey, *Law of the Constitution*, pp. 202-3.
20. A.V. Dicey, quoted in E.C.S. Wade and A.W. Bradley, *Constitutional Law*, 8th ed. (London: Longmans, 1970), in Morris Manning, *Rights, Freedoms and the Courts: A Practical Analysis of the Constitution Act, 1982* (Toronto: Emond-Montgomery Limited, 1983), p. 60. (The Manning volume is hereinafter referred to as *Rights, Freedoms and the Courts.*)
21. J.A. Corry, "Administrative Law in Canada," *Papers and Proceedings of the Fifth Annual Meeting of the Canadian Political Science Association*, 5 (1933), 191-92.
22. Herman Finer, "The Case for Subservience," in *Basic Issues in Public Administration*, ed. Donald C. Rowat (New York: Macmillan Company, 1961), p. 469.
23. War Measures Act, R.S.C. 1985, c. W-2; Emergencies Act, S.C. 1988, c. 29. Department of Justice Canada. Reproduced with the permission of the Minister of Supply and Services Canada, 1991.
24. Immigration Act, R.S.C. 1952, c. 325, s. 61(g).
25. John Philpot Curran, "Speech on the Right of Election of Lord Mayor of Dublin, 10 July, 1790," in *Oxford Dictionary of Quotations*, 2nd ed. (London: Oxford University Press, 1953), p. 167.
26. Dicey, *Law of the Constitution*, p. 198.
27. *Ibid.*, p. 200.

28. Hutchinson and Monahan, "Introduction," in Hutchinson and Monahan, *Rule of Law: Ideal or Ideology*, pp. ix-x.

29. Bernard Crick, *In Defence of Politics* (London: Penguin, 1964), p. 56, quoted by Robert J. Jackson and Doreen Jackson, *Politics in Canada: Culture, Institutions, Behaviour and Public Policy*, 2nd ed. (Scarborough, Ontario: Prentice-Hall Canada Inc., 1990), p. 23.

30. John Stuart Mill, *Considerations on Representative Government*, in John Stuart Mill, *Utilitarianism, On Liberty, and Considerations on Representative Government* (London: J.M. Dent & Sons Ltd., 1972), p. 300.

31. J.A. Corry and J.E. Hodgetts, *Democratic Government and Politics*, 3rd ed., rev. (Toronto: University of Toronto Press, 1959), pp. 25-26.

32. C.J. Friedrich, "The Nature of Administrative Responsibility," in Rowat, *Basic Issues in Public Administration*, p. 463.

33. Canada Elections Act, R.S.C., 1970, c.14, ss. 14, 20, 21 (1st Supp.).

34. Bagehot, *The English Constitution*, p. 14.

35. Marshall, *Constitutional Conventions*, p. 54.

36. Bagehot, *The English Constitution*, p. 4.

37. Eugene Forsey, "The Problem of 'Minority' Government in Canada," in *Freedom and Order: Collected Essays* ed. Eugene Forsey(Toronto: McClelland and Stewart Ltd., 1974), pp. 113-14. (This volume is hereinafter referred to as *Freedom and Order*.)

37a. Canada, House of Commons *Debates*, May 13, 1991, p. 5. (Hereinafter referred to as Commons, *Debates*.)

38. Bagehot, *The English Constitution*, p. 80.

39. Commons *Debates*, February 19, 1968, p. 6896; February 21, 1968, p. 6903; February 24, 1968, pp. 7077-78.

40. Dawson, *The Government of Canada*, 1963, 4th ed., p. 390; 1970, 5th ed., p. 357.

41. Eugene Forsey, "Government Defeats in the Canadian House of Commons, 1867-73," in Forsey, *Freedom and Order*, p. 123.

42. P.B. Waite, "The Quebec Resolutions and *Le Courier du Canada*," *Canadian Historical Review*, 40 (1959), especially 299.

43. K.C. Wheare, *Federal Government*, 4th ed. (London: Oxford University Press, 1963), p. 10.

44. Hogg, *Constitutional Law of Canada*, p. 56 (n. 29).

45. Mallory, *The Structure of Canadian Government*, pp. 407-8. Mallory is quoting the Privy Council (*Forbes v. A.G. Manitoba* [1937] A.C. 260, at 274; III Olmsted 160, at 173); and then F.R. Scott ("The Constitutional Background of Taxation Agreements," 2 *McGill L. J.* 2 [1955]).

46. *Re Silver Brothers* [1932] A.C. 514, at 521; III Olmsted 41, at 47. All citations of Privy Council decisions are, unless otherwise stated, from the verbatim *Decisions of the Judicial Committee of the Privy Council relating to the British North America Act, 1867, and The Canadian Constitution 1867-1954*, arr. by Richard A. Olmsted (Ottawa: Queen's Printer, 1954).
47. See for example Richard Simeon and Ian Robinson, *State, Society, and the Development of Canadian Federalism*, vol. 71 of The Collected research studies/Royal Commission on the Economic Union and Development Prospects for Canada (Toronto: University of Toronto Press, 1990), pp. 25-26, 262-68. This is an excellent treatment of Canadian federalism from an historical perspective.
48. Garth Stevenson, *Unfulfilled Union: Canadian Federalism and National Unity*, rev. ed. (Toronto: Gage Publishing Limited, 1982), pp. 40, 44-46.
49. Quoted in Simeon and Robinson, *State, Society, and the Development of Canadian Federalism*, p. 54.
50. Quoted *ibid.*, p. 53.
51. This is from the title of Reginald Whitaker's *The Government Party: Organizing and Financing the Liberal Party of Canada 1932-1958* (Toronto: University of Toronto Press, 1977).
52. Donald V. Smiley, *The Canadian Political Nationality* (Toronto: Methuen, 1967), pp. 35-39.
53. Province of Quebec, *Report of the Royal Commission of Inquiry on Constitutional Problems* (Tremblay Report), 1956, Vol. II, pp. 187ff. (Hereinafter referred to as *Tremblay* Report.)
54. Smiley, *The Canadian Political Nationality*, pp. 45-55.
55. Simeon and Robinson, *State, Society, and the Development of Canadian Federalism*, pp. 262-68.
56. Peter Russell, "The Political Purposes of the Canadian Charter of Rights and Freedoms," 61 *Canadian Bar Rev.* 41 (1983).
57. Hogg, *Constitutional Law of Canada*, p. 652 (n. 11).
58. Dicey, *Law of the Constitution*, pp. 39-40.
59. *Ibid.*, pp. 42, 43, quoting Blackstone and de Lolme, respectively.
60. Corry and Hodgetts, *Democratic Government and Politics*, pp. 93-94.
61. Hogg, *Constitutional Law of Canada*, p. 312 (n. 5).
62. Peter H. Russell, "The Effect of a Charter of Rights on the Policy-Making Role of Canadian Courts," *Canadian Public Administration*, 25 (1982), 32.
63. *Ibid.*

64. Patrick Monahan, *Politics and the Constitution: The Charter, Federalism and the Supreme Court of Canada* (Toronto: Carswell, 1987), p. 119.
65. Ian Greene, *The Charter of Rights* (Toronto: James Lorimer & Company, 1989), p. 107.
66. Two of the early discussions in recent years were Prime Minister Trudeau, *A Canadian Charter of Human Rights* (Ottawa: Queen's Printer, 1968); and Donald V. Smiley, "The Case against the Canadian Charter of Human Rights," *Canadian Journal of Political Science*, 2 (September 1989), 277-91.
67. Peter W. Hogg, *Canada Act 1982 Annotated* (Toronto: Carswell Company Limited, 1982), p. 11.

CHAPTER 5

1. Dawson, *The Government of Canada*, pp. 58-59.
2. Section II of 1947 Letters Patent, in Ollivier, *B.N.A. Acts*, p. 654.
3. Ollivier, *B.N.A. Acts*, p. 626 (n. 1).
4. Mallory, *The Structure of Canadian Government*, p. 46.
5. *Ref. re Legislative Authority of the Parliament of Canada in relation to the Upper House* [1980] 1 S.C.R. 54, at 66-68. (Hereinafter referred to as *Senate Reference.*)
6. Dawson, *The Government of Canada*, pp. 121-22. The texts of all amendments but the last are in Ollivier, *B.N.A. Acts*, pp. 109-44. The 1964 amendment was made after the Ollivier book was published.
7. Guy Favreau, *The Amendment of the Constitution of Canada* (Ottawa: Department of Justice, Queen's Printer, 1965), pp. 5-7. (Hereinafter referred to as *Amendment of the Constitution.*)
8. Paul Gérin-Lajoie, *Constitutional Amendment in Canada* (Toronto: University of Toronto Press, 1950), p. 47.
9. Dawson, *The Government of Canada*, p. 123 (n. 7).
10. Gérin-Lajoie, *Constitutional Amendment in Canada*, pp. 155-68.
11. The term was used by Geoffrey Marshall, "Beyond the B.N.A. Act: Amendment and Patriation," 19 *Alberta L. Rev.* 366 (1981). For a discussion of Britain's relationship to the patriation issue see Marshall's *Constitutional Conventions*, Chapter XI, "The Problem of Patriation."
12. Ollivier, *B.N.A. Acts*, p. 147 (n. 2).
13. Dawson, *The Government of Canada*, pp. 63-64.
14. Peter W. Hogg, "A Comparison of the Canadian Charter of Rights and Freedoms with the Canadian Bill of Rights," in *The Canadian Charter of Rights and Freedoms: Commentary*, ed. Walter S. Tarnopolsky and

Gérald-A. Beaudoin (Toronto: Carswell Company Limited, 1982), p. 23. (This volume is hereinafter referred to as *The Canadian Charter.*)

15. See also Andrew Heard, *Canadian Constitutional Conventions: The Marriage of Law and Politics*, (Toronto: Oxford University Press, 1991). This book published shortly before the present volume went to press, promises to be a valuable addition to the scanty literature on Canadian conventions.
16. *Ref. re Amendment of the Constitution of Canada* [1981] 1 S.C.R. 753, at 853. (Hereinafter referred to as *Patriation Reference.*)
17. Sir Ivor Jennings, *The Law and the Constitution*, 5th ed. (London: University of London Press Ltd., 1959), p. 74.
18. Hogg, *Constitutional Law of Canada*, p. 19.
19. *Patriation Reference* [1981] 1 S.C.R. 753, at 856, 882.
20. Marshall, *Constitutional Conventions*, p. 15.
21. John C. Courtney, "Recognition of Canadian Political Parties in Parliament and in Law," *Canadian Journal of Political Science*, 11 (March 1978), 33-60.
22. *Ref. re Power of Disallowance and Power of Reservation* [1938] S.C.R. 71, at 78. This was confirmed in *Patriation Reference* [1981] 1 S.C.R. 753, at 802.
23. Sir Ivor Jennings, *Cabinet Government*, 3rd ed. (Cambridge: Cambridge University Press, 1969), p. 6.
24. Jennings, *The Law and the Constitution*, p. 136.
25. Marshall, *Constitutional Conventions*, p. 9.
26. *Patriation Reference* [1981] 1 S.C.R. 753, at 893, 894.
27. Report of 1931 Dominion Provincial Conference, pp. 19-20, quoted in *Patriation Reference* [1981] 1 S.C.R. 753, at 907-8.
28. Peter Russell, "Bold Statescraft, Questionable Jurisprudence," in *And No One Cheered: Federalism, Democracy and the Constitution Act*, ed. Keith Banting and Richard Simeon (Toronto: Methuen, 1983), p. 223.
29. Commons *Debates*, 1940, p. 1122, quoted in *Patriation Reference* [1981] 1 S.C.R. 753, at 901.
30. Dawson, *The Government of Canada*, p. 125.
31. Commons *Debates*, 1943, p. 4366, quoted in *Patriation Reference* [1981] 1 S.C.R. 753, at 903.
32. Favreau, *Amendment of the Constitution*, p. 15. Reproduced with the permission of the Minister of Supply and Services Canada, 1990.
33. *Patriation Reference* [1981] 1 S.C.R. 753, at 905-6.
34. Marshall, *Constitutional Conventions*, p. 17.

35. Quoted in Harold W. Chase and Craig R. Ducat, *Edward S. Corwin's The Constitution and What it Means Today*, 14th ed. (Princeton: Princeton University Press, 1978), p. xiii.
36. Quoted in James MacGregor Burns, J.W. Peltason and Thomas E. Cronin, *Government by the People*, 12th alt. ed., nat. ed. (Englewood Cliffs, New Jersey: Prentice-Hall, Inc., 1985), p. 375.
37. Peter H. Russell, "The Supreme Court in the Eighties: Wrestling with the Charter," in *Politics: Canada*, 6th ed., ed. Paul Fox and Graham White (Toronto: McGraw-Hill Ryerson, 1987), p. 169.
38. Peter H. Russell, Rainer Knopff and Ted Morton, *Federalism and the Charter: Leading Constitutional Decisions, A New Edition* (Ottawa: Carleton University Press, 1989), p. 6. (Hereinafter referred to as *Federalism and the Charter.*)
39. *Ref. re Anti-Inflation Act* [1976] 2 S.C.R. 373; *Senate Reference* [1980] 1 S.C.R. 54.
40. Quoted in *Patriation Reference* [1981] 1 S.C.R. 753, at 763-64.
41. *Ibid.*, 753.
42. *A.G. Quebec v. A.G. Canada* [1982] 2 S.C.R. 793. (Hereinafter referred to as *Quebec Veto Reference.*)
43. *Ref. re Offshore Mineral Rights of British Columbia* [1967] S.C.R. 792. (Hereinafter referred to as *B.C. Offshore Mineral Rights Reference.*) *Ref. re Seabed and Subsoil of Continental Shelf Offshore Newfoundland* [1984] 1 S.C.R. 86. (Hereinafter referred to as *Nfld. Continental Shelf Reference.*)
44. *McEvoy v. A.G. New Brunswick* [1983] 1 S.C.R. 704, at 708. The Court noted four cases where it refused to answer (709-15), including the 1979 *Senate Reference* [1980] 1 S.C.R. 54.
45. Russell, Knopff, and Morton, *Federalism and the Charter*, p. 24.
46. *Senate Reference* [1980] 1 S.C.R 54, at 55.
47. *McEvoy v. A.G. New Brunswick* [1983] 1 S.C.R. 704, at 707. The following quotation is from p. 704.
48. *A.G. Ontario v. A.G. Canada* (Reference Appeal) [1912] A.C. 571, at 589; I Olmsted 622, at 640.
49. Gerald Rubin, "The Nature, Use and Effect of Reference Cases in Canadian Constitutional Law," in *The Courts and the Canadian Constitution*, ed. W.R. Lederman (Toronto: McClelland and Stewart Limited, 1964), p. 236.
50. Peter H. Russell, *Leading Constitutional Decisions* (Toronto: McClelland and Stewart, 1965), pp. xxvi-xxvii. Reprinted with permission from Carleton University Press.

51. Corry and Hodgetts, *Democratic Government and Politics*, p. 333. Corry and Hodgetts use the analogy to discuss the effectiveness of the legislature, especially the opposition, in influencing the cabinet.

52. Russell, Knopff and Morton, *Federalism and the Charter*, p. 8. Reprinted with permission from Carleton University Press.

53. Peter H. Russell, "The Supreme Court's Interpretation of the Constitution," in *Politics: Canada*, 5th ed., ed. Paul W. Fox (Toronto: McGraw-Hill Ryerson Limited, 1982), p. 604. (All later references to this book are to the 5th ed. unless otherwise stated.)

54. Hogg, *Constitutional Law of Canada*, pp. 312-13.

55. Neil Finkelstein, *Laskin's Canadian Constitutional Law*, 5th ed. (Toronto: Carswell, 1986), p. 283.

56. Hogg, *Constitutional Law of Canada*, p. 322; Albert Abel, 19 University of Toronto L. J. 494 (1969).

57. Alan C. Cairns, "The Judicial Committee and its Critics," *Canadian Journal of Political Science*, 4 (September 1971), 319.

58. Cairns, "The Living Canadian Constitution," p. 150.

59. *Russell v. R.* [1882] 7 A.C. 829, at 839, 842; I Olmsted 145, at 156, 158-59.

60. *Hodge v. R.* [1883] 9 A.C. 117, at 130; I Olmsted 184, at 197.

61. *A.G. Ontario v. A.G. Canada* (Local Prohibition) [1896] A.C. 348, at 360; I Olmsted 343, at 355-56.

62. *Re Board of Commerce Act, 1919, and Combines and Fair Prices Act, 1919* [1922] 1 A.C. 191, at 200; II Olmsted 245, at 253.

63. *Toronto Electric Commissioners v. Snider* [1925] A.C. 396, at 412; II Olmsted 394, at 409.

64. *Ref. re Proposed Federal Tax of Exported Natural Gas* [1982] 1 S.C.R. 1004, at 1044. (Hereinafter referred to as *Exported Natural Gas Tax Reference*.)

65. *Re Regulation and Control of Aeronautics in Canada* [1932] A.C. 54; II Olmsted 709. (Hereinafter referred to as *Aeronautics Reference*.) *Re Regulation and Control of Radio Communication in Canada* [1932] A.C. 304; III Olmsted 18. (Hereinafter referred to as *Radio Reference*.)

66. *A.G. Canada v. A.G. Ontario* [1937] A.C. 326, at 351-52, 354; III Olmsted 180, at 203-4, 206. (Hereinafter referred to as *Labour Conventions Reference*.)

67. *Co-operative Committee on Japanese Canadians v. A.G. Canada* [1947] A.C. 87, at 101, 108; III Olmsted 458, at 472, 480. *Canadian Federation of Agriculture v. A G. Quebec* (Margarine Reference) [1951] A.C. 179, at 198; III Olmsted 665, at 687.

68. Peter H. Russell, "The Supreme Court's Interpretation of the Constitution," in Fox, *Politics: Canada*, p. 605.
69. *A.G. Ontario v. Canada Temperance Federation* [1946] A.C. 193, at 205; III Olmsted 424, at 437.
70. *Ref. re Anti-Inflation Act* [1976] 2 S.C.R. 373.
71. Peter H. Russell, "The Supreme Court and Federal-Provincial Relations: The Political Use of Legal Resources," *Canadian Public Policy*, 11 (1985), 162-63.
72. Katherine E. Swinton, *The Supreme Court and Canadian Federalism: The Laskin-Dickson Years* (Toronto: Carswell, 1990), p.15.
73. Russell, "The Supreme Court's Interpretation of the Constitution," p. 609.
74. *Ref. re Alberta Statutes* [1938] S.C.R. 100, at 133. See also Greene, *The Charter of Rights*, p. 20.
75. *A.G. Canada v. Dupond* [1978] 2 S.C.R. 770, at 796.
76. *OPSEU [Ontario Public Service Employees' Union] v. A.G. Ontario* [1987] 2 S.C.R. 2, at 57. Justice Abbott's remarks are from *Switzman v. Elbling* [1957] S.C.R. 285, at 328.
77. *R. v. Drybones* [1970] S.C.R. 282.
78. *Singh v. Minister of Employment and Immigration* [1985] 1 S.C.R. 177, at 239, 185.
79. Greene, *The Charter of Rights*, pp. 132-33.
80. Justice Estey in *Law Society of Upper Canada v. Skapinker* [1984] 1 S.C.R. 357, at 366.
81. Russell, Knopff and Morton, *Federalism and the Charter*, p. 27.
82. *Singh v. Minister of Employment and Immigration* [1985] 1 S.C.R. 177, at 209.
83. Russell, Knopff and Morton, *Federalism and the Charter*, pp. 11 -12.
84. This is the organization of Chapter 2 of Greene, *The Charter of Rights*.

CHAPTER 6

1. The principles are in Edward McWhinney, *Canada and the Constitution 1979-1982: Patriation and the Charter of Rights* (Toronto: University of Toronto Press, 1982), Appendix C, pp. 165-66.
2. Quoted in Gérin-Lajoie, *Constitutional Amendment in Canada*, p. 229.
3. Favreau, *Amendment of the Constitution*, pp. 21-23.
4. *Ibid.*, p. 22. Reproduced with the permission of the Minister of Supply and Services Canada, 1990.
5. Stevenson, *Unfulfilled Union: Canadian Federalism and National Unity*, p. 204.

6. The Fulton Formula is in Favreau, *Amendment of the Constitution*, Appendix 2, pp. 106-9.
7. *Ibid.*, p. 27.
8. The Fulton-Favreau Formula is *ibid.*, Appendix 3, pp. 110-15.
9. The Lesage-Pearson correspondence is in Fox, *Politics: Canada*, pp. 146-49.
10. Donald V. Smiley, *Canada in Question: Federalism in the Eighties*, 3rd ed. (Toronto: McGraw-Hill Ryerson Limited, 1980), p. 77.
11. Roy Romanow, John Whyte, and Howard Leeson, *Canada...Notwithstanding: The Making of the Constitution, 1976-1982* (Toronto: Carswell/Methuen, 1984), p. 1. (Hereinafter referred to as *Canada... Notwithstanding.*)
12. October 14, 1976, letter from Alberta Premier Lougheed on behalf of the premiers to the Prime Minister. In Government of Alberta, *Harmony in Diversity: A New Federalism for Canada*, Position Paper on Constitutional Change, October, 1978, p. 26.
13. *Ibid.*
14. Romanow, Whyte, and Leeson, *Canada...Notwithstanding*, pp. 5-6.
15. *Ibid.*, pp. 21-51
16. Quoted *ibid.*, p. 53.
17. *Ibid.*, p. 61.
18. *Ibid.*, p. 66.
19. *Ibid.*, p. 94.
20. Quoted *ibid.*, p. 95.
21. *Ibid.*, p. 101.
22. *Ibid.*, pp. 130-31.
23. The formula is in McWhinney, *Canada and the Constitution, 1979-1982: Patriation and the Charter of Rights*, Appendix B, pp. 156-61.
24. Romanow, Whyte, and Leeson, *Canada...Notwithstanding*, p. 161.
25. *Ibid.*, p. 160.
26. *Ibid.*, p. 162.
27. Cited by *Patriation Reference* [1981] 1 S.C.R. 753, at 762-65.
28. *Ibid.*, p. 753.
29. *Ibid.*, at 880-81.
30. *Ibid.*, at 882-83.
31. Russell, "The Supreme Court in the Eighties—Wrestling with the Charter," p. 165.
32. Russell, "Bold Statescraft, Questionable Jurisprudence," p. 210.
33. *Ibid.*

34. Marshall, *Constitutional Conventions*, p. 198.
35. Romanow, Whyte, and Leeson, *Canada...Notwithstanding*, p. 193.
36. *Quebec Veto Reference* [1982] 2 S.C.R. 793, at 814.
37. Ronald I. Cheffins and Patricia A. Johnson, *The Revised Canadian Constitution: Politics as Law* (Toronto: McGraw-Hill Ryerson Limited, 1986), p. 147.
38. Gilbert Bouchard, *Journal* (Edmonton), August 13, 1986, p. A11.

CHAPTER 7

1. *Patriation Reference* [1981] 1 S.C.R. 753, at 805.
2. Mallory, *The Structure of Canadian Government*, p. 46.
3. Dawson, *The Government of Canada*, p. 152.
4. Jacques Monet "Governor General," *The Canadian Encyclopedia* (1985), 2, 758.
5. Information obtained through the office of Arnold Malone, M.P., April 16, 1991.
6. Dawson, *The Government of Canada*, p. 44.
7. W.H. McConnell, *Commentary on the British North America Act* (Toronto: Macmillan of Canada, 1977), p. 50. (Hereinafter referred to as *Commentary on the B.N.A. Act.*)
8. Mallory, *The Structure of Canadian Government*, p. 65.
9. Sir T. Erskine May, *A Treatise on the Law, Privileges, Proceedings and Usage of Parliament*, 14th ed., p. 41, quoted in Dawson, *The Government of Canada*, p. 337 (n. 34).
10. Commons Debates, 1876, p. 1142, quoted in Gérin-Lajoie, *Constitutional Amendment in Canada*, p. 60. See also pp. 58-59.
11. Based on *Canada Year Book, 1990* (Ottawa: Supply and Services, 1989), Table 19.2, p. 19-21.
12. [1928] S.C.R. 276. Cited by *Edwards v. A.G. Canada* [1930] A.C. 124, at 125; II Olmsted 630, at 631.
13. *Edwards v. A.G. Canada* [1930] A.C. 124; II Olmsted 630. The women who appealed the "Persons" decision to the Privy Council are Henrietta Muir Edwards, Alberta Judge Emily Murphy, Hon. Irene Parlby (an Alberta cabinet minister), Nellie McClung, and Louise McKinney (first woman elected to a Canadian legislature—Alberta).
14. Information obtained through the office of Arnold Malone, M.P., April 16, 1991.
15. Mallory, *The Structure of Canadian Government*, pp. 249-50.
16. Quoted in Forsey, "Appointment of Extra Senators under Section 26 of the British North America Act," in Forsey, *Freedom and Order*, pp. 53-54.

17. Mike Trickey and Jim Polling, "Additional senator OK with Ont. court," *Journal* (Edmonton), October 18, 1990; "B.C. Court backs Senate appointments," *Journal* (Edmonton) February 7, 1991; Joan Ramsay, "[New Brunswick] Court decision on N.B. senator pleases parties," *Journal* (Edmonton), November 21, 1990.
18. McConnell, *Commentary on the B.N.A. Act*, p. 75.
19. *Ibid.*, p. 76.
20. Gérin-Lajoie, *Constitutional Amendment in Canada*, pp. 73-74.
21. Mallory, *The Structure of Canadian Government*, pp. 208-9.
22. Representation Act, 1985, S.C., 1986, c. 8, s. 6.
23. John C. Courtney, "Parliament and Representation: The Unfinished Agenda of Electoral Redistributions," *Canadian Journal of Political Science*, 21 (December 1988), 680-81.
24. Andrew Sancton, "Eroding Representation-by-Population in the Canadian House of Commons: The Representation Act, 1985," *Canadian Journal of Political Science*, 23 (September 1990), 454.
25. Courtney, "Parliament and Representation: The Unfinished Agenda of Electoral Redistributions," p. 676.
26. *Ibid.*, p. 689.
27. Mallory, *The Structure of Canadian Government*, p. 203 (n. 4).
28. Dawson, *The Government of Canada*, pp. 320-22.
29. McConnell, *Commentary on the B.N.A. Act*, p. 83.
30. Dawson, *The Government of Canada*, pp. 321-22.
31. Commons *Debates*, December 12, 1988, p. 1.
32. Canada, *Standing Orders of the House of Commons* (Ottawa: Supply and Services Canada, November 1988).
33. Gary Levy, "A Night to Remember: The First Election of a Speaker by Secret Ballot," *Canadian Parliamentary Review*, 9 (Winter 1986-87), 13.
34. Denis Smith, "The Speakership of the Canadian House of Commons: Some Proposals," in *Contemporary Issues in Canadian Politics*, ed. Frederick Vaughan, Patrick Kyba, and O.P. Dwivedi (Scarborough, Ontario: Prentice-Hall, 1970), p. 180. The election of Lamoureux to a third term, and Jerome (1979) and Fraser (1988) to second terms, occurred after this article was published.
35. Levy, "A Night to Remember: The First Election of a Speaker by Secret Ballot," 14 (n. 1).
36. McConnell, *Commentary on the B.N.A. Act*, p. 96.
37. Canada, House of Commons Standing Committee on Privileges and Elections, *Minutes of Proceedings and Evidence*, October 17, 1985, App. p. 1. Column (4) includes adjustments according to the legislation as finally passed by Parliament. Column (5) is taken from Elections

Canada, Representation in the Federal Parliament (Ottawa: Supply and Services Canada, 1986), p. 17.

38. John Courtney, "Some Thoughts on Redistribution," *Canadian Parliamentary Review*, 9 (Spring 1986), 18.
39. Dawson, *The Government of Canada*, p. 309.
40. Mallory, *The Structure of Canadian Government*, p. 206.
41. Courtney, "Some Thoughts on Redistribution," 19.
42. Commons *Debates*, June 1, 1939, p. 4846.
43. Bagehot, *The English Constitution*, p. 57.
44. Dawson, *The Government of Canada*, p. 134.
45. *Ibid.*, p. 150.
46. *Liquidators of the Maritime Bank of Canada v. Receiver-General of New Brunswick* [1892] A.C. 437, at 443; I Olmsted 263, at 270.
47. Saywell, *The Office of Lieutenant-Governor: A Study in Canadian Government and Politics*, p. 255.
48. McConnell, *Commentary on the B.N.A. Act*, p. 116.
49. Legislative Assembly of Canada, *Scrapbook Hansard*, July 15, 1866, quoted ibid., p. 119.
50. Eugene Forsey, "The Canadian Constitution and its Amendment," in Forsey, *Freedom and Order*, p. 227 (n. 8).
51. Eugene Forsey, "Extension of the Life of Legislatures," in Forsey, *Freedom and Order*, pp. 205-6.
52. *Ref. re Power of Disallowance and Power of Reservation* [1938] S.C.R. 71, at 81.
53. Wheare, *Federal Government*, p. 10.
54. Mallory, *The Structure of Canadian Government*, p. 241 (n. 3).
55. G.V. La Forest, *Disallowance and Reservation of Provincial Legislation* (Ottawa: Queen's Printer, 1965), pp. 83-101.
56. *Ibid.*, pp. 102-15. To La Forest's total of 69 with 13 assents has been added the (later) 1961 instance.
57. Quoted in J.R. Mallory, "The Lieutenant-Governor's Discretionary Powers: The Reservation of Bill 56 in Saskatchewan," in Fox, *Politics: Canada*, p. 436.
58. John T. Saywell, "Reservation Revisited: Alberta, 1937," *Canadian Journal of Economics and Political Science*, 26 (1961), 368.
59. Quoted in Mallory, "The Lieutenant-Governor's Discretionary Powers: The Reservation of Bill 56 in Saskatchewan," p. 436.
60. *Ref. re Power of Disallowance and Power of Reservation* [1938] S.C.R. 71. *Patriation Reference* [1981] 1 S.C.R. 753, at 802; the following quotation is from 802.

61. Mallory, *The Structure of Canadian Government*, pp. 370-71.

62. Hogg, *Constitutional Law of Canada*, pp. 371-72.

63. See Hogg, *ibid.*, pp. 373-95, upon which is based the following discussion of the three broad criteria for p.o.g.g.'s use.

64. The five cases noted below to illustrate the "gap" are: *Citizens Insurance Co. v. Parsons* [1881] 7 A.C. 96; I Olmsted 94. *Radio Reference* [1932] A.C. 304; III Olmsted 18. *Labour Conventions Reference* [1937] A.C. 326; III Olmsted 180. *Nfld. Continental Shelf Reference* [1984] 1 S.C.R. 86. *B.C. Offshore Mineral Rights Reference* [1967] S.C.R. 792.

65. The four cases noted below to illustrate the "national concern" are: *A.G. Ontario v. Canada Temperance Federation* [1946] A.C. 193; III Olmsted 424. *Johannesson v. West St. Paul* [1952] 1 S.C.R. 292. *Munro v. National Capital Commission* [1966] S.C.R. 663. *R. v. Crown Zellerbach Canada Ltd.* [1988] 1 S.C.R. 401.

66. *Tremblay Report*, pp. 187ff.

67. *YMHA Jewish Community Centre of Winnipeg v. Brown* [1989] 1 S.C.R. 1532. The above quotation is from p. 1549.

68. *Citizens Insurance Co. v. Parsons* [1881] A.C. 96; I Olmsted 94. The following quotations are from pp. 112, 113; Olmsted pp. 110, 111.

69. *A.G. Canada v. A.G. Alberta* (Insurance Reference) [1916] 1 A.C. 588, at 596; II Olmsted 1, at 9. Other significant Privy Council rulings are *Re Board of Commerce Act, 1919, and Combines and Fair Prices Act, 1919* [1922] 1 A.C. 191; II Olmsted 245, regulating prices and profits. *Toronto Electric Commissioners v. Snider* [1925] A.C. 396; II Olmsted 394, regulating labour relations. *A.G British Columbia v. A.G. Canada* (Natural Products Marketing Reference) [1937] A.C. 377; III Olmsted 228, regulating marketing. *Canadian Federation of Agriculture v. A.G. Quebec* (Margarine Reference) [1951] A.C. 179; III Olmsted 665, prohibiting the manufacture, sale or possession of margarine. The *Margarine Reference* was allowed to proceed to the Privy Council because it was before the courts at the time appeals were abolished in 1949.

70. *R. v. Eastern Terminal Elevator Company* [1925] S.C.R. 434.

71. *General Motors of Canada v. City National Leasing* [1989] 1 S.C.R. 641, at 659.

72. Hogg, *Constitutional Law of Canada*, pp. 443-47.

73. *A.G. Canada v. Canadian National Transportation* [1983] 2 S.C.R. 206, at 261-62. The two cases are *John Deere Plow Co. v. Wharton* [1915] A.C. 330; I Olmsted 717. *A.G. Ontario v. A.G. Canada* (Canada Standard Trade Mark) [1937] A.C. 405; III Olmsted 253. In ruling on the cases noted above in the "interprovincial" category the Privy Council was also rejecting the applicability of a "general" trade and commerce power.

74. *General Motors of Canada v. City National Leasing* [1989] 1 S.C.R. 641, at 660. Dickson was quoting Viscount Haldane in *John Deere Plow Co. v. Wharton* [1915] A.C. 330, at 340; I Olmsted 717, at 727.
75. *MacDonald v. Vapor Canada* [1977] 2 S.C.R. 134.
76. *A.G. Canada v. Canadian National Transportation* [1983] 2 S.C.R. 206, at 268; quoted in *General Motors of Canada v. City National Leasing* [1989] 1 S.C.R. 641, at 663. Dickson had first suggested the two additional criteria as a minority opinion in the 1983 *C.N. Transportation* case.
77. *A.G. Canada v. A.G. Ontario* (Unemployment Insurance Reference) [1937] A.C. 355; III Olmsted 207.
78. John Stuart Mill, *Principles of Political Economy*, ed. W.J. Ashley (London: Longmans, Green and Co., 1909), p. 823. Quoted by Lord Hobhouse in *Bank of Toronto v. Lambe* [1887] 12 A.C. 575, at 582; I Olmsted 222, at 229.
79. *Bank of Toronto v. Lambe* [1887] 12 A.C. 575, at 583; I Olmsted 222, at 229-30.
80. *Caron v. R.* [1924] A.C. 999, at 1004; II Olmsted 376, at 381.
81. *Exported Natural Gas Tax Reference* [1982] 1 S.C.R. 1004. The quotations are from p. 1005.
82. McConnell, *Commentary on the B.N.A. Act*, p. 191.
83. Canada Privy Council Office, *Guide to Canadian Ministries Since Confederation, July 1, 1867-February 1, 1982* (Ottawa: Canadian Government Publishing Centre, 1982), pp. 3-4, 41-42; S.F. Wise, "Armed Forces—Air Force," *The Canadian Encyclopedia*, 1, 93; *Canada Year Book, 1976-77* (Special Edition) (Ottawa: Supply and Services, 1977), p. 144.
84. *MacKay v. R.* [1980] 2 S.C.R. 370, at 371.
85. McConnell, *Commentary on the B.N.A. Act*, p. 195.
86. *Montreal v. Montreal Harbour Commissioners* [1926] A.C. 299, at 312; II Olmsted 480, at 492.
87. Hogg, *Constitutional Law of Canada*, p. 495.
88. *Ibid.*, p. 494.
89. McConnell, *Commentary on the B.N.A. Act*, p. 201.
90. *A.G. Canada v. A.G. Ontario* [1898] A.C. 700, at 713; I Olmsted 418, at 431. (Hereinafter referred to as *Fisheries Reference*.)
91. *Fowler v. R.* [1980] 2 S.C.R. 213; *Northwest Falling Contractors v. R.* [1980] 2 S.C.R. 292.
92. *Fisheries Reference* [1898] A.C. 700, at 712; I Olmsted 418, at 431.
93. *Exported Natural Gas Tax Reference* [1982] 1 S.C.R. 1004, at 1051.
94. *Munro v. National Capital Commission* [1966] S.C.R. 663.

95. McConnell, *Commentary on the B.N.A. Act*, p. 217. The following historical account is from pp. 203-4.
96. Lord Watson in *Tennant v. Union Bank of Canada* [1894] A.C. 31, at 46; I Olmsted 287, at 302. Viscount Simon in *A.G. Alberta v. A.G. Canada* (Alberta Bill of Rights Reference) [1947] A.C. 503, at 515-16; III Olmsted 539, at 553-54.
97. *Canadian Pioneer Management v. Labour Relations Board of Saskatchewan* [1980] 1 S.C.R. 433, at 461, 465-66.
98. *A.G. Alberta v. A.G. Canada* (Alberta Bank Taxation Reference, or Alberta Statutes Reference) [1939] A.C. 117; III Olmsted 294.
99. *McCulloch v. Maryland.* Excerpt in Peter Woll, ed., *American Government: Readings and Cases*, 10th ed. (Glenview, Illinois: Scott, Foresman and Company, 1990), p. 95.
100. *Bank of Montreal v. Hall* [1990] 1 S.C.R. 121.
101. *A.G. Saskatchewan v. A.G. Canada* (Saskatchewan Farm Security) [1949] A.C. 110; III Olmsted 582. The following quotations are from pp. 125, 123, 122; Olmsted pp. 598, 595-96, 594-95.
102. *A.G. Ontario v. Barfried Enterprises* [1963] S.C.R. 570, at 577.
103. McConnell, *Commentary on the B.N.A. Act*, p. 216.
104. *Ibid.*, p. 218.
105. Hogg, *Constitutional Law of Canada*, p. 552.
106. *Ibid.*, p. 553.
107. Indian Act. R.S.C. 1970, c. I-6. Sections include 42 (property of deceased Indians), 51 (property of mentally incompetent Indians), 52 (property of infant Indians), and 114ff (education).
108. *Derrickson v. Derrickson* [1986] 1 S.C.R. 285.
109. The three Natural Resources acts are in Ollivier, *B.N.A. Acts*, at pp. 361 (Alberta), 392 (Manitoba), 408 (Saskatchewan).
110. *Elk v. R.* [1980] 2 S.C.R. 166.
111. *R. v. Sparrow* [1990] 1 S.C.R. 1075, at 1076.
112. Hogg, *Constitutional Law of Canada*, p. 476.
113. *Re Certain Questions Concerning Marriage* [1912] A.C. 880, at 887; I Olmsted 650, at 657.
114. Hogg, *Constitutional Law of Canada*, pp. 535-36.
115. Peter H. Russell, *The Judiciary in Canada: The Third Branch of Government* (Toronto: McGraw-Hill Ryerson Limited, 1987), p. 226. (Hereinafter referred to as *The Judiciary in Canada*.)
116. Hogg, *Constitutional Law of Canada*, p. 398 (n. 1).
117. *Ibid.*, pp. 434-35.

118. Sir Montague Smith, *Citizens Insurance Co. v. Parsons* [1881] 7 A.C. 96, at 108; I Olmsted 94, at 106.

119. Lord Watson, *A.G. Ontario v. A.G. Canada* (Local Prohibition) [1896] A.C. 348, at 359; I Olmsted 343, at 354-55.

120. *Ibid.*, at 366; at 361.

121. Albert S. Abel, *Laskin's Canadian Constitutional Law*, 4th ed., rev. (Toronto: Carswell Company Ltd., 1975), p. 24.

122. Wheare, *Federal Government*, p. 74.

123. Justice Dickson in *Multiple Access v. McCutcheon* [1982] 2 S.C.R. 161, at 191. See also Hogg, *Constitutional Law of Canada*, pp. 355-56.

124. *Re Silver Brothers* [1932] A.C. 514, at 521; III Olmsted 41, at 47.

125. Hogg, *Constitutional Law of Canada*, pp. 290-95. The two cases noted below are *Re Initiative and Referendum Act* [1919] A.C. 935; II Olmsted 103. *R. v. Nat Bell Liquors* [1922] 2 A.C. 128; II Olmsted 268.

126. *OPSEU [Ontario Public Service Employees' Union] v. A.G. Ontario* [1987] 2 S.C.R. 2. Dickson's comment is on p. 15; Beetz's remarks are on pp. 37-47. The following two quotations in this section 92(1) commentary are from p. 4.

127. *Canadian Industrial Gas & Oil [CIGOL] v. Saskatchewan* [1978] 2 S.C.R. 545.

128. Hogg, *Constitutional Law of Canada*, p. 617.

129. *Ibid.*, pp. 613-14.

130. William D. Moull, "The Legal Effect of the Resource Amendment—What's New in Section 92A," in J. Peter Meekison, Roy J. Romanow and William D. Moull, *Origins and Meanings of Section 92A: The 1982 Constitutional Amendment on Resources* (Montreal: The Institute for Research on Public Policy, 1985), p. 41. (This volume is hereinafter referred to as *Origins and Meanings of Section 92A.*)

131. Robert J. Jackson, Doreen Jackson, and Nicolas Baxter-Moore, *Politics in Canada: Culture, Institutions, Behaviour and Public Policy*, 1st ed. (Scarborough, Ontario: Prentice-Hall Canada Inc., 1986), pp. 610-11.

132. *Bell Canada v. Quebec (Commission de la Santé et de la Sécurité du Travail)* [1988] 1 S.C.R. 749, at 750. Two other cases were decided the same day: *Canadian National Railway Co. v. Courtois, 868; Altrans Express v. British Columbia (Workers' Compensation Board),* 897.

133. Quoted in Finkelstein, *Laskin's Canadian Constitutional Law*, p. 628.

134. *YMHA Jewish Community Centre of Winnipeg v. Brown* [1989] 1 S.C.R. 1532.

135. *Aeronautics Reference* [1932] A.C. 54; II Olmsted 709.

136. *Johannesson v. West St. Paul* [1952] 1 S.C.R. 292.

137. Hogg, *Constitutional Law of Canada*, p. 496.

138. *Alberta Government Telephones v. Canada (Canadian Radio-television and Telecommunications Commission)* [1989] 2 S.C.R. 225, at 227.

139. *IBEW [International Brotherhood of Electrical Workers] v. Alberta Government Telephones* [1989] 2 S.C.R. 318.

140. *Canadian Pacific Railway v. A.G. British Columbia* (Empress Hotel Reference) [1950] A.C. 122; III Olmsted 637.

141. *Ref. re Validity of Industrial Relations and Disputes Act and Applicability in Respect of Certain Employees of Eastern Canada Stevedoring* (Stevedores Reference) [1955] S.C.R. 529.

142. Hogg, *Constitutional Law of Canada*, p. 485.

143. *Justice Mignault* in *Luscar Collieries v. McDonald* [1925] S.C.R. 460, at 480.

144. Finkelstein, *Laskin's Canadian Constitutional Law*, p. 627. The following quotation is from pp. 628-29.

145. *Jorgenson v. A.G. Canada* [1971] S.C.R. 725. Excerpt *ibid.*, pp. 629-30.

146. *R. v. Eastern Terminal Elevator Company* [1925] S.C.R. 434.

147. Finkelstein, *Laskin's Canadian Constitutional Law*, p. 629.

148. A. Lajoie, *Le pouvoir déclaratoire du Parlement* (Montreal: Université Montreal, 1969), cited by Hogg, *Constitutional Law of Canada*, pp. 92 (n. 58), 491-92.

149. *Citizens Insurance Co. v. Parsons* [1881] 7 A.C. 96, at 116-17; I Olmsted 94, at 114-15.

150. *Bonanza Creek Gold Mining Co. v. R.* [1916] 1 A.C. 566, at 583-85; II Olmsted 16, at 33-35.

151. This is the implication of *Canadian Pioneer Management v. Labour Relations Board of Saskatchewan* [1980] 1 S.C.R. 433. See Hogg, *Constitutional Law of Canada*, p. 532.

152. Hogg, *Constitutional Law of Canada*, p. 28.

153. *Ibid.*, p. 455.

154. Russell, *The Judiciary in Canada*, pp. 254, 291.

155. Peter H. Russell, "Constitutional Reform of the Judicial Branch: Symbolic vs. Operational Considerations," *Canadian Journal of Political Science*, 17 (June 1984), 249.

156. *Ritcey v. R.* [1980] 1 S.C.R. 1077.

157. *O'Hara v. British Columbia* [1987] 2 S.C.R. 591, at 606.

158. *A.G. Canada v. Canadian National Transportation* [1983] 2 S.C.R. 206, at 207. A companion case decided the same day was *R. v. Wetmore,* 284.

159. Hogg, *Constitutional Law of Canada*, p. 418.

160. Abel, *Laskin's Canadian Constitutional Law*, p. 827.
161. *Schneider v. R.* [1982] 2 S.C.R. 112. The following quotations are from p. 113.
162. J. Peter Meekison and Roy J. Romanow, "Western Advocacy and Section 92A of the Constitution," in Meekison, Romanow and Moull, *Origins and Meanings of Section 92A*, p. 4.
163. *Ibid.* The Turner quotation, p. 7, is from Commons *Debates*, May 6, 1974, p. 2079.
164. Allan Blakeney, opening statement at the October 1978 First Ministers' Conference (Verbatim Transcript, Canadian Government Conference Secretariat). Quoted in Meekison and Romanow, "Western Advocacy and Section 92A of the Constitution," p. 12.
165. *Canadian Industrial Gas & Oil [CIGOL] v. Saskatchewan* [1978] 2 S.C.R. 545, at 560, 562; *Central Canada Potash and A.G. Canada v. Saskatchewan* [1979] 1 S.C.R. 42, at 72.
166. Hogg, *Constitutional Law of Canada*, p. 472.
167. Meekison and Romanow, "Western Advocacy and Section 92A of the Constitution," p. 7.
168. *Ibid.*, pp. 14-23.
169. Hogg, *Canada Act 1982 Annotated*, p. 102.
170. J. Murray Beck, *Pendulum of Power: Canada's Federal Elections* (Scarborough, Ontario: Prentice-Hall of Canada, Ltd., 1968), p. 76.
171. *Ottawa Roman Catholic Separate School Trustees v. Mackell* [1917] A.C. 62, at 69; II Olmsted 57, at 64.
172. *Greater Montreal Protestant School Board v. A.G. Quebec* [1989] 1 S.C.R. 377; the quotation in the next paragraph is from p. 379. *Mahe v. Alberta* [1990] 1 S.C.R. 342; the quotation in the next paragraph is from p. 382.
173. *A.G. Quebec v. Greater Hull School Board* [1984] 2 S.C.R. 575.
174. *Greater Montreal Protestant School Board v. A.G. Quebec* [1989] 1 S.C.R. 377, at 414.
175. *Ref. re Bill 30, an Act to Amend the Education Act (Ont.)* [1987] 1 S.C.R. 1148.
176. Abel, *Laskin's Canadian Constitutional Law*, pp. 253-54.
177. Senator Ryan, Canada, Senate *Debates*, May 7, 1868, p. 256.
178. *R. v. Foundation Company of Canada Ltd.* [1980] 1 S.C.R. 695, at 706-7.
179. *Toronto v. York* [1938] A.C. 415, at 426; III Olmsted 266, at 276.
180. *Martineau & Sons v. Montreal* [1932] A.C. 113, at 121; III Olmsted 1, at 8.
181. Russell, *The Judiciary in Canada*, p. 121.

182. *Ibid.*, pp. 58-59.

183. Romanow, Whyte, and Leeson, *Canada...Notwithstanding*, pp. 37-38.

184. Russell discusses possibilities in Chapter 5 of *The Judiciary in Canada*.

185. *Ref. re Residential Tenancies Act* [1981] 1 S.C.R. 714, at 728.

186. *Ibid.*, at 734-36.

186a. *Ref. re Young Offenders Act (P.E.I.)*, May 31, 1990. Reported in *Supreme Court News*, vol. 7, no. 2, February 7, 1991, p. 18. The Court added that "even if such jurisdiction had existed at Confederation, it would have been in the nature of powers exercised by inferior courts, since offences that were less stigmatized and which carried light sentences were already within their jurisdiction in 1867."

187. *A.G. Ontario v. A.G. Canada* (B.C. Family Relations Act Reference) [1982] 1 S.C.R. 62. The following quotation is from p. 63.

188. *McEvoy v. A.G. New Brunswick* [1983] 1 S.C.R. 704. The following quotations are from pp. 704-5, 721, 722.

189. Finkelstein, *Laskin's Canadian Constitutional Law*, p. 114.

190. Russell, *The Judiciary in Canada*, p. 60.

191. *The Constitution of Canada: A Suggested Amendment Relating to Provincial Administrative Tribunals* (Ottawa: Department of Justice, 1983). Quoted in Gilles Pepin, "The Problem of Section 96 of the Constitution Act, 1867," in *The Courts and the Charter*, ed. Clare F. Beckton and A. Wayne MacKay (Toronto: University of Toronto Press, 1985), p. 250. This is vol. 58 of The Collected research studies/Royal Commission on the Economic Union and Development Prospects for Canada.

192. Commons *Debates*, March 12, 1976, p. 11771. Quoted in Russell, *The Judiciary in Canada*, p. 80.

193. Russell, *ibid.*, p. 176.

194. Dawson, *The Government of Canada*, p. 397.

195. Quoted in Russell, *The Judiciary in Canada*, p. 178.

196. *Ibid.*, p. 85.

197. *Ibid.*, p. 83.

198. Judges Act, S.C. 1987, c. 21, s. 4.

199. Hogg, *Constitutional Law of Canada*, p. 140.

200. Russell, *The Judiciary in Canada*, p. 82.

201. Frank MacKinnon, "The Establishment of the Supreme Court of Canada," *Canadian Historical Review*, 27 (1946), 260.

202. Hogg, *Constitutional Law of Canada*, pp. 170-71.

203. Supreme Court Act, R.S.C. 1985, c. S-26, s. 9(1)(2).

204. *Nadan v. R.* [1926] A.C. 482; II Olmsted 447.

205. *British Coal Corporation v. R.* [1935] A.C. 500; III Olmsted 121.

206. *Labour Conventions Reference* [1937] A.C. 326, at 328; III Olmsted 180, at 182.

207. *A.G. Ontario v. A.G. Canada* (Privy Council Appeals Reference) [1947] A.C. 127, at 153; III Olmsted 508, at 535.

208. Hogg, *Constitutional Law of Canada*, p. 142.

209. *A.G. Canada v. Law Society of British Columbia* [1982] 2 S.C.R. 307, at 309.

210. Judges Act, S.C. 1987, c. 21, ss. 4, 7, 8.

211. Russell, *The Judiciary in Canada*, p. 316.

212. However, the narrow interpretations of section 101 by the Supreme Court raise questions about the extent of Parliament's creative power. See *ibid.*, pp. 68-70; and Hogg, *Constitutional Law of Canada*, pp. 142-48.

213. *B.C. Offshore Mineral Rights Reference* [1967] S.C.R. 792; *Nfld. Continental Shelf Reference* [1984] 1 S.C.R. 86.

214. A. Milton Moore, J. Harvey Perry and Donald I. Beach, *The Financing of Canadian Federation: The First Hundred Years* (Toronto: Canadian Tax Foundation, 1966), p. 2.

215. *Ibid.*, p. 3.

216. Dawson, *The Government of Canada*, p. 102.

217. McConnell, *Commentary on the B.N.A. Act*, p. 358.

218. *Ref. re Interprovincial Trade Restrictions on Agricultural Commodities* [1971] 18 D.L.R. (3d) 326, at 341 (Man. C.A.).

219. *A.G. Manitoba v. Manitoba Egg and Poultry Association* [1971] S.C.R 689.

220. Justice Rand's statement is in *Murphy v. C.P.R.* [1958] S.C.R. 626, at 642. Chief Justice Laskin's statements are in *Ref. re Agricultural Products Marketing Act* [1978] 2 S.C.R. 1198, at 1268 (including the Rand quotation), 1267.

221. C.B.C. "Venture," November 18, 1990.

222. Susan Delacourt, "Premiers agree to provincial free trade," *The Globe and Mail* (Toronto), August 15, 1990, p. A1.

223. McConnell, *Commentary on the B.N.A. Act*, p. 363.

224. *Ibid.*, pp. 363-65.

225. Hogg, *Constitutional Law of Canada*, pp. 41-42 (n. 24).

226. British Columbia, Term 10 of the Schedule to the order-in-council; Prince Edward Island, a provision similar to British Columbia's but the terms are not numbered; Manitoba, section 2 of the Manitoba Act; Saskat-

chewan and Alberta, section 16 of the Saskatchewan Act and Alberta Act; Newfoundland, Term 18 of the Schedule to the Terms of Union of Newfoundland with Canada Act.

227. *Labour Conventions Reference* [1937] A.C. 326, at 351, 352; III Olmsted 180, at 203, 204.

228. Wright in 33 *Canadian Bar Rev.* 1125-28 (1955); cited by Hogg, *Constitutional Law of Canada*, p. 252 (n. 48).

229. B.J. McKinnon, letter to the editor, 34 *Canadian Bar Rev.* 117 (1956).

230. *Francis v. R.* [1956] S.C.R. 618, at 621. Quoted by Chief Justice Laskin in *MacDonald v. Vapor Canada* [1977] 2 S.C.R. 134, at 168.

231. *MacDonald v. Vapor Canada* [1977] 2 S.C.R. 134, at 169.

232. Justice Rand, "Some Aspects of Canadian Constitutionalism," 38 *Canadian Bar Rev.* 142-43 (1960).

233. *MacDonald v. Montreal* [1986] 1 S.C.R. 460, at 496. On the same day the Supreme Court delivered a similar judgement, ruling that a summons issued by a Manitoba court need not be bilingual—in this case it could be in English only—under section 23 of the Manitoba Act: *Bilodeau v. A.G. Manitoba* [1986] 1 S.C.R. 449.

234. *MacDonald v. Montreal* [1986] 1 S.C.R. 460, at 523.

235. Dickson was referring to Charter section 19(2). *Société des Acadiens du Nouveau-Brunswick Inc. v. Association of Parents for Fairness in Education* [1986] 1 S.C.R. 549, at 566 (hereinafter referred to as *Société des Acadiens v. Association of Parents*). This case was decided the same day as *MacDonald v. Montreal* [1986] 1 S.C.R. 460.

236. *MacDonald v. Montreal* [1986] 1 S.C.R 460, at 462. The following quotation is from p. 463.

237. *Société des Acadiens v. Association of Parents* [1986] 1 S.C.R. 549, at 638.

238. *Jones v. A.G. New Brunswick* [1975] 2 S.C.R. 182, at 192-93.

239. *A.G. Quebec v. Blaikie* [1979] 2 S.C.R. 1016, at 1025.

240. *A.G. Quebec v. Blaikie* [1981] 1 S.C.R. 312, at 313.

241. *A.G. Quebec v. Brunet; A.G. Quebec v. Albert; A.G. Quebec v. Collier* [1990] 1 S.C.R. 260.

242. *A.G. Manitoba v. Forest* [1979] 2 S.C.R. 1032.

243. *Ref. re Manitoba Language Rights* [1985] 1 S.C.R. 721, at 724, 725.

244. *Ref. re Manitoba Language Rights (Order)* [1985] 2 S.C.R. 347, at 348-49.

245. *R. v. Mercure* [1988] 1 S.C.R. 234. *R. v. Paquette* [1990] 2 S.C.R. 1103; litigation had begun in the lower courts in 1985.

246. North-West Territories Act, R.S.C. 1886, c. 50, s. 110. Department of Justice Canada. Reproduced with the permission of the Minister of Supply and Services Canada, 1991.

247. Alberta Act, S.C. 1905, c. 3; Saskatchewan Act, S.C. 1905, c. 42. Department of Justice Canada. Reproduced with the permission of the Minister of Supply and Services Canada, 1991.

248. *R. v. Mercure* [1988] 1 S.C.R. 234. The following quotations are from pp. 255, 280-81.

249. Canada, Department of Justice, *A Consolidation of the Constitution Acts, 1867 to 1982* (Ottawa: Canadian Government Publishing Centre, 1986), p. 48 (n. 73).

250. James Marsh, "Intercolonial Railway," *The Canadian Encyclopedia*, 2, 889.

CHAPTER 8

1. SI/82-97, May 12, 1982, in *Canada Gazette* Part II, Vol. 116, No. 9, p. 1808.
2. *Ref. re Public Service Employee Relations Act, Labour Relations Act, and Police Officers Collective Bargaining Act (Alta)* [1987] 1 S.C.R. 313, at 394. (Hereinafter referred to as *Alberta Labour Reference.*)
3. *R. v. Stevens* [1988] 1 S.C.R. 1153 at 1158. Three of the eight judges who participated in the decision dissented.
4. F.L. Morton, cited by Greene, *The Charter of Rights*, p. 217.
5. Hogg, *Canada Act 1982 Annotated*, pp. 14-15.
6. *R. v. Amway* Corp. [1989] 1 S.C.R. 21.
7. *Tremblay v. Daigle* [1989] 2 S.C.R. 530, at 532-33.
8. *R. v. Sullivan*, Supreme Court of Canada, March 21, 1991, unpublished.
9. Romanow, Whyte, and Leeson, *Canada...Notwithstanding*, p. 243.
10. *R. v. Therens* [1985] 1 S.C.R. 613, at 645.
11. *Ibid.*, is a case in point.
12. *R. v. Oakes* [1986] 1 S.C.R. 103, at 136.
13. *A.G. Quebec v. Quebec Association of Protestant School Boards* [1984] 2 S.C.R. 66, at 67.
14. *R. v. Big M Drug Mart* [1985] 1 S.C.R. 295. The following quotations are from p. 352.
15. *R. v. Oakes* [1986] 1 S.C.R. 103, at 138-40. The quotations within this statement are from ibid.

15a. *Committee for the Commonwealth of Canada v. Canada*, January 25, 1991. Reported in *Supreme Court News*, vol. 7, no. 1, p. 3.

16. Russell, Knopff and Morton, *Federalism and the Charter*, p. 453. Reprinted with permission from Carleton University Press.
17. *R. v. Edwards Books and Art* [1986] 2 S.C.R. 713.
18. *R. v. Big M Drug Mart* [1985] 1 S.C.R. 295, at 336-37.

19. *Walter v. A.G. Alberta; Fletcher v. A.G. Alberta* [1969], S.C.R. 383. Quoted in Irwin Colter, "Freedom of Assembly, Association, Conscience and Religion (s. 2(a), (c), and (d))," in Tarnopolsky and Beaudoin, *The Canadian Charter*, p. 195.
20. *R. v. Big M Drug Mart* [1985] 1 S.C.R. 295, at 296. The other case, judged the same day and with identical reasoning, was *Plantation Indoor Plants v. A.G. Alberta* [1985] 1 S.C.R. 366.
21. *R. v Edwards Books and Art* [1986] 2 S.C.R. 713. The following quotation is from p. 715.
22. *Ibid.*, at 772.
23. Tarnopolsky, J.A., quoted by Chief Justice Dickson, *ibid.*, at 761.
24. *R. v. Edwards Books and Art* [1986] 2 S.C.R. 713, at 770.
25. *R. v. Jones* [1986] 2 S.C.R. 284, at 285.
26. Mill, *On Liberty*, in Mill, *Utilitarianism, On Liberty, and Considerations on Representative Government*, p. 79.
27. Quoted in Noel Lyon, "The Teleological Mandate of the Fundamental Freedoms Guarantee: What to do with Vague but Meaningful Generalities," in The *New Constitution and the Charter of Rights: Fundamental Issues and Strategies*, ed. Edward P. Belobaba and Eric Gertner (Toronto: Butterworths, 1983), p. 72. (Hereinafter this article is referred to as "The Teleological Mandate.")
28. Justice Lamer for the Court in *RWDSU [Retail, Wholesale and Department Store Union] v. Dolphin Delivery* [1986] 2 S.C.R. 573, at 583. (Hereinafter referred to as *RWDSU v. Dolphin Delivery*.)
29. *R. v. Keegstra*, December 13, 1990. Edited reprint (mimeograph): "Leading Constitutional Decisions of the Supreme Court of Canada," ed. Peter H. Russell, Rainer Knopff, and F.L. Morton (Calgary: The Research Unit for Socio-Legal Studies, Faculty of Social Sciences, University of Calgary). The following quotations are from pp. 6, 6-7, 7, 15, 17.
30. *RWDSU v. Dolphin Delivery* [1986] 2 S.C.R. 573.
31. *BCGEU [British Columbia Government Employees' Union] v. A.G. British Columbia* [1988] 2 S.C.R. 214, at 229.
32. *Canadian Newspapers Co. v. A.G. Canada* [1988] 2 S.C.R. 122.
33. *Edmonton Journal v. A.G. Alberta* [1989] 2 S.C.R. 1326.
34. *Ref. re ss. 193 and 195.1 (1) (c) of the Criminal Code (Man.)* [1990] 1 S.C.R. 1123. The following quotations are from pp. 1134, 1136. The other two cases are *R. v. Stagnitta* [1990] 1 S.C.R. 1226, and *R. v. Skinner* [1990] 1 S.C.R. 1235.
35. *Irwin Toy v. A.G. Quebec* [1989] 1 S.C.R. 927, at 933.
36. *Rocket v. Royal College of Dental Surgeons of Ontario* [1990] 2 S.C.R. 232. The following quotations are from pp. 248, 251.

37. *Devine v. A.G. Quebec* [1988] 2 S.C.R. 790, at 792.
38. *Ibid.; Ford v. A.G. Quebec* [1988] 2 S.C.R. 712.
39. Quoted in *Ford v. A.G. Quebec* [1988] 2 S.C.R. 712, at 750.
40. *Ibid.*, at 778.
41. *Slaight Communication v. Davidson* [1989] 1 S.C.R. 1038, at 1040.

41a. *Committee for the Commonwealth of Canada v. Canada*, January 25, 1991. Reported in *Supreme Court News*, vol. 7, no. 1, p. 3.

41b. *Osborne v. Canada (Treasury Board)*, Supreme Court of Canada, June 6, 1991, unpublished, mimeograph unpaged.

42. *National Citizens' Coalition v. A.G. Canada* [1984] 11 D.L.R. (4th) 481 (Alta. Q.B.); cited by Hogg, *Constitutional Law of Canada*, p. 718.
43. Manning, *Rights, Freedoms and the Courts*, p. 211.
44. Lyon, "The Teleological Mandate," p. 72.
45. SOR/70-443, October 16, 1970, in *Canada Gazette* Part II, Vol. 104, No. 20, pp. 1127-30.
46. *Roncarelli v. Duplessis* [1959] S.C.R. 121.
47. Quoted in Colter, "Freedom of Assembly, Association, Conscience and Religion (s. 2(a), (c), and (d))," p. 179.
48. Quoted *ibid.*, p. 181.
49. *Alberta Labour Reference* [1987] 1 S.C.R. 313. *PSAC [Public Service Alliance of Canada] v. Canada* [1987] 1 S.C.R. 424. *RWDSU [Retail, Wholesale and Department Store Union] v. Saskatchewan* [1987] 1 S.C.R. 460. The following quotations are from the *Alberta Labour Reference*, pp. 397, 410.
50. Justice Sopinka for the majority in *Professional Institute of Public Service of Canada v. Northwest Territories (Commissioner)* [1990] 2 S.C.R. 367, at 402.
51. *Alberta Labour Reference* [1987] 1 S.C.R. 313, at 390.
52. *R. v. Skinner* [1990] 1 S.C.R. 1235, at 1244. The following quotations are from pp. 1243, 1244. Justice Wilson's remarks are on pp. 1253-54.
53. *Muldoon v. Canada* [1988] 3 F.C. 628; *Canadian Disability Rights Council v. Canada* [1988] 3 F.C. 622.
54. *Belczowski v. R.*, Federal Court of Canada (T.D.), February 28, 1991, unpublished, pp. 14, 16-17. Stephen Bindman, "Federal government appeals court ruling giving prisoners right to vote," *Journal* (Edmonton), March 27, 1991, p. A3.
55. Greene, *The Charter of Rights*, p. 124.

55a. *Carter v. A.G. Saskatchewan* Supreme Court of Canada, June 6, 1991, unpublished, mimeograph unpaged.

56. Hogg, *Constitutional Law of Canada*, p. 730.
57. Greene, *The Charter of Rights*, p. 46.
58. *United States of America v. Cotroni; United States of America v. El Zein* [1989] 1 S.C.R. 1469, at 1471.
59. *Law Society of Upper Canada v. Skapinker* [1984] 1 S.C.R. 357. The following quotation is from p. 382.
60. *Black v. Law Society of Alberta* [1989] 1 S.C.R. 591. The following quotations are from pp. 593, 599.
61. Romanow, Whyte, and Leeson, *Canada...Notwithstanding*, p. 208.
62. F.L. Morton and M.J. Withey, cited by Greene, *The Charter of Rights*, p. 126. F.L. Morton, Peter H. Russell, and Michael J. Withey, "Judging the Judges: The Supreme Court's First One Hundred Charter Decisions," in *Politics: Canada*, 7th ed., ed. Paul W. Fox and Graham White (Toronto: McGraw-Hill Ryerson, 1991), p. 67.
63. *R. v. Hebert* [1990] 2 S.C.R. 151, at 180.
64. *Operation Dismantle v. R.* [1985] 1 S.C.R. 441. The following quotations are from pp. 442-43.
65. *Singh v. Minister of Employment and Immigration* [1985] 1 S.C.R. 177, at 179.
66. *Irwin Toy v. A.G. Quebec* [1989] 1 S.C.R. 927, at 935.
67. *Borowski v. A.G. Canada* [1989] 1 S.C.R. 342.
68. *Tremblay v. Daigle* [1989] 2 S.C.R. 530.
69. *R. v. Sullivan*, Supreme Court of Canada, March 21, 1991, unpublished.
70. Chief Justice Dickson, *R. v. Edwards Books and Art* [1986] 2 S.C.R. 713, at 786.
71. *Ref. re B.C. Motor Vehicle Act* [1985] 2 S.C.R. 486, at 524.
72. *Canada v. Schmidt* [1987] 1 S.C.R. 500, at 523. Similar comments were made in *Argentina v. Mellino* [1987] 1 S.C.R. 536, decided the same day.
73. John D. Whyte, "Fundamental Justice," 13 *Manitoba L. J.* 474 (1983).
74. Justice Wilson in *Singh v. Minister of Employment and Immigration* [1985] 1 S.C.R. 177, at 207, quoting the Law Reform Commission and the Universal Declaration of Human Rights.
75. *R. v. Morgentaler* [1988] 1 S.C.R. 30.
76. Greene, *The Charter of Rights*, p. 153.
77. *R. v. Morgentaler* [1988] 1 S.C.R. 30, at 32-33.
78. *Ibid.*, at 36-37.
79. The following statements are from *ibid.*, at 33-37.
80. B.L. Strayer (Assistant Deputy Minister, Department of Justice) appearing before the Special Joint Committee of the Senate and House of

Commons on the Constitution of Canada, *Minutes of Proceedings and Evidence*, January 27, 1981, p. 46:32. (Hereinafter referred to as Committee on the Constitution, Minutes.)

81. Justice Lamer, *Ref. re B.C. Motor Vehicle Act* [1985] 2 S.C.R. 486, at 509, 501-2, 513.
82. *R. v. Hess; R. v. Nguyen* [1990] 2 S.C.R. 906, at 939-40.
83. *R. v. Jones* [1986] 2 S.C.R. 284, at 287-88.
84. Manning, *Rights, Freedoms and the Courts*, p. 264.
85. *R. v. Hebert* [1990] 2. S.C.R. 151. The quotations in this and the following paragraph are from pp. 176, 153.
86. *Singh v. Minister of Employment and Immigration* [1985] 1 S.C.R. 177. The quotation is from Morton, Russell, and Withey, "Judging the Judges: The Supreme Court's First One Hundred Charter Decisions," p. 71.
87. *R. v. Lyons* [1987] 2 S.C.R. 309, at 329.

87a. *R. v. Swain*, May 2, 1991. Reported in *Supreme Court News*, vol. 7 no. 6, pp. 66-67.

88. *R. v. Cornell* [1988] 1 S.C.R. 461, at 462.
89. *R. v. Beare; R. v. Higgins* [1988] 2 S.C.R. 387, at 389.
90. *Krug v. R.* [1985] 2 S.C.R. 255.
91. *Thomson Newspapers v. Canada (Director of Investigation and Research, Restrictive Trade Practices Commission)* [1990] 1 S.C.R. 425. (Hereinafter referred to as *Thomson Newspapers v. Canada.*) The following comments of individual judges are from pp. 428, 483, 549.
92. *Ref. re ss. 193 and 195.1(1) (c) of the Criminal Code* (*Man.*) [1990] 1 S.C.R. 1123, at 1126.
93. Justice Lamer for a Court majority, *Ref. re B.C. Motor Vehicle Act* [1985] 2 S.C.R. 486, at 502-3.

93a. *R. v. Collins* [1987] 1 S.C.R. 265, at 278.

94. *Hunter v. Southam* [1984] 2 S.C.R. 145. The following quotations are from pp. 155, 146-47, 150.
95. *Thomson Newspapers v. Canada* [1990] 1 S.C.R. 425, at 497-98.
96. *R. v. Simmons* [1988] 2 S.C.R. 495. The following quotations are from pp. 497-98.
97. *Hunter v. Southam* [1984] 2 S.C.R. 145, at 159-60.
98. *R. v. Duarte* [1990] 1 S.C.R. 30, at 39, 42; *R. v. Wiggins* [1990] 1 S.C.R. 62.
99. *R. v. Thompson* [1990] 2 S.C.R. 1111, at 1154.
100. *R. v. Wong*, November 22, 1990. Edited reprint (mimeograph): "Leading Constitutional Decisions of the Supreme Court of Canada," ed. Peter H. Russell, Rainer Knopff, and F.L. Morton, p. 5.

101. *R. v. Hufsky* [1988] 1 S.C.R. 621, at 638.
102. *R. v. McKinlay Transport* [1990] 1 S.C.R. 627, at 648.
103. *R. v. Sieben* [1987] 1 S.C.R. 295; *R. v. Hamill* [1987] 1 S.C.R. 301.
104. *R. v. Dyment* [1988] 2 S.C.R. 417.
105. Manning, *Rights, Freedoms and the Courts*, pp. 322-23.
106. *R. v. Hufsky* [1988] 1 S.C.R. 621, at 623.
107. *R. v. Storrey* [1990] 1 S.C.R. 241.
108. *R. v. Hufsky* [1988] 1 S.C.R. 621; *R. v. Ladouceur* [1990] 1 S.C.R. 1257.
109. *R. v. Lyons* [1987] 2 S.C.R. 309; *R. v. Milne* [1987] 2 S.C.R. 512.
110. Justice La Forest quoting the Crown's counsel with La Forest's "complete agreement." *R. v. Lyons* [1987] 2 S.C.R. 309, at 348. The following quotation is from p. 349.
110a. *R. v. Swain*, May 2, 1991. Reported in *Supreme Court News*, vol. 7, no. 6, pp. 69-70.
111. *R. v. Luxton* [1990] 2 S.C.R. 711, at 723.
112. *R. v. Therens* [1985] 1 S.C.R. 613. The following quotations are from pp. 642, 644.
113. *Clarkson v. R.* [1986] 1 S.C.R. 383.
114. *R. v. Manninen* [1987] 1 S.C.R. 1233.
115. *R. v. Smith* [1989] 2 S.C.R. 368, at 369. The requirement of "diligence" was first enunciated in *R. v. Tremblay* [1987] 2 S.C.R. 435.
116. *R. v. Ross* [1989] 1 S.C.R. 3. The following quotation is from p. 11.
117. Justice Minister Chrétien appearing before the Committee on the Constitution, *Minutes*, January 27, 1981, p. 46:125.
118. *R. v. Brydges* [1990] 1 S.C.R. 190.
119. *R. v. Thomsen* [1988] 1 S.C.R. 640.
120. *R. v. Therens* [1985] 1 S.C.R. 613.
121. *R. v. Simmons* [1988] 2 S.C.R. 495.
122. *R. v. Black* [1989] 2 S.C.R. 138, at 139. See also *R. v. Evans*, Supreme Court of Canada, April 18, 1991, unpublished.
122a. *R. v. Evans*, Supreme Court of Canada, April 18, 1991, unpublished, p. 4.
123. *Mills v. R.* [1986] 1 S.C.R. 863, at 918, 920.
124. *R. v. Askov* [1990] 2 S.C.R. 1199, at 1221.
125. *Ibid.*, 1199. The following quotations from this case are from pp. 1240, 1243.
126. *R. v. Rahey* [1987] 1 S.C.R. 588, at 613.
127. Florence Loyie, "Trial delays could terminate 3000 youth-court cases," *Journal* (Edmonton), March 22, 1991, p. A1. A later report stated that

Alberta was hiring additional judges, crown prosecutors and other staff to unclog the province's judicial system generally. Richard Helm, "Alberta justice system bailed out," *Journal* (Edmonton), April 9, 1991, p. A1.

128. Hogg, *Constitutional Law of Canada*, p. 766.
129. *R. v. Amway Corp.* [1989] 1 S.C.R. 21.
130. *R. v. Oakes* [1986] 1 S.C.R. 103, at 119-20.
131. See, for example, Hogg, *Constitutional Law of Canada*, pp. 768-69.
132. *R. v. Whyte* [1988] 2 S.C.R. 3, at 4.
133. *Ibid.*, at 4-5.
134. *R. v. Oakes* [1986] 1 S.C.R. 103.
135. *R. v. Whyte* [1988] 2 S.C.R. 3.
136. *R v. Penno* [1990] 2 S.C.R. 865. The following quotations are from pp. 885, 896.
137. *R. v. Keegstra*, December 13, 1990. Edited reprint (mimeograph): "Leading Constitutional Decisions of the Supreme Court of Canada," ed. Peter H. Russell, Rainer Knopff, and F.L. Morton, pp. 13-14.
138. *R. v. Vaillancourt* [1987] 2 S.C.R. 636, at 636-37 (s. 213 of the Criminal Code), 638-39. The quotations in brackets are from *R. v. Martineau* [1990] 2 S.C.R. 633, at 647.

138a. *R. v. Chaulk*, December 20, 1990. Reported in *Supreme Court News*, vol. 6, no. 20, p. 267.

139. *R. v. Schwartz* [1988] 2 S.C.R. 443. The following quotations are from pp. 485, 445.
140. *R. v. Corbett* [1988] 1 S.C.R. 670, at 671-72.
141. *R. v. Vermette* [1988] 1 S.C.R. 985, at 986.
142. David C. McDonald, *Legal Rights in the Canadian Charter of Rights and Freedoms: A Manual of Issues and Sources* (Toronto: Carswell Company Limited, 1982), p. 104.
143. *Canadian Newspapers Co. v. A.G. Canada* [1988] 2 S.C.R. 122.
144. *Valente v. R.* [1985] 2 S.C.R. 673. The following quotations are from pp. 675, 712, 674.
145. Greene, *The Charter of Rights*, p. 148.

145a. *R. v. Lippe*, Supreme Court of Canada, December 5, 1990, unpublished, mimeograph unpaged.

146. Hogg, *Constitutional Law of Canada*, p. 771.
147. Justice Wilson for the Court, *R. v. Turpin* [1989] 1 S.C.R. 1296, at 1310.
148. *R. v. Lyons* [1987] 2 S.C.R. 309. The following quotations are from pp. 313, 362.

149. *R. v. Turpin* [1989] 1 S.C.R. 1296, at 1297.
150. United States Justice Frankfurter, quoted by Justice Wilson, *ibid.*, 1313.
151. Justice Lamer for the Court, *R. v. Lee* [1989] 2 S.C.R. 1384, at 1390. He was quoting Justice Wilson who, however, dissented as to the applicability of section 1.
152. Hogg, *Constitutional Law of Canada*, pp. 772-73. The case was *R. v. S.B.*, heard by the British Columbia Court of Appeal.
153. *MacKay v. R.* [1980] 2 S.C.R. 370. The following quotations are from pp. 408, 379-80.
154. *R. v. McDonald* [1983] 150 D.L.R. (3d) 620 (Court Martial Appeal Court), cited by Hogg, *Constitutional Law of Canada*, p. 774 (n. 193).
155. *R. v. Wigglesworth* [1987] 2 S.C.R. 541. The following quotation is from p. 561.
156. *R. v. Van Rassel* [1990] 1 S.C.R. 225, at 240.
157. *R. v. Shubley* [1990] 1 S.C.R. 3.
158. *Corporation professionnelle des médecins du Québec v. Thibault* [1988] 1 S.C.R. 1033. The following quotations are from pp. 1044, 1045.
159. Laskin in *Miller and Cockreill v. R.* [1977] 2 S.C.R. 680, at 688-90. Quoted by Justice Lamer in *R. v. Smith (Edward Dewey)* [1987] 1 S.C.R. 1045, at 1067.
160. *R. v. Smith (Edward Dewey)* [1987] 1 S.C.R. 1045, at 1072. The following quotation is from p. 1073.
161. *Ibid.*, at 1074. The quotation from this case in the next paragraph is from p. 1077.

161a. Chief Justice Lamer in *R. v. Luxton* [1990] 2 S.C.R. 711, at 724.

162. *R. v. Lyons* [1987] 2 S.C.R. 309, at 312.
163. *Steele v. Mountain Institution* [1990] 2 S.C.R. 1385, at 1412, 1415, 1417.
164. *R. v. Milne* [1987] 2 S.C.R. 512.
165. *Miller and Cockreill v. R.* [1977] 2 S.C.R. 680, noted by Justice Lamer in *R. v. Smith (Edward Dewey)* [1987] 1 S.C.R. 1045, at 1066.
166. Manning, *Rights, Freedoms and the Courts*, p. 453.
167. This is suggested by Ed Ratushny, "The Role of the Accused in the Criminal Process (ss. 10(a), 11(a), (c), and (d), and 13)," in Tarnopolsky and Beaudoin, *The Canadian Charter*, p. 365.
168. *Dubois v. R.* [1985] 2 S.C.R. 350. The following quotations are from p. 351. This position was confirmed in *R. v. Mannion* [1986] 2 S.C.R. 272.

168a. *R. v. Kuldip*, December 7, 1990. Reported in *Supreme Court News*, vol. 6, no. 18, p. 234.

169. Walter S. Tarnopolsky, "The Equality Rights (ss. 15, 27 and 28)," in Tarnopolsky and Beaudoin, *The Canadian Charter*, p. 396.

170. "Consolidation of Proposed Resolution and Possible Amendments as Placed before the Special Joint Committee [of the Senate and House of Commons on the Canadian Constitution] by the Minister of Justice, January, 1981, Together with Explanatory Notes," p. 7. (Mimeographed.)
171. *Andrews v. Law Society of British Columbia* [1989] 1 S.C.R. 143.
172. *A.G. Canada v. Lavell and Bedard* [1974] S.C.R. 1349.
173. *Bliss v. A.G. Canada* [1979] 1 S.C.R. 183.
174. *Brooks v. Canada Safeway* [1989] 1 S.C.R. 1219, at 1221.
175. *Andrews v. Law Society of British Columbia* [1989] 1 S.C.R. 143, at 166.
176. *R. v. Drybones* [1970] S.C.R. 282.
177. *Andrews v. Law Society of British Columbia* [1989] 1 S.C.R. 143, at 174-75.
178. *Ibid.*, at 182.
179. Justice Wilson in *R. v. Big M Drug Mart* [1985] 1 S.C.R. 295, at 360. For a discussion of this issue see Rainer Knopff, "What do Constitutional Equality Rights Protect Canadians Against?", *Canadian Journal of Political Science*, 20 (June 1987), 265-86.
180. *R. v. Turpin* [1989] 1 S.C.R. 1296. The following quotations are from pp. 1326, 1332-33.
181. *R. v. Hess; R. v. Nguyen* [1990] 2 S.C.R. 906. The following quotations are from pp. 928-29, 929-30, 930-31, 944.
182. *Ref. re Bill 30, an Act to Amend the Education Act (Ont.)* [1987] 1 S.C.R. 1148. The following quotations are from pp. 1206-7.
183. *Rudolph Wolff & Co. v. Canada* [1990] 1 S.C.R. 695; *Dywidag Systems International, Canada Ltd. v. Zutphen Brothers Construction Ltd.* [1990] 1 S.C.R. 705. The following quotation is from *Wolff* at 696.
184. *Borowski v. A.G. Canada* [1989] 1 S.C.R. 342.
185. *McKinney v. University of Guelph*, Supreme Court of Canada, December 6, 1990, unpublished, mimeograph unpaged.
186. *Tetreault-Gadoury v. Canada (Canada Unemployment and Immigration Commission)*, Supreme Court of Canada, June 6, 1991, unpublished, mimeograph unpaged.
187. *R. v. S.* (s.) [1990] 2 S.C.R. 254, at 260, 256-57.
188. Tarnopolsky, "The Equality Rights (ss. 15, 27 and 28)," p. 437.
189. *Jones v. A.G. New Brunswick* [1975] 2 S.C.R. 182.
190. *Ibid.*, at 192-93.
191. André Tremblay, "The Language Rights (ss. 16 to 23)," in Tarnopolsky and Beaudoin, *The Canadian Charter*, p. 458 (n. 21).
192. *Société des Acadiens v. Association of Parents* [1986] 1 S.C.R. 549. The following quotations are from pp. 565, 578, 579, 580.

193. *MacDonald v. Montreal* [1986] 1 S.C.R. 460; *Bilodeau v. A.G. Manitoba* [1986] 1 S.C.R. 449; *Société des Acadiens v. Association of Parents* [1986] 1 S.C.R. 549.
194. *Quebec Protestant School Boards v. A.G. Quebec* [1982] 140 D.L.R. (3d) 33 (Que. S.C.), at 71-90. Cited by Hogg, *Constitutional Law of Canada*, p. 682 (nn. 171, 172).
195. *A.G. Quebec v. Quebec Association of Protestant School Boards* [1984] 2 S.C.R. 66.
196. *Mahe v. Alberta* [1990] 1 S.C.R. 342. The quotation below is from p. 387.
197. *Ibid.*, at 394-95.
198. *Borowski v. A.G. Canada* [1989] 1 S.C.R. 342, at 367.
199. *R. v. Rahey* [1987] 1 S.C.R. 588, at 619.
200. *Operation Dismantle v. R.* [1985] 1 S.C.R. 441, at 450. This opinion was confirmed in *R. v. Vermette* [1988] 1 S.C.R. 985, at 992.
201. *R. v. Rahey* [1987] 1 S.C.R. 588, at 590.
202. *Mills v. R.* [1986] 1 S.C.R. 863.
203. *Argentina v. Mellino* [1987] 1 S.C.R. 536; *United States v. Allard* [1987] 1 S.C.R. 564.
204. *Mills v. R.* [1986] 1 S.C.R. 863, at 965.
205. Justice Lamer in *R. v. Rahey* [1987] 1 S.C.R. 588, at 614.
206. *R. v. Therens* [1985] 1 S.C.R. 613, at 647-48.
207. Russell, Knopff and Morton, *Federalism and the Charter*, p. 426.
208. *R. v. Simmons* [1988] 2 S.C.R. 495, at 534.
209. *R. v. Collins* [1987] 1 S.C.R. 265.
210. Yves-Marie, Morisette, "The Exclusion of Evidence under the *Canadian Charter of Rights and Freedoms*: What to Do and What Not to Do," 29 *McGill L. J.* 538 (1984); quoted *ibid.*, at p. 282.
211. *R. v. Collins* [1987] 1 S.C.R. 265, at 282-83.
212. *Ibid.*, at 288.
213. *Ibid.*, at 286.
214. *R. v. Manninen* [1987] 1 S.C.R. 1233.
215. *R. v. Greffe* [1990] 1 S.C.R. 755. The following quotations are from pp. 793, 770, 784.

215a. Quoted in *R. v. Garfoli* [1990] 2 S.C.R. 1421, at 1440.

216. Dale Gibson, "Enforcement of the Canadian Charter of Rights and Freedoms (section 24)," in Tarnopolsky and Beaudoin, *The Canadian Charter*, p. 514.
217. Wigmore, *Treatise on the Law of Evidence* (1961), vol. 8, 31. Quoted by Hogg, *Constitutional Law of Canada*, p. 699 (n. 254).

218. Hogg, *Constitutional Law of Canada*, p. 565. See also p. 563.
219. Chief Justice Dickson, *R. v. Sparrow* [1990] 1 S.C.R. 1075, at 1103.
220. Greene, *The Charter of Rights*, p. 58.
221. Hogg, *Canada Act 1982 Annotated*, pp. 70-71.
222. *R. v. Big M Drug Mart* [1985] 1 S.C.R. 295, at 302.
223. *Ibid.*, at 337.
224. *Société des Acadiens v. Association of Parents* [1986] 1 S.C.R. 549, at 621.
225. *R. v. Keegstra*, December 13, 1990. Edited reprint (mimeograph): "Leading Constitutional Decisions of the Supreme Court of Canada," ed. Peter H. Russell, Rainer Knopff, and F.L. Morton, p. 5.
226. *R. v. Edwards Books and Art* [1986] 2 S.C.R. 713, at 808-9.
227. Romanow, Whyte and Leeson, *Canada...Notwithstanding*, p. 213.
228. *Ref. re Bill 30, an Act to Amend the Education Act (Ont.)* [1987] 1 S.C.R. 1148, at 1198.
229. *Mahe v. Alberta* [1990] 1 S.C.R. 342.
230. *Greater Montreal Protestant School Board v. A.G. Quebec* [1989] 1 S.C.R. 377, at 378.
231. *RWDSU v. Dolphin Delivery* [1986] 2 S.C.R. 573, at 574.
232. Hogg, *Constitutional Law of Canada*, pp. 674-75.
233. Fred Jordan, Department of Justice, appearing before the Committee on the Constitution, *Minutes*, January 29, 1981, p. 48:27.
234. *Operation Dismantle v. R.* [1985] 1 S.C.R. 441, at 463-64.
235. *RWDSU v. Dolphin Delivery* [1986] 2 S.C.R. 573. The following quotations are from pp. 598, 603, 602.
236. *McKinney v. University of Guelph*, Supreme Court of Canada, December 6, 1990, unpublished, mimeograph unpaged. The Court reached similar conclusions in three analogous cases decided the same day: *Harrison v. University of British Columbia*, *Stoffman v. Vancouver General Hospital*, and *Douglas/ Kwantlen Faculty Association v. Douglas College*.
237. Robert J. Jackson and Doreen Jackson, *Politics in Canada: Culture, Institutions, Behaviour and Public Policy*, 2nd ed., p. 212.
238. See Hogg, *Constitutional Law of Canada*, p. 690 (n. 213), for a review of the literature.
239. Gil Rémillard, quoted by Darrel R. Reid and Christopher Kendall, "Chronology of Events 1986-1987," in *Canada: The State of the Federation 1987-88*, ed. Peter M. Leslie and Ronald L. Watts (Kingston, Ontario: Institute of Intergovernmental Relations, 1988), p. 201.
240. *Ford v. A.G. Quebec* [1988] 2 S.C.R. 712, at 741.

241. *Alberta Labour Reference* [1987] 1 S.C.R. 313; *PSAC [Public Service Alliance of Canada] v. Canada* [1987] 1 S.C.R. 424; *RWDSU [Retail, Wholesale and Department Store Union] v. Saskatchewan* [1987] 1 S.C.R. 460.

242. Rainer Knopff and F.L. Morton, "Judicial Statesmanship and the Charter of Rights and Freedoms," in Morton, *Law, Politics and the Judicial Process in Canada*, pp. 327-34.

243. Romanow, Whyte, and Leeson, *Canada...Notwithstanding*, pp. 212-13.

244. *Ibid.*, p. 214.

245. *R. v. Sparrow* [1990] 1 S.C.R. 1075.

246. *Ibid.*, at 1091.

247. Brian Slattery, "Understanding Aboriginal Rights," 66 *Canadian Bar Rev.* 781-82 (1987); quoted *ibid.*, at 1092.

248. *R. v. Sparrow* [1990] 1 S.C.R. 1075, at 1095. The following quotations in this paragraph are from pp. 1097, 1099.

249. *Ibid.*, at 1103, 1105.

250. Noel Lyon, "An Essay on Constitutional Interpretation," 26 *Osgood Hall L. J.* 100 (1988); quoted *ibid.*, at 1106.

251. *R. v. Sparrow* [1990] 1 S.C.R. 1075, at 1109. The quotations in the next two paragraphs are from pp. 1119, 1121.

252. Michael Mandel, *The Charter of Rights and the Legalization of Politics in Canada* (Toronto: Wall & Thompson, 1989), p. 251.

253. Michael D. Behils, Introduction to chapter 10, "Aboriginal and Northern Rights: Integrating the First Peoples into the Constitution," *The Meech Lake Primer: Conflicting Views of the 1987 Constitutional Accord*, ed. Michael D. Behils (Ottawa: University of Ottawa Press, 1989), p. 415.

254. Quoted by Mandel, *The Charter of Rights and the Legalization of Politics in Canada*, p. 251.

255. Chief George Erasmus appearing before the Special Joint Committee of the Senate and of the House of Commons on the 1987 Constitutional Accord, *Minutes of Proceedings and Evidence*, August 19, 1987, p. 9:50.

256. "Constitution Amendment Proclamation, 1983," SI/84-102, July 11, 1984, in *Canada Gazette* Part II, Vol. 118, No. 14, pp. 2984-86.

257. D. Marc Kilgour, "A Formal Analysis of the Amending Formula of Canada's Constitution Act, 1982," *Canadian Journal of Political Science*, 16 (December 1983), 773.

258. Gordon Robertson, "Meech Lake—The myth of the time limit," supplement to The Institute for Research on Public Policy *Newsletter*, vol. 11, no. 3, May/June 1989.

259. For an account of this episode see Andrew Sancton, "Eroding Representation-by-Population in the Canadian House of Commons: The Representation Act, 1985," *Canadian Journal of Political Science*, 23 September 1990), 441.

260. Hogg, *Constitutional Law of Canada*, pp. 66-67.

261. *Ibid.*, pp. 67-68.

261a. *Douglas/Kwantlen Faculty Association v. Douglas College*, December 6, 1990. Reported in *Supreme Court News*, vol. 6, no. 18, p. 229.

262. *RWDSU v. Dolphin Delivery* [1986] 2 S.C.R. 573, at 574-75, 592-93.

263. *Operation Dismantle v. R.* [1985] 1 S.C.R. 441, at 485.

264. Hogg, *Constitutional Law of Canada*, p. 666.

CONCLUSION/EPILOGUE

1. *Osborne v. Canada (Treasury Board)*, Supreme Court of Canada, June 6, 1991, unpublished, mimeograph unpaged.
2. Morton, Russell, and Withey, "Judging the Judges: The Supreme Court's First One Hundred Charter Decisions," p. 63.
3. *Ibid.*, p. 64.
4. *Ibid.*, p. 67.
5. Swinton, *The Supreme Court and Canadian Federalism: The Laskin-Dickson Years*, p. 323.
6. Swinton's consideration of this question forms the basis of the following discussion. *Ibid.*, pp. 338-49.
7. *Andrews v. Law Society of British Columbia* [1989] 1 S.C.R. 143, at 198.
8. Government of Alberta, *Alberta in a New Canada*, undated. The following quotations are from pp. 1, 2, 20.
9. Quoted in the *Journal* (Edmonton), June 29, 1991, "The Forum: A Report to the People from the Citizens' Forum on Canada's Future," p. 4.
10. Commons *Debates*, May 13, 1991, p. 3.
11. Joe Clark, quoted in Susan Delacourt, "Constituent assembly plea rejected," *The Globe and Mail* (Toronto), June 28, 1991, p. A4.
12. The following three lists are from the *Journal* (Edmonton), January 31, 1991, p. A3.
13. Quoted in "Quebec open to proposals from the rest of Canada," *Journal*, (Edmonton), March 24, 1991.

INDEX OF CASES

Cases which might logically be identified by more than one name are cross listed. For example, *Hunter v. Southam* is also listed under *Southam* with the statement "See *Hunter v. Southam.*"

Although many cases are officially titled "*R. v. . . .*" they are indexed below as "*. . ., R. v.*" (e.g., *Swain, R. v.*) in order to avoid much needless cross listing, or searching by the reader.

Similarly, reference cases identified as "*Ref. re*" or "*Re*" are alphabetized by the name of the reference.

GENERAL INDEX

An indexed heading which is also a section topic within the 1867 or 1982 Constitution Act states the relevant section of that Act—e.g., (1867:93). This is to be interpreted as "*See* the page references under Constitution Act, 1867, s. 93."

The listing of 1867 and 1982 Constitution Act sections shows the locations of Chapter 7 and 8 commentaries in bold type.

G

N

O